ATLA BIBLIOGRAPHY SERIES
edited by Dr. Kenneth E. Rowe

1. *A Guide to the Study of the Holiness Movement,* by Charles Edwin Jones. 1974.
2. *Thomas Merton: A Bibliography,* by Marquita E. Breit. 1974.
3. *The Sermon on the Mount: A History of Interpretation and Bibliography,* by Warren S. Kissinger. 1975.
4. *The Parables of Jesus: A History of Interpretation and Bibliography,* by Warren S. Kissinger. 1979.
5. *Homosexuality and the Judeo-Christian Tradition: An Annotated Bibliography,* by Tom Horner. 1981.
6. *A Guide to the Study of the Pentecostal Movement,* by Charles Edwin Jones. 1983.
7. *The Genesis of Modern Process Thought: A Historical Outline with Bibliography,* by George R. Lucas, Jr. 1983.
8. *A Presbyterian Bibliography,* by Harold B. Prince. 1983.
9. *Paul Tillich: A Comprehensive Bibliography . . .,* by Richard C. Crossman. 1983.
10. *A Bibliography of the Samaritans,* by Alan David Crown. 1984.
11. *An Annotated and Classified Bibliography of English Literature Pertaining to the Ethiopian Orthodox Church,* by Jon Bonk. 1984.
12. *International Meditation Bibliography, 1950 to 1982,* by Howard R. Jarrell. 1984.

INTERNATIONAL MEDITATION BIBLIOGRAPHY 1950-1982

by

Howard R. Jarrell

ATLA Bibliography Series No. 12

The American Theological Library Association

and

The Scarecrow Press, Inc.

Metuchen, N.J., and London, 1985

Library of Congress Cataloging in Publication Data
Jarrell, Howard R.
    International meditation bibliography, 1950 to 1982.
    (ATLA bibliography series ; no. 12)
    Includes indexes.
    1. Meditation--Bibliography. I. Title. II. Series.
Z7815.7.J37   1985   [BL627]   016.158'12   84-21691
ISBN 0-8108-1759-4

To Mike Driscoll, Tom Lennon, and Steve McCarthy

for friendships that are appreciated and cherished.

■ CONTENTS ■

Foreword   vii

User's Guide   ix

Articles   1

Books   145

Doctoral Dissertations and Master's Theses   251

Motion Pictures   289

Recordings   295

Societies and Associations   311

Author Index   325

Title Index   346

Subject Index   408

The American Theological Library Association Bibliography Series is designed to stimulate and encourage the preparation of
reliable bibliographies and guides to the literature of religious
studies in all of its scope and variety. Compilers are free to
define their field, make their own selections and work out internal organization as the unique demands of the subject indicate. We are pleased to publish Howard R. Jarrell's international meditation bibliography as Number 12 in the series.

Mr. Jarrell took his undergraduate studies at the University of Dayton and studied librarianship at Case-Western
Reserve University. He has held several positions in libraries in Ohio and Florida and currently serves as Senior Reference Librarian at Wright State University in Dayton, Ohio.

Kenneth E. Rowe
Series Editor

Drew University
Madison, New Jersey

■ FOREWORD ■

Our traditional system of education focuses on objects of
knowledge. Students are exposed to various facts, ideas,
and works of artistic creation, and they are expected to determine the validity of these objects of knowledge and the
meaningful relationships among them. In addition to satisfy-
ing natural curiosity about the relative universe, this system
forces the student to think on quieter levels of the mind. As
a result, through practice, the efficiency of the process of
gaining knowledge is enhanced.

Howard Jarrell's bibliography is an ideal aid to such
scholarship. This comprehensive tool brings together the
very diverse literature in one area of inquiry: the many techniques and systems of thought that have been categorized as
meditation.

This book has an even greater value as a guide to
practical action for the scholar. It gives easy access to numerous reports of scientific research in this area, most of them
on the Transcendental Meditation program of Maharishi Mahesh
Yogi. This simple, natural technique, systematically taught
and easily learned at over 1500 Capitals of the Age of Enlightenment in almost every part of the world, has been shown
to have many benefits. Hundreds of scientific studies show
that regular practice of this technique for just twenty minutes,
morning and evening, leads to increased creative intelligence
and orderliness of thinking, better physical and mental health,
and the development of a state of inner fulfilment conducive
to harmonious human relationships. Thus this bibliography
provides evidence that it would be beneficial for the reader
to seek the experience of the Transcendental Meditation technique, not just to view it as an interesting object of knowledge.

Regular practice of this technique will lead the seeker to the supreme value of education: complete knowledge. Knowledge has two components: the object of knowledge, and the Knower, or the field of pure consciousness. Knowledge is structured in consciousness just as waves are structured in the ocean. Without the experience of the Knower, objective knowledge is baseless and superficial. The Transcendental Meditation technique is unique in the world today. Not a philosophy, not a religion, neither concentration nor contemplation, during its practice the mind effortlessly settles to its state of least excitation. This is the most direct method for experiencing pure consciousness, the field of pure subjectivity. With regular practice of the technique, the nervous system is so cultured that this field is permanently established in the awareness. With both the object of inquiry and the subject lively in the awareness, knowledge is complete.

Knowledge is for action. Action is for achievement. Achievement is for fulfilment. Thus, in the final analysis, Howard Jarrell's bibliography has its greatest value as a beacon to lead the seeker to complete fulfilment in the state of enlightenment.

William S. Baker
Miami University
Oxford, Ohio

■ USER'S GUIDE ■

The purpose of this work is to provide readers and researchers interested in meditation with an index and guide to resource material. Annotations for the articles and dissertations should be particularly useful, as well as the Author, Title, and Subject Indexes. The work can be used to verify titles for interlibrary loan of material not available at local libraries. The bibliography is basically descriptive and is not primarily intended for collection development. No evaluation of the references has been made.

The bibliography encompasses material on all forms and techniques of meditation published from 1950 to 1982, with some references in 1983. It includes Christian meditation, Zen Buddhist meditation, Relaxation techniques, Yoga meditation, and Transcendental Meditation. Most available research has been in the area of TM.

Articles are in English. Books include works written in English and German, with some titles in French, Spanish, Portuguese, Italian, or Dutch languages. Dissertations and theses are in English or German.

Provided in separate lists are 900 journal and magazine articles, 1000 books, over 200 dissertations and master's theses, 32 motion pictures, 93 recordings, and names and addresses of 32 societies and associations.

Each citation has been numbered within each of the format sections and these numbers are used in the indexes. In addition to the names of authors, the Author Index includes those of other persons involved in the production of the works. The Title Index includes subtitles for many of the English language books. Titles of journals and magazines are also given in the Title Index.

Entries in the Subject Index under the heading of "Bibliographies" can be useful for additional information. For related material see the International Yoga Bibliography, 1950 to 1980, also by this author and published by Scarecrow Press in 1981.

■ ARTICLES ■

A1   Aaronson, Bernard S. "The Hypnotic Induction of the Void."
     Journal of the American Society of Psychosomatic Dentistry
     and Medicine, 26 (1979): 22-30.
     The void experience of Eastern and Western mysticism was
     analyzed as a state resulting from a separation of self from
     one's senses, from one's concept of self, and a loss of oppo-
     sites and polarities.

A2   Abdullah, Syed, and Helen Schucman. "Cerebral Lateraliza-
     tion, Bimodal Consciousness, and Related Developments in
     Psychiatry." Research Communications in Psychology,
     Psychiatry and Behavior, 1 (1976): 671-679.
     Explains the therapeutic benefits arising from regular medita-
     tion with aspects of cerebral hemispheric dominance.

A3   Abrams, Allan I. "Paired-Asssociate Learning and Recall: A
     Pilot Study of the Transcendental Meditation Program." In
     Scientific Research on the Transcendental Meditation Pro-
     gram: Collected Papers, Vol. 1. Edited by David W.
     Orme-Johnson and John T. Farrow. 2nd ed., Weggis,
     Switzerland: Maharishi European Research University
     Press, 1977, p. 377-381.
     Subjects practicing the TM technique were reported to have
     quicker acquisition of information and superior recall.

A4   _____, and Larry M. Siegel. "Transcendental Meditation
     and Rehabilitation at Folsom Prison: Response to a Cri-
     tique." Criminal Justice and Behavior, 6 (March 1979):
     13-21. Tentatively scheduled for inclusion in Scientific
     Research on the Transcendental Meditation Program: Col-
     lected Papers, Vol. 2. Rheinweiler, West Germany:
     Maharishi European Research University Press, (in press).
     The article responds to the challenge posed by Don Allen's
     article [A13] as to the validity of their study [A5] and its
     findings.

A5   _____, and _____. "Transcendental Meditation Program
     and Rehabilitation at Folsom State Prison: A Cross-Valida-
     tion Study." Criminal Justice and Behavior, 5 (March
     1978): 3-20. Tentatively scheduled for inclusion in Sci-

1

entific Research on the Transcendental Meditation Program:
Collected Papers, Vol. 2. Rheinweiler, West Germany:
Maharishi European Research University Press, (in press).
This study indicates reduction in anxiety, neuroticism, hostil-
ity, and insomnia as effects of the Transcendental Meditation
program.

A6   Aerthayil, James. "The Hesychast Method of Prayer." Jour-
       nal of Dharma, 2 (April 1977): 204-216.
Historical-theological survey of how the invocation of the name
of Jesus has been associated with Hesychast meditation.

A7   Agarwal, B.L., and A. Kharbanda. "Effect of Transcendental
       Meditation on Mild and Moderate Hypertension." Journal of
       the Association of Physicians of India, 29 (August 1981):
       591-596. Tentatively scheduled for inclusion in Scientific
       Research on the Transcendental Meditation Program:
       Collected Papers, Vol. 2. Rheinweiler, West Germany:
       Maharishi European Research University Press, (in press).
Most of the reduction in blood pressure took place in the first
two months. Suggested that drugs be added or substituted
after two months if results are not satisfactory.

A8   Ahuja, M.M.S.; M.G. Karmarkar; and S. Reddy. "TSH, LH,
       Cortisol Response to TRH and LH-RH and Insulin Hypo-
       glycaemia in Subjects Practising Transcendental Meditation."
       Indian Journal of Medical Research, 74 (November 1981):
       715-720.
Evaluates the effects of transcendental meditation on hormonal
profile.

A9   Akers, Thomas K.; Don M. Tucker; Randy S. Roth; and John
       S. Vidiloff. "Personality Correlates of EEG Change During
       Meditation." Psychological Reports, 40 (April 1977): 439-
       442.
The result is discussed in terms of previous research, the
premeditation level of alpha, and the implications for the use
of meditation as a therapeutic procedure.

A9K   Akishige, Yoshiharu. "The Principles of Psychology of Zen."
       In Meditation: Classic and Contemporary Perspectives,
       edited by Deane H. Shapiro, Jr. and Roger N. Walsh.
       Hawthorne, N.Y.: Aldine Pub. Co., 1984.

A10   Albert, Ira B., and Barbara McNeece. "The Reported Sleep
       Characteristics of Meditators and Nonmeditators." Bulletin
       of the Psychonomic Society, 3 (January 1974): 73-74.
Meditators reported that they awakened in the morning more
rested than nonmeditators. Meditators also reported more
dreaming and a more positive quality in their dream content.

A11   Aldrich, Virgil C. "Meditation on the New-Theory and Prac-
       tice of Meditation." Western Humanities Review, 29 (Winter
       1975): 1-15.
       A critical essay on Transcendental Meditation.

A12   Alexander, C.N., and E.J. Marks. "Development and Per-
       sonality in Practitioners of the Transcendental Meditation
       Program in Comparison to Members of Other Programs in
       a Male Inmate Population: Preliminary Summary of Cross-
       Sectional Findings." Tentatively scheduled for inclusion in
       Scientific Research on the Transcendental Meditation Pro-
       gram: Collected Papers, Vol. 2. Rheinweiler, West Ger-
       many: Maharishi European Research University Press,
       (in press).
       Subjects compared favorably to other institutional programs
       in terms of psychopathology, ego and cognitive development,
       and higher consciousness.

A13   Allen, Don. "TM at Folson Prison: A Critique of Abrams
       and Siegel." Criminal Justice and Behavior, 6 (March
       1979): 9-12.
       It is suggested that if there are any rehabilitative effects
       from Transcendental Meditation, they are not documented by
       Abrams and Siegel's paper [A5]. See also [A4] for reply.

A14   Allison, John. "Respiratory Changes During Transcendental
       Meditation." Lancet, No. 7651 (1970): 833. In Scientific
       Research on the Transcendental Meditation Program: Col-
       lected Papers, Vol. 1. Edited by David W. Orme-Johnson
       and John T. Farrow. 2nd ed., Weggis, Switzerland:
       Maharishi European Research University Press, 1977, p.
       92-93.
       A decrease in breath rate was observed during the practice
       of Transcendental Meditation.

A15   Anand, B.K., and G.S. Chhina. "Investigations on Yogis
       Claiming to Stop Their Heartbeats." Indian Journal of
       Medical Research, 49 (January 1961): 90-94.
       Heart sounds could not be heard and pulse could not be felt.
       EKG showed that heart was contracting normally. X-ray
       screenings revealed the heart contracting normally.

A16   _____; _____; and Baldev Singh. "Some Aspects of
       Electroencephalographic Studies in Yogis." Electroen-
       cephalography and Clinical Neurophysiology, 13 (1961):
       452-456. Also in Meditation: Classic and Contemporary
       Perspectives, edited by Deane H. Shapiro, Jr. and Roger
       N. Walsh. Hawthorne, N.Y.: Aldine Pub. Co., 1984.
       Four Yogis who practiced samadhi were investigated electro-
       encephalographically. It was observed that their resting

records showed persistent alpha activity with increased am-
plitute modulation during samadhi. The alpha activity could
not be blocked by various sensory stimuli during meditation.

A17   Anchor, Kenneth N.; Sharon E. Beck; Nicholas Sieveking;
and Joyce Adkins. "A History of Clinical Biofeedback."
American Journal of Clinical Biofeedback, 5 (Spring-
Summer 1982): 3-16.
A literature review that includes references to meditation,
yoga and zen.

A18   Anderson, Douglas J. "Transcendental Meditation as an Alternative to Heroin Abuse in Servicemen." American Journal
of Psychiatry, 134 (November 1977): 1308-1309.
Concludes that TM is not an alternative to drug abuse for all
populations. For those who seem to benefit, TM may be no
better than any alternative such as a hobby or a sport that
requires motivation.

A19   Andrews, Gavin; S.W. MacMahon; Anne Austin; and D.G.
Byrne. "Hypertension Comparison of Drug and Nondrug
Treatments." British Medical Journal, 284 (1982): 1523-
1526.
Drugs produced the greatest decrease in blood pressure.
Weight reduction, yoga and muscle relaxation each produced
smaller yet significant decreases. Meditation, exercise, bio-
feedback, and salt restriction were not significantly effective.

A20   Appelle, Stuart, and Lawrence E. Oswald. "Simple Reaction
Time as a Function of Alertness and Prior Mental Activity."
Perceptual and Motor Skills, 38 (June 1974): 1263-1268.
In Scientific Research on the Transcendental Meditation
Program: Collected Papers, Vol. 1. Edited by David W.
Orme-Johnson and John T. Farrow. 2nd ed., Weggis,
Switzerland: Maharishi European Research University Press,
1977, p. 312-315.
Simple reaction time to light onset was measured before and
after twenty minute periods of differing mental activity, in-
cluding meditation.

A21   Aron, Arthur, and Elaine N. Aron. "The Transcendental
Meditation Program's Effect on Addictive Behavior." Addictive Behaviors, 5 (1980): 3-12.
Reviews research and considers possible explanations for the
positive effects of TM in reducing addictive behavior. Discusses practical issues in implementing TM programs.

A22   _____; David Orme-Johnson; and Paul Brubaker. "The
Transcendental Meditation Program in the College Curriculum: A 4-Year Longitudinal Study of Effects on Cognitive
and Affective Functioning." College Student Journal, 15

(Summer 1981): 140-146.
Students in the first class of an undergraduate program at
Maharishi International University were studied. The value
of including the TM program in the college curriculum appears
to receive some support.

A23   Aron, Elaine N., and Arthur Aron. "An Introduction to Ma-
           harishi's Theory of Creativity: Its Empirical Base and
           Description of the Creative Process." Journal of Creative
           Behavior, 16 (1982): 29-49.
Discusses research on the effect of the TM program on creativity, the creative process, and implications of the Maharishi's theory of creativity.

A24   _____, and _____. "The Transcendental Meditation Pro-
           gram and Marital Adjustment." Psychological Reports, 51
           (December 1982): 887-890. Tentatively scheduled for in-
           clusion in Scientific Research on the Transcendental Medi-
           tation Program: Collected Papers, Vol. 2. Rheinweiler,
           West Germany: Maharishi European Research University
           Press, (in press).
Research results presented at the 6th Annual Family Research
Conference, Provo, Utah, 1977. Higher marital adjustment
was demonstrated by married women practicing the TM program than for matched controls.

A25   _____, and _____. "The Transcendental Meditation Pro-
           gram for the Reduction of Stress-Related Conditions."
           Journal of Chronic Diseases and Therapeutics Research, 3
           (January 1979): 11-21.
Considers research on the TM program which could imply a
change in the ability of individuals to cope with stressors and
the use of TM in the treatment of stress-related social problems of mental disorder, substance abuse, and criminal behavior.

A26   Ashbrook, James B. "Praying for the Spirit." Religion in
           Life, 46 (Spring 1977): 62-71.
Gives a simple technique for Christian meditation.

A27   Avila, Donald, and Renate Nummela. "Transcendental Medita-
           tion: A Psychological Interpretation." Journal of Clinical
           Psychology, 33 (July 1977): 842-844.
Suggests that meditation should become one of the basic tools
of the helping professions.

A28   Bache, Christopher M. "On the Emergence of Perinatal Symp-
           toms in Buddhist Meditation." Journal for the Scientific
           Study of Religion, 20 (December 1981): 339-350.
Advanced Zen meditators occasionally experience physical seizures and disruptive emotions. Using data from LSD research,

the author suggests the seizures are emerging birth-trauma memories.

A29   Badaoui, K.; A.M. Rouzere; and David W. Orme-Johnson. "Electrophysiological Changes During Periods of Respiratory Suspension During the Transcendental Meditation Technique." Tentative scheduled for inclusion in Scientific Research on the Transcendental Meditation Program: Collected Papers, Vol. 2. Rheinweiler, West Germany: Maharishi European Research University Press, (in press).
Heart rate decreased and EEG coherence increased during periods of respiratory suspension correlated with pure consciousness.

A30   Badaracco, Marie R. "Psychoanalysis as Altering States of Consciousness." Journal of the American Academy of Psychoanalysis. 3 (April 1975): 205-210.
The article shows how the process of psychoanalysis is akin to that of meditation and how they are identical in underlying nature.

A31   Bagga, O.P., and A. Gandhi. "A Comparative Study of the Effect of Transcendental Meditation (T.M.) and Shavasana Practice on Cardiovascular System." Indian Heart Journal, 35 (January-February 1983): 39-45.
Both techniques lowered the heart rate and blood pressure, and increased skin resistance. The effects were relatively more significant in subjects practicing TM than Shavasana.

A32   Bahrke, Michael S. "Exercise, Meditation and Anxiety Reduction: A Review." American Corrective Therapy Journal, 33 (March-April 1979): 41-44.
Reviews research suggesting that exercise, meditation and relaxation techniques are capable of reducing tension and anxiety.

A33   _____, and William P. Morgan. "Anxiety Reduction Following Exercise and Meditation." Cognitive Therapy and Research, 2 (December 1978): 323-333.
The investigation suggests acute physical activity, Benson's Relaxation Response, and a quiet rest session are equally effective in reducing state anxiety.

A34   Bailey, Judi. "Slow Me Down, Lord!" St. Anthony Messenger, 89 (May 1982): 20-23.
A personal account of how a simple meditative technique of breath concentration helped the writer with Christian meditation.

A35   Bainbridge, William Sims, and Daniel H. Jackson. "The Rise and Decline of Transcendental Meditation." In The Social

Impact of New Religious Movements. Edited by Bryan Wilson. Barrytown, N.Y.: Unification Theological Seminary; New York: dist. by Rose of Sharon Press, 1981. p. 135-158.
Gives an ethnographic description of the Transcendental Meditation movement from 1966 to 1977.

A36   , and Rodney Stark. "Client and Audience Cults in America." Sociological Analysis, 41 (Fall 1980): 199-214.
The paper examines the prevalence and location of several kinds of cults and cult interests including Transcendental Meditation.

A37   Baird, Robert D. "Religious or Non-Religious: TM in American Courts." Journal of Dharma, 7 (October-December 1982): 391-407.
Discusses various court cases involving the question of whether or not TM is a religion.

A38   Bakker, Robert. "Decreased Respiratory Rate During the Transcendental Meditation Technique: A Replication." In Scientific Research on the Transcendental Meditation Program: Collected Papers, Vol. 1. Edited by David W. Orme-Johnson and John T. Farrow. 2nd ed., Weggis, Switzerland: Maharishi European Research University Press, 1977, p. 140-141.
A decrease in respiration rate was reported for subjects practicing the TM technique, supporting the findings of Wallace, Benson and Wilson, and Allison.

A39   Ballou, David. "The Transcendental Meditation Program at Stillwater Prison." In Scientific Research on the Transcendental Meditation Program: Collected Papers, Vol. 1. Edited by David W. Orme-Johnson and John T. Farrow. 2nd ed., Weggis, Switzerland: Maharishi European Research University Press, 1977, p. 569-576.
Prisoners who practiced TM showed reduced anxiety and increased social stability.

A40   Baltazar, Eulalio R. "TM and the Religion-in-School Issue." Christian Century, 93 (18 August 1976): 708-709.
Argues that schools should not be hampered by considerations as to whether a teaching is religious or secular. See [A75].

A41   Bamrungtrakul, Ratna. "You Can Change Yourself and the World with Christian-Asian Meditation." East Asian Pastoral Review, 19 (1982): 32-37.
Explains the technique of Christian-Asian meditation. Lists the natural and spiritual effects of the meditation.

A42   Banquet, Jean-Paul. "EEG and Meditation." Electroencephalog-

raphy and Clinical Neurophysiology, 33 (1972): 454. In
Scientific Research on the Transcendental Meditation Pro-
gram: Collected Papers, Vol. 1. Edited by David W.
Orme-Johnson and John T. Farrow. 2nd ed., Weggis,
Switzerland: Maharishi European Research University Press,
1977, p. 151.
This study suggests an orderly state of restful alertness oc-
curs during the TM technique as registered by EEG changes.

A43   . "Spectral Analysis of the EEG in Meditation."
Electroencephalography and Clinical Neurophysiology, 35
(August 1973): 143-151. In Scientific Research on the
Transcendental Meditation Program: Collected Papers, Vol.
1. Edited by David W. Orme-Johnson and John T. Farrow.
2nd ed., Weggis, Switzerland: Maharishi European Research
University Press, 1977, p. 152-159. Also in Meditation:
Classic and Contemporary Perspectives, edited by Deane
H. Shapiro, Jr. and Roger N. Walsh. Hawthorne, N.Y.:
Aldine Pub. Co., 1984.
This study showed distinctive EEG changes for subjects prac-
ticing the TM technique.

A44   ; J.C. Bourzeix; and N. Leseure. "Potentiels évoques
et états de vigilance induits qu' cours d'épreuves de temps
de réaction de choix." Revue d'Electroencéphalographie et
de Neurophysiologie Clinique, 19 (1979): 221-227. Text in
French. Summary in English. Tentatively scheduled for
inclusion in Scientific Research on the Transcendental
Meditation Program: Collected Papers, Vol. 2. Rheinweiler,
West Germany: Maharishi European Research University
Press, (in press).
TM participants showed fewer mistakes on a simple visual reaction time task than control subjects.

A45   ; C. Haynes; H. Russel; and B. Reber. "Analysis
of Sleep in Altered States of Consciousness by Classical
Electro Encephalogram and Coherence Spectra." Electroencephalography and Clinical Neurophysiology, 43 (October
1977): 503. Tentatively scheduled for inclusion in Scientific Research on the Transcendental Meditation Program:
Collected Papers, Vol. 2. Rheinweiler, West Germany:
Maharishi European Research University Press, (in press).
Abstract of an experiment in which subjects practiced Transcendental Meditation. Dramatic changes occurred in the duration of different sleep stages.

A46   , and Maurice Sailhan. "EEG Analysis of Spontaneous
and Induced States of Consciousness." Revue d'Electroencéphalographie et de Neurophysiologie Clinique, 4 (1974):
445-453. In Scientific Research on the Transcendental
Meditation Program: Collected Papers, Vol. 1. Edited by

David W. Orme-Johnson and John T. Farrow. 2nd ed., Weggis, Switzerland: Maharishi European Research University Press, 1977, p. 165-172.
The state produced during the practice of TM was compared to sleep, relaxation, and arousal. It was found to be a unique state of wakefulness and less activation.

A47   _____, and _____. "Quantified EEG Spectral Analysis of Sleep and Transcendental Meditation." In Scientific Research on the Transcendental Meditation Program: Collected Papers, Vol. 1. Edited by David W. Orme-Johnson and John T. Farrow. 2nd ed., Weggis, Switzerland: Maharishi European Research University Press, 1977, p. 182-186.
Awareness seems to become independent of any mental state and can carry over into sleep states by long-term participants of Transcendental Meditation.

A48   Barmark, Susanne M., and Samuel C. Gaunitz. "Transcendental Meditation and Heterohypnosis as Altered States of Consciousness." International Journal of Clinical and Experimental Hypnosis, 27 (July 1979): 227-239.
Neither heterohypnosis nor Transcendental Meditation were identified as low-arousal states. Changes in the distribution of attention and in body image were discussed.

A49   Barnes, Michael. "Light from the East: A Typology of Meditation Techniques." Month (Second New Series), 14 (May 1981): 149-154.
Part one of two parts. Discusses Zen, Bhakti Yoga, and Vedanta meditation techniques.

A50   _____. "Light from the East: Aid from the East for Christian Prayer." Month (Second New Series), 14 (June 1981): 202-206.
Part two of a two part series. Discusses TM meditation. Considers how this and other techniques can be an aid to Christian prayer.

A51   Barwood, T.J.; J.A. Empson; S.G. Lister; and A.J. Tilley. "Auditory Evoked Potentials and Transcendental Meditation." Electroencephalography and Clinical Neurophysiology, 45 (November 1978): 671-673.
The primary hypothesis, that there should be some change consistent with the subjective accounts of non-attention to stimuli was rejected. There was no difference between the EEPs elicited during meditation and baseline periods. Also, there were AEP changes after meditation.

A52   Battelle, Phyllis. "TM vs. RR." Ladies' Home Journal, 93 (March 1976) 111, 172, 174, 176.

Reported by a person who has tried both Transcendental Meditation and Benson's Relaxation Response to ease tension.

A53   Bauhofer, U. "Physiological Cardiovascular Effects of the Transcendental Meditation Technique." Tentatively scheduled for inclusion in Scientific Research on the Transcendental Meditation Program: Collected Papers, Vol. 2. Rheinweiler, West Germany: Maharishi European Research University Press, (in press).
Meditation was shown to significantly decrease cardiac output, heartbeat, volume, and blood pressure amplitude. An increase in diastolic blood pressure was found.

A54   Beary, John F.; Herbert Benson; and Helen P. Klemchuk. "A Simple Psychophysiologic Technique Which Elicits the Hypometabolic Changes of the Relaxation Response." Psychosomatic Medicine, 36 (March 1974): 115-120.
Oxygen consumption, carbon dioxide production, and respiratory rate were shown to decrease during the practice of the Relaxation Response.

A55   Becker, David E., and David Shapiro. "Physiological Responses to Clicks During Zen, Yoga, and TM Meditation." Psychophysiology, 18 (November 1981): 694-699.
A replicated experiment that failed to indicate differing states of consciousness in Zen, Yoga, and TM meditators as suggested in earlier studies.

A55K   Beiman, Irving; Stephan A. Johnson; Antonio E. Puente; Henry W. Majestic; and Lewis E. Graham. "The Relationship of Client Characteristics to Outcome for Transcendental Meditation, Behavior Therapy, and Self-Relaxation." In Meditation: Classic and Contemporary Perspectives, edited by Deane H. Shapiro, Jr. and Roger N. Walsh. Hawthorne, N.Y.: Aldine Pub. Co., 1984.

A56   Bennett, James E., and John Trinder. "Hemispheric Laterality and Cognitive Style Associated with Transcendental Meditation." Psychophysiology, 14 (May 1977): 293-296. Tentatively scheduled for inclusion in Scientific Research on the Transcendental Meditation Program: Collected Papers, Vol. 2. Rheinweiler, West Germany: Maharishi European Research University Press, (in press). Also in Meditation: Classic and Contemporary Perspectives, edited by Deane H. Shapiro, Jr. and Roger N. Walsh. Hawthorne, N.Y.: Aldine Pub. Co., 1984.
Left and right hemispheres of the brain were tested for alpha activity during meditation, with analytical tasks, and with spatial tasks.

A57   Benson, Herbert. "Decreased Alcohol Intake Associated with

the Practice of Meditation: A Retrospective Investigation."
Annals of the New York Academy of Sciences, 233 (April
1974): 174-177.
Uncontrolled data showed there was a marked decrease in alcohol intake by TM practitioners. No data was available concerning the prevalence of alcoholism in these subjects.

A58   _____. "Systemic Hypertension and the Relaxation Response." New England Journal of Medicine, 296 (19 May
1977): 1152-1156. Critique by Mac Meuhlman and reply by
H. Benson, 297 (1 September 1977): 513.
The Relaxation Response appears to be a valuable adjunct to
pharmacologic therapy for hypertension. It may also be useful
as a preventive measure.

A59   _____. "Yoga for Drug Abuse." New England Journal of
Medicine, 281 (13 November 1969): 1133.
A letter reporting positive effects of Transcendental Meditation
in treating drug abuse.

A60   _____. "Your Innate Asset for Combating Stress." Harvard Business Review, 52 (July-August 1974): 49-60.
Compares methods for inducing relaxation. Outlines the author's Relaxation Response technique. Surveys the historical
background of meditation and Relaxation Response in religious
practices.

A61   _____, and Robert L. Allen. "How Much Stress Is Too
Much." Harvard Business Review, 58 (September-October
1980): 86-92.
Suggests what chief executives can do to balance both the
value and dangers of stress in their organizations. Includes
his Relaxation Response.

A62   _____; Patricia A. Arns; and John W. Hoffman. "The
Relaxation Response and Hypnosis." International Journal
of Clinical and Experimental Hypnosis, 29 (July 1981):
259-270.
Finds that a physiological state exists before experiencing
hypnotic phenomena that is comparable to the Relaxation Response. It is characterized, in part, by decreased heart
rate, respiratory rate, and blood pressure.

A63   _____; John F. Beary; and Mark P. Carol. "The Relaxation Response." Psychiatry, 37 (February 1974): 37-46.
Subjective and objective data supports the hypothesis that an
integrated central nervous system reaction underlies this
altered state of consciousness. Suggests possible health benefits.

A64   _____; Thomas Dryer; and Howard L. Hartley. "Decreased

$\dot{V}O_2$ Consumption During Exercise with Elicitation of the Relaxation Response." Journal of Human Stress, 4 (June 1978): 38-42.
Shows that oxygen consumption at a fixed work intensity was decreased with the Relaxation Response technique.

A65 _____; Martha M. Greenwood; and Helen Klemchuk. "The Relaxation Response: Psychophysiological Aspects and Clinical Applications." International Journal of Psychiatry in Medicine, 6 (1975): 87-98.
Describes the basic elements of techniques which elicit the Relaxation Response and discusses the results of clinical investigations which employ the Relaxation Response as a therapeutic intervention.

A66 _____, and Miriam Z. Klipper. "Relax Your Way to Better Health." Reader's Digest, 108 (April 1976): 132-134.
Condensed from the book, Relaxation Response. The technique is explained.

A67 _____; Jamie B. Kotch; Karen D. Crassweller; and Martha M. Greenwood. "Historical and Clinical Considerations of the Relaxation Response." American Scientist, 65 (July-August 1977): 441-445.
Because of the physiologic changes observed during the elicitation of the Relaxation Response, it may have significance in counteracting overactivity of the sympathetic nervous system.

A68 _____; John W. Lehmann; M.S. Malhotra; Ralph F. Goldman; Jeffrey Hopkins; and Mark D. Epstein. "Body Temperature Changes During the Practice of G Tum-mo Yoga." Nature, 295 (January 1982): 234-236.
Advanced Tibetan-Buddhist meditators exhibited the capacity to increase the temperature of their fingers and toes by as much as 8.3°C.

A69 _____; Bonnie P. Malvea; and John R. Graham. "Physiologic Correlates of Meditation and Their Clinical Effects in Headache: An Ongoing Investigation." Headache, 13 (1973): 23-24.
Many subjects claimed decrease or cessation of headache after starting regular practice of TM. Data is regarded as preliminary.

A69K _____; Bernard A. Rosner; Barbara R. Marzetta; and Helen M. Klemchuk. "Decreased Blood Pressure in Pharmacologically Treated Hypertensive Patients Who Regularly Elicited the Relaxation Response." In Meditation: Classic and Contemporary Perspectives, edited by Deane H. Shapiro, Jr. and Roger N. Walsh. Hawthorne, N.Y.: Aldine Pub. Co., 1984.

A70   ; Roger F. Steinert; Martha M. Greenwood; Helen M. Klemchuk; and Norman H. Peterson. "Continuous Measurement of O_2 Consumption and CO_2 Elimination During a Wakeful Hypometabolic State." Journal of Human Stress, 1 (March 1975): 37-44.
The study reports statistically significant decreases of O_2 consumption and CO_2 elimination for the entire twenty minutes of the meditation period.

A71   , and Robert Keith Wallace. "Decreased Blood Pressure in Hypertensive Subjects Who Practiced Meditation." In Scientific Research on the Transcendental Meditation Program: Collected Papers, Vol. 1. Edited by David W. Orme-Johnson and John T. Farrow. 2nd ed., Weggis, Switzerland: Maharishi European Research University Press, 1977, p. 266.
This study shows that elevated systemic arterial blood pressure may be reduced by practicing Transcendental Meditation.

A72   , and   . "Decreased Drug Abuse with Transcendental Meditation: A Study of 1,862 Subjects." In Drug Abuse: Proceedings of the International Conference on Drug Abuse, University of Michigan, 1970. Edited by Chris J.D. Zarafonetis. Philadelphia: Lea & Febiger, 1972, p. 369-378. Also in Scientific Research on the Transcendental Meditation Program: Collected Papers, Vol. 1. Edited by David W. Orme-Johnson and John T. Farrow. 2nd ed., Weggis, Switzerland: Maharishi European Research University Press, 1977, p. 498-505. Also in Meditation: Classic and Contemporary Perspectives, edited by Deane H. Shapiro, Jr. and Roger N. Walsh. Hawthorne, N.Y.: Aldine Pub. Co., 1984.
After starting Transcendental Meditation there was a significant decrease in the amount of drug use, a decrease or cessation in engaging in drug-selling activity, and changed attitudes in the direction of discouraging others from abusing drugs. Consumption of alcoholic beverages decreased and fewer cigarettes were smoked.

A73   , et al. "Treatment of Anxiety: A Comparison of the Usefulness of Self-Hypnosis and a Meditational Relaxation Technique: An Overview." Psychotherapy and Psychosomatics, 30 (1978): 229-242.
Both techniques were beneficial in the therapy of anxiety. There was improvement both on the psychiatric tests and in systolic blood pressure.

A74   Berg, Willem P. van den, and Bert Mulder. "Psychological Research on the Effects of the Transcendental Meditation Technique on a Number of Personality Variables." Gedrag: Tijdschrift voor Psychologie, 4 (1976): 206-218. In Scientific Research on the Transcendental Meditation Program: Collected Papers, Vol. 1. Edited by David W. Orme-Johnson and John T. Farrow. 2nd ed., Weggis, Switzerland: Maharishi European Research University Press, 1977, p. 428-433.

The results of this study indicate that the practice of the Transcendental Meditation technique allows development of a more harmonious personality in the direction of self-actualization.

A75 Bergfalk, Lynn, et al. "TM Opponents: Which Battle to Fight?" Christian Century, 94 (16 February 1977): 150-154.

Replies to E.R. Baltazar's article, "TM and the Religion-in-School Issue." [A40]

A76 Berker, Ennis. "Stability of Skin Resistance Responses One Week After Instruction in the Transcendental Meditation Technique." In Scientific Research on the Transcendental Meditation Program: Collected Papers, Vol. 1. Edited by David W. Orme-Johnson and John T. Farrow. 2nd ed. Weggis, Switzerland: Maharishi European Research University Press, 1977, p. 243-247.

After one week of practice of the TM technique there is evidence of increased stability in the autonomic nervous system.

A77 Berrettini, R.B. "The Effect of the Transcendental Meditation Program on Short-Term Recall Performance." Tentatively scheduled for inclusion in Scientific Research on the Transcendental Meditation Program: Collected Papers, Vol. 2. Rheinweiler, West Germany: Maharishi European Research University Press, (in press).

Short-term recall performance was facilitated by the practice of Transcendental Meditation.

A78 Besnard, Albert Marie. "The Influence of Asiatic Methods of Meditation." In The Prayer Life. Edited by Christian Duquoc and Claude Geffré. New York: Herder and Herder, 1972, p. 91.

Discusses the need of Christians to give prayer greater freedom and increased seriousness by the integration of the body into prayer, using Yoga and Zen.

A79 _____. "Meditation Starting from the Word." Studies in Formative Spirituality, 1 (November 1980): 419-447.

Discusses the following five forms of Christian meditation: Meditation of the Word, Meditation of the Presence, Meditation of the Divine Vibration, Meditation of the Breath, and Meditation of the Mysteries.

A80 Bevan, A.J.W. "Endocrine Changes in Transcendental Medi-

tation." Clinical and Experimental Pharmacology and Physiology, 7 (January-February 1980): 75-76.
Abstract of a study to examine short-term changes in some
serum hormone levels associated with stress and the practice
of TM.

A81   . "Endocrine Changes in Transcendental Meditation."
Proceedings of the Australian Society for Medical Research,
11 (1978): 56. Tentatively scheduled for inclusion in Scientific Research on the Transcendental Meditation Program:
Collected Papers, Vol. 2. Rheinweiler, West Germany:
Maharishi European Research University Press, (in press).
Reports that Transcendental Meditation was contrasted with
ordinary relaxation. Meditators showed significant reductions
in serum hormone, cortisol, and trüodothyronine.

A82   ; R.G. Symons; C.G. Berg; and M.L. Wellby. "Short-
Term Endocrine Changes in Transcendental Meditation."
Proceedings of the Endocrine Society of Australia, 22
(1979): 56. Tentatively scheduled for inclusion in Scien-
tific Research on the Transcendental Meditation Program:
Collected Papers, Vol. 2. Rheinweiler, West Germany:
Maharishi European Research University Press, (in press).
Experienced meditators showed a significant reduction in
growth hormone during the practice of the TM technique.

A83   ; P.M. Young; M.L. Welby; P. Nenandovic; and J.A.
Dickins. "Endocrine Changes in Relaxation Procedures."
Proceedings of the Endocrine Society of Australia, 19
(1976): 59. Tentatively scheduled for inclusion in Scien-
tific Research on the Transcendental Meditation Program:
Collected Papers, Vol. 2. Rheinweiler, West Germany:
Maharishi European Research University Press, (in press).
Meditators showed immediate and cumulative decreases in plasma
and urinary free cortisol.

A84   Beyer, Stephan V. "The Doctrine of Meditation in the Hinayana." In Buddhism: A Modern Perspective. Edited by
Charles S. Prebish. University Park: Pennsylvania State
University Press, 1975, p. 137-147.
Discusses Buddhist techniques in the practice of calm; including those involved in trance and those used to eliminate distractions. Also discusses the practice of insight meditation.

A85   . "The Doctrine of Meditation in the Mahayana." In
Buddhism: A Modern Perspective. Edited by Charles S.
Prebish. University Park: Pennsylvania State University
Press, 1975, p. 148-158.
Discusses the standard structure of meditation, visionary and
ecstatic techniques, and the development of new techniques of
spontaneity of the Mahayana religious and social phenomenon.

A86   Bhajanananda, Swami. "Hindu Upasana vis-à-vis Christian
            Meditation." Journal of Dharma, 2 (April 1977): 217-230.
        Comparative study of Hindu and Christian meditation focusing
        on three kinds of Hindu meditation: pratikopasana, namopa-
        sana, and ahamgrahopassana.

A87   Bibbee, Richard, and Julian B. Roebuck. "The Meditation
            Movement: Symbolic Interactionism and Synchronicity."
            Studies in Symbolic Interaction, 1 (1978): 205-240.
        Examines the effect that the meditation movement has and is
        likely to have on society in the United States.

A88   Birmingham, Frederic A. "There's No Use Talking to Me—I'm
            Meditating." Saturday Evening Post, 247 (March 1975).
        The author's personal account of taking a course in Tran-
        scendental Meditation.

A89   Black, Henry R. "Nonpharmacologic Therapy for Hyperten-
            sion." American Journal of Medicine, 66 (May 1979): 837-
            842.
        Suggests that clinicians consider nonpharmacologic therapy
        for all types of hypertensive patients as a valuable adjunct
        to pharmacologic treatment. Discusses relaxation techniques,
        biofeedback, exercise, weight reduction, salt restriction, and
        Transcendental Meditation.

A90   Blackwell, Barry; Saul Bloomfield; Peter Gartside; Ann Robin-
            son; Irwin Hanenson; Herbert Magenheim; Sanford Nidich;
            and Ronald Zigler. "Transcendental Meditation in Hyper-
            tension: Individual Response Patterns." Lancet, 1, no.
            7953 (1975): 223-226. Tentatively scheduled for inclusion in
            Scientific Research on the Transcendental Meditation Pro-
            gram: Collected Papers, Vol. 2. Rheinweiler, West Ger-
            many: Maharishi European Research University Press, (in
            press).
        Subjects showed psychological changes and reduced anxiety
        scores. Some subjects showed reductions in blood pressure.

A91   _____; Irwin B. Hanenson; Saul S. Bloomfield; Herbert G.
            Magenheim; Sanford I. Nidich; and Peter Gartside. "Ef-
            fects of Transcendental Meditation on Blood Pressure: A
            Controlled Pilot Experiment." Psychosomatic Medicine, 37
            (1975): 86. In Scientific Research on the Transcendental
            Meditation Program: Collected Papers, Vol. 1. Edited by
            David W. Orme-Johnson and John T. Farrow. 2nd ed.
            Weggis, Switzerland: Maharishi European Research Univer-
            sity Press, 1977, p. 267.
        Results suggest that Transcendental Meditation can decrease
        blood pressure and anxiety.

A92   Blasdell, Karen S. "The Effects of the Transcendental Medi-

tation Technique Upon a Complex Perceptual-Motor Task."
In Scientific Research on the Transcendental Meditation
Program: Collected Papers, Vol. 1. Edited by David W.
Orme-Johnson and John T. Farrow. 2nd ed. Weggis,
Switzerland: Maharishi European Research University Press,
1977, p. 322-325.
It was found that subjects practicing TM demonstrated greater
speed and accuracy of complex perceptual-motor tasks.

A93 Block, Bruce. "Transcendental Meditation as a Reciprocal Inhibitor in Psychotherapy." Journal of Contemporary Psychotherapy, 9 (Summer 1977): 78-82.
The advantages of TM over other anxiety inhibitors commonly
used is discussed in relation to psychotherapy.

A94 Bloomfield, Harold H. "Some Observations on the Uses of the
Transcendental Meditation Program in Psychiatry." In Scientific Research on the Transcendental Meditation Program:
Collected Papers, Vol. 1. Edited by David W. Orme-Johnson
and John T. Farrow. 2nd ed. Weggis, Switzerland:
Maharishi European Research University Press, 1977, p.
605-622.
The use of the TM program with in-patients of a psychiatric
hospital indicated it was a successful adjunct to therapy.

A95 Boals, Gordon F. "Toward a Cognitive Reconceptualization
of Meditation." Journal of Transpersonal Psychology, 10
(1978): 143-182.
The thesis of this review is that the conceptualization of meditation as a relaxation technique has outlived its usefulness.
A reconceptualization from a cognitive perspective is proposed,
and its implications for psychotherapy and future research are
explored.

A96 Bolen, Jean S. "Meditation and Psychotherapy in the Treatment of Cancer." Psychic, 4 (July 1973): 19-22.
In addition to being treated with cobalt radiation, patients
learn meditation and are involved in psychotherapy.

A97 Bolley, Alfons. "Recent Research into the Psychology of God-
Consciousness in Meditation." Lumen Vitae, 16 (June
1961): 223-232.
This article describes certain positive results from systematic
research on Christian meditation with five men and five wom-
en.

A97K Bono, Joseph, Jr. "Psychological Assessment of Transcendental Meditation." In Meditation: Classic and Contemporary Perspectives, edited by Deane H. Shapiro, Jr. and
Roger N. Walsh. Hawthorne, N.Y.: Aldine Pub. Co.,
1984.

A98   Borland, Candace, and Garland Landrith, III. "Improved
       Quality of City Life Through the Transcendental Meditation
       Program: Decreased Crime Rate." In Scientific Research
       on the Transcendental Meditation Program: Collected Pa-
       pers, Vol. 1. Edited by David W. Orme-Johnson and
       John T. Farrow. 2nd ed., Weggis, Switzerland: Maha-
       rishi European Research University Press, 1977, p. 639-
       648.
       Suggests that crime rate decreased in cities where one per-
       cent of their populations began practicing the TM technique.

A99   Boswell, Philip C., and Edward J. Murray. "Effects of
       Meditation on Psychological and Physiological Measures of
       Anxiety." Journal of Consulting and Clinical Psychology,
       47 (June 1979): 606-607.
       There was no evidence that meditation reduced anxiety.

A100   Boudreau, Léonce. "Transcendental Meditation and Yoga as
       Reciprocal Inhibitors." Journal of Behavior Therapy and
       Experimental Psychiatry, 3 (June 1972): 97-98.
       In two cases, one of claustrophobia, the other of profuse
       perspiration, Transcendental Meditation and yoga were thera-
       peutically successful.

A101   Bourne, Peter G. "Non-Pharmacological Approaches to the
       Treatment of Drug Abuse." American Journal of Chinese
       Medicine, 3 (July 1975): 235-244.
       Acupuncture, Transcendental Meditation, electrosleep, bio-
       feedback and hypnotism are methods discussed to help some
       addicts.

A102   Bowker, John. "Worlds of Faith: A Feeling of Peace--Prayer
       and Meditation." Listener, 109 (10 February 1983): 13-14.
       Discusses what people of various faiths do when they pray
       or meditate.

A103   Bradley, Brian W., and Thomas R. McCanne. "Autonomic
       Responses to Stress: The Effects of Progressive Relaxa-
       tion, the Relaxation Response, and Expectancy of Relief."
       Biofeedback and Self-Regulation, 6 (June 1981): 235-251.
       Examination of positive and negative expectations toward
       progressive relaxation techniques. Showed the heart rate
       is lowered for progressive relaxation, and that although ex-
       pectancy may affect cardiovascular response to stress, medi-
       tation appears not to.

A104   Bradshaw, David. "Yoga." Teaching Adults, 9 (April 1975):
       4-6.
       Describes concentrative meditation, self-expressive or open-
       ing meditation, and insight meditation techniques.

A105   Bräutigam, Eva. "Effects of the Transcendental Meditation
        Program on Drug Abusers: A Prospective Study." In
        Scientific Research on the Transcendental Meditation Pro-
        gram: Collected Papers, Vol. 1. Edited by David W.
        Orme-Johnson and John T. Farrow. 2nd ed., Weggis,
        Switzerland: Maharishi European Research University Press,
        1977, p. 506-514.
        The use of hashish by subjects practicing TM decreased.
        Meditators showed increased self-acceptance and psychologi-
        cal stability.

A106   Bright, Deborah; Victor A. Buccola; William J. Stone; and
        Jack V. Toohey. "What School Physicians, Nurses and
        Health Educators Should Know About Transcendental
        Meditation." Journal of School Health, 43 (March 1973):
        192-194.
        Suggests that TM claims deserve consideration as positive
        implications for education.

A107   Brofman, Martin. "Meditation Took Me Past Cancer." Pre-
        vention, 32 (March 1980): p. 150+
        A personal account of a cancer patient using meditation and
        eventual healing.

A108   Brown, Clinton C.; R. Fischer; A.M.I. Wagman; N. Horrom;
        and P. Marks. "EEG in Meditation and Therapeutic Touch
        Healing." Journal of Altered States of Consciousness, 3
        (1977): 169-180.
        Five subjects who actively practice Therapeutic Touch Heal-
        ing were physiologically monitored during conditions of rest--
        eyes closed, meditation, mental arithmetic, and Therapeutic
        Touch Healing. EEG measurements are given.

A109   Brown, Daniel P. "A Model for the Levels of Concentrative
        Meditation." International Journal of Clinical and Experi-
        mental Hypnosis, 25 (October 1977): 236-273. Also in
        Meditation: Classic and Contemporary Perspectives, edited
        by Deane H. Shapiro, Jr. and Roger N. Walsh. Haw-
        thorne, N.Y.: Aldine Pub. Co., 1984.
        Certain similarities are noted between Yogic texts and the
        constructivist theories of perception, information processing,
        and affect. The overall direction of change in concentrative
        meditation follows as invarient sequence of levels of conscious-
        ness.

A109K   _____, and Jack Engler. "A Rorschach Study of the Stages
        of Mindfulness Meditation." In Meditation: Classic and
        Contemporary Perspectives, edited by Deane H. Shapiro,
        Jr. and Roger N. Walsh. Hawthorne, N.Y.: Aldine Pub.
        Co., 1984.

A110 _____, and _____. "The Stages of Mindfulness Meditation: A Validation Study." Journal of Transpersonal
Psychology, 12 (1980): 143-192.
The purpose of this study has been to illustrate an approach
to the empirical validation of accounts and reports of meditation attainments using the Rorschach test as a measure of
cognitive and perceptual change.

A111 Brown, Reeve. "Karme-Choling." Blair and Ketchum's Coun-
try Journal, 4 (December 1977): p. 51+
Describes activities at Karme-Choling, a Tibetan Buddhist
Meditation Center in Barnet, Vermont.

A112 Buchanan, Franklin R. "Living the Life of a Zen Monk."
Social Education, 43 (November-December 1979): 522-526.
The author shares his direct experiences with Zen priests
and temples of both the Soto and Rinzai sects. Meditation
periods are described in detail.

A113 Buckler, W. "Transcendental Meditation." Canadian Medical
Association Journal, 115 (1976): 607.
A letter suggesting that TM can be effective in the treatment
of muscle tension pain attributed to arthritis, disc degenera-
tion, or entrapment of a nerve or a spinal root.

A114 Bujatti, M., and P. Riederer. "Serotonin, Noradrenaline,
Dopamine Metabolites in Transcendental Meditation-Technique." Journal of Neural Transmission, 39 (1976): 257-
267. Tentatively scheduled for inclusion in Scientific
Research on the Transcendental Meditation Program:
Collected Papers, Vol. 2. Rheinweiler, West Germany:
Maharishi European Research University Press, (in press).
A comparison of biogenic amine metabolites in subjects practicing Transcendental Meditation showed higher serotonin
levels and lower levels of noradrenaline, indicating orderly
brain activity and lower physiological arousal.

A115 Burns, Douglas, and Ron J. Ohayv. "Psychological Changes
in Meditating Western Monks in Thailand." Journal of
Transpersonal Psychology, 12 (1980): 11-24.
An interview with Dr. Douglas Burns on Buddhism and meditation as a form of psychological self-therapy. Discusses
changes in personality.

A116 Burns, John E. "Transcendental Meditation in the Boardroom." Industrial Management (Des Plaines), 17 (April
1975): 13-15.
Discusses the usefulness of TM in the business community.

A117 Busby, Keith, and Joseph DeKoninck. "Short-Term Effects
of Strategies for Self Regulation on Personality Dimensions

and Dream Content." Perceptual and Motor Skills, 50
(1980): 751-765.
Findings suggest there are no major differences between the
effectiveness of Transcendental Meditation and relaxation
techniques in producing psychological change.

A118   Buttrick, George A., et al. "Disharmony About TM."
        Christian Century, 93 (17 March 1976): 259-262.
        Replies to articles on Transcendental Meditation in the De-
        cember 10, 1975 issue of Christian Century [A204, A275].

A119   Cairns, Grace E. "The Philosophy and Psychology of the
        Oriental Mandala." Philosophy East and West, 11 (Janu-
        ary 1962): 219-230.
        Examines the symbolic form of the mandala as a function for
        the reintegration of the aspirant and his unification with the
        total cosmic reality.

A120   Calandra, Alexander. "Science and Meditation." Journal of
        College Science Teaching, 5 (May 1976): 301-302.
        Discusses Benson's Relaxation Response and its modification,
        the Harvard Meditation Technique, in contrast with TM.

A121   Calian, Carnegie Samuel. "Hesychasm and Transcendental
        Meditation: Sources for Contemporary Theology?" East-
        ern Churches Review, 10 (1978): 126-140.
        The author finds no need for Transcendental Meditation since
        its benefits are available through hesychasm and Christian
        meditation in other forms.

A122   Campbell, Colin. "The Facts on Transcendental Meditation:
        Part 1. Transcendence Is as American as Ralph Waldo
        Emerson." Psychology Today, 7 (April 1974): 37-38.
        Part 1 of 3 parts. A look at Maharishi Mahesh Yogi and his
        TM movement. Discusses its history, scope and striking re-
        semblance to the 19th century New England Transcendental-
        ists.

A123   Candelent, Thomas, and Gillian Candelent. "Teaching Tran-
        scendental Meditation in a Psychiatric Setting." Hospital
        and Community Psychiatry, 26 (March 1975): 156-159.
        Tentatively scheduled for inclusion in Scientific Research
        on the Transcendental Meditation Program: Collected Pa-
        pers, Vol. 2. Rheinweiler, West Germany: Maharishi
        European Research University Press, (in press).
        Meditation lowered anxiety, decreased insomnia, and lessened
        over-active or impulsive behavior of psychiatric patients.

A124   Carmody, James. "Meditation." Sponsa Regis, 33 (January
        1962): 127-135.
        On the value of mental prayer and some difficulties involved.

A125 Carpenter, J. Tyler. "Meditation, Esoteric Traditions: Contributions to Psychotherapy." _American Journal of Psychotherapy_, 31 (July 1977): 394-404.
A brief introduction to several different Eastern systems of philosophy and therapy. Suggests that meditative exercises produce insight into repetitive, self-defeating patterns of behavior, desensitization of painful thoughts, and the conditioning of the central nervous system.

A126 Carr-Kaffashan, Lucille, and Robert L. Woolfolk. "Active and Placebo Effects in Treatment of Moderate and Severe Insomnia." _Journal of Consulting and Clinical Psychology_, 47 (December 1979): 1072-1080.
This study examines the efficacy of relaxation training and a highly credible placebo in the treatment of both severe and moderate sleep onset insomnia.

A127 Carrington, Patricia; Gilbeart H. Collings, Jr.; Herbert Benson; Harry Robinson; Loring W. Wood; Paul M. Lehrer; Robert L. Woolfolk; and Jean W. Cole. "The Use of Meditation Relaxation Techniques for the Management of Stress in a Working Population." _Journal of Occupational Medicine_, 22 (April 1980): 221-231.
The study compared relaxation and control conditions as part of a program of stress-reduction for employees of the New York Telephone Co. Clinically standardized meditation, respiratory one method meditation, and progressive relaxation were compared. The conclusion is that meditation has considerable value for stress-management programs in organizational settings.

A128 _____, and Harmon S. Ephron. "Meditation and Psychoanalysis." _Journal of the American Academy of Psychoanalysis_, 3 (January 1975): 43-57.
Considers the effects of TM on personality, as an adjunct to psychoanalysis for the patient, and value to the psychoanalyst who learns to meditate.

A129 Carsello, Carmen J., and James W. Creaser. "Does Transcendental Meditation Training Affect Grades." _Journal of Applied Psychology_, 63 (October 1978): 644-645.
No effect upon grades was demonstrated for TM training.

A130 Cassel, Russel N. "Basic Fundamentals of Mind Control and Transcendental Meditation." _Psychology_, 11 (May 1974): 26-33.
Defines fourteen stages for developing competencies in the art of mind control and Transcendental Meditation.

A131 _____. "Fostering Transcendental Meditation Using Bio-Feedback Eliminates Hoax and Restores Creditability to

Art." Psychology, 13 (May 1976): 58-64.
Suggests that TM must be combined with biofeedback to be
effective.

A132   Castillo, J.A. "Sociological Studies of the TM and TM-Sidhi
        Program in the Philippines." Tentatively scheduled for in-
        clusion in Scientific Research on the Transcendental Medi-
        tation Program: Collected Papers, Vol. 2. Rheinweiler,
        West Germany: Maharishi European Research University
        Press, (in press).
A paper presented to the International Congress on Research
on Higher States of Consciousness, Bangkok, Thailand, January, 1980. Reports that crime rate in Manila decreased after
the TM-Sidhi program began.

A133   Cauthen, Nelson R., and Carole A. Prymak. "Meditation
        Versus Relaxation: An Examination of the Physiological
        Effects of Relaxation Training and of Different Levels of
        Experience with Transcendental Meditation." Journal of
        Consulting and Clinical Psychology, 45 (June 1977): 496-
        497.
The two more experienced groups of meditators showed decreases in heart rate during meditation while the relaxation
group showed decreases after relaxing. There were no
significant changes in skin conductance or respiration.

A134   Chailak, Seumor D. "Sociological Effects of the TM-Sidhi Pro-
        gram in Thailand." Tentatively scheduled for inclusion in
        Scientific Research on the Transcendental Meditation Pro-
        gram: Collected Papers, Vol. 2. Rheinweiler, West Ger-
        many: Maharishi European Research University Press,
        (in press).
A paper presented at the International Congress on Research
on Higher States of Consciousness, Bangkok, Thailand, January, 1980. Crime rate and accident rates decreased in Bangkok after the TM-Sidhi program began.

A135   Chang, Suk C. "The Psychology of Consciousness." Amer-
        ican Journal of Psychotherapy, 32 (January 1978): 105-
        116.
Suggests the study of meditation as a viable approach to the
exploration of the meaning of consciousness.

A136   Chen, C.M. "Comment on Samatha, Samapatti, and Dhyana
        in Ch'an." Philosophy East and West, 16 (January-April
        1966): 84-89.
Discusses the three stages of meditation in which there is
stopping or silencing, attaining calmness, and unperturbed
abstraction.

A137   Chenard, J.R. "A Controlled Study of the Influences of

Transcendental Meditation on a Specific Value of the H-
Reflex (Hoffmann) Recruitment Curve and the Surface
EMG." Tentatively scheduled for inclusion in Scientific
Research on the Transcendental Meditation Program: Col-
lected Papers, Vol. 2. Rheinweiler, West Germany:
Maharishi European Research University Press, (in press).
A paper presented to the Association Canadienne Française
pour l'Advancement des Sciences, University of Québec,
Canada, 1979. TM practitioners showed a significant de-
crease in the electromypographic activity of the frontalis
muscle and in the amplitude of the Hoffmann reflex.

A138   Chethimattam, John B. "Meditation: A Discriminating Real-
            ization." Journal of Dharma, 2 (April 1977): 164-172.
        Analyzes the meditation involved in the Middle Path of the
        Buddha and the Advaita Vedanta technique of Samkara.

A139   Ch'ien, Anne. "Meditation and Rituals in Neo-Confucion
            Tradition." Journal of Dharma, 2 (April 1977): 173-188.
        The complementary dimensions of meditation and ritual in a
        Chinese setting are studied focusing on self-cultivation.

A140   Childs, John P. "The Use of the Transcendental Meditation
            Program as a Therapy with Juvenile Offenders." In
            Scientific Research on the Transcendental Meditation Pro-
            gram: Collected Papers, Vol. 1. Edited by David W.
            Orme-Johnson and John T. Farrow. 2nd ed., Weggis,
            Switzerland: Maharishi European Research University
            Press, 1977, p. 577-584.
        Reduced anxiety, increased self-regard, and improved be-
        havior were shown by juvenile offenders practicing TM.
        [Cf. D40]

A141   Christine, Shirley. "Ma Bell Gets De-Stressed." New Real-
            ities, 3 (February 1980): 23.
        Reports on Patricia Carrington's project to help employees
        at the New York Telephone Co. reduce stress.

A142   Clark, Matt, and Sylvester Monroe. "Meditation Therapy:
            Treatment of High Blood Pressure." Newsweek, 85 (28
            April 1975): 51.
        Reports on Dr. Herbert Benson's work using meditation to
        reduce high blood pressure.

A143   Clarke, W. Norris. "Be Still and Contemplate." New Catho-
            lic World, 215 (November 1972): 246-248+
        Suggests the technique of quiet sitting, asking yourself
        "Who am I?" or turning toward God in silence with deep
        openness and receptivity of love and trust.

A144   Clasper, P.D. "Meditation and Prayer in Theological Educa-

tion in South-East Asia." International Review of Missions, 51 (July 1962): 291-302.
Gives suggestions for Christian meditation and describes the effects of meditation in areas of Christian life.

A145   Clements, Geoffrey, and Stephen L. Milstein. "Auditory Thresholds in Advanced Participants in the Transcendental Meditation Program." In Scientific Research on the Transcendental Meditation Program: Collected Papers, Vol. 1. Edited by David W. Orme-Johnson and John T. Farrow. 2nd ed., Weggis, Switzerland: Maharishi European Research University Press, 1977, p. 719-722.
Unusually sensitive hearing thresholds were found in advanced participants in the TM program.

A146   Clutterback, David. "How I Learned to Stop Worrying and Love the Job." International Management, 28 (August 1973): 27-29.
Example of Transcendental Meditation to help managers cope with stress at work.

A147   Cognet, Louis. "Meditation." Cistercian Studies, 8 (1973): 243-252.
Discusses the value of Christian meditation in bringing the soul nearer to God.

A148   Cohen, Irving J. "Meditating on Stress." Inc., 4 (July 1982): 113-114.
Example of Benson's relaxation method used at the New York Telephone Co.

A149   Collier, Roy W. "The Effect of the Transcendental Meditation Program Upon University Academic Attainment." In Scientific Research on the Transcendental Meditation Program: Collected Papers, Vol. 1. Edited by David W. Orme-Johnson and John T. Farrow. 2nd ed., Weggis, Switzerland: Maharishi European Research University Press, 1977, p. 393-395.
Improved academic performance of students in the TM program was demonstrated.

A150   Collons, Rodger, and James S. Bingay. "Meditation and Problem Solving." Best's Review (Life/Health Ed.), 82 (February 1982): 106, 108.
Reports on H.S. Kindler's research. Shows that a meditation-relaxation technique reduces anxiety, stress, and weariness. It also improves problem-solving ability.

A151   Cooper, Michael J., and Maurice M. Aygen. "Effect of Meditation on Serum Cholesterol and Blood Pressure." Journal of the Israel Medical Association, 95 (1978): 1-2. Tentatively scheduled for inclusion in <u>Scientific Research on the</u> <u>Transcendental Meditation Program: Collected Papers,</u> <u>Vol. 2.</u> Rheinweiler, West Germany: Maharishi European Research University Press, (in press).

Blood pressure and serum cholesterol levels were significantly lowered after subjects with slightly elevated blood pressure started the TM technique.

A152 _____, and _____. "A Relaxation Technique in the Management of Hypercholesterolemia." <u>Journal of Human</u> <u>Stress</u>, 5 (December 1979): 24-27. Tentatively scheduled for inclusion in <u>Scientific Research on the Transcendental</u> <u>Meditation Program: Collected Papers, Vol. 2.</u> Rhein- weiler, West Germany: Maharishi European Research Uni- versity Press, (in press).

This investigation indicates that Transcendental Meditation can significantly reduce levels of serum cholesterol in highly motivated hypercholesterolemic individuals.

A153 Corby, James C.; Walton T. Roth; Vincent P. Zarcone; and Bert S. Kopell. "Psychophysiological Correlates of the Practice of Tantric Yoga Meditation." <u>Archives of General</u> <u>Psychiatry</u>, 35 (May 1978): 571-577. Critique by B.D. Elson and reply by J.C. Corby, 36 (1979): 605-606. Also in <u>Meditation: Classic and Contemporary Perspectives</u>, edited by Deane H. Shapiro, Jr. and Roger N. Walsh. Hawthorne, N.Y.: Aldine Pub. Co., 1984.

Unlike previous studies, proficient meditators demonstrated increased autonomic activation during meditation while unex- perienced meditators demonstrated autonomic relaxation. During meditation, proficient meditators increased alpha and theta power, minimal evidence of EEG-defined sleep, and de- creased autonomic orienting to external stimulation. An epi- sode of the Yogic state of intense concentration was ob- served.

A154 Corcoran, Kevin J. "Experiential Empathy: A Theory of a Felt-Level Experience." <u>Journal of Humanistic Psychology</u>, 21 (Winter 1981): 29-38.

A new theoretical view of experiential empathy is presented. Support for the theory is found in the research on medita- tion.

A155 Corey, Paul W. "Airway Conductance and Oxygen Consump- tion Changes Associated with Practice of the Transcen- dental Meditation Technique." In <u>Scientific Research on</u> <u>the Transcendental Meditation Program: Collected Papers,</u> <u>Vol. 1.</u> Edited by David W. Orme-Johnson and John T. Farrow. 2nd ed., Weggis, Switzerland: Maharishi Euro- pean Research University Press, 1977, p. 94-107.

Airway conductance increased during and after the practice

of TM. There was also a decrease in heart rate and oxygen consumption during meditation.

A156   Corlin, Claes. "The Lama and the Jumbo-Jet: Report on a
        Tibetan Meditation-Group in Switzerland." Ethos, 42
        (1977): 3-4, 149-155.
        Report on the visit of Lama Duchung Rinpoche to a Tibetan
        meditation group in Switzerland.

A157   Costa, Eugenio, and Kevin Donovan. "Music and Meditation."
        Music and Liturgy, 1 (Summer 1975): 170-174.
        Explores the relationship between Christian meditation and
        music.

A158   Cousins, Ewert. "Franciscan Meditation: The Mind's Journey
        Into God." Journal of Dharma, 2 (April 1977): 137-151.
        Concentrates on the writings of Bonaventure.

A159   Cousins, L.S. "Buddhist Jhana: Its Nature and Attainment
        According to the Pali Sources." Religion, 3 (Autumn
        1973): 115-131.
        Meditation according to the Theravada school is explained.

A160   Cowger, Ernest L., and Paul E. Torrance. "Further Exam-
        ination of the Quality of Changes in Creative Functioning
        Resulting from Meditation (Zazen) Training." Creative
        Child and Adult Quarterly, 7 (Winter 1982): 211-217.
        Meditators experienced statistically significant gains in many
        creative functioning measures. Changes of the meditation
        group exceeded those of the relaxation group.

A161   Cox, Harvey. "Pool of Narcissus: The Psychologizing of
        Meditation." Cross Currents, 27 (Spring 1977): 16-28.
        Argues that as it becomes psychologized, meditation loses its
        capacity to move us away from our narcissism.

A162   Credidio, Steven G. "Comparative Effectiveness of Patterned
        Biofeedback Versus Meditation Training on EMG and Skin
        Temperature Changes." Behaviour Research and Therapy,
        20 (1982): 233-241.
        The most positive subjective reports came from subjects in the
        meditation group. Suggests that meditation offers an alter-
        native as a relaxation procedure.

A163   Cummins, Norbert. "Training of the Student in the Life of
        Prayer." Doctrine and Life, 12 (July 1962): 354-364.
        Discusses the importance of instructing ecclesiastical students
        in meditation and affective prayer.

A164   Cunningham, Monte, and Walter Koch. "The Transcendental
        Meditation Program and Rehabilitation: A Pilot Project at

the Federal Correctional Institution at Lompoc, California."
In Scientific Research on the Transcendental Meditation
Program: Collected Papers, Vol. 1. Edited by David W.
Orme-Johnson and John T. Farrow. 2nd ed. Weggis,
Switzerland: Maharishi European Research University
Press, 1977, p. 562-568.
A reduction in anxiety and an increase in positive behavior
were shown by prisoners practicing TM.

A165   Curtis, William D., and Harold W. Wessberg. "A Comparison
of Heart Rate, Respiration, and Galvanic Skin Response
Among Meditators, Relaxers, and Controls." Journal of
Altered States of Consciousness, 2 (1975-76): 319-324.
Examination of meditators, deep muscle relaxers, and control
groups demonstrated no statistical differences in heart rate,
respiration, or galvanic skin response. Subjectively, meditators were more positive of the stress reaction.

A166   Cuthbert, Bruce; Jean Kristeller; Robert Simons; Robert
Hodes; and Peter J. Lang. "Strategies of Arousal Control: Biofeedback, Meditation, and Motivation." Journal
of Experimental Psychology: General, 110 (December
1981): 518-546.
A series of four experiments assessed the effects of instructions to lower heart rate and reduce general arousal.

A167   Dalal, Abdulhusein S., and Theodore X. Barber. "Yoga,
'Yogic Feats,' and Hypnosis in the Light of Empirical Research." American Journal of Clinical Hypnosis, 11
(January 1969): 155-166.
A literature review suggesting that yogic samadhi and hypnotic trance cannot be viewed as scientific concepts and that
observable phenomena are not mysterious, but can be readily
explained.

A168   Daniels, D. "Comparison of the Transcendental Meditation
Technique to Various Relaxation Procedures." Tentatively
scheduled for inclusion in Scientific Research on the
Transcendental Meditation Program: Collected Papers,
Vol. 2. Rheinweiler, West Germany: Maharishi European
Research University Press, (in press).
Greater autonomic stability and greater ability to process in-
formation at higher speed were shown by subjects practicing
the TM technique than controls and practitioners of other re-
laxation procedures.

A169   Daniels, Lloyd K. "The Treatment of Psychophysiological
Disorders and Severe Anxiety by Behavior Therapy,
Hypnosis and Transcendental Meditation." American
Journal of Clinical Hypnosis, 17 (April 1975): 267-270.
A case history in which TM was part of the therapy to re-
duce acute stress.

A170   Dardes, J.A. "Psychological Changes Associated with the Practice of Transcendental Meditation and Personality Characteristics of Self-Selected Meditators." Tentatively scheduled for inclusion in Scientific Research on the Transcendental Meditation Program: Collected Papers, Vol. 2. Rheinweiler, West Germany: Maharishi European Research University Press, (in press).
College students practicing the TM technique reported an improvement in physical and mental health, and a more integrated and creative personality than non-meditators.

A171   Dash, P., and C.N. Alexander. "Electrophysiological Characteristics During Transcendental Meditation and Napping." Tentatively scheduled for inclusion in Scientific Research on the Transcendental Meditation Program: Collected Papers, Vol. 2. Rheinweiler, West Germany: Maharishi European Research University Press, (in press).
EEG characteristics showed that sleep is distinguishable from Transcendental Meditation.

A172   Datta, G.P., and R.K. Upadhyay. "Transcendental Meditation." Indian Journal of Psychiatric Social Work, 6 (July 1977): 18-27.
Presents the historical development of Transcendental Meditation and the prospects of it having a longer appeal than other non-professional psychotherapies.

A173   Davidson, Julian M. "The Physiology of Meditation and Mystical States of Consciousness." Perspectives in Biology and Medicine, 19 (Spring 1976): 345-379. Also in Meditation: Classic and Contemporary Perspectives, edited by Deane H. Shapiro, Jr. and Roger N. Walsh. Hawthorne, N.Y.: Aldine Pub. Co., 1984.
A literature review of studies directed at physiological events during meditation.

A174   Davidson, Richard J., and Daniel J. Goleman. "The Role of Attention in Meditation and Hypnosis: A Psychobiological Perspective on Transformations of Consciousness." International Journal of Clinical and Experimental Hypnosis, 25 (October 1977): 291-308. Also in Meditation: Classic and Contemporary Perspectives, edited by Deane H. Shapiro, Jr. and Roger N. Walsh. Hawthorne, N.Y.: Aldine Pub. Co., 1984.
A temporal-developmental scheme was outlined and employed to organize data on changes in consciousness arising from the practice of meditation and the induction of hypnosis.

A175   _____; _____; and Gary E. Schwartz. "Attentional and Affective Concomitants of Meditation: A Cross-Sectional Study." Journal of Abnormal Psychology, 85 (April 1976):

235-238. Also in Meditation: Classic and Contemporary Perspectives, edited by Deane H. Shapiro, Jr. and Roger N. Walsh. Hawthorne, N.Y.: Aldine Pub. Co., 1984. The data from this study reveal reliable increases in measures of attentional absorption in conjunction with a reliable decrement in trait anxiety across groups as a function of length of time meditating.

A175K _____, and Gary E. Schwartz. "Matching Relaxation Therapies to Types of Anxiety: A Patterning Approach." In Meditation: Classic and Contemporary Perspectives, edited by Deane H. Shapiro, Jr. and Roger N. Walsh. Hawthorne, N.Y.: Aldine Pub. Co., 1984.

A176 Davies, John. "The Transcendental Meditation Program and Progressive Relaxation: Comparative Effects on Trait Anxiety and Self-Actualization." In Scientific Research on the Transcendental Meditation Program: Collected Papers, Vol. 1. Edited by David W. Orme-Johnson and John T. Farrow. 2nd ed., Weggis, Switzerland: Maharishi European Research University Press, 1977, p. 449-452.
Those practicing the TM technique showed more comprehensive positive changes.

A177 Davies, Stevan L.; Jeffrey A. Goldstein; and Zalman M. Schachter. "The Kabbalah of the Nations: Anglicization of Jewish Kabbalah." Studia Mystica, 3 (Fall 1980): 34-47.
A literature review of popular books to help the reader practice Kabbalistic meditation.

A178 Day, Judith. "Buddhist Meditation and Christian Contemplative Prayer: A Comparison." Contemplative Review, 14 (Spring 1981): 28-33.
Discusses the commonality of Buddhist meditation in the Theravada tradition with Christian contemplative prayer and their lack of conflict.

A179 Day, Richard C., and Samia N. Sadek. "The Effect of Benson's Relaxation Response on the Anxiety Levels of Lebanese Children Under Stress." Journal of Experimental Child Psychology, 34 (October 1982): 350-356.
Results indicated that the subjects in the treatment group scored lower on general anxiety scale and a test anxiety scale than did the control group.

A180 Deatherage, Gary. "The Clinical Use of 'Mindfulness' Meditation Techniques in Short-Term Psychotherapy." Journal of Transpersonal Psychology, 7 (1975): 133-143.

The techniques described here are adopted from the Buddhist Satipatthana or "mindfulness meditation." The client is instructed to observe and concentrate on his own breathing while noting and labeling thought interruptions. Five cases are presented.

A181   DeGrâce, Gaston. "Effects of Meditation on Personality and Values." Journal of Clinical Psychology, 32 (October 1976): 809-813.
The study demonstrated a decrease in the tendency to dominate and the search of social status after five months of Zen meditation.

A182   Deikman, Arthur J. "Experimental Meditation." Journal of Nervous and Mental Diseases, 136 (April 1966): 329-343.
The hypothesis is supported that through contemplative meditation de-automatization occurs and permits a different perceptual and cognitive experience.

A183   _____. "Implication of Experimentally Induced Contemplative Meditation." Journal of Nervous and Mental Diseases, 142 (February 1966): 101-116.
Reports some results of a phenomenological investigation of meditation phenomena and attempts to explain the data and relate it to a broader context.

A183K   _____. "The State-of-the-Art of Meditation." In Meditation: Classic and Contemporary Perspectives, edited by Deane H. Shapiro, Jr. and Roger N. Walsh. Hawthorne, N.Y.: Aldine Pub. Co., 1984.

A184   Deliz, Antonio J. "Meditation, Protein, Diet, and Mega-Vitamins in Treatment of a Progressive, Iatrogenic Cardiac and Psychotic Condition." Journal of Orthomolecular Psychiatry, 6 (1977): 44-49.
A doctor presents his own case history focusing on an orthomolecular program.

A185   Delmonte, M.M. "Expectation and Meditation." Psychological Reports, 49 (December 1981): 699-709.
Subjects were tested to ascertain their present perceived-selves and their expectations of Transcendental Meditation just before introductory talks on meditation, just after these talks, and seven months later on follow-up.

A186   _____. "Personality Characteristics and Regularity of Meditation." Psychological Reports, 46 (June 1980): 703-712.
Personality scores taken prior to Transcendental Meditation were used to predict responses to meditation.

A187 _____. "Pilot Study of Conditioned Relaxation During
Stimulation Meditation." Psychological Reports, 45 (August 1979): 169-170.
Significantly lower frontalis EMG occurred while subjects repeated a mantra, although the actual difference was too small
to be of clinical value.

A188 _____. "Suggestibility and Meditation." Psychological
Reports, 48 (June 1981): 727-737.
Similarities between meditation and hypnosis are discussed.

A189 _____, and M. Braidwood. "Treatment of Retarded Ejaculation with Psychotherapy and Meditative Relaxation: A
Case Report." Psychological Reports, 47 (August 1980):
8-10.
The treatment was successful and led to conception.

A190 DeVol, Thomas I. "Ecstatic Pentecostal Prayer and Meditation." Journal of Religion and Health, 13 (October 1974):
285-288.
Recommends the Pentecostal experience of prayer and meditation that induces glossolalia, i.e., speaking in other
tongues.

A191 Dhanaraj, V. Hubert. "Influence of Transcendental Meditation
on Drug Abuse." Tentatively scheduled for inclusion in
Scientific Research on the Transcendental Meditation Program: Collected Papers, Vol. 2. Rheinweiler, West Germany: Maharishi European Research University Press,
(in press).
Subjects practicing the TM technique decreased drug usage.

A192 _____, and Mohan Singh. "Reduction in Metabolic Rate
During the Practice of the Transcendental Meditation
Technique." In Scientific Research on the Transcendental
Meditation Program: Collected Papers, Vol. 1. Edited by
David W. Orme-Johnson and John T. Farrow. 2nd ed.
Weggis, Switzerland: Maharishi European Research Uni-
versity Press, 1977, p. 137-139.
During the TM technique a significantly larger drop in meta-
bolic rate occurred than during simple rest. Based on Ph.D.
thesis by the first author, Dept. of Physical Education, Uni-
versity of Alberta, Edmonton, Alberta, Canada.

A193 Dhavamony, Mariasusai. "Transcendental Meditation." Clergy
Review, 63 (November 1978): 418-425.
Explains how TM can be made of use in religious meditation
as a force and means of fostering and increasing the life of
Christian faith and morality.

A194 _____. "Vedantic Philosophy of Religion." International

Philosophical Quarterly, 21 (March 1981): 51-69.
Includes a discussion of Ramanuja's and Sankara's philosophies of religion relative to meditation.

A195   Dick, Leah Dell, and Robert E. Ragland. "A Study of the Transcendental Meditation Program in the Service of Counseling." In _Scientific Research on the Transcendental Meditation Program: Collected Papers_, Vol. 1. Edited by David W. Orme-Johnson and John T. Farrow. 2nd ed., Weggis, Switzerland: Maharishi European Research University Press, 1977, p. 600-604.
The general conclusion was that the Transcendental Meditation program seemed to foster self-directedness for counselees.

A196   DiGiusto, Eros L., and Nigel W. Bond. "Imagery and the Autonomic Nervous System: Some Methodological Issues." _Perceptual and Motor Skills_, 48 (April 1979): 427-438.
Conclusions have relevance to research into techniques such as biofeedback, Transcendental Meditation, and progressive relaxation where imagery may have an influence.

A197   Dillbeck, Michael C. "The Effect of the Transcendental Meditation Technique on Anxiety Level." _Journal of Clinical Psychology_, 33 (October 1977): 1076-1078. Tentatively scheduled for inclusion in _Scientific Research on the Transcendental Meditation Program: Collected Papers_, Vol. 2. Rheinweiler, West Germany: Maharishi European Research University Press, (in press).
Suggests the anxiety-reducing effect of the practice of TM cannot be attributed merely to sitting quietly, although additional research must determine the extent to which expectations for change contributed to this effect.

A198   _____. "Meditation and Flexibility of Visual Perception and Verbal Problem Solving." _Memory and Cognition_, 10 (May 1982): 207-215.
This study investigates the effects of the regular practice of the TM technique on habitual patterns of visual perception and verbal problem solving. TM had a positive influence on visual perception. The verbal problem solving hypothesis was not supported.

A199   _____; Arthur P. Aron; and Susan L. Dillbeck. "Transcendental Meditation Program as an Educational Technology: Research and Applications." _Educational Technology_, 19 (November 1979): 7-13.
This article reviews laboratory and applied research on the TM program relevant to the educational process. A bibliography is included.

A200   _____; T.W. Bauer; and S.I. Seferovich. "The Transcendental Meditation Program as a Predictor of Crime Rate Changes in the Kansas City Metropolitan Area." Tentatively scheduled for inclusion in Scientific Research on the Transcendental Meditation Program: Collected Papers, Vol. 2. Rheinweiler, West Germany: Maharishi European Research University Press, (in press).

Crime rate decreased in the Kansas City metropolitan area after the TM program began, conforming accurately to that predicted by a mathematical model of the Maharishi Effect.

A 201 _____, and Edward C. Bronson. "Short-Term Longitudinal Effects of the Transcendental Meditation Technique on EEG Power and Coherence." International Journal of Neuroscience, 14 (1981): 147-151.

Suggests that EEH coherence may be a more sensitive parameter than alpha power to distinguish between the TM technique and general relaxation.

A 202 _____; Garland Landrith, III; and David W. Orme-Johnson. "The Transcendental Meditation Program and Crime Rate Change in a Sample of Forty-Eight Cities." Journal of Crime and Justice, 4 (1981): 25-45. Tentatively scheduled for inclusion in Scientific Research on the Transcendental Meditation Program: Collected Papers, Vol. 2. Rheinweiler, West Germany: Maharishi European Research University Press, (in press).

A five year follow-up of Borland and Landrith's study [A98] on the Maharishi Effect. Confirms that the crime rate decreases when Transcendental Meditation is practiced by one percent of the city population. This trend continues through the follow-up period.

A 203 _____; David W. Orme-Johnson; and R. Keith Wallace. "Frontal EEG Coherence, H-Reflex Recovery, Concept Learning, and the TM-Sidhi Program." International Journal of Neuroscience, 15 (1981): 151-157.

Frontal EEG coherence and H-reflex recovery were significantly correlated with flexible performance on the concept learning task following the reversal. Instruction in the TM-Sidhi program significantly improved efficiency of concept-learning performance before the concept was reversed, although not afterward.

A 204 Dilley, John R. "TM Comes to the Heartland of the Midwest: Maharishi International University." Christian Century, 92 (10 December 1975): 1129-1132. See [A118] for critique.

A Presbyterian minister's account of how he helped open the way for Maharishi International University to move to Fairfield, Iowa. Reports on the benefits of TM practice for his family.

A 205   DiNardo, Peter A., and Jayne B. Raymond. "Locus of Con-
        trol and Attention During Meditation." Journal of Consult-
        ing and Clinical Psychology, 47 (December 1979): 1136-
        1137.
        Results showed that an internal locus of control was related
        to fewer intrusions than was an external locus of control.

A 206   Dinklage, H.A. "Personal Prevention: Meditation May Be
        the Answer." Journal of the American Society for Pre-
        ventive Dentistry, 5 (May-June 1975): 23.
        Recommends meditation to reduce stress among dentists and
        their auxiliaries.

A 207   Dodds, Dinah, et al. "The Effect of Transcendental Medita-
        tion on Language Learning and GPA." (ERIC ED 138
        048).
        A paper presented to the Pacific Northwest Conference on
        Foreign Languages, Portland, Oregon, 1975. This study
        suggests that TM does not affect academic performance over
        an extended period of time.

A 208   Doerr, Edd. "TM Goes to School." Humanist, 34 (November
        1974): 32.
        A report critical on the teaching of Transcendental Meditation
        in public schools. The New Jersey case is discussed.

A 209   _____. "Transcendental Meditation Goes to School."
        Church and State, 27 (October 1974): 3, 6. Condensed
        in Education Digest, 40 (January 1975): 44-45.
        Reviews court litigation and the issue of teaching Transcen-
        dental Meditation in public schools.

A 210   Domash, Lawrence H. "The Transcendental Meditation Tech-
        nique and Quantum Physics: Is Pure Consciousness a
        Macroscopic Quantum State in the Brain?" In Scientific
        Research on the Transcendental Meditation Program:
        Collected Papers, Vol. 1. Edited by David W. Orme-
        Johnson and John T. Farrow. 2nd ed., Weggis, Switzer-
        land: Maharishi European Research University Press,
        1977, p. 652-670.
        Puts forward the hypothesis that a form of superconductivity
        in the brain may underlie the physiology of the TM technique.

A 211   Domino, George. "Transcendental Meditation and Creativity:
        An Empirical Investigation." (ERIC ED 141 710).
        A paper presented at the Annual Meeting of the Western
        Psychological Association, Los Angeles, California, April 8-
        11, 1976. The claim that the practice of meditation leads to
        increased creativity is not supported by the study.

A 212   Don, Norman S. "The Transformation of Conscious Experi-

ence and Its EEG Correlates." <u>Journal of Altered States of Consciousness</u>, 3 (1977-78): 147-168.
Examined the EEG correlates of changes of conscious experience in subjects using the technique of focusing.

A213   Doner, David Winston, Jr. "The Transcendental Meditation Program: New Dimension in Living for the Dialysis/Transplant Client." <u>Journal of the American Association of Nephrology Nurses and Technicians</u>, 3 (1976): 119-125. Tentatively scheduled for inclusion in <u>Scientific Research on the Transcendental Meditation Program: Collected Papers, Vol. 2</u>. Rheinweiler, West Germany: Maharishi European Research University Press, (in press).
The TM program is shown to be a useful therapeutic adjunct for patients with long-term chronic illness by decreasing levels of anxiety and improving a positive self image, independency, and a sense of overall well-being.

A214   Donohue, John W. "New Jersey Mantra." <u>America</u>, 137 (19 November 1977): 360.
Reports on the court litigation in New Jersey that prohibited the teaching of Transcendental Meditation in public schools.

A215   Donovan, Dale. "Meditation and Surfing: In Search of the Elusive." <u>Surfer</u>, 21 (June 1980): 26.
Describes the state of meditation that some surfers experience while surfing.

A216   Doren, David M. "Tonic of Wildness." <u>Scandinavian Review</u>, 67 (March 1979): 58-67.
The author writes about his experiences with walking meditation in Lapland.

A217   Dostalek, C.; J. Faber; H. Krasa; E. Roldan; and F. Vele. "Yoga Meditation Effect on the EEG and EMG Activity." <u>Activas Nervosa Superior</u>, 21 (1979): 41.
Swami Maheshwarananda was monitored in three sessions of yoga meditation exercises. Effects on respiration, EEG, EMG and GSR are reported.

A218   Dreher, John. "Can a Christian Practice TM?" <u>Our Sunday Visitor</u>, 67 (13 August 1978): 8. (Reprinted from <u>The Providence Visitor</u>.)
Concludes that a Catholic cannot reconcile his faith with TM.

A219   Drennen, William, and Brian Chermol. "Relaxation and Placebo-Suggestion as Uncontrolled Variables in TM Research." <u>Journal of Humanistic Psychology</u>, 18 (Fall 1978): 89-93.
No evidence was found that TM was more effective than another relaxation technique in effecting personality change.

A220   Driscoll, Francis. "TM as a Secondary School Subject."
        Phi Delta Kappan, 54 (December 1972): 236-237.
        A New York superintendent tells how he installed a TM
        course in school and with what results.

A221   Dukhan, Hamlyn, and K. Ramakrishna Rao. "Meditation and
        ESP Scoring." In Research in Parapsychology, 1972.
        Edited by W.G. Roll, R.L. Morris, and J.D. Morris.
        Metuchen, N.J.: The Scarecrow Press, Inc., 1973, p.
        148-151.
        Explores the relationship between the practice of yogic medi-
        tation and ESP scoring.

A222   Dumitrescu, Ioan Florin. "An Electronographic Study of
        Psychic States Obtained by Yoga." Journal of Holistic
        Health, 3 (1978): 57-59.
        Subjects' hands and feet were photographed using an electo-
        luminescent method before and after practicing relaxation
        and concentration techniques used in Hatha Yoga. Electron-
        ographs registered the modifications of the psychic states
        produced by the yoga techniques.

A223   Dwivedi, K.N.; V.M. Gupta; and K.N. Udupa. "A Prelimi-
        nary Report on Some Physiological Changes Due to Vipash-
        yana Meditation." Indian Journal of Medical Sciences, 31
        (March 1977): 51-54.
        The study shows that Vipashyana meditation can produce
        changes in blood pressure levels, pulse rates and respiration.

A224   Dworkin, Susan. "Jews Who Seek Eastern Mysticism."
        Hadassah Magazine, (May, 1974). Condensed in Jewish
        Digest, (January 1975): 9-14.
        Discusses the presence of Jews in Transcendental Meditation
        and Zen Buddhism.

A224K   Earle, Jonathan B. "Cerebral Laterality and Meditation: A
        Review of the Literature." Journal of Transpersonal Psy-
        chology, 13 (1981): 155-173. Also in Meditation: Classic
        and Contemporary Perspectives, edited by Deane H.
        Shapiro, Jr. and Roger N. Walsh. Hawthorne, N.Y.:
        Aldine Pub. Co., 1984.
        Reviews the role both hemispheres play in the production of
        meditative states of consciousness.

A225   Edmiston, Susan. "My Search to Find Happiness in 40 Min-
        utes a Day." Redbook, 140 (January 1973): 74-75, 121-
        122.
        A personal account expressing some reservation about
        Transcendental Meditation.

A226   Egan, James M. "Meditation and the Search for God."

Thomist Reader, 1 (1957): 71-89.
Explains why meditation is necessary for any progress in
spiritual life.

A 227   Ehrlich, Milton P. "Family Meditation." Journal of Family
        Counseling, 4 (Fall 1976): 40-45.
        A personal account of the author's own family unit meditating
        together every morning for fifteen minutes.

A 228   _____. "Self-Acceptance and Meditation." Journal of
        Pastoral Counseling, 11 (Fall-Winter 1976-77): 37-41.
        The author believes that meditation can provide a most use-
        ful contribution to the process of psychotherapy for both the
        patient and therapist in the goal of self acceptance.

A 229   "Elected Silence: New Jersey School Meditation." America,
        138 (4 February 1978): 72-73.
        An editorial on the New Jersey court litigation to prevent
        the teaching of TM in public schools.

A 229K Ellis, Albert. "The Place of Meditation in Cognitive-Behavior
        Therapy and Rational-Emotive Therapy." In Meditation:
        Classic and Contemporary Perspectives, edited by Deane
        H. Shapiro, Jr. and Roger N. Walsh. Hawthorne, N.Y.:
        Aldine Pub. Co., 1984.

A 230   Elson, Barry D.; Peter Hauri; and David Cunis. "Physio-
        logical Changes in Yoga Meditation." Psychophysiology,
        14 (January 1977): 52-57.
        Findings suggest that Ananda Marga meditation produces a
        physiological effect different from that observed in controls
        who try to relax with their eyes closed.

A 231   Emery, Pierre-Yves. "Scripture Meditated." Lumen Vitae,
        21 (March 1966): 37-49.
        Gives examples of scriptural references as objects of medita-
        tion.

A 232   Engel, Allison. "Maharishi International University Mixes
        Meditation and Education." Change, 7 (May 1975): 19-22.
        A report on the administration, educational program, and
        students of MIU.

A 233   Erskine-Milliss, Julie, and Malcolm Schonell. "Relaxation
        Therapy in Asthma: A Critical Review." Psychosomatic
        Medicine, 43 (1981): 365-372.
        A review article showing that autogenic training and Tran-
        scendental Meditation, systematic desensitization, and bio-
        feedback-assisted relaxation can produce improvement in res-
        piratory function with variable responses.

A234   "Executive's Guide to Living with Stress." Business Week,
2446 (23 August 1976): 75-80.
Discusses various methods of coping with stress, including
Transcendental Meditation, est, transactional analysis, biofeedback, yoga, encounter groups, and behavior modification.

A235   Eyerman, James. "Transcendental Meditation and Mental Retardation." Journal of Clinical Psychiatry, 42 (January
1981): 35-36. Tentatively scheduled for inclusion in Scientific Research on the Transcendental Meditation Program: Collected Papers, Vol. 2. Rheinweiler, West Germany: Maharishi European Research University Press,
(in press).
A 26-year old moderately mentally retarded woman was taught
the Transcendental Meditation technique. She experienced
improvements in her verbal and social behavior and physiological functioning over a period of three years.

A236   Faber, Phillip A.; Graham S. Saayman; and Stephen W.
Touyz. "Meditation and Archetypal Content of Nocturnal
Dreams." Journal of Analytical Psychology, 23 (January
1978): 1-22.
The dreams of meditators contained significantly more archetypal elements, reflecting universal and moral themes, than
did those of non-meditators, which were characterized by
personal and everyday issues. There was a higher recall
rate and amount of content in the dreams of meditators.

A237   Falk, William. "Meditation Merges with the Mainstream."
Esquire, 99 (March 1983): 249-250.
A short report on the meditation techniques of Relaxation
Response and Clinically Standardized Meditation.

A238   Farge, E.J.; G.H. Hartung; and C.M. Borland. "Runners
and Meditators: A Comparison of Personality Profiles."
Journal of Personality Assessment, 43 (October 1979):
501-503.
The meditators were more assertive and enthusiastic than the
runners. They also appear less conscientious and controlled
than runners, as well as more experimenting and suspicious.

A239   Farrow, John T. "Physiological Changes Associated with
Transcendental Consciousness, the State of Least Excitation of Consciousness." In Scientific Research on the
Transcendental Meditation Program: Collected Papers, Vol.
1. Edited by David W. Orme-Johnson and John T. Farrow.
2nd ed., Weggis, Switzerland: Maharishi European Research University Press, 1977, p. 108-133.
A variety of physiological changes were correlated with the
practice of the TM technique.

A 240   _____, and J. Russell Hebert. "Breath Suspension During the Transcendental Meditation Technique." Psychosomatic Medicine, 44 (May 1982): 133-53.
Breath suspension, a correlate of pure consciousness experience, was studied in a large group of subjects practicing the TM technique.

A 241   Fehr, Theo. "A Longitudinal Study of the Effect of the Transcendental Meditation Program on Changes in Personality." In Scientific Research on the Transcendental Meditation Program: Collected Papers, Vol. 1. Edited by David W. Orme-Johnson and John T. Farrow. 2nd ed., Weggis, Switzerland: Maharishi European Research University Press, 1977, p. 476-483.
This study shows that personality develops in stages as a result of the practice of the TM technique.

A 242   _____; Uwe Nerstheimer; and Sibille Törber. "Study of Personality Changes Resulting from the Transcendental Meditation Program: Freiburger Personality Inventory." In Scientific Research on the Transcendental Meditation Program: Collected Papers, Vol. 1. Edited by David W. Orme-Johnson and John T. Farrow. 2nd ed., Weggis, Switzerland: Maharishi European Research University Press, 1977, p. 420-424.
A variety of positive personality changes were correlated with the practice of the TM technique.

A 243   Fenton, J.C. "Priestly Meditation and Theology." American Ecclesiastical Review, 144 (June 1961): 406-417.
An essay on the function and meaning of meditation for priests.

A 244   Fenwick, P.B., et al. "Metabolic and EEH Changes During Transcendental Meditation: An Explanation." Biological Psychology, 5 (January 1977): 101-118. Also in Meditation: Classic and Contemporary Perspectives, edited by Deane H. Shapiro, Jr. and Roger N. Walsh. Hawthorne, N.Y.: Aldine Pub. Co., 1984.
A drop in oxygen consumption and carbon dioxide production, found by previous authors during TM was confirmed, but not in a significant amount. No support was found for the concept that TM is a fourth stage of consciousness.

A 245   Ferguson, Phillip C. "The Psychobiology of Transcendental Meditation: A Review." Journal of Altered States of Consciousness, 2 (1975): 15-36.
A literature review that highlights the influence of TM in areas of oxygen consumption, cardiac output, blood lactate concentrations, stress, anxiety and neuroticism. Implications in psychotherapy, prisoner rehabilitation, and personality are noted.

A 246   _____. "Transcendental Meditation and Its Potential Application in the Field of Special Education." Journal of Special Education, 10 (Summer 1976): 211-220.
The general physiological, perceptual, personality, and medical benefits noticed and researched among practitioners of TM suggests that the technique may have potential use in the field of special education.

A 247   _____, and John C. Gowan. "TM: Some Preliminary Findings." Journal of Humanistic Psychology, 16 (Summer 1976): 51-60. Published later as "Psychological Findings on Transcendental Meditation" in Scientific Research on the Transcendental Meditation Program: Collected Papers, Vol. 1. Edited by David W. Orme-Johnson and John T. Farrow. 2nd ed., Weggis, Switzerland: Maharishi European Research University Press, 1977, p. 484-488.
Results suggest that the regular practice of TM appears to reduce anxiety, depression, and neurotic levels and to increase self-actualization.

A 248   Ferguson, R.E. "The Transcendental Meditation Program at MCI Walpole: An Evaluation Report." Tentatively scheduled for inclusion in Scientific Research on the Transcendental Meditation Program: Collected Papers, Vol. 2. Rheinweiler, West Germany: Maharishi European Research University Press, (in press).
Prisoners practicing the TM program at the Massachusetts Corrections Institute Walpole exhibited a reduction in anxiety and hostility, improvement in sleep and reduction of disciplinary reports.

A 249   Fiebert, Martin S. "Responsiveness to an Introductory Meditation Method." Perceptual and Motor Skills, 45 (December 1977): 849-850.
Results moderately suggest those favoring personal growth will favor meditation.

A 250   _____, and Travis M. Mead. "Meditation and Academic Performance." Perceptual and Motor Skills, 53 (October 1981): 447-450.
The results suggest that actualism meditation techniques had a mildly facilitative effect on academic effectiveness.

A 251   Fischer, Roland. "Cartography of the Ecstatic and Meditative States." Science, 174 (26 November 1971): 897-904.
Varieties of conscious states are mapped on a perception-hallucination continuum of increasing ergotropic arousal and the perception-meditation (Zazen) continuum of increasing trophotropic arousal.

A 252   _____. "Healing as a State of Consciousness: Cartography

of the Passive Concentration Stage of Autogenic Training."
Journal of Altered States of Consciousness, 4 (1978-79):
57-61.
Comparisons are made to Theravada Buddhist meditation.

A253 _____. "On Images and Pure Light: Integration of East
and West." Journal of Altered States of Consciousness, 3
(1977-78): 205-212.
Examines varieties of Western and Eastern (Christian and
non-Christian) forms of contemplation in which the meditator
experiences a pure white light.

A254 _____. "Transformations of Consciousness: A Cartography, Part I; The Perception-Meditation Continuum."
Confinia Psychiatrica, 18 (1975): 221-244; Part II, 19
(1976): 1-23.
The Japanese Zen and Indian Yoga meditation techniques are
cartographed on a perception-meditation continuum of increasing trophotropic arousal. A two part article.

A255 Flanagan, Finbarr. "TM: Self-Transcendence or Self-
Deception." Clergy Review, 64 (May 1979): 167-172.
A critical analysis of Transcendental Meditation from a Chris-
tian perspective.

A256 Fling, Sheila; Anne Thomas; and Michael Gallaher. "Participant Characteristics and the Effects of Two Types of
Meditation Versus Quiet Sitting." Journal of Clinical
Psychology, 37 (October 1981): 784-790.
Practice time correlated with anxiety reduction for the combined treatment groups. Other characteristic measures varied
between groups.

A257 Floyd, W.T., and J. Haynes. "The Influence of Transcendental Meditation on Anxiety." Tentatively scheduled for
inclusion in Scientific Research on the Transcendental
Meditation Program: Collected Papers, Vol. 2. Rheinweiler, West Germany: Maharishi European Research
University Press, (in press).
After 18 weeks of practicing the TM technique subjects
showed significant anxiety reduction.

A258 Flygare, Thomas J. "Federal Court Upholds Minute of Silent
Prayer or Meditation in Public Schools." Phi Delta Kappan,
58 (December 1976): 354-355.
Reports on the lawsuit filed by the Civil Liberties Union of
Massachusetts on behalf of twelve Framington school children
and their parents against a Massachusetts law requiring a
period of silence in the public schools.

A259 Fox, Matthew. "The Case for Extrovert Meditation." Spirit-

uality Today, 30 (June 1978): 164-177.
Two kinds of extrovert meditation are discussed. One, that
of concentrating on outside images not as objects but as experiences of communion, and two, of centering by way of
making or doing.

A260   Frankel, Bernard L.; Dali J. Patel; David Horwitz; William
         T. Friedewald; and Kenneth R. Gardner. "Treatment of
         Hypertension with Biofeedback and Relaxation Techniques."
         Psychosomatic Medicine, 40 (June 1978): 276-293.
Reports that their treatment of hypertension with biofeedback
and relaxation techniques failed to produce the anticipated
reduction of blood pressure.

A261   Franklin, R.L. "On Taking New Beliefs Seriously: A Case
         Study." Theoria to Theory, 14 (June 1980): 43-64.
Includes a description of levitation or hopping in the TM
program.

A262   _____. "A Science of Pure Consciousness." Religious
         Studies, 19 (June 1983): 185-204.
Discusses TM and the TM-Sidhi program in terms of what the
author calls a new science of pure consciousness that could
transform the whole framework of our current scientific and
religious thought.

A263   Frederick, A.B. "The Tension Literature." (ERIC ED 115
         638).
A paper presented at the Annual Meeting of the American
Association for the Advancement of Tension Control, 2nd,
Chicago, Illinois, 1975. This bibliography of books, films,
and periodicals bearing on stress, relaxation, anxiety, and/
or methods of controlling stress. Includes references to
Transcendental Meditation.

A264   French, Alfred P.; Albert C. Schmid; and Elizabeth Ingalls.
         "Transcendental Meditation, Altered Reality Testing, and
         Behavioral Change: A Case Report." Journal of Nervous
         and Mental Disease. 161 (July 1975): 55-58.
This paper presents the case of a 39-year-old woman who,
several weeks following initiation into TM, experienced altered
reality testing and behavior. Appropriate treatment is discussed.

A265   _____, and Joe P. Tupin. "Therapeutic Application of a
         Simple Relaxation Method." American Journal of Psycho-
         therapy, 28 (April 1974): 282-287.
Consists of muscular relaxation followed by the use of a
pleasant relaxing memory as a center on which attention may
be focused.

A266   Frew, David R. "Transcendental Meditation and Productivity." Academy of Management Journal, 17 (June 1974):
362-368. In Scientific Research on the Transcendental
Meditation Program: Collected Papers, Vol. 1. Edited by
David W. Orme-Johnson and John T. Farrow. 2nd ed.,
Weggis, Switzerland: Maharishi European Research University Press, 1977, p. 625-629.
Reports that TM would appear to be positively related to
productivity with meditators higher in the organizational level
having greater gains. Gains in productivity would also appear
to be related to the type of organizational structure.

A267   _____. "Unstressing the Stressed Up Executive." Conference Board Record, 12 (July 1975): 57-60.
The author suggests cautious optimism in judging the success
of TM in U.S. industry. His own research is positive.

A268   Friend, Kenneth E. "Effects of the Transcendental Meditation
Program on Work Attitudes and Behavior." In Scientific
Research on the Transcendental Meditation Program: Collected Papers, Vol. 1. Edited by David W. Orme-Johnson
and John T. Farrow. 2nd ed., Weggis, Switzerland:
Maharishi European Research University Press, 1977, p.
630-638.
Supports previous findings that TM meditators show increased
job satisfaction and performance, and improved relationships
with supervisors and co-workers.

A269   _____. "Report on a Mental Health Center Transcendental
Meditation Program for Staff." Tentatively scheduled for
inclusion in Scientific Research on the Transcendental
Meditation Program: Collected Papers, Vol. 2. Rheinweiler, West Germany: Maharishi European Research University Press, (in press).
Workers who practiced the TM technique were found to have
more job satisfaction and improved work behavior.

A270   _____, and Michael Maliszewski. "More on the Reliability
of the Kinesthetic Aftereffects Measure and Need for
Stimulation." Journal of Personality Assessment, 42 (Au-
gust 1978): 385-391. Tentatively scheduled for inclusion
in Scientific Research on the Transcendental Meditation
Program: Collected Papers, Vol. 2. Rheinweiler, West
Germany: Maharishi European Research University Press,
(in press).
Kinesthetic aftereffects scores suggest that the practice of
Transcendental Meditation reduces the need for stimulation.

A271   Fromm, Erika. "Altered States of Consciousness and Hypnosis: A Discussion." International Journal of Clinical and
Experimental Hypnosis, 25 (October 1977): 325-334.

This discussion summarizes, critically evaluates, and attempts to integrate the findings of a few meditative researchers.

A272   _____. "Primary and Secondary Process in Waking and in Altered States of Consciousness." Academic Psychology Bulletin, 3 (March 1981): 29-45.
For each state, including the beginning states of various forms of meditation, the prevailing balance between primary and secondary process is explicated.

A273   Frumkin, Kenneth; Robert J. Nathan; Maurice F. Prout; and Mariam C. Cohen. "Nonpharmacologic Control of Essential Hypertension in Man: A Critical Review of the Experiment Literature." Psychosomatic Medicine, 40 (June 1978): 294-320.
A review article on biofeedback and relaxation methodologies in which the strengths and weaknesses of various authors' research designs, data, and conclusions are discussed. Suggestions for further experimentation are offered.

A274   Frumkin, Lynn R., and Robert R. Pagano. "The Effect of Transcendental Meditation on Iconic Memory." Biofeedback and Self-Regulation, 4 (December 1979): 313-322.
Three experiments investigated the effects of TM on iconic memory. The performance of the meditators was significantly lower in two of the three experiments.

A275   Fulton, Robert B. "Public Funding for TM?" Christian Century, 92 (10 December 1975): 1124-1125. See [A118] for critique.
Opposes the teaching of TM in public schools.

A276   Fuson, J.W. "The Effect of the Transcendental Meditation Program on Sleeping and Dreaming Patterns." Tentatively scheduled for inclusion in Scientific Research on the Transcendental Meditation Program: Collected Papers, Vol. 2. Rheinweiler, West Germany: Maharishi European Research University Press, (in press).
Improved quality of sleeping and dreaming was reported by subjects practicing the TM technique.

A277   Galanter, Marc, and Peter Buckley. "Evangelical Religion and Meditation: Psychotherapeutic Effects." Journal of Nervous and Mental Disease, 166 (October 1978): 685-691.
Members of the Divine Light Mission were evaluated for psychological effects. A significant decline in the incidence of neurotic symptoms and of alcohol and drug use was observed after joining the sect.

A278   Ganguli, H.C. "Meditation Program and Modern Youth: Dynamics of Initiation." Human Relations, 35 (October

1982): 903-925.
This study analyzes the motivational factors that led subjects
to join an organized meditation group program.

A279   Gannon, Linda, and Richard A. Sternbach. "Alpha Enhance-
        ment as a Treatment for Pain: A Case Study." Journal
        of Behavior Therapy and Experimental Psychiatry, 2
        (1971): 209-213.
This case study provides some evidence that it is possible
for a patient to learn to prevent the onset of pain by means
of operant alpha conditioning techniques that include yoga
meditation.

A280   Garfield, Charles A. "Consciousness Alteration and Fear of
        Death." Journal of Transpersonal Psychology, 7 (1975):
        147-175.
Attitudes toward death by groups practicing Zen meditation
and Tibetan meditation are studied.

A281   Garrison, John. "Stress Management Training for the Handi-
        capped." Archives of Physical Medicine and Rehabilitation,
        59 (December 1978): 580-585.
The procedure combines progressive muscle relaxation and
clinical meditation for effectiveness.

A282   _____, and Patricia A. Scott. "A Group Self-Care Ap-
        proach to Stress Management." Journal of Psychiatric
        Nursing and Mental Health Services, 17 (June 1979): 9-14.
Reports on progressive relaxation, clinical meditation, and
Stress Management Training as techniques for stress manage-
ment.

A283   Gash, Arnold, and Joel S. Karliner. "No Effect of Tran-
        scendental Meditation on Left Ventricular Function." An-
        nals of Internal Medicine, 88 (February 1978): 215-216.
Findings suggest that TM has no major immediate effects on
the heart, but cannot exclude the possibility that TM has
beneficial effects on the cardiovascular system.

A284   Gaylin, Jody. "I'm the Maharishi: Fly Me." Psychology
        Today, 11 (August 1977): 29, 85.
Reports on levitation claims of Transcendental Meditation in-
structors.

A285   Geisler, Matthias. "The Therapeutic Effects of Transcendental
        Meditation on Drug Users." Zeitschrift für Klinische Psy-
        chologie, 7 (1978): 235-255. (Text in German; summary
        in English) Tentatively scheduled for inclusion in Scien-
        tific Research on the Transcendental Meditation Program:
        Collected Papers, Vol. 2. Rheinweiler, West Germany:
        Maharishi European Research University Press, (in press).

A further analysis and elaboration of the original study by Schenkluhn and Geisler reported in Scientific Research on the Transcendental Meditation Program: Collected Papers, Vol. 1 [A708]. Drug rehabilitation occurred subsequent to improvement in psychological health.

A286   Gellhorn, Ernst, and William F. Kiely. "Mystical States of
        Consciousness: Neurophysiological and Clinical Aspects."
        Journal of Nervous and Mental Disease, 154 (June 1972):
        399-405. Critique by Gary K. Mills and Ken Campbell,
        in the Journal, 159 (September 1974): 191-195. Reply by
        Kiely, 196-197.
The relationship of the trophotropic and ergotropic systems of autonomic-somatic integration and their relevance to a variety of emotional states and levels of consciousness is reviewed, including Yoga and Zen meditation.

A287   Gersten, Dennis J. "Meditation as an Adjunct to Medical and
        Psychiatric Treatment." American Journal of Psychiatry,
        135 (May 1978): 598-599.
A case report in which the author believes meditation was probably a significant factor in the healing process.

A288   Gerus, Claire. "Relax Today, Tomorrow the World."
        Macleans, (12 February 1979): 45-46.
Reports on the practice of Transcendental Meditation.

A289   Gibbons, Gerald. "Transcendental Meditation and Christian
        Prayer: How Different Are They?" Liguorian, 64 (June
        1976): 13-15.
A short comparison favoring Christian prayer over TM.

A290   Gilbert, Albin R. "Pseudo Mind-Expansion Through Psyche-
        delics and Brain-Wave-Programming Versus True Mind-
        Expansion Through Life Conditioning to the Absolute."
        Psychologia: An International Journal of Psychology in
        the Orient, 14 (December 1971): 187-192.
Explains how daily living can be enhanced by meditating on the Absolute.

A291   Gilbert, Gary S.; Jerry C. Parker; and Charles D. Claiborn.
        "Differential Mood Changes in Alcoholics as a Function of
        Anxiety Management Strategies." Journal of Clinical Psy-
        chology, 34 (January 1978): 229-232.
The results indicated that progressive relaxation training, meditation training, and quiet rest produced qualitatively different patterns.

A292   Giles, S. "Analysis of Decreased Crime Trends in 56 Major
        US Cities Due to the Transcendental Meditation Program."
        Tentatively scheduled for inclusion in Scientific Research

on the Transcendental Meditation Program: Collected Papers, Vol. 2. Rheinweiler, West Germany: Maharishi European Research University Press, (in press).
A mathematical model of the Maharishi Effect accurately predicted a decrease in crime rate in major U.S. cities in 1975-76. See also the report by M. Weinless [A870].

A 293 Gilles, Anthony. "Teilhard and the Maharishi: The Thoughts of Teilhard and the Teachings of Maharishi." Teilhard Review, 12 (February 1977): 10-14.
Shows the thought of Teilhard and the teachings of the Maharishi as complementary approaches to providing fulfillment for the most basic human desires, including the meaning and purpose to existence.

A 294 _____. "Three Modes of Meditation." America, 139 (July 29-August 5, 1978): 52-54.
A former student of the Maharishi Mahesh Yogi describes his passage through TM, centering-prayer, and Ignatian contemplation.

A 295 Ginder, Richard. "Meditation." Sponsa Regis, 29 (April 1958): 212-217.
Essay on the rewards of Christian meditation. Suggestions are given for simple techniques.

A 296 Girodo, Michel. "Yoga Meditation and Flooding in the Treatment of Anxiety Neurosis." Journal of Behavior Therapy and Experimental Psychiatry, 5 (September 1974): 157-160.
Analysis of patient characteristics suggested that yoga meditation was beneficial for patients with a short history of illness and that flooding was effective in those with a long history.

A 296K Globus, Gordon G. "Potential Contributions of Meditation to Neuroscience." In Meditation: Classic and Contemporary Perspectives, edited by Deane H. Shapiro, Jr. and Roger N. Walsh. Hawthorne, N.Y.: Aldine Pub. Co., 1984.

A 297 Glueck, Bernard C., and Charles F. Stroebel. "Biofeedback and Meditation in the Treatment of Psychiatric Illnesses." Comprehensive Psychiatry, 16 (July-August, 1975): 303-321.
The most appropriate technique to use with psychiatric patients, in an attempt to produce an increase in generalized relaxation response, appears to be a mantra-type passive Transcendental Meditation.

A 297K _____, and Charles F. Stroebel. "Meditation in the Treatment of Psychiatric Illness." In Meditation: Classic and

Contemporary Perspectives, edited by Deane H. Shapiro, Jr. and Roger N. Walsh. Hawthorne, N.Y.: Aldine Pub. Co., 1984.

A297R   , and   . "Psychophysiological Correlates of Meditation: EEG Changes During Meditation." In Meditation: Classic and Contemporary Perspectives, edited by Deane H. Shapiro, Jr. and Roger N. Walsh. Hawthorne, N.Y.: Aldine Pub. Co., 1984.

A298   Goldberg, Lois S., and Gloria Meltzer. "Arrow-Dot Scores of Drug Addicts Selecting General or Yoga Therapy." Perceptual and Motor Skills, 40 (1975): 726.
Subjects associated with yoga therapy showed a greater motivation toward rehabilitation.

A299   Goldberg, Phil. "Maharishi International University." Interface Journal, 1 (February 1975): 41-45.
Gives a brief history of MIU, an overview of its curriculum development, and the benefits of the TM technique.

A300   Goldberg, Richard J. "Anxiety Reduction by Self-Regulation: Theory, Practice, and Evaluation." Annals of Internal Medicine, 96 (April 1982): 483-487.
Provides the medical practitioner with the underlying theories and methodologic issues involved in assessing the efficacy of such self-regulatory therapies as relaxation, biofeedback, and meditation.

A301   Goldhaber, Amos N. "Transcendental Meditation." Congressional Record, 120, Part 10 (6 May 1974): 13219-13223.
An article summarizing the scientific research on the therapeutic value of Transcendental Meditation.

A302   Goldman, Barbara L.; and Paul J. Dormitor; and Edward J. Murray. "Effects of Zen Meditation on Anxiety Reduction and Perceptual Functioning." Journal of Consulting and Clinical Psychology, 47 (June 1979): 551-556.
Measures of self-reported anxiety showed a decrease after meditation, but no more than the two control groups. State anxiety after stress showed no effect of meditation. No improvement of perceptual functioning was measured.

A303   Goleman, Daniel. "The Buddha on Meditation and States of Consciousness, Part I: The Teachings." Journal of Transpersonal Psychology, 4 (1972): 1-44. Also in Meditation: Classic and Contemporary Perspectives, edited by Deane H. Shapiro, Jr. and Roger N. Walsh. Hawthorne, N.Y.: Aldine Pub. Co., 1984.
This paper begins in Part I with a detailed discussion of the

Visuddhimagga account of Gotama Buddha's teachings on meditation and higher states of consciousness.

A304 _____. "The Buddha on Meditation and States of Consciousness, Part II: A Typology of Meditation Techniques."
Journal of Transpersonal Psychology, 4 (1972): 151-210.
In Part II, a threefold dynamic typology is generated, using
Buddha's account and map as a reference point. This typology is used as a pattern in a survey of many meditation
systems.

A305 _____. "An Eastern Toe in the Stream of Consciousness."
Psychology Today, 15 (January 1981): 84, 86-87.
A report on the Buddhist form of mindfulness meditation as
an aid in therapy.

A306 _____. "Meditation and Consciousness: An Asian Approach
to Mental Health." American Journal of Psychotherapy,
30 (January 1976): 41-54.
In light of Abhidhamma psychology and empirical findings,
applications of meditation are suggested for inducing an op-
timal mode of responsiveness to environmental demands, and
as a complementary adjunct to psychotherapy.

A307 _____. "Meditation as Meta-Therapy: Hypothesis Toward
a Proposed Fifth State of Consciousness." Journal of
Transpersonal Psychology, 3 (1971): 1-25.
Several hypotheses relate meditation to systematic desensitization, reduction of anxiety, and improved performance of
tasks. Characteristics of a fifth state of consciousness or
enlightenment are described.

A308 _____. "Meditation: Concentration and Insight." Journal
of Dharma, 2 (April 1977): 129-136.
A psychologist's view of meditation as a process of mental
re-training.

A309 _____. "Meditation Helps Break the Stress Spiral."
Psychology Today, 9 (February 1976): 82-84, 86, 93.
Suggests that people who meditate can move serenely from
one trying situation to the next.

A310 _____. "Meditation Without Mystery." Psychology Today,
10 (March 1977): 54-56, 58, 60, 65, 67, 88.
This is an excerpt from the author's book, The Varieties of
the Meditative Experience, which discusses the many schools
of meditation, where they are from, and for what they
strive.

A311 _____. "Mental Health in Classical Buddhist Psychology."
Journal of Transpersonal Psychology, 7 (1975): 176-181.

Healthy and unhealthy mental factors mentioned in classical
Buddhist psychology are described relevant to the Abhidhamma system of psychology.

A312 _____. "A Taxonomy of Meditation-Specific Altered
     States." Journal of Altered States of Consciousness, 4
     (1978-79): 203-213.
Classical Buddhist sources are used to describe the typogra-
phy of states of consciousness created by concentration and
mindfulness strategies in meditation.

A313 _____. "Transcendental Meditation Goes Public." Psy-
     chology Today, 9 (November 1975): 90-91.
Discusses popular books on Transcendental Meditation and
Benson's, The Relaxation Response.

A314 _____, and Mark Epstein. "Meditation and Well-Being:
     An Eastern Model of Psychological Health." In Beyond
     Health and Normality: Explorations of Exceptional Psycho-
     logical Well-Being. Edited by Roger Walsh and Deane H.
     Shapiro, Jr. New York: Van Nostrand Reinhold, 1983,
     p. 229-252.

A315 _____; Jean Houston; and Ewert Cousins. "Importance
     of Meditation." Journal of Dharma, 2 (April 1977): 231-
     239.
A discussion forum on the value of meditation.

A316 _____, and Gary E. Schwartz. "Meditation as an Inter-
     vention in Stress Reactivity." Journal of Consulting and
     Clinical Psychology, 44 (June 1976): 456-466. Tentatively
     scheduled for inclusion in Scientific Research on the
     Transcendental Meditation Program: Collected Papers, Vol.
     2. Rheinweiler, West Germany: Maharishi European Re-
     search University Press, (in press). Also in Meditation:
     Classic and Contemporary Perspectives, edited by Deane
     H. Shapiro, Jr. and Roger N. Walsh. Hawthorne, N.Y.:
     Aldine Pub. Co., 1984.
Comparison between the abilities of meditation and relaxation
in the reduction of stress reactions in a laboratory setting.
Shows how meditators habituated more quickly to stressor
impact and experienced less subjective anxiety. Further research indicates that meditation state effects may become
meditator traits.

A317 Gopi Krishna. "Meditation: Is It Always Beneficial? Some
     Positive and Negative Views." Journal of Altered States
     of Consciousness, 2 (1975): 37-47.
The notion that techniques for training brain waves will enable unpracticed meditators to duplicate the physiological
states of Zen and Yoga is disputed.

A318   Gowan, John Curtis. "The Facilitation of Creativity Through Meditational Procedures." Journal of Creative Behavior, 12 (Summer 1978): 156-160.
Surveys research studies on Transcendental Meditation and creativity.

A319   Goyeche, John R.; T. Chihara; and H. Shimizu. "Two Concentration Methods: A Preliminary Comparison." Psychologia: An International Journal of Psychology in the Orient, 15 (June 1972): 110-111.
A direct comparison of the effects of Zen concentration and cotention.

A320   Graham, T.; R. Webb; A. DeLyzer; M. Stokes; and D. Willis. "The Effect of Transcendental Meditation on Heart Rate Response to a Startle." Tentatively scheduled for inclusion in Scientific Research on the Meditation Program: Collected Papers, Vol. 2. Rheinweiler, West Germany: Maharishi European Research University Press, (in press).
Practitioners of the TM technique recovered more quickly from a fright-startle than control subjects.

A321   Grassi, Joseph. "Meditation: What? Why? How?" St. Anthony Messenger, 83 (March 1976): 34-40.
Explains the place of meditation in Christian tradition and offers simple exercises to start meditating.

A322   Greaves, George. "Meditation as an Adjunct to Psychotherapy." Voices: The Art and Science of Psychotherapy, 8 (Fall 1972): 50-52.
Suggests the use of mandalas, yogic breathing exercises, and mantras in meditation as a valuable adjunct to psychotherapy. Zazen is also discussed.

A323   Greenberg, Jerrold S. "Stress, Relaxation, and the Health Educator." Journal of School Health, 47 (November 1977): 522-525.
The relationship of the mind to the body, the reaction of the body to stress, and stress-reducing techniques are studied.

A324   Greenwood, Martha M., and Herbert Benson. "The Efficacy of Progressive Relaxation in Systematic Desensitization and a Proposal for an Alternative Competitive Response: The Relaxation Response." Behaviour Research and Therapy, 15 (1977): 337-343.
Suggests that studies of progressive relaxation have not substantiated that its practice is associated with decreased autonomic activity and the use of the Relaxation Response should be a more appropriate method of systematic desensitization.

A325   Griffiths, Paul. "Buddhist Jhana: A Form-Critical Study."
        Religion, 13 (January 1983): 55-68.
        Textual and contextual analyses of meditative techniques
        known as the four Jhanani, found in Pali sources.

A326   _____. "Concentration or Insight: The Problematic of
        Theravada Buddhist Meditation-Theory." Journal of the
        American Academy of Religion, 49 (December 1981): 605-
        624.
        This paper examines some of the attempts at reconciliation
        and combination of two separate sets of meditative practice
        described in Pali sources.

A327   Grim, Paul F. "Relaxation, Meditation, and Insight." Psy-
        chologia: An International Journal of Psychology in the
        Orient, 18 (September 1975): 125-133.
        Discusses the experience of learning autogenic training and
        progressive relaxation with particular reference to holding
        an image completely still.

A328   Grubb, P.H.W. "Healing Through Meditation." London
        Quarterly and Holborn Review, 181 (July 1956): 186-190.
        The teachings of Dr. Porter Mills and Marian Dunlop on con-
        templative meditation as it relates to healing are discussed.

A329   Gruber, Louis N. "Simple Techniques to Relieve Anxiety."
        Journal of Family Practice, 5 (October 1977): 641-644.
        Five techniques derived from Gestalt therapy and Zen medi-
        tation are described.

A330   Guenther, H.V. "Buddhist Metaphysics and Existential
        Meditation." Studies in Religion/Sciences Religieuses, 1
        (Spring 1972): 291-297.
        Explores the relationship between metaphysics and meditation
        in the context of Buddhist philosophy.

A331   Gupta, N.C. "Effects of Transcendental Meditation on Anxi-
        ety and Self-Concept." Tentatively scheduled for inclu-
        sion in Scientific Research on the Transcendental Meditation
        Program: Collected Papers, Vol. 2. Rheinweiler, West
        Germany: Maharishi European Research University Press,
        (in press).
        Subjects practicing the TM technique showed decreased anxi-
        ety and increased self-concept.

A332   Gutfeldt, H. "Meditation and the New Church." New
        Church Magazine, 95 (January/April 1976): 20-28.
        Explains that meditation can lead to a more mature applica-
        tion of the principles of the New Church.

A333   Haddon, David. "New Plant Thrives in a Spiritual Desert:

Transcendental Meditation." Christianity Today, 18 (21
December 1973): 9-12.
Critical of the use of Transcendental Meditation in schools.
Argues that it is a religion incompatible with Christian faith.

A334 _____. "Transcendental Meditation Challenges the
Church." Christianity Today, 20 (26 March 1976): 15-18.
Part one concerns the religious significance of TM and its
conflicts with Christianity. Part two (9 April 1976, p. 17-
19) suggests that the practice of TM may have an anti-
Christian character.

A335 Hafner, R. Julian. "Psychological Treatment of Essential
Hypertension: A Controlled Comparison of Meditation and
Meditation Plus Biofeedback." Biofeedback and Self-
Regulation, 7 (September 1982): 305-306.
Three hypotheses were tested with varying results. Suggests
further study about the influence of meditation or relaxation
training on hypertension.

A336 Hahn, H.R., and T.E. Whalen. "The Effects of the Transcendental Meditation Program on Levels of Hostility,
Anxiety, and Depression." Tentatively scheduled for inclusion in Scientific Research on the Transcendental Meditation Program: Collected Papers, Vol. 2. Rheinweiler,
West Germany: Maharishi European Research University
Press, (in press).
Levels of hostility, anxiety, and depression were reduced in
participants of the Transcendental Meditation program.

A337 Haimes, Leonard, and Richard Tyson. "How to Meditate."
Cosmopolitan, 184 (March 1978): 88.
Progressive relaxation and Zen breathing techniques are ex-
plained.

A338 Haines, Aubrey B. "Taking a Flier with TM." Christian
Century, 95 (16-23 August 1978): 770-771.
Critical of Transcendental Meditation devotees who claim
levitation feats.

A339 Hampton, Peter J. "TM and the Salesman." Agency Sales
Magazine, 7 (October 1977): 26-28.
Explains how by means of Transcendental Meditation, the
salesman is able to gain access to his internal source of creative intelligence, which can help him be successful.

A340 Hanley, Charles P., and James L. Spates. "Transcendental
Meditation and Social Psychological Attitudes." Journal
of Psychology, 99 (July 1978): 121-127. Tentatively
scheduled for inclusion in Scientific Research on the
Transcendental Meditation Program: Collected Papers,

Vol. 2. Rheinweiler, West Germany: Maharishi European
Research University Press, (in press).
Meditating students indicated more positive attitudes.

A341   Hanson, Bradley. "Transcendental Meditation: Technique
        and Interpretation." Dial: A Journal of Theology, 17
        (Autumn 1978): 300-303.
        Suggests Christians should be cautious about learning TM
        or recommending it to others because the evidence does not
        support assurances that TM is a religiously neutral tech-
        nique.

A342   Harding, S.D. "The Transcendental Meditation Program in
        British Secondary Schools." Tentatively scheduled for
        inclusion in Scientific Research on the Transcendental
        Meditation Program: Collected Papers, Vol. 2. Rhein-
        weiler, West Germany: Maharishi European Research
        University Press, (in press).
        Neuroticism was reduced in secondary school students who
        practiced the TM technique.

A343   Hart, Daniel E., and John R. Means. "Effects of Meditation
        Versus Professional Reading on Students' Perceptions of
        Paraprofessional Counselors' Effectiveness." Psychological
        Reports, 51 (October 1982): 479-482.
        Showed a positive effect of meditation on self-actualization of
        subjects.

A344   Hassett, James. "Caution: Meditation Can Hurt; Study by
        Leon Otis." Psychology Today, 12 (November 1978):
        125-126.
        Reports on research by Leon Otis that Transcendental Medi-
        tation can have severe side effects in a small number of those
        who meditate.

A345   Hatchard, G. "Influence of the Transcendental Meditation
        Program on Crime Rate in Suburban Cleveland." Tenta-
        tively scheduled for inclusion in Scientific Research on
        the Transcendental Meditation Program: Collected Pa-
        pers, Vol. 2. Rheinweiler, West Germany: Maharishi
        European Research University Press, (in press).
        A correlation was found between the percentage of the popu-
        lation instructed in the TM technique and crime rate change
        in the suburbs of Cleveland, Ohio.

A346   Haynes, Christopher T.; J. Russell Hebert; William Reber;
        and David Orme-Johnson. "The Psychophysiology of
        Advanced Participants in the Transcendental Meditation
        Program: Correlations of EEG Coherence, Creativity,
        H-Reflex Recovery, and Experience of Transcendental
        Consciousness." In Scientific Research on the Transcen-

dental Meditation Program: Collected Papers, Vol. 1.
Edited by David W. Orme-Johnson and John T. Farrow.
2nd ed., Weggis, Switzerland: Maharishi European Research University Press, 1977, p. 208-212.
Advanced meditators were correlated with high EEG coherence, high creativity, rapid neuromuscular recovery, and experience of transcendental consciousness.

A347   Heaton, Dennis, and David W. Orme-Johnson. "The Transcendental Meditation Program and Academic Achievement."
In Scientific Research on the Transcendental Meditation
Program: Collected Papers, Vol. 1. Edited by David W.
Orme-Johnson and John T. Farrow. 2nd ed., Weggis,
Switzerland: Maharishi European Research University
Press, 1977, p. 396-399.
An increase in grade point average was shown by students practicing the TM technique.

A348   Hebert, J. Russell. "Periodic Suspension of Respiration
During the Transcendental Meditation Technique." In
Scientific Research on the Transcendental Meditation Program: Collected Papers, Vol. 1. Edited by David W.
Orme-Johnson and John T. Farrow. 2nd ed., Weggis,
Switzerland: Maharishi European Research University
Press, 1977, p. 134-136.
Ten of the 95 subjects studied for breath patterns during meditation showed periods of breath suspension from 10 to 45 seconds.

A349   _____, and D. Lehmann. "Theta Bursts: An EEG Pattern in Normal Subjects Practising the Transcendental
Meditation Technique." Electroencephalography and Clinical Neurophysiology, 42 (March 1977): 397-405. Tentatively scheduled for inclusion in Scientific Research on
the Transcendental Meditation Program: Collected Papers,
Vol. 2. Rheinweiler, West Germany: Maharishi European
Research University Press, (in press).
Theta bursts found in meditators were different from theta activity in pathological states or sleep. Suggests the experience of satisfaction.

A350   Hedgepeth, William. "Non-Drug Turn-On Hits Campus."
Look, 32 (6 February 1968): 68-78.
Reports on the practice of Transcendental Meditation at the University of California at Berkeley, Yale, and other universities.

A351   Heery, Myrtle. "When Doctors Meditate." Yoga Journal,
(May/June 1981): 31-34.
A report on the International Health Conference sponsored by the Siddha Yoga Dham Foundation in Santa Monica, Cali-

fornia, in December, 1980. A two-day program of seminars, lectures, group discussions and meditations.

A352   Heide, Frederick J. "Habituation of Alpha Blocking During Meditation." Psychophysiology, 16 (March 1979): 198.
Abstract of a study suggesting that the TM technique produces a pattern of responsiveness unlike Zen or Yoga but similar to simple relaxed wakefulness.

A353   _____, and T.D. Borkovec. "Relaxation-Induced Anxiety: Paradoxical Anxiety Enhancement Due to Relaxation Training." Journal of Consulting and Clinical Psychology, 51 (April 1983): 171-182.
Subjects practicing progressive relaxation and mantra meditation were studied for the possibility of paradoxical increases in cognitive, physiological, or behavioral components of anxiety. Based on a dissertation by the first author. [Cf. D91K]

A354   _____; W.L. Wadlington; and Richard M. Lundy. "Hypnotic Responsivity as a Predictor of Outcome in Meditation." International Journal of Clinical and Experimental Hypnosis, 28 (October 1980): 358-366.
Concluded that hypnotic responsivity is moderately predictive of outcome in meditation and that hypnotic responsivity is not increased by practice in meditation.

A355   Heidelberg, R. "Transcendental Meditation in the Obstetrical Psychoprophylaxis." Tentatively scheduled for inclusion in Scientific Research on the Transcendental Meditation Program: Collected Papers, Vol. 2. Rheinweiler, West Germany: Maharishi European Research University Press, (in press).
Mothers practicing the TM technique experienced less pain and anxiety during pregnancy and during birth. A shorter duration of birth and fewer impairments to the children from the delivery were also noted.

A356   Helminiak, Daniel A. "How Is Meditation Prayer?" Review for Religious, 41 (September/October 1982): 774-782.
Explains the psychological and theological aspects of meditation. Concludes that meditative practice is prayer.

A357   _____. "Meditation: Psychologically and Theologically Considered." Pastoral Psychology, 30 (Fall 1981): 6-20.
Summarizes research under six topic headings, moving from the most common effects of regular meditation to the most subtle and rare.

A358   Hendlin, Steven J. "Initial Zen Intensive (Sesshin): A Subjective Account." Journal of Pastoral Counseling, 14

(Fall-Winter 1979): 27-43.
Experimental analysis of the effects of intensive meditation practice on a beginning student.

A359   Hendricks, C.G. "Meditation as Discrimination Training: A Theoretical Note." Journal of Transpersonal Psychology, 7 (1975): 144-146.
The author has found that clients who meditate on a mantra learn to discriminate thought from other stimuli.

A360   Henry, James P. "Relaxation Methods and the Control of Blood Pressure." Psychosomatic Medicine, 40 (June 1978): 273-275.
An editorial discussing the results of various researchers in the use of relaxation methods to control blood pressure.

A361   Herbst, Winfrid. "The Priest and His Daily Meditation." Pastoral Life, 8 (August 1960): 26-31.
Discusses the necessity of daily meditation for priests and offers some suggestions for variety.

A362   Hewitt, Jay, and Ralph Miller. "Relative Effects of Meditation Versus Other Activities on Ratings of Relaxation and Enjoyment of Others." Psychological Reports, 48 (April 1981): 395-398.
Concluded that Transcendental Meditation was not better than some alternative techniques. Subjects were more likely to engage in alternative techniques. Meditation had no effect on ratings of social relations.

A363   Heyes, Anthony David. "Blindness and Yoga." New Outlook for the Blind, 68 (November 1974): 385-393.
The author suggests it would be appropriate to encourage blind people in Yogic practices of exercise and meditation.

A364   Hickman, James L.; Michael Murphy; and Mike Spino. "Psychophysical Transformations Through Meditation and Sport." Simulation and Games, 8 (March 1977): 49-60.
This study explores the effect of meditation on runners.

A365   Hjelle, Larry A. "Transcendental Meditation and Psychological Health." Perceptual and Motor Skills, 39 (August 1974): 623-628. In Scientific Research on the Transcendental Meditation Program: Collected Papers, Vol. 1. Edited by David W. Orme-Johnson and John T. Farrow. 2nd ed., Weggis, Switzerland: Maharishi European Research University Press, 1977, p. 437-441.
Experienced meditators were less anxious and more internally controlled than beginning meditators. They were also more self-actualized.

A366   Hoffer, William. "A Way to Cope with Executive Stress."
        Association Management, 27 (August 1975): 57-59.
        The usefulness of Transcendental Meditation by executives in
        dealing with stress is discussed.

A367   Hoffman, John W.; Herbert Benson; Patricia A. Arns; Gene
        L. Stainbrook; Lewis Landsberg; James B. Young; and
        Andrew Gill. "Reduced Sympathetic Nervous System Re-
        sponsivity Associated with the Relaxation Response."
        Science, 215 (January 1982): 190-192.
        Suggests that subjects eliciting the Relaxation Response may
        be less responsive to stress.

A368   Holeman, Richard, and Gary Seiler. "Effects of Sensitivity
        Training and Transcendental Meditation on Perception of
        Others." Perceptual and Motor Skills, 49 (August 1979):
        270.
        This study compared the effects of six weeks of sensitivity
        training and TM on perception of others.

A369   Holmes, David S.; Sheldon Solomon; Bruce M. Cappo; and
        Jeffrey L. Greenberg. "Effect of Transcendental Meditation
        Versus Resting on Physiological and Subjective Arousal."
        Journal of Personality and Social Psychology, 44 (June
        1983): 1245-1252.
        Both meditation and resting were associated with decreases
        in physiological and subjective arousal. There was no evi-
        dence that TM has a greater influence than resting.

A370   Holmgren, Carl A. "An Assessment of the Possible Relation-
        ship of the Practice of Meditation to Increases in Attentive-
        ness to Learning." (ERIC ED 085 608).
        This 1972 study suggests that Zen meditation facilitates
        greater attentiveness to learning, at time of training. How-
        ever, six months after the experience no significance was
        found.

A371   Holt, William R.; John L. Caruso; and James B. Riley.
        "Transcendental Meditation versus Pseudo-Meditation on
        Visual Choice Reaction Time." Perceptual and Motor
        Skills, 46 (June 1978): 726. Tentatively scheduled for
        inclusion in Scientific Research on the Transcendental
        Meditation Program: Collected Papers, Vol. 2. Rhein-
        weiler, West Germany: Maharishi European Research Uni-
        versity Press, (in press).
        The facilitative effect of Transcendental Meditation was demon-
        strated on visual choice reaction time.

A372   Honsberger, Ronald W., and Archie F. Wilson. "The Effect
        of Transcendental Meditation Upon Bronchial Asthma."
        Clinical Research, 21 (1973): 278. In Scientific Research

on the Transcendental Meditation Program: Collected Papers, Vol. 1. Edited by David W. Orme-Johnson and John T. Farrow. 2nd ed., Weggis, Switzerland: Maharishi European Research University Press, 1977, p. 279. Suggests that TM is a beneficial adjunct in the treatment of asthma and deserves further evaluation.

A373   _____, and _____. "Transcendental Meditation in Treating Asthma." Respiratory Therapy: The Journal of Inhalation Technology, 3 (1973): 79-80. In Scientific Research on the Transcendental Meditation Program: Collected Papers, Vol. 1. Edited by David W. Orme-Johnson and John T. Farrow. 2nd ed., Weggis, Switzerland: Maharishi European Research University Press, 1977, p. 280-282.
The results indicate that TM is useful in the treatment of asthma.

A374 Horn, Paul. "A Visit with India's High-Powered New Prophet." Look, (6 February 1968): 64-66.
A report of an American jazz musician's visit with the Maharishi Mahesh Yogi.

A375 "How Companies Cope with Executive Stress." Business Week, (21 August 1978): 107-108.
Discusses training in biofeedback and meditation for executives to reduce stress.

A376 Howard, Jane. "Year of the Guru: With Report by Jane Howard." Life, 64 (9 February 1968): 52-59.
Examines the influence of Maharishi Mahesh Yogi and Transcendental Meditation, Swami Bhaktivedanta and The Society for Krishna Consciousness, Yogi Dinkar, and Swami Satchidananda.

A377 Incorvaia, Joel. "Teaching Transcendental Meditation in Public Schools: Defining Religion for Establishment Purposes." San Diego Law Review, 16 (March 1979): 325-354.
Reviews the case of Malmak v. Maharishi Mahesh Yogi concerning the teaching of TM in New Jersey public schools.

A378 Ingleside, John J. "Profitable Meditation." Priest, 9 (April 1953): 272-277.
Gives analyses of meditation and suggestions for successful meditation. Directed to priests.

A379 Isaacs, Ken. "Your Very Own Meditator." Popular Science, 197 (November 1970): 92-94, 134.
Explains how to build a dodecahedral structure to use for meditation.

A380   James, Nancy A. "How to Do Everything by Learning to Do
        Nothing." Mademoiselle, 84 (June 1978): 156-157, 202.
        An introduction to Zen meditation.

A381   Janby, Jørn. "Immediate Effects of the Transcendental Medi-
        tation Technique: Increased Skin Resistance During First
        Meditation After Instruction." In Scientific Research on
        the Transcendental Meditation Program: Collected Papers,
        Vol. 1. Edited by David W. Orme-Johnson and John T.
        Farrow. 2nd ed., Weggis, Switzerland: Maharishi Euro-
        pean Research University Press, 1977, p. 213-215.
        Skin resistance was measured before and after instruction in
        TM. A mean increase of 300 percent was observed. Indi-
        cates a decrease in stress and anxiety.

A382   Javalgekar, R.R. "Transcendental Meditation in the Manage-
        ment of Heart Failure." Journal of Molecular and Cellular
        Cardiology, 12, Suppl. 1 (August 1980): 62.
        Abstract of a study suggesting TM as a simple, safe, non-
        toxic therapeutic measure for cardiac patients.

A383   Jerome, Jim. "From India with 'Shakti': A Swami Lights Up
        His Disciples Lives." People, 12 (3 December 1979):
        131-132.
        Reports on the life of Swami Muktananda.

A384   Jevning, Ron. "Major Change in Intermediary Metabolism by
        Behavioral Rest States." Psychophysiology, 19 (May
        1982): 327.
        Abstract of a study where Transcendental Meditation was em-
        ployed for in-depth examination of changes in intermediary
        metabolism.

A384K   _____, and James P. O'Halloran. "Metabolic Effects of
        Transcendental Meditation: Toward a New Paradigm of
        Neurobiology." In Meditation: Classic and Contemporary
        Perspectives, edited by Deane H. Shapiro, Jr. and Roger
        N. Walsh. Hawthorne, N.Y.: Aldine Pub. Co., 1984.

A385   _____; H.C. Pirkle; and A.F. Wilson. "Behavioral Alter-
        ation of Plasma Phenylalamine Concentration." Physiology
        and Behavior, 19 (November 1977): 611-614. Tentatively
        scheduled for inclusion in Scientific Research on the
        Transcendental Meditation Program: Collected Papers,
        Vol. 2. Rheinweiler, West Germany: Maharishi European
        Research University Press, (in press).
        Increased phenylalamine concentration was noted during TM
        practice with no change during relaxation practice.

A386   _____; W.R. Smith; A.F. Wilson; and M.E. Morton. "Al-

terations in Blood Flow During Transcendental Meditation."
Psychophysiology, 13 (March 1976): 168 (Abstract).
Tentatively scheduled for inclusion in Scientific Research
on the Transcendental Meditation Program: Collected Pa-
pers, Vol. 2. Rheinweiler, West Germany: Maharishi
European Research University Press, (in press).
An experiment indicating that the physiology of TM is funda-
mentally different from simple relaxation or sleep.

A 387   , and A.F. Wilson. "Altered Red Cell Metabolism in
Transcendental Meditation." Psychophysiology, 14 (January 1977): 94 (Abstract). Tentatively scheduled for inclusion in Scientific Research on the Transcendental Meditation Program: Collected Papers, Vol. 2. Rheinweiler,
West Germany: Maharishi European Research University
Press, (in press).
Lactate generation in the blood decreased by thirty percent
during Transcendental Meditation. No change was found
during relaxation.

A 388   , and   . "Behavioral Increase of Cerebral
Blood Flow." Physiologist, 21 (August 1978): 60 (Ab-
stract). Tentatively scheduled for inclusion in Scientific
Research on the Transcendental Meditation Program:
Collected Papers, Vol. 2. Rheinweiler, West Germany:
Maharishi European Research University Press, (in press).
A study showing that Transcendental Meditation significantly
increases cerebral blood flow as measured in subjects having
practiced the technique regularly for more than five years.

A 389   ;   ; and J.M. Davidson. "Adrenocortical
Activity During Meditation." Hormones and Behavior, 10
(February 1978): 54-60. Tentatively scheduled for inclu-
sion in Scientific Research on the Transcendental Meditation
Program: Collected Papers, Vol. 2. Rheinweiler, West
Germany: Maharishi European Research University Press,
(in press).
Long-term practitioners of the Transcendental Meditation
technique showed a significant decrease in cortisol.

A 390   ;   ; and J.P. O'Halloran. "Muscle and Skin
Blood Flow and Metabolism During States of Decreased
Activation." Physiology and Behavior, 29 (August 1982):
343-348.
Acute decline of forearm oxygen consumption was observed
in subjects during Transcendental Meditation.

A 391   ;   ; and W.R. Smith. "Plasma Amino Acids
During the Transcendental Meditation Technique: Comparison to Sleep." In Scientific Research on the Transcendental Meditation Program: Collected Papers, Vol. 1.

Edited by David W. Orme-Johnson and John T. Farrow.
2nd ed., Weggis, Switzerland: Maharishi European Research University Press, 1977, p. 145-147.
Long-term TM participants experienced an increase in plasma
phenylalamine. There was no significant change in amino
acid level.

A392 _____; _____; and _____. "The Transcendental
Meditation Technique, Adrenocortical Activity, and Implications for Stress." Experientia, 34 (15 May 1978):
618-619.
The practice of the Transcendental Meditation technique in
subjects eliciting this state regularly for three to five years
is correlated with acute decline of adrenocortical activity not
associated with sleep during the practice.

A393 _____; _____; _____; and M.E. Morton. "Redistri-
bution of Blood Flow in Acute Hypometabolic Behavior."
American Journal of Physiology, 235 (1979): R89-R92.
Tentatively scheduled for inclusion in Scientific Research
on the Transcendental Meditation Program: Collected Papers, Vol. 2. Rheinweiler, West Germany: Maharishi
European Research University Press, (in press).
The study noted considerable increase of nonrenal, nonhepa-
tic blood flow during TM and to a lesser extent during rest
after the practice.

A394 _____; _____; and Eileen F. VanderLaan. "Plasma
Prolactin and Growth Hormone During Meditation." Psychosomatic Medicine, 40 (June 1978): 329-333. Tentatively
scheduled for inclusion in Scientific Research on the
Transcendental Meditation Program: Collected Papers, Vol.
2. Rheinweiler, West Germany: Maharishi European Research University Press, (in press).
Both short-term and long-term practitioners of the Transcendental Meditation technique showed increases in plasma pro-
lactine towards the end or soon after the practice.

A395 _____; _____; _____; and S. Levine. "Plasma Pro-
lactin and Cortisol During Transcendental Meditation." In
Scientific Research on the Transcendental Meditation Pro-
gram: Collected Papers, Vol. 1. Edited by David W.
Orme-Johnson and John T. Farrow. 2nd ed., Weggis,
Switzerland: Maharishi European Research University
Press, 1977, p. 143-144.
Plasma cortisol decreased during the TM technique. Plasma
prolactin increased after the technique. This indicates a
reduction in stress.

A396 Johansson, F.P. "The Effect of the Practice of the Transcendental Meditation Program on the Degree of Neuroticism

as Measured by DMT [Defense Mechanism Test]." Tentatively scheduled for inclusion in Scientific Research on the Transcendental Meditation Program: Collected Papers, Vol. 2. Rheinweiler, West Germany: Maharishi European Research University Press, (in press).
Deep rooted stresses were resolved through six months of TM practice.

A397   Johnson, Janis. "Court Challenge to TM." Christian Century, 93 (31 March 1976): 300-302.
Reports on court litigation in New Jersey to stop the teaching of Transcendental Meditation in public schools.

A398   Johnston, Hank. "Marketed Social Movement: A Case Study of the Rapid Growth of TM." Pacific Sociological Review, 23 (July 1980): 333-354.
Analyzes the causal factors in TM's rapid growth, including strategies of the organization, needs of participants, and media coverage.

A399   Johnston, William. "Superthinking: An Introduction to Christian Zen." America, 125 (24 July 1971): 28-30.
This article appears as a chapter in his book, Christian Zen.

A400   Jonsson, C. "Organizational Development Through the Transcendental Meditation Program: A Study of Relationships Between the Transcendental Meditation Program and Certain Efficiency Criteria." Tentatively scheduled for inclusion in Scientific Research on the Transcendental Meditation Program: Collected Papers, Vol. 2. Rheinweiler, West Germany: Maharishi European Research University Press, (in press).
Subjects practicing the TM technique were more alert and active, were less tired and angry, had more self-confidence, and had a better ability to assign correct priorities to different tasks when compared to non-meditators.

A401   Justin Lucian, Bro. "St. LaSalle and Transcendental Meditation." Review for Religious, 36 (January 1977): 91-96.
The meditation techniques of St. John Baptist de LaSalle is compared to the Transcendental Meditation method.

A402   Kabat-Zinn, Jon. "An Outpatient Program in Behavioral Medicine for Chronic Pain Patients Based on the Practice of Mindfulness Meditation: Theoretical Considerations and Preliminary Results." General Hospital Psychiatry, 4 (April 1982): 33-47.
Concluded that this form of meditation can be used effectively in self-regulation for chronic pain patients.

A403   Kanas, Nick, and Mardi J. Horowitz. "Reactions of Tran-

scendental Meditators and Nonmeditators to Stress Films:
A Cognitive Study." Archives of General Psychiatry, 34
(December 1977): 1431-1436.
The article examines the claim that Transcendental Meditation
reduces stress. Meditators and non-meditators were examined
on cognitive and affective measures. Meditators did not show
less stress than non-meditators.

A404   Kanellakos, Demetri P. "Transcendental Consciousness: Ex-
        panded Awareness as a Means of Preventing and Eliminat-
        ing the Effects of Stress." In Stress and Anxiety, Vol.
        5. Edited by Charles D. Spielberger and Irwin G. Sara-
        son. New York: Wiley & Sons, 1978, p. 262-315.
A literature review of research on the TM program and its
effectiveness in the elimination of anxiety and stress and the
expansion of individual consciousness.

A405   Kaplan, Stephen. "Appraisal of a Psychological Approach to
        Meditation." Zygon, 13 (March 1978): 83-101.
Discusses psychological-scientific theories of meditation and
the presuppositions on which they are based.

A406   Kasamatsu, Akira, and Tomio Hirai. "An Electroencephalo-
        graphic Study of the Zen Meditation (Zazen)." Journal of
        the American Institute of Hypnosis, 14 (May 1973): 107-
        114. Also in Meditation: Classic and Contemporary Per-
        spectives, edited by Deane H. Shapiro, Jr. and Roger N.
        Walsh. Hawthorne, N.Y.: Aldine Pub. Co., 1984.
The EEG changes accompanied with Zen meditation have been
described in detail. Changes were also compared with that
of hypnotic trance and sleep.

A407   Katz, David. "Decreased Drug Use and Prevention of Drug
        Use Through the Transcendental Meditation Program."
        In Scientific Research on the Transcendental Meditation
        Program: Collected Papers, Vol. 1. Edited by David W.
        Orme-Johnson and John T. Farrow. 2nd ed., Weggis,
        Switzerland: Maharishi European Research University
        Press, 1977, p. 536-543.
Subjects practicing the TM technique significantly decreased
their use of marijuana, wine and beer, and liquor.

A408   Keating, Thomas. "Contemplative Prayer in the Christian
        Tradition." America, 138 (8 April 1978): 278-281.
A history of contemplative prayer showing that it has been
generally disregarded in seminaries, religious life, and on
the parish level.

A409   _____. "Prayer and Spirituality: Meditative Prayer."
        Today's Catholic Teacher, 12 (February 1979): 32-33.
Explains the need for silence in daily contemplative prayer.

A410   Keefe, Jeffrey. "Stress and Meditation." Catechist, 14
          (February 1981): 3.
          A brief report on a few meditation methods.

A411   Kelly, Hugh. "In Defense of Meditation." Doctrine and Life,
          14 (December 1964): 599-607.
          Contends that Christian meditation is still important and nec-
          essary for spiritual development.

A412   Kelsey, Morton. "Teaching Religious Experience Through
          Meditation." Council on the Study of Religion, Bulletin,
          8 (February 1977): 1, 3-6.
          Description of a class at the University of Notre Dame offer-
          ing experiences in some of the better known meditative tech-
          niques as an approach to religious experience.

A413   Kemmerling, T. "Effect of Transcendental Meditation on
          Muscular Tone." Psychopathometric, 4 (1978): 437-440.
          Tentatively scheduled for inclusion in Scientific Research
          on the Transcendental Meditation Program: Collected Pa-
          pers, Vol. 2. Rheinweiler, West Germany: Maharishi
          European Research University Press, (in press).
          Muscular relaxation was significantly higher during meditation
          than during the normal relaxation level.

A414   Kennedy, Raymond B. "Self-Induced Depersonalization Syn-
          drome." American Journal of Psychiatry, 133 (November
          1976): 1326-1328.
          The author reports on two cases in which depersonalization
          occurred during the waking consciousness of individuals who
          had engaged in meditative techniques designed to alter con-
          sciousness.

A415   Kenton, Leslie, and Chris Phillips. "Coping with Stress."
          Industrial Management (London), (November 1975): 32-35.
          Examines Transcendental Meditation and Relaxation for Living
          techniques for reducing stress and promoting relaxation among
          managers.

A416   Kim, Young Mi. "Meditation and Behavioral Therapy." In-
          terciencia, 5 (1980): 157-158.
          Zen Buddhism and Transcendental Meditation are considered
          for possible use with behavior therapy.

A417   Kindler, Herbert S. "The Influence of a Meditation-Relaxation
          Technique on Group Problem-Solving Effectiveness." Jour-
          nal of Applied Behavioral Science, 15 (October/November/
          December 1979): 527-533.
          This research was in conjunction with his dissertation. Re-
          sults are interpreted as encouragement for organizations to
          offer meditation-relaxation programs to employees on a volun-
          tary basis. [Cf. D112]

A418   King, Winston L. "Comparison of Theravada and Zen Bud-
        dhist Meditational Methods and Goals." History of Reli-
        gions, 9 (May 1970): 304-315.
        Examines and evaluates some salient features of the contrasts
        and likenesses of the two forms of meditation.

A419   _____. "Experience in Buddhist Meditation." Journal of
        Religion, 41 (January 1961): 51-61.
        An empirical study of Buddhist meditation in a meditation
        center in Burma.

A420   _____. "Structure and Dynamics of Attainment of Cessa-
        tion in Theravada Meditation." Journal of the American
        Academy of Religion, 45 (June 1977): 226.
        Abstract of a study which discusses the necessary compon-
        ents and methodology of attaining cessation, the highest
        meditational state possible in Theravada Buddhism. Article
        available from Scholars Press, Missoula, Mt.

A421   Kirkland, Karl, and James G. Hollandsworth. "Effective
        Test Taking: Skills-Acquisition Versus Anxiety-Reduction
        Techniques." Journal of Consulting and Clinical Psychol-
        ogy, 48 (August 1980): 431-439.
        Skills-acquisition was found to be superior over cue-controlled
        relaxation and meditation for each of the variables measured.
        [Cf. D115]

A422   Kirsch, Irving, and David Henry. "Self-Desensitization and
        Meditation in the Reduction of Public Speaking Anxiety."
        Journal of Consulting and Clinical Psychology, 47 (June
        1979): 536-541.
        All treatments were equally effective in reducing anxiety.

A423   Kirtane, L.T. "Transcendental Meditation: A Multipurpose
        Tool in Clinical Practice." Tentatively scheduled for in-
        clusion in Scientific Research on the Transcendental Medi-
        tation Program: Collected Papers, Vol. 2. Rheinweiler,
        West Germany: Maharishi European Research University
        Press, (in press).
        The TM technique was effective in contributing to the restor-
        ation of good health in many cases of severe mental and
        physical illness.

A424   Kitagawa, Joseph M. "Experience, Knowledge and Under-
        standing." Religious Studies, 11 (June 1975): 201-213.
        Discusses the openness in the West toward Eastern religious
        insights as well as their meditation techniques.

A425   Klemons, Ira M. "Changes in Inflammation in Persons Prac-
        ticing the Transcendental Meditation Technique." In
        Scientific Research on the Transcendental Meditation Pro-

gram: Collected Papers, Vol. 1. Edited by David W.
Orme-Johnson and John T. Farrow. 2nd ed., Weggis,
Switzerland: Maharishi European Research University
Press, 1977, p. 287-291.
Periodontal inflamation was decreased among participants in
a TM program. Suggests the TM program increases resist-
ance to disease through a general strengthening process.

A426   Kline, Kenneth S.; Edward M. Docherty; and Frank H. Farley. "Transcendental Meditation, Self-Actualization, and
Global Personality." Journal of General Psychology, 106
(January 1982): 3-8.
Reasons for failing to find a significant change in global personality or self-actualization due to the practice of Transcendental Meditation were discussed. Cautions in conducting this type of research.

A427   Kobal, G.; A. Wandohoefer; and K.-H. Plattig. "EEG Power
Spectra and Auditory Evoked Potentials in Transcendental
Meditation." Pflüger's Archiv: European Journal of
Physiology, 359 (1975): R96.
Abstract of experiments computing amplitudes and areas of
the averaged potentials compared by variance analysis in TM
subjects. A follow-up study.

A428   Koh, T.C. "Tai Chi Chuan." American Journal of Chinese
Medicine, 9 (1981): 15-22.
Tai Chi is briefly described as an exercise, a practice of
meditation, and a means of self-defense.

A429   Kohr, Richard L. "Changes in Subjective Meditation Experience During a Short-Term Project." Journal of Altered
States of Consciousness, 3 (1978): 221-234.
Results show that close adherence to meditation procedures
was important to a higher quality experience. Levels of
anxiety and personal problems are also discussed.

A430   _____. "Dimensionality in Meditative Experience: A
Replication." Journal of Transpersonal Psychology, 9
(1977): 193-203. Also in Meditation: Classic and Contemporary Perspectives, edited by Deane H. Shapiro, Jr.
and Roger N. Walsh. Hawthorne, N.Y.: Aldine Pub.
Co., 1984.
This study reports on an effort to replicate the findings of
Karlis Osis and his associates, which sought to test the util-
ity of Edgar Cayce's meditation technique.

A431   Kolsawalla, Maharukh B. "An Experimental Investigation into
the Effectiveness of Some Yogic Variables as a Mechanism
of Change in the Value-Attitude System." Journal of
Indian Psychology, 1 (January 1978): 59-68.

Along with becoming more open-minded an individual practicing meditation felt relaxed and tends toward greater emotional maturity and self-control.

A432 Kornfield, Jack. "Intensive Insight Meditation: A Phenomenological Study." Journal of Transpersonal Psychology,
11 (1979): 41-58.
A study to record and examine the range and patterns of
experiences reported by students of Vipassana or insight
meditation.

A433 Kory, Robert B. "TM: An Investment with Positive Returns." Management World, 5 (November 1976): 8-11.
Reports on the popularity of Transcendental Meditation among
business people.

A434 _____, and Pat Hufnagel. "The Effect of the Science of
Creative Intelligence Course on High School Students: A
Preliminary Report." In Scientific Research on the Tran-
cendental Meditation Program: Collected Papers, Vol. 1.
Edited by David W. Orme-Johnson and John T. Farrow.
2nd ed., Weggis, Switzerland: Maharishi European Re-
search University Press, 1977, p. 400-402.
Academic performance and psychological health improved
among high school students enrolled in Science of Creative
Intelligence courses.

A435 Koseki, Aaron K. "Concept of Practice in San-lun Thought:
Chi-Tsang and the 'Concurrent Insight' of the Two
Truths." Philosophy East and West, 31 (October 1981):
449-466.
Discusses the emergence of a San-lun tradition of meditation
masters.

A436 Kotchabhakdi, N., and T. Chentanez. "Biochemical Effects
of the TM and TM-Sidhi Program." Tentatively scheduled
for inclusion in Scientific Research on the Transcendental
Meditation Program: Collected Papers, Vol. 2. Rheinweiler, West Germany: Maharishi European Research University Press, (in press).
A paper presented at the International Congress on Research
on Higher States of Consciousness, Bangkok, Thailand, January, 1980. Various biochemical measures were recorded during and after meditation.

A437 Krahne, W., and G. Tenoli. "EEG and Transcendental Meditation." Pflüger's Archiv: European Journal of Physiology, 359 (1975): R95.
Abstract of a report showing that EEG changes during TM
were different from those seen in states of wakefulness,
drowsiness and sleep, but showed some similarities to other
forms of relaxation.

A 438   Kral, Mary. "Christian Meditation: It's the Real Thing."
      Our Sunday Visitor, 64 (14 March 1976): 16.
      Explains what traditional Christian meditation is and how one
      does it. First in a series of articles.

A 439   _____. "A Guide to Christian Meditation." Our Sunday
      Visitor, 64 (21 March 1976): 3.
      A practical outline in seven steps of how Christian meditation
      can be done. Part two in a series of articles.

A 440   _____. "Meditation: Affair of the Heart." Our Sunday
      Visitor, 64 (28 March 1976): 3+
      The author tells you how you can know if you're ready for
      advanced meditation. Last part in a series of articles.

A 441   Kras, Diana J. "The Transcendental Meditation Technique
      and EEG Alpha Activity." In Scientific Research on the
      Transcendental Meditation Program: Collected Papers,
      Vol. 1. Edited by David W. Orme-Johnson and John T.
      Farrow. 2nd ed., Weggis, Switzerland: Maharishi
      European Research University Press, 1977, p. 173-181.
      An increase of alpha activity in the EEG was found in par-
      ticipants in the TM program.

A 442   Krippner, Stanley, and Michael Maliszewski. "Meditation and
      the Creative Process." Journal of Indian Psychology, 1
      (January 1978): 40-58.
      Many research articles on meditation and creativity are re-
      viewed. Evidence indicates a complex relationship.

A 443   Kroll, Una M. "Doctor's View of TM." Frontier, 17 (Spring
      1974): 31-33.
      Discusses the physiological and psychological benefits of
      practicing Transcendental Meditation. Also examines its re-
      lationship to the Christian church.

A 444   Kubose, Sunnan K. "An Experimental Investigation of Psy-
      chological Aspects of Meditation." Psychologia: An In-
      ternational Journal of Psychology in the Orient, 19
      (March 1976): 1-10.
      Investigates the description, production, and utilization as-
      pects of meditation, with special attention to the concentra-
      tive aspect of meditation.

A 445   _____, and Takao Umemoto. "Creativity and the Zen
      Koan." Psychologia: An International Journal of Psy-
      chology in the Orient, 23 (March 1980): 1-9.
      It is proposed that both creative problem solving and Zen
      koan study share common stages of preparation, incubation,
      illumination, and evaluation.

A446   No entry.

A447   No entry.

A448   Kukulan, J.C.; A. Aron; and A.I. Abrams. "The Transcendental Meditation Program and Children's Personality." Tentatively scheduled for inclusion in Scientific Research on the Transcendental Meditation Program: Collected Papers, Vol. 2. Rheinweiler, West Germany: Maharishi European Research University Press, (in press).
A paper presented at the meeting of the Canadian Psychological Association, Ottawa, Canada, 1978. Children practicing the TM program scored lower on anxiety level and higher on internal locus of control than non-meditators.

A449   Kulandai, Victor. "Transcendental Meditation, and the Great Night Festival of Shiva, March 11, 1975." Social Justice Review, 68 (February 1976): 345-346.
Critical of an address by Maharishi Mahesh Yogi in New Delhi.

A450   _____. "The Trap: Transcendental Meditation." Social Justice Review, 68 (December 1975): 249-252.
Critical of TM from a Christian point of view.

A451   Kuna, Daniel J. "Meditation and Work." Vocational Guidance Quarterly, 23 (June 1975): 342-345.
Research results are used to conclude that meditation leads to a number of physiological and psychological changes that are conducive to work adjustment and performance.

A452   Lahr, J.J. "Relationship Between Experience in Transcendental Meditation and Adaption to Life Events and Related Stress." Tentatively scheduled for inclusion in Scientific Research on the Transcendental Meditation Program: Collected Papers, Vol. 2. Rheinweiler, West Germany: Maharishi European Research University Press, (in press).
Experienced practitioners of the TM program adapted better to changes in their lives than non-meditators.

A453   LaMore, George E. "Secular Selling of a Religion." Christian Century, 92 (10 December 1975): 1133-1137. See [A118] for critique.
Critical of Transcendental Meditation claims. Disputes the claim that it is a technique compatible with all faiths.

A454   Landrith, G., III. "The Maharishi Effect and Invincibility: The Influence of the TM Program on the Variables of Crime, Automobile Accidents and Fires." Tentatively scheduled for inclusion in Scientific Research on the Transcendental Meditation Program: Collected Papers,

Vol. 2. Rheinweiler, West Germany: Maharishi European
Research University Press, (in press).
A positive effect on the variables was found in cities with
one percent of the population practicing the TM technique.

A455   Lang, R.; K. Dehof; K.A. Meurer; and W. Kaufmann.
"Sympathetic Activity and Transcendental Meditation."
Journal of Neural Transmission, 44 (1979): 117-135.
Tentatively scheduled for inclusion in Scientific Research
on the Transcendental Meditation Program: Collected Pa-
pers, Vol. 2. Rheinweiler, West Germany: Maharishi
European Research University Press, (in press).
Concludes that effects of Transcendental Meditation on the
autonomic nervous system are more obvious in advanced medi-
tators.

A456   Lapham, Lewis H. "There Once Was a Guru from Rishikesh."
Saturday Evening Post, 241 (4 May 1968): 23-29, and
(18 May 1968): 28-33, 88.
A two part article. The writer learns about Transcendental
Meditation, travels to India, and meets the Maharishi Mahesh
Yogi, the Beatles, and other notables.

A457   Larkin, Vincent, et al. "Health Instruction Packages: Con-
sumer--Behavior/Emotions." (ERIC ED 202 524).
"Eliciting the Relaxation Response Through Self-Hypnosis"
by Richard L. Bunning, describes the common elements of
all relaxation techniques.

A458   Lasden, Martin. "Before You Reach Your Breaking Point."
Computer Decisions, 14 (February 1982): 84-98.
Includes a brief report on the use of Transcendental Medita-
tion to reduce stress for employees at various companies.

A459   Laurie, Gina. "An Investigation Into the Changes in Skin
Resistance During the Transcendental Meditation Tech-
nique." In Scientific Research on the Transcendental
Meditation Program: Collected Papers, Vol. 1. Edited by
David W. Orme-Johnson and John T. Farrow. 2nd ed.,
Weggis, Switzerland: Maharishi European Research Uni-
versity Press, 1977, p. 216-223.
Subjects experienced a significant increase in basal skin re-
sistance during the TM technique.

A460   Lazar, Zoe; Lawrence Farwell; and John T. Farrow. "The
Effects of the Transcendental Meditation Program on Anxi-
ety, Drug Abuse, Cigarette Smoking, and Alcohol Con-
sumption." In Scientific Research on the Transcendental
Meditation Program: Collected Papers, Vol. 1. Edited by
David W. Orme-Johnson and John T. Farrow. 2nd ed.,
Weggis, Switzerland: Maharishi European Research Uni-

versity Press, 1977, p. 524-535.

Subjects showed a reduction in anxiety and substance abuse after they began the practice of the TM technique. The reduction increased in those who practiced TM over longer periods of time.

A460K   Lazarus, Arnold A. "Meditation: The Problems of Any Unimodel Technique." In Meditation: Classic and Contemporary Perspectives, edited by Deane H. Shapiro, Jr. and Roger N. Walsh. Hawthorne, N.Y.: Aldine Pub. Co. 1984.

A461   _____. "Psychiatric Problems Precipitated by Transcendental Meditation." Psychological Reports,, 39 (October 1976): 601-602.

TM proves extremely effective when applied to properly selected cases by informed practitioners. When used indiscriminately it can precipitate serious psychiatric problems.

A462   Lefferts, Barney. "Chief Guru of the Western World." New York Times Magazine, (17 December 1967): 44-45, 48, 50, 52, 54, 57, 60.

A report on the Maharishi Mahesh Yogi.

A463   Legrand, P.; M. Toubol; J. Barrabino; G. Darcourt; and A. Fadeuilhe. "Contingent Negative Variation in Meditation." Electroencephalography and Clinical Neurophysiology, 43 (1977): 532-533. Tentatively scheduled for inclusion in Scientific Research on the Transcendental Meditation Program: Collected Papers, Vol. 2. Rheinweiler, West Germany: Maharishi European Research University Press, (in press).

The modification of the amplitude and terminal phase of the CNV was shown to persist after Transcendental Meditation.

A464   Lehmann, John W., and Herbert Benson. "Nonpharmacologic Treatment of Hypertension: A Review." General Hospital Psychiatry, 4 (1982): 27-32.

Reviews the literature about the benefits of nonpharmacologic interventions, including relaxation-meditation techniques, reduction of salt intake, weight loss, and regular vigorous exercise for reducing hypertension.

A465   Lehrer, Paul M.; Saundra Schoicket; Patricia Carrington; and Robert L. Woolfolk. "Psychophysiological and Cognitive Responses to Stressful Stimuli in Subjects Practicing Progressive Relaxation and Clinically Standardized Meditation." Behaviour Research and Therapy, 18 (1980): 293-303.

Article examines differences between the two methods. Heart rate, integrated frontalis EMG activity, and muscular relaxation were measured.

A466   Leighton, Sally M. "Invitation to Meditation." Grail, 38
        (October 1956): 50-54.
        Shows that meditation and mental prayer are useful ways to
        deepen one's spiritual life.

A467   Lesh, Terry V. "Zen Meditation and the Development of
        Empathy in Counselors." Journal of Human Psychology,
        10 (Spring 1970): 39-74. Also in Meditation: Classic
        and Contemporary Perspectives, edited by Deane H.
        Shapiro, Jr. and Roger N. Walsh. Hawthorne, N.Y.:
        Aldine Pub. Co., 1984.
        This study suggests that, after formal training in Zen medi-
        tation, counselors' empathic ability tends to decrease.

A468   LeShan, Lawrence. "The Case for Meditation." Saturday
        Review, 2 (22 February 1975): 26-27.
        A report on the popularity of meditation and its contribution
        to society.

A469   Lester, David. "Transcendental Meditation in Correctional
        Settings: A Review and Discussion." Corrective and
        Social Psychiatry and Journal of Behavior Technology
        Methods and Therapy, 28 (1982): 63-64.
        Discusses the advantages and disadvantages of TM as com-
        pared with relaxation techniques in prisons.

A469K   Leung, Paul. "Comparative Effects of Training in External
        and Internal Concentration on Two Counseling Behaviors."
        Journal of Counseling Psychology, 20 (May 1973): 227-
        234. Also in Meditation: Classic and Contemporary Per-
        spectives, edited by Deane H. Shapiro, Jr. and Roger N.
        Walsh. Hawthorne, N.Y.: Aldine Pub. Co., 1984.
        Zen techniques significantly increased subjects' ability to
        have empathic understanding of the client and the ability to
        respond selectively to client statements during a counseling
        interview.

A470   Levander, V.L.; H. Benson; R.C. Wheeler; and R.K. Wal-
        lace. "Increased Forearm Blood Flow During a Wakeful
        Hypometabolic State." Federation Proceedings, 31 (1972):
        405 (Abstract). In Scientific Research on the Transcen-
        dental Meditation Program: Collected Papers, Vol. 1.
        Edited by David W. Orme-Johnson and John T. Farrow.
        2nd ed., Weggis, Switzerland: Maharishi European Re-
        search University Press, 1977, p. 142.
        A study which shows there was an increase in forearm blood
        flow of subjects during the practice of the TM technique.
        Suggests decreased sympathetic activity and deep relaxation.

A471   Levin, Susan. "The Transcendental Meditation Technique in
        Secondary Education." (ERIC ED 186 775). Tentatively

scheduled for inclusion in Scientific Research on the Transcendental Meditation Program: Collected Papers, Vol. 2.
Rheinweiler, West Germany: Maharishi European Research
University Press, (in press).
A paper presented at the Annual Convention of the American
Psychological Association (87th, New York, N.Y., Sept. 1-5,
1979). High school students who practiced the TM technique
showed significantly less neuroticism and improvement in self-
concept. [Cf. D130]

A472   Levine, Paul H. "Transcendental Meditation and the Science
        of Creative Intelligence." Phi Delta Kappan, 54 (Decem-
        ber 1972): 231-235.
Surveys the research literature on TM and discusses the implications for education.

A473   _____; J. Russell Hebert; Christopher T. Haynes; and
        Urs Strobel. "EEG Coherence During the Transcendental
        Meditation Technique." In Scientific Research on the
        Transcendental Meditation Program: Collected Papers,
        Vol. 1. Edited by David W. Orme-Johnson and John T.
        Farrow. 2nd ed., Weggis, Switzerland: Maharishi Euro-
        pean Research University Press, 1977, p. 187-207.
Recorded increases in EEG coherence suggesting increased
ordering of brain wave activity during Transcendental Meditation.

A474   Lewis, Shawn D. "Transcendental Meditation." Ebony, 31
        (July 1976): 100-102, 104-106.
Reports on the benefits and claims of Transcendental Meditation.

A475   Lin, M.T., and A. Chandra. "Effects of Transcendental
        Meditation on the Physiological Functions in Chinese Peo-
        ple." Tentatively scheduled for inclusion in Scientific
        Research on the Transcendental Meditation Program:
        Collected Papers, Vol. 2. Rheinweiler, West Germany:
        Maharishi European Research University Press, (in press).
A paper presented at the International Congress on Research
on Higher States of Consciousness, Bangkok, Thailand, January, 1980. Subjects showed reductions in metabolic rate and
other physiological functions as well as increased auditory
acuity and tolerance to cold.

A476   Linden, William. "Practicing of Meditation by School Chil-
        dren and Their Levels of Field Dependence-Independence,
        Text Anxiety, and Reading Achievement." Journal of
        Consulting and Clinical Psychology, 41 (August 1973):
        139-143. Also in Meditation: Classic and Contemporary
        Perspectives, edited by Deane H. Shapiro, Jr. and Roger
        N. Walsh. Hawthorne, N.Y.: Aldine Pub. Co., 1984.

Subjects became more field independent and less anxious.
No effect on level of reading achievement was apparent.

A477   Lintel, Albert G., III. "Physiological Anxiety Response in
        Transcendental Meditators and Nonmeditators." Perceptual
        and Motor Skills, 50 (February 1980): 295-300.
        Concluded that Transcendental Meditation is not an effective
        means of reducing autonomic responses to stress.

A478   Lionel, N.D. "Meditation and Medicine." Ceylon Medical
        Journal, 21 (March 1976): 1-2.
        An editorial reviewing findings on the therapeutic value of
        Transcendental Meditation. Expresses cautious optimism.

A479   Lock, Mary C. "Can Meditation Improve Your Management
        Performance." Manage, 29 (November/December 1977):
        22-23.
        Reports on the use of meditation to reduce stress.

A480   Lourdes, P.V., and M.S. Silverman. "The Transcendental
        Meditation Program and a Basic Paradigm Shift in Science
        and Psychotherapy." Tentatively scheduled for inclusion
        in Scientific Research on the Transcendental Meditation
        Program: Collected Papers, Vol. 2. Rheinweiler, West
        Germany: Maharishi European Research University Press,
        (in press).
        Describes how the Science of Creative Intelligence could be
        an alternate paradigm to account more comprehensively for
        human phenomena and how the TM technique will bring about
        this shift in science and psychotherapy.

A481   Love, Mike. "Transcendental Meditation." Senior Scholastic,
        101 (25 September 1972): 35, 39-40.
        Beach Boy Mike Love writes of his personal experience with
        TM and the Maharishi Mahesh Yogi.

A482   Lovell-Smith, D.H. "Transcendental Meditation: Treating
        the Patients as Well as the Disease." New Zealand Family
        Physician, 9 (April 1982): 62-64.
        The writer feels that the TM program is an ideal therapy for
        promoting better health.

A483   Lukas, Jerome S. "The Effects of TM on Concurrent Heart
        Rate, Peripheral Blood Pulse Volume, and the Alpha Wave
        Frequency." (ERIC ED 091 627).
        A paper presented at the Annual Meeting of the American
        Psychological Association, Montreal, Canada, August 1973.
        Results suggested that TM had little effect on heart rate,
        peripheral blood pulse volume, or alpha wave frequency.

A484   MacCallum, Michael J. "The Transcendental Meditation Pro-

gram and Creativity." In Scientific Research on the Transcendental Meditation Program: Collected Papers, Vol. 1. Edited by David W. Orme-Johnson and John T. Farrow. 2nd ed., Weggis, Switzerland: Maharishi European Research University Press, 1977, p. 410-419.
Subjects practicing the TM technique showed increases in creativity.

A485   MacCormick, Chalmers. "Zen Catholicism of Thomas Merton." Journal of Ecumenical Studies, 9 (Fall 1982): 802-818.
Suggests that Merton found Zen and Catholicism not only compatible, but complementary, which made him more rather than less a Catholic.

A486   Madsen, W.C. "Meditation and the Flexibility of Constructions of Reality." Tentatively scheduled for inclusion in Scientific Research on the Transcendental Meditation Program: Collected Papers, Vol. 2. Rheinweiler, West Germany: Maharishi European Research University Press, (in press).
Transcendental Meditation was shown to increase the open-mindedness of the meditators.

A487   Magarey, Christopher. "Healing and Meditation in Medical Practice." Medical Journal of Australia, 1 (April 1981): 338, 340-341.
Suggests that with daily meditation, medical practitioners can expect to become not only more effective healers but also to find increasing equanimity, health, and happiness in their own lives.

A488   Main, John. "An Introduction to Christian Meditation." Cistercian Studies, 14 (1979): 232-241.
This is the first in a series of four talks intended to serve as an introduction to the practice of Christian meditation, using a mantra.

A489   Majumdar, Sachindra K. "Meditation: An Open Way to Serenity of Mind and Body." Vogue, 156 (July 1970): 105, 107-108, 110.
An introduction to the meaning and value of meditation.

A490   "Making Brain Waves." Newsweek, 75 (23 March 1970): 92-93.
A short report on the physiological testing of Zen meditators.

A491   Malec, James, and Carl N. Sipprelle. "Physiological and Subjective Effects of Zen Meditation and Demand Characteristics." Journal of Consulting and Clinical Psychology, 45 (April 1977): 339-340. Also in Meditation: Classic and Contemporary Perspectives, edited by Deane H.

Shapiro, Jr. and Roger N. Walsh. Hawthorne, N.Y.: Aldine Pub. Co., 1984.
Results show that Zen meditation produces small physiological changes in naive, unpracticed subjects.

A 492   Manchester, Harland. "Transcendental Meditation: What's It All About?" Reader's Digest, 107 (December 1975): 114-116.
A brief explanation of Transcendental Meditation.

A 493   Manickam, P. Kambar. "Mental Health and Meditation." Religion and Society, 26 (June 1979): 14-20.
Explains the philosophical and psychological basis of Indian understanding of mental health in relationship to meditation and the Church.

A 494   Mano, D. Keith. "Transcendental Meditation." National Review, 27 (6 June 1975): 618-619.
A satirical report on Transcendental Meditation

A 495   Maquet, Jacques. "Bhavana in Contemporary Sri Lanka: The Idea and Practice." In Buddhist Studies in Honour of Walpola Rahula. Edited by Somaratna Balasooriya. London: Gordon Fraser, and Sri Lanka: Vimamsa, 1980, p. 139-153. Orig. pub. as "Meditation in Contemporary Sri Lanka: Idea and Practice." Journal of Transpersonal Psychology, 7 (1975): 182-196.
Includes a personal acocunt of the author's participation in the life of a meditation monastery for one month, where he visited, listened to, and observed the activities of monks and lay persons involved in the Buddhist life and meditation. Meditation remains largely unpracticed by Buddhist monks in Sri Lanka.

A 496   Maraldo, John C. "The Hermeneutics of Practice in Dogen and Francis of Assisi: An Exercise in Buddhist-Christian Dialogue." Eastern Buddhist, New Series, 14 (Autumn 1982): 22-46.
Discusses the Zen practice of zazen and the practice of St. Francis. Includes "The Canticle of Brother Sun."

A 497   Marchand, Roger. "New Light on TM." Liguorian, 66 (September 1978): 38-43, and (October 1978): 19-24.
A two part, critical article discussing TM and Benson's Relaxation Response. Recommends instead a method by Karl Rahner.

A 498   Marcus, Jay B. "Transcendental Meditation: A New Method of Reducing Drug Abuse." Drug Forum, 3 (Winter 1974): 113-136.
Describes the physiological and psychological effects of Tran-

scendental Meditation. Surveys investigations into treating and preventing drug abuse.

A499 _____. "Transcendental Meditation: Consciousness Expansion as a Rehabilitation Technique." Journal of Psychedelic Drugs, 7 (April/June 1975): 169-179.
The article focusses on TM as a rehabilitation technique in drug abuse.

A500 _____. "What the Supervisor Should Know About Transcendental Meditation." Supervisory Management, 23 (June 1978): 31-41, and (July 1978): 33-39.
A two part article adapted from the author's book, TM and Business: Personal and Corporate Benefits of Inner Development. New York: McGraw-Hill, 1977. Concentrates on brain wave activity.

A501 Marechal, Paul. "Transcendental Meditation and Its Potential Value in the Monastic Life." Cistercian Studies, 8 (1973): 210-237.
Concerned with the definition, effects, and mechanics of TM, as well as the value and feasibility of including meditation in the monastic horarium.

A501K Marlatt, C. Alan; Robert R. Pagano; Richard M. Rose; and Janice K. Marques. "Effects of Meditation and Relaxation Upon Alcohol Use in Male Social Drinkers." In Meditation: Classic and Contemporary Perspectives, edited by Deane H. Shapiro, Jr. and Roger N. Walsh. Hawthorne, N.Y.: Aldine Pub. Co., 1984.

A502 Martinetti, Raymond F. "Influence of Transcendental Meditation on Perceptual Illusion: A Pilot Study." Perceptual and Motor Skills, 43 (December 1976): 822. Tentatively scheduled for inclusion in Scientific Research on the Transcendental Meditation Program: Collected Papers, Vol. 2. Rheinweiler, West Germany: Maharishi European Research University Press, (in press).
Preliminary findings do not permit a definitive statement on whether TM improves perceptual awareness.

A503 Matas, Francine, and Lee Pantas. "A PK Experiment Comparing Meditating Versus Non-Meditating Subjects." Proceedings of the Parapsychological Association, 8 (1971): 12-13.
Experiment showed the increased ability to concentrate acquired through the practice of meditation may be related to the production of psychokinetic phenomena.

A504 Maupin, Edward W. "Individual Differences in Response to a Zen Meditation Exercise." Journal of Consulting Psy-

chology, 29 (1965): 139-145.
Increased capacity for regression and tolerance for unrealistic experience were measurable. Attention measures were not significant. See also the author's dissertation [D145].

A505   Mazzarella, Pat. "The Maharishi's Spiritual Novocaine."
        Sign, 56 (April 1977): 12-13.
        Critical of Transcendental Meditation from a Christian point of view. Suggests Christian meditation.

A506   McBride, Alfred. "From Zen to the Cloud of Unknowing."
        Momentum, 7 (May 1976): 31-33.
        Suggests that meditation is a means by which educators can help students gain control of their lives.

A507   McCormick, Anne. "The Extent to Which Relaxation Techniques Are Taught at Community Colleges in California."
        (ERIC ED 186 074).
        This study includes relaxation training, centering, hypnosis, Transcendental Meditation, and yoga.

A508   McCuaig, Larry W. "Salivary Electrolytes, Protein and pH During Transcendental Meditation." Experientia, 30 (1974): 988-989. Tentatively scheduled for inclusion in Scientific Research on the Transcendental Meditation Program: Collected Papers, Vol. 2. Rheinweiler, West Germany: Maharishi European Research University Press, (in press).
        It was found that meditation produced a general increase in salivary minerals. The protein content of the saliva was also increased. Salivary pH was decreased.

A509   McDonagh, John M. "The Double Mantra Technique." Journal of Contemporary Psychotherapy, 8 (Winter-Spring 1976-77): 109-111.
        Recommended for individuals who have difficulty in focusing on a single mantra.

A510   _____, and Thomas Egenes. "The Transcendental Meditation Technique and Temperature Homeostasis." In Scientific Research on the Transcendental Meditation Program: Collected Papers, Vol. 1. Edited by David W. Orme-Johnson and John T. Farrow. 2nd ed., Weggis, Switzerland: Maharishi European Research University Press, 1977, p. 261-263.
        Skin temperature after exercise returned more rapidly to the baseline degree for meditators than nonmeditators.

A511   McEvoy, T.M.; L.R. Frumkin; and S.W. Harkins. "Effects of Meditation on Brain-Stem Auditory Evoked Potentials." International Journal of Neuroscience, 10 (1980): 165-170.

Tentatively scheduled for inclusion in Scientific Research
on the Transcendental Meditation Program: Collected Papers, Vol. 2. Rheinweiler, West Germany: Maharishi
European Research University Press, (in press).
Suggests an improved signal to noise processing by practitioners of Transcendental Meditation.

A512 McGeveran, William A., Jr. "Meditation at the Telephone
Company." Wharton Magazine, 6 (Fall 1981): 28-32.
Reports on the use of Clinically Standardized Meditation by
Dr. Patricia Carrington at the New York Telephone Company
to reduce stress.

A513 McIntyre, Mary E.; Franklin H. Silverman; and William D.
Trotter. "Transcendental Meditation and Stuttering: A
Preliminary Report." Perceptual and Motor Skills, 39
(August 1974): 294. In Scientific Research on the Tran-
scendental Meditation Program: Collected Papers, Vol. 1.
Edited by David W. Orme-Johnson and John T. Farrow.
2nd ed., Weggis, Switzerland: Maharishi European Re-
search University Press, 1977, p. 300.
Subjective impressions suggest TM may enable some stutterers
to speak more fluently.

A514 McLaughlin, Mary. "Why Pay to Meditate?" McCalls, 103
(January 1976): 45-46.
Compares TM with Benson's Relaxation Response.

A515 McLeod, John. "The Social Context of TM." Journal of Humanistic Psychology, 21 (Summer 1981): 17-33.
It is suggested that much of the impact which TM has on
people is a result of entering a social group with its own
characteristic language, rules, and world view.

A516 McQuade, Walter. "Doing Something About Stress." Fortune, 87 (May 1973): 250-258, 260-261.
Discusses the benefits of TM, biofeedback training, and Zen
meditation in reducing stress.

A517 Meany, John O. "On Meditation and Sensory Awareness."
Review for Religious, 29 (March 1970): 276-279.
Examines the importance of being aware of our own bodies
and its relationship to Christian meditation.

A518 Meares, Ainslie. "Atavistic Regression as a Factor in the
Remission of Cancer." Medical Journal of Australia, 2 (23
July 1977): 132-133.
It is suggested that the atavistic regression of the mind in
intensive meditation is accompanied by a similar physiological
regression, and that this may involve the immune system and
so influence the patient's defenses against cancer.

A519   _____. "A Form of Intensive Meditation Associated with the Regression of Cancer." American Journal of Clinical Hypnosis, 25 (October–January 1982-83): 114-121.
Describes this type of meditation, how it is used, and the way in which the patient is brought to experience it.

A520   _____. "Meditation: Psychological Approach to Cancer Treatment." Practitioner, 222 (January 1979): 119-122.
Suggests that an effort should be made to explore in depth the possibility that meditation may prove effective, either on its own or in combination with existing forms of cancer treatment. Cases are briefly summarized.

A521   _____. "The Psychological Treatment of Cancer: The Patient's Confusion of the Time for Living and the Time for Dying." Australian Family Physician, 8 (July 1979): 801-805.
Suggests that meditation may be able to enhance the immune defenses and increase the quality of life during the course of living and dying for cancer patients.

A522   _____. "The Quality of Meditation Effective in the Regression of Cancer." Journal of the American Society of Psychosomatic Dentistry and Medicine, 25 (1978): 129-132.
The purpose of this article is to describe that particular type of meditation which is most successful in its effect on cancer growth.

A523   _____. "Regression of Cancer After Intensive Meditation." Medical Journal of Australia, 2 (31 July 1976): 184.
A case history suggesting intensive meditation as a treatment for cancer.

A524   _____. "Regression of Cancer of the Rectum After Intensive Meditation." Medical Journal of Australia, 10 (17 November 1979): 539-540.
A case report suggesting intensive meditation as a possible alternative treatment of cancer.

A525   _____. "Regression of Osteogenic Sarcoma Metastases Associated with Intensive Meditation." Medical Journal of Australia, 2 (21 October 1978): 433.
A case history on the successful use of intensive meditation in the treatment of cancer.

A526   _____. "Regression of Recurrence of Carcinoma of the Breast at Mastectomy Site Associated with Intensive Meditation." Australian Family Physician, 10 (March 1981): 218-219.
A case history of the use of meditation to treat a cancer patient.

A527   . "The Relief of Anxiety Through Relaxing Meditation." Australian Family Physician, 5 (August 1976):
906-910.
Explains the technique of a relaxing meditation known as
Mental Ataraxis.

A528   . "Remission of Massive Metastastis from Undifferentiated Carcinoma of the Lung Associated with Intensive
Meditation." Journal of the American Society of Psychosomatic Dentistry and Medicine, 27 (1980): 40-41.
The therapeutic process in the present case is confused by
the patient's subsequent physical treatment, but is reported
to record the initial seven month's remission.

A529   . "Stress, Meditation and the Regression of Cancer."
Practitioner, 226 (September 1982): 1607-1609.
Discusses the nature of meditation and the effect of meditation on stress. Includes brief summaries of case reports of
regression of cancer after intensive meditation.

A530   . "Vivid Visualization and Dim Visual Awareness in
the Regression of Cancer in Meditation." Journal of the
American Society of Psychosomatic Dentistry and Medicine,
25 (1978): 85-88.
A patient with advanced cancer made a dramatic remission
following intense meditation.

A531   . "What Can the Cancer Patient Expect from Intensive Meditation." Australian Family Physician, 9 (May
1980): 322-325.
Patients experienced a significant reduction in anxiety and
depression, together with much less discomfort and pain. A
ten percent change of regression of the growth was indicated.

A532 "Meditation for Managers." Industry Week, 178 (6 August
1973): 37-39.
Reports on Transcendental Meditation as a technique to reduce stress and increase productivity among managers.

A533 "Meditation Gets an A-Okay in Ma Bell Tryout." Training,
17 (May 1980): 17-18.
A comparison of Dr. Patricia Carrington's Clinically Standardized Meditation, progressive muscle relaxation, and the
Respiratory "One" Method in reducing symptoms of stress.

A534 "Meditation: Let's Sleep on It." Science News, 109 (24
January 1976): 54.
Briefly surveys studies comparing TM and sleep.

A535 Melzer, F. "Meditation in the Service of Theological Training." International Review of Missions, 49 (October

1960): 393-400.
Shows the significance meditation can have when the theological teacher himself as a private individual practices meditation.

A536   Merton, Thomas. "Meditation: Action and Union." Sponsa Regis, 31 (March 1960): 191-198.
An excerpt from his Spiritual Direciton and Meditation. Suggests that in order for mental prayer to achieve the full effect for which it is intended, it must awaken a consciousness of union with God, of our dependence on Him, and His constant loving presence in our souls.

A537   _____. "Presuppositions to Meditation." Sponsa Regis, 31 (April 1960): 231-240.
Explains universal requirements of a sense of indigence, proper atmosphere, leisure, sincerity, and love, for the practice of meditation or mental prayer.

A538   _____. "The Subject of Meditation." Sponsa Regis, 31 (May 1960): 268-274.
Suggests an approach to meditation by deep reflective reading of the liturgical texts as they are presented Sunday in the Missal.

A539   _____. "Temperament and Meditation." Sponsa Regis, 31 (June 1960): 296-299.
Shows how the way individuals meditate depends in large measure upon their temperament and natural gifts.

A540   _____. "What Is Meditation?" Sponsa Regis, 31 (February 1960): 180-187.
Examples are given of the meaning of meditation in the gospels and scripture.

A541   Meserve, Harry C. "Meditation and Health." Journal of Religion and Health, 19 (Spring 1980): 3-6.
An editorial showing the many benefits achieved by regular meditation for both preventive and curative significance.

A542   Meyer, Richard. "Practice of Awareness as a Form of Psychotherapy." Journal of Religion and Health, 10 (October 1971): 333-345.
A meditation technique is described and views of relating it to psychotherapy are discussed. The writer explores his own experience with meditation.

A543   Michaels, Ruth R.; M.J. Huber; and Daisy S. McCann. "Evaluation of Transcendental Meditation as a Method of Reducing Stress." Science, 192 (18 June 1976): 1242-1244.
Defines the effects of Transcendental Meditation and the

physiological effects of stress upon the human body. Stressful physiological states were reproduced and meditation was
compared to a resting state. It was shown that meditation
does not induce a unique metabolic state but is biochemically
similar to resting. Therefore, rest may be responsible for
the physiological changes during TM.

A544   _____; Juan Parra; Daisy S. McCann; and Arthur J. Van-
        der. "Renin, Cortisol, and Aldosterone During Transcen-
        dental Meditation." Psychosomatic Medicine, 41 (February
        1979): 50-54.
Results did not support the hypothesis that TM induces a
unique state characterized by decreased sympathetic activity
or release from stress, but suggests that meditators may be
less responsive to acute stress.

A545   Mikulas, William L. "Buddhism and Behavior Modification."
        Psychological Record, 31 (Summer 1981): 331-342.
Meditation is discussed and related to behavior modification
practice.

A546   _____. "Four Noble Truths of Buddhism Related to Be-
        havior Therapy." Psychological Record, 28 (Winter 1978):
        59-67.
Basic tenets of Buddhist psychology are related to the theory
and practice of behavior therapy with emphasis on self-
control. Discussion includes meditation as a therapeutic tool.

A547   Miller, Alan L. "The Buddhist Monastery as a Total Institu-
        tion." Journal of Religious Studies, 7 (Fall 1979): 15-29.
The meditation process of Mindfulness, Samadhi and Bodhi in
Buddhist monasticism are studied.

A548   Mills, Walter W., and John T. Farrow. "The Transcendental
        Meditation Technique and Acute Experimental Pain." Psy-
        chosomatic Medicine, 43 (April 1981): 157-164. Tentative-
        ly scheduled for inclusion in Scientific Research on the
        Transcendental Meditation Program: Collected Papers, Vol.
        2. Rheinweiler, West Germany: Maharishi European Re-
        search University Press, (in press).
The TM technique was found to decrease the distress associated with the experience of acute experimental pain.

A549   "Mind Over Drugs." Time, 98 (25 October 1971): 51.
Reports on the study by Dr. Herbert Benson and R. Keith
Wallace on the physiological changes occurring during medi-
tation.

A550   "Mind Over Matter." Chemistry, 45 (April 1972): 22.
A short report on physiological changes studied by Robert
K. Wallace and Herbert Benson on Transcendental Meditation
subjects.

A551   Miskiman, Donald E. "The Effect of the Transcendental
        Meditation Program on Compensatory Paradoxical Sleep."
        In Scientific Research on the Transcendental Meditation
        Program: Collected Papers, Vol. 1. Edited by David W.
        Orme-Johnson and John T. Farrow. 2nd ed., Weggis,
        Switzerland: Maharishi European Research University
        Press, 1977, p. 292-295.
        Subjects who practiced the TM technique showed faster re-
        covery from sleep deprivation.

A552   _____. "The Effect of the Transcendental Meditation Pro-
        gram on the Organization of Thinking and Recall (Second-
        ary Organization)." In Scientific Research on the Tran-
        scendental Meditation Program: Collected Papers, Vol. 1.
        Edited by David W. Orme-Johnson and John T. Farrow.
        2nd ed., Weggis, Switzerland: Maharishi European Re-
        search University Press, 1977, p. 385-392.
        The organizational ability of the mind was enhanced by the
        Transcendental Meditation program.

A553   _____. "Long-Term Effects of the Transcendental Medita-
        tion Program in the Treatment of Insomnia." In Scientific
        Research on the Transcendental Meditation Program: Col-
        lected Papers, Vol. 1. Edited by David W. Orme-Johnson
        and John T. Farrow. 2nd ed., Weggis, Switzerland:
        Maharishi European Research University Press, 1977, p.
        299.
        This is a follow-up study which shows that the TM program
        remained effective throughout the first year of treatment for
        insomnia.

A554   _____. "Performance on a Learning Task by Subjects Who
        Practice the Transcendental Meditation Technique." In
        Scientific Research on the Transcendental Meditation Pro-
        gram: Collected Papers, Vol. 1. Edited by David W.
        Orme-Johnson and John T. Farrow. 2nd ed., Weggis,
        Switzerland: Maharishi European Research University
        Press, 1977, p. 382-384.
        Meditators displayed superior learning ability as a result of
        decreased anxiety and improved ability to focus attention ef-
        fectively.

A555   _____. "The Treatment of Insomnia by the Transcendental
        Meditation Program." In Scientific Research on the Tran-
        scendental Meditation Program: Collected Papers, Vol. 1.
        2nd ed., Weggis, Switzerland: Maharishi European Re-
        search University Press, 1977, p. 296-298.
        Results indicated that subjects, after learning TM, required
        a significantly shorter time to fall asleep.

A556   Mitchell, Kenneth R., and Ronald G. White. "Control of

Migraine Headache by Behavioral Self-Management: A
Controlled Time Study." Headache, 16 (1976): 178-184.
Critical of Transcendental Meditation as a technique for the
treatment of migraine.

A557   Moffett, James. "Reading and Writing as Meditation." Language Arts, 60 (March 1983): 315-322, 332.
Discusses ways that reading and writing influence consciousness. Suggests the relationship between reading and writing
is a form of meditation.

A558   _____. "Writing, Inner Speech, and Meditation." College
English, 44 (March 1982): 231-246. Discussion, 45 (April
1983): 400-406.
Proposes that staff development for teachers include the
teaching and practice of meditation to improve their writing
while fostering their general adult growth.

A559   Mokusen, Miyuki. "The Psychodynamics of Buddhist Meditation: A Jungian Perspective." Eastern Buddhist, New
Series, 10 (October 1977): 155-168.
Suggests that to be an individual in the Jungian sense of
self-acceptance shares the same underlying processes found
in Zen.

A560   Moltmann, Jürgen. "Theology of Mystical Experience." Scottish Journal of Theology, 32 (1979): 501-520.
Includes a discussion of the following stages of mystical experience: action and meditation, meditation and contemplation, contemplation and mystical union, mystical union and
martyrdom, and the vision of the world in God.

A561   Monahan, Raymond J. "Secondary Prevention of Drug Dependence Through the Transcendental Meditation Program
in Metropolitan Philadelphia." International Journal of
the Addictions, 12 (1977): 729-754. Tentatively scheduled
for inclusion in Scientific Research on the Transcendental
Meditation Program: Collected Papers, Vol. 2. Rheinweiler, West Germany: Maharishi European Research University Press, (in press).
For most substances the amount of decrease was positively
correlated with the degree of participation in the TM program
and length of time meditating.

A562   Montgomery, Randal. "TM & Science: Friends or Foes?"
Fate, 33 (June 1980): 63+
Criticizes the Transcendental Meditation movement.

A563   Morando, Dante. "Education: Meditation/Contemplation/Re-
collection." Philosophy Today, 3 (Summer 1959): 94-109.
An article translated from Rivista Rosminiano, vol. 51, 1957.

Discusses meditation in relationship to education, character, involvement, chance, anxiety, and activism.

A564   Morris, Joseph. "Meditation in the Classroom." Learning, 5 (December 1976): 22-27.
Discusses sensory awareness, physical movement, concentrative meditation, and guided fantasy.

A565   Morse, Donald R. "An Exploratory Study of the Use of Meditation Alone and in Combination with Hypnosis in Clinical Dentistry." Journal of the American Society of Psychosomatic Dentistry and Medicine, 24 (1977): 113-120.
The study showed that Transcendental Meditation by itself is effective to help control fear, reduce tension, decrease pain, and diminish salivation. It is more effective when combined with hypnosis.

A566   _____. "Meditation in Dentistry." General Dentistry, 24 (September-October, 1976): 57-59.
The use of TM with hypnosis for patients, the use of TM by dentists, and a physiological study of TM and hypnosis.

A567   _____. "Overcoming 'Practice Stress' Via Meditation and Hypnosis." Dental Survey, 53 (July 1977): 32-36.
The author devised a combination meditation-hypnosis technique for self-use in coping with stress.

A568   _____. "Stress and Bruxism: A Critical Review and Report of Cases." Journal of Human Stress, 8 (March 1982): 43-54.
Reports on a case where the patient used meditation for bruxism control.

A569   _____. "Variety, Exercise, Meditation Can Relieve Practice Stress." Dental Student, 56 (December 1977): 26-29.
Suggestions for dental students in dealing with anxiety and stress in school by using relaxation and meditation techniques.

A570   _____, and Merrick L. Furst. "Meditation: An In Depth Study." Journal of the American Society of Psychosomatic Dentistry and Medicine, 29 (Special Issue, No. 5, 1982): 4-96.
This lengthy article on meditation includes a discussion of relaxation techniques, psychological adaptation, arousal, stress, and personality.

A571   _____; John S. Martin; Merrick L. Furst; and Louis L. Dubin. "A Physiological and Subjective Evaluation of Meditation, Hypnosis, and Relaxation." Psychosomatic Medicine, 39 (September-October 1977): 304-324. Also in

Meditation: Classic and Contemporary Perspectives,
edited by Deane H. Shapiro, Jr. and Roger N. Walsh.
Hawthorne, N.Y.: Aldine Pub. Co., 1984.
A literature review is presented and comparative evaluations
of each state are examined.

A572 _____ ; _____ ; _____ ; and _____ . "A Physiological
and Subjective Evaluation of Neutral and Emotionally-
Charged Words for Meditation: Part I." Journal of the
American Society of Psychosomatic Dentistry and Medicine,
26 (1979): 31-38.
Part one of a three part series investigating the effectiveness
and possible differences between neutral and emotionally-
charged words used as mantras for meditation.

A573 _____ ; _____ ; _____ ; and _____ . "A Physiological
and Subjective Evaluation of Neutral and Emotionally-
Charged Words for Meditation: Part II." Journal of the
American Society of Psychosomatic Dentistry and Medicine,
26 (1979): 56-62.
This part presents detailed results of the statistical measures.

A574 _____ ; _____ ; _____ ; and _____ . "A Physiological
and Subjective Evaluation of Neutral and Emotionally-
Charged Words for Meditation: Part III." Journal of the
American Society of Psychosomatic Dentistry and Medicine,
26 (1979): 106-112.
The study demonstrated that neutral and emotionally-charged
words produce no physiological differences but different subjective effects, and should be individually selected.

A575 _____ ; George R. Schacterle; M. Lawrence Furst; Jordon
Goldberg; Brian Greenspan; David Swiecinski; and James
Susek. "The Effect of Stress and Meditation on Salivary
Protein and Bacteria: A Review and Pilot Study." Journal of Human Stress, 8 (December 1982): 31-39.
Meditation subjects showed increased salivary translucency,
decreased salivary protein, and reduced subjective evaluation of stress. Findings of high bacteria levels under stress
and lower bacterial levels under relaxation indicate that
stress may contribute to dental caries and relaxation may
have an anti-caries effect.

A576 _____ , and James M. Wilcko. "Nonsurgical Endodontic
Therapy for a Vital Tooth with Meditation-Hypnosis as the
Sole Anesthetic: A Case Report." American Journal of
Clinical Hypnosis, 21 (April 1979): 258-262.
A combined meditation-hypnosis technique was used effective-
ly in this case history as the analgesic method. The patient
reported no pain or discomfort.

A577   Muinz, Arthur J. "Transcendental Meditation: Some Implica-
           tions for Education." New Jersey Education Association
           Review, 48 (January 1975): 28-29.
        Points out that students who meditate have reported steady
        improvement in their academic activities and generally im-
        proved attitudes toward learning.

A578   Murdock, Maureen H. "Meditation with Young Children."
           Gifted Child Quarterly, 23 (1979): 195-206. Reprinted
           from Journal of Transpersonal Psychology, 10 (1978):
           29-44.
        Describes meditative techniques used at the kindergarten
        level and the children's responses.

A579   Murphy, Suzanne. "Take a Relaxation Break!" House and
           Garden, 153 (May 1981): 68+
        An introduction to relaxation techniques.

A580   Murray, John B. "What Is Meditation? Does It Help?"
           Genetic Psychology Monographs, 106 (August 1982): 85-
           115.
        Reviews current research on meditation. Suggests that no
        convincing evidence indicates a psychotherapeutic superior-
        ity of one type of meditation over another. Discusses meth-
        odological limitations of meditation research.

A581   Nadel, Gerry. "It Will Help You Cope." Good Housekeeping,
           182 (March 1976): 79, 124, 126.
        An interview with Dr. Herbert Benson, author of The Re-
        laxation Response. The technique is explained.

A582   Naifeh, Kaifeh, and Joe Kamiya. "Changes in Alveolar Car-
           bon Dioxide Tension During Meditation." Biofeedback and
           Self-Regulation, 5 (1980): 378-379.
        Abstract of a paper suggesting that during meditation there
        is an alteration in the usual neural interaction between res-
        piratory centers and those centers governing level of arousal.

A583   Naranjo, Claudio. "Gestalt Conference Talk 1981." Gestalt
           Journal, 5 (Spring 1982): 3-19.
        Discusses the relationship and common factors between Ges-
        talt therapy and meditation. Such factors are a search for
        self-awareness, the suspension of conceptualization, and en-
        gagement in action without logical thinking.

A584   Nash, Carroll B. "Hypnosis and Transcendental Meditation
           as Inducers of ESP." Parapsychology Review, 13 (Janu-
           ary-February 1982): 19-20.
        Suggests there is a greater occurrence of ESP during hypno-
        sis than during Transcendental Meditation.

A585   Nataraj, P., and M.G. Radhamani. "The Transcendental
        Meditation Program and Its Effects on Psychological Func-
        tionings in Secondary School Students of a Rural Indian
        High School." Tentatively scheduled for inclusion in
        Scientific Research on the Transcendental Meditation Pro-
        gram: Collected Papers, Vol. 2. Rheinweiler, West Ger-
        many: Maharishi European Research University Press,
        (in press).
        Improvement in reading comprehension and memory was shown
        by students practicing the TM technique. A paper presented
        at the Vedas and Modern Science International Conference,
        Bangalore, India, 1975.

A586   Nearing, Peter. "New Mode of Meditation." Commonweal, 51
        (27 January 1950): 439.
        Excerpt from an article in Orate Frates (Collegeville, Minn.),
        January 1950, suggesting the formation of meditation groups.

A587   Nebelkopf, E. "Holistic Program for the Drug Addict and
        Alcoholic." Journal of Psychoactive Drugs, 13 (1981):
        345-352.
        Contains a short section on the benefits of yoga and medita-
        tion for some substance abusers.

A588   Nelson, Harold. "The Art of Christian Meditation." Bulletin
        of the American Protestant Hospital Association, 43 (1979):
        25-27.
        A basic technique of breath-counting and the use of a Chris-
        tian mantra.

A589   Nevins, Albert J. "The Spiritual Life: Meditation." Our
        Sunday Visitor, 67 (14 January 1979): 15.
        Points out the benefits and importance of Christian meditation
        to spiritual life.

A590   Nicet Joseph, Bro. "Advantages of Meditation." LaSallian
        Digest, 4 (Summer 1962): 7-12.
        Suggests a daily effort at Christian meditation and prayer.

A591   Nidich, Sanford; William Seeman; and Thomas Dreskin. "In-
        fluence of Transcendental Meditation: A Replication."
        Journal of Counseling Psychology, 20 (November 1973):
        565-566. In Scientific Research on the Transcendental
        Meditation Program: Collected Papers, Vol. 1. Edited by
        David W. Orme-Johnson and John T. Farrow. 2nd ed.,
        Weggis, Switzerland: Maharishi European Research Uni-
        versity Press, 1977, p. 442-443.
        For ten of the twelve variables significant differences be-
        tween experimental and control subjects appeared in the di-
        rection of self-actualization. [Cf. A720]

A592   _____ ; _____ ; and Mary Seibert. "Influence of the
         Transcendental Meditation Program on State Anxiety." In
         Scientific Research on the Transcendental Meditation Pro-
         gram: Collected Papers, Vol. 1. Edited by David W.
         Orme-Johnson and John T. Farrow. 2nd ed., Weggis,
         Switzerland: Maharishi European Research University
         Press, 1977, p. 434-436.
         Subjects practicing the TM technique effectively reduced
         anxiety.

A593   "Nirvana in a Dank, Dark Tank." Time, 115 (24 March
         1980): 77.
         Reports on the use of float tanks as a technique for relaxa-
         tion and meditation.

A594   Nordberg, Robert B. "Meditation: Future Vehicle for Ca-
         reer Exploration." Vocational Guidance Quarterly, 22
         (June 1974): 267-271.
         The author believes that heightened self-understanding can
         be achieved through meditation and other mystical approaches
         and that this knowledge can be applied to choosing and ad-
         vancing a career.

A595   Noyes, Humphrey F. "Meditation: The Doorway to Whole-
         ness." Humanitas, 3 (Fall 1967): 171-184. Reprinted
         from Main Currents in Modern Thought, 22 (1965): 35-40.
         Discusses meditation as a preventive approach to the prob-
         lems of ego-centeredness and the emotive state.

A596   Nystul, Michael S., and Margaret Garde. "Comparison of
         Self-Concepts of Transcendental Meditators and Nonmedi-
         tators." Psychological Reports, 41 (August 1977): 303-
         306. Tentatively scheduled for inclusion in Scientific
         Research on the Transcendental Meditation Program:
         Collected Papers, Vol. 2. Rheinweiler, West Germany:
         Maharishi European Research University Press, (in press).
         Showed that meditators had significantly more positive self-
         concepts.

A597   _____ , and _____ . "The Self-Concepts of Regular
         Transcendental Meditators, Dropout Meditators, and Non-
         meditators." Journal of Psychology, 103 (September
         1979): 15-18.
         Findings provide a personality description of the groups in
         relation to each other.

A598   Oakley, E.M. "The Brothers Speak: The Ray Stanford
         Tapes." New Realities, 1 (2 November 1977): 39+
         Discusses attitudes of the mind, preparation of the body,
         and the goal of meditation as regards The Association for the
         Understanding of Man.

A599   Oates, Bob J. "To Shine During Meetings, Enliven the
         Mind." Administrative Management, 43 (September 1982):
         71.
         A short report on the benefits of Transcendental Meditation
         in business.

A600   O'Brien, Bartholomew J. "Practical Techniques in Teaching
         the Art of Prayer." Spiritual Life, 6 (September 1960):
         243-248.
         Gives techniques for teaching meditation in a seminary.

A601   O'Haire, Trula D., and James E. Marcia. "Some Personality
         Characteristics Associated with Ananda Marga Meditators:
         A Pilot Study." Perceptual and Motor Skills, 51 (October
         1980): 447-452.
         A number of personality characteristics were studied with
         varying degrees of differences between meditators and non-
         meditators.

A602   O'Hanlon, Daniel J. "Cultivating Contemplation." America,
         140 (24 March 1979): 230-232.
         A personal account of the author's experiences with medita-
         tion during a two-week retreat.

A603   _____. "Zen and the Spiritual Exercises: A Dialogue Be-
         tween Faiths." Theological Studies, 39 (December 1978):
         737-768.
         Compares the differences and similarities between Zen and
         concepts found in Spiritual Exercises by St. Ignatius Loyola.

A604   Ohayv, Ron J. "Field Interview with a Theravada Teaching
         Master." Journal of Transpersonal Psychology, 12 (1980):
         1-10.
         Excerpts from a series of interviews conducted in 1973 with
         various Theravada meditation teachers at a monastery in
         Thailand.

A605   Olson, Steven D. "Silence: Forming and Transforming
         Ministry." Currents in Theology and Mission, 10 (Febru-
         ary 1983): 14-20.
         Discusses the value of silence for Christians from personal
         experience as a pastor.

A606   Orme-Johnson, David W. "Autonomic Stability and Tran-
         scendental Meditation." Psychosomatic Medicine, 35 (July
         1973): 341-349. In Scientific Research on the Transcen-
         dental Meditation Program: Collected Papers, Vol. 1.
         Edited by David W. Orme-Johnson and John T. Farrow.
         2nd ed., Weggis, Switzerland: Maharishi European Re-
         search University Press, 1977, p. 233-238.
         A greater autonomic stability was shown by subjects practic-
         ing the TM technique.

A607 _____. "The Dawn of the Age of Enlightenment: Experimental Evidence that the Transcendental Meditation Technique Produces a Fourth and Fifth State of Consciousness
in the Individual and a Profound Influence of Orderliness
in Society." In Scientific Research on the Transcendental
Meditation Program: Collected Papers, Vol. 1. Edited by
David W. Orme-Johnson and John T. Farrow. 2nd ed.,
Weggis, Switzerland: Maharishi European Research University Press, 1977, p. 671-691.
An extensive review of scientific research on the TM program
was made to support the hypotheses expressed in the title.

A608 _____. "The World Peace Project: An Experimental Analysis of Achieving World Peace Through the TM-Sidhi
Program." Tentatively scheduled for inclusion in Scientific Research on the Transcendental Meditation Program:
Collected Papers, Vol. 2. Rheinweiler, West Germany:
Maharishi European Research University Press, (in press).
A research project suggesting that a few individuals can increase the coherence of collective consciousness of society by
means of the TM-Sidhi program, resulting in a reduction of
violence and social disorder.

A609 _____; Gary K. Arthur; Lavelle Franklin; and James
O'Connell. "The Transcendental Meditation Technique and
Drug Abuse Counselors." In Scientific Research on the
Transcendental Meditation Program: Collected Papers, Vol.
1. Edited by David W. Orme-Johnson and John T. Farrow.
2nd ed., Weggis, Switzerland: Maharishi European Research University Press, 1977, p. 597-599.
Counselors who participated in the TM program reported gaining more energy and relaxation. They showed a significant
decrease in anxiety.

A610 _____; Geoffrey Clements; Christopher T. Haynes; and
Kheireddine Badaoui. "Higher States of Consciousness:
EEG Coherence, Creativity, and Experiences of the Sid-
his." In Scientific Research on the Transcendental Medi-
tation Program: Collected Papers, Vol. 1. Edited by
David W. Orme-Johnson and John T. Farrow. 2nd ed.,
Weggis, Switzerland: Maharishi European Research Uni-
versity Press, 1977, p. 705-712.
Positive correlations were found for EEG coherence, creativ-
ity, and experiences of higher states of consciousness.

A611 _____; Michael C. Dillbeck; R. Keith Wallace; and Garland
S. Landrith, III. "Intersubject EEG Coherence: Is Consciousness a Field?" International Journal of Neuroscience, 16 (1982): 203-209. Tentatively scheduled for inclusion in Scientific Research on the Transcendental Meditation Program: Collected Papers, Vol. 2. Rheinweiler,

West Germany: Maharishi European Research University
Press, (in press), under the title, "Coherent Field Effects in Collective Consciousness Measured by the EEG."
Decreased social disorder in the vicinity of TM and TM-Sidhi
participants is discussed in terms of a field theoretical view
of consciousness.

A612 _____, and Brigitte Duck. "Psychological Testing of MIU
Students: First Report." In Scientific Research on the
Transcendental Meditation Program: Collected Papers, Vol.
1. Edited by David W. Orme-Johnson and John T. Farrow.
2nd ed., Weggis, Switzerland: Maharishi European Research University Press, 1977, p. 470-475.
College students practicing the TM technique at Maharishi
International University scored higher than other students
on scales of self-actualization.

A613 _____, and Barbara Granieri. "The Effects of the Age of
Enlightenment Governor Training Courses on Field Independence, Creativity, Intelligence, and Behavioral Flexibility." In Scientific Research on the Transcendental
Meditation Program: Collected Papers, Vol. 1. Edited by
David W. Orme-Johnson and John T. Farrow. 2nd ed.,
Weggis, Switzerland: Maharishi European Research University Press, 1977, p. 713-718.
Studies showed that field independence, creativity, intelligence, and behavioral flexibility increased by participants in
the courses.

A614 _____, and Christopher T. Haynes. "EEG Phase Coherence, Pure Consciousness, Creativity, and TM-Sidhi Experiences." International Journal of Neuroscience, 13
(1981): 211-218.
Found higher levels of coherence associated with TM-Sidhi
experiences and creativity, indicating common psychophysiological processes.

A615 _____; John Kiehlbauch; Richard Moore; and John Bristol.
"Personality and Autonomic Changes in Prisoners Practicing the Transcendental Meditation Technique." In Scientific Research on the Transcendental Meditation Program:
Collected Papers, Vol. 1. Edited by David W. Orme-
Johnson and John T. Farrow. 2nd ed., Weggis, Switzerland: Maharishi European Research University Press,
1977, p. 556-561.
Prisoners practicing the TM technique showed an increase in
physiological stability and psychological adaptability.

A616 _____; David Kolb; and J. Russell Hebert. "An Experimental Analysis of the Effects of the Transcendental Meditation Technique on Reaction Time." In Scientific Re-

search on the Transcendental Meditation Program: Collected Papers, Vol. 1. Edited by David W. Orme-Johnson and John T. Farrow. 2nd ed., Weggis, Switzerland: Maharishi European Research University Press, 1977, p. 316-321.
Simple reaction time was faster for subjects after a period of the TM technique than after a period of rest.

A617 _____; R. Keith Wallace; Michael C. Dillbeck; C.N. Alexander; and O. Ball. "Longitudinal Effects of the TM-Sidhi Program on EEG Coherence, Creativity, Intelligence and Moral Reasoning." Tentatively scheduled for inclusion in Scientific Research on the Transcendental Meditation Program: Collected Papers, Vol. 2. Rheinweiler, West Germany: Maharishi European Research University Press, (in press).
Beneficial changes in coherence and creativity were produced by a four-month TM-Sidhi course.

A618 Orsy, Ladislas M. "From Meditation to Contemplation." Review for Religious, 22 (March 1963): 172-179.
Discusses the period of transition from meditation to contemplation and shows the theological background of the change that takes place in the soul.

A619 Osis, Karlis, and Edwin Bokert. "ESP and Changed States of Consciousness Induced by Meditation." Journal of the American Society for Psychical Research, 65 (1971): 17-65.
An experiment designed to explore the relationship between ESP processes and changed states of consciousness induced by meditation.

A620 _____; _____; and Mary Lou Carlson. "Dimensions of the Meditative Experience." Journal of Transpersonal Psychology, 5 (1973): 109-135.
Reports on four experiments in an attempt to discover the psychological dimensions of the meditative state. ESP was evaluated.

A620K Otis, Leon S. "Adverse Effects of Transcendental Meditation." In Meditation: Classic and Contemporary Perspectives, edited by Deane H. Shapiro, Jr. and Roger N. Walsh. Hawthorne, N.Y.: Aldine Pub. Co., 1984.

A621 _____. "The Facts on Transcendental Meditation: Part III. If Well-Integrated but Anxious, Try TM." Psychology Today, 7 (April 1974): 45-46.
Part three of three parts. Scholars at Stanford Research Institute assigned people randomly to control groups or to the practice of TM. They found that TM does help some people. However, so does sitting quietly twice a day.

A622   Ottens, Allen J. "The Effect of Transcendental Meditation
        Upon Modifying the Cigarette Smoking Habit." Journal of
        School Health, 45 (December 1975): 577-583.
        Both TM and self control groups significantly decreased their
        cigarette consumption. It was not possible to conclude that
        one treatment was more effective than the other. [Cf. D168]

A623   "Our Catholic Faith: Saint Ignatius Loyola on Meditation."
        Our Sunday Visitor, 66 (8 May 1977): 13.
        An outline of St. Loyola's treatise on prayer, the Spiritual
        Exercises.

A624   Overbeck, K.D. "Effects of the Transcendental Meditation
        Technic on the Psychological and Psychosomatic State."
        Psychotherapie, Psychosomatik, Medizinische, Psychologie,
        32 (November 1982): 188-192.
        Meditators experienced a reduction of nervous somatic com-
        plaints and enhancement of emotional stability and flexibility.
        Article in German. Abstract in English.

A625   _____, and S.E. Tönnies. "Some Effects of Transcendental
        Meditation on Children with Learning Problems." Tenta-
        tively scheduled for inclusion in Scientific Research on
        the Transcendental Meditation Program: Collected Papers,
        Vol. 2. Rheinweiler, West Germany: Maharishi European
        Research University Press, (in press).
        Test anxiety and school dislike were decreased in children
        with learning disorders who practiced the TM technique.

A626   Owens, Claire M. "Self-Realization: Induced and Spontane-
        ous." Journal of Altered States of Consciousness, 2
        (1975): 59-73.
        Compares Buddhist and Zen meditation with the spontaneous
        mystical experience.

A627   Pagano, Robert R., and Lynn R. Frumkin. "The Effect of
        Transcendental Meditation on Right Hemispheric Function-
        ing." Biofeedback and Self-Regulation, 2 (December
        1977): 407-415. Tentatively scheduled for inclusion in
        Scientific Research on the Transcendental Meditation Pro-
        gram: Collected Papers, Vol. 2. Rheinweiler, West Ger-
        many: Maharishi European Research University Press,
        (in press). Also in Meditation: Classic and Contemporary
        Perspectives, edited by Deane H. Shapiro, Jr. and Roger
        N. Walsh. Hawthorne, N.Y.: Aldine Pub. Co., 1984.
        The results of this study support the hypothesis that medi-
        tation facilitates right hemispheric functioning.

A628   _____; Richard M. Rose; and Robert M. Stivers; and
        Stephen Warrenburg. "Sleep During Transcendental Medi-

tation." Science, 191 (23 January 1976): 308-310. (Critique by R.K. Wallace and reply by R. Pagano, Science, 193 [27 August 1976]: 718, 720.) Also in Meditation: Classic and Contemporary Perspectives, edited by Deane H. Shapiro, Jr. and Roger N. Walsh. Hawthorne, N.Y.: Aldine Pub. Co., 1984.
The range of states observed during sleep and meditation did not support the view that meditation produces a single unique state of consciousness.

A629   Palmer, D.K. "Inspired Analgesia Through Transcendental Meditation." New Zealand Dental Journal, 76 (April 1980): 61-64.
Teeth were removed using Transcendental Meditation instead of conventional analgesia.

A630   Palmer, John; Karen Khamashta; and Kathy Israelson. "An ESP Ganzfeld Experiment with Transcendental Meditators." Journal of the American Society for Psychical Research, 73 (October 1979): 333-348.
The most extreme ESP deviations occurred among subjects reporting the most pronounced alterations of consciousness.

A631   Palmer, Susan. "Performance Practices in Meditation Rituals Among the New Religions." Studies in Religion, 9 (1980): 403-413.
Examples are given of performance practices of four religious movements in Montreal, the Sivananda Yoga Society, the American Sufi Order, Dharmadatu, and a Tai Chi Chuan class.

A632   Paratparananda, Swami. "Meditation According to Spanish Mystics." Vedanta Kesari, 66 (November-December 1979): 435-440.
Explains the philosophy and methodology of meditation as practiced by St. Theresa of Jesus and St. John of the Cross.

A633   Parker, Jerry C., and Gary S. Gilbert. "Anxiety Management in Alcoholics: A Study of Generalized Effects of Relaxation Techniques." Addictive Behaviors, 3 (1978): 123-127.
The measures of arousal employed in this study were state anxiety, systolic and diastolic blood pressure, heart rate, and spontaneous GSR. Results revealed generalized effects for blood pressure, but not for the other dependent measures.

A634   _____; _____; and Richard W. Thoreson. "Reduction of Autonomic Arousal in Alcoholics: A Comparison of Relaxation and Meditation Techniques." Journal of Consulting and Clinical Psychology, 46 (October 1978): 879-886.

Results indicate both progressive relaxation training and meditation training are useful in reducing blood pressure in alcoholics.

A635 Parmisano, A. Stanley. "Alien Methods of Meditation." Cross and Crown, 29 (September 1977): 275-284. Suggests that elements of oriental and secular meditation may be useful for those immersed in one or another Christian tradition of prayer shaped and oriented by the Eucharist.

A636 Pas, Julian F. "Shan-tao's Interpretation of the Meditative Vision of Buddha Amitayus." History of Religions, 14 (November 1974): 96-116. Among various commentaries on the Amitayur-Buddhanusmrti-sutra, Shan-tao's work is considered to be the most outstanding because of his personal approach.

A637 Patel, Chandra H. "Biofeedback-Aided Relaxation and Meditation in the Management of Hypertension." Biofeedback and Self-Regulation, 2 (March 1977): 1-41. Based on clinical, epidemiological, and experimental work, a possible pathogenesis of essential hypertension is outlined. A treatment program is suggested which centers on the regular use of systematic relaxation. Includes a lengthy bibliography.

A638 _____. "Meditation in General Practice." British Medical Journal, 282 (14 February 1981): 528-529. Suggests meditation as a therapy for keeping patients alert and yet relaxed.

A639 _____. "12-Month Follow-Up of Yoga and Bio-Feedback in the Management of Hypertension." Lancet, 1, 7898 (11 January 1975): 62-64. Reduction in blood pressure was satisfactorily maintained in the treatment group monthly for twelve months.

A640 _____, and M. Carruthers. "Coronary Risk Factor Reduction Through Biofeedback-Aided Relaxation and Meditation." Journal of the Royal College of General Practitioners, 27 (July 1977): 401-405. Showed significant reduction in blood pressure and number of cigarettes smoked by smokers. Reduction in the lipids in the hypertensive group was measured.

A641 Patricca, Nicholas A. "Meditation and Self-Realization." Listening, 13 (Winter 1978): 48-58. This essay is a theoretical rather than technical exposition of Zen meditation.

A642 Paty, J.; P. Brenot; C. Bensch; J.M.A. Faure; and J.D.

Vincent. "Electrophysiology of Transcendental Meditation: Contingent Negative Variation and Evoked Response Studies." Tentatively scheduled for inclusion in Scientific Research on the Transcendental Meditation Program: Collected Papers, Vol. 2. Rheinweiler, West Germany: Maharishi European Research University Press, (in press). The states induced by TM were shown to be different from that of sleep.

A643 _____ ; J.D. Vincent; and J.M.A. Faure. "Contingent Negative Variation Studies During Meditation." Electroencephalography and Clinical Neurophysiology, 43 (October 1977): 540.
Abstract report of an experiment showing important CNV changes in relation to meditation.

A644 Peerbolte, M. Leitert. "Meditation as Re-Minding Oneself." Darshana International, 15 (April 1975): 38-42.
This paper forms a chapter on how to meditate in the author's unpublished work, Transpersonal Psychology and Snydic-Energy.

A645 Pelletier, Kenneth R. "The Effects of the Transcendental Meditation Program on Perceptual Style: Increased Field Independence." In Scientific Research on the Transcendental Meditation Program: Collected Papers, Vol. 1. Edited by David W. Orme-Johnson and John T. Farrow. 2nd ed., Weggis, Switzerland: Maharishi European Research University Press, 1977, p. 337-345.
Increased perceptual acuity, increased field independence, and increased ego-distance were demonstrated by subjects practicing the TM technique.

A646 _____ . "Influence of Transcendental Meditation Upon Autokinetic Perception." Perceptual and Motor Skills, 39 (December 1974): 1031-1034. In Scientific Research on the Transcendental Meditation Program: Collected Papers, Vol. 1. Edited by David W. Orme-Johnson and John T. Farrow. 2nd ed., Weggis, Switzerland: Maharishi European Research University Press, 1977, p. 335-336. Also in Meditation: Classic and Contemporary Perspectives,, edited by Deane H. Shapiro, Jr. and Roger N. Walsh. Hawthorne, N.Y.: Aldine Pub. Co., 1984.
Transcendental Meditation was shown to increase ego-distance and field independence in subjects practicing the technique.

A647 Penner, Wes J.; Harvey W. Zingle; Ron Dyke; and Steve Truch. "Does an In-Depth Transcendental Meditation Course Effect Change in the Personalities of the Participants." Western Psychologist, 4 (1973): 104-111. In Scientific Research on the Transcendental Meditation Pro-

gram: Collected Papers, Vol. 1. Edited by David W.
Orme-Johnson and John T. Farrow. 2nd ed., Weggis,
Switzerland: Maharishi European Research University
Press, 1977, p. 444-448.
The study was inconclusive in attributing significant changes
in personality among TM participants. However, some posi-
tive changes were demonstrated.

A648   Peters, Ruanne K., and Herbert Benson. "Time Out from
        Tension." Harvard Business Review, 56 (January-
        February 1978): 120-124.
        Gives instruction to elicit the Relaxation Response.

A649   Phelan, Michael. "Transcendental Meditation: A Revitaliza-
        tion of the American Civil Religion." Archives de Sci-
        ences Sociales des Religions, 24 (July-September 1979):
        5-20.
        The author's hypothesis is that TM disciples are ethically
        oriented, culturally conservative individuals who have se-
        lected Transcendental Meditation as a means of dealing with
        stress because alternative counter-culture groups are opposed
        to traditional values.

A650   Piggins, David, and Douglas Morgan. "Note Upon Steady
        Visual Fixation and Repeated Auditory Stimulation in Medi-
        tation and the Laboratory." Perceptual and Motor Skills,
        44 (April 1977): 357-358.
        The techniques of steady visual fixation and repetitious audi-
        tory input are used for investigating perceptual phenomena
        and in yoga and meditation for facilitating altered states of
        awareness.

A651   _____, and _____. "Perceptual Phenomena Resulting
        from Steady Visual Fixation and Repeated Auditory Input
        Under Experimental Conditions and in Meditation." Jour-
        nal of Altered States of Consciousness, 3 (1977-78): 197-
        203.
        Comparable perceptual phenomena are reported by laboratory
        subjects and meditators resulting from steady visual fixation
        and repetitious auditory stimulation. Author is mistakenly
        identified as Douglas Piggins in the article.

A652   Pine, Devera. "Meditation: Medicine?" Health, 14 (July
        1982): 16.
        A brief report on meditation and its ability to block the ef-
        fects of norepinephrine, an "emergency" hormone that raises
        blood pressure and increases heart rate.

A653   Pirot, Michael. "The Effects of the Transcendental Meditation
        Technique Upon Auditory Discrimination." In Scientific
        Research on the Transcendental Meditation Program:

Collected Papers, Vol. 1. Edited by David W. Orme-Johnson and John T. Farrow. 2nd ed., Weggis, Switzerland: Maharishi European Research University Press, 1977, p. 331-334.
An increase in perceptual acuity relating to auditory discrimination was found in those who practiced Transcendental Meditation.

A654　Podgorski, Frank. "Samkhya-Yoga Meditation: Psycho-Spiritual Transvaluation." Journal of Dharma, 2 (April 1977): 152-163.
Details four steps on the samkhya-yogic path to samadhi.

A655　Polidora, Jim. "A Reading Guide to the Biology of the Mind/Body." Somatics, 1 (Fall 1977): 14-24.
An annotated reading list for use in courses taught by Dr. Polidora at the University of California. Arranged in sections identified as: I. Theory and Background; II. Yoga, Stretching, Exercise and Play; III. Relaxation, Centering and Meditation; IV. Health and Healing; V. Body-Work; VI. Know Thyself; and VII. Transpersonal and Humanistic Psychology and Education.

A656　Pollack, Albert A.; David B. Case; Michael A. Weber; and John H. Laragh. "Limitations of Transcendental Meditation in the Treatment of Essential Hypertension." Lancet, 1, 8002 (8 January 1977): 71-73. (Critique by J.A. Bralley and reply by A. Pollack, Lancet, 1, 8011 [12 March 1977]: 604-605.)
The study found no significant change in blood pressure after a six month program of Transcendental Meditation in a group of patients with essential hypertension.

A657　"Power of Positive Non-Thinking." Newsweek, 83 (7 January 1974): 73-75.
Report on Transcendental Meditation in the United States.

A658　Preston, David L. "Becoming a Zen Practitioner." Sociological Analysis, 42 (Spring 1981): 47-55.
Concerned with the processes of conversion-commitment to a new religious form and how it is actually accomplished by the individual.

A659　_____. "Meditative Ritual Practice and Spiritual Conversion-Commitment: Theoretical Implications Based on the Case of Zen." Sociological Analysis, 43 (Fall 1982): 257-270.
An analysis of meditational rituals in Zen as a means of approaching the nature of spiritual conversion and commitment.

A660　Preston, Paul. "Strategies for Coping with Stress." Asso-

ciation Management, 28 (November 1976): 46–49.
Explains the benefits of meditation for the executive and
gives four basic steps of a meditation technique.

A661   Price, John F. "Sets of Arrows: A Foundational Duality?"
        Epistemologia, 2 (1979): 269–296. Tentatively scheduled
        for inclusion in Scientific Research on the Transcendental
        Meditation Program: Collected Papers, Vol. 2. Rhein-
        weiler, West Germany: Maharishi European Research Uni-
        versity Press, (in press).
Suggests the Transcendental Meditation program could lead
to a unified way of formulating the foundations of mathematics and to new creative patterns of thinking because of
increased EEG coherence between hemispheres of the brain.

A662   Prince, Raymond. "Meditation: Some Psychological Specula-
        tions." Psychiatric Journal of the University of Ottawa,
        3 (September 1978): 202–209.
The author examines a number of typologies of meditation
available and speculates on the relationship of the meditative
state to differential cerebral hemispheric function.

A663   Puente, Antonio E. "Psychophysiological Investigations on
        Transcendental Meditation." Biofeedback and Self-Regula-
        tion, 6 (September 1981): 327–342.
Evaluates the psychophysiological changes occurring during
the practice of Transcendental Meditation including respiration rate, heart rate, electromyogram, electroencephalogram,
and skin conductance level.

A664   _____, and Irving Beiman. "The Effects of Behavior
        Therapy, Self-Relaxation, and Transcendental Meditation
        on Cardiovascular Stress Response." Journal of Clinical
        Psychology, 36 (January 1980): 291–295.
Behavior therapy, self-relaxation, Transcendental Meditation,
and a control were compared on measures of cardiovascular
and stress response. Behavior therapy and self-relaxation
were more effective than Transcendental Meditation and the
control in reducing cardiovascular stress.

A665   Puligandla, R. "Phenomenological Reduction and Yogic Medi-
        tation." Philosophy East and West, 20 (January 1970):
        19–33.
Examines and shows parallels between Husserl's phenomenological reduction and yogic meditation as expounded by Patanjali.

A666   Puryear, Herbert B.; Charles T. Cayce; and Mark A.
        Thurston. "Anxiety Reduction Associated with Meditation:
        Home Study." Perceptual and Motor Skills, 43 (October
        1976): 527–531.

Meditation group reported highly significant reduction on the IPAT Anxiety Scale scores after twenty-eight days of daily meditation.

A667   Qian, Xue Sen. "Some Theoretical Ideas on the Development of Basic Research in Human Body Science." PSI Research, 1 (June 1982): 4-15.
Discusses similarities between Qigong meditation, which involves movement and breath exercises, and ESP abilities. Acupuncture is also considered.

A668   Rabinoff, R.; M. Dillbeck; and R. Deissler. "The Effect of Coherent Collective Consciousness on the Weather." Tentatively scheduled for inclusion in Scientific Research on the Transcendental Meditation Program: Collected Papers, Vol. 2. Rheinweiler, West Germany: Maharishi European Research University Press, (in press).
Discusses the correlation between good weather and construction periods when the Golden Dome was built at Maharishi International University.

A669   Radford, John. "What Can We Learn from Zen? A Review and Some Speculations." Psychologia: An International Journal of Psychology in the Orient, 19 (June 1976): 57-66.
Suggests that Zen can be usefully characterized as a set of techniques designed to bring about specific changes in behavior and experience.

A670   Rahav, Giora. "TM and Rehabilitation: Another View." Criminal Justice and Behavior, 7 (March 1980): 11-16.
Critical of the Abrams and Siegal evaluation of the Transcendental Meditation program at Folsom prison [A5].

A671   Ramirez, J. "The Transcendental Meditation Program as a Possible Treatment Modality for Drug Offenders: Evaluation of a Pilot Project at Milan Federal Correctional Institution." Tentatively scheduled for inclusion in Scientific Research on the Transcendental Meditation Program: Collected Papers, Vol. 2. Rheinweiler, West Germany: Maharishi European Research University Press, (in press).
Subjects developed greater emotional stability and maturity and self-concept improvement while they decreased aggression and showed less concern with physical symptoms.

A672   Rao, K. Ramakrishna, and Irpinder Puri. "Subsensory Perception (SSP), Extrasensory Perception (ESP) and Transcendental Meditation (TM)." Journal of Indian Psychology, 1 (January 1978): 69-74.
Did not give evidence of any significant effect of TM on the subjects' ESP or SSP scores. Suggested that TM may have enhanced psi ability in the post-meditation session.

A673   Rao, P.V. Krishna, and K. Ramakrishna Rao. "Two Studies
of Extrasensory Perception and Subliminal Perception."
Journal of Parapsychology, 46 (1983): 185-208.
A comparison of SP and ESP scores of TM subjects and control groups showed the TM group did better than the control
group on the SP task, but not the ESP task. However, the
subjects in the TM group who obtained more SP hits than the
group mean obtained significantly more ESP hits than the
high-SP subjects in the control group.

A674   Rappaport, A.F., and L. Cammer. "Breath Meditation in
Treatment of Essential Hypertension." Behavior Therapy,
8 (1977): 269-270.
A letter describing a case study in which a client was able
to reduce his blood pressure with this meditational technique.

A675   Raskin, Majorie; Lekh R. Bali; and Harmon V. Peeke.
"Muscle Biofeedback and Transcendental Meditation: A
Controlled Evaluation of Efficacy in the Treatment of
Chronic Anxiety." Archives of General Psychiatry, 37
(January 1980): 93-97.
Compares muscle biofeedback, Transcendental Meditation, and
relaxation therapy as a treatment for chronic anxiety. No
differences were found between treatments. Considers re-
laxation therapies as a sole treatment as limited in the treat-
ment of chronic anxiety.

A676   Reddy, M. Kesav; A. Jhansi Lakshmi Bai; and V. Raghavender Rao. "The Effects of the Transcendental Meditation
Program on Athletic Performance." In Scientific Research
on the Transcendental Meditation Program: Collected Papers, Vol. 1. Edited by David W. Orme-Johnson and
John T. Farrow. 2nd ed., Weggis, Switzerland: Maharishi European Research University Press, 1977, p. 346-
358.
A broad range of qualities essential to athletic performance
was improved by the TM program.

A677   Redfering, David L., and Mary J. Bowman. "Effects of a
Meditative-Relaxation Exercise on Non-Attending Behaviors
of Behaviorally Disturbed Children." Journal of Clinical
Child Psychology, 10 (Summer 1981): 126-127.
Reports significant reduction in the number of non-attending
behaviors for the treatment group.

A678   Reed, Henry. "Improved Dream Recall Associated with Meditation." Journal of Clinical Psychology, 34 (January
1978): 150-156.
It was found that when a subject had meditated the day before, there was significantly greater completeness of dream
recall on the following morning. Regularity of the subject's

meditation was also significant. Results were discussed in terms of Edgar Cayce's attunement model of meditation.

A679   Richter, Rainer, and Bernhard Dahme. "Bronchial Asthma in Adults: There Is Little Evidence for the Effectiveness of Behavioral Therapy and Relaxation." Journal of Psychosomatic Research, 26 (1982): 533-540.
Although some evidence shows that meditation and autogenic training brings improvement in adults with bronchial asthma, the authors suggest they do not yield general beneficial effects. Critical of the methodology used by other investigators.

A680   Riedesel, Brian C. "Toward Full Development of the Person." Personnel and Guidance Journal, 57 (March 1979): 332-337. (Critique by R. McDonald, P&GJ, 58 (October 1979): 87.)
The Science of Creative Intelligence is presented as a theoretical model for the promotion of more complete development of the individual. Research data on TM and counseling modalities are discussed. Includes a lengthy bibliography.

A681   Riepe, Dale. "Indian Philosophical Influences on Recent American Thought and Life-Styles." Revolutionary World, 33 (1979): 9-21.
Indian influences on nineteenth-century American thought are summarized. Contemporary impact of Transcendental Meditation and Krishna Consciousness is discussed.

A682   Rigby, Byron P. "Enlightenment in Nursing Through Transcendental Meditation." Lamp, 40 (January-February 1983): 52-56.
Discusses TM and stress release, improved job satisfaction, and improved creativity and intelligence. Collective consciousness, reduction in crime, and improved health trends are also examined.

A683   _____. "Higher States of Consciousness Through the Transcendental Meditation Program: A Literature Review." Journal of Chronic Diseases and Therapeutics Research, 1 (1977): 35-55.
Describes the phenomenology of TM practice and relates this to its probable mode of action. Research findings are discussed. Includes a lengthy bibliography.

A684   Rimol, Andrew G.P. "The Transcendental Meditation Technique and Its Effects on Sensory-Motor Performance." In Scientific Research on the Transcendental Meditation Program: Collected Papers, Vol. 1. Edited by David W. Orme-Johnson and John T. Farrow. 2nd ed., Weggis, Switzerland: Maharishi European Research University

Press, 1977, p. 326-330.
Both short-term and long-term improvement of sensory-motor
performance was produced by the TM technique.

A685   Rivers, Steven M., and Nicholas P. Spanos. "Personal Vari-
         ables Predicting Voluntary Participation in and Attrition
         from a Meditation Program." Psychological Reports,, 49
         (December 1981): 795-801.
Meditating volunteers scored higher on the pretest absorption
measure than non-volunteers. Ninety-one percent of the
volunteers had stopped meditating one month after training.
The pretest self-esteem and psychosomatic symptoms measures predicted attrition from meditation.

A686   Robertson, Debra Warshal. "The Short and Long Range Ef-
         fects of the Transcendental Meditation Technique on Frac-
         tionated Reaction Time." Journal of Sports Medicine and
         Physical Fitness, 23 (March 1983): 113-120.
TM subjects indicated no significant immediate pretreatment
or posttreatment effect on fractionated reaction time components, but a significant cumulative effect over days was found.

A687   Rodier, David F.T. "Meditative States in the Abhidharma
         and in Pseudo-Dionysius." In Neoplatonism and Indian
         Thought. Edited by R. Baine Harris. Norfolk: Inter-
         national Society for Neoplatonic Studies, 1982, p. 121-136.
Suggests that some problems of meditative states in the Buddhist philosophy's Abhidharma tradition can be illuminated,
if not solved, by a comparison with the account of meditative
states in the Neoplatonic mysticism of Pseudo-Dionysius.

A688   Rogers, Cecil A., and Diane D. Livingston. "Accumulative
         Effects of Periodic Relaxation." Perceptual and Motor
         Skills, 44 (June 1977): 690.
Transcendental Meditation was used as a relaxation technique.
Results on the whole were negative.

A689   Roggenbuck, Peggy. "Insight Meditation: A Spiritual Prac-
         tice Without the Trappings; An Interview with Joseph
         Goldstein and Jack Kornfield." Yoga Journal, (May/June
         1979): 40-43.
A discussion of insight or Vipassana Meditation, which is
the basic spiritual practice of the Theravadin school of Buddhism as set forth in the early teachings of the Buddha.

A690   Roll, William G. "Science Looks at the Occult." Psychic, 4
         (June 1973): 50-55.
Reports on research concerning the relationship of meditation
and ESP.

A691   _____, and Gerald F. Solfvin. "Meditation and ESP." In

Research in Parapsychology 1975. Edited by J.D. Morris, W.G. Roll, and R.L. Morris. Metuchen, N.J.: The Scarecrow Press, 1976, p. 92-97.
Explores the relationship between ESP and meditation. Also looks at personality traits which might be related to the ESP and meditation responses.

A692   _____ ; _____ ; Joan Krieger; David Ray; and Lee Younts. "Group ESP Scores, Mood, and Meditation." Journal of Parapsychology, 44 (1980): 74-75.
Abstract of a paper presenting three analyses on ESP and meditation.

A693   Rosenthal, J.M. "The Effect of the Transcendental Meditation Program on Self-Actualization, Self-Concept, and Hypnotic Susceptibility." Tentatively scheduled for inclusion in Scientific Research on the Transcendental Meditation Program: Collected Papers, Vol. 2. Rheinweiler, West Germany: Maharishi European Research University Press, (in press).
TM practitioners showed greater self-actualization and higher self-concept than non-meditators and subjects practicing relaxation or contemplation.

A694   Ross, Jean. "The Effects of the Transcendental Meditation Program on Anxiety, Neuroticism, and Psychoticism." In Scientific Research on the Transcendental Meditation Program: Collected Papers, Vol. 1. Edited by David W. Orme-Johnson and John T. Farrow. 2nd ed., Weggis, Switzerland: Maharishi European Research University Press, 1977, p. 594-596.
There was a decrease in anxiety, neuroticism, and psychoticism in people who regularly practiced the TM technique.

A695   Routt, Thomas. "Low Heart and Respiration Rates in Individuals Practicing the Transcendental Meditation Technique." In Scientific Research on the Transcendental Meditation Program: Collected Papers, Vol. 1. Edited by David W. Orme-Johnson and John T. Farrow. 2nd ed., Weggis, Switzerland: Maharishi European Research University Press, 1977, p. 256-260.
Subjects practicing the TM technique measured lower levels of heart rate and respiratory rate.

A696   Rouzere, A.M.; K. Badaoui; and R. Hartmann. "Higher Amplitude Fronto-Central Alpha and Theta Activity During the Transcendental Meditation Technique." Tentatively scheduled for inclusion in Scientific Research on the Transcendental Meditation Program: Collected Papers, Vol. 2. Rheinweiler, West Germany: Maharishi European Research University Press, (in press).

Higher alpha and theta bursts were shown by meditators than non-meditating controls during TM.

A697   Rowan, John. "The Real Self and Mystical Experience."
        Journal of Humanistic Psychology, 23 (Spring 1983): 9-27.
        Critical of meditation as a technique for self-actualization and
        mystical experiences.

A698   Rubottom, Al E. "Transcendental Meditation and Its Potential
        Uses for Schools." Social Education, 36 (December 1972):
        851-857.
        Quoting from various studies, the author explains why there
        is a need for the practice of TM and the Science of Creative
        Intelligence in junior and senior high schools.

A699   Russell, Kenneth C. "A Medieval Dynamic Understanding of
        Meditation." Review for Religious, 41 (May-June 1982):
        411-418.
        Discusses the views of Guigo II, ninth prior of the Grande
        Chartreuse, on the importance of meditation in Christian
        faith.

A700   Sabel, Bernhard A. "Transcendental Meditation and Con-
        centration Ability." Perceptual and Motor Skills, 50
        (June 1980): 799-802.
        Transcendental Meditation had no measurable short-term ef-
        fects on concentration.

A701   Sacks, Howard L. "The Effect of Spiritual Exercises on the
        Integration of Self-System." Journal for the Scientific
        Study of Religion, 18 (March 1979): 46-50.
        Spiritual Exercises of Saint Ignatius Loyola show a significant
        integrative effect on the self-systems of individuals in the
        sample.

A702   Sailer, Heather R.; John Schlacter; and Mark R. Edwards.
        "Stress: Causes, Consequences, and Coping Strategies."
        Personnel, 59 (July/August 1982): 35-48.
        Discusses various strategies designed to cope with stress,
        including the Relaxation Response and meditation.

A703   Sallis, James F., Jr. "Issues in the Therapeutic Use of
        Meditation." (ERIC ED 181 358).
        A paper presented at the Annual Convention of the American
        Psychological Association (87th, New York, N.Y., Sept. 1-5,
        1979). Observations, findings, and suggestions from the
        literature are gathered to produce a listing of problem areas
        and unresolved issues. Includes a bibliography of clinical
        and research references.

A704   _____. "Meditation and Self-Actualization: A Theoretical

Comparison." Psychologia: An International Journal of Psychology in the Orient, 25 (March 1982): 59-64.
Theoretical foundations of meditation are discussed as they relate to the goals of humanistic psychotherapy, specifically self-actualization and the work of A.H. Maslow.

A705   Scarf, Maggie. "Tuning Down with TM." New York Times Magazine, (9 February 1975): 12-13, 52-55, 63.
Reports on the personal experience of the author with Transcendental Meditation.

A706   Schaeffer, Edith. "Meditation or Meditation." Christianity Today, 18 (30 August 1974): 20-21.
Biblical quotations regarding Christian meditation.

A707   _____. "Testing TM." Christianity Today, 20 (26 March 1976): 29-30.
Critical of the use of TM by Christians. Biblical references cited.

A708   Schenkluhn, Hartmut, and Matthias Geisler. "A Longitudinal Study of the Influence of the Transcendental Meditation Program on Drug Abuse." In Scientific Research on the Transcendental Meditation Program: Collected Papers, Vol. 1. Edited by David W. Orme-Johnson and John T. Farrow. 2nd ed., Weggis, Switzerland: Maharishi European Research University Press, 1977, p. 544-555.
The TM program was shown to be effective in reducing drug abuse. A further analysis of this study was done by Matthias Geisler [A285].

A709   Schilling, Peter B. "The Effect of the Regular Practice of the Transcendental Meditation Technique on Behavior and Personality." In Scientific Research on the Transcendental Meditation Program: Collected Papers, Vol. 1. Edited by David W. Orme-Johnson and John T. Farrow. 2nd ed., Weggis, Switzerland: Maharishi European Research University Press, 1977, p. 453-461.
A decrease in drug and alcohol use was measured by subjects practicing the TM technique. More effective psychosocial functioning was also demonstrated.

A710   Schimmel, David. "Supreme Court: Silent Meditation OK but No Transcendental Meditation in Schools." American School Board Journal, 166 (March 1979): 32-33.
Reports on the U.S. Supreme Court decision prohibiting the teaching of Transcendental Meditation in public schools.

A711   Schultz, Edward L. "Meditation and Ministry." The Christian Ministry, 11 (March 1980): 28-29.
Shows how Christian meditation can be an important source for the enhancement of Christian spirituality.

A712 Schultz, Terri. "What Science Is Discovering About the Potential Benefits of Meditation: Transcendental Meditation." Today's Health, 50 (April 1972): 34-37, 64-67.
Reports on physiological and psychological changes that take place with TM meditators.

A713 Schur, Edwin, and Lawrence LeShan. "Two Faces of Meditation." Parent's Magazine, 52 (November 1977): 70-71+
Two articles presenting the pros and cons of meditation from different points of view.

A714 Schuster, Richard. "Empathy and Mindfulness." Journal of Humanistic Psychology, 19 (Winter 1979): 71-77.
Suggests that therapist empathy is enhanced and strengthened by Satipatthana or mindfulness meditation.

A715 _____. "Meditation: Philosophy and Practice in a Drug Rehabilitation Setting." Drug Forum, 5 (1975-76): 163-170.
This paper is concerned with the beginning phases of integrating meditation into the treatment program in an intramural adolescent drug treatment facility.

A716 Schwartz, Gary E. "The Facts on Transcendental Meditation: II. TM Relaxes Some People and Makes Them Feel Better." Psychology Today, 7 (April 1974): 39-44.
Part two of three parts. A TM researcher surveys the data from current studies, describes the physiology of TM, discusses its relationship to drugs and creativity, and points out the problems of TM research.

A717 _____; Richard J. Davidson; and Daniel J. Goleman. "Patterning of Cognitive and Somatic Processes in the Self-Regulation of Anxiety: Effects of Meditation Versus Exercise." Psychosomatic Medicine, 40 (June 1978): 321-328. Also in Meditation: Classic and Contemporary Perspectives, edited by Deane H. Shapiro, Jr. and Roger N. Walsh. Hawthorne, N.Y.: Aldine Pub. Co., 1984.
Subjects practicing physical exercise reported relatively less somatic and more cognitive anxiety than meditators.

A718 Sciacca, Michelle F. "Meaningful Silence." Philosophy Today, 1 (Winter 1957): 250-254.
An essay on the value of Christian meditation.

A719 Scully, Malcolm. "Maharishi U." Saturday Review of Education, 1 (May 1973): 11.
A very brief report on TM and education at Maharishi International University.

A720 Seeman, William; Sanford Nidich; and Thomas Banta. "In-

fluence of Transcendental Meditation on a Measure of Self-Actualization." Journal of Counseling Psychology, 19 (May 1972): 184-187. In Scientific Research on the Transcendental Meditation Program: Collected Papers, Vol. 1. Edited by David W. Orme-Johnson and John T. Farrow. 2nd ed., Weggis, Switzerland: Maharishi European Research University Press, 1977, p. 417-419.
For six of the twelve variables there were differences between experimental and control subjects in the direction of self-actualization. The study was replicated later by Sanford Nidich [A591].

A721   Seer, Peter. "Psychological Control of Essential Hypertension: Review of the Literature and Methodological Critique." Psychological Bulletin, 86 (September 1979): 1015-1043.
A review of recent studies (1971-1978) that investigated psychological approaches, including relaxation/meditation, to the treatment of essential hypertension. Includes a bibliography.

A722   _____, and John M. Raeburn. "Meditation Training and Essential Hypertension: A Methodological Study." Journal of Behavioral Medicine, 3 (March 1980): 59-71.
Results showed modest reductions in blood pressure. There was considerable subject variation in responses. Critical of other studies.

A723   "Seer of Flying: Supernatural Powers." Time 110 (8 August 1977): 75.
Includes a photograph of a Transcendental Meditation practitioner levitating.

A724   Seiler, Gary, and Victoria Seiler. "The Effects of Transcendental Meditation on Periodontal Tissue." Journal of the American Society of Psychosomatic Dentistry and Medicine, 26 (1979): 8-12.
Meditators showed a significantly better periodontal health.

A725   Sethi, Amarjit Singh. "Sikh Meditation." Journal of Comparative Sociology, 4-5 (1977-78): 75-92.
Shows the importance of Nam, and the necessity of experiencing Nam through the practice of various meditational exercises.

A726   _____. "Stress Coping." Canadian Journal of Public Health, 73 (July-August 1982): 267-271. Critique by D.R. Loewen, CJPH, 73 (November-December 1982): 435.
Presents an analysis of the stress concept, and outlines strategies that can be used to cope with and utilize stress effectively, including meditation.

A727 _____. "Using Meditation in Stress Situations." Dimensions in Health Service, 57 (January 1980): 24-26.
Defines the actual method of coping that was discussed in the
author's article, "Management and Meditation" [A728].

A728 _____, and A. Daya. "Management and Meditation." Dimensions in Health Service, 55 (July 1978): 32-33.
Suggests meditation as a means of coping with stress by
hospital executives and physicians.

A729 Severeide, C.J. "Physiological and Phenomenological Aspects
of Transcendental Meditation." Tentatively scheduled for
inclusion in Scientific Research on the Transcendental
Meditation Program: Collected Papers, Vol. 2. Rheinweiler, West Germany: Maharishi European Research University Press, (in press).
Suggests the TM technique brings about a fourth state of
consciousness, called pure consciousness. Respiratory rate,
heart rate, and skin resistance were measured.

A730 Shafii, Mohammad. "Adaptive and Therapeutic Aspects of
Meditation." International Journal of Psychoanalytic Psychotherapy, 2 (August 1973): 364-382.
Shows how meditation can help correct maladaptive behavior
and suggests that early childhood traumas can be re-experi-
enced and mastered during meditation.

A731 _____. "Silence in the Service of Ego: Psychoanalytic
Study of Meditation." International Journal of Psycho-
Analysis, 54 (1973): 431-443.
Discusses silence and quiescence in meditation as a temporary
and controlled but deep regression in the service of ego.

A732 _____; Richard A. Lavely; and Robert D. Jaffe. "Meditation and Marijuana." American Journal of Psychiatry,
131 (January 1974): 60-63. In Scientific Research on the
Transcendental Meditation Program: Collected Papers, Vol.
1. Edited by David W. Orme-Johnson and John T. Farrow.
2nd ed., Weggis, Switzerland: Maharishi European Research University Press, 1977, p. 515-519.
Found that the longer a person had practiced meditation, the
more likely it was that he had decreased or stopped his use
of marijuana.

A733 _____; _____; and _____. "Meditation and the Prevention of Alcohol Abuse." American Journal of Psychiatry, 132 (September 1975): 942-945, and Alcohol Health
and Research World, (Summer 1976): 18-21. In Scientific
Research on the Transcendental Meditation Program: Collected Papers, Vol. 1. Edited by David W. Orme-Johnson
and John T. Farrow. 2nd ed., Weggis, Switzerland:

Maharishi European Research University Press, 1977, p. 520-523.
Suggests that Transcendental Meditation could be an effective preventive tool in the area of alcohol abuse.

A734 _____ ; _____ ; and _____ . "The Transcendental Meditation Program and Cigarette Smoking." Tentatively scheduled for inclusion in Scientific Research on the Transcendental Meditation Program: Collected Papers, Vol. 2. Rheinweiler, West Germany: Maharishi European Research University Press, (in press).
Cigarette smoking was significantly decreased or discontinued by persons practicing the TM technique.

A735 Shainberg, David. "Long Distance Running as Meditation." Annals of the New York Academy of Sciences, 301 (1977): 1002-1009.
The author shares his personal experience of long distance running as a body-brain-space-time event that is a form of meditation for him.

A736 Shainberg, Lawrence. "Violence of Just Sitting." New York Times Magazine, (10 October 1976): 16-17+
Reports on Zen practice at the International Dai Bosatsu Zendo near Livingston Manor, N.Y.

A737 Shapiro, Deane H., Jr. "Behavioral and Attitudinal Changes Resulting from a Zen Experience Workshop and Zen Meditation." Journal of Humanistic Psychology, 18 (Summer 1978): 21-29.
Although this research suggests the possible self-control applications of meditation to an individual's covert behavior, the author recommends further investigaiton.

A737K _____ . "Classic Perspectives of Meditation: Toward an Empirical Understanding of Meditation as an Altered State of Consciousness." In Meditation: Classic and Contemporary Perspectives, edited by Deane H. Shapiro, Jr. and Roger N. Walsh. Hawthorne, N.Y.: Aldine Pub. Co., 1984.

A738 _____ . "Instructions for a Training Package Combining Formal and Informal Zen Meditation with Behavioral Self-Control Strategies." Psychologia: An International Journal of Psychology in the Orient, 21 (June 1978): 70-76.
Includes a brief introduction to Zen meditation, a description of formal Zen breath meditation, and a description of informal meditation combined behavioral self-control techniques used in the author's previous studies.

A739 _____ . "Overview: Clinical and Physiological Comparison of Meditation with Other Self-Control Strategies." American Journal of Psychiatry, 139 (March 1982): 267-274. Critique by D.A. Switkes and reply by D.H. Shapiro, 139 (September 1982): 1217-1218. Also in Meditation: Classic and Contemporary Perspectives, edited by Deane H. Shapiro, Jr. and Roger N. Walsh. Hawthorne, N.Y.: Aldine Pub. Co., 1984.

Provides a definition of meditation and then cites literature comparing meditation with such self-regulation strategies as biofeedback, hypnosis, and progressive relaxation. Discusses meditation as a clinical intervention strategy as well as the adverse effects. Offers guidelines and suggestions for future research.

A739K   _____. "A Systems Approach to Meditation Research: Guidelines and Suggestions." In Meditation: Classic and Contemporary Perspectives, edited by Deane H. Shapiro, Jr. and Roger N. Walsh. Hawthorne, N.Y.: Aldine Pub. Co., 1984.

A740   _____. "Zen Meditation and Behavioral Self-Control: Some Similarities and Differences." (ERIC ED 108 084). A paper presented at the Annual Meeting of the American Education Research Association, Washington, D.C., March 30-April 3, 1975. An attempt is made to understand behaviors involved in the two self-control strategies mentioned in the title. Clinical outcome literature is reviewed. Rehabilitative and preventive benefits are discussed.

A741   _____. "Zen Meditation and Behavioral Self-Control Strategies Applied to a Case of Generalized Anxiety." Psychologia: An International Journal of Psychology in the Orient, 19 (September 1976): 134-138.

Discusses self-control techniques of Zen meditation and behavioral self-management. These techniques were used to reduce feelings of anxiety, stress, and tension in females. Suggests guidelines for integration of Eastern and Western methods of self-control in psychotherapy.

A742   _____, and David Giber. "Meditation and Psychotherapeutic Effects: Self-regulation Strategy and Altered State of Consciousness." Archives of General Psychiatry, 35 (March 1978): 294-302. Also in Meditation: Classic and Contemporary Perspectives, edited by Deane H. Shapiro, Jr. and Roger N. Walsh. Hawthorne, N.Y.: Aldine Pub. Co., 1984.

Review of studies in which meditation is considered a self-regulatory strategy for clinical problems in avoiding stress. Another section covers reviews of meditation as an altered state of consciousness. Evaluations of past studies are presented and suggestions for possible research and design are mentioned.

A743 _____; Johanna Shapiro; Roger N. Walsh; and Dan Brown. "Effects of Intensive Meditation on Sex-Role Identification: Implications for a Control Model of Psychological Health." Psychological Reports, 51 (August 1982): 44-46.
This study assessed the impact of a three-month meditation retreat on fifteen respondents' self-perceived masculinity and femininity.

A744 _____, and Steven M. Zifferblatt. "An Applied Clinical Combination of Zen Meditation and Behavioral Self-Control Strategies: Reducing Methadone Dosage in Drug Abuse." Behavior Therapy, 7 (1976): 694-695.
A letter suggesting that much more refinement and evaluation of the strategies needs to be undertaken to understand the effectiveness of these treatment techniques.

A745 _____, and _____. "Zen Meditation and Behavior Self-Control: Similarities, Differences, and Clinical Applications." American Psychologist, 31 (July 1976): 519-532.
Also in Meditation: Classic and Contemporary Perspectives, edited by Deane H. Shapiro, Jr. and Roger N. Walsh. Hawthorne, N.Y.: Aldine Pub. Co., 1984.
After briefly reviewing the clinical outcome literature for both strategies, the article concludes with a discussion of the rehabilitative and preventive benefits that may be gained from a combination of the two techniques.

A746 Shapiro, Jonathan. "The Relationship of the Transcendental Meditation Program to Self-Actualization and Negative Personality Characteristics." In Scientific Research on the Transcendental Meditation Program: Collected Papers, Vol. 1. Edited by David W. Orme-Johnson and John T. Farrow. 2nd ed., Weggis, Switzerland: Maharishi European Research University Press, 1977, p. 462-467.
Increased self-actualization, decreased aggression, decreased neuroticism, and decreased depression were demonstrated by subjects who practiced the TM technique.

A747 Shaw, Robert, and David Kolb. "Reaction Time Following the Transcendental Meditation Technique." In Scientific Research on the Transcendental Meditation Program: Collected Papers, Vol. 1. Edited by David W. Orme-Johnson and John T. Farrow. 2nd ed., Weggis, Switzerland: Maharishi European Research University Press, 1977, p. 309-311.
The findings showed improved reaction time in meditators.

A748 Shea, Gordon F. "Cost Effective Stress Management Training." Training and Development Journal, 34 (July 1980): 25-33.
The rank order, from the most cost effective to least cost

effective, based on selected criteria appear to be: Self-hypnosis, Progressive relaxation, TM, Biofeedback, Yoga/Zen, and Physical exercise.

A749   Shear, Jonathan. "Maharishi, Plato, and the TM-Sidhi Pro-
        gram on Inner Structures of Consciousness." Metaphilos-
        ophy, 12 (January 1981): 72-84. Tentatively scheduled
        for inclusion in Scientific Research on the Transcendental
        Meditation Program: Collected Papers, Vol. 2. Rhein-
        weiler, West Germany: Maharishi European Research Uni-
        versity Press, (in press).
        Discusses how the experience of a particular TM-Sidhi tech-
        nique sheds significant light on our understanding of Plato.

A750   _____. "Universal Structures and Dynamics of Creativity:
        Maharishi, Plato, Jung and Various Creative Geniuses on
        the Creative Process." Journal of Creative Behavior, 16
        (1982): 155-175.
        Suggests the techniques of the Transcendental Meditation
        program which produce experiences of awareness are capable
        of enhancing creativity systematically on a wide scale.

A751   Shecter, Howard. "The Transcendental Meditation Program
        in the Classroom: A Psychological Evaluation." In Sci-
        entific Research on the Transcendental Meditation Pro-
        gram: Collected Papers, Vol. 1. Edited by David W.
        Orme-Johnson and John T. Farrow. 2nd ed., Weggis,
        Switzerland: Maharishi European Research University
        Press, 1977, p. 403-409.
        High school students practicing the TM technique showed
        positive changes in creativity, intellectual performance, and
        other psychological variables.

A752   Shepherd, Massey H. "Implications of Liturgical Prayer for
        Personal Meditation and Contemplation." Studia Liturgica,
        9 (1973): 56-71.
        Gives examples of Scriptural passages characteristic of pri-
        vate prayer and meditation.

A753   Shimano, Eido T., and Donald B. Douglas. "On Research
        in Zen." American Journal of Psychiatry, 132 (December
        1975): 1300-1302.
        The authors discuss several aspects of Zen, such as the
        psychophysiological effects of meditation and the general im-
        pact of enlightenment, that are potential areas of research.
        They stress that researchers should practice Zen meditation
        themselves.

A754   Sime, Wesley E. "A Comparison of Exercise and Meditation
        in Reducing Physiological Response to Stress." (ERIC
        ED 141 339).

A paper presented at the Annual meeting of the American College of Sports Medicine, Chicago, Ill., May 1977. Results indicated that brief mild exercise may be to a slight degree more effective in coping with stress than quiet meditation.

A755   Simon, David B.; Suzanne Oparil; and Chase P. Kimball. "The Transcendental Meditation Program and Essential Hypertension." In Scientific Research on the Transcendental Meditation Program: Collected Papers, Vol. 1. Edited by David W. Orme-Johnson and John T. Farrow. 2nd ed., Weggis, Switzerland: Maharishi European Research University Press, 1977, p. 268-269.
Borderline hypertensives experienced decreased systolic and diastolic blood pressure after practicing the TM technique.

A756   Simon, Jane. "Creativity and Altered States of Consciousness." American Journal of Psychoanalysis, 37 (Spring 1977): 3-12.
Examines the relationship between creativity and therapy, dreams, meditation, hypnosis, and biofeedback.

A757   "A Simple, Cost-Free and Comfortable Way to Combat Job Tension." Nation's Business, 64 (December 1976): 29-36.
An interview with Dr. Herbert Benson on his system, the Relaxation Response.

A758   Sinari, Ramakant. "The Method of Phenomenological Reduction and Yoga." Philosophy East and West, 15 (July-October 1965): 217-228.
Examines Husserl's transcendental reduction. Concludes that yoga carries it to its logical end.

A759   Sinha, S.N.; S.C. Prasad; and K.N. Sharma. "An Experimental Study of Cognitive Control and Arousal Processes During Meditation." Psychologia: An International Journal of Psychology in the Orient, 21 (December 1978): 227-230.
Attentiveness, alertness, and behavior arousal before and after cognitive control practices in the form of Vipashyana meditation training are evaluated.

A760   Smith, Adam. "Meditation Game." Atlantic, 236 (October 1975): 33-45.
This is an excerpt from the author's book, Powers of Mind, dealing with Transcendental Meditation.

A761   _____. "Sport Is a Western Yoga." Psychology Today, 9 (October 1975): 45+
An excerpt from the author's book, Powers of Mind, discussing the relationship of sports to meditation and the personal experiences of some athletes. Includes an introduction by T. George Harris.

A762   Smith, Jonathan C. "Meditation as Psychotherapy: A Review of the Literature." Psychological Bulletin, 82 (July 1975): 558-564. Also in Meditation: Classic and Contemporary Perspectives, edited by Deane H. Shapiro, Jr. and Roger N. Walsh. Hawthorne, N.Y.: Aldine Pub. Co., 1984.
Suggests there is no conclusive evidence that meditation is therapeutic. Benefits found could be the result of expectation of relief or of simply sitting on a regular basis.

A762K   _____. "Meditation Research: Three Observations on the State-of-the-Art." In Meditation: Classic and Contemporary Perspectives, edited by Deane H. Shapiro, Jr. and Roger N. Walsh. Hawthorne, N.Y.: Aldine Pub. Co., 1984.

A763   _____. "Personality Correlates of Continuation and Outcome in Meditation and Erect Sitting Control Treatments." Journal of Consulting and Clinical Psychology, 46 (April 1978): 272-279. Also in Meditation: Classic and Contemporary Perspectives, edited by Deane H. Shapiro, Jr. and Roger N. Walsh. Hawthorne, N.Y.: Aldine Pub. Co., 1984.
It was concluded that differing treatment rationales rendered the treatments appealing, credible, and effective for different types of individuals.

A764   _____. "Psychotherapeutic Effects of Transcendental Meditation with Controls for Expectation of Relief and Daily Sitting." Journal of Consulting and Clinical Psychology, 44 (August 1976): 630-637. Also in Meditation: Classic and Contemporary Perspectives, edited by Deane H. Shapiro, Jr. and Roger N. Walsh. Hawthorne, N.Y.: Aldine Pub. Co., 1984.
Differences between groups did not approach significance. The results support the conclusion that the crucial therapeutic component of TM is not the TM exercise. Based on the author's dissertation [D204].

A765   Smith, Terrance R. "The Transcendental Meditation Technique and Skin Resistance Response to Loud Tones." In Scientific Research on the Transcendental Meditation Program: Collected Papers, Vol. 1. Edited by David W. Orme-Johnson and John T. Farrow. 2nd ed., Weggis, Switzerland: Maharishi European Research University Press, 1977, p. 248-250.
Meditators showed more rapid habituation to loud tones than nonmeditators.

A766   Snell, Vincent. "Transcendental Meditation: Stressing Natural Harmony." Nursing Mirror, 149 (22 November 1979): 30-31.

Asks for recognition of Transcendental Meditation as a valuable ally to orthodox medicine for the maintenance of perfect mental and physical health.

A767   Solfvin, Gerald; W.G. Roll; and Joan Krieger. "Meditation and ESP: Remote Viewing." Journal of Parapsychology, 41 (1977): 261-263.
Abstract of a paper. As part of a series of projects studying the effect of group meditation on ESP performance, this study tested the effects of subjects' and agents' attitudes toward one another.

A768   Solomon, Earl G., and Ann K. Bumpus. "The Running Meditation Response: An Adjunct to Psychotherapy." American Journal of Psychotherapy, 32 (October 1978): 583-592.
Slow, long distance running and the mental centering devices of TM are combined, using hypnosis in some cases, to enhance altered state of consciousness. Indications and contraindications to this technique are described.

A769   Soskis, David A. "Teaching Meditation to Medical Students." Journal of Religion and Health, 17 (April 1978): 136-143.
Describes and evaluates a course in meditation and healing offered to second-year students at Temple University School of Medicine.

A770   Spanos, Nicholas P.; Jack Gottlieb; and Stephen M. Rivers. "The Effects of Short-Term Meditation Practice on Hypnotic Responsivity." Psychological Record, 30 (1980): 343-348.
Neither the meditation nor the listening treatments enhanced hypnotic responsivity or absorption.

A771   _____; Stephen M. Rivers; and Jack Gottlieb. "Hypnotic Responsivity, Meditation, and Laterality of Eye Movements." Journal of Abnormal Psychology, 87 (October 1978): 566-569.
Measures of hypnotic responsivity, meditating skill, imaginal abilities, and attitudes toward hypnosis are discussed. Laterality of eye movements did not correlate significantly with any of the variables.

A772   _____; Henderikus J. Stam; Stephen M. Rivers; and H. Lorraine Radtke. "Meditation, Expectation and Performance on Indexes of Nonanalytic Attending." International Journal of Clinical and Experimental Hypnosis, 28 (July 1980): 244-251.
Intrusion rate correlated significantly with hypnotic susceptibility. Meditation practice failed to produce either an overall reduction in rate of intrusions or an increment in hypnotic susceptibility.

A773 _____; Shawn Steggles; H. Lorraine Radtke-Bodorik; and
Stephen M. Rivers. "Nonanalytic Attending, Hypnotic
Susceptibility, and Psychological Well-Being in Trained
Meditators and Nonmeditators." Journal of Abnormal Psychology, 88 (February 1979): 85-87.
Meditators signaled fewer intrusions and reported deeper
levels of meditating than nonmeditators. However, meditators
and nonmeditators did not differ on hypnotic susceptibility,
absorption, or indices of psychopathology.

A774 Speeth, Kathleen R. "On Psychotherapeutic Attention."
Journal of Transpersonal Psychology, 14 (1982): 141-160.
Considers problems and techniques of attentional focus in
psychotherapeutic practice.

A775 Spino, Mike, and James L. Hickman. "Beyond the Physical
Limits." Runner's World, 12 (March 1977): 52-53.
Reports how runners add an extra dimension to both the
physical and psychological experiences associated with running by combining running with meditation.

A776 Stanford, Rex G., and John Palmer. "Meditation Prior to
the ESP Task: An EEG Study with an Outstanding ESP
Subject." In Research in Parapsychology 1972. Edited
by W.G. Roll, R.L. Morris, and J.D. Morris. Metuchen,
N.J.: The Scarecrow Press, Inc., 1973, p. 34-36.
Measured high alpha frequency in the meditation period pre-
ceding the ESP session.

A777 Stek, Robert J., and Barry A. Bass. "Personal Adjustment
and Perceived Locus of Control Among Students Interested
in Meditation." Psychological Reports,, 32 (June 1973):
1019-1022. In Scientific Research on the Transcendental
Meditation Program: Collected Papers, Vol. 1. Edited by
David W. Orme-Johnson and John T. Farrow. 2nd ed.,
Weggis, Switzerland: Maharishi European Research University Press, 1977, p. 425-427.
Level of interest in Transcendental Meditation was not related either to perceived locus of control or to personal adjustment.

A778 Stern, Maureen. "The Effects of the Transcendental Meditation Program on Trait Anxiety." In Scientific Research
on the Transcendental Meditation Program: Collected Papers, Vol. 1. Edited by David W. Orme-Johnson and
John T. Farrow. 2nd ed., Weggis, Switzerland: Maharishi European Research University Press, 1977, p. 468-
469.
General anxiety was decreased by those practicing the TM
technique.

A779   Stevens, Clifford. "The Fine Art of Meditation." Our Sun-
            day Visitor, 62 (17 February 1974): 3.
        Explains the tradition and method of Christian meditation as
        a preparation for prayer.

A780   Stevens, Mary Martha. "Transcendental Meditation and Den-
            tal Hygiene." Dental Hygiene, 54 (April 1980): 165-168.
        Explains how Transcendental Meditation may benefit the den-
        tal hygienist and can be easily incorporated into the daily
        routine.

A781   Stewart, Robert A. "Self-Realization as the Basis of Psycho-
            therapy: A Look at Two Eastern-Based Practices, Tran-
            scendental Meditation and Alpha Brain Wave Biofeedback."
            Social Behavior and Personality, 2 (1974): 191-200.
        Surveys the research in Transcendental Meditation, Zen, and
        biofeedback training.

A782   _____. "States of Human Realization: Some Physiological
            and Psychological Correlates." Psychologia: An Inter-
            national Journal of Psychology in the Orient, 17 (Septem-
            ber 1974): 126-134.
        This paper looks at some of the physiological, psychological,
        and social research on the Zen tradition of meditation and
        Transcendental Meditation.

A783   Stigsby, Bent; Jennifer C. Rodenberg; and Hanne B. Moth.
            "Electroencephalographic Findings During Mantra Medita-
            tion (Transcendental Meditation): A Controlled, Quanti-
            tative Study of Experienced Meditators." Electroencepha-
            lography and Clinical Neurophysiology, 51 (April 1981):
            434-442.
        The EEGs during TM were not different from those recorded
        during wakefulness and drowsiness, but clearly different
        from those recorded during sleep onset and sleep.

A784   Stone, Richard A., and James Deleo. "Psychotherapeutic
            Control of Hypertension." New England Journal of Medi-
            cine, 294 (8 January 1976): 80-84. Also in Meditation:
            Classic and Contemporary Perspectives, edited by Deane
            H. Shapiro, Jr. and Roger N. Walsh. Hawthorne, N.Y.:
            Aldine Pub. Co., 1984.
        Buddhist meditation was demonstrated to provide improved
        blood pressure control in certain patients with mild or mod-
        erate hypertension.

A785   Strassman, R.J., and M. Galanter. "The Abhidarma: A
            Cross-Cultural Model for the Psychiatric Application of
            Meditation." International Journal of Social Psychiatry,
            26 (Winter 1980): 293-299.
        The clinical relevance of the Buddhist Abhidharma psycho-
        logical system of meditation is presented.

A786   Strenski, Ivan. "Gradual Enlightenment, Sudden Enlighten-
        ment and Empiricism." Philosophy East and West, 30
        (January 1980): 3-20.
        Compares the structures of institutionalized theories of knowl-
        edge with the structures of meditational practices and beliefs
        to see whether one might understand their characteristics in
        terms of their underlying epistemological structure.

A786K   Stroebel, Charles F., and Bernard C. Glueck. "Passive
        Meditation: Subjective, Clinical Comparison with Biofeed-
        back." In Meditation: Classic and Contemporary Per-
        spectives, edited by Deane H. Shapiro, Jr. and Roger
        N. Walsh. Hawthorne, N.Y.: Aldine Pub. Co., 1984.

A787   Subrahmanyam, Sarada. "Clinical and Biochemical Effects of
        the TM Program." Tentatively scheduled for inclusion in
        Scientific Research on the Transcendental Meditation Pro-
        gram: Collected Papers, Vol. 2. Rheinweiler, West Ger-
        many: Maharishi European Research University Press,
        Hyperaggressive patients, mental retardates, epileptics, and
        normals all experienced beneficial changes in various bio-
        chemical levels. A paper presented at the meeting of the
        International Congress on Higher States of Consciousness,
        Bangkok, Thailand, January, 1980.

A788   _____. "Neurohumoral Correlates of Behavior." Annals
        of the National Academy of Medical Sciences, (India), 16
        (April-June 1980): 73-88.
        Yoga and meditation were included in the therapy of epileptic,
        aggressive hyperkinetic, and mental retardation patients.

A789   Sudbrack, Josef. "The Challenge of Eastern Meditation."
        Monastic Studies, 12 (Winter 1976): 121-150.
        A comparison of Zen meditation and Christian meditation.

A790   Suflita, Jeanette. "How to Teach Children to Meditate."
        Catechist, 13 (February 1980): 56-57.
        The author explains a simple method of teaching third-
        graders to meditate.

A791   Sultan, S.E. "A Study of the Ability of Individuals Trained
        in the Transcendental Meditation Technique to Achieve
        and Maintain Levels of Physiological Relaxation." Tenta-
        tively scheduled for inclusion in Scientific Research on
        the Transcendental Meditation Program: Collected Papers,
        Vol. 2. Rheinweiler, West Germany: Maharishi European
        Research University Press, (in press).
        A deeper level of relaxation was experienced by subjects
        practicing the TM technique than control groups. [Cf. D211]

A792   Surwillo, Walter W., and Douglas P. Hobson. "Brain Electrical Activity During Prayer." Psychological Reports,, 43 (1978): 135-143.
Findings did not show any evidence of EEG slowing in prayer. Also discussed in relation to Yoga and Transcendental Meditation.

A793   Surwit, Richard S.; David Shapiro; and Michael I. Good. "Comparison of Cardiovascular Biofeedback, Neuromuscular Biofeedback, and Meditation in the Treatment of Borderline Essential Hypertension." Journal of Consulting and Clinical Psychology, 46 (April 1978): 252-263.
All groups showed only moderate reductions in blood pressure.

A794   Swearer, Donald K. "Control and Freedom: The Structure of Buddhist Meditation in the Pali Suttas." Philosophy East and West, 23 (October 1973): 435-455.
Contends that the structure of Buddhist meditation is built around the two foci of control and freedom.

A795   Swinyard, Chester A.; Shakuntala Chaube; and David B. Sutton. "Neurological and Behavioral Aspects of Transcendental Meditation Relevant to Alcoholism: A Review." Annals of the New York Academy of Sciences, 233 (April 1974): 162-173.
Suggests that TM will eventually be found to have a very significant potential in combating alcoholism. A literature review.

A796   Tabak, Lawrence. "Maharishi U.: Learning to Levitate in Fairfield, Iowa." Moment, 4 (January-February 1979): 26-32.
Discusses the influence of Judaism at Maharishi International University.

A797   Tambiah, S.J. "The Cosmological and Performative Significance of a Thai Cult of Healing Through Meditation." Culture, Medicine, and Psychiatry, 1 (April 1977): 97-132.
The various ramifications of the cosmology are discussed. The features of the ritual as they contribute to its performative efficacy are highlighted. Suggests a single scheme underlying religious ideas and applications of knowledge such as meditation, medicine, alchemy, and astrology.

A798   Tart, Charles T. "A Psychologist's Experience with Transcendental Meditation." Journal of Transpersonal Psychology, 3 (1971): 135-140.
The author reports on his personal psychological and physiological experiences after practicing TM for one year.

A799   Tasler, Susan. "TM: A Prescription to Cure Stress."
        Canadian Business Magazine, 48 (February 1975): 40-46.
        Discusses the effect of TM on job performance, job satisfac-
        tion, productivity, and stress.

A800   Taylor, Rodney L. "Meditation in Ming Neo-Orthodoxy:
        Kao P'an-lung's Writings on Quiet-Sitting." Journal of
        Chinese Philosophy, 6 (1979): 149-182.
        A thorough explanation and analysis of Kao's method in the
        practice of quiet-sitting.

A801   _____. "Sudden/Gradual Paradigm and Neo-Confucian
        Mind-Cultivation." Philosophy East and West, 33 (January
        1983): 17-34.
        Discusses mind cultivation and quiet-sitting during the Sung
        Dynasty, Wang Yang-ming and the decreasing relevancy of
        quiet-sitting, late Ming Ch'eng-Chu quiet-sitting, and the
        relevancy of a Buddhist paradigm.

A802   Teahan, John F. "Meditation and Prayer in Merton's Spirit-
        uality." American Benedictine Review, 30 (June 1979):
        107-133.
        Examines Merton's understanding of prayer and the need for
        meditation and prayer in the Christian life.

A803   Tebecis, Andris K. "Eye Movements During Transcendental
        Meditation." Folia Psychiatrica et Neurologica Japonica,
        30 (1976): 487-493.
        Shows that the changes in eye movements which occurred in
        a proportion of subjects experienced in TM are similar to
        those during passive hypnosis.

A804   "Tempest Over TM: Question of TM Courses in New Jersey
        Schools." Time, 107 (1 March 1976): 34, 37.
        Reports on court litigation in New Jersey to prohibit the
        teaching of TM in public schools.

A805   Thelle, Notto R. "Zen for Missionaries: A Report of a
        Seminar for Missionaries at Eiheiji." Japanese Religions,
        12 (December 1981): 65-71.
        A critical discussion of the strengths and weaknesses of Zen
        for Christians.

A806   Thomas, D., and K.A. Abbas. "Comparison of Transcendental
        Meditation and Progressive Relaxation in Reducing Anxi-
        ety." British Medical Journal, 2, 6154 (23-30 December
        1978): 1749. Critiques by K. McPherson and M. Peet, 1,
        6157 (20 January 1979): 201.
        A short report on a study showing that TM and PR are
        equally effective in reducing anxiety.

A807   Thompson, Era Bell. "Meditation Can Solve Race Problem."
        Ebony, 23 (May 1968): 78-80, 82-84, 86-88.
An interview with the Maharishi Mahesh Yogi.

A808   Throll, D.A. "The Effects of the Transcendental Meditation
        Technique Upon Adolescent Personality." Tentatively
scheduled for inclusion in Scientific Research on the Transcendental Meditation Program: Collected Papers, Vol. 2.
Rheinweiler, West Germany: Maharishi European Research
University Press, (in press).
Positive personality changes were found in TM practitioners
in areas of psychological adjustment, self-actualization, and
drug consumption. Physical health was also improved.

A809   _____. "Transcendental Meditation and Progressive Re-
        laxation: Their Physiological Effects." Journal of Clinical
Psychology, 38 (July 1982): 522-530.
The TM group displayed more significant decreases in measured physiological rates during meditation and during activity
than did the PR group. Both groups displayed significantly
lowered metabolic rates during TM or PR.

A810   _____. "Transcendental Meditation and Progressive Re-
        laxation: Their Psychological Effects." Journal of Clini-
cal Psychology, 37 (October 1981): 776-781.
At posttest the TM group displayed more significant and
comprehensive results on psychological variables. Both
groups demonstrated significant decreases in state and trait
anxiety.

A811   _____, and L.A. Throll. "The Effect of a Three Month
        Residence Course Upon the Personalities of Experienced
Meditators." Tentatively scheduled for inclusion in Scientific Research on the Transcendental Meditation Program: Collected Papers, Vol. 2. Rheinweiler, West Germany: Maharishi European Research University Press,
(in press).
Experienced meditators showed improved health, increased
creativity, and decreased anxiety. Drug usage was minimal.

A812   Tibblin, Gösta, and Carl-Gunnar Eriksson. "The Prevention
        of Hypertension." Acta Medica Scandinavica Supplemen-
tum, 606 (1977): 101-106.
Focuses on salt, control of obesity, physical exercise, and
meditation.

A813   Tjoa, André. "Meditation, Neuroticism and Intelligence: A
        Follow-Up." Gedrag: Tijdschrift voor Psychologie, 3
(1975): 167-182. Also published as "Increased Intelligence
and Reduced Neuroticism Through the Transcendental

Meditation Program." In Scientific Research on the Transcendental Meditation Program: Collected Papers, Vol. 1.
Edited by David W. Orme-Johnson and John T. Farrow.
2nd ed., Weggis, Switzerland: Maharishi European Research University Press, 1977, p. 368-376.
The results tend to support the thesis that regular meditation enhances intelligence and both neurotic and psychosomatic stability.

A814 _____. "Some Evidence That the Transcendental Meditation
Program Increases Intelligence and Reduces Neuroticism
as Measured by Psychological Tests." In Scientific Research on the Transcendental Meditation Program: Collected Papers, Vol. 1. Edited by David W. Orme-Johnson
and John T. Farrow. 2nd ed., Weggis, Switzerland:
Maharishi European Research University Press, 1977, p.
363-367.
Increased intelligence and decreased neuroticism were demonstrated by meditators.

A815 "TM Course Entangles Church, State: Fed Court." Phi
Delta Kappan, 60 (May 1979): 690.
A short report on the ruling of a federal appeals court that
the teaching of TM at five New Jersey public schools vio-
lated the U.S. Constitution.

A816 "TM Craze: Forty Minutes to Bliss." Time, 106 (13 October 1975): 70-74.
Reports on the popularity of Transcendental Meditation in
the U.S.

A817 "TM Grounded: Federal District Court Ruled the Govern-
ment-Funded Teaching of TM Unconstitutional." Christianity Today, 22 (18 November 1977): 56.
Mentions the results of litigation in New Jersey to prohibit
the teaching of TM in public schools.

A818 "TM in the Pen." Time, 112 (13 November 1978): 84.
A short report on the use of Transcendental Meditation in
prisons.

A819 "TM: Management Finds a New Technique to Increase Productivity." Commerce America, 2 (17 January 1977):
8-10.
Reports on a number of companies offering the TM program
to their employees.

A820 "TM: The Drugless High." Time, 100 (23 October 1972):
102, 105, K13, K17.
Discusses the effects of Transcendental Meditation.

A821   "To Ease Your Mind." Mademoiselle, 81 (April 1975): 143,
        206-207.
        A short explanation of Transcendental Meditation.

A822   Toane, E.B. "Transcendental Meditation Program." Cana-
        dian Medical Association Journal, 114 (19 June 1976):
        1095-1096. Critiques and reply, 115 (9 October 1976):
        607, 609.
        The author believes that TM should be considered in the
        treatment of psychosomatic disorders and any illness associ-
        ated with stress, and the technique used as a method of
        preventive medicine.

A823   "Tools for Transformation." New Realities, 2 (June 1978):
        32-33.
        Gives a technique for contacting your inner voice.

A824   Törber, S.; F. Mertesdorf; and E. Hiesel. "Effects of the
        Transcendental Meditation Technique on Mood and Body
        Sensation." Tentatively scheduled for inclusion in Sci-
        entific Research on the Transcendental Meditation Pro-
        gram: Collected Papers, Vol. 2. Rheinweiler, West Ger-
        many: Maharishi European Research University Press,
        (in press).
        TM meditators experienced less depression, anxiety, ner-
        vousness, anger, fatigue, and dreaminess; and more relax-
        ation, activation, and elation than controls.

A825   "Transcendental Meditation and Meaning of Religion Under
        Establishment Clause." Minnesota Law Review, 62 (1978):
        887-948.
        Concerns the case of Malmak versus Maharishi Mahesh Yogi
        regarding the teaching of TM in New Jersey public schools.

A826   Travis, Frederick. "The Transcendental Meditation Tech-
        nique and Creativity: A Longitudinal Study of Cornell
        University Undergraduates." Journal of Creative Be-
        havior, 13 (1979): 169-180. Tentatively scheduled for
        inclusion in Scientific Research on the Transcendental
        Meditation Program: Collected Papers, Vol. 2. Rhein-
        weiler, West Germany: Maharishi European Research
        University Press, (in press).
        The increased brain wave synchrony reported in TM prac-
        titioners offers an explanation for the observed improvements
        in figural creativity scores.

A827   Truch, S., and J. Hritzuk. "The Effects of Transcendental
        Meditation on Several Psychological Variables Associated
        with Teacher Effectiveness." Tentatively scheduled for
        inclusion in Scientific Research on the Transcendental
        Meditation Program: Collected Papers, Vol. 2. Rhein-

weiler, West Germany: Maharishi European Research University Press, (in press).
School teachers showed significant changes in anxiety, attitude, self-actualization, and self-concept after eight weeks of practicing the TM technique.

A828   Turnbull, Michael J., and Hugh Norris. "Effects of Transcendental Meditation on Self-Identity Indices and Personality." British Journal of Psychology, 73 (February 1982): 57-68.
Subjects practicing Transcendental Meditation appear to have experienced consistent and definable changes of a generally beneficial nature. The value of TM as a therapeutic tool is suggested.

A829   Tyson, Paul D. "A General Systems Theory Approach to Consciousness, Attention, and Meditation." Psychological Record, 32 (Fall 1982): 491-500.
Attention and meditation are used to illustrate how a nondichotomous approach yields implications and possibilities commonly found in daily experience, but excluded by traditional dichotomous approaches.

A829K Vahia, N.S.; D.R. Doongaji; D.V.Jeste; S.N. Kapoor; Indubala Ardhapurkar; and S. Ravindra Nath. "Further Experience with Therapy Based Upon Concepts of Patanjali in the Treatment of Psychiatric Disorders." In Meditation: Classic and Contemporary Perspectives, edited by Deane H. Shapiro, Jr. and Roger N. Walsh. Hawthorne, N.Y.: Aldine Pub. Co., 1984.

A830   Van Dusen, Wilson. "Meditation." New-Church Magazine, 96 (Spring 1977): 5-14.
Discusses the writings of Emanuel Swedenborg on meditation.

A831   Van Horn, Phyllis Battelle. "How Transcendental Meditation Changed Our Family's Life." Ladies' Home Journal, 92 (November 1975): 97, 160, 162, 164.
Personal account of how a wife and mother found relaxation and renewed energy through TM.

A832   Van Nuys, David. "Meditation, Attention, and Hypnotic Susceptibility: A Correlational Study." International Journal of Clinical and Experimental Hypnosis, 21 (April 1973): 59-69.
A correlation was shown between meditation measures of attention and hypnotizability.

A833   _____. "A Novel Technique for Studying Attention During Meditation." Journal of Transpersonal Psychology, 3 (1971): 125-133.

This study employed the technique of having the subject report each intrusion during meditation.

A834   Varni, James W. "Self-Regulation Techniques in the Management of Chronic Arthritic Pain in Hemophilia." Behavior Therapy, 12 (March 1981): 185-194.
The self-regulation techniques, including meditation, resulted in clinically significant reduction in arthritic pain.

A835   Vattano, Anthony J. "Self-Management Procedures for Coping with Stress." Social Work, 23 (March 1978): 113-119. Critique by Stewart Moore, 23 (July 1978): 329-330.
This article describes the research on stress and anxiety that relates to relaxation training, systematic desensitization, and meditation. The implications for social work education and practice are examined.

A836   Vieg, Elizabeth Lam. "Lure of Novel Religious Forms: Three Autobiographical Sketches." Soundings, 57 (Winter 1974): 403-419.
Discusses characteristics common to the three autobiographies.

A837   Vizbara-Kessler, Barbara. "Transpersonalizing Education in the '80s." Educational Horizons, 59 (Summer 1981): 192-194.
Lists the benefits that relaxation and meditation have to offer students.

A838   Vonnegut, Kurt, Jr. "Yes, We Have No Nirvanas." Esquire, 69 (June 1968): 78-79, 176, 178-179. Reprinted, 99 (June 1983): 284-286+
An account by the author of his meeting with the Maharishi Mahesh Yogi.

A839   Vrolijk, Arie. "Transcendental Meditation and Dianetics." Gedrag: Tijdschrift voor Psychologie, 6 (1978): 181-206.
The article attempts to conceptualize what is known about TM and Dianetics, and to indicate what they have to offer to psychology.

A840   Waal-Manning, Henrika, and D.A. Jenkins. "Systolic Blood-Pressure and Pulse-Rate During Transcendental Meditation." Proceedings of the University of Otago Medical School, 57 (1979): 75-76.
The mean systolic blood pressure remained unchanged during TM in subjects who meditate regularly, though they found a decrease in heart rate of three beats per minute.

A841   Wadler, Joyce. "Can TM Work for You?" Seventeen, 35 (February 1976): 112-113, 131-132.
Gives personal accounts of TM practice and examples of mantras.

A842   Wainwright, Loudon. "Invitation to Instant Bliss." Life, 63
        (10 November 1967): 26.
        An interview with the Maharishi Mahesh Yogi.

A843   Walker, C.R. "Personal Discipline and William Law." Ex-
        pository Times, 73 (November 1961): 35-38.
        Concludes that the writings of William Law confirms the need
        for a disciplined life of prayer and meditation in the Chris-
        tian ministry.

A844   Wallace, Robert Keith. "Neurophysiology of Enlightenment."
        In Scientific Research on the Transcendental Meditation
        Program: Collected Papers, Vol. 1. Edited by David W.
        Orme-Johnson and John T. Farrow. 2nd ed., Weggis,
        Switzerland: Maharishi European Research University
        Press, 1977, p. 692-697.
        Outlines the broad historical implications of scientific research
        on the TM program.

A845   _____. "Physiological Effects of Transcendental Meditation."
        Science, 167 (27 March 1970): 1751-1754. In Scientific
        Research on the Transcendental Meditation Program:
        Collected Papers, Vol. 1. Edited by David W. Orme-John-
        son and John T. Farrow. 2nd ed., Weggis, Switzerland:
        Maharishi European Research University Press, 1977, p.
        38-42.
        Oxygen consumption, heart rate, skin resistance, and elec-
        troencephalograph measurements all recorded significant
        changes. [Cf. B951, D222]

A846   _____, and Herbert Benson. "Physiology of Meditation."
        Scientific American, 226 (February 1972): 84-90. Re-
        printed in Altered States of Awareness. San Francisco:
        W.H. Freeman & Co., 1972, p. 125-131. Also in Scientific
        Research on the Transcendental Meditation Program: Col-
        lected Papers, Vol. 1. Edited by David W. Orme-John-
        and John T. Farrow. 2nd ed., Weggis, Switzerland:
        Maharishi European Research University Press, 1977, p.
        86-91.
        Studies the effects of meditation on decreasing oxygen con-
        sumption, concentration of blood lactate, and respiratory
        rate while increasing skin resistance and alpha waves. No
        change was observed in blood pressure.

A847   _____; _____; and Archie Wilson. "A Wakeful Hypo-
        metabolic Physiologic State." American Journal of Physi-
        ology, 221 (1971): 795-799. In Scientific Research on
        the Transcendental Meditation Program: Collected Papers,
        Vol. 1. Edited by David W. Orme-Johnson and John T.
        Farrow. 2nd ed., Weggis, Switzerland: Maharishi
        European Research University Press, 1977, p. 79-85.

Also in <u>Meditation: Classic and Contemporary Perspectives</u>, edited by Deane H. Shapiro, Jr. and Roger N. Walsh. Hawthorne, N.Y.: Aldine Pub. Co., 1984.
Describes hypometabolic and other physiological correlates during Transcendental Meditation.

A848 _____; Michael Dillbeck; Eliha Jacobe; and Beth Harrington. "The Effects of the Transcendental Meditation and TM-Sidhi Program on the Aging Process." <u>International Journal of Neuroscience</u>, 16 (February 1982): 53-58.
Tentatively scheduled for inclusion in <u>Scientific Research on the Transcendental Meditation Program: Collected Papers, Vol. 2</u>. Rheinweiler, West Germany: Maharishi European Research University Press, (in press), as "Reversal of Biological Aging in Subjects Practicing the Transcendental Meditation and TM-Sidhi Program."
A paper that suggests that the TM and TM-Sidhi programs may produce certain physiological changes opposite to those characterizing the aging process.

A849 _____; Paul J. Mills; David W. Orme-Johnson; Michael Dillbeck; and Eliha Jacobe. "Modification of the Paired H Reflex Through the Transcendental Meditation and TM-Sidhi Program." <u>Experimental Neurology</u>, 79 (January 1983): 77-86. Tentatively scheduled for inclusion in <u>Scientific Research on the Transcendental Meditation Program: Collected Papers, Vol. 2</u>. Rheinweiler, West Germany: Maharishi European Research University Press, (in press), as "The Effect of the TM-Sidhi Program on the Paired Hoffmann Reflex Response."
The amplitude of the paired H reflex for those in the TM-Sidhi program was significantly facilitated in the experimental male subjects. The experimental female subjects and the control group, (TM technique only), showed no significant change. The results extend previous studies showing distinct physiological differences between subjects practicing these two programs. Presented at the 4th Congress of the International Society of Electrophysiological Kinesiology, Boston, 1979.

A850 _____; Joel Silver; Paul J. Mills; Michael C. Dillbeck; and Dale E. Wagoner. "Systolic Blood Pressure and Long-Term Practice of the Transcendental Meditation and TM-Sidhi Program: Effects of TM on Systolic Blood Pressure." <u>Psychosomatic Medicine</u>, 45 (March 1983): 41-46.
Findings suggest beneficial effects of the long-term practice of the TM and TM-Sidhi programs on systolic blood pressure.

A851 Walrath, Larry C., and David H. Hamilton. "Autonomic Correlates of Meditation and Hypnosis." <u>American Journal of Clinical Hypnosis</u>, 17 (January 1975): 190-197.

Also in Meditation: Classic and Contemporary Perspectives, edited by Deane H. Shapiro, Jr. and Roger N.
Walsh. Hawthorne, N.Y.: Aldine Pub. Co., 1984.
Results suggest that meditation and hypnosis do not differ
markedly from each other, nor from instructed relaxation.

A852   Walsh, Roger N. "The Consciousness Disciplines and the
Behavioral Sciences: Questions of Comparison and Assessment." American Journal of Psychiatry, 137 (June
1980): 663-673.
Attention is drawn to the relevance of recent findings assessing consciousness disciplines, including meditation studies.

A852K   _____. "An Evolutionary Model of Meditation Research."
In Meditation: Classic and Contemporary Perspectives,
edited by Deane H. Shapiro, Jr. and Roger N. Walsh.
Hawthorne, N.Y.: Aldine Pub. Co., 1984.

A853   _____. "Initial Meditative Experiences: Part I." Journal
of Transpersonal Psychology, 9 (1977): 151-192. Also in
Meditation: Classic and Contemporary Perspectives,
edited by Deane H. Shapiro, Jr. and Roger N. Walsh.
Hawthorne, N.Y.: Aldine Pub. Co., 1984.
This is an account of the author's experiences of two years
of Vipassana or Insight meditation. First of two parts.

A854   _____. "Initial Meditative Experiences: Part II." Journal of Transpersonal Psychology, 10 (1978): 1-28. Also
in Meditation: Classic and Contemporary Perspectives,
edited by Deane H. Shapiro, Jr. and Roger N. Walsh.
Hawthorne, N.Y.: Aldine Pub. Co., 1984.

A855   _____. "Meditation: An Introduction and Review."
Journal of Transpersonal Psychology, 11 (1979): 161-174.
Presents an overview for the nonspecialist of the evolution
and state of the art of empirical research on meditation.
Includes a bibliography.

A856   _____. "Meditation Practice and Research." Journal of
Humanistic Psychology, 23 (Winter 1983): 18-50.
Gives an introduction and overview of meditation practice,
theory, and research. Reviews various Eastern and Western
psychological and physiological models that have been used
to account for the effects of meditation. Discusses meditation as self-regulation strategy and surveys the research
literature.

A857   _____. "A Model for Viewing Meditation Research." Journal of Transpersonal Psychology, 14 (1982): 69-84.
An evolutionary model of meditation research is given that
represents a specific application of a more general stimulus-
response model. Parameters and variables are discussed.

A858　　　　　　; Daniel Goleman; Jack Kornfield; Corrado Pensa;
　　　　　　and Deane Shapiro. "Meditation: Aspects of Research
　　　　　　and Practice." Journal of Transpersonal Psychology, 10
　　　　　　(1978): 113-133.
This is the edited transcription of a discussion presented at
the Sixth Annual Conference of the Association for Transpersonal Psychology, Asilomar Conference Grounds, Pacific
Grove, Calif., September 12, 1978.

A859　　　　　　, and Lorin Roche. "Precipitation of Acute Psychotic
　　　　　　Episodes by Intensive Meditation in Individuals with a
　　　　　　History of Schizophrenia." American Journal of Psychia-
　　　　　　try, 136 (August 1979): 1085-1086.
Reports on three cases that show possible etiologic similarities that may be useful in identifying a population at risk
for pathologic reactions to intensive meditation.

A860　　　Wampler, Larry D., and Stephen B. Amira. "Transcendental
　　　　　　Meditation and Assertive Training in the Treatment of So-
　　　　　　cial Anxiety." (ERIC ED 189 521).
A paper presented at the Annual Meeting of the Western
Psychological Association, 60th, Honolulu, Hawaii, May 5-9,
1980. Single and combined TM and assertive training programs were compared for effectiveness in the treatment of
socially anxious college students. [Cf. D223]

A861　　　Wandhoefer, A., and K.-H. Plattig. "Stimulus-Linked DC-
　　　　　　Shift and Auditory Evoked Potentials in Transcendental
　　　　　　Meditation." Pflüger's Archiv: European Journal of
　　　　　　Physiology, 343 (1973): R79.
Abstract for a study reporting a shortening of latencies for
auditory slow evoked potentials in subjects before and dur-
ing performance of TM compared with a control group and
subjects in a dozing state.

A862　　　Warm, J.S.; W. Seeman; L.H. Bean; N. Chin; and N.F.
　　　　　　Wessling. "Meditation and Sustained Attention." Bulletin
　　　　　　of the Psychonomic Society, 10 (1977): 245.
Abstract for a paper reporting greater attentiveness among
subjects experienced in Transcendental Meditation.

A863　　　Warrenburg, Stephen; Robert R. Pagano; Marcella Woods;
　　　　　　and Michael Hlastala. "A Comparison of Somatic Relaxa-
　　　　　　tion and EEG Activity in Classical Progressive Relaxation
　　　　　　and Transcendental Meditation." Journal of Behavioral
　　　　　　Medicine, 3 (March 1980): 73-93.
Despite similar state effects, the long-term PR group manifested lower levels of somatic activity across all conditions
compared to both novice PR and long-term TM groups.

A864　　　Warshal, Debra. "Effects of the Transcendental Meditation

Technique on Normal and Jendrassik Reflex Time." Perceptual and Motor Skills, 50 (1980): 1103-1106. Tentatively scheduled for inclusion in Scientific Research on
the Transcendental Meditation Program: Collected Papers,
Vol. 2. Rheinweiler, West Germany: Maharishi European
Research University Press, (in press).
While no significant differences in reflex times were observed
pretreatment and posttreatment, a significant reduction in
reflex times was found over sessions during the six-week
test period.

A 865 _____, and J.W. Peterson. "Change in Cardiac Output
During Transcendental Meditation as Measured by Nonin-
vasive Impedance Plethysmography." Tentatively scheduled for inclusion in Scientific Research on the Transcendental Meditation Program: Collected Papers, Vol. 2.
Rheinweiler, West Germany: Maharishi European Research
University Press, (in press).
An increase of six percent in both cardiac output and stroke
volume were measured during meditation.

A 866 Washburn, Michael C. "Observations Relevant to a Unified
Theory of Meditation." Journal of Transpersonal Psychology, 10 (1978): 45-65.
Discusses the relationship and goals between concentrative
meditation and receptive meditation.

A 867 Waxman, Jerry. "A Finite State Model for Meditation Phenomena." Perceptual and Motor Skills, 49 (August 1979):
123-127.
Suggests that reports of brain wave synchrony during Transcendental Meditation rather than indicating greater integration of brain function might be an artifact of parts of the
brain acting like a finite state machine.

A 868 Wayman, Alex, et al. "Meditation in Christianity and Other
Religions: Meditation dans le Christianisme et les autres
religions." Studia Missionalia, 25 (1976): 1-304.
A comprehensive study of meditation in Christianity compared with meditation in other religions.

A 869 Weinberger, David. "Bouncing Up the Road to Nirvana."
Macleans, 93 (7 July 1980): 9.
Includes a picture of TM students levitating.

A 870 Weinless, M. "The Influence of the Transcendental Meditation
Program on Crime in Major U.S. Cities." Tentatively
scheduled for inclusion in Scientific Research on the
Transcendental Meditation Program: Collected Papers, Vol.
2. Rheinweiler, West Germany: Maharishi European Research University Press, (in press).

Crime rates decreased in 56 major U.S. cities as demonstrated by a mathematical model of the Maharishi Effect. See also the report by S. Giles [A292].

A871   Weiss, C. "The Immediate Effect of the Transcendental Meditation Technique and Theoretical Reflections Upon the Psychology and Physiology of Subjective Well-Being." Tentatively scheduled for inclusion in Scientific Research on the Transcendental Meditation Program: Collected Papers, Vol. 2. Rheinweiler, West Germany: Maharishi European Research University Press, (in press).
TM meditators showed improvement of subjective well-being as measured by alertness, happiness, and activeness.

A872   Weldon, James T., and Arthur Aron. "The Transcendental Meditation Program and Normalization of Weight." In Scientific Research on the Transcendental Meditation Program: Collected Papers, Vol. 1. Edited by David W. Orme-Johnson and John T. Farrow. 2nd ed., Weggis, Switzerland: Maharishi European Research University Press, 1977, p. 301-306.
Underweight subjects gained weight and overweight subjects lost weight after starting the TM technique.

A873   Weldon, John F. "Sampling of the New Religions: Four Groups Described." International Review of Mission, 67 (October 1978): 407-426.
Discusses the Unification Church, Children of God, Scientology, and Transcendental Meditation.

A874   Welwood, John. "Meditation and the Unconscious: A New Perspective." Journal of Transpersonal Psychology, 9 (1977): 1-26.
This paper proposes a new way of looking at unconscious process that may be useful in perceiving meditation more accurately in a psychological framework.

A875   _____. "Reflections on Psychotherapy, Focusing, and Meditation." Journal of Transpersonal Psychology, 12 (1980): 127-141.
Explores the relationship among psychotherapy, focusing, and meditation as it relates to psychotherapists and their clients.

A876   _____. "Vulnerability and Power in the Therapeutic Process: Existential and Buddhist Perspectives." Journal of Transpersonal Psychology, 14 (1982): 125-139.
Shows how meditation can help a person get through moments of dread and crisis.

A877   Werner, O.; E. Arnold; B. Rigby; B. Charles; and G.

Clements. "Endocrinological Changes Following Instruction in the TM-Sidhi Program." Tentatively scheduled for inclusion in Scientific Research on the Transcendental Meditation Program: Collected Papers, Vol. 2. Rheinweiler, West Germany: Maharishi European Research University Press, (in press).
A paper presented at the International Congress on Research on Higher States of Consciousness, Bangkok, Thailand, January, 1980. Reductions in ACTH, cortisol, TSH, T4, and prolactin were measured in subjects practicing the TM-Sidhi program.

A878   West, Michael A. "Changes in Skin Resistance in Subjects Resting, Reading, Listening to Music, or Practicing the Transcendental Meditation Technique." In Scientific Research on the Transcendental Meditation Program: Collected Papers, Vol. 1. Edited by David W. Orme-Johnson and John T. Farrow. 2nd ed., Weggis, Switzerland: Maharishi European Research University Press, 1977, p. 224-229.
The TM technique produced a deeper rest than the other forms of relaxation.

A879   _____. "Meditation." British Journal of Psychiatry, 135 (November 1979): 457-467.
A literature review covering the psychophysiological correlates of meditation, personality change associated with learning and regularly practicing meditation, and the use of meditation as a therapy in psychiatric units in cases of drug addiction, insomnia, and hypertension.

A880   _____. "Meditation and the EEG." Psychological Medicine, 10 (1980): 369-375.
Previous research on meditation and the EEG is described and findings are discussed. Comparisons of meditation with other altered states are reviewed.

A881   _____. "Meditation, Personality and Arousal." Personality and Individual Differences, 1 (1980): 135-142.
The results suggest that a significant proportion of people give up meditating and that the subjective experience of meditation was similar to that of the hypnagogic state. Reported effects were generally physiological and psychological benefits related to relaxation.

A882   _____. "Physiological Effects of Meditation: A Longitudinal Study." British Journal of Social and Clinical Psychology, 18 (June 1979): 219-226.
The results indicate that regular meditation practice might be effective in producing some physiological relaxation outside of the meditation state itself.

A883   _____. "The Psychosomatics of Meditation." Journal of
            Psychosomatic Research, 24 (1980): 265–273.
            Meditation is defined and a brief history is given. Meditation
            as a relaxation technique and problems of carrying out re-
            search are discussed. Research results are reviewed in areas
            of psychological correlates of meditation, personality change,
            and meditation as therapy in stress-related disorders. Dan-
            gers are also mentioned.

A884   Westcott, B.A. "Hemispheric Symmetry of the EEG During
            the Transcendental Meditation Technique." In Scientific
            Research on the Transcendental Meditation Program: Col-
            lected Papers, Vol. 1.   Edited by David W. Orme-Johnson
            and John T. Farrow. 2nd ed., Weggis, Switzerland:
            Maharishi European Research University Press, 1977, p.
            160–164.
            It was found that persons practicing the TM technique showed
            increased orderliness of brain functioning.

A885   Whalen, William J. "TM: Expensive Meditation." U.S.
            Catholic, 42 (January 1977): 32–36.
            A critical comparison of TM with other forms of meditation,
            including Dr. Herbert Benson's Relaxation Response.

A886   Whelan, Joseph. "Contemplation Is Companionship." New
            Catholic World, 215 (November 1972): 271–274.
            Discusses prayer, contemplation, and meditation as a way to
            experience companionship with God.

A887   White, John. "Introduction to Meditation." Fields Within
            Fields, No. 13 (Fall 1974): 49–53.
            An extract from the author's book, What Is Meditation?
            Examines various types of meditation.

A888   White, Ken D. "Salivation: The Significance of Imagery in
            Its Voluntary Control." Psychophysiology, 15 (May 1978):
            196–203.
            It was shown that salivation can be controlled by Transcen-
            dental Meditation.

A889   Whitman, Ardis. "Art of Meditation." Reader's Digest, 103
            (September 1973): 130–134.
            A short article on technique and value of meditation.

A890   Wienpahl, Paul. "Wang Yang-ming and Meditation." Journal
            of Chinese Philosophy, 1 (March 1974): 199–227.
            An analysis of meditation as described in The Instructions
            for Practical Living, by Wang Yang-ming.

A891   Wilcox, Gregory G. "Autonomic Functioning in Subjects
            Practicing the Transcendental Meditation Technique." In

Scientific Research on the Transcendental Meditation Program: Collected Papers, Vol. 1. Edited by David W. Orme-Johnson and John T. Farrow. 2nd ed., Weggis, Switzerland: Maharishi European Research University Press, 1977, p. 239-242.
Suggests that the TM technique has a stabilizing effect on autonomic functioning.

A892   Williams, Gurney. "Sit Back, Close Your Eyes, Turn Off." Science Digest, 76 (November 1974): 70-75.
Reports on Dr. Herbert Benson's work with Transcendental Meditation at Harvard.

A893   _____. "Transcendental Meditation: Can It Fight Drug Abuse?" Science Digest, 71 (February 1972): 74-79.
Examines research by Dr. Herbert Benson on Transcendental Meditation.

A894   Williams, L.R. "Transcendental Meditation and Mirror-Tracing Skill." Perceptual and Motor Skills, 46 (April 1978): 371-378.
Learning, performance and patterns of inter-individual and intra-individual variability of 32 experienced TM meditators were compared to those of 32 non-meditators. The results provided no support for TM in this regard.

A895   _____, and P.G. Herbert. "Transcendental Meditation and Fine Perceptual-Motor Skill." Perceptual and Motor Skills, 43 (August 1976): 303-309.
Certain reported physiological and psychological benefits that are attributed to the practice of Transcendental Meditation, such as less anxiety, greater consistency, more awareness, alertness, and attention are not manifested in this behavioral test of perceptual-motor function.

A896   _____; B. Lodge; and P.S. Reddish. "Effects of Transcendental Meditation on Rotary Pursuit Skill." Research Quarterly, 48 (March 1977): 196-201.
The results did not support the expectations that the meditators would demonstrate superior learning and performance and less reactive inhibition than the nonmeditators.

A897   _____, and B.L. Vickerman. "Effects of Transcendental Meditation on Fine Motor Skill." Perceptual and Motor Skills, 43 (October 1976): 607-613.
Concludes that the practice of Transcendental Meditation does not benefit acquisition of fine perceptual-motor skill.

A898   Williams, Paul; Anthony Francis; and Robert Durham. "Personality and Meditation." Perceptual and Motor Skills, 43 (December 1976): 787-792.

The relationship of psychoticism, extraversion-introversion, and neuroticism to the practice of Transcendental Meditation was studied.

A 899   , and Michael A. West. "EEG Responses to Photic Stimulation in Persons Experienced at Meditation." Electroencephalography and Clinical Neurophysiology, 39 (November 1975): 519–522. In Scientific Research on the Transcendental Meditation Program: Collected Papers, Vol. 1. Edited by David W. Orme-Johnson and John T. Farrow. 2nd ed., Weggis, Switzerland: Maharishi European Research University Press, 1977, p. 251–255. Also in Meditation: Classic and Contemporary Perspectives, edited by Deane H. Shapiro, Jr. and Roger N. Walsh. Hawthorne, N.Y.: Aldine Pub. Co., 1984.
Greater alertness was shown by participants in the TM program.

A 900 Willis, Robert J. "Meditation to Fit the Person: Psychology and the Meditative Way." Journal of Religion and Health, 18 (April 1979): 93–119.
Discussion of what meditation is and a review of its positive effects.

A 901 Wilson, Archie F.; Ronald W. Honsberger; John T. Chiu; and Harold S. Novey. "Transcendental Meditation and Asthma." In Scientific Research on the Transcendental Meditation Program: Collected Papers, Vol.1. Edited by David W. Orme-Johnson and John T. Farrow. 2nd ed., Weggis, Switzerland: Maharishi European Research University Press, 1977, p. 283–286.
Suggests the TM program is a useful adjunct in treating asthma.

A 902 Wilson, Bradford. "On Meditation and Self-Parenting." Journal of Pastoral Counseling, 12 (Spring-Summer 1977): 16–19.
Explains how meditation can prove to be a useful centering exercise for some individuals.

A 903 Winquist, W. Thomas. "The Transcendental Meditation Program and Drug Abuse: A Retrospective Study." In Scientific Research on the Transcendental Meditation Program: Collected Papers, Vol.1. Edited by David W. Orme-Johnson and John T. Farrow. 2nd ed., Weggis, Switzerland: Maharishi European Research University Press, 1977, p. 494–497.
Drug abuse was stopped or greatly decreased by subjects practicing the TM technique.

A 904 Wolkomir, Richard. "Unique Way to a Better Life." Mechanix

Illustrated, 71 (December 1975): 24+
A personal account of the writer's Transcendental Meditation
lessons.

A905   Wong, Martin R., et al. "Effects of Meditation on Anxiety
        and Chemical Dependency." Journal of Drug Education,
        11 (1981): 91-105.
        Significant differences established upon the termination of a
        two to three week treatment phase were no longer evident
        after six months. Subjects who continued at least minimal
        meditative practice showed positive changes. Comparisons
        were made with Alcoholics Anonymous members.

A906   Woodrum, Eric. "The Development of the Transcendental
        Meditation Movement." The Zetetic, 1-2 (Spring-Summer
        1977): 38-48.
        This essay describes and examines the Transcendental Medi-
        tation movement's particular pattern of growth in light of
        three developmental periods in the movement's history and
        of two subpopulations in the movement. An earlier version
        of this paper was presented at the Southwestern Sociological
        Association Meeting in Dallas, Texas, in April, 1976.

A907   _____. "Religious Organizational Change: An Analysis
        Based on the TM Movement." Review of Religious Re-
        search, 24 (December 1982): 89-103.
        Traces the sociological history of the TM movement during
        the Spiritual Mystical period (1959-1965), the Counter Cul-
        ture period (1965-1969), and the Secularized, Popular Reli-
        gious period (1970-present). An earlier version of this pa-
        per was presented at the Southern Sociological Society Meet-
        ings in Louisville, Kentucky, in April, 1981.

A908   Woodward, Kenneth L., and Pamela Abramson. "Maharishi
        Over Matter." Newsweek, 89 (13 June 1977): 98, 100.
        Reports on some of the claims of Transcendental Meditation.

A909   Woolfolk, Robert L. "Psychophysiological Correlates of Medi-
        tation ..." Archives of General Psychiatry, 32 (October
        1975): 1326-1333. Also in Meditation: Classic and Con-
        temporary Perspectives, edited by Deane H. Shapiro, Jr.
        and Roger N. Walsh. Hawthorne, N.Y.: Aldine Pub.
        Co., 1984.
        A literature review of research that has investigated the
        physiological changes associated with meditation as it is
        practiced by adherents of Indian Yoga, Transcendental
        Meditation, and Zen Buddhism.

A909K   _____. "Self-Control Meditation and the Treatment of
        Chronic Anger." In Meditation: Classic and Contempo-
        rary Perspectives, edited by Deane H. Shapiro, Jr. and

Roger N. Walsh. Hawthorne, N.Y.: Aldine Pub. Co., 1984.

A910   _____; Lucille Carr-Kaffashan; Terrence F. McNulty; and Paul M. Lehrer. "Meditation Training as a Treatment for Insomnia." Behavior Therapy, 7 (May 1976): 359-365.
Showed both meditation and progressive relaxation to be superior to no treatment in reducing latency of sleep onset.

A910K   _____, and Cyril M. Franks. "Meditation and Behavior Therapy." In Meditation: Classic and Contemporary Perspectives, edited by Deane H. Shapiro, Jr. and Roger N. Walsh. Hawthorne, N.Y.: Aldine Pub. Co., 1984.

A911   _____; Paul M. Lehrer; Barbara S. McCann; and Anthony J. Rooney. "Effects of Progressive Relaxation and Meditation on Cognitive and Somatic Manifestations of Daily Stress." Behaviour Research and Therapy, 20 (1982): 461-467.
Little evidence was generated for differential effects of treatments. Both resulted in the significant reduction of stress.

A912   _____, and Anthony J. Rooney. "The Effect of Explicit Expectations on Initial Meditation Experiences." Biofeedback and Self-Regulation, 6 (December 1981): 483-491.
Results indicate that meditation can lower physiological arousal and produce feelings of calm regardless of expectations or the suggestions of the experimenter.

A913   Woolley-Hart, Ann. "Meditation and Cancer: Slowing Down the Inevitable." Nursing Mirror, 149 (4 October 1979): 36-39.
Against a background of the relationship between stress and cancer, the author discusses the use of meditation in ameliorating and slowing down terminal carcinoma.

A914   Wortz, Edward. "Application of Awareness Methods in Psychotherapy." Journal of Transpersonal Psychology, 14 (1982): 61-68.
Suggests a listening meditation and a breathing meditation as therapeutic tools in the context of psychotherapy.

A915   Yaego, David. "Meditation and Self-Examination: Reflections on Spirituality." Dialog: A Journal of Theology, 21 (Summer 1982): 184-189.
Stresses the need for Christian meditation as a means of self-examination.

A916   Yergin, Daniel. "Have Mantra Will Meditate." Harper's Magazine, 247 (October 1973): 115.
A short report on Transcendental Meditation.

A917   Younger, Joel; Wayne Adriance; and Ralph J. Berger.
        "Sleep During Transcendental Meditation." Perceptual and
        Motor Skills, 40 (June 1975): 953-954.
        Six of the eight subjects spent considerable portions of their
        meditation periods in unambiguous physiological sleep.

A918   "Youth Discovers Meditation." Liguorian, 56 (June 1968):
        3-4.
        Critical of Transcendental Meditation from a Christian point
        of view.

A919   Yu, Chun-Fang. "Buddha-Invocation (nien-fo) as Koan."
        Journal of Dharma, 2 (April 1977): 189-203.
        An historical survey showing the complimentary nature of
        and joint practice of Ch'an koans and Pure Land Buddhism
        nien-fo practiced by Chinese monks.

A920   Yuille, John C., and Lynn Sereda. "Positive Effects of
        Meditation: A Limited Generalization." Journal of Applied
        Psychology, 65 (June 1980): 333-340.
        The practice of meditation had no systematic effect on the
        variables assessed in this study.

A921   Zaffarano, Joan. "Transcendental Meditation: New Tool of
        Management?" Administrative Management, 35 (May 1974):
        28-31.
        Reports of positive and negative opinions concerning the use
        of Transcendental Meditation in business.

A922   Zaichkowsky, Leonard D., and Randy Kamen. "Biofeedback
        and Meditation: Effects on Muscle Tension and Locus of
        Control." Perceptual and Motor Skills, 46 (June 1978):
        955-958.
        Biofeedback training, Transcendental Meditation, and Relax-
        ation Response all resulted in significant decreases in frontalis
        muscle tension.

A923   Zamarra, John W.; Italo Besseghini; and Stephen Wittenberg.
        "The Effects of the Transcendental Meditation Program on
        the Exercise Performance of Patients with Angina Pectoris."
        In Scientific Research on the Transcendental Meditation
        Program: Collected Papers, Vol. 1. Edited by David W.
        Orme-Johnson and John T. Farrow. 2nd ed., Weggis,
        Switzerland: Maharishi European Research University
        Press, 1977, p. 270-278.
        Angina pectoris patients improved tolerance to exercise after
        participating in the TM program.

A924   Zimmermann, W. "Improved Quality of Life During the Rhode
        Island Ideal Society Campaign from June 12 to September
        12, 1978." Tentatively scheduled for inclusion in Scien-

tific Research on the Transcendental Meditation Program: Collected Papers, Vol. 2. Rheinweiler, West Germany: Maharishi European Research University Press, (in press). Suggests the concentration of TM practitioners in Rhode Island at that time resulted in the improvement of the quality of life and social well being for the entire state.

A925 Zullo, Allan. "Relax with Transcendental Meditation." Marriage (St. Meinrad, Ind.), 55 (March 1973): 10-16.
Reports on the benefits of Transcendental Meditation.

A926 Zuroff, David C., and J. Conrad Schwarz. "Effects of Transcendental Meditation and Muscle Relaxation on Trait Anxiety, Maladjustment, Locus of Control, and Drug Use." Journal of Consulting and Clinical Psychology, 46 (April 1978): 264-271.
It was concluded that both treatments may reduce trait anxiety. There were no significant measures of locus of control, maladjustment, and drug use.

A927 _____, and _____. "Transcendental Meditation versus Muscle Relaxation: A Two-Year Follow-Up of a Controlled Experiment." American Journal of Psychiatry, 137 (October 1980): 1229-1231.
Both meditation and muscle relaxation groups radically reduced their frequency of practice within a year of training. The authors concluded that although some subjects do enjoy and continue to practice Transcendental Meditation, it is not universally beneficial.

■ BOOKS ■

B1 Addington, Jack Ensign, and Cornelia Addington. The Joy of Meditation. Marina del Rey, Calif.: DeVorss, 1979. 129p. LC 78-75078

B2 _____, and _____. Your Needs Met: More than 150 Scientific Prayers That Will Work for You. Rev. ed. San Diego, Calif.: Abundant Living Foundation, 1973. 156p.

B3 Agard, Roy. The Still Mind: A Western Interpretation of Patanjali's Yoga. London: Thorsons Publishers, 1961. 64p. LC 62-847

B4 Aïvanhov, Omraam Mickhaël. A New Earth: Methods, Exercises, Formulas, Prayers. Lyon: Editions Prosveta, 1975. 183,[52]p. (His Complete Works; v. 13) Translation of La nouvelle terre. LC 78-363082

B5 _____. La nouvelle terres: Méthodes, exercises, formules, prières. Lyon: Editions Prosveta, 1975. 207,[51]p. (His Oeuvres complètes; t.13) LC 77-484354 (French)

B6 Ajaya, Swami, 1940- . A Practical Guide to Meditation. Completely rev. ed. Glenview, Ill.: Himalayan International Institute of Yoga Science and Philosophy, 1976. Orig. pub., 1974. 115p. (His Yoga Psychology; v.1) LC 76-374539

B7 Akins, W.R., and H. George Nurnberg. How to Meditate Without Attending a TM Class: Easy Step by Step Instructions Plus Frequently Asked Questions and Their Answers!: Including Instructions for Selecting a Personal Mantra. New York: Amjon; distributed by Crown Publishers, 1976. 136p. Includes bibliographical references. LC 76-2995

B8 Alberts, Ton. Yoga en meditatie. Haarlem: Het Boekenfonds Stichting Yoga Nederland, 1974. 152p. LC 75-576334 (Dutch)

B9 Albrecht, Alois. Neuwerden aus seinem Wort: Meditationsgottesdienste. Stuttgart: Verlag Katholisches Bibelwerk, 1976. 75p. (German)

145

B10 _____ . Sinn erfahren aus dem Wort: 9 Meditationsgottesdienste zu Bildern d. Johannes. Stuttgart: Verlag Katholisches Bibelwerk, 1977. 81p. (German)

B11 Alder, Vera Stanley. The Fifth Dimension: The Future of
Mankind. London: Rider, 1983. Also, London: Rider &
Co. and New York: Weiser, 1970. Orig. pub., London:
Rider, 1940. 240p. (1940 ed. published under title: The
Fifth Dimension and the Future of Mankind.) LC 76-491329
and LC 78-16459
Explains what meditation is and how it works as part of a com-
plete way of life. Suggests that it will help humanity as a
whole to advance. Instructions are included.

B12 Alibrandi, Tom. The Meditation Handbook. Chatsworth,
Calif.: Major Books, 1976. 157p. Bibliography: p.143.
LC 75-36083

B13 Allan, John. TM: A Cosmic Confidence Trick: Transcendental
Meditation Analysed. Leicester: Inter-Varsity Press, 1980.
61p. Bibliography: p.61.

B14 Allen, Mark, 1946- , and Shakti Gawain, 1948- , with Noj
Bernoff, 1953- . Reunion, Tools for Transformation.
Cover art and other artwork by Rebecca Donicht. Berkely,
Calif.: Whatever Pub., 1978.

B15 Alschuler, Alfred, et al. Teacher Burnout. Washington, D.C.:
National Education Association, 1980. 96p. (Analysis and
Action Series) (ERIC ED 201 640)
Deals with identifying signs of stress and methods of reducing
work-related stressors. Includes a section on "How to Bring
Forth the Relaxation Response."

B16 Amaldas, Brahmachari. Yoga and Contemplation. Foreword
by Bede Griffiths. London: Darton Longman & Todd,
1981. xiii,146p.

B17 Antes, Michael. Transzendentale Meditation, TM-Sidhi-Programm und Rigidität-Flexibilität: e. systemat. theoret.
Analyse u. empir. Ergebnisse. Bielefeld: B.-K.-Verlag,
1979. xv,308p. (German) [Cf. D6]

B18 Antes, Peter, 1942- , and Bernhard Uhde, 1948- . Aufbruch
zur Ruhe: Texte u. Gedanken über Meditation in Hinduis-
mus, Buddhismus, Islam. Mainz: Matthias Grünewald-
Verlag and Düsseldorf: Patmos-Verlag, 1974. 155p.
(Series: Topos-Taschenbücher; Bd.27) Bibliography:
p.154-155. LC 75-528437 (German)

B19 Appelkvist, Claes, 1952- . Friheten är din: medvetandeutveckling och samhälle: transcendental meditation. Stockholm: Askild & Kharnekull, 1979. 192p. Bibliography: p.191. LC 80-501821 (Swedish)

B 20 Approaches to Meditation. Edited by Virginia Hanson. Wheaton, Ill., London and Madras: Theosophical Pub. House, 1976. Orig. pub., 1973. Dist. by DeVorss, Marina del Rey, Calif. x,147p. First published as a special issue of the journal, The American Theosophist. Includes bibliographical references. LC 73-80
Includes works by Lama Govinda, Simons Roof, I.K. Taimni, and Chogyam Trungpa.

B 21 Argüelles, José, 1939- , and Miriam Argüelles, 1943- . Mandala. Foreword by Chögyam Trungpa. Berkeley, Calif.: Shambala, 1972. 140p. Bibliography: p.130-134. LC 70-189856

B 22 Arintero, Juan González, 1860-1928. Stages of Prayer. Translated by Kathleen Pond. St. Louis: Herder, 1957. 178p. LC 58-487

B 23 Arnáiz Barón, Rafael, 1911-1938. To Know How to Wait. Translated by Mairin Mitchell. Westminster, Md.: The Newman Press, 1964. xvii,381p. LC 64-55964

B 24 Arnold, Seraphin. Das innere Beten; Anregungen zur Betrachtung. Zürich: Thomas-Verlag, 1959. 183,[1]p. (Series: Franziskanische Lebenswerte; 3) LC 59-45449 (German)

B 25 The Art & Science of Meditation. Edited by L.K. Misra. Glenview, Ill.: Himalayan Institute, 1976. 112p. (Dawn Series; 2) Includes bibliographies. LC 77-361768

B 26 Arya, Usharbudh. Mantra & Meditation. Honesdale, Pa.: Himalayan International Institute of Yoga Science & Philosophy of the U.S.A., 1981. xxxiii,237,[1]p. Continues: Superconscious Meditation [B 28]. Bibliography: p.238. LC 81-84076

B 27 _____. Meditation and the Art of Dying. Honesdale, Pa.: Himalayan International Institute of Yoga Science and Philosophy, 1979. xii,179p. LC 78-78252

B 28 _____. Superconscious Meditation. 2nd ed. Honesdale, Pa.: Himalayan International Institute, 1977, c1978. Orig. pub., 1974. Dist. by DeVorss & Co., Marina del Rey, Calif. 132p. LC 78-102982
Dr. Arya is a disciple of Swami Rama. This is an explanation of a traditional Indian meditation technique for the Westerner.

B29 Atkinson, William Walker, 1862-1932. A Series of Lessons in
     Raja Yoga, by Yogi Ramacharaka [pseud.]. Jacksonville,
     Fla.: The Yoga Publication Society, date? Also, Bombay:
     D.B. Taraporevala, 1973 and 1966; and London: L.N.
     Fowler, 1964. Orig. pub., Chicago: The Yogi Publication
     Society, 1906. vi,299p. (Cover title: Raja Yoga.) (Yogi
     Philosophy, v.3)

B30 Atlanteans. Atlantean Meditation Course. 3rd ed. Chelten-
     ham: Atlanteans, 1976. 21p.

B31 Atmananda, Swami. The Four Yogas; or, The Four Paths to
     Spiritual Enlightenment, in the Words of the Ancient Rishis.
     Bombay: Bharatiya Vidya Bhavan, 1966. xiv,236p. LC
     67-268

B32 Aufderbeck, Hugo. Die geistliche Stunde. Ein Weg z. Bildung
     d. Gemeindekernes. Freiburg (i. Br.): Seelsorge-Verl.,
     1968. 188p. (German)

B33 Badzong, Hans-Joachim. Seins-Prinzipien. Engelberg/Schweiz,
     München: Drei-Eichen-Verlag. Bd. 1. Selbst-Erkenntnis,
     Bewusstseins-Lenkung, Lotusblumen-Kraftzentren. 1979.
     108p. Bd.2. Seins-Strukturen ins Ur; Der Weg zum Logos-
     Bewusstein; Weisheit des Logos. 1980. 112p. (German)

B34 Bailey, Alice Anne (LaTrobe-Bateman), 1880-1949. From In-
     tellect to Intuition. 3rd paperback ed. London and New
     York: Lucis Pub. Co., 1978, c1960. Orig. pub., 1932.
     vii,275p. Includes bibliographical references.

B35 _____. Jüngerschaft im Neuen Zeitalter. Übers. von Ger-
     trud Labes. Genf: Lucis, und Bietigheim (Württemberg):
     Rohm, 1975. Bd. 2, 924p. Einheitssacht.: Discipleship in
     the New Age. (German)

B36 _____. Letters on Occult Meditation. Received and edited
     by Alice A. Bailey. New York: Lucis Pub. Co., 1974 and
     previous editions. Also, London: Lucis Press, 1972 and
     previous editions. Orig. pub., New York: Lucifer Pub.
     Co., 1922. Dist. in U.S. by DeVorss & Co., Marina del
     Rey, Calif. 375p.
     The technique of occult meditation is described, in which the
     personality makes contact with the soul and inspiration.

B37 _____. Seed Thoughts for Meditation. Distilled from Alice
     A. Bailey's Discipleship in the New Age, Vol. 1, by C.E.
     Willis. Tisbury: Compton Russell, 1976. 64p. Disciple-
     ship in the New Age, Vol. 1, orig. pub., New York:
     Lucis Pub. Co., 1944; Also, London: Lucis Press, 1972.

B38   Baker, Douglas. Theory and Practice of Meditation. Essendon, Eng.: Douglas Baker, 1975. 297,[26]p. (Cover title: Meditation) (Seven Pillars of Ancient Wisdom Series; v.2)
The nature, types, and stages of meditation are extensively discussed. Exercises are presented with many full color and black and white illustrations.

B39   _____, and Celia Hansen. Superconsciousness Through Meditation. Wellingborough: Aquarian Press, 1978. 127[1]p. Bibliography: p.128. LC 79-311706

B40   Baker, Mary Ellen Penny. La meditación: Un paso al más allá con Edgar Cayce. México: Editorial Diana, 1977. 174p. Translation of Meditation: A Step Beyond with Edgar Cayce. Bibliography: p.173-174. (Spanish)

B41   _____. Meditation: A Step Beyond with Edgar Cayce. Foreword by Hugh Lynn Cayce. New York: Pinnacle Books, 1975. Orig. pub., Garden City, N.Y.: Doubleday, 1973. 166p. Bibliography: p.[165]-166.
Contains many quotations from the readings of Edgar Cayce considered to be relevant to meditation.

B42   Balan, George. Einführung in die Musikmeditation: d. weltanschaul. Grundlagen: Musik-d. wahre Philosophie. Neustadt/Aisch: Kunsthandel-Verlag Schmelzer, 1982. 161p. (German)

B43   Balsamo, Ignatius. An Instruction How to Pray and Meditate Well, 1622. Translated out of French into English by John Heigham. Menston: Scolar Press, 1972. [4],336p. (English Recusant Literature, 1558-1640; v.102) LC 73-157408

B44   Barth, Friedrich K. Menschlichkeit probieren: [Malen u. Meditieren in Gruppen]. Gelnhausen; Berlin; and Stein: Burckhardthaus-Laetare-Verlag, and Frieburg i. Br.: Christophorus-Verlag, 1979. 158p. (German)

B45   Bartholomae, Wolfgang. Gott ist da: Hilfen z. betrachtenden Gebet. Wuppertal: Theologischer Verlag Brockhaus, 1974. 69p.

B46   Barton, Winifred G., 1923- . Meditation and Astral Projection. Ottawa: Psi Science Productions, 1974. 169p. (Psi-Science Series; no.9)

B47   _____. La méditation et la projection astrale: la plus grande aventure de tours les temps. Montréal: Editions Sélect, 1980. (French)

B48   Beard, Rebecca. Was jedermann sucht: Gesundung durch
       Einheit d. Lebens. Bietigheim/Württ.: Turm-Verlag,
       1976. 163p. (German)

B49   Beier, Peter. Meditationsgottesdienste. Gütersloh: Güters-
       loher Verlagshaus Mohn, 1976. 144p. (German)

B50   Bélorgey, Godefroid. The Practice of Mental Prayer. Fore-
       word by M. Eugene Boylan. Translated from the French.
       Westminster, Md.: Newman Press, 1952. Also, Cork:
       The Mercier Press, 1951. 184p.
       Discusses the various degrees of mental prayer from medita-
       tive to mystical.

B51   Benares, Camden. Zen Without Zen Masters. Commentary
       by Robert Anton Wilson. Illustrated by Deborah M. Cot-
       ter. Berkeley, Calif.: And/Or Press, 1977. 127p.
       Bibliography: p.125. LC 77-151928

B51K   Benson, Herbert, with Miriam Z. Klipper. Relajación.
       Traducción: Iris Menéndez. Barcelona: Editorial Pro-
       maire, 1977. 176p. Translation of: The Relaxation
       Response. Bibliography: p.153-176. (Spanish)

B52   _____, with _____. The Relaxation Response. New
       York: Avon Books, 1976. Orig. pub., New York: Mor-
       row, 1975. Also pub. in large print, Boston: G.K. Hall,
       1976. 222p. Bibliography: p.183-212. LC 75-14309
       Gives instructions in a technique which has been shown to
       reduce hypertension and induce a sense of peace, calm, and
       well-being, enabling the practitioner to deal with daily stress
       more effectively.

B52K   _____, with William Proctor. Beyond the Relaxation Re-
       sponse: How to Harness the Healing Power of Your Per-
       sonal Beliefs. New York: Times Books, 1984.

B53   Benz, Ernst. Meditation, Musik und Tanz: über d. "Hand-
       psalter", e. spätmittelalterl. Meditationsform aus d. Rose-
       tum d. Mauburnus. Mainz: Akademie der Wiss. u.d.
       Literatur, und Wiesbaden: Steiner [in Komm.], 1976.
       37p. (German)

B54   Bernard, Theos. Hatha Yoga Ein Erfahrungsbericht aus In-
       dien und Tibet. Stuttgart: Günther, 1970, 1957. 123p.
       (German)

B55   Betz, Otto, Hrsg. Das Leben meditieren: e. Lesebuch. 2.
       Aufl. 7.-10. Tsd. München: Pfeiffer, 1972. 207p.
       (German)

B56 _____, Hrsg. Die Welt meditieren: Texte f. e. Jahr. 4.
Aufl. 13.-15. Tsd. München: Pfeiffer, 1971. 207p.
(German)

B57 Bewusstsenserweiterung durch Meditation, mit Beitr. von
Ladislaus Boros [u.a.]. 3. Aufl. Freiburg (im Breisgau),
Basil, and Wien: Herder, 1975. Orig. pub., 1973.
159p. Includes bibliographical references. LC 74-313274
(German)

B58 Beyond Ego: Transpersonal Dimensions in Psychology.
Edited by Roger N. Walsh and Frances Vaughan. Los
Angeles: J.P. Tarcher; New York: distributed by St.
Martin's Press, 1980. 272p. Includes bibliographies.
LC 79-56299

B59 Bhaktivedanta Swami, A.C., 1896-1977. The First Step in
God Realization. Boston, Mass.: Iskon Press, 1970.
60p. Running title: Srimad Bhagavatam. "Continuation
of A.C. Bhaktivedanta Swami's ... project of translating
and commentating upon the twelve cantos of the Srimad
Bhagavatam." English and Sanskrit. Commentary in
English. LC 70-127183

B60 Bibliography and Reprint Catalog, Maharishi International
University: Scientific Research on the Transcendental
Meditation and TM-Sidhi-Program. Revised ed. Fairfield,
Iowa: Reprint Service, Maharishi International University,
1982. 61p.
A guide to research materials available from the Maharishi
International University on the subject of Transcendental
Meditation.

B61 Biesinger, Albert, Hrsg. Meditation im Religionsunterricht:
theoret. u. schulprakt. Perspektiven. Düsseldorf, Patmos-
Verlag, 1981. 236p. (German)

B62 Bill, Josef, and Franz-Josef Steinmetz, Hrsg. Aus der Mitte
leben: Wege bibl. Meditation. Stuttgart: KBW-Verlag,
1973. 152p. (German)

B63 Bitter, Wilhelm, 1893- , Hrsg. Meditation in Religion und
Psychotherapie. München: Kindler, 1967. 331p.
(Kindler-Taschenbücher, 2025/2026. Geist und Psyche)
LC 67-68558 (German)

B64 _____, Hrsg. Meditation in Religion und Psychotherapie:
ein Tagungsbericht. 2., verhanderte Aufl. Stuttgart: E.
Klett, 1973. Orig. pub., 1958. 212p. Includes bibliographical references. LC 73-346540 (German)

B65   Bjornstad, James. The Transcendental Mirage. Minneapolis:
       Bethany Fellowship, 1976. 93p. Bibliography: p.[91]-
       93. LC 76-6614

B66   Blavatsky, Helene Petrovna (Hahn-Hahn), 1831-1891. Raja-
       Yoga, or Occultism. 3rd ed. Bombay: Theosophy Co.,
       1973. Orig. pub., 1931. xii,255p.

B67   _____. Raja yoga ou occultisme. Paris: Compagnie
       théosophie, 196-? 6 vols. (Les Cahiers théosophiques;
       no.55-60) LC 79-361343 (French)

B68   Bleistein, Roman. Junge Menschen meditieren. Würzburg:
       Echter, 1976. 93p. (German)

B69   _____. Türen nach innen: Gebrauchsanweisung f. e.
       vertieftes Leben u. Anl. z. Meditation. Gelnhausen:
       Burckhardthaus-Verlag; Berlin: Christlicher Zeitschriften-
       verlag; Freiburg (Breisgau): Christophorus-Verlag, 1974.
       64p. (German)

B70   _____, Hrsg. Türen nach innen: Weg zur Meditation.
       Gelnhausen: Burckhardthaus-Verlag; Berlin: Christ-
       licher Zeitschrifenverlag; Freiburg (Breisgau): Christo-
       phorus-Verlag, 1974. 335p. (German)

B71   Blofeld, John Eaton Calthorpe, 1913- . Gateway to Wisdom:
       Taoist and Buddhist Contemplative and Healing Yogas
       Adapted for Western Students of the Way. Boulder, Colo.:
       Shambhala; New York: distr. by Random House, 1980.
       Also, London: Allen and Unwin, 1980. x,214p. LC 79-
       6785
       Presents the author's experiences in meditation and healing
       techniques adapted from Chinese and Tibetan teachings for
       the use of the Westerner.

B72   _____. Mantras: Sacred Words of Power. London [etc.]:
       Mandala Books, 1978. Orig. pub., London: Allen & Un-
       win, and New York: Dutton, 1977. xiv,106p.
       The author explains the significance of mantras and how they
       operate. He also discusses his personal experience with the
       use of mantras.

B73   _____. Selbstheilung durch die Kraft der Stille: Übungs-
       anleitungen zur Wiedergewinnung d. inneren Gleichgewichts
       mit altbewährten Meditationsmethoden. Bern und München:
       Barth im Scherz-Verlag, 1981. 303p. Einheitssacht.:
       Gateway to Wisdom. (German)

B74   _____. The Tantric Mysticism of Tibet: A Practical Guide.
       Boulder, Colo.: Prajna Press, 1982. Also, New York:

Causeway Books, 1974. Orig. pub., New York: Dutton, 1970. 257p. Reprint of 1970 ed., pub. by Dutton. Bibliography: p.253. LC 82-300

B75 Bloomfield, Harold H., 1944- , Michael Peter Cain, 1941- , and Dennis T. Jaffe. MT [i.e. Meditação transcendental]: Descoberta da energia interior e domínio da tensão. Em colaboração com Robert Bruce Kory. A presentação por Hans Selye. Introdução por R. Buckminster Fuller. Tradução de Sônia Coutinho. Prefáçio de Charlotte Minoga Kikoler. Rio de Janeiro: Nova Fronteira, 1976. 312p. Título original: TM: Discovering Inner Energy and Overcoming Stress. (Portuguese)

B76 _____, _____, and _____. Rentoudu. Helsinki, Finland: Weilin & Göös, 1976. 280p. Translation of TM: Discovering Inner Energy and Overcoming Stress. Bibliography in English: p.261-280. (Finnish)

B77 _____, _____, and _____. TM*: Descubrimiento de la energía interna y superación del stress. Colaboración de Robert Bruce Kory. Prólogo de Hans Selye. Introducción de R. Buckminster Fuller. Traducido por Isabel Ugarte. Barcelona: Grijalbo, 1977. 370p. Título original: TM*: Discovering Inner Energy and Overcoming Stress. Bibliography: p.351-370. (Spanish)

B78 _____, _____, and _____. TM*: Discovering Inner Energy and Overcoming Stress. In collaboration with Robert Bruce Kory. Foreword by Hans Selye. Introduction by R. Buckminster Fuller. London [etc.]: Unwin Paperbacks, 1978. Also, London: Allen and Unwin, 1976, and New York: Dell Pub. Co., 1975. Orig. pub., New York: Delacorte Press, 1975. Also pub. in large print, Boston: G.K. Hall & Co., 1976. xxvii,292p. Bibliography: p.263-282.
A detailed discussion of results that are being obtained by Transcendental Meditation.

B79 _____, _____, and _____. (TM) Transcendental Meditation: Hur man finner den inre energin och övervinner stress. I samarbete med Robert Bruce Kory. Översatt av Philippa Wiking. Stockholm: P A Norstedt & Sönes förlag, 1975. 261p. Translation of TM: Discovering Inner Energy and Overcoming Stress. Bibliography: p.243-261. (Swedish)

B80 _____, _____, and _____. Transzendentale Meditation: TM; Lebenskraft aus neuen Quellen. Düsseldorf and Wien: Econ-Verlag, 1976. 327p. Einheitssacht.: TM: Discovering Inner Energy and Overcoming Stress. (German)

B81 _____, and Robert B. Kory. Das Glückspotential: Psychotherapie u. Transzendentale Meditation; e. grundlegend neues Denkmodell. Bielefeld: Kleine, 1980. 340p. Einheitssacht.: Happiness: The TM Program, Psychiatry, and Enlightenment. (German)

B82 _____, and _____. Happiness: The TM Program, Psychiatry, and Enlightenment. Introduction by Maharishi Mahesh Yogi. Foreword by Bernard C. Glueck. New York: Pocket Books, 1977. Orig. pub., New York: Dawn Press, 1976, xxviii,304p. Includes bibliographical references. LC 76-3754
Based on Dr. Bloomfield's use of the TM program with his patients in dealing with anxiety, tension, high blood pressure, insomnia and marital strife.

B83 Boden, Liselotte M. Meditation und pädagogische Praxis: Methoden, Vorstufen, Modelle. München: Kösel, 1978. 215p. (German)

B84 _____. Meditieren, sich entfalten. Limburg: Lahn-Verlag, 1980. 150p. Literaturverz.: p.142-144. (German)

B85 Bodmershof, Wilhelm. Geistige Versenkung, eine Studie. Zürich: Kober, 1965. 169p. LC 78-264311 (German)

B86 Boeckel, Johannes F. Meditationspraxis: Techniken u. Methoden. München: Goldmann, 1981, und München: Mosaik-Verlag, 1977. 191p. (German)

B87 Bonarjee, Hector. Yoga Mysticism for Modern Man. Chichester: Janay Publishing Co., 1972. [10],64p. LC 72-193643

B88 Börner-Kray, Brunhild. Meditation: Betrachtungen u. Hinweise. Pforzheim: Verlag Dem Wahren, Schönen, Guten, 1974. 79p. (German)

B89 Bowers, Margaret, and David Haddon. Two New Cults: TM and Sun Myung Moon. Philadelphia: Eternity Magazine, 1976. 18p.

B90 Bowness, Charles. The Practice of Meditation. 2nd ed., revised, enlarged. Wellingborough: Aquarian Press, 1979. Orig. pub., London: Aquarian Press, and New York: Samuel Weiser, 1971. 96p.

B91 Boxerman, David. Alpha-Wellen: d. Technik d. elektron. Meditation. Basel: Sphinx-Verlag, 1977. 126p. (German)

B92 Boylan, Eugene. Difficulties in Mental Prayer. Westminster, Md.: Newman Press, 1965 and previous editions; dist. by

Paulist Press. Also, Dublin: M.H. Gill, 1953 and previous editions. Orig. pub., 1943. xiv,127p. LC 66-1533

B 93   Braden, Klaus, and Hans Nagel, compilers. Achtung, Mitmensch. Wohlstandsgesellschaft herausgenfordert. 2. verb. Aufl. Stuttgart: Evangelishes Bibelwerk; Katholisches Bibelwerk, 1970. 189p. (Bibel provokativ, Bd. 3) Literaturverz.: p.174-183. LC 79-890061 (German)

B 94   Brooke, Avery. Doorway to Meditation. Drawings by Robert Pinart. New York: Seabury Press, 1978. Orig. pub., Norton, Conn.: Vineyard Books, 1973. 111p. LC 78-51941
A handwritten text with many pictures showing how meditation and prayer can be practiced in different ways during daily life.

B 95   _____. Hidden in Plain Sight: The Practice of Christian Meditation. Art by Carol Aymar Armstrong. New York: Seabury Press, 1978. 143p. LC 77-17548

B 96   _____. How to Meditate Without Leaving the World. New York: Seabury Press, 1976. Orig. pub., Norton, Conn.: Vineyard Books, 1975. 96p. Sequel to Doorway to Meditation. LC 75-327279
Teaches meditation in the Judaeo-Christian tradition with many references to the Bible.

B 97   Brosse, Jacques. Satori: ou, Un début en zazen. Paris: R. Laffont, 1976. 362p. LC 78-348064 (French)

B 98   Bruijn, Erik. De weg van zazen: Inleiding tot Zen-meditatie. Met tekeningen van Noni Lichtveld. Deventer: Ankh-Hermes, 1976. 160p. LC 76-506780 (Dutch)

B 99   Bruno, Vincenzo S.J. An Abridgement of Meditations. Translated from the Italian by R.G., i.e. Richard Gibbons. And, Censurs of Certaine Propositions. Translated from the Latin. Ikley: Scolar Press, 1975. [61],244,[10],123p. (English Recusant Literature, 1558-1640; v.246) LC 76-361313

B 100   Brunton, Paul, 1898- . Discover Yourself. New York: E.P. Dutton, 1960 and previous editions. Orig. pub., 1939. 322p. Also pub. as The Inner Reality.

B 101   _____. Entdecke dich selbst. Freiburg im Breisgau: Bauer, 1981 and 1977. Also, Zürich und Stuttgart: Rascher, 1968. 348p. Einheitssacht.: Discover Yourself. (German)

B102   . A Hermit in the Himalayas: The Journal of a
Lonely Exile. New York: Samuel Weiser, 1972. Also,
London: Rider, 1969. Orig. pub., London: Rider, and
New York: E.P. Dutton, 1937. 187p.

B103   . Hidden Teaching Beyond Yoga. New York:
Samuel Weiser, 1977 and 1972. Also, New Delhi: B.I.
Publications, 1973; London: Rider, 1969 and 1950; and
New York: Dutton, 1946. Orig. pub., London: Rider,
and New York: E.P. Dutton, 1941. 365p.

B104   . The Inner Reality. New York: Samuel Weiser,
1972. Also, London: Rider, 1970 and previous editions.
Orig. pub. as Discover Yourself, New York: E.P. Dutton, 1939, and as The Inner Reality, London: Rider,
1939. 244p.

B105   . Die Philosophie der Wahrheit; tiefster Grund des
Yoga. Aus dem Englischen übertragen von Karin Eckhart.
Zürich: Rascher, 1951. 556p. Einheitssacht.: Hidden
Teaching Beyond Yoga. (German)

B106   . The Quest of the Overself. New York: Samuel
Weiser, 1975 and 1972. Also, London: Rider, 1970;
New York: Dutton, 1953, 1946; and Philadelphia: The
Blakiston Co., 1943. Orig. pub., London: Rider, 1937,
and New York: E.P. Dutton, 1938.

B107   . La réalité intérieure. Traduit de l'anglais par R.
Jouan. Paris: Payot, 1955. 267p. Translation of
Discover Yourself. (French)

B108   . A Search in Secret India. New York: Samuel
Weiser 1977, 1972 and 1970. Also, Bombay: B.I. Publications, 1970; London and New York: Rider, 1970 and
1951; and New York: E.P. Dutton, 1959. Orig. pub.,
New York: E.P. Dutton, 1935, and London: Rider,
1934. 312p.

B109   . The Secret Path: A Technique of Spiritual Self-
Discovery for the Modern World. London: Rider, 1969
and previous editions. Also, New York: Dutton, 1958.
Orig. pub., New York: Dutton, 1935, and London:
Rider, 1934. 176p. LC 70-410609

B110   . Das Überselbst. 5., überarb. Aufl. Freiburg im
Breisgau: Bauer, 1976. Orig. pub., Zürich u. Stuttgart:
Rascher, 1962. 360p. Einheitssacht.: The Quest of the
Overself. (German)

B111   . Der Weg nach innen: prakt. Anleitung zur geistigen Selbstfindung in d. heutigen Zeit. 9. Aufl. München: Barth, 1981 and previous editions. 173p. Einheitssacht.: The Secret Path. (German)

B112 _____. Die Weisheit des Überselbst. Freiburg i. Br., 1977 und 1971. 6120. Einheitssacht.: The Wisdom of the Overself. (German)

B113 _____. The Wisdom of the Overself. New York: Samuel Weiser, 1972 and 1970. Also, London: Rider, 1972 and 1969; and New York: E.P. Dutton, 1962. Orig. pub., London: Rider, and New York: E.P. Dutton, 1943. 276p.

B114 Buchinger, Otto. Geistige Vertiefung und religiöse Verwirklichung durch Fasten und meditative Abgeschiedenheit. Bietigheim/Württ.: Turm-Verl., 1967. 88p. (German)

B115 Budberg, Kurt. A chave dos mistérios; Os segredos do extremo Oriente, a prática dos exercícios para obter os podêres extrasensoriais. Com pref. do mestre Narmacaláya Swan. Rio de Janeiro: Ed. Fon-Fon e Seleta, 1967. 242p. LC 68-142058 (Portuguese)

B116 Ein Buddhistisches Yogalehrbuch. Hrsg. von Dieter Schlingloff. Berlin: Akademie-Verlag, 1964-1966. 2 vols. Includes facsim. of original text with romanization and German translation and German commentary. Bibliography: v.1, p[256]-259. LC 80-454194 (German)

B117 Bugault, Guy. La notion de "Prajna" ou de sapience selon les perspectives du "Mahayana"; part de la connaissance et de l'inconnaissance dans l'analogie bouddhique. Paris: E. de Boccard, 1968. 289p. Bibliography: p.[233]-244. LC 73-356950 (French)

B118 Bühler, Walther. Meditation als Erkenntnisweg; Bewusstseinserweiterung mit der Droge. 2. erw. Aufl. Stuttgart: Verlag Freies Geistesleben, 1980 and 1972. Orig. pub., 1962. 55p. (German)

B119 Buksbazen, John Daishin, 1939- . To Forget the Self: An Illustrated Guide to Zen Meditation. Photography by John Daido Loori. Foreword by Peter Matthiessen. Preface by Chotan Aitken Roshi. Los Angeles: Zen Center of Los Angeles, 1977. xix,70p. (The Zen Writings Series; 3) Includes bibliographical references. LC 76-9463
An artistic, conversational, and authoritative guide to Zen meditation with detailed instructions.

B120 Byles, Marie Beuzeville. Journey into Burmese Silence.

London: Allen & Unwin, 1962. [3],220p. Includes bibliography. LC 63-5867

B121 _____. Paths to Inner Calm. London: G. Allen & Unwin, 1965. 208p. Bibliography: p.14. LC 65-6317

B122 Caballero, Nicolás. El camino de la libertad. Valencia: Comercial Editora de Publicaciones, 1975?-1979? 6 vols. Includes bibliographical references. LC 76-462665 (Spanish)

B123 _____. La meditación: Una técnica oriental y un contenido cristiano. Valencia: Comercial Editora de Publicaciones, 1976? 255p. (His El camino de la libertad; v.3) (Colección CP; no.79-80) Includes bibliographical references. LC 77-482142 (Spanish)

B124 _____. The Way to Freedom: Meditation, Oriental Approach and Christian Content. Translated by Colette Joly Dees. New York: Paulist Press, 1982. 152p. Includes bibliographical references. Translation of El camino de la libertad; v.3)

B125 Calquist, Jan, and Henrik Ivarsson. Herr, führe mich in die Stille: e. Buch für Meditation u. Gebet. Hammersbach: Wort im Bild, 1979. 63p. (German)

B126 Campbell, Anthony. Seven States of Consciousness: A Vision of Possibilities Suggested by the Teaching of Maharishi Mahesh Yogi. London: Gollancz, 1980. Also, New York and London: Harper and Row, 1974. Orig. pub., London: Gollancz, 1973. 175p. Bibliography: p.175. Includes quotations from the writings of the Maharishi and humanistic psychologists and scientists. The author also describes his personal experiences with TM.

B127 _____. TM and the Nature of Enlightenment: Creative Intelligence and the Teachings of Maharishi Mahesh Yogi. London: Gollancz, 1975. Bibliography: p.[213]-215. LC 76-362221
Attempts to reconcile the separation between the spiritual and the material. Examines the mystical thought of the Maharishi and the TM process.

B128 Caprile, Giovanni. Appunti su l'orazione mentale. Firenze: Edizioni di spiritualità, 1953. 190p. Piccola guida bibliografia: p.169-181. (Italian)

B129 Carlsen, Robin Woodsworth. What Is Enlightenment? Sutras of the Personal. Victoria, B.C.: Snow Man Press, 1979. 79p.

B130   Carlson, Ronald L., 1950- . Transcendental Meditation:
        Relaxation or Religion? Chicago: Moody Press, 1978.
        156p. Bibliography: p.151-156. LC 78-1886

B131   Carrington, Patricia. Freedom in Meditation. Garden City,
        N.Y.: Anchor Press, 1978, c1977. xii,384p. Includes
        bibliographical references. LC 76-6240
        A clinical psychologist analyzes different types of meditation
        with a concentration on Transcendental Meditation, the Ben-
        son method of relaxation response, and her own Clinically
        Standardized Meditation.

B132   _____. Das grosse Buch der Meditation. Übers. aus d.
        Amerikan von Margret Meilwes. 2. Aufl. Bern, Müchen
        and Wien: Scherz, 1982. Orig. pub., 1980. Einheits-
        sacht.: Freedom in Meditation. (German)

B133   Cataldi, Oscar B., Jr. Psychophysiology and Its Thera-
        peutic Effects on Stress: An Annotated Bibliography.
        Dayton, Ohio: Wright State University, 1982. 4p.
        Provides references to the therapeutic effectiveness of relax-
        ation techniques including meditation, progressive relaxation,
        biofeedback training, and behavior therapy.

B134   Cayce, Edgar, 1877-1945. Meditation, Endocrine Glands,
        Prayer, and Affirmations. Prepared by the Readings
        Research Department and the Editorial Department, under
        the direction of the Library Series Committee. Virginia
        Beach, Va.: Association for Research and Enlightenment,
        1975. viii,274p. (His Meditation; pt.2) (The Edgar
        Cayce Readings; v.3) LC 76-354632

B135   Center for Self Sufficiency, Learning Institute. At Your
        Own Pace Bibliography on Meditation. Houston: The
        Center, Box 7234, 1983.

B136   Chaitow, Leon. Relaxation and Meditation Techniques.
        Wellingborough: Thorsons, Pub. Ltd., 1983. 128p.
        Examines the major causes of stress, looks at the physiologi-
        cal and pathological effects which prolonged stress can pro-
        duce, and sets out relaxation methods, meditation and visual-
        ization techniques and advice on nutrition and exercise.

B137   Chaman Lal, 1903- . Yoga of Meditation. Fort Lauderdale,
        Fla.: The Author, 1971. 253p. LC 72-179424

B138   Chandraprabhsagar, Muni, 1922- . Realize What You Are:
        The Dynamics of Jain Meditation, by Gurudev Shree
        Chitrabhanu [i.e. M. Chandraprabhsagar]. Edited by
        Leonard M. Marks. Drawings by Jeffrey R. Webb.
        New York: Dodd, Mead, 1978. xiii,125p. LC 78-9461

B139   Chaney, Robert Galen, 1913- . The Inner Way. Los Ange-
        les: Astara, 1975. Orig. pub., Los Angeles: DeVorss,
        1962. 145p. LC 75-32234

B140   Chang, Lit-sen. Transcendental Meditation: A Mystic Cult
        of Self-Intoxication; A Former T.M. Promoter Speaks.
        Nutley, N.J.: Presbyterian and Reformed Pub. Co.,
        1978. x,92p.

B141   Chantal, Jeanne Françoise (Frémiot) de Rabutin, Baronne de,
        Saint, 1572-1641. St. Chantal on Prayer: A Translation
        of Her Writings on Prayer, by A. Durand. Boston: St.
        Paul Editions, 1968. 63p. LC 67-31593

B142   Chao Khun, Sobhana Dhammasudhi. Beneficial Factors for
        Meditation: An Elementary Guide to Vipassana Meditation,
        Preferably for Beginners. 2nd and enlarged ed. Hindhead
        (Linkside West, Beacon Hill, Hindhead, Surrey): The
        Vipassana Foundation, 1970. Orig. pub., 1968. 72p.

B143   Chapman, A.H. (Arthur Harry), 1924- . What TM Can and
        Cannot Do for You. With Elza M. Almeida and Jeffrey C.
        Chapman. New York: Berkley Publishing Corporation,
        1976. 208p. Bibliography: p.195-200.
        Questions and answers based on a psychiatrist's experience
        with patients and the use of TM for its possible benefits.

B144   Chase, Loriene, and Clifton W. King. The Human Miracle:
        Transcendent Psychology. New York: Hawthorne Books,
        1974. xii,206p. LC 74-2573

B145   Chaudhuri, Haridas. Philosophy of Meditation. 2nd ed.
        San Francisco, Calif.: Cultural Integration Fellowship,
        1974. Dist. by Auromere, Pomona, Calif. Orig. pub.,
        New York: Philosophical Library, 1965. 88p.

B146   Chen, Chien-min, 1904- . Buddhist Meditation, Systematic
        and Practical; A Talk by the Buddhist Yogi, C.M. Chen,
        Written Down By Rev. B. Kantipalo. Rev. and enlarged
        ed. New York: C.T. Shen, 1980. Also, 1976. Orig.
        pub., 1966. xxvi,486p.

B147   Chih-i. Die Kunst der Versenkung: d. Anweisungen zur
        Meditation d. Grossen Meisters Chi-Chi aus d. China d.
        6. Jh. Bern, München, and Wien: Barth, 1975. 109p.
        (German)

B148   Chilson, Richard. Geschenk des Geistes: Übungen zur
        Selbsterfahrung u. Bibelmeditation. Graz, Wien, and
        Köln: Verlag Styria, 1981. 256p. (German)

B149   Chinmayananda, Swami. Meditation and Life. Madras:
        Chinmaya Publications Trust, 1967? xi,154p. LC 73-
        901755

B150   Chinmoy. Meditation: God Speaks and I Listen. Jamaica,
        N.Y.: Sri Chinmoy Lighthouse, 1974. 2 vols.

B151   _____. Meditation: God's Blessing-Assurance. Jamaica,
        N.Y.: Agni Press, 1974. 72p.

B152   _____. Meditation: God's Duty and Man's Beauty.
        Jamaica, N.Y.: Agni Press, 1974. 60p.

B153   _____. Meditation: Humanity's Race and Divinity's Grace.
        Jamaica, N.Y.: Agni Press, 1974. 2 vols.

B154   _____. Meditation: Man-Perfection in God-Satisfaction.
        Jamaica, N.Y.: Agni Press, 1978. Dist. by Aum Publi-
        cations, Jamaica, N.Y. 304p. LC 80-65399

B155   _____. Meditation: Man's Choice and God's Voice.
        Jamaica, N.Y.: Agni Press, 1974. Dist. by Aum Publi-
        cations, Jamaica, N.Y. 2 vols.

B156   _____. The Meditation-World. Jamaica, N.Y.: Agni
        Press, 1977. 54p. (His Miscellanies; v.11)

B157   Christensen, Chuck, and Winnie Christensen. How to Listen
        When God Speaks: Helps for the Daily Quiet Time.
        Wheaton, Ill.: H. Shaw Publishers, 1978. 79p. LC 78-
        73294

B158   Das Christentum in der antiken Welt. Stuttgart, Württem-
        berg: Verein d. Freunde d. Humanist. Gymnasiums,
        1981. viii,107p. Literaturverz.: p.97-101. (German)

B159   Christus und die Gurus: asiatische-religiöse Gruppen im
        Westen: Information u. Orientirung. Hrsg. von Lothar
        Schreiner und Michael Mildenberger. Stuttgart und Ber-
        lin: Kreuz-Verlag, 1980. 192p. LC 81-454605 (German)

B160   Chuang, Chou. Lebe bewusst!: Wegweisungen zur Sinner-
        füllung d. Daseins. Engelberg/Schweiz, München: Drei-
        Eichen-Verlag, 1978? 96p. (German)

B161   Churches' Fellowship for Psychical and Spiritual Studies.
        Mysticism Committee. Guide-Lines for Meditation. London:
        The General Secretary, St. Mary Abchurch, Abchurch
        La., EC4N 7BA: The Committee, 1971. 26p. Bibliogra-
        phy: p.26.

B162   Clowney, Edmund P. CM, Christian Meditation. Nutley,
        N.J.: Craig Press, 1979. Dist. by Presbyterian & Re-
        formed Pub. Co., Phillipsburg, N.J. 103p. Includes
        bibliographical references. Also published in digest form:
        Nutley, N.J.: Craig Press, 1978, 42p. Also pub. as
        Christian Meditation. Leicester: Inter-Varsity Press,
        1980. 48p.

B163   Cohen, Daniel. Meditation: What It Can Do For You. New
        York: Dodd, Mead, 1977. 144p. Bibliography: p.135-
        137. LC 77-7499
        Defines meditation, surveys its history and various forms,
        and focuses on Transcendental Meditation. Juvenile litera-
        ture.

B164   Coleman, John E., 1930- . The Quiet Mind. New York:
        Harper & Row, and London: Rider, 1971. 239p. LC
        71-148446 and LC 70-569839
        A personal account of the author's experiences with various
        types of meditation.

B165   Contemplation and Action in World Religions: Selected Papers
        from the Rothko Chapel Colloquium "Traditional Modes of
        Contemplation and Action." Edited by Yusuf Ibish and
        Ileana Marculescu. Houston: Rothko Chapel; Seattle:
        distributed by University of Washington Press, 1978.
        274p. Includes bibliographical references. LC 78-61504
        [Cf. B909]

B166   Conze, Edward, 1904- . Buddhist Meditation. Edited and
        translated by Edward Conze. New York: Harper & Row,
        and London: Unwin Books, 1975. Also, London: Allen
        & Unwin, 1972, and New York: Harper & Row, 1969.
        Orig. pub., London: Allen & Unwin, 1956. 183p. In-
        cludes bibliographical references.
        The bulk of the selections are derived from the Old Wisdom
        school [i.e. of the Theravadin and Sarvastivadin schools]
        and in particular from Buddhaghosa's Path of Purity. Con-
        tinued by Buddhist Thought in India.

B167   Cooke, Grace. Christliche Meditation: transzendentale
        Übungspraxis, von Grace Cooke und White Eagle. Autoris.
        Übers.: Walter Ohr u. Gerti Schmid-Curtius. Zürich:
        Origo-Verlag, 1972. 117p. Einheitssacht.: Meditation.
        (German)

B168   _____ . The Jewel in the Lotus. Liss (New Lands, Liss,
        Hants. GU33 7HY): White Eagle Publishing Trust, 1973.
        Dist. in U.S. by DeVorss, Marina del Rey, Calif. 156p.
        Grace Cooke is a medium through whom White Eagle presents
        his teaching on the place of meditation in everyday life.

B169   _____. Meditation. 2nd ed. Liss: White Eagle Publishing Trust, 1965, 1980 printing. Orig. pub., 1955. Dist.
in U.S. by DeVorss & Co., Marina del Rey, Calif. 167p.
Sets forth a technique of meditation and spiritual unfoldment
which can be used by individuals or groups. Presents the
philosophy of White Eagle, Mrs. Cooke's spiritual guide.

B170   Cooper, Joan. Guided Meditation and the Teaching of Jesus.
Tisbury: Element, 1982. 80p.

B171   Corless, Roger. The Art of Christian Alchemy: Transfigur-
ing the Ordinary Through Holistic Meditation. New York:
Paulist Press, 1981. 118p. Bibliography: p.105-118.
LC 81-80872

B172   Costain, Edward E. Comment méditer? Traduit par Jacque-
line Lenclud. Montréal: Editions Sélect, 1980. 95p.
(Guides Sélect; 11) Traduction de: How to Meditate.
(French)

B173   Cox, Harvey Gallagher. Turning East: The Promise and
Peril of the New Orientalism. New York: Simon & Schus-
ter, 1977. 192p. Bibliography: p.177-180. Also pub.
as Turning East: Why Americans Look to the Orient for
Spirituality, and What that Search Can Mean to the West.
LC 77-8600

B174   Craig, Philippa. Living from Within. Pinner: Grail Publications, 1979. 64p. Music. Bibliography: p.62. List
of music: p.60-61.

B175   Crasset, Jean. Anleitung zum innerlichen Gebet mit einer
neuen Art von Betrachtungen. Übers.: Hermann Zurhausen. Neu hrsg. von Jakob Philippi. 3. Aufl. Kevelaer: Butzon & Bercker, 1954. 190p. Einheitssacht.:
Méthode d'oraison, avec une nouvelle forme de méditations.
(German)

B176   Crom, Scott. Quaker Worship and Techniques of Meditation.
Wallingford, Pa.: Pendle Hill Publications, 1974. 30p.
(Pendle Hill Pamphlet; 195) LC 74-82795

B177   Curran, Jo, 1933- . Who Are You?: Know Thyself. San
Antonio: Naylor Co., 1975. 52p. LC 75-35536

B178   Cuvelier, André. Comme une terre desséchée; de la méditation orientale à l'oraison chrétienne. Paris: Apostolat
des éditions, and Sherbrooke (Canada): Editions paul-
ines, 1972. 158p. (Collection Ressourcement; 3) LC
74-326663 (French)

B179   Dancer, Jay. <u>The Transcendental Meditation Experience.</u> New York: Award Books, 1976. 176p.

B180   Davis, Roy Eugene. <u>An Easy Guide to Meditation</u>. Lakemont, Ga.: CSA Press, 1978. Dist. by DeVorss & Co., Marina del Rey, Calif. 74p. LC 78-103655

B181   _____. <u>Einfache Einführung in die Meditation: e. einfache Methode, d. hilft, sich von Spannung u. Stress zu befreien, Bewusstsein zu entfalten u. sich besser zu konzentrieren.</u> Frankfurt/Main: Verlag CSA Deutschland Schneider, 1978. 88p. Einheitssacht.: <u>An Easy Guide to Meditation</u>. (German)

B182   _____. <u>How You Can Use the Technique of Creative Imagination</u>. Revised ed. Lakemont, Ga.: CSA Press, 1974. Orig. pub., Lakemont, Ga.: CSA Press, and Miami, Fla.: Marshall-Davis Publishers, 1961. 112p.

B183   _____. <u>Die Macht der Seele als erlebte Wirklichkeit.</u> Ubertr. ins Dt. von Annemarie Leypold. Friedrichsdorf: Verlag CSA, 1981. Orig. pub., 1978. 199p. Einheitssacht.: <u>This Is Reality</u>. (German)

B184   _____. <u>So kannst Du Deine Träume verwirklichen: d. Technik d. schöpfer. Imagination.</u> Friedrichsdorf und Frankfurt am Main: Verlag CSA, 1978. 128p. Einheitssacht.: <u>How You Can Use the Technique of Creative Imagination</u>. (German) [Cf. B188]

B185   _____. <u>Studies in Truth</u>. Lakemont, Ga.: CSA Press, 1969. 165p. LC 73-77611

B186   _____. <u>This Is Reality</u>. Lakemont, Ga.: CSA Press, 1967, c1962. 211p.

B187   _____. <u>Wahrheitsstudien.</u> Frankfurt am Main: Verlag CSA, 1979. 141p. Einheitssacht.: <u>Studies in Truth</u>. (German)

B188   _____. <u>Wie Sie die Technik der schopferischen Imagination anwenden konnen, um Ihre Traume zu verwirklichen.</u> Frankfurt am Main: Verlag CSA, 1978. 112p. Einheitssacht.: <u>How You Can Use the Technique of Creative Imagination</u>. (German) [Cf. B184]

B189   Déchanet, Jean Marie, 1906- . <u>Christian Yoga</u>. Translated by Roland Hindmarsh. London: Search Press, 1972 and 1970. Dist. in U.S. by Christian Classics, Westminster, Md. Also, New York: Harper & Row, 1972 and 1960; London: Burns & Oates, 1964 and 1960. vi,196p.

Translation of La voie du silence.
Explains how the technique of Yoga and meditation can be
used to facilitate contemplative prayer for the Christian.

B190   . Journal d'un yogi. Préface du Dr. Paul Minelli.
Paris: le Courrier du livre, 1967-1978. 3 vols. (Vol. 3
published by Epi) Includes bibliographical references.
(t.1. Mon corps et moi. t.2. Mon coeur et Dieu. t.3.
L'autre et les autres.) LC 68-71246 (French)

B191   . La voie du silence: l'expérience d'un moine.
Suive de Note sur la prière du coeur, par F. Gouillard.
Paris: Desclée De Brouwer, 1978, c1963. 232p. Bib-
liography; p. 37. LC 79-391436 (French)

B192   . Yoga and God: An Invitation to Christian Yoga.
Translated by Sarah Fawcett. Meinrad, Ind.: Abbey
Press, 1975, and London: Search Press, 1974. viii,161p.
Translation of Journal d'un yogi [B190]. Includes bib-
liographical references. LC 75-19918
Includes a discussion of Kundalini and a general survey of
meditational practices.

B193   Deikman, Arthur. Finding Your Way to the Real World:
The Key to Personal Freedom. London: Souvenir Press,
1977. xi,163p. Orig. pub. as Personal Freedom. New
York: Grossman Publishers, 1976.

B194   DelCor, Christa. Christliche Meditation für alle. München:
Verl. Ars Sacra, 1966. 31p. (German)

B195   . Meditation der Liebe. München: Verlag Ars
Sacra, 1974. 31p. (German)

B196   Denniston, Denise, and Peter McWilliams. El libro de la TM*
(meditación transcendental): cómo gozar el resto de su
vida. Illustraciones de Barry Geller. Traducido por
Ricardo De Frutos. Barcelona: Grijalbo, 1978. 351p.
(Edibolsillo paperback Grijal; 168) On spine: TM, meditación transcendental. Translation of The TM Book.
(Spanish)

B197   , and   . The Transcendental Meditation TM
Book: How to Enjoy the Rest of Your Life. Illustrated
by Barry Geller. New York: Warner Books, 1975. Al-
so, Allen Park, Mich.: Three Rivers Press (Versemonger
Press), 1975. Dist. by Price/Stern/Sloan, New York and
Los Angeles. 351p. On spine: The TM Book. LC 75-
13848
The material is presented in a question and answer format.
The areas covered are: What TM is not; What TM is; What

TM does; Learning TM; and TM Solution to all problems.
Instructions are not included.

B198   Desbuquoit, Achille M. How to Meditate. Translated and
        arranged by G. Protopapas. Milwaukee: Bruce Pub. Co.,
        1955. 75p. LC 55-7861
        Discusses the need for meditation and the conditions of men-
        tal prayer.

B199   Deshimaru, Taisen. Vrai Zen, source vive, révolution in-
        térieure. Sho do ka, chant de l'immédiat satori, [poème
        de Yoka Daishi]. Traduit et commenté par T. Deshimaru.
        Paris: le Courrier du livre, 1969. 288p. LC 73-321964
        (French)

B200   _____. Za-Zen: la pratique du Zen. Présenté par Janine
        Monnot et Vincent Bardet. Paris: Seghers, 1974. 166p.
        LC 75-503963 (French)

B201   Deshpande, R.R. The Dhyanayoga in the Bhagavadgita.
        Foreword by S.G. Hulyalkar. Bijapur, Mysore State,
        1969. xiii,120p. LC 75-918069
        Includes copious quotations in Sanskrit.

B202   Dessauer, Phillip. Meditation im christlichen Dasein. Hrsg.
        von Irmgard Wild. München: Kösel-Verlag, 1968. 229p.
        LC 68-104531 (German)

B203   _____. Natural Meditation. Translated from the German
        by J. Holland Smith. Foreword by Aelred Graham. New
        York: P.J. Kenedy, 1965. 128p. Orig. pub. as Die
        naturale Meditation. LC 65-14319

B204   _____. Die naturale Meditation. München: Kösel, 1961.
        139p. (German)

B205   Dhammarantana, U. Guide Through Visuddhimagga. Vara-
        nasi: Maha Bodhi Society, Sarnath, 1964. vi,163p.
        LC 67-1735

B206   Dhiravamsa. Agenommen, Sie fühlen sich elend: Meditation
        als Mittel zur Wandlung. Wien: Octopus-Verlag, 1979.
        260p. Einheitssacht.: The Way of Non-Attachment.
        (German)

B207   _____. The Dynamic Way of Meditation: The Release &
        Cure of Pain & Suffering Through Vipassana Meditative
        Techniques. Wellingborough: Thorsons Publishers, 1983.
        Dist. in U.S. by Sterling Pub. Co., New York. Orig.
        pub., Northamptonshire: Turnstone Press Limited, 1982.

B 208 _____ . The Way of Non-Attachment: The Practice of In-
sight Meditation. New York: Schocken Books, 1977.
Orig. pub., London: Turnstone Books, 1975. 160p.
LC 76-48761
A discussion of meditation and an introduction to the prin-
ciples of Vipassana Meditation or the practice of Insight
Meditation.

B 209 Dieball, Werner. Biotranszendenz: d. sichere Weg zu wirk-
samer Lebenshilfe, zu mehr Schwung u. Kreativität. Freiburg im Breisgau: Bauer, 1981. 276p. Literaturverz.:
p.275-277. (German)

B 210 Diefenbach, Gabriel. Common Mystic Prayer. Boston, Ma.:
St. Paul Editions, 1978. 137p. Reprint of the 1947 ed.
pub. by St. Anthony Guild Press, Paterson, N.J. Bibliography: p.135-137. LC 78-5672

B 211 No entry.

B 212 A Directory of Ashrams in India and Abroad. Edited by
R.P. Saxena and Vinay Lakshmi. Mathura: Ashram
Publications, 197-? 103p. LC 77-903982

B 213 Diskin, Eve. Yoga Meditation. Miami, Fla.: American Institute of Yoga, 1969. xiii,70p.

B 214 Dorje, Konchok. Marxismus und Meditation. München,
Trikont-Verlag, 1980. 177p. (German)

B 215 Douval, H.E. Wiedergeburt durch innere Sekretion: Umwandlung der Zeugungskraft; Entwicklung, Speicherung
und Anwendung ungewandelter Liebeskraft für Lebenser-
folg und Magie als Schlüssel für okkulte Phänomene und
Lebensglück. Gelnhausen: H. Schwab, 1964. 62p. LC
77-250725 (German)

B 216 Dowman, Keith. Calm and Clear. Translations and com-
mentary written by Keith Dowman. Berkeley, Calif.:
Tibetan Nyingma Meditation Center, 1974, c1973. 127p.
LC 73-79058 [Same as B 544]

B 217 Downing, George. Massage & Meditation. Illustrated by
Anne Kent Rush. New York: Random House, 1974.
85p. LC 73-20585
The book shows that massage and meditation are very much
alike in their aspects and can be integrated. Philosophy and
instructions are included.

B 218 _____ . Massage & [und] Meditation. 3. Aufl., Berlin:
Ki-Buch-Verlag, 1981. Orig. pub., 1976. 85p. Einheitssacht.: Massage and Meditation. (German)

B219   Downing, Jim. Meditation: The Bible Tells You How. Fore-
        word by Betty Lee Skinner. Colorado Springs, Colo.:
        Navpress, 1977, c1976. 96p. LC 76-24064

B220   Dumoulin, Heinrich. Östliche Meditation und chrisliche My-
        stik. Freiburg (i. Br.) und München: Alber, 1966.
        339p. Includes bibliographical references. LC 67-82534
        (German)

B221   Dürckheim, Karlfried Graf. Meditieren, wozu und wie: d.
        Wende zum Initiatischen. 6. Aufl. Freiburg im Breis-
        gau, Basel, und Wien: Herder, 1981. 237p. Litera-
        turverz: p.236-238. (German)

B222   _____. Übung des Leibes auf dem inneren Weg. München:
        Lurz, 1978. 87p.

B223   Dutta, Rex. Reality of Occult, Yoga, Meditation, Flying
        Saucers. London: Pelham, 1974. 199p. Bibliography:
        p.194-195. LC 75-305351

B224   Eastcott, Michael J. The Silent Path: An Introduction to
        Meditation. London: Rider, 1983. Also, New York:
        Samuel Weiser, 1976. Orig. pub., London: Rider, 1969.
        ix,166p. Bibliography: p.159-160.
        Includes sections on vision, concentration, and planes of
        consciousness. Reflective, receptive, creative, and prayer-
        ful meditation are also covered. The author is a student of
        Alice Baily.

B225   _____. Weg der Stille: eine Einf. in d. Meditation. Die
        dt. Übers. besorgte Ernst G. Techow. Weilheim (Obb.):
        Barth, 1972. 244p. Einheitssacht.: The Silent Path.
        (German)

B226   Easwaran, Eknath. Instructions in Meditation. Berkeley,
        Calif.: Blue Mountain Center of Meditation, 1972. Dist.
        by Nilgiri Press, Petaluma, Calif., and DeVorss & Co.,
        Marina del Rey, Calif.

B227   _____. The Mantram Handbook. Introduction by Richard
        B. Applegate. London [etc.]: Routledge and Kegan
        Paul, 1978. Orig. pub., Berkeley, Calif.: Nilgiri Press,
        1977. Dist. by DeVorss & Co., Marina del Rey, Calif.
        260p. Bibliography: p.249-250.
        Examples of mantrams are given from many different religions.
        The author explains what a mantram is and how it can be
        used in daily life.

B228   _____. Meditation: Commonsense Directions for an Un-
        common Life. London [etc.]: Routledge and Kegan Paul,

1979. Orig. pub., Petaluma, Calif.: Nilgiri Press, 1978.
Dist. by DeVorss & Co., Marina del Rey, Calif. 237p.
Bibliography: p.220-223.
This book also includes a chapter on mantras.

B229 _____. A Meditation Manual. Berkeley, Calif.: Blue
Mountain Center of Meditation, Sadhana Press, 1972. 16p.

B230 Ebon, Martin, comp. Maharishi: The Founder of Transcendental Meditation. New York: New American Library,
c1968, 1975 printing. Orig. pub. as Maharishi, the
Guru: An International Symposium. New York: New
American Library, and Bombay: Indian Book House,
1968. Dist. in India by Pearl Books, Bombay.
A variety of essays and articles dealing with the life, times,
teachings and impact of the Maharishi Mahesh Yogi.

B231 Edwards, F. Henry (Francis Henry), 1807- . Meditation
& Prayer. Independence, Mo.: Herald Pub. House,
1980. 272p. Includes bibliographical references. LC
79-23708

B232 Edwards, Tilden. Living Simply Through the Day: Spiritual
Survival in a Complex Age. New York: Paulist Press,
1977. viii,225p. Includes bibliographical references.
LC 77-14855

B233 Egdom, Richard van, 1947- . Het speelse geweten: teorie
en metode van sofrologie. Bloemendaal: Nelissen, 1978.
111p. Bibliography: p.105-106. LC 81-459340 (Dutch)

B234 Eggiman, Ernst, 1936- . Meditation mit offensen Augen.
München: C. Kaiser, 1974. 79p. (Kaiser Traktate;
12) Bibliography: p.6. LC 75-539895 (German)

B235 Ellis, George A., 1947- . Inside Folsom Prison: Transcendental Meditation and TM-Sidhi Program. Palm Springs,
Calif.: ETC Publications; Chicago: distributed by Chicago Review Press, 1979. xxv,254p. Bibliography: p.
235-240. LC 78-16774

B235K Ellwood, Robert S., 1933- . Finding the Quiet Mind.
Wheaton, Ill.: Theosophical Pub. House, 1983. xi,155p.
(A Quest Book) LC 83-615

B236 Emery, Pierre Yves. La Méditation de l'Ecriture. 4e édition
augmentée. Les Psaumes, prière pour l'Eglis. Taizé:
les Presses de Taizé, 1967. 80p. LC 68-77202 (French)

B237 Emmons, Michael L. The Inner Source: A Guide to Meditative Therapy. San Luis Obispo, Calif.: Impact Publish-

ers, 1978. Dist. by DeVorss & Co., Marina del Rey, Calif.: ix,291p. Bibliography: p.279–286. LC 78–466

B 238 Faces of Meditation, by Swami Rama ... [et al.]. Edited by S.N. Agnihotri and Justin O'Brien. Honesdale, Pa.: Himalayan International Institute, 1978. 97p.

B 239 Falconí, Juan, 1596–1638. Camino derecho para el cielo. ed. e introd. de Elfas Gómez. Barcelona: J. Flors, 1960. xi,321p. (Espirituales españoles: Serie A, Textos; L3) Includes bibliographical references. LC 79–371765 (Spanish)

B 240 Fast, Howard Melvin, 1914- . The Art of Zen Meditation. Culver City, Calif.: Peace Press, 1977. Dist. by De-Vorss, Marina del Rey, Calif. LC 77–6222 An introduction to Zen meditation with photographs and direct instructions.

B 241 Fenhagen, James C. More than Wanderers: Spiritual Disciplines for Christian Ministry. New York: Seabury Press, 1978. xiii,105p. Includes bibliographical references. LC 77–17974

B 242 Fenn, Mair. An Introduction to T.M. Dublin: Mercier, 1978, 1979 printing. 96p. Bibliography: p.95.

B 243 Fichtl, Friedemann, Hrsg. Materialien zur Bildmeditation: Dias, Anregungen, Entwürfe. Freiburg i. Br.: Christophorus-Verlag; Gelnhausen and Berlin: Burckhard-thaus-Verlag, 1976. 128p. (German)

B 244 Filocalia: la pregària del cor. Por Sants Pares. Barcelona: Editorial Claret, 1979. 191p. (Col·lecció Els Daus; no. 33) Bibliography: p.189–190. LC 80–113634 (Spanish) The Greek Philokalia was compiled in the eighteenth century by Macarius of Corinth and Nicodemus of the Holy Mountain, and first published in Venice in 1782.

B 245 Firkel, Eva. Praktische Hilfen zum Gebet. Bergen-Enkheim bei Frankfurt und Main: Kaffke, 1976. 38p. (German)

B 246 Flor, Margherita. Maharishi Mahesh Yogi og transcendental meditation. København: Thaning & Appel, 1968. 101p. LC 75–379065 (Danish)

B 247 Forem, Jack, 1943- . Meditación transcendental: Maharishi Mahesh Yogi y la ciencia de la intelligencia creativa. Traductor, René Cárdenas Barrios. México: D.F. Diana, 1975. 300p. Título original. Transcendental Meditation... Includes bibliographical references. (Spanish)

B 248 _____. Transcendental Meditation: Maharishi Mahesh Yogi and the Science of Creative Intelligence. Rev. ed. New York: Bantam Books, 1976. Also, London: Allen and Unwin, 1974. Orig. pub., New York: Dutton, 1973. 283p.
A TM instructor provides an introduction to TM and the Science of Creative Intelligence. The growth of the movement and the principles of SCI are explained. There is a review of scientific research about TM and a discussion of the practical application of SCI and TM.

B 249 The Foundations of Mindfulness. Edited by Chögyam Trungpa Rinpoche. Associate editor, Michael H. Kohn. Boulder, Colo.: Vajradhau, and New York: distributed by Random House, 1976. 88p. (Garuda; v.4) LC 75-40263

B 250 Frew, David R. The Management of Stress: Using TM at Work. Chicago: Nelson-Hall, 1977. xxiii,235p. Includes bibliographical references. LC 76-18164
The three main parts of this book deal with: management, stress, and the worker; the impact of stress; and the effect of TM on productivity and stress.

B 251 Friede, Martin. Durch Krankheit zur Genesung. Elgg: Volksverlag, 1977. 155p. Includes bibliographical references. LC 78-387326 (German)

B 252 Fröbe-Kapteyn, Olga, Hrsg. Yoga und Meditation im Osten und im Western. Zürich: Rhein-Verlag, 1956, c1934. 348p. (Eranos Jahrbuch; Bd.1) Includes Bibliographical references. (German)

B 253 Frontiers of the Spirit: Studies in the Mystical and Psychical Areas in Observance of the Twentieth Anniversary of the Founding of Spiritual Frontiers Fellowship. Edited by Paul Lambourne Higgins. Minneapolis: T.S. Denison, 1976. 133p. LC 76-358476

B 254 Fuchs, Joseph, 1912- , and Anneliese Harf. Meditieren im Alltag. Hinführung und Anleitungen. 2. Aufl. Frieberg b. Augsburg: Palloti-Verlag, 1973. Orig. pub., 1969. 215p. (Sammulung Pallotti; Bd.11) (German)

B 255 Fujimoto, Rindō, 1894- . The Way of Zazen. Translated by Tetsuya Inoue and Yoshihiko Tanigawa. Introduction by Elsie P. Mitchell. Cambridge, Mass.: Buddhist Association, 1961. xiv,26p. LC 79-221042

B 256 Funderburk, James, 1947- . Science Studies Yoga: A Review of Physiological Data. Introduction by Barbara B. Brown. Glenview, Ill.: Himalayan International Institute of Yoga Science & Philosophy, 1977. xiv,257p.

B257   Gardner, Adelaide. Meditation: A Practical Study with
        Exercises. Rev. ed. Wheaton, Ill.: Theosophical Pub.
        House, 1968, 1979 printing. Dist. by DeVorss, Marina
        del Rey, Calif. 116p. LC 68-5856 Includes bibliograph-
Includes bibliographical references.

B258   Gaus, Hans, and Albert Schlereth, Bearb. Meditation.
        München: Kösel, 1971. 79p. (Alternativen; Heft 8)
        "Die Verfasser (Auswahl)": p.77-78. LC 72-364104
        (German)

B259   Gawain, Shakti. Creative Visualization. Toronto and New
        York: Bantam Books, 1982. Orig. pub., Berkeley,
        Calif.: Whatever Publishing, 1978. xii,127p. Bibliog-
        raphy: p.124-127.

B260   Gent, John. Yoga Seeker. Mansfield, Notts.: The Author,
        19--. Part 8: Dhyana, the Yoga of Meditation, 1977,
        14p. Part 9: Mantra Yoga, the Music of the Mind, 1977.
        12p.

B261   Gerberding, Kieth A. How to Respond to ... Transcendental
        Meditation. St. Louis: Concordia Pub. House, 1977.
        31p. (Response Series) Bibliography: p.31. LC 77-
        22212

B262   Gibson, William, 1914- . A Season in Heaven: Being the
        Log of an Expedition After the Legendary Beast, Cosmic
        Consciousness. New York: Bantam Books 1975. Orig.
        pub., New York: Atheneum, 1974. 133p.
The author relates his experiences in Spain studying Transcendental Meditation with the Maharishi Mahesh Yogi.

B263   Gijsen, Wim. Leven dat het een lieve lust is. Kruiden,
        homeopathie, markrobiotiek, yoga, meditatie. Teken.
        Lux Buurman. Den Haag: Bakker/Daamen, 1971. 105p.
        LC 73-872935 (Dutch)

B264   Gill, Jean. Images of My Self: Meditation and Self Explor-
        ation Through the Jungian Imagery of the Gospels. New
        York: Paulist Press, 1982. 88p. LC 82-81188
Offers techniques for practicing meditation as a way of
prayer.

B265   Gillies, Jerry, 1940- . Transcendental Sex: A Meditative
        Approach to Increasing Sensual Pleasure. Drawings by
        Teri L. Misrach. New York: Holt, Rinehart, and Win-
        ston, 1978. xiv,176p. LC 77-15202
The author believes that meditation can enhance sex and
that sex can be a form of meditation. A series of meditative
exercises are presented.

B266   Glasser, William. Positive Addiction. New York: Harper & Row, 1976. 159p. Includes bibliographical references. LC 75-15305

B267   Glaube, Erfahrung, Meditation. Hrsg. von Gerhard Ruhbach mit Beitr. von Josef Bill ... [et al]. [1.-4. Tsd.]. München: Kösel, 1977. 111p. Includes bibliographical references. LC 78-388450 (German)

B268   Glaubenserfahrung und Meditation: Wege e. neuen Spiritualitat. Hrsg. von Joseph Sauer mit Beitr. von Klaus Hemmerle ... [et al.]. Freiburg im Breisgau, Basel, und Wien: Herder, 1975. 134p. Includes bibliographic references. LC 76-463896 (German)

B269   Godrèche, Dominique. Santana: l'enseignement d'un maître bouddhiste en Inde. Paris: Seghers, 1975. 190p. LC 80-460729 (French)

B270   Goichon, Amélie Marie. Beschauliches Leben inmitten der Welt. Übertr. von Hugo Harder. Einsiedeln, Zürich, Köln: Benziger, 1953. 230p. Einheitssacht.: La Vie contemplative est-elle possible dans le monde? (German)

B271   Goldberg, Philip. Programma di MT, mediazione transcendentale: la via per la realizzione: che cosa è, come funziona, che cosa si ottiene. Traduzione di Claudia Cossio. Roma: Edizioni mediterranee, 1978. 223p. Translation of The TM Program. Bibliography: p.217-218. LC 80-462471 (Italian)

B272   _____. The TM Program: The Way to Fulfillment: The Transcendental Meditation Program Is a Proven Approach to Developing the Full Human Potential: What It Is, How It Works, What It Does. New York: Holt, Rinehart and Winston, 1976. xiv,178p. Bibliography: p.168-169. LC 76-11747
A TM instructor explains the benefits of TM. Case studies are presented.

B273   Goldhaber, Nat. TM: An Alphabetical Guide to the Transcendental Meditation Program. Special sections by Denise Denniston and Peter McWilliams. New York: Ballantine Books, 1976. 221,[56]p. Includes bibliographical references. LC 76-8830

B274   Goldsmith, Joel Solomon, 1892- . The Art of Meditation. London: Mandala Books, 1977. Orig. pub., London: Allen and Unwin, 1957, and New York: Harper & Row, 1956. Dist. by DeVorss, Marina del Rey, Calif. [5],154p. The reader is introduced to a regular program of daily meditation adapted to his needs and situation with instructions, examples and specifically written meditations.

B275 _____ . Der Geist, der in uns lebt. Dt. Übers.: Sigrid von Glasenapp. Gelnhausen-Gettenbach: Schwab, 1961. 168p. Einheitssacht.: Practicing the Presence. (German)

B276 _____ . Die Kunst der Meditation. Gelnhausen: Schwab, 1964. 186p. Einheitssacht.: The Art of Meditation. (German)

B277 _____ . Meditation and Prayer. San Gabriel, Calif.: Willing Pub., 1947. Dist. by DeVorss, Marina del Rey, Calif. 26p.

B278 _____ . Practicing the Presence. 9th ed. Romford: L.N. Fowler, 1976 and previous editions. Also, New York: Harper & Row, 1958. 200p.

B279 Goldstein, Joseph, 1944- . The Experience of Insight: A Natural Unfolding. Introduction by Ram Dass. Preface by Robert Hall. Boulder, Colo.: Shambhala, 1983. Dist. in U.S. by Random House. Also, London: Wildwood House, 1981. Orig. pub., Santa Cruz, Calif.: Unity Press, 1976. 185p. Includes bibliographical references. LC 82-42682
Practical instruction for the practice of Buddhist meditation including sitting and walking meditation, how one relates with the breath, feelings, consciousness, and everyday activity.

B280 _____ . Vipassana-Meditation: d. Entfaltung d. Bewusstseinsklarheit. Berlin: Schickler, 1978. Einheitssacht.: The Experience of Insight Meditation. (German)

B281 Goleman, Daniel. The Varieties of the Meditative Experience. London: Rider, 1978. Also, New York: Dutton, and Toronto & Vancouver: Clarke, Irwin & Co., 1977. Orig. pub., New York: Irvington Publishers; dist. by Halsted Press, 1977. Also dist. by DeVorss, Marina, del Rey, Calif. xxvii,131p. Bibliography: p. 119-122.
Discusses all the major forms of meditation, including those of Tibetan Buddhism, Sufism, Christianity and Judaism.

B282 Goosen, Marilyn May Mallory, 1943- . Christian Mysticism: Transcending Techniques: A Theological Reflection on the Empirical Testing of the Teaching of St. John of the Cross. Assen: Van Gorcum, 1977. xix,304p. Summary in Dutch. Includes bibliographical references.
Originally presented as a thesis, Catholic University, Nijmegen. Studies the contemplative traditions of Spanish mysticism.

B283   Gopi Krishna, 1903- . The Awakening of Kundalini. New
       York: Dutton, 1975. xii,129p. LC 74-28323

B284   Gössmann, Wilhelm. Die Kunst, Blumen zu stecken: e.
       Schule d. Lebendigen u. Meditativen, ostasiat.-europ.
       Frankfurt am Main: Insel-Verlag, 1980. 99p. (German)

B285   Govinda, Anagarika Brahmacari. Creative Meditation and
       Multi-Dimensional Consciousness, by Lama Amagrika
       Govinda (Anagavajra Knamsum Wangchuk). Wheaton, Ill.:
       Theosophical Pub. House, 1978. Also, London: Mandala
       Books, 1977. Orig. pub., Wheaton, Ill.: Theosophical
       Pub. House, 1976. Dist. by DeVorss & Co., Marina del
       Rey, Calif.: xii,294p. Includes bibliographical references.
       Also pub. in German as Schöpferische Meditation und
       multidemensionales.
       A variety of topics related to the contemplative life are pre-
       sented in a series of essays. Does not give rules or tech-
       niques for meditation.

B286   _____. Foundations of Tibetan Mysticism, According to
       the Esoteric Teachings of the Great Mantra, Om Mani
       Padme Hûm. Photographic plates by Li Gotami. New
       York: Samuel Weiser, 1974 and previous editions. Also,
       London: Rider, 1970 and previous editions. Orig. pub.,
       London: Rider, 1960. 311p. Translation of Grundlagen
       tibetischer Mystik. Bibliography: p.293-297.

B287   _____. Grundlagen tibetischer Mystik: nach d. esoter,
       Lehren d. Grossen Mantra Om Mani Padme Hûm. Frank-
       furt am Main: Fischer-Taschenbuch-Verlag, 1979 und
       1975. Also, Bern, München, und Wein: Barth, 1975;
       Weilheim/Obb.: Barth, 1972; und Zürich und Stuttgart:
       Rascher, 1966. 385p. (German)

B288   _____. Mandala: Meditationsgedichte und Betrachtungen.
       Mit fünfzehn Reproduktionen von Gemälden und Zeich-
       nungen des Verfassers. 3. erw. Aufl. Zürich: Origo,
       1978. Orig. pub., 1960. 168p. Cover title: Mandala:
       der heilige Kreis: Stufen der Meditation. (German)

B289   _____. Schöpferische Meditation und multidimensionales
       Bewusstsein. 2. Aufl. Freiburg im Breisgau: Aurum-
       Verlag, 1982. Orig. pub., 1977. 330. Includes bib-
       liographical references. Also pub. in English as Creative
       Meditation and Multi-Dimensional Consciousness. (German)

B290   Green, Elmer, 1917- , and Alyce Green. Beyond Biofeed-
       back. New York: Dell Publishing Co., 1978. Orig.
       pub., New York: Delacorte Press/S. Lawrence, 1977.
       xiv,369p. Bibliography: 344-354. LC 77-3256

B291   , and   . Biofeedback, eine neue Möglichkeit zu heilen. Freiburg i.Br.: Bauer, 1978. 394p. Einheitssacht: Beyond Biofeedback. (German)

B292   Gregg, Richard Bartlett, 1885- . Self-Transcendence. London: Gollancz, 1956. 224p. LC 57-41652

B293   Gregorius I, the Great, Saint, Pope, 540(ca.)-604. Prière pure et pureté du coeur; textes de saint Grégoire le Grand et saint Jean de la Croix, groupés et illustrés par dom Georges Lefebvre. Paris: Desclée, De Brouwer, 1953. 154p. (French)

B294   Gstrein, Heinz, 1941- . Islamische Sufi-Meditation für Christen. Wien, Freiburg, und Basel: Herder, 1977. 75p. LC 78-400751 (German)

B295   Guillerand, Augustin, 1877-1945. The Prayer of the Presence of God. Translated from the French by a monk of Parkminster. Wilkes-Barre, Pa.: Dimension Books, 1966. 191p. Translation of Face à Dieu. Includes bibliographical references. LC 66-22876

B296   Guimarães, Iris Fossati. Tua mente é um foco irradiante. Porto Alegre: [s.n.], 1974. 72p. LC 75-566359 (Portuguese)

B297   Gunther, Bernard. Dying for Enlightenment: Living with Bhagwan Shree Rajneesh. Photographed by Swami Krishna Bharti. San Francisco: Harper & Row, 1979. 151p. LC 78-15841

B298   Haack, Friedrich-Wilhelm. Transzendentale Meditation: Maharishi Mahesh Yogi; Weltplan; RRAe.V. München: Evangelischer Presseverband für Bayern, 1980, and 1976. 48p. (German)

B299   Haas, Harry. Leben wird es geben: Beispiele zur Meditation in d. Liturgie. Graz, Wien, and Köln: Verlag Styria, 1977. 125p. (German)

B300   Haddon, David. Transcendental Meditation: A Christian View. Madison, Wisconsin: Inter-Varsity Press, 1975, 1976 printing. 30p. Bibliography: p.30.

B301   , and Vail Hamilton. TM Wants You! A Christian Response to Transcendental Meditation. Grand Rapids, Mich.: Baker Book House, 1976. 204p. Includes bibliographical references.

B302   Haendler, Otto, 1890- . Meditation als Lebenspraxis. Mit einem Geleitwort von Joachim Scharfenberg. Göttingen: Vandenhoeck und Ruprecht, 1977. 119p. LC 77-556993 (German)

B303 Hall, Manly Palmer, 1901- . Meditation Disciplines and Personal Integration. Los Angeles, Calif.: Philosophical Research Society, 1979. Dist. by DeVorss & Co., Marina del Rey, Calif. 76p. LC 79-3691

B304 Halpern, Steven. Tuning the Human Instrument: An Owner's Manual. Palo Alto, Calif.: Spectrum Research Institute, 1978. 172p. Bibliography: p.151-158.

B305 Hamilton-Merritt, Jane. A Meditator's Diary: A Western Woman's Unique Experiences in Thailand Monasteries. Harmondsworth [etc.]: Penguin, 1979. Also, New York: Pocket Books, 1977. Orig. pub., London: Souvenir Press, and New York: Harper & Row, 1976. 156p. Bibliography: p.149.

B306 _____. Wandlung durch Meditation: d. einzigartigen Erfahrungen e. Frau aus d. Westen in Thailands Klöstern. Olten und Freiburg im Breisgau: Walter, 1981. 186p. Einheitssacht.: A Meditator's Diary. (German)

B307 Hanson, Bradley. The Call of Silence: Discovering Christian Meditation. Minneapolis: Augsburg, 1980. 140p. LC 80-67794

B308 Hanssen, Olav, and Reinhard Deichgräber. Leben heisst sehen: Anleitung zur Meditation. 4. Aufl. Göttingen: Vandenhoeck und Ruprecht, 1976 and previous editions. Orig. pub., 1968. 115p. Includes music. Includes bibliographical references. LC 72-357542 (German)

B309 Happold, Frederick Crossfield, 1893- . The Journey Inwards: A Simple Introduction to the Practice of Contemplative Meditation by Normal People. Atlanta: Knox Press, 1975. 142p. Reprint of 1968 ed. pub. by Darton, Longman & Todd, London. Bibliography: p.137-142. LC 75-13460
Drawing on Eastern mysticism, the author provides practical exercises for this type of prayer, with an emphasis on the Christian experience.

B310 _____. Prayer and Meditation: Their Nature and Practice. Harmondsworth: Penguin, 1971. 381p. Includes music. Includes bibliographical references. LC 72-176065

B311 Hari Dass, Baba. A Child's Garden of Yoga. Photographs by Steven N. Thomas (Mukund). Santa Cruz, Calif.:

Sri Rama Pub., 1980. 108p. LC 80-80299
Illustrates the three basic locks, deep breathing, exercises,
meditation, and simple portures of Yoga practice. Juvenile
literature.

B312 Harrington, John, 1923- . The Teaching of William Joseph
Chaminade on Mental Prayer. Dayton, Ohio: Marianist
Press, 1961. 173p.

B313 Harrison, Alan, 1920- . Watch and Pray. London: Guild
of Health, 1975. [2],9p. (Guild of Health Publications;
n.15)

B314 Harrison, Alton, Jr., and Diann Musial. Other Ways Other
Means: Altered Awareness Activities for Receptive Learning: Practical Teaching Strategies for the Use of Relaxation, Imagery, Dreams, Suggestology-Hypnosis, Meditation. Santa Monica, Calif.: Goodyear Pub. Co., 1978.
112p. Includes bibliographies. LC 77-14045

B315 Hauth, Rüdiger. Transzendentale Meditation, neue Wege zum
Heil? Gladbeck: Schrifenmissions-Verlag, 1979. 44p.
(German)

B316 Hayden, Eric William. Meditation: The Key to Expanded
Consciousness. Bognor Regis, W. Sussex: New Horizon,
1978. [5],ii,80p.

B317 Healing Implications for Psychotherapy. Edited by James L.
Fosshage and Paul Olsen, with Kenneth A. Frank ... [et
al.]. New York: Human Science Press, 1978. 388p.
(New Directions in Psychotherapy; v.2) Includes bib-
liographies. LC 77-25917
Includes two chapters on meditation.

B318 Heidelberg, Rainer. Transzendentale Meditation in der
geburtshilflichen Psychoprophylaxe: e. retrospektive
Unters. an 108 TM-Geburten u. 231 Kontrollen. Husum:
Hannesmann, 1981. 86p. (German)
This book on child-bearing and Transcendental Meditation
was the author's 1979 dissertation at Freie Univ., Berlin.
[Cf. D92]

B319 Heimler, Adolf. Selbsterfahrung und Glaube: Gruppendy-
namik, Tiefenpsychologie u. Meditation als Wege zur
religiösen Praxis. München: Pfeiffer, 1976. 358p.
(Pfeiffer-Werkbücher; Nr.132) Bibliography: p.353-354.
LC 77-450283 (German)

B320 Heinrichsbauer, Johannes. Buch der Besinnung. Anregungen
zu Betrachtung u. priesterl. Werk. Köln: Verl. Wort u.
Werk, 1954. 316p. (German)

B321 Heitmann, Claus: Gelebte Wahrheit: Stationen im Christus-
jahr; e. Leitf. zur bibl. Besinnung. Neukirchen-Vluyn,
Neukirchener Verlag, 1976. 174p. (German)

B322 Helleberg, Marilyn Morgan. Beyond TM: A Practical Guide
to the Lost Traditions of Christian Meditation. New York:
Paulist Press, 1980. x,129p. LC 80-82811

B323 Hemingway, Patricia Drake. The Transcendental Meditation
Primer: How to Stop Tension and Start Living. New
York: Dell Pub. Co., 1976. Orig. pub., New York:
D. McKay, 1975. xviii,264p. Bibliography: p.252-254.
Presents an overview of scientific research on TM and her
own experiences and observations. Statements from other
practitioners are included.

B324 Herausforderung, religiöse Erfahrung: vom Verhältnis
evangelischer Frömmigkeit zu Meditation und Mystik.
Hrsg. von Horst Reller und Manfred Seitz. Göttingen:
Vandenhoeck & Ruprecht, 1980. 212p. Includes bibliographies. LC 81-104300 (German)
Chiefly papers of the 23rd Pastoralkolleg of the VELKD held
in Bergkirchen-Lippe, Sept. 1976.

B325 Hertzog, Stuart P., 1945- . An Introduction to Meditation:
From the Teachings of Namgyal Rimpoche. Edmonton:
Pegasus, 1982.

B326 Herz, Stephanie M. My Words Are Spirit and Life: Meeting
Christ Through Daily Meditation. Garden City, N.Y.:
Image Books, 1979. 144p. Includes bibliographical ref-
erences. LC 78-4790

B327 Hewitt, James, 1928- . The Complete Yoga Book: Yoga of
Breathing, Yoga of Posture, and Yoga of Meditation. New
York: Schocken Books, 1978. xiv,550p. Bibliography:
p.544-550. LC 77-15934

B328 _____. Meditation. Illustrations by John Herring. Sev-
enoaks: Teach Yourself Books, and New York: David
McKay, 1978. [8],198p. Bibliography: p.187-181.

B329 _____. Yoga and Meditation. London: Barrie & Jenkins,
1977. vi,163p. Bibliography: p.161-163. LC 78-304270

B330 Hills, Christopher B. Into Meditation Now: A Course on
Direct Enlightenment. Boulder Creek, Calif.: University
of the Trees Press, 1979. xiii,100p. At head of title:
Introduction and Section Zero. LC 79-5124

B331 Hintersberger, Benedikta. Mit Jugendlichen meditieren:

Methoden, Einstiege, Texte. München: Don-Bosco-Verlag, 1981. 124p. (German)

B332　Hirai, Tomio, 1927- . Psychophysiology of Zen. With a postscript by William Johnston. Tokyo: Igaku Shoin, 1974. vi,147p. Bibliography: p.135-141. LC 74-175971
Combines a description of physiological changes during meditation with an historical overview to the religious and spiritual nature of Zen.

B333　＿＿＿＿. Zen and the Mind: Scientific Approach to Zen Practice. Tokyo: Japan Publications, 1978. 144p.

B334　＿＿＿＿. Zen Meditation Therapy. Tokyo: Japan Publications, 1975. Dist. in U.S. by Japan Publications Trading Co., Elmsford, N.Y. 103p. Orig. ed. pub. in Japanese by the Goma Shobo, Ltd., Tokyo, in 1974.
A Japanese psychiatrist presents findings concerning Zen meditation in the treatment of neuroses along with techniques and exercises.

B335　Hittleman, Richard L. Richard Hittleman's Guide to Yoga Meditation. New York: Bantam Books, 1969. 192p.

B336　＿＿＿＿. Richard Hittleman's 30 Day Yoga Meditation Plan. Photography by Thomas Burke. Illustrated by Robert Carlon. New York: Bantam Books, and London: Corgi, 1978. 215p. LC 78-104904
A daily meditation guide explaining techniques of visualization, breathing, yantra, mantra, and asanas.

B337　＿＿＿＿. Yoga Philosophy and Meditation: An Interpretation. Los Angeles: Hittleman, 1974. 37p.

B338　Ho, Van H. Moving Meditation: Enlightenment of the Mind and Total Fitness. Harbor City, Calif.: Van H. Ho, Assocs., 1979. 214p. LC 79-88748

B339　Hodgson, Joan. Planetary Harmonies: An Astrological Book of Meditation. Illustrated by Margaret Clarke. Liss: White Eagle Publishing Trust, 1980. 151p.

B340　Hof, Hans, and Wilfrid Stinissen, Utg., Meditation och mystik. En antologi on djupmeditation, mystik erfarenhet, avspänning. Stockholm: Verbum, 1972. 292p. Includes bibliographical references. LC 72-366781 (Swedish)

B341　Die Höhle des Herzens: Mantra-Praxis u. Namensgebet. Hrsg. von Willi Massa. Beitr. von Franz Xaver Jans. Kevelaer: Butzon und Bercker, 1982. 129p. (German)

B342 Hollings, Robert. Transcendental Meditation: An Introduction to the Practice and Aims of TM. Wellingborough: Aquarian, 1982. 96p.

B343 Holmes, Stewart Walker, and Chimyo Horioka. Zen Art for Meditation. Rutland, Vt.: C.E. Tuttle Co., 1973. 115p. LC 73-78279

B344 Hoppenworth, Klaus. Neue Heilswege aus Fernost, Hilfen oder Gefahren?: Information u. Auseinandersetzung mit Yoga, Autogenem Training, Transzendentaler Meditation u. Hare Krishna. Bad Liebenzell: Verlag der Liebenzeller Mission, 1978. 127p. (German)

B345 Hübener, Christian. Meditation. Düsseldorf: Georgs-Verlag, 1973. 22p. (German)

B346 Huber, Jack T. Psychotherapy and Meditation. London: Victor Gollancz, 1965. 128p. LC 66-93074

B347 _____. Through an Eastern Window. New York: St. Martin's Press, 1975? Also, Toronto and New York: Bantam, 1968, and Boston: Houghton Mifflin, 1967, c1965. 121p. LC 75-29928

B348 Huelsman, Richard J. Pray: Participant's Handbook. New York: Paulist Press, 1976. 129p. LC 78-322675

B349 Hulme, William Edward, 1920- . Let the Spirit In: Practicing Christian Devotional Meditation. Nashville: Abingdon, 1979. 94p. LC 78-26739

B350 Humphreys, Christmas, 1901- . Concentration and Meditation: A Manual of Mind Development. New York: Penguin Books, 1976 and previous editions. Also, London: Stuart and Watkins, 1973 and previous editions. Orig. pub., London: The Buddhist Lodge, 1935. xvi,343,[1]p. The greater part of this book was previously published in serial form between September, 1933 and March, 1935, in the magazine, Buddhism in England.

B351 _____. The Search Within: A Course in Meditation. London: Sheldon Press, and New York: Oxford University Press, 1977. 160p. Bibliography: p.159-160.

B352 Huntley, Frank Livingstone, 1902- . Bishop Joseph Hall and Protestant Meditation in Seventeenth-Century England: A Study with Texts of "The Art of Divine Meditation" (1606) and "Occasional Meditations" (1633). Binghampton, N.Y.: Center for Medieval & Early Renaissance Studies, 1981. 219p. (Medieval & Renaissance

Texts & Studies; v.1)   Includes bibliographical references.
LC 81-183427

B353   Hyatt, Christopher S.   Undoing Yourself with Energized
Meditation and Other Devices.   Phoenix, Ariz.:   Falcon
Press, 1982.   112p.

B354   Ichazo, Oscar, 1931-   .   The Human Process for Enlightenment and Freedom: A Series of Five Lectures.   Limited
edition.   New York: Arica Institute, Inc., for Simon &
Schuster, N.Y., 1976.   120p.   LC 75-37075

B355   Imbert, Jean Claude.   L'exploration de la conscience.   Paris:
Tchou, 1978.   274p.   Includes bibliographical references.
LC 78-392252   (French)

B356   Inayat Khan, (Pir-Zade) Vilayat.   Stufen einer Meditation.
Nach Zeugnissen der Sufi.   Vorw. von Henry Corbin.
Autoris.   Übers. d₀ Franz.   Original-Ms.:   Ursula v.
Mangoldt.   Weilheim Obb.:   O.W₀ Barth, 1962.   124p.
(German)

B357   Ingraham, E.V.   Meditation in the Silence.   Lee's Summit,
Mo.:   Unity School of Christianity, 1969.   Dist. by De-
Vorss & Co., Marina del Rey, Calif.   59p.
A textbook discussing the principles and practices of the
use of silence as a form of meditation bringing man into an
understanding relationship with God.

B358   Iranschähr, Hossein Kazemzadeh.   Konzentration und Meditation.   Eine Einf.   Olten: Amadeo-Verl., 1951.   78p.
(German)

B359   Isbert, Otto Albrecht.   Heilkraft im Yoga für Körper un
Geist.   Ein Kompendium für die tägliche Praxis.   München:
Drei Eichen Verlag, 1964.   73p.   (Heilwissen für jeder-
mann, Folge 11)   LC 68-69664   (German)

B360   _____.   Konzentration und schöpferisches Denken.   Praktische Übungswege.   Heidenheim: E. Hoffmann, 1962.
250p.   Mit Literaturverz: p.247-250.   (German)

B361   _____.   Raja-Yoga, der königliche Weg er Selbstmeisterung
in westlicher Sicht und Praxis.   Büdingen-Haingründau:
Verlags-Union, 1955.   107p.   (German)

B362   _____.   Yoga, Arbeit am Selbst.   Raja-Kriya-Praxis mit
einem Atemzyklus.   Mitwirkung von Irene Horbat.   Heidenheim: E. Hoffmann, 1960,.   179p.   (German)

B363   _____, and Irene Horbat, Hrsg.   Sadhana; Studien- und

Übungshefte zum Raja- und Kriya-Yoga. Heidenheim und
Brenz: E. Hoffmann, 1960- (German)

B364 Isherwood, Christopher, 1904- . My Guru and His Disciple.
New York: Penguin Books, 1981. Orig. pub., London:
Eyre Methuen, and New York: Farrar, Straus & Giroux,
1980. 338p. LC 80-29158
The author discusses his relationship with Swami Prabhava-
nanda.

B365 _____. Ramakrishna and His Disciples. 2nd ed. Hollywood, Calif.: Vedanta Press, 1980. Also, New York:
Simon and Schuster, 1970; and Calcutta: Advaita Ashram,
1969. Orig. pub., Methuen, and New York: Simon and
Schuster, 1965. 337p. Bibliography: p.335-337. LC
65-17100

B366 Ital, Gerta. Auf dem Wege zu Satori. Übersinnl. Erfahrungen
u. d. Erlebnis d. Erleuchtung. Weilheim/Obb.: O.W.
Barth, 1971. 272p. On spine: Satori. LC 79-25073
(German)

B367 _____. Meditationen aus dem Geist des Zen: d. grosse
Umwandlung zur Selbstbefreiung. Olten und Freiburg im
Breisgau: Walter, 1977. 228p. (German)

B367K Jacobson, Edmund, 1888- . Progressive Relaxation: A
Physiological and Clinical Investigation of Muscular States
and Their Significance in Psychology and Medical Practice.
Midway reprint. Chicago: The University of Chicago
Press, 1974, c1929. Also, 1968 and 1959 reprints of the
2nd ed., 1938. Orig. pub., 1929. xvii,493p. Bibliography: p.432-476.

B368 Janakananda Saraswati, Swami, 1939- . Yoga, Tantra and
Meditation in Daily Life. Translated from the Swedish by
Sheila LaFarge. Photographs by Chris Stuhr. London:
Rider, 1978. Orig. pub. as Yoga, Tantra and Meditation
in Your Daily Life, New York: Ballantine Books, 1976.
112p. Translation of Yoga, tantra, och meditation i min
vardag. Stockholm: Bonniers Förlag, 1975. LC 76-13536

B369 Jefferson, William. The Story of the Maharishi. New York:
Pocket Books, 1976. 128p.
Discusses the Maharishi Mahesh Yogi and his movement.

B370 Johne, Karin. Meditation für Kranke: e. Anleitung.
Zürich, Einsiedeln und Köln: Benziger, 1979. 132p.
(German)

B371 _____. Ökumenische Meditationsbriefe: für Kranke u.

Körperbehinderte u. für Gesunde. Berlin: Evangelische Verlagsanstalt, 1977. 123p. (German)

B372 Johnson, Willard L. Riding the Ox Home: A History of Meditation from Shamanism to Science. London: Rider, 1982. 261p. Bibliography: p.242-246.

B373 Johnston, William, 1925- . Christian Zen. 2nd rev. ed. San Francisco: Harper & Row, 1981, c1979. Also, Dublin: Gill and Macmillan, 1979, and New York: Harper & Row, 1974. Orig. pub., New York and London: Harper & Row, 1971. 134p. Includes bibliographical references. LC 80-8430
Provides guidelines for a way of Christian meditation that incorporates Eastern traditions.

B374 _____. Klang der Stille: Meditation in Medizin u. Mystik. Mainz: Matthias-Grünewald-Verlag, 1978. 172p. Einheitssacht.: Silent Music.

B375 _____. Silent Music: The Science of Meditation. New York and San Francisco: Harper & Row, and London: Fontana, 1976. Also, New York: Harper & Row, 1975. Orig. pub., London: Collins, and New York: Harper & Row, 1974.
A comparative study of religious meditation in the Zen and Christian traditions. Discusses experimental and scientific exploration of altered states of consciousness.

B376 Jones-Ryan, Maureen. Meditation Without Frills: A Woman's Workbook. Cambridge, Mass.: Schenckman Pub. Co., 1976. Dist. by Two Continents Pub. Group, New York. 145p. Bibliography: p.140-143. LC 76-16206

B377 Jorban, E. Meet Your Guru: How to Unlock Your Soul. Hicksville, N.Y.: Exposition Press, 1977. 48p.

B378 Joubert, L.E. Au bout de la pensée. Paris: Les Editions du Scorpion, Promotion et Edition, 1967. 96p. LC 68-95490 (French)

B379 Jungclaussen, Emmanuel. De innerlijke grond: de wereld in ons innerlijk ontdekken aan de hand van Johan Tauler. Haarlem: J.H. Gottmer, 1976. 85p. Translation of Der Meister in dir. (Dutch)

B380 _____. Der Meister in dir: Entdeckungen der inneren Welt nach Johannes Tauler. 3. Aufl. Freiburg im Breisgau: Herder, 1977. Orig. pub., 1975. 142p. (German)

B381 Jyotirmayananda Saraswati, Swami, 1943- . Meditate the

Tantric Yoga Way. Translated and edited by Lilian K.
Donat. London: Allen and Unwin, and New York:
Dutton, 1973. 117p. LC 73-161755

B382 _____. Praxis der Meditation. Theorie und Anleitung zu
10 Techniken. Hrsg. vom Österr. Yogaverband. Wein:
Verl. d. Palme, 1970. 111p. LC 79-866995 (German)

B383 Kamalaśila, fl. 762. La progression dans la méditation
(Bhāvanākrama de Kamalaśila). Traduit du sanscrit et
du tibétain par José van den Broeck. Bruxelles: Institut belge des hautes études boudhiques, 1977. xii,59p.
(Publications de l'Institut belge des hautes études boudhiques: Série Etudes et textes; no.6) Bibliography:
leaves 57-59. LC 78-389148 (French)

B384 Kampf, Harold. In Search of Serenity: A Guide to Suc-
cessful Meditation. Wellingborough: Thorsons, 1976.
Orig. pub., 1974. Dist. in U.S. by British Book Center,
Elmsford, N.Y. 63p. Bibliography: p.63.

B385 Kanellakos, Demetri P., and Jerome S. Lukas, 1930- . The
Psychobiology of Transcendental Meditation: A Literature
Review. Menlo Park, Calif., and London [etc.]: W.A.
Benjamin, 1974. xiii,158p. Orig. pub. as The Psycho- /
biology of Transcendental Meditation: A Literature Review:
Final Report. Menlo Park, Calif.: Stanford Research In-
stitute, 1973.
A comprehensive review of the published and unpublished
scientific and popular literature available up to about January
1974 in the field of Transcendental Meditation.

B386 _____, and Phillip C. Ferguson. The Psychobiology of
Transcendental Meditation: An Annotated Bibliography:
Spring 1973. Los Angeles: Maharishi International Uni-
versity, 1973? 29p. At head of title: International
Center for Scientific Research.

B387 Kaplan, Aryeh. Meditation and the Bible. New York:
Samuel Weiser, 1981, c1978. 179p. Includes bibliographical references. LC 79-101522

B388 Kapur, Teg Bahadur, 1922- . Dhyana Mandala: Meditating
for Self Realisation. Delhi: Shiksa Bharati, 1978. 120p.

B389 Karg, Cassian. Das kleine Geheimnis. Unser Herzensgebet.
Kirnach-Villigen/Schwarzw.: Verl. der Schulbrüder,
1967. 47p. (German)

B390 Kasdin, Simon. Mantra Yoga: 3000 Years of Great Cosmic
Echoes. Convent, N.J.: Emerson Society, 1964. 128p.

B391   Kaushik, R.P., 1926- . Energy Beyond Thought: Self-
        Enquiry Retreat, Sora, Italy, 1975. Ipswich, Mass.:
        Journal Publications, 1977. 123p. LC 76-39623

B392   . Light of Exploration: Talks on Meditation, San
        Francisco, 1975. Ipswich, Mass.: Journey Publications,
        1977. Dist. by DeVorss & Co., Marina del Rey, Calif.
        69p. LC 76-39622

B393   Kauz, Herman. Tai Chi Handbook: Exercises, Meditation,
        and Self-Defense. Garden City, N.Y.: Dolphin Books,
        1974. 174p. Includes bibliographical references. LC
        73-10552

B394   Keck, L. Robert, 1935- . The Spirit of Synergy: God's
        Power and You. Nashville: Abingdon, 1978. 159p.
        Bibliography: p.157-159. LC 78-732
        Suggests that Christians should make use of meditative
        prayer and suggests techniques. Describes his personal
        experience with pain.

B395   Kelsey, Morton T. The Other Side of Silence: A Guide to
        Christian Meditation. London: S.P.C.K., 1977. Orig.
        pub., New York: Paulist Press, 1976. viii,314p.
        Shows how Christian meditation is available to any ordinary
        person who wishes to use it. Discusses attitudes and meth-
        ods of meditation within the Christian tradition and modern
        depth psychology.

B396   Keshavadas, Swami, 1934- . This Is Wisdom: Mystical
        Teachings of Yoga, Meditation, and Love. Detroit, Mich.:
        Temple of Cosmic Religion, 1975. 96p.

B397   Khantipalo, Bhikku. Calm and Insight: A Buddhist Manual
        for Meditators. London: Curzon Press, 1981. Dist. in
        U.S. by Humanities Press, Atlantic Highlands, N.J.
        viii,152p.

B398   King, Winston Lee, 1907- . Theravada Meditation: The
        Buddhist Transformation of Yoga. University Park:
        Pennsylvania State University Press, 1980. viii,172p.
        Bibliography: p.163-166. LC 79-25856

B399   Kirpal Singh, 1894-1974. The Teachings of Kirpal Singh.
        Compiled and selected from the writings of Kirpal Singh
        by Ruth Seader. Bowling Green, Va.: Sawan Kirpal
        Publications, 1981. 3 vols. in 1. Includes bibliographi-
        cal references. V.1. The Holy Path. V.2. Self-
        Introspection & Meditation. V.3. The New Life. Also
        pub. in 3 vols., Sanbornton, N.Y.: Sant Bani Ashram,
        1974-1976.

B400 Klang, Gary. La méditation transcendantale: l'enseignement de Maharishi Mahesh Yogi. Préf. de Roger Marcaurelle. Montréal: A. Stanké, 1975, tirage de 1976. 174p. Includes bibliographical references. (French)

B401 Klein, Aaron E., and Cynthia L. Klein. Mind Trips: The Story of Consciousness-Raising Movements. Garden City, N.Y.: Doubleday, 1979. 110p. LC 78-2231
Discusses the background of the consciousness revolution, the many philosophies connected with it, including TM, est, and hari krishna, and its effect on the American way of life. Juvenile literature.

B402 Klon-chen-pa Dri-med-od-zer, 1308-1367. Kindly Bent to Ease Us. Translated from the Tibetan and annotated by Herbert V. Guenther. Emeryville, Calif.: Dharma Pub., 1976- (Tibetan Translation Series) Includes bibliographies. (Part 2: Meditation) LC 75-29959

B403 Kniffki, Christa, 1944- . Transzendentale Meditation und Autogenes Training: e. Vergleich. Mit e. Vorw. von Hans Selye u. e. Nachw. "Erfahrungen mit dem TM-Sidhi-Programm," von B.F. Zeiger. München: Kindler, 1979. 192p. Bibliography: p.143-149. LC 79-395686 (German) [Cf. D118]

B404 Knight, Harry G. An Introduction to Ethical Meditation. London: South Place Ethical Society, 1968. 13p. LC 68-113582

B405 Kohler, Mariane. La quête du gourou. Paris: Epi, 1977. 147p. LC 77-550497 (French)

B406 Kollander, Kathy, 1958- . TM Is for Kids, Too!: "Inside & Outside": A Story. Illustrated by Connie Sorensen. Designed, edited and compiled by Cielle Kollander. Mill-brae, Calif.: Celestial Arts, 1977. 72p. Includes bibliography. LC 76-53335
A simple introduction to the techniques of Transcendental Meditation. Juvenile literature.

B407 Kongtrul, Jamgon. Das Licht der Gewissheit. Freiburg im Breisgau: Aurum-Verlag, 1979. 219p. (German)

B407K _____. The Torch of Certainty. Translated from the Tibetan by Judith Hanson. Foreword by Chogyam Trung-pa. Boulder, Colo.: Prajna Press, 1983. Orig. pub., Boulder, Colo.: Shambhala, 1977. xvii,161p. (The Clear Light Series) LC 82-24522

B408 Kornfield, Jack, 1945- A Brief Guide to Meditation Tem-

ples of Thailand, by Sunno Bhikkhu [i.e. J. Kornfield].
Bangkok: Thaikasen Press, 1972. 62p. (World Fellowship of Buddhists Books Series; no.44)

B409 _____. Living Buddhist Masters. Boulder, Colo.: Prajna
Press/Shambhala Publications, Inc., 1983. xiii,334p.
Reprint. Orig. pub.: Santa Cruz, Calif.: Unity Press,
1977. LC 83-2260
Includes interviews and discourses by such masters of the
Theravada Buddhist school of meditation as Achaan Chaa,
Mahasi Sayadaw and U Ba Khin. Gives biographical infor-
mation on their particular techniques.

B410 Kory, Robert B. The Transcendental Meditation Program
for Business People. New York: AMACOM, 1976. 91p.
Bibliography: p.89-91. LC 76-3696
Cites scientific studies which show the effects of TM on the
brain, nervous system and heart. Compares the effects of
TM and non-meditation practices. Discusses management theory and the relationship of TM to the future of business.

B411 Köster, Peter. Ich gebe euch ein neues Herz: Einf. u.
Hilfen zu d. Geistlichen Übungen d. Ignatius von Loyola.
Stuttgart: Verlag Katholisches Bibelwerk, 1978. 175p.
(German)

B412 _____. Lebensorientierung an der Bibel: Meditationsim-
pulse zum Exerzitienbuch d. Ignatius von Loyola. Stuttgart: Verlag Katholisches Bibelwerk, 1978. 248p.
(German)

B413 Kramer, Joel, 1937- . The Passionate Mind: A Manual for
Living Creatively with One's Self. Assisted by Jules
Kanarek. Drawings by Dora Cornwall Kramer. Millbrae,
Calif.: Celestial Arts, 1974. vi,122p. LC 74-6047

B414 Kranenborg, R. Transcendente meditatie: velangen naar
zinvol leven en religie. Kampen: Kok, 1977. 132p.
Bibliography: p.129-132. LC 79-37822 (Dutch)

B415 Kravette, Steve. Complete Meditation. Rockport, Mass.:
Para Research, 1982. 320p.
Presents a broad range of metaphysical concepts and medi-
tation techniques.

B416 Kripalvanandji, Swami, 1913-1981. Science of Meditation.
Kayavarohan, India: Sri Kayavarohan Tirth Seva Samaj,
1977. Dist. in U.S. by Kripalu Yoga Retreat, Summit
Station, Pa. xx,208p. Includes bibliographical references. LC 77-906482

B417   Krishnamurti, Jiddu, 1895- . Meditationen. Berlin: Arbeitsgemeinschaft Krishnamurti; Berlin: E. Schmidt [in Komm.], 1969. 35p. (German)

B418   _____. The Only Revolution. Edited by Mary Lutyens. New York: Harper & Row, 1977. Orig. pub., London: Gollancz, and New York: Harper & Row, 1970. 175p.

B419   _____. Revolution durch Meditation. Bern, Frankfurt am Main, und Salzburg: Humata-Verlag Blume, 1981. 188p. Einheitssacht.: The Only Revolution. (German)

B420   Krishnananda, Swami. Meditation: Its Theory and Practice. 2nd ed. Shivanandanagar, U.P.: Divine Life Society, 1974. vi,80p. LC 77-911322

B421   Kroll, Una. The Healing Potential of Transcendental Meditation. Atlanta: John Knox Press, 1974. 176p. Orig. pub. as TM: A Signpost for the World. London: Darton, Longman & Todd, 1974. Includes bibliographical references. LC 74-7615
Discusses the similarities and differences between Christian prayer and TM. Strongly suggests the benefits of TM in healing. The author is an English physician.

B422   _____. La méditation transcendantale: une méthode de relaxation et de prière pour tous. Traduit de l'anglais par Jean Prignaud. 2e ed. Paris: Editions du Cerf, 1976, c1975. 150p. Bibliography: p.147. (French)

B423   Kühlewind, Georg. Die Wahrheit tun: Erfahrung u. Konsequenzen d. intuitiven Denkens. 2. Aufl., Stuttgart: Verlag Freies Geistesleben, 1982. Orig. pub., 1978. 205p. Includes bibliographical references. LC 80-461843 (German)

B424   Kurtz, Waldemar. Das Kleinod in der Lotos-Blüte: Zen-Meditation heute. Stuttgart: Günther, 1972. 150p. (German)

B425   Kushi, Michio. Michio Kushi's Do-In-Buch: Übungen zur körperl. u. geistigen Entwicklung. Frankfurt am Main: Martin; und Werbeln: Ost-West-Bund e. V., 1980. 312p. (German)

B426   Lalita. Choose Your Own Mantra. Drawings by Kevin Miller. New York, Toronto and London: Bantam, 1978. xii,212p. Bibliography: p.211-212.

B427   Lalitananda, Swami. Yoga Mystic Songs for Meditation. Miami, Fla.: Swami Lalitananda, 1975. Dist. by Yoga Research Foundation, Miami, Fla. 4 vols.

B428   Lamott, Kenneth Church, 1923- . Escape from Stress: How
        to Stop Killing Yourself. New York: Putnam, 1974. Dist.
        by Berkely Pub. Corp., New York. 211p. Bibliography:
        p.209-211. LC 74-79655

B429   Langen, Dietrich. Archaische Ekstase und asiatische Medi-
        tation mit ihren Beziehungen zum Abendland. Stuttgart:
        Hippokrates-Verlag, 1963. 128p. (German)

B430   Lanphear, Roger G., 1936- . Freedom from Crime Through
        the TM--Sidhi Program. New York: Nellen Pub. Co.,
        1979. xvi,205p. Bibliography: p.191-201. LC 78-2647

B431   Lanza del Vasto, Joseph Jean, 1901- . Approches de la vie
        Intérieure. Paris: Denoël, 1962. 333p. LC 65-46358
        (French)

B432   Lapauw, Camillus. Christliche Tiefenmeditation. München:
        Verlag Ars Sacra, 1974. 31p. (German)

B433   Lassalle, Hugo, 1898- . Erfahrungen eines Christen mit
        der Zen-Meditation. Bearb. und eingeführt von Waltraud
        Herbstrith (Teresia a Matre Dei OCD). Bergen-Enheim
        bei Frankfurt/M.: G. Kaffke, 1975. 46p. (Schriften-
        reihe zur Meditation; Nr.16) (German)

B434   _____ . Meditation als Weg zur Gotteserfahrung. Mainz:
        Matthias-Grünewald-Verlag, 1980. Nachdr. d. Ausg.
        Köln: Bachem, 1972. 107p. (German)

B435   _____ . El Zen. Bilbao: Mensajero, 1974. 244p. (Co-
        lección hombre y misterio; 3) Translation of Zen-Meditation
        für Christen. Includes bibliographical references.
        (Spanish)

B436   _____ . Zen-Meditation: eine Einfuhrung. Mit dem
        Protokoll eines Zen-Symposions zusgest. von Ruth Seu-
        bert. Zürich, Einsiedeln und Köln: Benziger, 1975.
        164p. LC 75-522508 (German)

B437   _____ . Zen Meditation for Christians. Translated by
        John C. Maraldo. LaSalle, Ill.: Open Court, 1974.
        175p. Includes bibliographical references. Translation
        of Zen Meditation für Christen.
        A comparison of Christian and Zen mysticism. Emphasizes
        the practice of Zazen. Discusses great Christian mystics
        and their mystical experiences similar to Zen masters.

B438   _____ . Zen-Meditation für Christen. Bern, München
        und Wien: Barth, 1976. Also, 1971. Orig. pub., 1969.
        208p. (German)

B439   . Zen, un camino hacia la propia identidad. 2. ed. Bilbao: Ediciones Mensajero, 1975. 154p. Translation of Zen, Weg zur Erleuchtung. (Spanish)

B440   . Zen unter Christen: östl. Meditation u. christl. Spiritualität. 2. Aufl. Graz, Wien und Köln: Verlag Styria, 1974. Orig. pub., 1973. 78p. (German)

B441   . Zen-Way to Enlightenment. London: Sheed & Ward, 1973. Also, New York: Taplinger, 1968; and London: Burns & Oates, and Montreal: Palm Publishers, 1967, c1966. 126p. Translation of Zen, Weg zur Erleuchtung.

B442   . Zen, Weg zur Erleuchtung. Hilfe z. Verständnis. Einf. in d. Meditation. Wien, Freiburg [i.Br.] und Basel: Herder, 1971 und 1969. Orig. pub., 1960. 132p. (German)

B443 Laurie, Sanders G., and Melvin J. Tucker. Centering, Your Guide to Inner Growth. New York: Destiny Book, 1983. Orig. pub., New York: Warner Books, 1978. Also pub. as Centering: The Power of Meditation. Wellingborough: Excalibur Books, 1982. 299p. LC 83-18899

B444 Lay, Rupert. Meditationstechniken für Manager. Reinbek bei Hamburg: Rowohlt, 1979. Und, München: Wirtschafsverlag Langen-Müller-Herbig, 1976. 249p. (German)

B445 Leen, Edward, 1885-1944. Progress Through Mental Prayer. New York: Arena Lettres, 1978. Earlier editions pub. by Sheed & Ward, New York. x,276p. Reprint of the ed. pub. by Sheed & Ward, London, 1935. LC 78-51560

B446 Lehodey, Vital, Fr., 1857-1948. The Ways of Mental Prayer. Translated from the French by a monk of Mount Melleray. Dublin: M.H. Gill, 1960 and previous editions. Orig. pub., 1912. Dist. in U.S. by TAN Books & Pubs., Inc., Rockford, Ill. xxxii,408p. Translation of Les voies de l'oraison mentale.

B447 Leiste, Heinrich. Vom Wesen der Meditation. 4., durchges. Aufl. Dornach: Philosophisch-Anthroposophischer Verlag, 1973. 61p. LC 74-333588 (German)

B448 Lercaro, Giacomo, Cardinal, 1891- . Methods of Mental Prayer. Translated from the Italian by T.F. Lindsay. Westminster, Md.: Newman Press, 1975. 308p. Translation of Metodi di orazione mentale. Includes bibliography. LC 57-8614
Sets forth various historical methods of Christian prayer and meditation.

B449   . Metodi di orazione mentale. 2. ed. Genova:
Bevilacqua e Solari, 1957. xix,361p. (Italian)

B450   Lerner, Eric. Journey of Insight Meditation: A Personal
Experience of the Buddha's Way. London: Turnstone
Books, and New York: Schocken Books, 1978. Orig.
pub., New York: Schocken Books, 1977. 185p.

B451   Lesh, Terry. Meditation for Young People. New York:
Lothrop, Lee & Shepard Co., 1977. 128p. LC 77-2215
Compares popular methods of meditation such as zazen,
transcendental meditation, and yoga and discusses their effects on stress and general mental health. Juvenile literature.

B452   LeShan, Lawrence L., 1920- . How to Meditate: A Guide
to Self-Discovery. Wellingborough: Turnstone, 1983.
Also, London: Sphere, 1978; London: Wildwood House,
1976; and New York: Bantam, 1975. Orig. pub., Boston: Little, Brown, 1974. Also, large print ed., Boston: G.K. Hall, 1974. Also dist. by DeVorss & Co.,
Marina del Rey, Calif. 144p.
Zen, Sufism, Yoga, and Christian and Jewish mysticism are
discussed. Breath counting, mantras, and sensory awareness are described. The author is a psychologist and parapsychological researcher.

B453   . Meditation als Lebenshilfe: [hilfreiche Methoden
zur Überwindung von berufl. u. privaten Problemen].
Bergisch Gladbach: Lübbe, 1978. Und Rüschlikon-
Zürich, Stuttgart u. Wien: Müller, 1977. 157p. Einheitssacht.: How to Meditate. (German)

B454   Levine, Stephen. A Gradual Awakening. Garden City,
N.Y.: Anchor Press, 1979. xv,173p. Bibliography:
p.161-163. LC 77-27712
The Americanization of Eastern ideas concerning meditation.

B455   Lewis, Gordon Russell, 1926- . What Everyone Should
Know About Transcendental Meditation. New York:
Pillar Books, 1977. Orig. pub., Glendale, Calif.: G/L
Regal Books, 1975. 95p. Bibliography: p.80-82.
LC 74-32326

B456   Liguori, Alfonso Maria de', Saint, 1696-1787. How to Converse Continually and Familiarly with God. Translated
by L.X. Aubin. Boston: St. Paul Editions, 1963. 75p.
LC 63-13908

B457   Lindenberg, Wladimir, 1902- . Meditation and Mankind:
Practices in Prayer and Meditation Throughout the World.

Translated from the German by Betty Collins. London: Rider, 1959. 206p. Translation of Die Menschheit betet.

B458 _____ . Die Menschheit betet: Praktiken d. Meditation in d. Welt. München und Basel: E. Reinhardt, 1977, and previous editions. 233p. (German)

B459 Linnewedel, Jürgen. Mystik, Meditation, Yoga, Zen: wie versteht man sie, wie übt man sie, wie helfen sie, heute? Mit einer Einführung von Michael Mildenberger. Stuttgart: Quell Verlag, 1975. 167p. Bibliography: p.163-168. LC 75-516598 (German)

B460 Linssen, Robert. La Méditation véritable: étude des pulsions pré-mentales. Paris: le Courrier du livre, 1976. 177p. Includes bibliographical references. LC 78-387333 (French)

B461 Loeckle, Werner. Das Frankfurter Paradiesgärtlein als Meditationsbild. 2., erw. Aufl. Freiburg i. Br.: Verlag Die Kommenden, 1976. 169p. (German)

B462 Löffler, Johann H. Durch die Sinne zum Sinn. Obernhain: Irisiana-Verlag, 1977. 94p. (German)

B463 Long, Barry. Meditation: A Foundation Course. London: Barry Long Centre, 1969, 1982 printing. 25p.

B464 Lotz, Johannes Baptist, 1903- . Einübung ins Meditieren am Neuen Testament. Frankfurt am Main: Knecht, 1965. 287p. Bibliography: p.283-287. LC 66-75735 (German)

B465 _____ . Interior Prayer: The Exercise of Personality. Translated by Dominic B. Gerlach. New York: Herder and Herder, 1968. 255p. Translation of Einübung ins Meditieren am Neuen Testament. LC 68-22451

B466 _____ . Kurze Anleitung zum Meditieren. Frankfurt am Main: Knecht, 1973. 298p. (German)

B467 _____ . Meditation, der Weg nach innen; philosophische Klärung, Anweisung zum Volzug. Frankfurt am Main: J. Knecht, Carolusdruckerei, 1954. 167p. (German)

B468 _____ . Meditation im Alltag. 3., (erw.) Aufl. Frankfurt a. M.: Knecht, 1959. 254p. (German)

B469 Lounsbery, Grace Constant. Buddhist Meditation in the Southern School; Theory and Practice for Westerners. Foreword by W.Y. Evans-Wentz. Tucson, Ariz.: Omen Press, 1973, c1935. Also, London: Luzac, 1950, and

New York: Knopf, 1936. Orig. pub., London: K. Paul, Trench, Trubner & Co., Ltd., 1935. xvii,177p. Bibliography: p.171-172. LC 73-76994

B470 _____. La Méditation bouddhique: étude de sa théorie et de sa pratique selon l'école du Sud. Préface du Dr. W.Y. Evans-Wentz. Paris: J. Maisonneuve, 1976. 186p. Translation of Buddhist Meditation in the Southern School. Reprint of 2d ed. (1935) pub. by Librairie d'Amérique et d'Orient, Paris. LC 79-390212 (French)

B471 Lu, K'uan Yü (Charles Luk), 1898- . Geheimnisse der chinesischen Meditation. Selbstgestaltung durch Bewusstseinskontrolle, nach d. Lehren d. Ch'an d. Mahayana u. d. taoist. Schulen in China. Zürich u. Stuttgart: Rascher, 1967. 296p. Einheitssacht.: The Secrets of Chinese Meditation. LC 72-354761 (German)

B472 _____. The Secrets of Chinese Meditation: Self-Cultivation by Mind Control as Taught in the Ch'an, Mahayana and Taoist Schools in China. New York: Samuel Weiser, 1980 and previous editions. Also, London: Rider, 1972, 1969 and 1964. 240p. Includes bibliographical references.

B473 Luis de Granada, 1504-1588. Of Prayer and Meditation, 1582. Translated from the Spanish by R. Hopkins. Menston: Scolar Press, 1971. 662p. (English Recusant Literature, 1558-1640; v.64) LC 72-179055

B474 Lyman, Frederick C. The Posture of Contemplation. New York: Philosophical Library, 1969. 123p. LC 68-54973

B475 Lysebeth, André van. Durch Yoga zum eigenen Selbst. München und Bern: O.W. Barth, 1973. 330p. Einheitssacht.: Je perfectionne mon yoga. (German)

B476 MacHovec, Frank J. OM: A Guide to Meditation and Inner Tranquility. Mount Vernon, N.Y.: Peter Pauper Press, 1973. 64p. LC 75-305040

B477 Maharishi International University. Science of Creative Intelligence for Secondary Education First-Year Course: Theme: Perceiving the Fullness of Life; Student Coursebook. Bremen, West Germany: MIU Press, 1975. 295p.

B478 _____. Science and Creative Intelligence for Secondary Education: Three-Year Curriculum. Rheinweiler, West Germany: MIU Press, 1974. 211p.

B479 Mahayana Buddhist Meditation: Theory and Practice. Edited

by Minoru Kiyota. Assisted by Elvin W. Jones. Honolulu: University Press of Hawaii, 1978. xv,312p. Bibliography: p.297-305. LC 78-60744
These studies and essays are representative of the work of
modern Buddhist scholarship in meditation.

B480   Mahesh Yogi, Maharishi. Creating an Ideal Society: A
        Global Undertaking. Rheinweiler, West Germany: MERU
        Press, 1976. 168p.

B481   _____. Love and God. Los Angeles: Maharishi Interna-
        tional University, and Livingston Manor, N.Y.: Age of
        Enlightenment Press, 1973. Also, Oslo: Spiritual Re-
        generaiton Movement in Norway, 1965. 54p.

B482   _____. Maharishi Mahesh Yogi on the Bhagavad-Gita: A
        New Translation and Commentary with Sanskrit Text;
        Chapters 1 to 6. Harmonsworth: Penguin, 1969. Also
        pub. as Bhagavad-Gita, a New Translation and Commen-
        tary with Sanskrit Text by His Holiness Maharishi Mahesh
        Yogi; Chapters 1 to 6. London and Los Angeles: Inter-
        national SRM Publications, 1967. 494p. LC 72-449366

B483   _____. Meditations of Maharishi Mahesh Yogi. New York:
        Bantam Books, 1968. 188p.

B484   _____. La science de l'être et l'art de vivre. Paris:
        Editions Robert Laffont, 1976. 409p. Translation of The
        Science of Being and Art of Living. (French)

B485   _____. The Science of Being and Art of Living. New
        rev. ed. New York: Maharishi International University,
        1976, c1966. Also, New York: New American Library,
        1968; Los Angeles: International SRM Publications, 1967;
        London: International SRM Pub., 1966; and Livingston
        Manor, N.Y.: Age of Enlightenment Press, 1966. Orig.
        pub., New Delhi and New York: Allied Publishers, 1963.
        334p. Also pub. as Transcendental Meditation.

B486   _____. Transcendental Meditation. New York: New
        American Library, 1975 and previous editions. Also,
        London: Allied Publishers Private Ltd., 1968. 320p.
        Orig. pub. in 1963 as The Science of Being and Art of
        Living.

B487   _____. Verwirklichung der idealen Gesellschaft: e. welt-
        weites Unternehmen; 1977, d. Jahr d. idealen Gesellschaft,
        3. Jahr d. Zeitalters d. Erleuchtung. Bad Bellingen:
        Verlag des Zeitalters d. Erleuchtung, 1977. 140p. (Ger-
        man)

B488   _____. Yoga Asanas. Los Angeles: Spiritual Regeneration Movement, 1965. 37p.

B489   Main, John, 1926- . Christian Meditation: Prayer in the
Tradition of John Cassian; Three Conferences Given by
John Main at the Abbey of Getsemani in November 1976.
Derby: The Grail, 1978. 24p.

B490   _____. Word Into Silence. New York: Paulist Press,
1981. Orig. pub., London: Darton, Longman & Todd,
1980. xiii,82p. Includes bibliographical references.
LC 80-84660

B491   Maitland, Robert. Essentials of Meditation. Lakemont, Ga.:
CSA Press, 1975. 139p. LC 75-11136

B492   Malone, A. Hodge. Mending the Ragged Edges. Bend, Or.:
Maverick Publications, 1979. 219p. LC 79-89338

B493   Mandus, Brother. All About You. London: Turnstone
Books, 1976. 197p. LC 77-361479

B494   _____. 'Relaxit,' and Get Fit! London: L.N. Fowler,
1974. 159p.

B495   Mangalo, Bhikkhu. The Practice of Recollection: A Guide
to Buddhist Meditation. Boulder, Colo.: Prajna, 1978.
Dist. by Great Eastern Book Co., Boulder, Colo. Orig.
pub., London: Buddhist Society, 1970. 25p.
Satipatthana, one of the basic practices of Buddhism, is explained. This is the practice of keeping the mind focused
on the present, on what is, here and now.

B496   Mangoldt, Ursula von. Meditation; Heilkraft im Alltag.
Weilheim/Obb.: O.W. Barth, 1960. 97p. (German)

B497   _____. Meditation und Kontemplation aus christlicher
Tradition. Anregungen für alle Suchenden. Weilheim/
Obb.: O.W. Barth, 1966. 303p. LC 66-7523 (German)

B498   _____. Östliche und westliche Meditation: Einf. u. Ab-
grenzung. München: Kösel, 1977. 101p. Includes
bibliographic references. LC 77-471508 (German)

B499   Marcus, Jay B. TM and Business: Personal and Corporate
Benefits of Inner Development. New York: McGraw-Hill,
1977. xviii,245p. Includes bibliographical references.
LC 77-23365
Draws a picture of how the TM (the Transcendental Meditation Program) technique systematically enhances the abilities most needed in business situations.

B500   Massa, Willi. Schweigen und Wort: Vorträge zur Meditation
         im Stil d. Zen. Kevelaer: Butzon und Bercker, 1977
         und 1974. 136p. (German)

B501   Masters, Roy. How to Control Your Emotions. Los Angeles:
         Foundation Books of Human Understanding, 1975. xxii,
         325p. LC 75-15708

B502   Matthew, Father, O.D.C. Contemplative Meditation for All:
         How to Do It. Dublin: Veritas Publications, and London:
         Catholic Truth Society, 1979. 24p.

B503   May, Gerald G. The Open Way: A Meditation Handbook.
         Illustrated by Richard Rossitter. New York: Paulist
         Press, 1977. 182p. LC 77-70641
         Explains what meditation is, its general rules and bases in
         terms of Eastern and Western systems.

B504   _____. Der sanfte Weg: e. Meditationshandbuch. Ham-
         burg: Isko Press, 1980. 263p. Einheitssacht.: The
         Open Way. (German)

B505   McAlpine, Campbell. Alone with God: A Manual of Biblical
         Meditation. Minneapolis: Bethany Fellowship, 1981.
         184p.

B506   McCormick, Thomas, and Sharon Fish. Meditation: A Prac-
         tical Guide to a Spiritual Discipline: Quiet Times for
         Forty Days. Downers Grove, Ill.: InterVarsity Press,
         1983. 120p. Includes bibliographical references.

B507   McSorley, Joseph, 1874- . A Primer of Prayer. New York:
         Deus Books, Paulist Press, 1961. Orig. pub., London
         and New York: Longmans, Green, and Co., 1934. viii,
         120p.

B508   McWilliams, Peter. The TM Program: A Basic Handbook.
         Greenwich, Conn.: Fawcett Publications, Inc., 1976.
         128p. LC 76-1363

B509   Meares, Ainslie. The Wealth Within: Self-Help Through a
         System of Relaxing Meditation. Melbourne: Hill of Con-
         tent, 1977. xii,162p. LC 79-309986

B510   _____. Dialogue on Meditation. Melbourne: Hill of Con-
         tent, 1979. 96p.

B511   Meditation and Kabbalah: Containing Relevant Texts from
         The Greater Hekhelot, Textbook of the Merkava School,
         the Works of Abraham Abulafia, Joseph Gikatalia's Gates
         of Light, The Gates of Holiness, Gate of the Holy Spirit,

Textbook of the Lurianic School, Hasidic Classics. Selected and translated by Aryeh Kaplan. York Beach, Me.: Samuel Weiser, 1982. 355p. Includes bibliographical references. LC 81-70150

B512 Meditation in Christianity. Edited by Swami Rama ... [et al.]. Rev. and enl. ed. Honesdale, Pa.: Himalayan International Institute of Yoga Science and Philosophy of the U.S.A., 1983. Also, 1979 and 1973. viii,128p. LC 83-32

B513 Meditation in Christianity and Other Religions = Meditation dans le Christianisme et les autres religions. Articles by Alex Wayman ... [et al.]. Rome: Gregorian University Press, 1976. 304p. (Studia Missionalia; 25)

B514 Meditation, Weg zur Mitte: Bild- u. Textmeditationen für d. Jugend- u. Gemeindearbeit. München: Calig; und Meitingen u. Freising: Kyrios-Verlag, 1975. 82p. (German)

B515 Meditational Therapy. Edited by Swami Ajaya. Glenview, Ill.: Himalayan International Institute of Yoga Science & Philosophy of USA, 1977. vii,92p. LC 80-105520
Focuses on the use of yoga and meditation in the treatment of stress, drug dependency, tension headaches, anxiety and a variety of psychosomatic dysfunctions.

B516 Meeting of the Ways: Explorations in East/West Psychology. Edited by John Welwood. New York: Schocken Books, 1979. xvi,240p. Bibliography: p.229-233. LC 78-26509
A collection of essays including a section that examines Eastern and Western concepts and theories of meditation.

B517 Mehta, Rohit. The Science of Meditation. Delhi: Motilal Banarsidass, 1978. Dist. in U.S. by Orient Book Distributors, Livingston, N.J. vi,199p. Bibliography: p.197-199.

B518 Melançon, Ovila, 1910- . L'oraison catholique et les techniques orientales de méditation. Montréal: Impr. Gagné, 1977. 187p. Bibliographie: p.171-175. (French)
Discusses Yoga, Zen meditation, and Transcendental Meditation.

B519 Melton, J. Gordon. The Encyclopedia of American Religions. Wilmington, N.C.: McGrath Pub. Co., 1978. 2 vols. Includes bibliographical references. LC 78-78210
Volume two contains the history and development of about ninety groups that practice and teach meditation.

B520   Melzer, Frisco, 1907- . Anleitung zur Meditation. 2.,
        veränd. u. erw. Aufl. Stuttgart: Evang. Verl.-Werk,
        1959. 142p. (German)

B521   _____. Der Guru als Seelenführer; abendländische Bege-
        gnung mit östlicher Geistigkeit. Mit einem Vorwort von
        Erich Schlick. Wuppertal: R. Brockhous, 1963. 47p.
        LC 67-121408 (German)

B522   _____. Innerung. Stufen u. Wege d. Meditation. Grund-
        legung und Übungen. Kassel: Johannes-Stauda-Verlag,
        1968. 215p. Bibliography: p.179-200. LC 74-358090
        (German)

B523   _____. Konzentration, Meditation, Kontemplation. Kassel:
        Stauda, 1974. 187p. Bibliography: p.163-173. LC 74-
        355694 (German)

B524   _____. Konzentration. Vom Wege, von d. Nachfolge, vom
        lebendigen Wort. Stuttgart: Evang. Verlagswerk, 1955.
        160p. (German)

B525   _____. Meditation. Eine Lebenshilfe. Stuttgart: Evang.
        Werlagswerk, 1954. 184p. (German)

B526   _____. Meditation in Ost und West. Stuttgart: Evang.
        Verl.-Werk, 1957. 170p. (German)

B527   Mental Prayer and Modern Life, a Symposium. Translated
        by Francis C. Lehner. Preface by Walter Farrell. New
        York: P.J. Kenedy, 1950. xi,202p. Translation of
        L'Oraison (Cahiers de la vie spirituelle). Includes bib-
        liographical references. LC 50-2547
        Presents historical, theological and practical considerations
        of mental prayer.

B528   Merton, Thomas, 1915-1968. The Asian Journal of Thomas
        Merton. Edited from his original notebooks by Naomi
        Burton, Patrick Hart & James Laughlin. Consulting
        editor, Amiya Chakravarty. New York: New Directions
        Pub. Corp., 1975. Also, London: Sheldon Press, 1974.
        Orig. pub., New York: New Directions Pub. Corp.,
        1973. xxviii,445p. Bibliography: p.357-361.
        This volume is based on notes written during Thomas Mer-
        ton's visit to the monasteries of the Orient prior to his ac-
        cidental death in Bangkok.

B529   _____. Beschouwend gebed. Translated into Netherlandic
        by R. Leys. Antwerp: Patmos, 1972. 115p. Transla-
        tion of Contemplative Prayer. (Dutch)

B530   _____. Contemplative Prayer. Foreword by Douglas V.
Steere. London: Darton, Longman and Todd, 1973,
c1969. Also, Garden City, N.Y.: Doubleday/Image
Books, 1971. Orig. pub., New York: Herder and Herder, 1969. 144p.

B531   _____. Meditationen eines Einsiedlers: über d. Sinn von
Meditationen u. Einsamkeit. 2. Aufl., 8. Tsd. Zürich,
Einsiedeln u. Köln: Benziger, 1979. Orig. pub., 1976.
141p. (German)

B532   _____. Spiritual Direction and Meditation: And, What Is
Contemplation? Wheathampstead: A. Clarke, 1975. 112p.
Spiritual Direction and Meditation originally published:
Collegeville, Minn.: Liturgical Press, 1960. What Is
Contemplation? originally published: Holy Cross: St.
Mary's College, 1948.

B533   _____. Vom Sinn der Kontemplation. Übertr. von Alfred
Kuoni. Zürich: Verl. d. Arche, 1955. 64p. Einheitssacht.: What Is Contemplation? (German)

B534   _____. Wahrhaftig beten. Übertr. von Margret Weilwes.
Freiberg: Paulusverlag, 1971. 137p. Einheitssacht.:
Contemplative Prayer. (German)

B535   _____. Wie der Mond stirbt: d. letzte Tagebuch d.
Thomas Merton. Hrsg. u. übertr. von Heinz G. Schmidt.
Wuppertal: Hammer, 1976. 231p. Einheitssacht.: Asian
Journal of Thomas Merton. (German)

B536   Meserve, Harry C. The Practical Meditator. New York:
Human Sciences Press, 1981. 137p. Bibliography: p.
131-134. LC 80-15631

B537   Michael, Russ. Why and How of Meditation. Washington,
D.C.: Milennium Publishing House, 1975. Orig. pub.,
Lakemont, Ga.: CSA Press, 1971. 165p.

B538   Michaëlle. Yoga and Prayer. Translated and adapted from
the French by Diana Cumming. Illustrated by Poor
Clare. London: Search Press Ltd., and Westminster,
Md.: Christian Classics, 1980. 109p. Translation of
Yoga et prière.

B539   _____. Yoga et prière. Paris: Editions du Cerf, 1977.
182p. LC 77-577324 (French)

B540   Mildenberger, Michael, 1934- , and Albrecht Schöll. Die
Macht der süssen Worte: Zauberformel TM; d. Bewe-
gung d. transzendentalen Meditation; Information u.

Kritik. Wuppertal: Aussaat-Verlag, 1977. 152,xvip.
Includes bibliographical references. LC 77-571940 (German)

B 541   Miller, Calvin. Transcendental Hesitation: A Biblical Appraisal of TM and Eastern Mysticism. Grand Rapids, Mich.: Zondervan Pub. House, 1977. 185p. Bibliography: p.181-185. LC 76-49979

B 542   Miller, John P., 1943- . The Compassionate Teacher: How to Teach and Learn with Your Whole Self. Englewood Cliffs, N.J.: Prentice-Hall, 1981. x,180p. Bibliography: p.172-176. LC 81-784

B 543   Minger, Fritz. Meditation ohne Geheimnis: Beitr. zur Psychologisierung, Entmystifizierung u. Popularisierung d. Meditation. Engelberg/Schweiz u. München: Drei-Eichen-Verlag, 1976. 87p. (German)

B 544   Mi-pham-rgya-mtsho, Jam-mgon Ju, 1846-1912. Calm and Clear: The Wheel of Analytic Meditation, [and] Instructions on Vision in the Middle Way. Commentary and interpretation by Tarthang Tulku, translated and edited by Keith Dowman, Mervin V. Hanson and John Reynolds. Foreword by Herbert V. Guenther. Emeryville, Calif.: Dharma Publishing, 1973. 110[17]p. LC 73-79058
[Same as B 216]
Two Tibetan meditational texts which present a step-by-step guide to the practice of meditation.

B 545   _____ . Ruhig und klar. Obernhain: Irisiana-Verlag, 1977. 120p. Einheitssacht.: Calm and Clear. (German)

B 546   Miura, Issheu, 1903- , and Ruth Fuller Sasaki, 1893- . Zen Dust: The History of the Koan and Study in Rinzai (Lin-chi) Zen. New York: Harcourt, Brace & World, 1967, c1966. Also, Kyoto: First Zen Institute of America in Japan, 1966. xxii,574p. An expanded version of the authors' The Zen Koan. New York: Harcourt, Brace & World, 1965. Bibliography: p.335-479. LC 66-10044

B 547   Moffatt, Doris. Christian Meditation the Better Way. Chappaqua, N.Y.: Christian Herald Books, 1979. 96p. LC 78-64842

B 548   Mojica Sandoz, Luis. La meditación según la más antiqua tradición budista. Río Piedras: University of Puerto Rico Press, 1979. ix,92p. (Colección Uprex: Serie Manuales; 54) Bibliography: 89-92. LC 78-31595 (Spanish)

B549   Molina, Antonio de, d. 1619? A Treatise of Mental Prayer,
        1617. Menston: Scolar Press, 1970. [17],371p. (Eng-
        lish Recusant Literature, 1558-1640; v.15) Reprint of the
        St. Omer, 1617 ed. LC 70-558337

B550   Molinero, José Ramon. A procura do deus interno no yoga.
        São Paulo: Mandála, 1971 or 2. 272p. LC 73-315461
        (Portuguese)

B551   _____. Raja yoga secreto. São Paulo: Mandála, 1971.
        251p. LC 72-313022 (Portuguese)

B552   Monléon, Jean de, 1890- . Traité sur l'oraison. Paris:
        Nouvelles Editions latines, 1950. 156p. (French)

B553   Moser, Georg. Meditation: e. Weg in d. Freiheit. Ruit bei
        Stuttgart: Schwabenverlag, 1979 and previous editions.
        48p. (German)

B554   Mountain, Marian. The Zen Environment: The Impact of
        Zen Meditation. Introduction by Dainin Katagiri Roshi.
        Foreword by Robert M. Pirsig. New York: W. Morrow,
        1982. 264p. Includes bibliographical references. LC
        81-11210

B555   Mouradian, Kay, 1933- . Reflective Meditation. Wheaton,
        Ill.: Theosophical Pub. House, 1982. 175p. Bibliogra-
        phy: p.169-175. LC 82-50163

B556   Mukerji, A.P., Swami. Yoga Lessons for Developing Spiritual
        Consciousness. Jacksonville, Fla.: Yoga Publication So-
        ciety, date? Orig. pub., Chicago, Ill.: Yogi Publication
        Society, 1911. 191p.

B557   Muktananda Paramhamsa, Swami, 1908-1982. Light on the
        Path. Ganeshpuri, India: Shree Gurudev Ashram, 1972.
        Dist. in U.S. by SYDA Foundation, South Fallsburg,
        N.Y. xii,108p.

B558   _____. Meditate. Foreword by Joseph Chilton Pearce.
        Preface by Marsha Mason. Albany: State University of
        New York Press, 1980. xi,84p. Bibliography: p.77-78.
        LC 80-20477
        Offers a specific and practical understanding of meditation
        using the mantra method.

B559   _____. Siddha Meditation: Commentaries on the Shiva
        Sutras and Other Sacred Texts. Oakland, Calif.:
        S.Y.D.A. Foundation, 1975. 117p.

B560   Müller-Elmau, Bernhard. Kräfte aus der Stille: d.

transzendentale Meditation. Düsseldorf u. Wien: Econ-
Verlag, 1977. 160p. (German)

B561 . Leben aus der Fülle: transzendentale Meditation
nach Maharishi Mahesh Yogi. Schloss Elmau: Verlag Der
Grünen Blätter, 1979? 52p. (German)

B562 Munen muso: Ungegenständliche Meditation: Festschr. für
Peter Hugo M. Enomiya-Lassalle SJ zum 80. Geburtstag.
Hrsg. von Günter Stachel. Mainz: Matthias Grünewald-
Verlag, 1978. 464p. Bibliography of H.M. Enomiya-
Lassalle's works: p.456-459. Includes bibliographic
references. LC 79-368114 (German)

B563 Muñoz Malagarriga, Concepción, 1949- . Guía de la meditación trascendental. Barcelona: Barral, 1977. 299p.
(Ediciones des bolsillo; v.515) American ed. published
under title: Meditación transcendental. Bibliography:
p.292-299. LC 79-378966 (Spanish)

B564 Muppathyil, Cyriac. Meditation as a Path to God-Realization:
A Study in the Spiritual Teachings of Swami Prabhavananda and His Assessment of Christian Spirituality. Roma:
Università Gregoriana, 1979. ix,159p. (Documenta missionalia; 13) Bibliography: p.155-159. LC 79-321050

B565 Murphy, Carol R. The Available Mind. Wallingford, Pa.:
Pendle Hill Pubications, 1974. 30p. Bibliography:
27p. LC 73-94186

B566 . O Inward Traveller. Wallingford, Pa.: Pendle
Hill Publications, 1977. 31p. Bibliography: p.30-31.
LC 77-91637

B567 Nagel, Hajo. Die Bio-Meditation: der neue Weg z. Meditation durch Training d. Hirnwellenaktivität mit elektron.
Hilfe; Intensiv-Methode mit Lehr-Gerät u. laufender in-
strumenteller Erfolgskontrolle. Baden-Baden: Inst. f.
Bio-Dynamik, 1973. 97p. (German)

B568 Nanda, Jyotir Maya, Swami, 1931- . Concentration and
Meditation. Miami: Swami Lalitananda, 1971. Dist. by
Yoga Research Foundation, Miami, Fla. 198p.

B569 . Mantra, Kirtana, Yantra & Tantra. Miami:
Swami Lalitananda, 1975. Dist. by Yoga Research Foundation, Miami, Fla. 64p.

B570 . Raja Yoga: Study of Mind. Miami: Swami Lalitananda, 1970. Dist. by Yoga Research Foundation,
Miami, Fla. vi,108p.

B571 _____. Raja Yoga Sutras. Miami: Yoga Research Foundation, 1978. 264p. LC 79-113723

B572 Naranjo, Claudio, and Robert E. Ornstein. On the Psychology of Meditation. New York and Harmondsworth, Eng.:
Penguin Books, 1976. Also, London: Allen & Unwin,
1972. Orig. pub., New York: Viking Press, 1971. Also
dist. by DeVorss & Co., Marina del Rey, Calif. 248p.
Bibliography: p.247-248. LC 77-2052
Examines the methods and goals of meditation. Surveys
psychological investigations that link the phenomena of
religious mind control with the results of experimental
psychology.

B573 _____. Psychologie der Meditation. Frankfurt am Main:
Fischer-Taschenbücher-Verlag, 1980 and previous edi-
tions. 222p. Einheitssacht.: On the Psychology of
Meditation. (German)

B574 Narayanananda, Swami. The Secrets of Mind-Control. 4th
rev. ed. Gylling, Denmark: Narayananada Universal
Yoga Trust, 1976. Also, Rishikesh, U.P.: Narayanan-
anda Universal Yoga Trust, 1970, and Rishikesh: N.K.
Prasad, 1959. Orig. pub., Himalayas, India: N.K.
Prasad, 1954. 221p.

B575 Narayanaswami Aiyar, K. The Thirty-Two Vidya-s. Introduction by V. Raghavan. 2nd ed. Madras: Adyar Library and Research Centre, 1963. xxiii,147p. (The
Adyar Library Series; v.90) Includes bibliographical
references. LC 75-276686

B576 Nayak, Anand. La Méditation dans le Bhâgavata-Purana.
Paris: Dervy, 1978. 92p. Includes bibliographical references. LC 79-374166 (French)

B577 Newhouse, Flower Arlene Sechler, 1909- . Gateways Into
Light; Processes of Western Meditation. Escondido,
Calif.: Christward Ministry, 1974. 160p. LC 74-
75517

B578 _____. Meditation: The Way to Attainment. Escondido,
Calif.: The Christward Ministry, 1951. Dist. by De-
Vorss & Co., Marina del Rey, Calif. 48p.

B579 Nhat Hanh, Thich. The Miracle of Being Awake: A Manual
on Meditation for the Use of Young Activists. Translated by Mobi Quynh Hoa. Edited by Jim Jorest.
Bangkok: Sathirakoses-Nagapradipa Foundation, 1976.
Also, Nyack, New York: Fellowship Books, 1975.
66p.

B 580 _____. The Miracle of Mindfulness: A Manual on Meditation. Translated by Mobi Warren. Drawings by Vo
Dinh. Boston: Beacon Press, 1976. ix,108p. LC 76-
7747
Short essays by a Zen master with concentration and relaxation exercises.

B 581 Nicholas, Ted, 1934- . A.M.: Anthrocentric Meditation:
How to Teach Yourself Meditation. Foreword by Luanne
Ruona. Photography by George J. Fistrovich. Wilmington, Del.: Enterprise Pub. Co., 1975. 201p. Bibliography: p.190-192. LC 75-33602

B 582 Nishijima, Gudō, 1919- , and Joe Langdon, 1942- . How
to Practice Zazen. Tokorozawa, Japan: Bukkyosha,
1976. Dist. in U.S. by Japan Publications Trading Co.,
Elmsford, N.Y. vi,58p. Translation of Zazen no yari-
kata. LC 77-366784

B 583 Nivaldi, Mauro. Meditazione e posizioni yoga per un perfetto
equilibrio fisico e mentale. Milano: G. De Vecchi, 1976.
157p. LC 76-475825 (Italian)

B 584 Norvell, (i.e., Anthony Trupo), 1908- . The Miracle Power
of Transcendental Meditation. West Nyack, N.Y.: Parker
Pub. Co., 1972. 200p. LC 72-2892

B 585 _____. Teach Your Child Transcendental Meditation.
New York: Drake Publishers, 1976. xvi,155p. LC 75-
36162
Shows parents how to use alpha biofeedback techniques,
through Transcendental Meditation with their children.

B 586 _____. Die Zauberkraft der transzendentalen Meditation.
Übers. von Rudolf Meldau. Freiburg i. Br.: Bauer,
1975 und 1973. 284p. Einheitssacht.: Miracle Power of
Transcendental Meditation. (German)

B 587 Null, Gary, and Steve Null. Biofeedback, Fasting & Meditation. New York: Pyramid Books, 1974. 156p. Includes bibliographical references. LC 74-17725

B 588 _____, and _____. Bioinformacion, ayuno y meditacion.
Mexico: Diana, 1979. 164p. Includes bibliographical
references. Translation of: Biofeedback, Fasting &
Meditation. (Spanish)

B 589 Nyanaponika. Geistestraining durch Achtsamkeit: d.
buddhistische Satipatthana-Methode. Konstanz: Verlag Christiani, 1975 and 1970. 198p. LC 73-363546
(German)

B590   . The Heart of Buddhist Meditation (Satipatthana):
A Handbook of Mental Training Based on the Buddha's
Way of Mindfulness, with an Anthology of Relevant Texts
Translated from the Pali and Sanskrit. Rev. ed. Lon-
don: Rider, 1983. New York: Samuel Weiser, 1973 and
previous editions. London: Rider, and New York:
Citadel Press, 1969. Orig. pub., London: Rider, 1962.
Also dist. in U.S. by Wehman Brothers, Inc., Cedar
Knolls, N.J. 224p.

B591   . The Power of Mindfulness. San Francisco: Unity
Press, 1972. Also, Kandy, Ceylon: Buddhist Publication
Society, 1968. 56p.

B592 Nyanasamvara (Somdet Phra). Betrachtung des Körpers.
Wien: Octopus-Verlag, 1980. 106p. (German)

B593 Oates, Bob. Celebrating the Dawn: Maharishi Mahesh Yogi
and the TM Technique. Epilogue by Maharishi Mahesh
Yogi. New York: Putnam, 1976. 227p. LC 76-14884
In part one of the book a teacher of TM discusses traveling
with the Maharishi Mahesh Yogi. Parts two and three relate
the Maharishi's major concepts on the TM technique to independent scientific research.

B594 Oberhammer, Gerhard. Strukturen yogischer Meditation:
Ünters. zur Spiritualität d. Yoga. Wien: Verlag der
Osterr. Akad. d. Wiss., 1977. 244p. LC 78-382957
(German)

B595 O'Brien, Bartholomew J. Spurs to Meditation. Milwaukee:
Bruce Pub. Co., 1955. 116p.

B596 Odier, Daniel, 1945- . Nirvana Tao: techniques de méditation. Paris: R. Laffont, 1974. 205p. Bibliography:
p.205-206. LC 75-505999 (French)

B597 Oehlschlager, Stephen. Beyond Self and Time. Boston:
Branden Press, 1975. 76p. LC 74-81763

B598 Oki, Masahiro, 1921- . Meditation Yoga. Tokyo: Japan
Publications, 1978. 176p. LC 77-93244

B599 Olausson, Ingrid, 1934- . Meditation: magi eller terapi?:
en bok om transcendental meditation. Stockholm: Rabén
& Sjögren, 1974. 230p. Bibliography: p.228-231. LC
75-576447 (Swedish)

B600 Oliver, Fay Conlee. Christian Growth Through Meditation:
Beyond "Transcendental Meditation." Valley Forge, Pa.:

Judson Press, 1976. 124p. Bibliography: p.121-124.
LC 76-23252

B601 Olson, Helena. Maharishi at '433': The Story of Maharishi
Mahesh Yogi's First Visit to the United States. 2nd ed.
Los Angeles: R.R. Donnelley, 1979. 246p. Revised
from the 1967 edition of A Hermit in the House. LC 79-
120031

B602 On Zen Practice. Edited by Hakuyu Taizan Maezumi and
Bernard Tetsugen Glassman. Los Angeles: Zen Center of Los Angeles, 1976. 2 vols. (Zen Writings
Series; v.1-2) Vol.2 has subtitle: Body, Breath,
and Mind. Includes bibliographical references. LC
77-70251

B603 Ornstein, Robert Evans. The Mind Field: A Personal Essay.
New York: Grossman Publishers, 1976. xiv,141p. Bib-
liography: p.135-139. LC 76-27868
A critical survey of some of the spiritual and psychological
movements popular in the U.S. They are contrasted with
Sufism.

B604 _____. The Psychology of Consciousness. 2nd ed. New
York: Harcourt Brace Jovanovich, 1977. Also, New York:
Penguin Books, 1975, and New York: Viking Press, 1974.
Orig. pub., San Francisco: W.H. Freeman, and New
York: Viking Press, 1972. ix,255p. Includes biblio-
graphical references. LC 77-71699
Includes a description of meditation and self-control methods
of Eastern religions.

B605 Ott, Ulrich. Meditation, praktisch: Vorschläge u. Schritte.
Basel: F. Reinhardt, 1974. 48p. (German)

B606 Overbeck, Klaus-Dieter. Auswirkungen der Transzendentalen
Meditation auf die psychische und psychosomatische Befindlichkeit. Bielefeld: Klein, 1981. 262p. Orig. presented as a dissertation at the University of Hamburg,
1978. (German) [D169]

B607 Pálos, Stephan. Atem und Meditation: moderne chines.
Atemtherapie, e. Weg zur Meditation. Bern, München:
u. Wien: Barth, 1980 and previous editions. 237p.
(German)

B608 Pandit, Madhav Pundalik, 1918- . Dhyana. 3rd ed.
Pondicherry, India: DIPTI Publications, 1972. Also,
Madras: Jupiter Press Private for M.P. Pandit, 1960.
60p. Dist. in U.S. by Auromere, Pomona, Calif.

B 609 _____ . Dhyana. Wege d. Versenkung. Aus d. Engl.
übers. von Gertrude Lietz u. Christian Isbert. Zollikon-
Zürich: Sri Aurobindo Verl., 1965. 43p. Einheitssacht.:
Dhyana. (German)

B 610 _____ . Japan (Mantra Yoga). Pomona, Calif.: Auromere,
1979 reprint of 1959 edition. 41p.

B 611 Pandita, Indiradevi, and R.L. Landers. A Bo[u]quet of
Love: Yoga and Meditation for Everyone. Fort Lauderdale, Fla.: Pandita, 1975. xl,248p. LC 75-37396

B 612 Papentin, Frank. Ordnung, Intelligenz und Evolution: e.
interdisziplinärer Umriss d. Wiss. auf d. Grundlage von
Maharishi Mahesh Yogi's Wiss d. kreativen Intelligenz.
Bremen: MERU-Verlag, 1978. 131p. (German)

B 613 Paramananda, Swami, 1883-1940. Concentration and Meditation. 8th ed. Cohasset, Mass.: Vedante Centre, 1974
and previous editions. Also dist. by DeVorss & Co.,
Marina del Rey, Calif. 130p.
Discusses the traditional Hindu approach and philosophy of
meditation by a disciple of Swami Vivekananda.

B 614 _____ . Silence as Yoga. 4th ed. Cohasset, Mass.: The
Vedanta Centre, and La Crescenta, Calif.: Ananda Ash-
rama. 82p. Formerly pub. as Creative Power of Silence.
Orig. pub., Boston, Mass.: The Vedanta Centre, and
La Crescenta, Calif.: Ananda Ashrama, 1923.

B 615 Parampanthi, Puragra, Swami, 1928- . Creative Self-
Transformation Through Meditation: A Six Week Course.
Forewords by Earlyne and Robert Chaney. Los Angeles:
Phoenix House, 1974. 159p. LC 74-21803

B 616 Paths of Meditation: A Collection of Essays on Different
Techniques of Meditation According to Different Faiths.
By Swami Siddhinathananda ... [et al.]. Mylapore, Madras, India: Sri Ramakrishna Math, 1980. Dist. in U.S.
by Vedanta Press, Hollywood, Calif. iv,236p.

B 617 Patton, John E. The Case Against TM in the Schools.
Grand Rapids, Mich.: Baker Book House, 1976. 100p.

B 618 Payne, Buryl. Getting There Without Drugs: Techniques
and Theories for the Expansion of Consciousness. London: Wildwood House, 1974. Orig. pub., New York:
Viking Press, 1973. xvii,205p. Bibliography: p.203-205.

B 619 _____ , and Carmen T. Reitano. BioMeditation: The Scientific Way to Use the Energy of Your Mind. Brookline,

Mass.: BFI, 1977. viii,147p. in various pagings. Includes bibliographical references.

B620　Pe Maung Tin, 1888- . Buddhist Devotion and Meditation:
An Objective Description and Study. London: S.P.C.K.,
1964. ix,90p. LC 67-35019

B621　Pearce, Joseph Chilton. The Bond of Power. New York:
Dutton, 1981. 179p. Includes bibliographical references.
LC 80-22860

B622　Peck, Robert L. American Meditation and Beginning Yoga.
Windham Center, Conn.: Personal Development Center,
Inc., 1976. 108p. Bibliography: p.107-108.

B623　Pelletier, Kenneth R. Altered Attention Deployment in Meditation. [s.l.: s.n.], 1972. 64p. Bibliography: p.51-64.

B624　_____. Mind as Healer, Mind as Slayer: A Holistic Approach to Preventing Stress Disorders. Foreword by O.
Carl Simonton and Stephanie Matthews Simonton. London
and Boston: G. Allen & Unwin; and New York: Delacorte Press/S. Lawrence, and Dell Pub., 1977. xv,366p.
Bibliography: p.323-354. LC 78-40371

B625　Persinger, Michael A. TM and Cult Mania. With Normand
J. Carrey and Lynn A. Suess. North Quincy, Mass.:
Christopher Pub. House, 1980. 198p. Bibliography:
p.191-193. LC 79-56918

B626　Peter, of Alcantara, Saint, 1499-1562. A Golden Treatise
of Mental Prayer. Chicago: Franciscan Herald Press,
1978. Also, Ikley, Eng.: Scolar Press, 1977; London:
Mowbray, and New York: Morehouse-Gorhan, 1952;
Philadelphia: M. Fithian, 1844; and Liverpool: Printed
by Booker for C. Dolman, 1843. 179p.

B627　_____. Tratado de la oración y meditación. Madrid:
Ediciones Rialp, 1958. 165p. Includes bibliographical
references. (Spanish)

B628　_____. Treatise on Prayer & Meditation. Translated with
an introduction and sketch of the saint's life by Dominic
Devas, O.F.M.; together with a complete English version
of Pax animae by John of Bonilla. Darby, Pa.: Arden
Library, date? Also, Westminster, Md.: Newman Press,
1949. Orig. pub., London: Burns, Oates and Washbourne Ltd., 1926. xx,211p. Reprint of 1926 ed. pub.
by Burns, Oates and Washbourne Ltd., London.

B629　Petersen, W.P. Meditation Made Easy. Illustrated by Terry

Fehr. New York: Watts, 1979. 66p. LC 79-11812
Discusses the techniques and benefits of meditation, a state
of consciousness known as "deep rest." Also suggests exercises designed to help beginners enter this state. Juvenile
literature.

B 630   Petersen, William J. TM, Transcendental Meditation: A Do
         About Nothing. New Canaan, Conn.: Keats Pub., 1976.
         106p. Bibliography: p.104-106. LC 76-24503

B 631   Petite Philocalie de la prière du coeur. Traduite et pré-
         sentée par Jean Gouillard. Paris: Editions du Seuil,
         1968. Also, Paris: Editions des Cahiers du Sud, 1953.
         252p. LC 76-375740 (French)

B 632   Pfaltzgraff, Rogério. Yoga de meditação, de Maharishi Ma-
         hesh Yogi. Rio de Janeiro: Editôra Mandarino, 1969?
         177p. LC 76-241437 (Portuguese)

B 633   Phra Sobhana Dhammsaduhi (Vichitr), 1934- . Insight
         Meditation. 2nd ed. London: Committee for the Ad-
         vancement of Buddhism, 1968. 144p. LC 73-393152

B 634   _____. The Real Way to Awakening: Being the Talks
         Delivered After Meditation Sessions at the Buddhapadipa
         Temple, London. London: Buddhapadipa Temple, 1969.
         vii,96p.

B 635   No entry.

B 636   Pieper, Josef. Glück und Kontemplation. München: Kösel,
         1957. 135p. (German)

B 637   Pipkin, H. Wayne. Christian Meditation, Its Art and Prac-
         tice. New York: Hawthorn Books, 1977. xiii,176p.
         Bibliography: p.146-160. LC 76-19763
         This work analyzes the various types of Christian meditation
         and includes samples of techniques.

B 638   Poeppig, Fred. Briefe zur geistigen Schulung. Freiburg i.
         Br.: Verlag Die Kommenden, 1976. 2. Kontemplation
         und Meditation, die Stufen des Rosenkreuzerweges. 2.,
         überarb. Aufl. p.63-115. 7. Das geistige Fundament
         des Schulungweges. Wie stärken wir unser Ich? p.343-
         394. (German)

B 639   _____. Lebenshilfen durch Geistesschulung. Wege zur
         Pflege d. inneren Lebens. Freiburg/Br.: Verl. Die
         Kommenden, 1955. 154p. (German)

B 640   _____. Wege zu einem meditativen Leben: Sprüche,

Gebete u. meditative Texte. 2. Aufl. Freiburg i. Br.:
Verlag Die Kommenden, 1981. Orig. pub., 1968. 142p.
(German)

B 641 _____. Yoga oder Meditation, der Weg des Abendlandes.
2., erw. Aufl. Freiburg i. Br.: Verlag Die Kommenden,
1965. Orig. pub., 1953. 199p. (German)

B 642 Pohlmann, Constantin. Franziskanische Meditation: Erfahrungen für heute. Mainz: Matthias-Grünewald-Verlag,
1982. 116p. (German)

B 643 Popenoe, Cris. Inner Development. Washington: Yes!
Inc., 1979. Dist. by Random House, New York. Orig.
ed., 1976, pub. as Books for Inner Development. 654p.
LC 78-56250
This is an annotated bibliography of books available from
the Yes! Bookshop in Washington, D.C.

B 644 _____. Records & Cassettes: A Selected Guide: A Yes!
Bookshop Guide. Washington, D.C.: Yes! Bookshop.
date? 66p.
This is an annotated bibliography of records and cassettes
available from the Yes! Bookshop in Washington, D.C.

B 645 Prabhu Ashrit, Swami. Gayatri Rahasya; or, An Exposition
of the Gayatri. Translated by J. Krishna Chowdhury.
New Delhi: English Book Store, 1965. xii,248p. Bibliographical footnotes. LC 68-15848

B 646 Prana: Jahrbuch für Yoga u. ostasiat. Meditationstechniken
u. ihre Anwendung in d. westl. Welt. München: Barth,
1979- .

B 647 Progoff, Ira. The Practice of Process Meditation: The
"Intensive Journal" Way to Spiritual Experience. New
York: Dialogue House Library, 1980. 343p. LC 80-
68847
Examines the principle of continuity in the universe and its
application to meditation.

B 648 _____. The Well and the Cathedral: A Cycle of Process
Meditation: With an Introduction on Its Use in the Practice of Meditation. 2nd ed. enlarged. New York: Dialogue House Library, 1977 and previous editions. 166p.
LC 76-20823
A meditative text that assists the process of personal meditation.

B 649 Pulley, William S. Als Mönch in Burma. Wien: Octopus-
Verlag, 1981. 149p. (German)

B 650   Puryear, Herbert Bruce, and Mark A. Thurston. <u>Meditation</u>
        <u>and the Mind of Man: Based on the Edgar Cayce Read-</u>
        <u>ings</u>. Rev. ed. Virginia Beach, Va.: A.R.E. Press,
        1978, c1975. vi,130p.
        A study from the psychological point of view of Edgar Cayce
        information on meditation.

B 651   Puryear, Meredith Ann. <u>Healings Through Meditation &</u>
        <u>Prayer: Based on the Edgar Cayce Readings</u>. Virginia
        Beach, Va.: A.R.E. Press, 1978. v,108p. Bibliography:
        p.107-108. LC 78-107320

B 652   Puthiadam, Ignatius. <u>Geist der Wahrheit: christl. Exerzitien</u>
        <u>im Dialog mit d. Hinduismus; e. Lese- u. Übungsbuch.</u>
        Kevelaer: Butzon und Bercker, 1980. 226p. (German)

B 653   Quiery, William H., 1926- . <u>Facing God</u>. Foreword by Ber-
        nard J. Cooke. Garden City, N.Y.: Image Books, 1969.
        Orig. pub., New York: Sheed and Ward, 1967. 199p.
        Bibliographical footnotes.

B 654   Rabten, Geshe. <u>Enseignement oral du bouddhisme au Tibet:</u>
        <u>la lumière du Tibet</u>. Recueilli par M.T. Paulauski.
        Traduit du tibétain par Gonsar Rimpoché. Paris: J.
        Maisonneuve, 1976. 158p. LC 81-457537 (French)

B 655   _____ . <u>Mahamudra, der Weg zur Erkenntnis der Wirklich-</u>
        <u>keit</u>. Zürich: Theseus-Verlag, 1979. 255p. (German)

B 656   Raghunathrao, Sadashivrao, 1904- . <u>An Offering to Raman-</u>
        <u>achala</u>. Poona: Vanita Publication, 1974. 96p. LC 75-
        904778

B 657   Raguin, Yves, 1912- . <u>L'attention au mystère: une entrée</u>
        <u>dans la vie spirituelle</u>. Bellarmin: Desclée de Brouwer,
        1979. 183p. (French)

B 658   _____ . <u>Attention to the Mystery: Entry Into the Spiritual</u>
        <u>Life</u>. Translation by Kathleen England. New York:
        Paulist Press, 1982. 119p. Translation of <u>L'attention au</u>
        <u>mystère</u>. LC 82-60595
        Discusses the spiritual dimension of everyday life, the place
        of human relationships, and the practice of meditation.

B 659   Rajagopalachari, P. <u>Der Meister: Shri Ram Chandra, sein</u>
        <u>Leben u. sein Weg d. natürl. Meditation</u>. Bern, München
        u. Wien: Barth, 1977. 198p. Einheitssacht.: <u>My Mas-</u>
        <u>ter</u>.

B 660   Rajaneesh, Acharya, 1931- . <u>The Book of the Secrets:</u>
        <u>Discourses on "Vigyana Bhairava Tantra."</u> Compiled by

Ma Yoga Astha. Edited by Ma Ananda Prem and Swami Ananda Teerth. London: Thames and Hudson, 1976-; and New York: Harper & Row, and Poona: Rajnessh Foundation, 1974- The Harper Colophon edition is in 3 vols. LC 77-356775, LC 75-36733 and LC 75-901521

B 661 _____. The Dimensionless Dimension: [A collection of thirty five immortal letters written by Bhagwan Shree Rajneesh to Ma Yoga Tao (former Miss Elizabeth Ann Small), president, Neo-Sannyas International for U.S.A.] Edited by Swami Yoga Chinmaya. 2nd ed. Bombay: Jeevan Jagriti Kendra (Life Awakening Centre), 1974. 47p. LC 74-903389

B 662 _____. Dynamics of Meditation: [Twelve interview-discourses on the various aspects of meditation.] Compiled by Ma Yoga Laxmi. Edited by Ma Ananda Prem. Bombay: Jeevan Jagriti Kendra, 1972. 285p. LC 74-902216

B 663 _____. The Eternal Message: [A collection of thirty immortal letters written by Bhagwan Shree Rajneesh to Ma Yoga Bhakti, New York, U.S.A., now Ma Ananda Pratima, world president of Neo-Sannyas International.] Edited by Swami Yoga Chinmaya. 2nd ed. Bombay: Jeevan Jagriti Kendra, 1973. 39p. LC 74-903394

B 664 _____. Flight of the Alone to the Alone. Compiled by Swamy Yoga Chinmaya (Kriyananda) and Mahendra H. Thaker. Bombay: Ishwarlal N. Shah, 1970. 35p. LC 76-925005

B 665 _____. The Great Challenge: A Rajneesh Reader. New York: Grove Press, 1982. 211p. LC 81-47642

B 666 _____. LSD: A Shortcut to False Samadhi. Compiled by Ma Yoga Laxmi. Edited by Dolley Diddee. Bombay: Jeevan Jagriti Kendra, 1971. 25p. LC 73-925007

B 667 _____. Meditation; A New Dimension. Compiled by Swami Kriyananda Saraswati. Bombay: Ishwarlal Naranji Shah, 1970. 30p. LC 70-925009

B 668 _____. Meditation: die Kunst, zu sich selbst zu finden. 3. Aufl. München: Heyne, 1981 and previous editions. 254p. Bibliogr. Bhagwan Rajneesh u. Literaturverz: p.251-254. Einheitssacht.: Meditation: The Art of Ecstasy. (German)

B 669 _____. Meditation: The Art of Ecstasy. Edited by Ma Satya Bharti. New York: Harper & Row, 1978, c1976.

xxi,248p. Most of this material orig. appeared in the author's Dynamics of Meditation [B662]. LC 76-465

B670 _____. The Psychology of the Esoteric. Edited by Ma Satya Bharti. New York: Perennial Library, 1979, c1973. Also, New York: Harper & Row, 1978, c1973. viii,168p. Orig. pub. as The Inward Revolution. Bombay: Jeevan Jagriti Kendra, 1973.
A series of twelve discourses by Bhagwan Shree Rajneesh, in which he is interviewed by various sannyasins and visitors from Norway, the U.S.A., France, and Japan.

B671 _____. This Very Body, the Buddha. Edited by Ma Ananda Vandana. Poona: Rajneesh Foundation, 1978. 333p. LC 79-904227

B672 _____. Turning In. [A collection of thirty immortal letters written by Bhagwan Shree Rajneesh to H.H. Ma Yoga Mukta (Mrs. Catherine Venizelos), president, Neo-Sannyas International for North America.] Edited by Swami Yoga Chinmaya. Bombay: Jeevan Jagriti Kendra, 1971. 39p. LC 74-903392

B673 _____. Was ist Meditation? Margarethenried: Sannyas-Verlag, 1979. 72p. Einheitssacht.: What Is Meditation? (German)

B674 _____. What Is Meditation? Edited by Swami Yoga Chinmaya. Bombay: Jeevan Jagriti Kendra, 1971. 58p. LC 76-924694

B675 Ram Chandra, 1899- . Efficacy of Raj Yoga in the Light of Sahaj Marg. 3rd ed. Shahjahanpur, U.P.: Shri Ram Chandra Mission, 1968. Orig. pub., 1950. xxiv,71p. LC 71-901519

B676 Ram Dass. Journey of Awakening: A Meditator's Guidebook. Edited by Daniel Goleman with Dwarkanath Bonner and Ram Dev (Dale Borglum). Illustrated by Vincent Piazza. Toronto, London and New York: Bantam Books, 1978. Also dist. by DeVorss & Co., Marina del Rey, Calif. xiii,395p. Bibliography: p.393-395.
The author discusses a number of meditational techniques involving mantras, prayers, singing, visualization, and sitting. Offers guidance and advice on a suitable method, what to avoid and what to expect. Includes a directory of U.S. and Canadian meditation and retreat ashrams.

B677 Ramachandra Rao, Saligrama Krishna, 1926- . Tibetan Meditation: Theory and Practice. New Delhi: Arnold-Heinemann, 1979. 112p. LC 79-900596

B678   Ramakrishna Vedante Centre. Meditation. 2nd ed. By
monks of the Ramakrishna Order. London: Ramakrishna
Vedanta Centre, 1974. Orig. pub., 1972. Dist. in U.S.
by Auromere, Inc., Pomona, Calif. xxiv,161p. Bibliography: p.154-156. LC 77-363286
Presents meditation as taught by monastic disciples of Shri
Ramakrishna, who lived in Bengal from 1836 to 1886.

B679   Ray, David A. The Art of Christian Meditation: A Guide
to Increase Your Personal Awareness of God. New York:
Pocket Books, 1979. Orig. pub., Wheaton, Ill.: Tyndale
House Publishers, 1977. 121p. Includes bibliographical
references. LC 77-80736

B680   Regardie, Israel. Foundations of Practical Magic: An Introduction to Qabalistic, Magical and Meditative Techniques.
Wellingborough: Aquarian Press, 1979. 160p. Includes
bibliographical references. LC 80-476006

B681   Reichelt, Karl Ludvig, 1877-1952. Meditation and Piety in
the Far East: A Religious-Psychological Study. Translated from the Norwegian by Sverre Holth. New York:
Harper, and London: Lutterworth Press, 1954. 171p.
(Lutterworth Library; v.42. Missionary Research Series;
no.19) Orig. appeared as volume 1 of Fromhetstyper og
helligdommer i Ost-Asia. Bibliography: p.167-168. LC
55-782 and LC 54-3506

B682   Reiter, Udo, 1944- . Autorrealizacion: caminos hacia uno
mismo. Bilboa: Mensajero, 1977. 299p. Translation of
Meditation: Wege zum Selbst. (Spanish)

B683   _____. Erlösung im Lotussitz? Meditation heute. Hamburg: Furche-Verlag, 1974. 76p. (Studenbücher; Bd.
120) Includes bibliographical references. LC 75-553377
(German)

B684   _____, Hrsg. Meditation: Wege zum Selbst; Yoga, Zen,
christl. Meditation, transzendentale Meditation, Ananda
Marga, Meditation als Psychotherapie, Meditation u.
Naturwiss. München: Goldmann, 1981. Und, München:
Mosaik-Verlag, 1976. 192p. (German)

B685   _____, and Detlef Bendrath. Meditation: Wiederentdeckte
Wege zum Heil? Stuttgart: Evangelische Zentralstelle für
Weltanschauungsfragen, 1972. 27p. (German)

B686   Religiöse Themen der Gegenwart. By Hubert Tellenbach ...
[et al.]; hrsg. von Joseph Sauer. Karlsruhe: Badenia-
Verlag, 1977. 104p. Includes bibliographical references.
LC 77-570602 (German)

B 687   Reynolds, David K. <u>Naikan Psychotherapy: Meditation for</u>
<u>Self-Development</u>. Chicago: University of Chicago Press,
1983. x,170p. Bibliography: p.165-168. LC 82-21862

B 688   Rieker, Hans-Ulrich, 1920- . <u>Das Geheimnis der Meditation</u>.
Zürich: Rascher, 1953. 227p. (German)

B 689   _____. <u>Meditation. Übungen z. Selbstgestaltung</u>. Zürich
u. Stuttgart: Rascher, 1962. 291p. LC 67-118074
(German)

B 690   _____. <u>The Secret of Meditation</u>. Translated from the
German by A.J. Pomerans. New York: Samuel Weiser,
and London: Rider, 1974. Also, New York: Philosophical Library, 1957. Orig. pub., London: Rider, 1955.
Also dist. by DeVorss & Co., Marina del Rey, Calif.
176p. Translation of <u>Das Geheimnis der Meditation</u>. LC
74-194601
Zen, Tibetan and Christian meditation are discussed.

B 691   Riemkasten, Felix, 1894- . <u>Das Atembuch; der Atem, wie</u>
<u>er heilt und hilft; systematische Lehre über Atmen,</u>
<u>leichte Gymnastik, Entspannen und Meditation</u>. 4. verb.
und erweiterte Aufl. Büdingen-Gettenbach: Lebensweiser-Verlag, 1957. 78p. (German)

B 692   _____. <u>Das Geheimnis der Stille; der einzige Weg zur</u>
<u>Konzentration und Meditation</u>. 2. Aufl. Büdingen-
Gettenbach: Lebensweiser-Verlag, 1957. Orig. pub.,
1953. 128p. (German)

B 693   Rinpoche, Namgyal. <u>The Song of Awakening: A Guide to</u>
<u>Liberation Through Marananussati Mindfulness of Death</u>.
Edited by Karma Chime Wongmo. Boise, Idaho: Open
Path, 1979. xii,108p. LC 79-65090

B 694   Rinpoche, Sogyal. <u>Face to Face: Meditation Experience</u>.
Illustrated by Marol. London: Orgyen Cho Ling, 1978.
24p.

B 695   _____. <u>View, Meditation and Action</u>. 3rd ed. London,
(76 Princess Rd., NW6 5QX): Orygen Cho Ling, 1979
and previous editions. 23p.
A summary of the series of talks entitled "How to Actually
Meditate," given in the early part of 1977 at St. Marks Institute Hall, Balderton St., London.

B 696   Rittelmeyer, Friedrich. <u>Andacht</u>. Stuttgart: Verl. Urachhaus, 1955. 60p. (German)

B 697   _____. <u>Meditation: Guidance of the Inner Life</u>. Spring

Valley, N.Y.: Floris Books; St. George Book Service, 1981. 128p.

B698 _____ . Meditation: 12 Briefe über Selbsterziehung. Stuttgart: Urachhaus, 1980 and previous editions. 301p. (German)

B699 Ritter, Gerhard. Psycho-Yoga: autogenes Meditations-Training: Kurs für die eigenen vier Wände. Wörthsee-Steinebach: Ritter, 1976. 1 case. LC 81-459082 (German)
Case contains a book, Psycho-Yoga (144p.), a pamphlet "Erfolgskontrollheft zum Psycho-Yoga-Kurs" (30p.), and 6 cassettes (2-track. mono. 15min.)

B700 Robbins, Jhan, and David Fisher. Meditation: Glück in eigener Regie. Übers. von Ralf Friese. Stuttgart: Deutsche Verlags-Anstalt, 1973. 132p. Einheitssacht.: Tranquility Without Pills. (German)

B701 _____ . Tranquility Without Pills. New York: Bantam, and London: Corgi, 1975. Also, New York: Bantam Books, and London: Souvenir Press, 1973. Orig. pub., New York: P.H. Wyden, 1972. x,163p.

B702 Robertson, Irvine. Transcendental Meditation. Chicago: Moody Press, 1976. 30p.

B703 Robins, Alan, and Jane A. Himber. Dawn of a New Age: The TM Program and Enlightenment. New York: Berkley Pub. Corp., 1976. 148p.

B704 Robinson, Gweneth E. Prayer & Meditation for Spiritual Growth: The Teachings of Ir-a-qi, the Persian Mystic. Holsworthy: Speight Books for the Unity Teaching and Healing Trust, 1975. iii,59p. LC 76-364406

B705 Rodhe, Sten, 1915- . Att komma till sig själv: om olika former av meditation. Stockholm: Natur o. kultur, 1978. 167p. Bibliography: p.147-151. LC 79-391155 (Swedish)

B706 Rofidal, Jean. Do-in. Lausanne: Editions du Signal, R. Gaillard; Paris: Chiron; [Lausanne]: [diffusion Editions Foma], 1978. 110p. Bibliography: p.105. LC 80-514633 (French)

B707 _____ . Do-in: Eastern Massage and Yoga Techniques. Translated from the French. Wellingborough, Northhamptonshire: Thorsons Publishers, 1981. 160p. Translation of Do-in.

B708 _____ . Do-in: The Philosophy. Translated from the
French by David Louch. Wellingborough: Thorsons,
Pub. Ltd., 1983. 96p.
A system of yoga plus Zen manipulations, breathing and
meditation.

B709 Rogan, John. Meditation: How to Do It. London: Church
Literature Association, 1978. 12,[3]p.

B710 Rohrbach, Peter Thomas. Conversation with Christ: An
Introduction to Mental Prayer. London and Dublin: G.
Chapman, 1966. Also, Denville, N.J.: Dimension Books,
1965. Orig. pub., Chicago: Fides Publishers Association, 1956. xiii,171p. LC 66-66051
Portrays the concept of meditation popularized by St. Teresa
of Avila and employed in Discalced Carmelite monasteries.

B711 Romney, Rodney R., 1931- . Journey to Inner Space.
Nashville: Abingdon, 1980. 142p. LC 79-18822

B712 Roof, Simons Lucas, 1920- . Greatness of Being: A Guide
to Beginner-Intermediate Meditation. 2nd ed. [s.l.]:
Comparative Religious Studies Foundation, 1973. xi,149p.

B713 Roost, Jean Georges. Le yoga, science et connaissance de
l'homme. Confignon: Yogashram, Jean Roost, 1971.
200p. Bibliography: p.199. LC 74-165540 (French)

B714 Rooy, J. de. Tools for Meditation. Translated from the
Dutch by Y. Bosch van Drakestein. Pinner: Grail Publications, 1976. 60p. Translation and revision of Mediteren. Hilversum: Gooi en Sticht, 1974.

B715 Rosenberg, Alfons. Christliche Bildmeditation. München:
Kösel, 1975. Orig. pub., München-Planegg: Otto-
Wilhelm-Barth Verlag, 1955. 223p. Includes bibliograph-
ical references. LC 78-347960 (German)

B716 _____ . Kreuzmeditation: d. Meditation d. ganzen Mensch-
en. München: Kösel, 1976. 133p. (German)

B717 Roth, Ephrem. Monatliche Geisteserneuerung und Vorbereitung auf den Tod. 2. Aufl. Reimlingen u. Würzburg:
St. Josefs-Verl., 1957. 143p. (German)

B718 Rotthaus, Erich. Vom Wesen und Wert des meditierenden
Übens in der Psychotherapie. Vortrag. Stuttgart:
Gemeinschaft Arzt u. Seelsorger, 1957. 17p. (German)

B719 Rötting, Gerhard Jan. Still sein, schauen, Christ sein. Einf.
in d. Stille. Gnadenthal/Kr. Limburg/L.: Präsenz-Verl.,
1970. 44p. (Tiefgang-Reihe; Nr.11) (German)

B720 Roux, George, of Montfavet. Révélation de la joie, technique de la méditation. Préface de Jean-Marie Aubert. Paris: Beauchesne, 1968. 192p. LC 75-375973 (French)

B721 Rozman, Deborah. Meditation for Children. Photography by John Hills. Line illustrations by Mary Elizabeth Bruno. New York: Pocket Books, 1977. 175p. Orig. pub., Millbrae, Calif.: Celestial Arts, 1976. Bibliography: p.174-175. LC 75-28766
A guide to meditation, individually or with the family. Includes yoga and concentration exercises. Juvenile literature.

B722 _____. Meditating with Children: The Art of Concentration and Centering. Rev. & expanded ed. Photography and cover design by John Hills. Boulder Creek, Calif.: University of the Trees Press, 1977 and previous editions. 151p. LC 76-10480

B723 _____. Mit Kindern meditieren: d. Kunst d. Konzentration u. Verinnerlichung; e. Handbuch d. New-Age-Erziehungsmethoden. Aus d. Amerikan von Christl Klostermann. Frankfurt am Main: Fischer-Taschenbuch-Verlag, 1982, 1979. 146p. Einheitssacht.: Meditating with Children. (German)

B724 Rudhyan, Dane, 1895- . Astrological Themes for Meditation. Lakemont, Ga.: CSA Press, 1972. Also dist. by Wilshire Book Co., North Hollywood, Calif. 104p.

B725 Rudolph, Hermann. Meditationen. Ein theosoph. Andachtsbuch nebst Anleitung z. Meditation. 6. erw. Aufl. Buenos Aires: Ed. Fändrich, 1960. 118p. (German)

B726 Ruhbach, Gerhard, Hrsg. Meditation: Versuche-Wege, Erfahrungen. Göttingen: Vandenhoeck & Ruprecht; und Regensburg: Pustet, 1975. 111p. (German)

B727 Rupp, Walter, Hrsg. Beten, leben, meditieren. Würzburg: Echter-Verlag; München: Tyrolia; und Hamburg: Agentur des Rauhen Hauses, 1975. 142p. (German)

B728 Russell, Marjorie. A Handbook of Christian Meditation. Old Greenwich, Conn.: Devin-Adair Co., 1978. 119p. Bibliography: p.118-119. LC 77-90859

B729 Russell, Peter, 1946- . Meditation: Paths to Tranquility. Edited by Susan Paton. London: British Broadcasting Corp., 1979. 64p. To accompany the BBC Radio series, "Meditation."

B730 _____. The TM Technique: A Skeptic's Guide to the TM

Program. 3rd ed. Boston: Routledge & K. Paul, 1979 and previous editions. Also pub. as The TM Technique: An Introduction to Transcendental and the Teachings of Maharishi Mahesh Yogi. London and Boston: Routledge & K. Paul, 1978. Orig. pub., 1976. xii,201p. Includes bibliographical references.

A TM teacher discusses the philosophy of TM in the light of theoretical physics and psychology. The possible benefits of TM are explored.

B731   Sabha-pati Svami, 1840- . The Philosophy and Science of Vedanta and Raja Yoga, by Mahatma Jnana Guru Yogi Sabhapathy Swami. Edited by Siris Chandra Vasu. Mahim, Bombay: Chaitanya Prabja Mandali, 1950. 81p.

B732   _____. Vedantic Raj Yoga: Ancient Tantra Yoga of Rishies. New Delhi: Pankaj Publications; Dist. by Cambridge Book and Sty. Stores, 1977. viii,62p. Reprint of the 1880 ed. pub. in Lahore. "A Historical View of the Theories of the Soul" by Alexander Bain: p.46-62.

B733   Sadhu, Mouni. Concentration, a Guide to Mental Mastery. Hollywood, Calif.: Wilshire Book Co., 1977 and previous editions. Orig. pub., New York: Harper, 1959. Also pub. as Concentration, an Outline for Practical Study. London: G. Allen & Unwin, 1970 and 1959. 219p. Includes bibliography. Second book in trilogy: In Days of Great Peace/Concentration/Samadhi.

An introduction with exercises for concentration using both Western and Eastern sources.

B734   _____. In Days of Great Peace: The Highest Yoga as Lived. Foreword by M. Hafiz Syed. North Hollywood, Calif.: Wilshire Book Co., 1974. Also, London: Allen and Unwin, 1970 and 1957. Previous ed., Bangalore: Rammarayan Press, 1952. 212p. First book in trilogy: In Days of Great Peace/Concentration/Samadhi.

The technique of jnana yoga is described by a disciple of Ramana Maharshi. An autobiographical account of life with the Hindu yogi, Ramana Maharshi.

B735   _____. Konzentration und Verwirklichung. München: Barth, 1974. 199p. Einheitssacht.: Concentraiton, a Guide to Mental Mastery. (German)

B736   _____. Meditation: An Outline for Practical Study. North Hollywood, Calif.: Wilshire Book Co., 1978 and previous editions. Also, North Hollywood, Calif.: Melvin Powers, 1976. Orig. pub., London: Allen & Unwin, 1967. Also dist. by DeVorss & Co., Marina del Rey, Calif.

A manual for the experienced student. Introduces the meditator to contemplation with meditations taken from all the
world's scriptures.

B737   . Samadhi: The Superconsciousness of the Future.
London: Allen and Unwin, 1976. Orig. pub., 1962.
182p. Includes bibliography. Third book in trilogy:
In Days of Great Peace/Concentration/Samadhi.

B738   St. John, John Richard, 1917- . Travels in Inner Space:
One Man's Exploration of Encounter Groups, Meditation,
and Altered States of Consciousness. London: Gollancz,
1977. 207p. Includes bibliographies. LC 78-318912

B739   Samendra, Anand. The You Book. London [14 Mornington
Cresent, MW1]: Alchemy, 1981. 171p. Limited ed. of
500 copies.

B740   Sampaio, André Leme. Meditação: ensaio. São Paulo, 1968.
44p. LC 75-278270 (Portuguese)

B741   Sanjoy, 1929- . The Way and the Goal of Raja Yoga, by
Jagdish Chander (i.e. Sanjoy). 2nd ed. Mount Abu:
Prajapita Brahma Kumaris Ishwariya Vishwa-Vidyalaya,
1977. vii,232p. (On verso of t.p.: Published by Liter-
ature Dept., God-Fatherly University of Brahma Kumaris,
Mount Abu)

B742   Sarasvati, Satya Prakash, Swami, 1905- . Patanjala Raja
Yoga. New Delhi: S. Chand, 1975. x,347p. Includes
bibliographical references. LC 75-904330

B743   Saraydarian, Torkom. La ciencia de la meditación. Translated by H.V. Morel. Buenos Aires: Editorial Kier,
1979. 286p. Translation of The Science of Meditation.
Includes bibliographical footnotes. (Spanish)

B744   . Five Great Mantrams of the New-Age. Agoura,
Calif.: Aquarian Educational Group, 1975. 45p. LC
73-39431

B745   . Innenschau: e. Handbuch d. prakt. Meditation.
Freiburg i. Br.: Bauer, 1977. 467p. Einheitssacht.:
The Science of Meditation. (German)

B746   . The Science of Meditation. Reseda, Calif.:
Aquarian Educational Group, 1971. 364p. Includes bibliographical references. LC 77-158995

B747   Sartory, Thomas. Erfahrungen mit Meditation: e. Orient-
ierungshilfe für Christen. Freiburg im Breisgau, Basel,
und Wien: Herder, 1976. 142p. (German)

B748   Satchidananda, Swami. How to Succeed in Yoga and Other
       Talks. Compiled from Integral Yoga Magazine, 1966-1977.
       Pomfret Center, Conn.: Integral Yoga Publication, 1978.
       127p. LC 78-107902

B749   _____. Meditation: Excerpts from Talks. [s.l.]:
       Satchidananda Ashram-Yogaville, 1975. 32p.

B750   Sathya Sai Baba, 1926- . Dhyana Vahini: Discourses.
       Translated from the original Telugu. 4th ed. Kadugodi,
       Bangalore Dist., India: Shri Sathya Sai Education and
       Publication Foundation, 1975. Also, Prasanthi Nilayan:
       Sanathana Sarathi, 1966. 74p.

B751   Satprakashananda, Swami. Meditation: Its Process, Prac-
       tice, and Culmination. St. Louis: Vedanta Society of
       St. Louis, 1976. 264p. Includes bibliographical refer-
       ences. LC 76-15722

B752   Satya Bharti, Ma. Drunk on the Divine: An Account of
       Life in the Ashram of Bhagwan Shree Rajneesh. New
       York: Grove Press, 1981. Orig. pub. as The Ultimate
       Risk: Encountering Bhagwan Shree Rajneesh. London:
       Wildwood House, and Sydney: Bookwise Australia, 1980.
       xi,220p. LC 79-6168

B753   _____. Wagnis Orange, Bhagwan Shree Rajneesh: e.
       Blick aus nächster Nähe auf e. d. grossen psycholog. u.
       spirituellen Zentren unseres Jh. Frankfurt am Main:
       Fachbuchhandlung für Psychologie, Verlagsabt., 1980.
       227p. Einheitssacht.: The Ultimate Risk. Bibliogr.
       Bhagwan Shree Rajneesh p.4-10. (German)

B754   Satyanand Agnihotri, 1850-1929. The Dev Shastra. 2nd ed.
       New Delhi: Dev Samaj Prakashan, 1975- Pt. 1. Philos-
       ophy of Nature. Pt. 2. The Philosophy of Truth &
       Falsehood. Pt. 4. Study of Infra-Human Relationships.
       LC 80-902812

B755   Satyananda Rao, Vedula, 1925- . Sri Prabhuji's Lectures
       Divine on the Theory, Practice, and the Technology of
       the Science of Rajayoga. Edited by N. Sarojani. Ala-
       muru, East Godavart Dt.: Rajayogasadhanasham, 1969.
       v,236p. LC 72-922203

B756   Satyananda Saraswati, Swami, 1923- . Kundalini Yoga.
       Monghyr: Bihar School of Yoga, 1973. 117p. Title on
       jacket: Tantra of Kundalini Yoga. Transcribed and
       edited by Satyananda Aschram des Tantra, Wien, Austria.
       LC 75-905295

B757 _____. Meditations from the Tantras, with Live Class Transcriptions. Edited by Swami Nishchalananda Saraswati. 3rd ed. Monghyr: Bihar School of Yoga, 1977 and previous editions. Orig. pub., 1974. viii,312p. Bibliography: p.308.

B758 Satyavan. The Gayatri Mantra: Yoga for Beginners. Hayama, Kangawa-ken, Japan: Autumn Press, 1974. 50p. LC 73-93264

B759 Sauls, Lynn. TM or CM? Mountain View, Calif.: Pacific Press, 1977. 29p.

B760 Sax, Saville, and Sandra Hollander. Wake the Dragon: A Book on Awareness, Meditation, Centering, Self-Shaping. Designer, Sarah Linquist. Photographers, Bob Fishbone and Eleanor Colfesh-Schurr. Edwardsville, Ill.: Reality Games Institute, 1975. 47p. LC 75-31350

B761 Saxena, R.P. Transcendental Meditation: A Scientific Approach. Foreword by Hans Selye. Laindon [9 Suffolk Drive, Laindon, Essex SS15 6PL]: International Society for Prevention of Stress, 1978. [9],iii,120p. Includes bibliography.

B762 Sayadaw, Mahasi. Practical Insight Meditation. San Francisco: Unity Press, 1972. Also, Kandy: Buddhist Publication Society; printed at Angunawala by Supra Printers, date? 64p.

B763 Scabelloni, Antoni Massimo, 1906- . Manuale pratico della meditazione. Roma: Teseo, 1972? 152p. At head of title: Massimo Scallgero. LC 74-345420 (Italian)

B764 _____. Meditazione e miracolo. Roma: Edizioni mediterranee, 1977. 181p. LC 78-386970 (Italian)

B765 Schamoni, Wilhelm, 1905- , Hrsg。 Gebet und Hingabe, Ausführungen der Heiligan: Thersia vom Kinde Jesu, Johannes vom Kreuz, Franz von Sales, Theresia von Jesus. Paderborn: F. Schöningh, 1953. 351p. (German)

B766 Scharf, Siegfried. Das grosse Buch der Herzensmeditation: Wort-Meditation, Liebe-Strahlung, Heil-Meditation; Theorie u. Praxis mit zahlr. Übungsbeispielen; e. Weg für d. westl. Menschen zur inneren Führung u. Heilwerdung aus d. Synthese Christl. Gebetspraxis u. östl. Meditationsweisen. Freiburg im Breisgau: Aurum-Verlag, 1979. 275p. (German)

B767 _____. Die Praxis der Herzensmeditation: Wort-Meditation,

Liebe-Strahlung, Heil-Meditation; e. Weg für d. westl. Menschen als Synthese christl. Gebetspraxis u. östl. Meditationsweisen. Freiburg im Breisgau: Aurum-Verlag, 1976. 109p. (German)

B768 Scheihing, Theresa O'Callaghan, and Louis M. Savary. Our Treasured Heritage: Teaching Christian Meditation to Children. New York: Crossroad, 1981. 155p. LC 81-7818
Shows parents how to help their children build a relationship with God through simple meditation modeled on the Ignatian form.

B769 Scherer, Georg. Reflexion, Meditation, Gebet: ein philosoph. Versuch. Essen: Driewer, 1973. 99p. Includes bibliographical references. LC 74-356725 (German)

B770 Schinle, Gertrudis. Das kontemplative Leben. Kurze Betrachtungen. Leutesdorf a. Rh.: Johannes-Verl., 1965. 70p. (German)

B771 Schmidt, Karl Otto. Bücher des flammenden Herzens. Meditation u. Kontemplation als Führer kosmischen Bewusstseins. 3. Aufl. Pfullingen/Württ.: Baum-Verl. Bd. 1. Sonne um Mitternacht, 1961, 164p. Bd. 2. Das Licht der Seele, 1961, 162p. Bd. 3. Die unsichtbare Kirche. Bd. 4. Der Gott in dir., 1962, 159p. Bd. 5. Die grossen Liebenden, 1962, 156p. (German)

B772 _____. Das Erwachen der Seele. Meditation u. Kontemplation als Führer zum neuen Leben. München-Planegg: O.W. Barth, 1954. 316p. (German)

B773 _____. Der geheimnisvolle Helfer in dir: Dynamik geistiger Selbsthilfe; e. Brevier prakt. Lebenskunst. Freiburg im Breisgau: Bauer, 1981 and 1977. 271p. (German)

B774 _____. Lebensweiser zur Selbst- und Schicksalsmeisterung. Handbücker d. Erfolgs-Psychologie. Bd. 1-3. Büdingen-Gettenbach: Lebensweiser-Verl., 1954-1955. Bd. 2. Der Weg zur Vollendung. Technik d. Konzentration. Praxis d. Meditation. Dynamik d. Kontemplation, 1955. (German)

B775 _____. Der Weg zur Vollendung: durch Meditation u. Kontemplation. Engelberg/Schweiz und München: Drei-Eichen-Verlag, 1978. Und, Pfullingen/Württ.: Baum-Verl., 1968. 315p. (German)

B776 Schmitt, Winfried. Seelische Selbsthilfe durch Yoga und Meditation. Büdingen-Gettenbach: Verlagsunion, 1956. 53p. (German)

B777 _____. Yoga, Zen, Meditation. Büdingen-Gettenbach: Lebensweiser-Verlag, 1959. 94p. (German)

B778 Scholtz-Wiesner, Renate F. von. Grundlagen des meditativen Lebens. Heilbronn: Verlag Heilbronn, 1981. 92p. (German)

B779 _____. Hoffen und Erkennen: Aphorismen zur Meditation. Heilbronn: Verlag Heilbronn, 1981. 67p. (German)

B780 Schulte, Nico. De ethiek van verlichting: groei en vervulling door het transcendente meditatie programma zoals geleerd door Maharishi Mahesh Yogi. Den Haag: MIU Nederland Pers, 1977. 164p. Includes bibliographical references. LC 77-484171 (Dutch)

B781 _____. Onderwijs voor verlichting: de TM techniek en de ontwikkeling van het bewustzijn: de ontbrekende dimensie in het onderwijs. Den Haag: MIU Nederland Pers, 1978. 253p. Bibliography: p.227-232. LC 80-497874 (Dutch)

B782 _____. Siddhi's zweven naar ideaal leven. Den Haag: MIU Nederland Pers, 1977. 176p. Includes bibliographical references. LC 79-393559 (Dutch)

B783 Schulte, Therese. Transzendentale Meditation und wohin sie führt: Abschiedsdisput e. TM-Lehrerin. 2. Aufl. Stuttgart: Verlag Freies Geistesleben, 1981. 252p. (German)

B784 Schulz, Chrysostomus. Ich bin da, vor Ihm: Meditation u. ihre Auswirkung. Frankfurt/Main: Kaffke, 1977. 23p. (German)

B785 Schwäbisch, Lutz. Selbstenftaltung durch Meditation: e. prakt. Anleitung. Reinbek bei Hamburg: Rowohlt, 1981 and previous editions. 219p. Literaturverz.: p.216-218. (German)

B786 Schwarz, Jack. The Path of Action. New York: Dutton, 1977. xxii,132p. LC 77-2247
Discusses meditative practice that is part of daily living rather than contemplative, using a synthesis of Eastern and Western thought.

B787 _____. Voluntary Controls. New York: Dutton, 1978. Also dist. by DeVorss & Co., Marina del Rey, Calif. xiv,143p. LC 77-25347
Discusses exercises and techniques for creative meditation. Activation of the chakras is also covered.

B788   Schwemer, Hermann. <u>Östliche Meditation und westliche re-</u>
<u>ligiöse Erneuerung</u>. Kassel: Stauda, 1975. 64p. (Kirche
zwischem Planen und Hoffen; Heft 13) Includes bibliographical references. LC 75-516971 (German)

B789   <u>Scientific Research on the Transcendental Meditation Program</u>:
<u>Collected Papers, Vol. 1</u>. Edited by David W. Orme-
Johnson and John T. Farrow. Introduction by Lawrence
H. Domash. Foreword by Maharishi Mahesh Yogi. 2nd
ed. Weggis, Switzerland: Maharishi European Research
University Press, 1977. Dist. in U.S. by Maharishi European Research University Press, Livingston Manor, N.Y.
Orig. pub. 1976, and dist. in U.S. by Maharishi International University Press, Los Angeles (now Fairfield,
Iowa). 727p. LC 78-53048
Of the one hundred and one papers in this volume, thirty-
one were first published in journals. Fifteen other papers
were published elsewhere. Fifty-five of them appear in
print here for the first time. In the second edition three
additional reports were added. Each paper is included in
the Articles section and the Author, Title, and Subject Indexes.

B790   <u>Scientific Research on the Transcendental Meditation Program</u>:
<u>Collected Papers, Vol. 2</u>. Edited by Berndt Zeiger.
Rheinweiler, West Germany: Maharishi European Research
University Press, (in press).
The papers tentatively scheduled for inclusion in this volume
have been included in the Articles section and the Author,
Title, and Subject indexes. The information was obtained
from the <u>Bibliography and Reprint Catalog, Maharishi Inter-</u>
<u>national University</u>: <u>Scientific Research on the Transcendental</u>
<u>Meditation and TM-Sidhi-Program</u>. Revised ed. Fairfield,
Iowa: Reprint Service, Maharishi International University,
1982.

B791   <u>Scientific Research on the Transcendental Meditation Pro-</u>
<u>gramme</u>. Bremen: MIU Press, 1975. 128p. Includes
references. (MIU Press Publication Number G 205)

B792   Scott, R.D., 1950- . <u>Transcendental Misconceptions</u>. San
Diego: Beta Books, 1978. Dist. by Bobbs-Merrill, In-
dianapolis, Ind. 227p. Includes bibliographical references. LC 77-13503

B793   <u>Se guérir soi-même: par le yoga et la méditation</u>. Direction,
Claude Leclerc. Recherche, Linda Nantel, Elise Pouliot.
Westmount, Québec: Productions Amérique française,
1980? 72p. (Les Grands cahiers de la vie; 4) (French)

B794   Sechrist, Elsie. <u>Meditation: Gateway to Light</u>. Revised

edition. Virginia Beach, Va.: A.R.E. Press, 1974.
Orig. pub., 1972. iii,53p.
The author is associated with Edgar Cayce's work.

B795 Seifert, Harvey. Explorations in Meditation and Contemplation. Nashville, Tenn.: Upper Room, 1981. 126p.
LC 81-50601

B796 _____, and Lois Seifert. Liberation of Life: Growth Exercises in Meditation and Action. Nashville: The Upper
Room, 1976. 112p. LC 76-46880

B797 Sekida, Katsuki, 1893- . Zen Training: Methods and Philosophy. Edited with an introduction by A.V. Grimstone.
New York: Weatherhill, 1975. 258p. An expanded English version of An Introduction to Zen for Beginners,
originally written in Japanese. Includes bibliographical
references. LC 75-17573
A substantial part of the book is devoted to describing how
Zazen is performed and what its effects are. Detailed instructions are provided for the beginner and experienced
student of Zen meditation.

B798 Sekiguchi, Shindai, 1907- . Zen: A Manual for Westerners.
Tokyo: Japan Publications, 1970. 110p. LC 72-115845

B799 Sexton, Thomas G., and Donald R. Poling. Can Intelligence
Be Taught? Bloomington, Ind.: Phi Delta Kappa Educa-
tional Foundation, 1973. 34p. (PDK Fastbacks; v.29)
Bibliography: p.33-34. LC 75-321775
Suggests that intelligence can be trained. The educational
applications of meditation are explored.

B800 Shah, Douglas. The Meditators. Plainfield, N.J.: Logos
International, 1975. x,147p. LC 75-7478

B801 Shapiro, Deane H., Jr. Meditation, Self-Regulation Strategy
& Altered State of Consciousness: A Scientific/Personal
Exploration. New York: Aldine, 1980. xxiii,318p.
Bibliography: p.281-307. LC 81-167900
A comprehensive survey of current research demonstrating
that meditation can be an important tool for exploring human
consciousness and providing medical health care.

B802 _____, and Roger N. Walsh. Meditation: Classic and
Contemporary Perspectives. Hawthorne, N.Y.: Aldine
Pub. Co., 1984.
A reader representing those works which are classics in the
field, methodologically interesting, and clinically relevant.
Includes the clinical use of meditation in drug abuse, hyper-
tension, tension and stress management, as well as physio-

logical findings and phenomenological studies. Includes a
bibliography of meditation-related works.

B 803   Shastri, Hari Prasad, 1882-1956. Meditation, Its Theory
and Practice. 9th ed. London: Shanti Sadan, 1974
and previous editions. 64p.
Discusses the spiritual and psychological principles of meditation with instructions for the beginner and advanced student.

B 804   _____. Meditation: Theorie u. Praxis. Krün: Verlag
der Helfenden, 1974. Also, Frankfurt: M. Atharva-
Verl., 1960. 83p. Einheitssacht.: Meditation, Its Theory and Practice. (German)

B 805   Shattock, Ernest Henry. An Experiment in Mindfulness.
London: Rider, and New York: Samuel Weiser, 1970.
Also, New York: Dutton, 1960. Orig. pub., London:
Rider, 1958. 158p.
A personal account of experiences with the Satipatthana
method of Buddhist meditation while the author was at a
meditation center in Rangoon.

B 806   Shedd, Charlie W. Getting Through to the Wonderful You:
A Christian Alternative to Transcendental Meditation.
Old Tappan, N.J.: Revell, 1976. 128p. LC 75-43875

B 807   Shyam, Swami. Mastermind. Vancouver: Fforbez Enter-
prises, 1975. xviii,156p.

B 808   Siddheswarananda, Swami. Meditation According to Yoga-
Vedanta. Translated by V.A. Thyagarajan. 3rd ed.
Puranattukara, Trichur Dt.: Sri Ramakrishna Ashrama;
[label: Dist. by Vivekananda Vedanta Society, Chicago],
1973. Also dist. by Auromere, Pomona, Calif. Orig.
pub., 1966. xvi,187p.

B 809   _____. La méditation selon le Yoga-Védânta. Paris:
Maisonneuve, 1976. Also, 1945 and 1943. 153p.
(French)

B 810   Silva, José, 1914- , and Philip Miele. El metodo Silva de
control mental. Translated by Emilio E. Guzmban.
México: Editorial Diana, 1978. 224p. Bibliography:
p.215. Translation of The Silva Mind Control Method.
(Spanish)

B 811   _____. The Silva Mind Control Method. St. Albans,
Hertfordshire: Panther Books, 1980. Also, New York:
Pocket Books, 1978. Orig. pub., New York: Simon and
Schuster, 1977. 208p.

B812   Simard, Jean-Paul. Se concentrer pour être heureux: tech-
        nique d'épanouissement personnel. Montréal: Centre
        interdisciplinaire de Montréal, 1981. 213p. Bibliographie:
        p.211-213. (French)

B813   Singh, Charan, 1916 or 17- . Die to Live: Maharaj Charan
        Singh Answers Questions on Meditation. Beas: Radha
        Soami Satsang Beas, 1979. viii,386p. Bibliography:
        p.353-363. LC 80-900740

B814   _____. Spiritual Discourses. 3rd ed. Beas: Radha
        Soami Satsang, 1974. Also, 1970. Orig. pub., 1964.
        xiv,240,[6]p. Bibliography: p.244-246.

B815   Sivananda, Swami, 1887-1963. Concentration and Meditation.
        5th ed. Himalayas, India: Divine Life Society, 1975.
        Dist. in U.S. by Orient Book Distributors, Livingston,
        N.J. Also, 1969, and Sivanandanagar: Yoga Vedanta
        Forest Academy, 1964 and 1959. Orig. pub., Rishikesh:
        The Sivananda Publication League, 1945. xxxii,411p.
        A comprehensive text on the theory and practice of medita-
        tion with detailed instructions. Sivananda was the guru to
        Swamis Satchidananda and Vishnudevananda.

B816   _____. Dhyana Yoga. Shivananda Nagar, Rishikesh:
        Yoga-Vedanta Forest University, 1958. xv,200p.

B817   _____. Fourteen Lessons in Raja Yoga. Delhi: Motilal
        Banarsidass, 1976. Dist. in U.S. by Orient Book Dis-
        tributors, Livingston, N.J. Also, Sivanandanager:
        Divine Life Society, 1970, and Rishikesh: Yoga Vedanta
        Forest Academy, 1960. xx,135p.

B818   _____. Japa Yoga: A Comprehensive Treatise on Man-
        tra-Sastra. 8th ed. Sivanandanagar: Divine Life Soci-
        ety, 1978 and previous editions. Dist. in U.S. by Orient
        Book Distributors, Livingston, N.J. xl,192[2]p.

B819   _____. Practice of Yoga: Various Practical Methods in
        Yoga and Meditation. 3rd rev. and enl. ed. Buedingen:
        Sivananda Press, 1954. 279p.

B820   _____. Samadhi Yoga. Rishikesh: Sivananda Literature
        Research Institute, 1961. Orig. pub., Rishikesh: Sivan-
        anda Publication League, 1944. xl,415p.

B821   _____. Selbstverwirklichung. (Diene, liebe, meditiere,
        verwirkliche.) Die Ges. vom göttl. Leben. Yoga Vedanta
        Forest University in Ananda Kutir. Dornbirn: Lichtland-
        verl., 1955. 132p. (German)

B822   . Übungen zur Konzentration und Meditation.
          München: O.W. Barth, 1959, 1955 und 1952. 390p.
          Einheitssacht.: Concentration and Meditation. (German)

B823   Sivananda Radha, Swami, 1911- . Mantras: Words of
          Power. Porthill, Idaho: Timeless Books, 1980. ix,129p.
          Bibliography: p.121. LC 80-10293

B824   Slade, Herbert Edwin William. Meeting Schools of Oriental
          Meditation. Guildford: Lutterworth Press, 1973. 55p.
          Includes bibliographical references.

B825   Slater, Victor Wallace. Raja Yoga: A Simplified and Practi-
          cal Course. London and Wheaton, Ill.: Theosophical
          Pub. House, 1968. viii,105p. LC 71-3051

B826   Smedt, Marc de. 50 techniques de méditation. Ill. de Bar-
          bara Crépon. Montréal: Editions France-Amérique, and
          Paris: Retz, 1979. 255,[1]p. Bibliographie: p.254-256.
          LC 79-391912 (French)

B827   , and Jean-Michel Varenne. Etre Jésus. Paris: R.
          Laffont, 1974. 285p. Bibliographie: p.284-285. LC 74-
          186520 (French)

B828   Smith, Bradford, 1909-1964. A arte da meditação. Tradu-
          ção de Ruy Jungmann. Rio de Janeiro: Forense, 1968.
          212p. Translation of Meditation: The Inward Art.
          (Portuguese)

B829   . Meditation: The Inward Art. Philadelphia: Lip-
          pincott, 1968, and London: Allen & Unwin, 1964. Orig.
          pub., Philadelphia: Lippincott, and Toronto: McClelland
          & Stewart Ltd., 1963. 224p.
          A discussion of different forms of meditation with instructions
          on how to do it from a Quaker's point of view.

B830   Smith, Malcolm, 1938- . How I Learned to Meditate. Plain-
          field, N.J.: Logos Internaitonal, 1977. viii,127p. LC
          77-18482
          Includes biographical material about Pentecostal clergy in
          the United States and England.

B831   Sober, Victoria Parker. The Journey of the Soul. River-
          side, Calif.: Radha Soami Society Beas--America, 1976.
          40p. LC 78-311795
          Explains the creation of souls, their journeys through dif-
          ferent life forms on earth, and, as humans, their prepara-
          tion through meditation to rejoin their Creator in Eternity.
          Juvenile literature.

B832 Soni, R.L. The Only Way to Deliverance. Boulder: Prajna
      Press, 1980. xi,106p. Bibliography: p.105-106. LC
      78-13237
      Consists of a commentary, accompanied by the author's
      translation of Satipathana Sutta.

B833 Sonnet, André. Die Praxis der Konzentration und Meditation:
      Wege zur Verinnerlichung. Freiburg im Breisgau: H.
      Bauer, 1961. 190p. (German)

B834 Sopa, Geshe Lhundup, 1925- , and Jeffrey Hopkins. Prac-
      tice and Theory of Tibetan Buddhism. Foreword by His
      Holiness The Dalai Lama. New York: Grove Press, 1976.
      xxviii,164p. Bibliography: p.153-155. LC 75-42898

B835 _____, und _____. Der tibetische Buddhismus. Düs-
      seldorf: Köln, 1981 und 1977. 224p. Einheitssacht.:
      Practice and Theory of Tibetan Buddhism. Literaturverz.:
      p.212-214. (German)

B836 Spachtholz, Otto Josef. Poesien aus religiöser Innenschau
      mit einstimmenden Akkorden in Prosa: Religion aus Leben
      u. Dichtung; Gott Tao Brahma Betrachtungsbuch f.
      Menschen aller Bekenntnisse. Wien: Europäischer Ver-
      lag, 1971. 56p. (German)

B837 Speyr, Adrienne von. Das Licht und die Bilder. Elemente
      d. Kontemplation. Einsiedeln: Johannes-Verl., 1955.
      122p. (German)

B838 Spink, Peter. The Path of the Mystic: Steps in a Pilgrim's
      Progress with Seven Meditational Exercises Suitable for
      Use by Groups or Individuals. London: Darton, Long-
      man and Todd, 1983. 85p.

B839 Spiritual Community Guide. San Rafael, Calif.: Spiritual
      Community Publications, 1972- . LC 72-621784

B840 Splett, Jörg, und Ingrid Splett. Meditation der Gemeinsam-
      keit. Aspekte e. ehel. Anthropologie. München und
      Freiburg i Br.: Wewel, 1970. 139p. Literaturverz.:
      p.135-137. (German)

B841 Spotlights on Purity, Knowledge, and Raja Yoga. 2nd ed.
      Mount Abu: Prajapita Brahma Kumaris Ishwariya Vishwa-
      Vidyalaya, 1976? 86p.

B842 Sprenger, Werner. Schleichwege zum Ich. Freiburg i Br.:
      Nie-nie-sagen-Verlag, 1979. 2. Meditationstexte zur
      Selbsfindung: werde d., d. Du bist. 222p.

B843   Stachel, Günter. Aufruf zur Meditation. 2. Aufl. Graz,
        Wien, und Köln: Verlag Styria, 1973. Orig. pub.,
        1972. 68p. (German)

B844   Staehelin, Balthasar: Der finale Mensch: Therapie für
        Materialisten. Zürich: Theologischer Verlag, 1976.
        187p. (German)

B845   _____. Der psychosomatische Christus: e. medizinpsy-
        cholog. Begründung d. These von Gottes Wohnen im
        Menschen u.e. Drei-rote-Rosen-Meditation. Schaffhausen:
        Novalis-Verlag, 1980. 160p. (German)

B846   Staff, Vera Stuart. On Starting a Study Group with Practice
        of Meditation. London: Mysticism Committee of the
        Churches' Fellowship for Psychical and Spiritual Studies,
        1974. 18p. Bibliography: p.10-16.

B847   Stahl, Carolyn. Opening to God: Guided Imagery Meditation
        on Scripture for Individuals and Groups. Nashville: The
        Upper Room, 1977. 139p. Bibliography: p.123-130.
        LC 77-87403

B848   Stanietz, Walter. Zum Paradies des Menschen. Pfullingen/
        Württ.: Baum-Verl., 1965. 104p. (German)

B849   Steinbrecher, Edwin C. The Inner Guide Meditation. Rev.
        & enl. ed. Santa Fe, N.M.: Blue Feather Press; dist.
        by D.O.M.E. Services, 1978. Previous editions published
        as An Excerpt from The Guide Meditation and The Guide
        Meditation. xiv,281p. Bibliography: p.251-263. LC
        78-60489

B850   Steiner, Rudolf. Anweisungen für eine esoterische Schulung;
        aus d. Inh. d. "Esoter. Schule." Dornach/Schweiz:
        Rudolf-Steiner-Verlag, 1979. 176p. (German)

B851   Steinfeld, Ludwig, 1917- . Autogene Meditation: von d.
        Grundübungen d. autogenen Trainings zur meditativen
        Versenkung. Düsseldorf: Patmos-Verlag, 1978. 178p.
        Bibliography: p.175-178. LC 80-464174 (German)

B852   Stevens, Edward, 1928- . Oriental Mysticism. New York:
        Paulist Press, 1973. 186p. Cover title: An Introduction
        to Oriental Mysticism. Includes bibliographical references.
        LC 73-87030
        Discusses the psychological, philosophical and devotional
        aspects of meditation.

B853   Stillhetens psykologi: Transcendental meditasjon: Virkning
        og dynamikk. By Rolf Brandrud ... [et al.]. Oslo:

Dyede, 1976. 100p. Prepared under the auspices of ACEM. LC 79-386658 (Norwegian)

B854   Stone, Justin F. Climb the Joyous Mountain: Living the Meditative Way. Albuquerque, N.M.: Sun Pub., 1975. 95p.

B855   _____. The Joys of Meditation: A Do-It-Yourself Book of Instruction in Varied Meditation Techniques. Albuquerque, N.M.: Far West Pub. Co., 1973. 95p. (Sun Books) LC 73-88725
Includes chapters on What is Meditation?, Great Circle Meditation, Three Modes of Japa, Zen Meditation, Satipattana, Secret Nei Kung, Two Tibetan Meditations, and How and Why Does Meditation Work?

B856   _____. Meditation for Healing. Albuquerque: Sun Pub. Co., 1977. 184p.
Includes chapters on Many Meditations--Many Effects, What is Meditation?, Different Modes of Meditation, Circulating the Chi, Breath, Way of Mindfulness, Chih-K'uan, Visualization, Tibetan Dumo Heat, Chanting Zen, Mind Control, Moving Meditation, and Spiritual Side of Meditation.

B857   _____. Zen Meditation: A Broad View. Albuquerque, N.M.: Sun Pub. Co., 1975. 151p.

B858   Story, Francis. Buddhist Meditation. Enl. ed. Kandy, Ceylon: Buddhist Pub. Society, 1963. 26p.

B859   Straughn, R.A. Meditation Techniques of the Kabalists, Vedantins and Taoists. Bronx, N.Y.: Maat Pub. Co., 1976. viii,166p. LC 76-370959

B860   Street, Noel, and Judy Dupree. How to Meditate Perfectly: Develop Spiritually, Unfold Psychically. Lakemont, Ga.: Tarnhelm Press, 1973. 93p. LC 73-75097

B861   Stürmer, Ernst. Zen. Zauber oder Zucht? Wien: Herder, 1973. 111p. LC 73-358364

B862   Subramuniya, Master. Beginning to Meditate. 2nd ed. Kapaa, Hawaii: Wailua University of Contemplative Arts, 1972. 18p. LC 73-174898

B863   _____. Everything Is Within You. 5th ed. San Francisco: Comstock House, 1973. Dist. by DeVorss, Marina del Rey, Calif. 43p. (The Pathfinder's Library; 5)

B864   _____. The Fine Art of Meditation. San Francisco: Comstock House, 1973. Dist. by DeVorss, Marina del Rey, Calif. 40p. (The Pathfinder's Library; 1)

B865   _____. Master Course, Part One. 6th ed. Kapra, Hawaii: Wailua University of Contemplative Arts, 1972, c1971. Includes unpaged Seminar Guide for Master Course, Part One. Accompanied by cassette tapes to be used with the text.
A twelve-week course on meditation and the path of enlightenment crafted by the monks of the School of Monastic and Renunciate Life from twelve hours of recorded discussions with Master Subramuniya.

B866   _____. The Meditator. San Francisco: Comstock House, 1973. Dist. by DeVorss, Marina del Rey, Calif. 72p.

B867   _____. Raja Yoga. 5th ed. San Francisco: Comstock House, 1973. Dist. by DeVorss & Co., Marina del Rey, Calif. 191p.

B868 Sudbrack, Josef. Herausgefordert zur Meditation: christl. Erfahrung im Gespräch mit d. Osten. Freiburg im Breisgau, Basel, und Wien: Herder, 1977. 175p. (German)

B869   _____. Meditation: Theorie und Praxis. Würzburg: Echter Verlag, 1971. 171p. (Geist und Leben, Studien zur Verwirklichung der christlichen Botschaft; Bd.2) LC 76-888371 (German)

B870   _____. Worte sind Brücken: Hinführung zur Gedichtmeditation. Frankfurt/Main: Kaffke, 1977. 95p. (German)

B871 Sujata, Anagarika. Beginning to see: Anl. zur Meditation. Klingenbach: Überdruck, 1979. 96p. (German)

B872 Suzuki, Daisetz Teitaro, 1870-1966.
Dr. Suzuki's works are not ordinarily found listed under the subject heading, Meditation, in library catalogs. The following list of titles in English is provided as possible sources of information on Zen meditation. Many of these titles have appeared in various editions and translations.
Awakening of a New Consciousness in Zen. Awakening of Zen. Buddhism in the Life and Thought of Japan. Buddhist Philosophy and Its Effects on the Life and Thought of the Japanese People. Chain of Compassion. Collected Writings on Shin Buddhism. Essays in Zen Buddhism, (First, Second, & Third Series). Essence of Buddhism. Essentials of Zen Buddhism, Selected from the Writings of Daisetz T. Suzuki. Field of Zen. Introduction to Zen Buddhism. Japanese Buddhism. Japanese Spirituality. Living by Zen. Living in the Light of Eternity. Manual of Zen Buddhism. Meditation Hall and Ideals of the Monkish Discipline. Miscellany on the Shin Teaching of Buddhism. Mysticism: Christian and

Buddhist. On Indian Mahayana Buddhism. Outlines of Mahayana Buddhism. Sengali, the Zen Master. Shin Buddhism.
Some Aspects of Zen Buddhism. Studies in the Lankavatra
Sutra. Studies in Zen. Training of the Zen Buddhist Monk.
Way of Compassion. What Is Zen? Zen and Japanese Buddhism. Zen and Japanese Culture, orig. pub. as Zen Bud-
hism and Its Influence on Japanese Culture. Zen Buddhism
and Psychoanalysis. Zen Buddhism, Selected Writings. Zen
Doctrine of No-Mind. Zen Monk's Life.

B873   Suzuki, Shunryu. Zen Mind, Beginner's Mind. Edited by
        Trudy Dixon. Introduction by Richard Baker. New
        York: Weatherhill, 1980 and previous editions. Some
        editions also published in Tokyo by Weatherhill. Orig.
        pub., New York: Walker/Weatherhill, 1970. 138p. LC
        70-123326

B874   Swearer, Donald K., 1934- , Editor. Secrets of the Lotus:
        Studies in Buddhist Meditation. New York: Macmillan,
        and London: Collier-Macmillan, 1971. xii,242p. Bibliog-
        raphy: p.236-237. LC 75-150068
        Both the satipatthana (Theravada) and zazen (Zen) medita-
        tion techniques are discussed. Includes a report on an ex-
        perimental meditation workshop with a group of university
        students.

B875   Taimni, Iqbal Kishen, 1898- . Gayatri: The Daily Reli-
        gious Practice of the Hindus. 2nd ed. Adyar, India and
        Wheaton, Ill.: Theosophical Pub. House, 1974. Orig.
        pub., Allahabad: Anand Pub. House, 1961. vi,192p.

B876   Takeuchi, Yoshinori, 1913- . Probleme der Versenkung im
        Ur-Buddhismus. Leiden: Brill, 1972. 96p. Includes
        bibliography. (German)

B877   Target, George William. Watch with Me: Spiritual Exercises
        Toward Learning the Lessons of Penitence and Humiliation
        at the Foot of the Cross. Philadelphia: Westminster
        Press, 1961. 95p. LC 62-17396

B878   Tart, Charles T., 1937- , Editor. Altered States of Con-
        sciousness. Garden City, N.Y.: Doubleday, 1972. Orig.
        pub., New York: Wiley, 1969. ix,589p. Bibliography:
        p.531-570. LC 74-189947
        Section four of this book includes four chapters on medita-
        tion. Section eight has material on Zen Meditation and Yoga.

B879   _____. States of Consciousness. New York: E.P. Dut-
        ton, 1975. xi,305p. Bibliography: p.287-295. LC 75-
        5940

B880   _____, Editor. Transpersonal Psychologies. New York:
        Harper & Row, 1977. Orig. pub., New York: Harper
        & Row, and London: Routledge and Kegan Paul, 1975.
        [7],504p. (Harper Colophon Books; CN486) Bibliography:
        p.479-490.

B881   _____, Hrsg. Transpersonale Psychologie. Die Übers.
        besorgten Gisela Uellenberg u. Gisela Hesse. Olten und
        Freiburg im Breisgau: Walter, 1978. 610p. Einheits-
        sacht.: Transpersonal Psychologies. Literaturverz.
        p.603-610. (German)

B882   Tarthang Tulku. Gesture of Balance: A Guide to Aware-
        ness, Selfhealing, and Meditation. Emeryville, Calif.:
        Dharma Pub., 1977. xii,170p. LC 75-5255
        Essays on opening, relaxation, meditation, awareness, and
        teaching in the Nyingma Buddhist tradition.

B883   _____. Openness Mind. Emeryville, Calif.: Dharma
        Pub., 1978. xv,160p. LC 78-13659
        The Nyingma tradition of Tibetan Buddhism is emphasized in
        this approach to meditation.

B884   _____. Psychische Energie durch inneres Gleichgewicht:
        Wege zu höherem Bewusstsein, Selbstheilung u. Medita-
        tion. Mit e. Einf. von Anagarika Govinda u. e. Vorw.
        von Herbert V. Guenther. Die autorisierte dt. Übers.
        besorgte Matthias Dehne. Freiburg im Breisgau: Aurum-
        Verlag, 1979. 172p. Einheitssacht.: Gesture of Balance.
        (German)

B885   Tebbetts, Charles. Self Hypnosis and Other Mind Expand-
        ing Techniques. Los Angeles: Westwood Pub. Co., 1979,
        c1977. x,129p. LC 77-76206
        Includes a chapter on meditation.

B886   Temple, Sebastian. How to Meditate. Chicago: Radial
        Press, 1972. Also dist. by DeVorss & Co., Marina del
        Rey, Calif. 177p.
        Various techniques of mind control and meditation are dis-
        cussed. Yoga and kundalini are also covered.

B887   Tepperwein, Kurt. Geistheilung durch sich selbst: gesund
        u. glücklich durch Psychokybernetik u. Hypnomeditation.
        Genf: Ariston-Verlag, 1975. 220p. (German)

B888   Teresia (a Matre Dei et Sanctissimo Vultu). Verweilen vor
        Gott: mit Teresa von Avila, Johannes vom Kreuz,
        Theresia Lisieux, Edith Stein. Freiburg im Breisgau,
        Basel und Wien: Herder, 1979 and previous editions.
        111p. (German)

B889 Thakar, Vimala, 1931- . <u>Kraft der Stille: Selbsterziehung</u>
<u>z. meditativen Leben.</u> Übers. Gilda Remscheid u. Nelly
Roquette. Zürich: Origo-Verlag, 1974. 80p. (German)

B890 _____. <u>Life as Yoga: Discourses at Chorwad.</u> Trans-
lation into English from Hindi by Devendra Singh. Delhi:
Motilal Banarsidass, 1977. Dist. in U.S. by Lawrence
Verry, Mystic, Conn. and Orient Book Distributors,
Livingston, N.J. 286p.

B891 _____. <u>Meditation: A Way of Life.</u> 2nd ed. Ahmedabad:
New Order Book Co., 1977. Orig. pub., 1972. 138p.

B892 _____. <u>The Meditative Way.</u> Ahmedabad: Vimal Praka-
shan Trust, 1969. 60p. LC 73-909965

B893 _____. <u>Silence in Action.</u> Hilversum, Holland: E.A.M.
Frankena-Geraets and L.E. Frankena, 1968. 88p.

B894 _____. <u>Why Meditation? Five Talks Delivered at the</u>
<u>Blaisdell Institute, Claremont University, California,</u> 1974.
Delhi: Motilal Banarsidass, 1977. 82p. LC 77-905963

B895 <u>The Theory and Practice of Meditation.</u> Edited by Rudolf
Ballentine. Glenview, Ill.: Himalayan International In-
stitute of Yoga Science & Philosophy of USA, 1977.
Orig. pub., 1975. 106p.
A variety of essays on meditation by Indian scholars asso-
ciated with Swami Rama (i.e. Rudolf Ballentine).

B896 Thomas, Jesse James. <u>The Youniverse: Gestalt Therapy,</u>
<u>Non-Western Religions, and the Present Age.</u> La Jolla,
Calif.: Psychology and Consulting Associates Press,
1977. 126p. Bibliography: p.125-126. LC 77-89164

B897 Thomas, Klaus. <u>Meditation: in Forschung u. Erfahrung,</u>
<u>in weltweiter Beobachtung u. prakt. Anleitung.</u> Stutt-
gart: Steinkopf, und Stuttgart: Thieme, 1973. x,409p.
(Seelsorge und Psychotherapie; Bd.1) Includes bibliographies. LC 73-354552

B898 Thubten Yeshe, 1935- . <u>Lecture Given by Lama Thubten</u>
<u>Yeshe at the 7th Meditation Course, Ogmin Jangch'ub</u>
<u>Choling, Kopan, Kathmandu, November-December 1974.</u>
Bromley: Distributed by Manjushri Institute, 1975. 16p.
(Manjushri Institute Publication; no.1) LC 77-36426

B899 _____. <u>Lecture Given by Lama Thubten Yeshe at the 8th</u>
<u>Meditation Course, Ogmin Jangch'ub Choling, Kopan,</u>
<u>Kathmandu, November-December 1975.</u> Bromley: Man-
jushri Institute, 1976. 8p. (Manjushri Institute Publication; no.2) LC 77-373654

B 900 Tilmann, Klemens, 1904- . Die Führung der Kinder zur
       Meditation. 3. Aufl. Würzburg: Echter-Verlag, 1964.
       89p. (German)

B 901 _____ . Die Führung zur Meditation: ein Werkbuch.
       Zürich, Einsiedeln, und Köln: Benziger, 1981 and pre-
       vious editions. Vol. 1, 352p. Vol. 2, 413p. Bibliog-
       raphy: Vol. 1, p.349-352. (German)

B 902 _____ . Leben aus der Tiefe: kleine Anleitung zur inneren
       Versenkung u. christl. Meditation. Zürich, Einsiedeln,
       und Köln: Benziger, 1979 and previous editions. 80p.
       (German)

B 903 _____ . Leven vanuit de diepte. Vertaling, J.F. Brouwer.
       Haarlem: Gottmer, 1976. 76p. Translation of Leben aus
       der Tiefe. (Dutch)

B 904 _____ . Meditation in Depth. Translated from the German
       by David Smith. New York: Paulist Press, 1979. xi,131p.
       Translation of selections from Die Führung zur Meditation,
       v.1. LC 79-116763

B 905 _____ . The Practice of Meditation. Translated from the
       German by David Smith. London: Search Press, and
       New York: Paulist Press, 1977. 139p. Translation of
       Übungsbuch zur Meditation. LC 77-366171 and LC 77-
       72469

B 906 _____ . Übungsbuch zur Meditation: Stoffe, Anleitungen,
       Weiterführungen. 4. Aufl., Zürich, Einsiedeln und Köln:
       Benziger, 1982. Also, 1976 and 1973. 143p. (German)

B 907 Titmuss, Christopher, and Christina Feldman. Lasst alles
       völlig neu für Euch sein: e. bedeutsamer Schritt; Wege
       zum meditativen Leben. Wien: Octopus-Verlag, 1980.
       157p. (German)

B 908 TM: How to Find Peace of Mind Through Meditation. Edited
       by Martin Ebon. New York: New American Library,
       1975. 246p. Bibliography: p.245-246.

B 909 Traditional Modes of Contemplation and Action: A Colloquium
       Held at Rothko Chapel, Houston Texas. Edited by Yusuf
       Ibish and Peter Lamborn Wilson. Tehran: Imperial Iran-
       ian Academy of Philosophy, 1977. Dist. in U.S. by Great
       Eastern Book Co., Boulder, Colo. viii,477p. (Imperial
       Iranian Academy of Philosophy Publication; 24) Colloquium
       held July 22-31, 1973. [Cf. B165]

B 910 Trende, Wulf. Nach innen weggetreten?: Meditationen

zwischen Weltflucht u. Engagement. Berlin: Union-Verlag, 1975. 94p. Includes bibliographical references. LC 76-454896 (German)

B 911 Troeger, Thomas H., 1945- . Meditation: Escape to Reality. Philadelphia: Westminster Press, 1977. 120p. LC 76-45794
An account of the relationship between Western and Eastern spirituality in the form of Yoga meditation and Christian prayer.

B 912 Truch, Stephen. The TM Technique and the Art of Learning. Introduction by Hans Selye. Toronto: Lester and Orpen, and Totowa, N.J.: Littlefield, Adams, 1977. 250p. Includes bibliographical references. LC 77-375758 and LC 77-945
The nature of stress and its harmful effects are explained. The author suggests the use of TM in schools.

B 913 Trudinger, Ron. Cells for Life: Home Groups: God's Strategy for Church Growth. Basingstoke: Olive Tree, 1979. 123p.
A manual for organizing Christian meditation groups.

B 914 Trungpa, Chögyam, 1939- . Aktive Meditation. Frankfurt am Main: Fischer-Taschenbuch-Verlag, 1978. 92p. (German)

B 915 _____. Aktive Meditation: tibet. Weisheit. Die Übers. besorgte Ursula von Mangoldt. 4. Aufl. Olten und Freiburg im Breisgau: Walter, 1982. Orig. pub., 1972. 122p. Einheitssacht.: Meditation in Action. (German)

B 916 _____. Das Märchen von der Freiheit und der Weg der Meditation. Freiburg im Breisgau: Aurum-Verlag, 1978. 170p. (German)

B 917 _____. Meditación en accion. Traductora, Sherab V. Manoukian Pathé. México: Editorial Diana, 1976. 107p. Translation of Meditation in Action. (Spanish)

B 918 _____. Méditation et action; causeries au Centre tibétain Samyê-Ling. Mises en français par Armel Guerne. Paris: Fayard, 1973. 160p. (Documents spirituels, 9) Translation of Meditation in Action. LC 74-150260 (French)

B 919 _____. Meditation in Action. Berkeley: Shambhala, 1970. Dist. by Random House, Westminster, Md. Orig. pub., London: Stuart & Watkins, 1969. Also dist. by DeVorss & Co., Marina del Rey, Calif. 74p. LC 78-11846

Discusses the application of meditation in our everyday world
of action by a former abbot of a Tibetan monastery.

B 920 _____ . Mudra. Berkeley: Shambhala, and London:
Routledge and Kegan Paul, 1972. 105p.

B 921 _____ . The Myth of Freedom and the Way of Meditation.
Edited by John Baker and Marvin Casper. Illustrated by
Glen Eddy. Berkeley and London: Shambhala, 1976.
Dist. in London by Routledge and Kegan Paul. viii,176p.
LC 75-40264
Based on lectures given in various parts of the United States
between 1971 and 1973. Explains the role that meditation
and devotion play in uncovering the sources of frustration
and in allowing these negative forces to become vehicles for
the realization of true freedom.

B 922 Tson-kha-pa Blo-bzan-grags-pa, 1357-1419. Calming the
Mind and Discerning the Real: Buddhist Meditation and
the Middle View, from the Lam rim chen mo of Tson-kha-
pa. Translated from the Tibetan by Alex Wayman. New
York and Guildford: Columbia University Press, 1978.
xi,508p. Bibliography: p.493-498. LC 78-4535
A translation of two important sections of a Tibetan ency-
clopaedic text completed by Tson-kha-pa in 1402. The first
section deals with the correct method of meditation in the
Tibetan Buddhist tradition.

B 923 _____ . The Yoga of Tibet: The Great Exposition of the
Secret Mantra, 2 and 3. Introduction by Tenzin Gyatso,
the Fourteenth Dalai Lama. Translated and edited by
Jeffrey Hopkins. London and Boston: Allen & Unwin,
1981. xii,274p. (The Wisdom of Tibet Series; v.4)
Translated from Tibetan and Sanskrit. Bibliography:
p.253-259.

B 924 Tyson, Richard, and Jay R. Walker. How to Stop Smoking
Through Meditation. Chicago: Playboy Press Paper-
backs, 1977, c1976. viii,145p. Bibliography: p.143-145.
LC 76-26057

B 925 _____ , and _____ . The Meditation Diet: The Relaxation System for Easy Weight Loss. Chicago: Playboy
Press, 1976. 147p. LC 75-45295

B 926 Uchiyama, Kosho, 1912- . Approach to Zen: The Reality
of Zazen/Modern Civilization and Zen. Tokyo: Japan Publications, 1973. 122p. Translation of Seimei no jitsubutsu.
LC 73-83957

B 927 United States. District Court (New Jersey). TM in Court.

Berkeley, Calif.: Spiritual Counterfeits Project, 1978. xi,75p. LC 78-107034
The opinion and order and judgment of the U.S. District Court, District of New Jersey, in the case of Alan B. Malnak et al., plaintiffs v. Maharishi Mahesh Yogi et al., defendants.

B928 Vajiranana, Parawahera. Buddhist Meditation in Theory and Practice: A General Exposition According to the Pali canon of the Theravada School. Colombo: M.D. Gunasena, 1962. 498p. Bibliography: p.490-492. LC 68-5419

B929 Van de Wetering, Janwillem, 1931- . A Glimpse of Nothingness: Experiences in an American Zen Community. New York: Pocket Books, 1978. Orig. pub., London: Routledge & Kegan Paul, and Boston: Houghton-Mifflin, 1975. 221p. Translation of Het dagende niets. LC 74-31078
An account of the author's year and a half in a Japanese Zen Buddhist monastery.

B930 Van Over, Raymond. Total Meditation: Mind Control Techniques for a Small Planet in Space. New York: Collier Books, and London: Collier-Macmillan, 1978. xiii,207p. LC 78-1685
A guide to all popular forms of meditation. Zen, Yoga, T'ai Chi, TM, and other mind-control techniques are introduced, explained, and demonstrated.

B931 Varadachari, K.C. Lectures on Sahaj Marg: A First Selection. Madras: Shri Ram Chandra Mission, 1968. 133p. LC 78-901518

B932 _____, Editor. Sahaj Marg and Personality Problems & Yoga Psychology and Modern Physiological Theories. Tirupati: Sahaj Marg Research Institute, 1969- 2 vols. Vol. 2 has title: Sahaj Marg and Personality Problems: Superstition and Spirituality. Includes bibliographical references. LC 74-904448

B933 _____. Talks on Sri Ram Chandra's Efficacy of Raj Yoga. Shahjahanpur: Ram Chandra Mission, 1964. xxviii,43p.

B934 Vellal, B.G., 1912- . Self-Realisation Through Soham Sadhana. Coorg: B.S. Kushalappa, 1977. viii,156p. LC 78-903465

B935 Verwall, Ernst, and Robert The Tjong Tjioe. Zomaar een glimlach. Chinese Zenmeditatie. Deventer: Ankh-Hermes, 1974. 156p. Includes bibliographical references. LC 75-550734 (Dutch)

B936   Vianney, Jean Baptiste Marie, Saint, 1786-1859. Le Curé
        d'Ars, sa pensée, son coeur [textes choisis de Jean Marie
        Vianney] Présentés par l'abbé Bernard Nodet. Le Puy:
        X. Mappus, 1966. 303p. (Foi vivante, 23) LC 72-411427
        (French)

B936K   Vining, Elizabeth Gray, 1902- . Harnessing Pegasus: In-
        spiration and Meditation. Wallingford, Pa.: Pendle Hill
        Publications, 1978. 24p. LC 78-70883

B937   Vishadananda, Swami. Spiritual Science: Part I: Evolution
        of the Human Soul. Part II: Universal Principles for a
        Universal Religion. Ottapalam, India: Pub.?, 196-?
        223p. LC 73-244579

B938   Vishnudevananda, Swami. Meditation and Mantras. Rev. ed.
        New York: OM Lotus Pub. Co., 1981. Orig. pub.,
        1978. Dist. by Orient Book Distributors, Livingston,
        N.J. 255p.

B939   Vivekananda, Swami, 1863-1902. Meditation and Its Methods
        According to Swami Vivekananda. Compiled and edited
        by Swami Chetanananda. Foreword by Christopher Isher-
        wood. Hollywood, Calif.: Vendanta Press, 1976. Dist.
        by Auromere, Pomona, Calif. and DeVorss & Co., Marina
        del Rey, Calif. LC 75-36392

B940   _____. Raja-yoga; mit den Yoga-Aphorismen des Patan-
        jali. Übers. aus der Originalausgabe des Advaita Ash-
        rama, Mayavati, Almora und hrsg. von Emma von Pelet.
        Zürich: Rascher, 1951, c1937. xx,286p. Einheitssacht.:
        Raja Yoga: The Yoga Aphorisms of Patanjali. (German)

B941   _____. Raja-Yoga; or, Conquering the Internal Nature.
        15th impression. Calcutta: Advaita Ashrama, 1973 and
        previous editions. Dist. in U.S. by Auromere, Pomona,
        Calif. Also, New York: Ramakrishna-Vivekananda
        Center, 1973 and previous editions, and Calcutta: Pub-
        lished by Swami Visweswaranda from the Udbodhan Of-
        fice, label--London: Luzac: 1920. xii,280p.

B942   _____. Raja Yoga: The Yoga Aphorisms of Patanjali.
        Hollywood, Calif.: Vedanta Press, date? Dist. by Auro-
        mere, Pomona, Calif. 239p.

B943   _____. Six Lessons on Raja Yoga. 5th ed. Calcutta:
        Udbodhan Office, 1957 and previous editions. Orig. pub.,
        1928. 32p.

B944   _____. Les yogas pratiques (Karma, Bhakti, Raja).
        Traduction française de Lizelle Reymond et Jean Herbert.

Préf. de Jean Herbert. Paris: A. Michel, 1970. 575p.
LC 79-509907 (French)

B 945   Viziale, Enrica. Meditazione transcendentale. Torino: MEB,
1979. 146p. (Mondi sconosciuti; 50) Bibliography:
p.143-144. LC 80-462473 (Italian)

B 946   Volin, Michael. The Quiet Hour: Mental Exercises and Meditative Practices for Personal Growth. London: Pelham
Books, 1980. 158p.

B 947   Volk, Georg. Entspannung, Sammlung, Meditation: Ein-
übungen zur Erhaltung unserer Gesundheit. 4. Aufl.
Mainz: Matthias-Grünewald-Verlag, 1977 and previous
editions. 96p. (German)

B 948   Völker, Walter. Kontemplation und Ekstase bei Pseudo-
Dionysius Areopagita. Wiesbaden: Steiner, 1958. xv,
263p. (German)

B 949   Waldemar, Charles. Das Geheimnis des Kaiser-Yoga, mys-
tische Praxis der Energiekunst. Sersheim/Württ.:
Osiris, 1957. 116p. (German)

B 950   Waldenfels, Hans. Meditation, Ost und West. Einsiedeln,
Zürich, und Köln: Benziger, 1975. 87p. (Theologische
Meditationen; 37) Bibliography: p.86-88. LC 75-506340
(German)

B 951   Wallace, Robert Keith. The Physiological Effects of Transcendental Meditation: A Proposed Fourth Major State of
Consciousness. 4th ed. Los Angeles: Students' International Meditation Society, 1975 and previous editions.
xiii,79p. Bibliography: p.75-79.
A dissertation submitted for the degree, Doctor of Philosophy in Physiology, at the University of California, Los
Angeles. The physiological effects of transcendental meditation are used to distinguish meditation from other states
of consciousness. Suggests that meditation produces a fourth
state of consciousness which may have practical clinical applications. [Cf. A845, D222]

B 952   Walter, Eugen. Betrachten. Ansätze, Erfahrungen u. Entfaltungen. Düsseldorf: Patmos-Verlag, 1966. 112p.
(German)

B 953   Walter, Silja, und Karl H. Zeiss. Hol nich herein: Meditationen in der Messe. Würzburg: Echter-Verlag, 1973.
85p. (German)

B 954   Wangyal, Geshe, Comp. The Door of Liberation. Preface by Tenzin Gyatsho, the XIVth Dalai Lama. New York: M. Girodias Associates; dist. by L. Stuart, 1973. 323p. LC 73-82688 Consists of translations from Tibetan Buddhist teachings.

B955 _____, Hrsg. Tibetische Meditationen. Zürich: Theseus-Verlag, 1975. 224p. Einheitssacht.: The Door of Liberation. (German)

B956 Watts, Alan, 1915-1973. The Art of Contemplation. London: Village Press, 1974. Orig. pub., Sausalito, Calif.: Society for Comparative Philosophy, and New York: Pantheon Books, 1972. 14p.

B957 _____. Meditation. Photographs by Joseph McHugh. New York: Jove, 1980. Also, New York: Pyramid Books, 1976. Orig. pub., Millbrae, Calif.: Celestial Arts, 1974. 63p. (His The Essence of Alan Watts; Book 2)
The author provides thoughts to meditate upon. Chanting is also discussed.

B958 Webster, Nell. Eating and Living the TM Way. New York: Pocket Books, 1976. 160p.

B959 Wedemeyer, Inge von. Der Pfad der Meditation im Spiegel einer universalen Kunst. Freiburg im Breisgau: Aurum-Verlag, 1977. 182,[32]p. Bibliography: p.177-178. LC 78-346643 (German)

B960 Wedgwood, James Ingall. Meditation for Beginners. 4th ed. London: Theosophical Publishing House, 1971. Fourth ed. orig. pub., 1961. Previous edition, 1918. 59p. Bibliography: p.59.

B961 Wege der Meditation heut. Informationen u. Diskussion. Hrsg. von Ursula von Mangoldt. Weilheim/Obb.: O.W. Barth, 1970. 217p. LC 79-576103 (German)

B962 Weidelener, Herman. Einführung in die Meditation. Augsburg: Manu-Verl., 1958. 116p. (German)

B963 _____. Ergebnisse meditativer Arbeit. Augsburg: Manu-Verl., 1959. 93p. (German)

B964 Weiss, Bardo. Weg ins Leben: Meditationen über Bilder u. Symbole aus d. Johannesevangelium. Mainz: Matthias-Grünewald-Verlag, 1979. 117p. (German)

B965 Weiss, Harmut. Yoga-Meditation: Schulung zur Selbstverwirklichung. Düsseldorf und Wien: Econ-Verlag, 1978. 128p. (German)

B 966 Weldon, John, and Zola Levitt. The Transcendental Explosion. Foreword by Pat Boone. Irvine, Calif.: Harvest House Publishers, 1976. 218p. Includes bibliographical references. LC 76-17364

B 967 Weschke, Eugen. Übungen zur gegenständlichen Meditation. Kassel: Johannes-Stauda-Verlag, 1975. 60p. LC 75-520854 (German)

B 968 Wessler, M. Jenelyn, 1924- , and Daniel B. Wessler. The Gifts of Silence. Atlanta: John Knox Press, 1976. Dist. by DeVorss & Co., Marina del Rey, Calif. 90p. LC 75-32942

B 969 West, Serene, 1929- . Very Practical Meditation. Virginia Beach, Va.: Donning, 1981. 102p. LC 79-20249

B 970 When Fires Burn: Insights into the Devotional Life. Edited by Wilson O. Weldon. Nashville: The Upper Room, 1969. 70p. LC 72-81640

B 971 White, John, 1939- . Alles über TM, Transzendentale Meditation: d. neue Lehre d. Maharishi Mahesh Yogi. Dt. Übers. von Leni Sobez. München: Heyne, 1976. 141p. Einheitssacht.: Everything You Want to Know About TM, Including How to Do It. (German)

B 972 _____ . Everything You Want to Know About TM, Including How to Do It: A Look at Higher Consciousness and the Enlightenment Industry. New York: Pocket Books, 1976. 191p. Bibliography: p.189-190. LC 76-351823

B 973 _____ , Editor. What Is Meditation? Garden City, N.Y. Anchor Press, 1974. Dist. by DeVorss & Co., Marina del Rey, Calif. xxii,254p. Includes bibliographies. LC 73-81126
Includes essays by Alan Watts, Swami Chinmayananda, Gopi Krishna, Claudio Naranjo, Robert de Ropp, Chögyam Trungpa, and Joel Goldsmith.

B 974 Whitehead, Carleton. Creative Meditation. New York: Dodd, Mead, 1975. 154p. LC 75-4882

B 975 Whitehill, James. Enter the Quiet: Everyone's Way to Meditation. San Francisco and London [etc.]: Harper and Row, 1980. xiv,172p. Bibliography: p.170-172. LC 79-2996

B 976 Whitman, Evelyn Ardis, 1905- . Meditation: Journey to the Self. New York: Simon and Schuster, 1976. 189p. LC 75-44316

LC 75-44316
The author examines biofeedback, sensory awareness, cosmic consciousness, healing, and meditation.

B 977   Wieck, Carl Ernst. Meditationen. 1. Heidelberg: Meister, 1960. 78p. (German)

B 978   Wienpahl, Paul. The Matter of Zen: A Brief Account of Zazen. New York: New York University Press, 1964. xi,162p. Includes bibliographical references. LC 64-10525

B 979   Wijngaards, N.M. Over het TM [i.e. Transcendente Meditatie] programma en het TM-Sidhi programma: zoals geleerd door Maharishi Mahesh Yogi. Den Haag: MIU Nederland Pers, 1978. 144p. Bibliography: p.144. LC 79-339806 (Dutch)

B 980   _____. Wat is transcendente meditatie: Zoals geleerd door Maharishi Mahesh Yogi. Den Haag: MIU Nederland Pers, 1976. 96p. Bibliography: p.95-96. LC 77-452216 (Dutch)

B 981   Wilberforce, Bertrand Arthur Henry. An Easy Method of Mental Prayer. Westminster, Md.: Newman Press, 1955. 31p.

B 982   Willett, Robert F. Primer for Christian Meditation. Wilton, Conn.: Morehouse-Barlow, 1976. 63p.

B 983   Williams, Lillian. It's About Meditation!: The What? Why? Where? When? and How to Do It. Toronto: Spiritual Press, 1981. ii,145p. Bibliography. p.i.

B 984   Willis, Janice Dean, Comp. The Diamond Light: An Introduction to Tibetan Buddhist Meditations. New York: Simon and Schuster, 1973, c1972. 124p. Orig. pub. as The Diamond Light of the Eastern Dawn.

B 985   Wilson, Jim. Meditation and the Fulness of Life. Cambridge: J. Clarke, 1974. 76p.

B 986   Wise, Charles C., Jr. Mind Is It: Meditation, Prayer, Healing, and the Psychic. Penn Laird, Va.: Magian Press, 1978. 191p. Includes bibliographical references. LC 77-82923

B 987   Witzenmann, Herbert. Was ist Meditation?: Eine grundlegende Erörterung zur geisteswiss. Bewusstseinserweiterung. Dornach/Schweiz: Spicker, 1982. 83p. (Zeitbetrachtungen und Bewusstseinsfragen; Bd.1) (German)

B988   Wood, Ernest, 1883-1965. Concentration: An Approach to
        Meditation. Wheaton, Ill.: Theosophical Pub. House,
        1981 and previous editions. Also, Adyar Madras: The
        Theosophical Pub. House, 1966 and previous editions.
        xi,154p. Also pub. as Concentration: A Practical Course
        with a Supplement on Meditation. Wheaton, Ill.: Theo-
        sophical Pub. House, 1973 and previous editions. Also,
        Madras: Theosophical Pub. House, 1959 and previous
        editions. Orig. pub., 1913, Madras. Also dist. by De-
        Vorss & Co., Marina del Rey, Calif.

B989   Worldwide Directory of Meditation and Yoga Retreats. Edited
        by Frieda Carrol. Dover, Del.: Alpha Pyramis Pub. Co.,
        153 S. Bradford, (in press).

B990   Writings from the Philokalia on Prayer of the Heart. Trans-
        lated from the Russian by E. Kadlaubovsky and G.E.H.
        Palmer. London: Faber and Faber, 1975 and previous
        editions. 420p.
        The Greek Philokalia was compiled in the eighteenth century
        by Macarius of Corinth and Nicodemus of the Holy Mountain
        and first published in Venice in 1782.

B991   Wunderli, Jürg, 1934- . Meditation, Hilfe im Alltag: e.
        Arzt über Vorbereitung, Praxis u. Sinn d. Konzentration
        u. Meditation. Stuttgart: Fink, 1973. 93p. (German)

B992   _____ . Schritte nach innen: östl. Meditation u. westl.
        Mystik. 2. Aufl. Freiburg im Breisgau, Basel, und
        Wien: Herder, 1977. Orig. pub., 1975. 183p. Includes
        bibliographical references. LC 75-507528 (German)

B993   _____ . Yoga und Medizin: Atmung, Entspannung, Kon-
        zentration u. Meditation in ihren Beziehungen zu unserer
        Gesundheit; eine prekt. Einf. Ill. Frieder Knauss.
        Stuttgart: J. Fink, 1972. 82p. LC 73-328850 (German)

B994   Yamaoka, Haruo. Meditation Gut Enlightenment: The Way
        of Hara. South San Francisco: Heian International Pub.
        Co., 1976. 81p. Bibliography: p.73-75. LC 76-18413

B995   Yatiswarananda, Swami, 1889-1960. Meditation and Spiritual
        Life. Bangalore: Sri Ramakrishna Ashrama, 1979.
        Dist. in U.S. by Auromere, Pomona, Calif. xxxv,700p.
        Includes bibliographical references. LC 79-906555

B996   Yesudian, Selva Raja, and Elisabeth Haich. Raja Yoga.
        Translated by John P. Robertson. Foreword by T.
        Huzella. London and Boston: Unwin Paperbacks, 1980.
        Also, London: Allen and Unwin, 1970. This translation
        orig. pub. as Yoga Uniting East and West. London:

Allen and Unwin, and New York: Harper, 1956. 160p.
Translation of Yoga in den zwei Welten. LC 80-494557

B 997 _____, and _____. Raja-Yoga. 3.Aufl. von Yoga in
den zwei Welten. Thielle/NE: Fankhauser; (München-
Pasing: Drei-Eichen-Verlag in Kommission, 1966). 223p.
LC 67-68544 (German) [Cf. B 999]

B 998 _____, and _____. Raja Yoga, yoga royal: la voie
spirituelle. Traduction française de Francine Yesudian
Aegerter. Verdun, Québec: M. Broquet, 1979. 191p.
Traduction de Yoga in den zwei Welten. (French)

B 999 _____, and _____. Yoga in den zwei Welten. 2. Aufl.
Thielle: Fankhauser, 1955. Orig. pub., 1951. 230p.
(German) [Cf. B 997]

B 1000 Yogananda, Paramhansa, 1893-1952. Metaphysical Meditations.
8th ed. Los Angeles: Self-Realization Fellowship, 1974
and previous editions. Orig. pub., 1932. vi,115p.

B 1001 _____. Meditationen zur Selbstverwirklichung. 7. Aufl.
München: Barth, 1981 and previous editions. 119p.
Einheitssacht.: Metaphysical Meditations. (German)

B 1002 _____. Scientific Healing Affirmations: Theory and
Practice of Concentraiton; the Scientific Use of Concentration and Affirmations for Healing Inharmonies of Body,
Mind, and Soul Through Reason, Will, Feeling, and
Prayer. Los Angeles: Self-Realization Fellowship, 1974
and previous editions. Orig. pub., Boston: Satsanga,
1924. 76p.

B 1003 _____. Wissenschaftlich Heilmeditationen. Bern, Wien,
und München: Barth, 1981 and previous editions. 91p.
Einheitssacht.: Scientific Healing Affirmations. (German)

B 1004 Yogiji, Harbhajan Singh Khalsa. Kundalini Meditation Manual
for Intermediate Students: A Manual for the Total Balance of the Personality, Drawn from the teachings of
Yogi Bhajan. Pomona, Calif.: KRI, 1978. Dist. by
DeVorss, Marina del Rey, Calif. 70p.

B 1005 _____. Survival Kit: Meditations and Exercises for Stress
and Pressure of the Times. By Yogi Bhajan. San Diego,
Calif.: Vikram K. Khalsa & Dharm Darshan K. Khalsa,
1980. 74p.

B 1006 You: Prayer for Beginners and Those Who Have Forgotten
How. Compiled by Mark Link. Niles, Ill.: Argus Communications, 1976. 156p. Includes bibliographical references. LC 76-41584

B1007 Zen and Hasidism: The Similarities Between Two Spiritual Disciplines. Compiled by Harold Heifetz. Wheaton, Ill.: Theosophical Pub. House, 1978. 242p. Includes bibliographical references.

B1008 Zienswijze op occultisme, meditatie, spiritisme, reincarnatie, ufo's. Samengesteld door Jack van Belle. Laren: Luitingh, 1972. 207p. Bibliography: p.202-207. (Dutch)

DAI is the standard abbreviation for Dissertation Abstracts International, from which information about some of the following references was obtained. Microfiche, microfilm, or paper copies of dissertations in DAI may be purchased from University Microfilms International, Dissertation Copies, Post Office Box 1764, Ann Arbor, Michigan, 48106. Prices and ordering information can be found in DAI. Interlibrary loan policies are from American Doctoral Dissertations, also published by University Microfilms International, and are subject to change.

D1   Abrams, Allan I. "The Effects of Meditation on Elementary School Students." DAI, 37 (1977), 5689A (Ph.D. University of California, Berkeley. Will lend.) Tentatively scheduled for inclusion in Scientific Research on the Transcendental Meditation Program: Collected Papers, Vol. 2. Rheinweiler, West Germany: Maharishi European Research University Press, (in press).
Subjects were randomly assigned to one of four meditation instruction conditions: Transcendental Meditation, concentration, contemplation, and quiet meditation. Found that elementary school students generally benefited, in both the affective and cognitive domains, from a meditation program requiring only a few minutes per day.

D2   Alexander, Charles N. "Ego Development, Personality and Behavioral Change in Inmates Practicing the Transcendental Meditation Technique or Participating in Other Programs: A Cross-Sectional and Longitudinal Study." DAI, 43 (1982), 539B (Ph.D. Harvard University. Will lend.)
The study supported the hypothesis that TM may act to unfreeze stage of consciousness development. None of the other programs were significantly effective.

D3   Allen, Christine P. "Effects of Transcendental Meditation, Electromyographic (EMG) Biofeedback Relaxation, and Conventional Relaxation on Vasoconstriction, Muscle Tension, and Stuttering: A Quantitative Comparison." DAI, 40

251

(1979), 689B (Ph.D. University of Michigan. Will lend.)
The data obtained in this investigation indicate that further
research in the application of TM as an adjunct therapy with
stutterers is warranted.

D4   Allen, Roger J. "The Relative Effectiveness of Progressive
      Relaxation, Meditation, and GSR Biofeedback for Reducing
      Psychophysiological Stress." (M.S. Thesis. University
      of Kansas, 1977.)

D5   Anderson, Hilary. "A Study of the Principles and Methods
      of Self-Integration in Integral Yoga." DAI, 34 (1974),
      4649B (Ph.D. California Institute of Asian Studies. Now,
      California Institute of Integral Studies. Will lend.)
This investigation was conducted in order to identify the essential method found in the various principles and processes
utilized by the Integral Yoga of Sri Aurobindo to attain self-
realization and subsequently self-integration.

D6   Antes, M. "Transzendentale Meditation, TM-Sidhi-programm
      und Rigidität-flexibilität." [The Effects of the TM-Sidhi
      Program on Rigidity-Flexibility.] (Diploma Thesis. Uni-
      versität Saarbrücken, 1978.) Tentatively scheduled for
      inclusion in Scientific Research on the Transcendental
      Meditation Program: Collected Papers, Vol. 2. Rhein-
      weiler, West Germany: Maharishi European Research Uni-
      versity Press, (in press).
Greater psychophysiological flexibility and better body coordi-
nation were shown by participants in the TM-Sidhi program.
[Cf. B17]

D7   Armstrong, P.F. "Taking Knowledge: A Sociological Approach
      to the Study of Meditation and the Divine Light Mission."
      (Ph.D. Essex, 1978.)

D8   Bacher, Paula G. "An Investigation Into the Compatibility of
      Existential-Humanistic Psychotherapy and Buddhist Medita-
      tion." DAI, 42 (1981), 2565A (Ed.D. Boston University
      School of Education. Will not lend.)
It was found that a sequential approach, wherein psychotherapy precedes meditation, is of overall greater benefit to
the client and to both the disciplines of psychotherapy and
meditation, than a blended approach.

D9   Bahrke, Michael S. "Influence of Acute Physical Activity and
      Non-Cultic Meditation on State Anxiety." DAI, 38 (1978),
      5987A (Ph.D. University of Wisconsin, Madison. Will not
      lend.)
The present evidence suggests that acute physical activity,
non-cultic meditation, and a quiet rest session are equally
effective in reducing state anxiety.

D10 Ball, Orlow E. "The Effects of Transcendental Meditation
   (TM) and the TM Sidhis Program on Verbal and Figural
   Creativity (TTCT), Auditory Creativity (S&I), and Hemi-
   spheric Dominance (SOLAT)." DAI,, 40 (1980), 3880A
   (Ph.D. University of Georgia. Will not lend.) Tentatively
   scheduled for inclusion in Scientific Research on the Tran-
   scendental Meditation Program: Collected Papers, Vol. 2.
   Rheinweiler, West Germany: Maharishi European Research
   University Press, (in press).
 Significant increases in creativity were shown by students
 participating in the TM and TM-Sidhi program.

D11 Barish, J. "The Philosophy and Practice of TM and Its Relationship to Self-Actualization." (Master's Thesis.
   California State University, Hayward, 1973.)

D12 Barnes, Ronald M. "A Study of the Psychological Structures
   of Transcendental, Yoga, and Ignatian Meditation as Allied
   Phenomena." DAI,, 41 (1981), 4243B (Ph.D. Duquesne
   University. Will lend.)
 In addition to the dialogue of similarities and differences in
 the three forms, the study inquires into the role of bodily
 attunement, the achievement of "cosmic (empty) consciousness," and the use of technique.

D13 Barozzi, Ronald L. "The Influence of a Meditation Technique
   and an Eastern Ideology on the Value Orientations of College Students." DAI, 36 (1976), 6316A (Ph.D. Utah
   State University. Will lend.)
 Students exposed to the technique of meditation seemed to be
 unaffected as far as altering their value orientations was concerned. Students exposed to the Zen ideology seemed to pos-
 sess a greater probability for experiencing a countercultural
 effect than students not exposed to it.

D14 Barr, William H. "College Student Development and Transcendental Meditation: An Analysis and Comparison." DAI,
   35 (1975), 5840A (Ph.D. Michigan State University.
   Will lend.)
 A possible integration between the "student development philosophy" of Arthur Chickering and "meditational philosophy"
 (Transcendental Meditation) of Maharishi Mahesh Yogi is explored. The attempted integration of these two models is un-
 successful.

D15 Bartels, Wayne J. "The Effects of a Western Meditation on a
   Measure of Self-Actualization." DAI, 37 (1977), 5596A
   (Ed.D. Oklahoma State University. Will lend.)
 There were no significant differences on any of the variables
 between the control group and the experimental group.

D16   Bassford, R.D. "TM and Stress (Physiological and Subjective),
       Internal Versus External Locus of Control and Self-Concept."
       (Ph.D. Thesis. University of Western Ontario, 1973.)

D17   Bauhofer, U. "Die kreislaufphysiologischen Auswirkungen bei
       der Transzendentalen Meditation." [The Physiological Ef-
       fects on the Circulatory System During TM.] (Dissertation.
       Universität Würzburg, 1978.)

D18   Baxter, Elizabeth S. "The Growth Process Inventory: A
       Validation Study." DAI, 40 (1980), 4471B (Ph.D. United
       States International University. Will lend.)
       The main objective was to see whether the GPI could discrimi-
       nate between persons in different stages of a growth process
       (Transcendental Meditation) and individuals not in a formal
       growth process. It was concluded that the GPI was able to
       discriminate to a considerable degree.

D19   Beckwith, L.L. and L. Boissonnault. "Growth of Affective
       Learning in the Light of the Science of Creative Intelli-
       gence." (Master's Thesis. Maharishi International Uni-
       versity, 1976.)

D20   Berg, Ruth E. "The Art of Meditation as Defined by the
       Hesychasts from the Critical Perspective of Psychology."
       DAI, 38 (1977), 1379-1380B (Ph.D. United States Inter-
       national University. Will lend.)
       The major purpose of this study is to investigate in detail
       this early form of meditation known as Hesychasm. This
       study also concerns itself with many other roads to ecstasy
       such as St. Teresa, St. John, Yoga, Sufism, and Zen. The
       altered states of these special forms are examined in the light
       of Hesychasm and then examined psychologically.

D21   Berkowitz, Alan H. "The Effect of Transcendental Meditation
       on Trait Anxiety and Self-Esteem." DAI, 38 (1977), 2353-
       2354B
       In general, it was concluded that for the population tested,
       practicing TM for either one or three months appears to have
       a greater impact on trait anxiety than it does on self-esteem.

D22   Berlin, T. "TM und Industriegesellschaft: Selbstverstandnis
       und soziale Bedeutung einer neuen Bewegung." [TM and
       Industrial Society: Self-Comprehension and Social Signifi-
       cance of a New Movement.] (Diplomarbeit. Bielefeld,
       1976.)

D22K   Berry, George C. "Discriminating Groups of Hypnotized and
       Meditating Subjects from Normal Subjects with the Altered
       States of Consciousness Inventory." DAI, 43 (1982):
       1594B (Ph.D. United States International University.
       Will lend.)

The Inventory was shown to discriminate subjects in the normal, hypnotic, and meditative states of consciousness.

D23   Bielefeldt, Carl W. "The 'Fukan Zazen-gi' and the Meditation Teachings of the Japanese Zen Master Dogen." DAI, 41 (1981) 3147A (Ph.D. University of California, Berkeley. Will lend.)
This paper is a study of the Fukan Zazen-gi, a meditation text by the Japanese Zen master Dogen (1200-1253).

D24   Bitting, Anthony L. "Meditation and Biofeedback: A Comparison of Effects on Anxiety, Self-Actualization, Openness and Self-Esteem." (Ph.D. California School of Professional Psychology, Berkeley, 1976. Will lend.)

D25   Blanz, Larry T. "Personality Changes as a Function of Two Different Meditative Techniques." DAI, 34 (1974), 7035-7036A (Ed.D. University of Tennessee. Will lend.)
The two techniques chosen, Soto Zen and Mantra Yoga, reflect differing philosophies and have yielded differing EEG recordings. It was concluded that the results lend support to the position that meditation techniques yield similar personality changes.

D26   Blasdell, K.S. "Transcendental Meditation and the Tonic Vibration Reflex." (M.S. Thesis. University of California, Los Angeles, 1974.) Tentatively scheduled for inclusion in Scientific Research on the Transcendental Meditation Program: Collected Papers, Vol. 2. Rheinweiler, West Germany: Maharishi European Research University Press, (in press).
Significantly different measures of tonic vibration reflex were found during sleep, TM, and waking state.

D27   Blümlein, W. "Veränderungen spezifischer bzw. spezieller Leistungen (Aufmerksamkeit) und des subjektiven Erlebens nach Ausübung der Technik der TM im Vergleich zu einfacher Entspannung." [Changes of Specific/Special Abilities (Attention) and of Subjective Experience After the Practice of the TM Technique in Comparison to Ordinary Relaxation.] (Diplomarbeit. Universität Tübingen, Psychologisches Institut, 1977.)

D28   Bole, David N. "The Effect of the Relaxation Response on the Positive Personality Characteristics of Paraprofessional Counselors." DAI, 39 (1978), 2136A (Ph.D. University of Florida. Will not lend.)
It was concluded that the Benson Relaxation Response is one method for acquiring and developing the positive personality traits which have been linked to effective counseling and resulting client growth.

D29 Borelli, Marianne D. "The Effects of the Practice of Meditation by Eight to Eleven Year Old Children on Their Trait Anxiety and Self-Esteem." DAI, 43 (1982), 1040B (Ph.D. New York University. Will not lend.)
No significant decrease in trait anxiety or increase in self-esteem was demonstrated by this study.

D29K Brandon, Jeffrey E. "A Comparative Evaluation of Three Relaxation Training Procedures." DAI, 43 (1983): 2279A (Ph.D. Southern Illinois University at Carbondale. Will lend.)
Behavioral Relaxation Training, Meditation, and a Seashore Sounds "Attention Focusing" method were compared. All three groups showed significant reductions on electromyographic level and self-report. Reduction on the behavioral relaxation scales was significant only for the Behavioral Relaxation Training group.

D30 Bridgewater, Michael J. "The Relative Efficacy of Meditation in Reducing an Induced Anxiety Reaction." DAI, 40 (1979), 903-904B (Ph.D. New Mexico State University. Will not lend.)
This study failed to provide convincing evidence that meditation was more effective than muscle relaxation or practiced rest. However, the study did suggest that meditation may at least have an advantage in reducing immediate or short-term anxiety.

D30K Brown, Daniel P. "Mahamudra Meditation-Stages and Contemporary Cognitive Psychology: A Study in Comparative Psychological Hermeneutics." (Ph.D. University of Chicago, 1981. Will lend.)

D31 Brown, Melanie. "Higher Education for Higher Consciousness: A Study of Students at Maharishi International University." DAI, 38 (1977), 649A (Ph.D. University of California, Berkeley. Will lend.) Tentatively scheduled for inclusion in Scientific Research on the Transcendental Meditation Program: Collected Papers, Vol. 2. Rheinweiler, West Germany: Maharishi European Research University Press, (in press).
MIU students were found to be more intellectually oriented, more altruistic and psychologically stable, and more committed to higher education than students at the University of California, Berkeley, and at a private liberal arts college.

D32 Bruner, Richard L. "The Reduction of Anxiety and Tension States Through Learning the Relaxation Response: A Theoretical Study with Clinical Applications." DAI, 39 (1978), 370-371B (Psy.D. Rutgers University, The State University of New Jersey. Graduate School of Applied and

Professional Psychology. Will not lend.)
Subjects varied in degrees of anxiety reduction.

D33 Bühler, M. "Transzendentalen Meditation: Darstellung einer Entspannungsmethode und Überlegungen zu ihrer Anwendbarkeit in einem ausgewählten psychologischen Problembereich." [Transcendental Meditation: Performance of a Relaxation Method and Considerations for Its Application in a Selected Psychological Problem Area.] (Diplomarbeit. Psychologisches Institut der Freien Universität, Berlin, 1979.)

D34 Bunk, Brian E. "Effects of Hatha Yoga and Mantra Meditation on the Psychological Health and Behavior of Incarcerated Males." DAI, 40 (1979), 904B (Ph.D. University of Texas Health Science Center at Dallas. Will not lend.)
The overall results of the study suggest that yoga, meditation, and a combination of the two may be effective strategies for lowering anxiety and for facilitating an internal locus of control reinforcement in incarcerated males.

D35 Burgin, Victoria D. "Group Treatment of Test Anxiety in College Students by Undergraduate Group Leaders." DAI, 39 (1978), 1468-1469B (Ph.D. University of Rochester. Will not lend.)
The results indicated that both the cognitive behavior modification and the group meditation treatments failed to lead to significant anxiety reduction on self-report measures or to produce improvement on performance measures.

D36 Bynum, Jack L. "Christian Meditation and Biofeedback Training as Psychotherapeutic Agents in the Treatment of Essential Hypertension." DAI, 41 (1980), 2506A (Ed.D. Southwestern Baptist Theological Seminary. Will lend.)
The practice of Christian meditation produced the most significant results of the dissertation, although the raw data indicated a general lowering of blood pressure for subjects in all three treatment groups.

D37 Campbell, Richard E. "The Relationship of Arica Training to Self-Actualization and Interpersonal Behavior." DAI, 36 (1975), 1401b (Ph.D. United States International University. Will lend.)
This study suggests the possibility of a relationship between Arica training in meditation and related techniques to self-actualization. Conclusions were treated with caution.

D38 Cara, Arthur J. "Transcendental Meditation: An Analysis of the Rhetoric of a Social Movement as Innovation." DAI, 41 (1981), 3318A (Ph.D. Ohio State University. Will not lend.)

This study seeks to "recast" social scientific interpretations of the rhetoric of social movements, and introduce a new rhetorically coded lens with which to view the symbolic reality of the Transcendental Meditation social phenomenon.

D39   Carson, Linda G. "Zen Meditation in the Elderly." DAI, 36
        (1975), 903-904B (Ph.D. University of Nevada, Reno.
        Will lend.)
   Investigated the possibility of instituting Zazen in a sample of elderly people and the outcome of this practice as it relates to self-esteem, depression, death anxiety, and personality traits.

D40   Childs, John P. "The Use of Transcendental Meditation as
        Therapy with Juvenile Offenders." DAI, 34 (1974), 4732-
        4733A (Ed.D. University of Tennessee. Will lend.) Ex-
        tracted in Scientific Research on the Transcendental Medita-
        tion Program: Collected Papers, Vol. 1, 2nd ed., Weggis,
        Switzerland: Maharishi European Research University,
        1977. pp. 577-584.
   Sufficient progress was made to warrant recommendation of the technique to the use of those who counsel juvenile offenders.

D41   Comer, James F. "Meditation and Progressive Relaxation in
        the Treatment of Test Anxiety." DAI, 38 (1978), 6142-
        6143B (Ph.D₀ University of Kansas. Will lend.)
   It is concluded that in actual test performance, meditation may be as effective as relaxation in the treatment of test anxiety, depending on the type of instructions accompanying each of them.

D42   Cowger, Ernest L., Jr. "The Effects of Meditation (Zazen)
        Upon Selected Dimensions of Personal Development." DAI,
        34 (1974), 4734A (Ph.D. University of Georgia. Will not
        lend.)
   Meditation appears to be an effective means for self-actualiza-tion and reducing anxiety. It did not affect creative thinking abilities.

D43   Curtin, Thomas G. "The Relationship Between Transcendental
        Meditation and Adaptive Regression." DAI, 73 (1973),
        1696A (Ed.D. Boston University School of Education.
        Will not lend.)
   The study shows that Transcendental Meditation increases one's capacity for adaptive regression.

D44   Curtis, Miriam J. "The Relationship Between Bimodal Con-
        sciousness, Meditation and Two Levels of Death Anxiety."
        DAI, 41 (1980), 2314B (Ph.D. California School of Pro-
        fessional Psychology, Los Angeles. Will lend.)

The results of this study imply that meditation may have useful application to dying patients and their families.

D45   Cuthbert, Bruce N. "Voluntary Slowing of Heart Rate: A
       Comparison of Various Techniques." DAI, 37 (1976),
       3067B (Ph.D. University of Wisconsin, Madison. Will not
       lend.)
       It was concluded that Transcendental Meditation may be more
       effective than feedback in slowing the heart rate.

D46   Dean, P.J. "The Effects of the TM Technique on Concept
       Formation, Autonomic Stability and EEG Coherence."
       (Master's Thesis. Maharishi International University,
       1980.)

D47   DeBlassie, Paul A., III. "Christian Meditation: A Clinical
       Investigation." DAI, 42 (1981), 1167B (Ph.D. Colorado
       State University. Will not lend.)
       The results indicate that neither Christian meditation nor the
       relaxation response produce significant effects on anxiety,
       neurosis, or religious orientation.

D48   Deckarm, R. "Die psychotherapeutischen Wirkungen der
       TM." [The Psychotherapeutic Effect of TM.] (Diplomar-
       beit in Psychologie. Universität Saarbrücken, 1978.)

D49   Denmark, Ted H. "Approaches to Self-Realization in Adult
       Education Through Meditation." DAI, 37 (1976), 96A
       (Ph.D. University of California, Berkeley. Will lend.)
       It is held that meditation has valuable insights to offer the
       field of education for adults.

D50   Denny, Mary C. "Self-Hypnotic Absorption and Affective
       Change in a Program of Spiritual Exercises." DAI, 41
       (1981), 3917-3198B (Ph.D. Catholic University of Amer-
       ica. Will lend.)
       Process was based on the Spiritual Exercises of St. Ignatius
       Loyola. Findings support the use of a self-hypnosis ritual in
       conjunction with meditation series to induce positive affective
       change.

D51   Depping, F. "Behebung einiger sozialerzieherischer Probleme
       in der Schule im Rahmen von Selbstverwirlichungskon-
       zepten mit besonderer Berucksichtigung der TM." [Solu-
       tion of Some Social Educational Problems in School in the
       Context of Self-Actualization Concepts with Special Regard
       to TM.] (Diplomarbeit. Kiel, 1978.)

       Dhanaraj, V. Hubert. See A192.

D52   Dice, Marvin L., Jr. "The Effectiveness of Meditation on Selected Measures of Self-Actualization." DAI, 40 (1979), 2534A (Ph.D. Saint Louis University. Will lend.) Research indicated that for the three selected measures of self-actualization, there was no significant difference between persons who plan to practice Transcendental Meditation and persons who decide not to receive instruction in the practice.

D53　Dick, Leah D. "A Study of Meditation in the Service of Counseling." DAI, 34 (1974), 4037B (Ph.D. University of Oklahoma. Will lend.) The findings give support to the hypothesis that the practice Transcendental Meditation will aid the university counselee in experiencing a sense of well-being.

D54　Dieterle, W. "Methode der Ideenfindung zur Lösung von Gestaltungsprobleme: Ansatzpunkte für ein erweitertes Instrumentarium." [Methods to Find Ideas for Solutions of Problems in Formational Problems.] (Diplomarbeit. Technische Universität Berlin, 1976.)

D55　Diger, Michael J. "The Effect of Tai Chi Ch'uan Meditation on the Presence of Facilitative Factors in the Psychotherapist." (Ph.D. California School of Professional Psychology, Berkeley, 1973. Will lend.)

D56　Dillbeck, Michael C. "The Effects of the Transcendental Meditation Technique on Visual Perception and Verbal Problem Solving." DAI, 37 (1977), 5319-5320B (Ph.D. Purdue University. Will lend.) Tentatively scheduled for inclusion in Scientific Research on the Transcendental Meditation Program: Collected Papers, Vol. 2. Rheinweiler, West Germany: Maharishi European Research University Press, (in press). Statistical analyses supported the hypothesis of both immediate and two-week effects of TM on the perceptual tasks, while no effects were found on the anagram task of verbal problem solving.

D57　Diner, Martin D. "The Differential Effects of Meditation and Systematic Desensitization on Specific and General Anxiety." DAI, 39 (1978), 1950B (Ph.D. Temple University. Will lend.) It was concluded that the association of different personality traits with improvement in different treatments strongly suggests the importance of subject personality traits.

D58　Domitor, Paul J. "Zen Meditation, Expectancy, and Their Relative Contributions to Changes in Perceptual Flexibility." DAI, 38 (1978), 6145B (Ph.D. University of Miami. Will not lend.) The results provide no support for the hypothesis that meditation favorably affects perceptual change.

D59   Doxey, N.C.S. "A Comparative Multidisciplinary Investigation
      Into Three Hypothetical Altered States of Consciousness."
      (Ph.D. Thesis. University of Cape Town, S. Africa.)

D60   Edwards, John T. "The Effects of Induced Affect and Relax-
      ation Response Training on the Self-Management of Cigarette
      Smoking." DAI, 39 (1978) 1472-1473B (Ph.D. University
      of Georgia. Will not lend.)
      Suggests that both Induced Affect and Relaxation Response
      training can be effective in significantly reducing cigarette
      consumption.

D61   Elegant, John I. "The Relationship Between Transcendental
      Meditation and Dogmatism." DAI, 34 (1973), 1607A (Ed.D.
      Boston University School of Education. Will not lend.)
      It was found that there was no significant relationship between
      the practice of TM and level of dogmatism.

D62   Esser, P. "Meditation, Zen und TM." (Diplomarbeit in Psy-
      chologie. Universität Münster, 1975.)

D63   Fabick, Stephen D. "The Relative Effectiveness of Systematic
      Desensitization, Cognitive Modification, and Mantra Medita-
      tion in the Reduction of Test Anxiety." DAI, 37 (1977),
      4862A (Ed.D. West Virginia University. Will not lend.)
      Results showed that all three treatments significantly reduced
      test anxiety and general anxiety.

D64   Fagerstrom, M.F. "A Descriptive Study of Beginning Tran-
      scendental Meditators." (Master of Nursing Thesis. Uni-
      versity of Washington, 1973.)

D65   Faulkner, Michael H. "The Science of Creative Intelligence--
      Transcendental Meditation: A Correlated Study with the
      Art of Violin Playing." (D.M.A. University of Cincinnati,
      1980. Will not lend.)

D66   Ferguson, Phillip C. "An Integrative Meta-Analysis of Psy-
      chological Studies Investigating the Treatment Outcomes of
      Meditation Techniques." DAI, 42 (1981), 1547A (Ed.D
      University of Colorado at Boulder. Will lend.) Tentatively
      scheduled for inclusion in Scientific Research on the Tran-
      scendental Meditation Program: Collected Papers, Vol. 2.
      Rheinweiler, West Germany: Maharishi European Research
      University Press, (in press).
      The analysis suggests that the treatment effects of Transcen-
      dental Meditation produce a moderate effect outcome in both
      clinical and academic settings. Findings also suggest that
      other meditation modalities investigated produce negligible
      treatment effects.

D67   Fine, Lawrence B. "Techniques of Mystical Meditation for

Achieving Prophecy and the Holy Spirit in the Teachings of Isaac Lurie and Hayyim Vital." DAI, 37 (1976), 1039A (Ph.D. Brandeis University. Will lend.)
This study explores three different forms of ecstatic or illuminatory experience in their writings: the phenomenon of maggidism, the practice of yihudim, and Vital's technique of reading in the Mishnah.

D68   Flurer, James A. "The Development of a Christian Approach to Sport Meditation." (D.Min. Colgate Rochester Divinity School, Bexley Hall Crozer Theological Seminary, 1980. Will lend.)

D69   Forte, Michael A. "The Process of Meditation and the Retraining of Attention." (Ph.D. Harvard University, 1979. Will lend.)

D70   Frank, Marion R. "Transactional Analysis and Meditation Training as Interventions in Teacher Education: An Exploratory Study." DAI, 39 (1978), 823-824A (Ed.D. Temple University. Will lend.)
The study found some increase in the direction of self-actualization and degree of valuing a flexible teaching style and suggests teacher education might be redirected to incorporate these activities.

D71   French, Phyllis Elaine Walker. "A Study to Investigate the Effects of Meditation in Reducing Attentional Deficits in a Thirteen-Year-Old Male." (M.S. Thesis. Wright State University, Dayton, Ohio, 1977. Will lend.)
The results of this study were inconclusive.

D72   Fritz, George. "The Effects of Meditation Upon Peer Counselor Effectiveness." DAI, 40 (1980), 5730A (Ed.D. Lehigh University. Will not lend.)
It was concluded that two meditation strategies, the Relaxation Response and Open Focus, do not enhance the personal and professional qualities related to effective counseling.

D73   Gayten, Warren. "An Investigation of Physiological Changes During the Practice of Tai Chi Ch'uan: A Moving Meditation." DAI, 39 (1979), 6177B (Ph.D. California School of Professional Psychology, Berkeley. Will lend.)
Tai Chi could not be considered an altered state of consciousness when compared to Yoga and Zen meditation. Data did point towards it as being a visceral learning system that could lead to an altered state of biological awareness.

D74   Geisler, M. "Einstellungs und Verhaltensänderung bei Drogenkonsumenten nach TM." [Change of Attitude and Behavior of Drug Users After TM.] (Diplomarbeit. Ruhr-Universität Bochum, 1976.)

D75   Goldman, Barbara L. "The Efficacy of Meditation in the Re-
          duction of Reported Anxiety with Controls for Expectancy."
          DAI, 38 (1978), 6152-6153B (Ph.D. University of Miami.
          Will not lend.)
       No support was found for anxiety reducing effects of Zen
       breath meditation.

D76   Goleman, Daniel J. "Meditation and Stress Reactivity." (Ph.D.
          Harvard University, 1974. Will lend.)

D77   Gordin, Richard D. "Effects of Hypnosis, Relaxation Train-
          ing, or Music on State Anxiety and Stress in Female Ath-
          letes." DAI, 42 (1981), 598-599A (Ed.D. University of
          Utah. Will lend.)
       Examination of the effects of hypnosis, relaxation training,
       or music on state anxiety and stress in female athletes showed
       no relationship to state anxiety and motor performance.

D78   Gordon, Rikki L. "The Effects of Transcendental Meditation
          Upon Ego Permissiveness, Anxiety and Neuroticism." DAI,
          40 (1980), 4488A (Ph.D. California School of Professional
          Psychology, Los Angeles. Will lend.)
       Mean ego permissiveness did not change over time. Neuroti-
       cism decreased over time. Anxiety started high, decreased in
       the 2-4 month group and increased again in the 12-14 month
       group, though not as high as the control group.

D79   Green, David B. "The Relationship of a Counselor-Guided
          Meditation to Counselor Presence as Defined in Psychosyn-
          thesis." DAI, 41 (1980), 2450A (Ph.D. Indiana State
          University. Will lend.)
       No significant relationship was discovered in the study.

D80   Greenfield, Thomas K. "Individual Differences and Mystical
          Experience in Response to Three Forms of Meditation."
          DAI, 38 (1978), 5569-5570B (Ph.D. University of Michi-
          gan. Will lend.)
       Silent mantra, color visualization, and mind emptying were
       studied.

D81   Griffiths, Thomas J. "The Effects of Two Selected Relaxation
          Techniques on Levels of Anxiety, Stress, and Underwater
          Performance of Beginning Scuba Diving Students." DAI,
          41 (1980), 585A (Ed.D. University of Maryland. Will
          lend.)
       The purpose of this study was to investigate the effects of
       two types of relaxation training (EMG BFT and Meditation) on
       levels of self-reported anxiety, physiological measures of
       stress, and underwater performance of beginning scuba diving
       students.

D82   Griggs, Steven T. "Clairvoyance and the Transcendental

Meditation Sidhi Program." DAI, 43 (1982), 1980B (Ph.D. United States International University. Will lend.)
The possibility that practicing the Transcendental Meditation Sidhi Program leads to increased clairvoyance was not supported.

D83 _____. "A Preliminary Study Into the Effects of Transcendental Meditation on Empathy." (M.A. Thesis. United States Internaitonal University, 1976.) Tentatively scheduled for inclusion in Scientific Research on the Transcendental Meditation Program: Collected Papers, Vol. 2. Rheinweiler, West Germany: Maharishi European Research University Press, (in press).
Empathy was found in varying degrees in subjects practicing the TM technique, depending on the experience level of the meditators.

D84 Gunaratana, Henepola. "A Critical Analysis of the Jhanas in Theravada Buddhist Meditation." DAI, 41 (1981), 4420A (Ph.D. American University. Will lend.)
The primary purpose of this study was to determine the precise role of the jhanas in the Theravada Buddhist presentation of the way to liberation.

D85 Haines, John L. "The Effects of a Trans-rational Training Program on Affective Sensitivity." DAI, 38 (1978), 4583A (Ed.D. West Virginia University. Will not lend.)
This study supports the idea that Zen meditative techniques can be effective training aids in the development of empathic understanding in counselors.

D86 Handmacher, Barbara H. "Time in Meditation and Sex Differences Related to Intrapersonal and Interpersonal Orientation." DAI, 39 (1978), 676-677A (Ph.D. Ohio State University. Will not lend.) Tentatively scheduled for inclusion in Scientific Research on the Transcendental Meditation Program: Collected Papers, Vol. 2. Rheinweiler, West Germany: Maharishi European Research University Press, (in press).
The study assesses meditator personality traits in relation to years of practice in meditation, compares meditators with non-meditators, compares sex differences, and correlates the intrapersonal variables with the interpersonal variables.

D87 Hanschen, G. "Das Theorie-Praxis Verhältnis in der Wissenschaft der Kreativen Intelligenz." [The Relationship Between Theory and Practice in the Science of Creative Intelligence.] (Diplomarbeit. Berlin, 1976.)

D88 Harrow, R.J. "The Effects of the TM Technique on Fractionated Reflex and Reaction Times." (Master's Thesis. University of Massachusetts, 1976.)

D89   Hartgrove, J.L. and W.G. Braud. "Perception of Depth and
        Illusions During a 'Transcendental State'." (M.A. Thesis.
        University of Houston, 1975.)

D90   Hatch, Jeffrey M. "The Cheops Pyramidal Form: Its Influ-
        ence Upon Alpha and Theta Production During Meditation."
        DAI, 35 (1975), 4628B   (Ed.D. University of Northern
        Colorado. Will lend.)
        Results indicated that the Cheops Pyramidal Form was not in-
        strumental in altering the state of meditation.

D91   Hattauer, Edward A. "Clinically Standardized Meditation
        (CSM) and Counselor Behavior." DAI, 41 (1981), 3892B
        (Ph.D. Columbia University. Will lend.)
        The purpose of this study was to explore the potential effects
        of meditation on the interpersonal sensitivity of counselors.
        Test results were variable. The majority of the subjects felt
        that meditation had a positive impact.

D91K   Heide, Frederick J. "Relaxation-Induced Anxiety: A Psycho-
        physiological Investigation." DAI, 42 (1981): 1606B
        (Ph.D. Pennsylvania State University. Will lend.)
        In general, relaxation-induced anxiety was more prominent
        with the meditational procedure than with progressive relaxa-
        tion. Also reported in Journal of Consulting and Clinical
        Psychology, 51 (April 1983): 171-182. [Cf. A353]

D92   Heidelberg, Rainer. "Transzendentale Meditation in der ge-
        burtshilflichen Psychoprophylaxe." [Transcendental Medi-
        tation in the Child-Bearing Psychoprophylaxis.] (Dis-
        sertation. Freie Universität, Berlin, 1979.) Also pub-
        lished by Hannesmann in Husum, 1981. [B318]

D93   Heil, John. "Visual Imagery Change During Relaxation-
        Meditation Training." DAI, 43 (1983), 2338B   (D.A.
        Lehigh University. Will not lend.)
        Relaxation-meditation practice appears to be a route to the
        enhancement of visual imagery ability.

D94   Heinz, Brad R. "The Origins of Meditation: Perspectives
        Beyond the Scientific Research." DAI, 43 (1982), 232B
        (Ph.D. Loyola University of Chicago. Will lend.)
        Presents a comprehensive theoretical overview of meditation's
        dynamics by describing them from within the Indian Vedantic
        model of consciousness.

D95   Hendricksen, Norman E. "The Effects of Progressive Relaxa-
        tion and Meditation on Mood Stability and State Anxiety in
        Alcoholic Inpatients." DAI, 39 (1978), 981B (Ph.D.
        University of Missouri, Columbia. Will not lend.)
        It was concluded that the practice of progressive relaxation or

meditation, in a group setting, does not generally result in increased mood stability or significantly lower state anxiety levels.

D96   Hertner, H.D. "Der Einfluss der TM auf die Faktoren der menschlichen Arbeitskraft." [The Influence of TM on the Factors of Human Ability.] (Abschlussarbeit als Betriebswirt. Fachhochschule für Wirtschaft, Pforzheim, 1975.)

D97   Higuchi, Annette A. "Effects of Self-Induced Relaxation on Autonomic Responses and Subjective Distress of High- and Low-neuroticism Scorers to Adversive Baby Cries." DAI, 37 (1977), 4142-4143B (Ph.D. University of Hawaii. Will lend.)
This study investigated the efficacy of brief training in progressive muscle relaxation and meditation as self-control methods for coping with stress. Though neither resulted in significantly lower levels of stress, it was demonstrated that muscle relaxation training provided more reduction in stress.

D98   Hirss, Jean R.U. "A Comparison of Two Types of Meditation to Reduce Stress in a Teaching Population." DAI, 43 (1983), 3847A (Ph.D. University of Washington. Will lend.)
Those who meditated consistently reported higher mood levels, which in turn were related to lower anxiety scores on the posttests.

D99   Hoffmann, B. "Möglichkeiten und Grenzen der TM zur Behebung schulischer Insufficienzen im educaktiven Bereich." [Possibilities and Limits of TM Solving Deficiencies in School.] (Diplomarbeit fur Handelslehre. Köln, 1977.)

D100   Howald, W. "Meditation, ihre angsttherapeutischen und angstprophylaktischen Wirkungen, dargestellt am Beispiel der TM." [Meditation and Its Anxiety Therapeutic and Anxiety Prophylactic Effects: TM Used as an Example.] (Diplomarbeit. Universität Münster, Psychologisches Institut, 1975.)

D101   Jackson, Yvonne. "Learning Disorders and the Transcendental Meditation Program: Retrospects and Prospects (A Preliminary Study with Economically Deprived Adolescents)." DAI, 38 (1977), 3351-3352A (Ed.D. University of Massachusetts. Will lend.) Tentatively scheduled for inclusion in Scientific Research on the Transcendental

Meditation Program: Collected Papers, Vol. 2. Rheinweiler, West Germany: Maharishi European Research University Press, (in press).
The results indicated that the students developed significantly on the personality measure. Although meditators performed better in reading and arithmetic, the differences were
not significant.

D102   Jacobs, Jane A. "Psychological Change Through the Spiritual
       Teacher: Implications for Psychotherapy." DAI, 35
       (1975), 3582-3583B (Ph.D. California School of Profes-
       sional Psychology, Berkeley. Will lend.)
Concluded that the spiritual teacher needs to avail himself of
the knowledge of Western psychotherapies because there is a
discrepancy between the teacher's theories of how change
toward enlightenment takes place and what is actually hap-
pening psychologically between him and his students, and in
his group.

D103   Jain, Prabhachandra K. "Relations Between Interpersonal
       Styles and Mood States." DAI, 38 (1978), 5573B (Ph.D.
       Catholic University of America. Will lend.)
An attempt was made to identify reciprocal relations between
interpersonal styles and mood states. The results indicated
a need for more studies of the effects of different meditation
methods on specific personality types.

D104   Johnson, Stephen J. "Effects of Yoga-Therapy on Conflict
       Resolution, Self-Concept, and Emotional Adjustment."
       DAI, 34 (1974), 6385A (Ph.D. University of Southern
       California. Will lend.)
Conclusions seem to warrant using yoga-therapy as an effective method of stimulating positive changes in conflict resolution, self-concept and emotional adjustment.

D105   Jones, Roger C. "A Comparison of Aerobic Exercise, An-
       aerobic Exercise and Meditation on Multidimensional Stress
       Measures." DAI, 42 (1981), 2504B (Ph.D. Ohio Univer-
       sity. Will not lend.)
Subjects in aerobic exercises (running) reported decreases
in both somatic and cognitive anxiety. Subjects in the anaerobic exercise program reported decreases solely in somatic
anxiety. Subjects in the aerobic exercise treatment reported
a decrease in trait anxiety. Subjects in the anaerobic exercise demonstrated an increase in state anxiety. Subjects in
the meditation treatment program reported significant decreases for each of the six dependent variables.

D106   Joscelyn, Lela A. "The Effects of the Transcendental Medi-

tation Technique on a Measure of Self-Actualization."
DAI, 39 (1979), 4104B (Ph.D. University of Windsor,
Canada.)
No significant effect could be confirmed.

D107   Joseph, Arthur B. "The Influence of One Form of Zen Meditation on Levels of Anxiety and Self-Actualization." DAI,
40 (1979), 1335-1336B (Ed.D. State University of New
York at Albany. Will lend.)
The results indicated no significant effect of the zazen meditation technique upon the criterion measures of anxiety and
self-actualization.

D108   Kamholtz, John D. "The Effects of a Stress Reduction Program on Type A Behavior Pattern, Blood Pressure, Muscle
Tension, and Relaxation Practice Time." DAI, 40 (1980),
4908A (Ed.D. State University of New York at Buffalo.
Will lend.)
Groups were instructed in either meditation, autogenic training, biofeedback, or progressive relaxation. Improvement
was demonstrated on Relaxation Inventory test. No significant difference between groups was shown.

D109   Keithler, Mary A. "The Influence of the Transcendental
Meditation Program and Personality Variables on Auditory
Thresholds and Cardio-respiratory Responding." DAI,
42 (1981), 1662B (Ph.D. Washington University. Will
not lend.)
Little relationship was found between any of the variables
and measures.

D110   Kelton, Jeffrey J. "Perceptual and Cognitive Processes in
Meditation." DAI, 38 (1978), 3931B (Ph.D. University
of Georgia. Will not lend.)
This study examined the effect of short-term practice of a
visual concentrative meditation technique on various measures
of attention. Meditators demonstrated a significant improvement in their ability to resist distractions.

D111   Kemmerling, T. "Auswirkungen der Technik der Transzen-
dentalen Meditation auf den Muskeltonus." [Effect of the
Transcendental Meditation Technique on the Muscle Tone.]
(Diplomarbeit. Deutsche Sporthochschule Köln, 1976/77.)

D112   Kindler, Herbert S. "The Influence of a Meditation-Relaxation Technique on Group Problem-Solving Effectiveness."
DAI, 39 (1979), 4370-4371A (Ph.D. University of California, Los Angeles. Will lend.)
The results are interpreted to serve as encouragement for
organizations to offer meditation-relaxation to employees on
a voluntary basis. [Cf. A417]

D113   Kindlon, Daniel J. "The Relationship Between Meditation
        Practice and Components of Anxiety and Creativity."
        DAI, 42 (1982), 3511A (Ph.D. Cornell University. Will
        lend.)
        No significant relationship between meditation practice and
        components of anxiety and creativity could be demonstrated.

D114   King, Jeanne W. "Meditation and the Enhancement of Focus-
        ing Ability." DAI, 40 (1979), 2844B (Ph.D. Northwest-
        ern University. Will not lend.)
        The major finding was that meditation training and practice
        resulted in a significant improvement in "focusing" ability.

D115   Kirkland, Karl. "Effective Test-Taking: Skills Acquisition
        Versus Anxiety Reduction Techniques." DAI, 41 (1981),
        4265B (Ph.D. University of Southern Mississippi.
        Will not lend.)
        Results indicate that the skills acquisition technique was
        superior. [Cf. A421]

D116   Kirschner, Sam. "Zen Meditators: A Clinical Study." DAI,
        36 (1976), 3613-3614B (Ph.D. Adelphi University. Will
        lend.)
        The results indicated that the subjects perceived several im-
        portant changes in their lives dealing with emotional prob-
        lems, which they attributed to zazen practice.

D117   Kline, Kenneth S. "Effects of a Transcendental Meditation
        Program on Personality and Arousal." DAI, 36 (1976),
        6386-6387B (Ph.D. University of Wisconsin, Madison.
        Will not lend.)
        No significant effects on personality and arousal could be
        demonstrated.

D118   Kniffki, C. "Transzendentale Meditation und Autogenes
        Training: Vergleich ihrer Effekte auf einige Persönlich-
        keitsvariablen." [Transcendental Meditation and Autogenic
        Training: Comparison of their effects on some personal-
        ity variables.] (Diplomarbeit. Universität Göttingen,
        1975.) [Cf. B403]

D119   Kobayashi, Kazuo. "The Effect of Zen Meditation on the
        Valence of Intrusive Thoughts." DAI, 43 (1982), 280B
        (Ph.D. United States International University. Will
        lend.)
        The results showed that the valence of intrusions significant-
        ly decreased for two of the three subjects.

D120   Kongtawng, Thanom. "Effects of Meditation on Self-Concept."
        DAI, 38 (1977), 1230A (Ed.D. Memphis State University.
        Will lend.)

The study was able to determine a significantly greater positive change in self-concept.

D120K   Kornfield, Jack M. "The Psychology of Mindfulness Meditation." DAI, 44 (1983): 610B (Ph.D. Saybrook Institute. Will not lend.)
Describes in detail the background, setting, and instructions used to teach Mindfulness Meditation which is based on the Thereavada Buddhist tradition. Analyzes and compares patterns of "energy" flow, vision, time, dreams and other unusual perceptions in meditators and control group. Changes appear to result from the effect of the retreat environment combined with intensive meditation practice.

D121   Kraft, Charles G. "Eastern and Western Approaches for Mind-Body Integration." DAI, 39 (1979), 4039-4040B (Ed.D. University of Northern Colorado. Will lend.)
A control group, Gestalt group, combined Hatha Yoga & Meditation group, and a Bioenergetic exercise group were studied in terms of self-actualization, anxiety, neuromuscular activity, mind-body flexibility and health.

D122   Krahne, W. "Konventionelle und quantitative EEG-Analyse bei TM." [Conventional and Quantitative EEG Analysis During TM.] (Dissertation. Universität Göttingen, 1976.)

D123   Kretschmer, H. "Der Einfluss der Meditation auf die Veränderung psychotherapeutisch relevanter Persönlichkeitsmerkmale." [The Influence of Meditation in Changing Psychotherapeutically Relevant Personality Characteristics.] (Diplomarbeit. Universität Göttingen, Psychologisches Institut, 1976.)

D124   Krueger, Robert C. "The Comparative Effects of Zen Focusing and Muscle Relaxation Training on Selected Experiential Variables." DAI, 41 (1980), 1405A (Ph.D. University of Iowa. Will not lend.)
The study was directed at the subjects' ability to do experiential focusing, their orientation toward living in the present, and state-trait anxiety.

D125   Krüger, M. "Die Evolutionsstrategie." [The Evolution Strategy.] (Diplomarbeit. Universität Bremen, 1977.)

D126   Kvapil, Mary A. "A Model for Enabling Persons in the Spiritual Disciplines of Prayer and Meditation." DAI, 43 (1982), 1201A (D.Min. Drew University. Will not lend.)

The types of prayer include image prayer, contemplation, the Jesus Prayer, mindfulness, and Biblical prayers of thanksgiving, praise, intercession, conversation, etc.

D127   Landrith, G.B., III. "Comparisons of Feelings During and After Long Periods of Transcendental Meditation." (Master's Thesis. University of Kansas, Lawrence, 1971.)

D128   Laurie, James R. "A Model for Teaching Meditation Classes in a Christian Context." (D.Min. Southern Methodist University, 1978. Will lend.)

D129   Lesh, Terry V. "The Relationship Between Zen Meditation and the Development of Accurate Empathy." DAI, 30 (1970), 4778A (Ph.D. University of Oregon. Will not lend.)
The results of the study show significant improvement in empathic ability among meditators.

D130   Levin, Susan. "The Transcendental Meditation Technique in Secondary Education." DAI, 38 (1977), 706-707A (Ph.D. University of California, Berkeley. Will lend.)
The research examined the educational and psychological effects of an academic course for secondary educational students which includes the practice of the Transcendental Meditation technique. Positively correlated gains were demonstrated. [Cf. A471]

D131   Lewis, Jerome. "The Effects of a Group Meditation Technique Upon Degree of Test Anxiety and Level of Digit-Letter Retention in High School Students." DAI, 38 (1978), 6015-6016A (Ph.D. University of Southern California. Will lend.)
No statistically significant effects could be found.

D132   Lewis, John W. "Jungian Depth Psychology and Transcendental Meditation: Complementary Practices for the Realization of the Self." DAI, 39 (1978), 986-987B (Ph.D. University of California, Santa Cruz. Will lend.)
The study determined that both techniques are compatible as simultaneous practices.

D133   Linden, William. "The Relation Between the Practicing of Meditation by School Children and Their Levels of Field Dependence-Independence, Test Anxiety and Reading Achievement." DAI, 33 (1972), 1798B (Ph.D. New York University. Will not lend.)
An increase in level of field independence was shown. A decrease in test anxiety was demonstrated. An increase in reading grade was not found.

D134   Ling, Paul K. "The Intensive Buddhist Meditation Retreat and Self: Psychological and Theravadin Considerations." DAI, 42 (1982), 2992B (Ph.D. Boston University Graduate School. Will not lend.)
The study explores factors such as idealization, self-love, self-concepts, and experience of self and world.

D135   Lourdes, Peter V. "Implications of the Transcendental Meditation Program for Counseling: The Possibility of a Paradigm Shift." DAI, 39 (1978), 1343-1344A (Ph.D. Loyola University of Chicago. Will lend.)
It was argued that TM can be considered a viable treatment modality; that the Science of Creative Intelligence can fill a gap in counseling; and that if TM is adopted as a treatment modality, it will lead to an examination of the assumptions on which TM and conventional psychotherapy are based.

D136   Lukoff, David G. "Comparison of a Holistic and a Social Skills Training Program for Schizophrenics." DAI, 41 (1981), 4268B (Ph.D. Loyola University of Chicago. Will lend.)
While both groups showed substantial decreases in symptomology, analysis showed no significant differences between the groups. The pattern of differences favored the holistic group.

D137   MacIntosh, G.R. "Transcendental Meditation and Selected Life Attitudes." (Master's Thesis. University of Calgary, Alberta, Canada, 1972.)

D137K   Macrae, Janet A. "A Comparison Between Meditating Subjects and Non-Meditating Subjects on Time Experience and Human Field Motion." DAI, 43 (1983): 3537B (Ph.D. New York University. Will not lend.)
The mean score of the meditating subjects on the Time Metaphor Test was significantly lower than non-meditators, indicating a higher sense of timelessness. The mean score of the meditating subjects in the Human Field Motion Test was higher than non-meditators, indicating greater human field motion.

D138   Maher, Michael F. "Movement Exploration and Zazen Meditation: A Comparison of Two Methods of Personal-Growth-Group Approaches on the Self-Actualization Potential of Counselor Candidates." DAI, 39 (1979), 5329A (Ph.D. University of Idaho. Will not lend.)
Results indicate that both Movement Exploration and Zazen Meditation can be significant self-actualizing agents and neither method was judged to be superior.

D139   Maliszewski, Michael. "Need for Stimulation: Its Relation-
           ship to Interest in and the Practice of the Transcendental
           Meditation Technique." DAI, 38 (1978), 3932-3933B
           (Ph.D. University of Chicago. Will lend.)
        Findings show the efficacy of TM in the beginning meditator
        to be related to expectations and motivations of subjects,
        personality make-up of subjects, and contrasting reactions
        of individuals to treatment in psychotherapy.

D140   Marcus, Steven V. "The Influence of the Transcendental
           Meditation Program on the Marital Dyad." DAI, (1978),
           3895B (Ph.D. California School of Professional Psychol-
           ogy, Fresno. Will lend.) Tentatively scheduled for in-
           clusion in Scientific Research on the Transcendental Medi-
           tation Program: Collected Papers, Vol. 2. Rheinweiler,
           West Germany: Maharishi European Research University
           Press, (in press).
        Results show the TM Program to be an effective psychothera-
        peutic agent.

D141   Marr, S. "Transcendental Meditation as a Means of Trait
           Anxiety Reduction in a Correctional Setting." (Master's
           Thesis. Southern Illinois University, 1974.)

D142   Marron, Jay P. "Transcendental Meditation: A Clinical
           Evaluation." DAI, 34 (1974), 4051B (Ph.D. Colorado
           State University. Will not lend.)
        The technique of TM was shown to be an effective method of
        reducing state anxiety. Other personality correlates such
        as motivation, attitudes, and preference for novelty were al-
        so examined.

D143   Marshall, James P. "An Exploration of the Social Conse-
           quences and Implications of a Revelationary Movement."
           DAI, 39 (1978), 3175A (Ph.D. University of Colorado
           at Boulder. Will lend.) Tentatively scheduled for inclu-
           sion in Scientific Research on the Transcendental Medita-
           tion Program: Collected Papers, Vol. 2. Rheinweiler,
           West Germany: Maharishi European Research University
           Press, (in press).
        Suggests that the Transcendental Movement serves to in-
        crease the integration of the individual into the existing so-
        cial order.

D144   Matheson, Charlene M. "Exercise and Meditation as a Life-
           style Intervention for Addictive Behaviors." DAI, 42
           (1982), 4935B (Ph.D. University of Washington. Will
           lend.)
        The study shows that exercise and meditation together pro-
        duce a greater effect on cigarette and alcohol consumption
        than does either alone.

D145   Maupin, Edward W. "An Exploratory Study of Individual Differences in Response to a Zen Meditation Exercise." DAI, 23 (1963), 3978 (Ph.D. University of Michigan. Will lend.) Also reported in the Journal of Consulting Psychology, 29 (1965): 139-145. [Cf. 504]
Increased capacity for regression and tolerance for unrealistic experience were measurable. Attention measures were not significant.

D146   Mayer, Elizabeth L. "On the Psychological Nature of Resistances to Meditation Which Arise During the Meditation Process: A Study of a Form of Alternative Education." DAI, 35 (1975), 5929-5930A (Ph.D. Stanford University. Will lend.)
The investigation demonstrates that resistances to meditation may be usefully understood in terms of the psychoanalytic theory of resistance.

D147   McKenzie, N.C. "Prayer, Meditation and Religious Experience: An Empirical Study." (M.Phil. King's College, London, 1979.)

D148   Mengel, Gail S.E. "The Effects of Transcendental Meditation on the Reading Achievement of Learning Disabled Youngsters." DAI, 39 (1979), 6699A (Ph.D. University of Connecticut. Will lend.)
No significant effects of Transcendental Meditation on reading achievement were revealed.

D149   Miro, B. "Biochemische und physiologische Auswirkungen der Transcendentalen Meditation." [Biochemical and Physiological Effects of Transcendental Meditation.] (Diplomarbeit. Bonn, 1975.)

D150   Moles, Edward A. "Zen Meditation: A Study of Regression in Service of the Ego." DAI, 38 (1977), 2871-2872B (Ph.D. California School of Professional Psychology, Berkeley. Will lend.)
This study examined the effects of Zen meditation on reality testing, impulse control, sense of reality of self and world, adaptive regression, thought processes, defensive functioning, and synthetic-integrative functioning.

D151   Möller, S. "Der Einstaz von TM in der Rehabilitation Strafgefangener." [Application of TM in Rehabilitation of Prison Inmates.] (Diplomarbeit. Universität Münster, 1978.)

D151K   Moore, Richard H. "Changes in Psychological Functioning Through Contemplative Meditation." DAI, 43 (1983): 2319B (Ph.D. Nova University. Will lend.)

Results indicate that contemplative meditation significantly contributes to the improved psychological functioning of practitioners. It was most effective in areas of perception and personality. Anxiety was also studied.

D152   Morler, Edward E. "A Preliminary Study of the Effects of Transcendental Meditation on Selected Dimensions of Organization Dynamics." DAI, 35 (1974), 766A (Ph.D. University of Maryland. Will lend.)
It was concluded that TM may not have the immediate measurable effects on the psychological, attitudinal and behavioral dimensions that TM literature and many of its proponents imply, and that reported changes may be due to the placebo effect.

D153   Muller-Kainz, E. "Der Effekt der Transzendentalen Meditation auf Adipositas." [The Effect of Transcendental Meditation on Adipositas.] (Dissertation. Universität Würzburg, 1977.)

D154   Munk, H. "Primärtherapie und Transzendentalen Meditation Vergleichende Untersuchung über Methoden, Theorien, therapeutische Effekte." [Primal Therapy and TM: Comparable Research on Methods, Theories, Therapeutic Effects.] (Diplomarbeit. Universität Marburg, 1975.)

D155   Murphy, Martha J. "Exploration in the Use of Group Meditation with Persons in Psychotherapy." DAI, 33 (1973), 6089B (Ph.D. California School of Professional Psychology, Berkeley. Will lend.)
This study reports on how successfully persons in psychotherapy meditate, what experiences they report, and what effects it has on their daily lives.

D156   Neidenbach, S.L. "Transcendental Meditation and the Self-Reported Incidence of Psychosomatically Related Symptoms." (M.S. Thesis. University of Illinois Medical Center, 1974.)

D157   Neptune, Calvin, III. "An Investigation of the Effect of Meditation Training in a Cigarette Smoking Extinguishment Program." DAI, 39 (1978), 416B (Ph.D. Kansas State University. Will lend.)
A significantly higher abstention rate was demonstrated in a group trained in the human relaxation response combined with a behavioral chain interruption smoking modification technique than other groups tested.

D158   Nidich, Sanford I. "The Science of Creative Intelligence as a Theory of Education." (M.S. Thesis. University of Cincinnati, 1973.)

D159 _____. "A Study of the Relationship of Transcendental
Meditation to Kohlberg's Stages of Moral Reasoning."
DAI, 36 (1976), 4361-4362A (Ed.D. University of Cincinnati. Will not lend.) Extracted in Scientific Research
on the Transcendental Meditation Program: Collected Papers, Vol. 1, 2nd ed., Weggis, Switzerland: Maharishi
European Research University, 1977. pp. 585-593.
This study found that a positive relationship exists between
the practice of Transcendental Meditation and moral reasoning.

D160 Nolly, Gerald A. "The Immediate Aftereffects of Meditation
on Perceptual Awareness." DAI, 36 (1975), 919B (Ph.D.
University of Kansas. Will lend.)
The results of the study indicated significant differences in
perceptual awareness between experienced meditators and in-
experienced meditators.

D161 Norwood, Jean E. "An Investigation of a Zen Meditation
Procedure and Its Effect on Selected Personality and Psychotherapeutic Variables." DAI, 43 (1983), 3721B (Ph.D.
North Texas State University. Will lend.)
Analysis indicated no treatment effect for three personality
variables; time-competence, inner-direction, and locus of control. There was significant effect on the field-independence
measure.

D162 Nourse, James C. "A Phenomenological Approach to Self-
Knowledge." DAI, 36 (1976), 4173B (Ph.D. University
of Tennessee. Will lend.)
A study of the author's personal experience with Transcendental Meditation and the phenomenon of Existenz.

D163 Nowak, W. "Asthetischer Zustand und Transzendentales Bewusstsein: Zur Interpretation der Briefe Über die äs-
thetische Erziehung des Menschen von Freidreich Schiller."
[The State of the Aesthetic and Transcendental Consciousness: Interpretation of the letters, On the Aesthetic
Education of Man by Friedrich Schiller.] (Hausarbeit zur
Erlangeung des Magistergrades. Universität Göttingen,
1980.)

D164 Nuernberger, Edwin P. "The Use of Meditation in the Treatment of Alcoholism." DAI, 38 (1977), 1413B (Ph.D.
University of Minnesota. Will lend.)
Significant change or improvement was reported on most of
the test battery given to 143 male subjects who completed a
four week treatment program.

D165 Oldfield, Richard R. "The Effects of Meditation on Selected
Measures of Human Potential." DAI, 42 (1982), 4717A

(Ph.D. University of Nebraska, Lincoln. Will not lend.)
Self-concept, aggression, and psychophysiological response
were studied. The results supported two of the five hypotheses employed. However, the investigator indicated that
data warranted the consideration of meditation as an educational methodology for enhancing human potential.

D166   Orth, Deborah K. "Clinical Treatments of Depression." DAI,
        40 (1980), 6154A (Ed.D. West Virginia University. Will
        not lend.)
        In general there was more improvement seen in subjects as-
        signed to the meditation, jogging, or self-chosen activity
        treatment than self-monitoring treatment.

D167   Osbelt, U. "Stressbewältigung und Transzendentalen Medi-
        tation." [Overcoming Stress and Transcendental Medita-
        tion.] (Diplomarbeit. Universität Bochum, 1979.)

D168   Ottens, Allen J. "The Effect of Transcendental Meditation
        Upon Modifying the Cigarette Smoking Habit." DAI, 35
        (1975), 7131A (Ph.D. University of Illinois at Urbana-
        Champaign. Will lend.)
        Both TM and self control groups significantly reduced their
        cigarette consumption over ten weeks to the same degree.
        [Cf. A622]

D169   Overbeck, Klaus-Dieter. "Auswirkungen der Transzenden-
        talen Meditation auf die psychische und psychosomatische
        Befindlichkeit." [Effects of Transcendental Meditation on
        the Psychic and Psychosomatic State of Health.] (Ph.D.
        Dissertation. Universität Hamburg, 1978.) Also pub-
        lished by Kleine Verlag, Bielefeld, 1981.

D170   Parker, Jerry C. "The Effects of Progressive Relaxation
        Training and Meditation on Autonomic Arousal in Alco-
        holics." DAI, 37 (1977), 4697-4698B (Ph.D. University
        of Missouri, Columbia. Will not lend.)
        The study was an investigation of the comparative effects of
        progressive relaxation training and meditation training on
        self-report and physiological indices of autonomic arousal in
        alcoholics.

D171   Phillips, Susan K. "Yoga Psychology and Dimensions of
        Counseling Practice." DAI, 40 (1980), 4902A (Ph.D.
        University of Wisconsin, Madison. Will not lend.)
        There is support for the contention that a new orientation to
        counseling practice, a "yoga therapy" orientation, is develop-
        ing.

D172   Polowniak, William A.J. "The Meditation-Encounter-Growth
        Group." DAI, 34 (1973), 1732B (Ph.D. United States

International University. Will lend.)
The study is an investigation of the effectiveness of a program in concentration, meditation and various yoga experiences in producing changes in self-concept, self-actualizing,
and the feeling of purpose and meaningfulness in life.

D173   Puente, Antonio E. "Psychophysiological Investigations on
        Transcendental Meditation." DAI, 39 (1979), 3571B
        (Ph.D. University of Georgia. Will not lend.)
        The results do not suggest that meditation experience pro-
        duces greater reductions in physiological arousal than Ben-
        son's relaxation response or no treatment.

D174   Rankin, G. "The Transcendental Meditation Movement: A
        Discussion of Perspectives in the Study of Religious and
        Quasi-Religious Movements." (M.A. University of Keele,
        1977.)

D175   Reddy, M.K. "Acute Effects of Transcendental Meditation
        on Selected Psychophysiological Parameters and Athletic
        Performance." (Degree of Idrettskandidat. Norwegian
        College of Physical Education and Sport, Oslo, 1976.)
        Tentatively scheduled for inclusion in Scientific Research
        on the Transcendental Meditation Program: Collected Pa-
        pers, Vol. 2. Rheinweiler, West Germany: Maharishi
        European Research University Press, (in press).
        This investigation showed that the rest produced by TM is
        greater than during relaxed sitting. Performance improved
        more after TM.

D176   Reed, Jeanette I.T. "The Impact of Transcendental Medita-
        tion on Cognitive Flexibility, Field Dependence, and Di-
        rectional Priorities in Attention Deployment." DAI, 37
        (1976), 475-476B (Ph.D. University of California,
        Berkeley. Will lend.)
        The results of this study suggest that the practice of TM
        does not lead to increased cognitive flexibility or greater
        field independence. Change did occur in attention develop-
        ment.

D177   Riddle, Alexander G. "Effects of Selected Elements of Medi-
        tation on Self-Actualization, Locus of Control, and Trait
        Anxiety." DAI, 40 (1980), 3149B (Ph.D. University of
        South Carolina. Will lend.)
        No changes occurred in locus of control. Decreases in trait
        anxiety were shown.

D178   Riedesel, Brian C. "Meditation and Empathic Behavior: A
        Study of Clinically Standardized Meditation and Effective
        Sensitivity." DAI, 43 (1983), 3274A (Ph.D. University
        of Utah. Will lend.)

Treatment had no significant effect on Affective Sensitivity
Scale performance. Other beneficial subjective effects were
reported.

D179   Rios, Robert J. "The Effect of Hypnosis and Meditation on
        State and Trait Anxiety and Locus of Control." DAI, 40
        (1980), 6209A (Ph.D. Texas A&M University. Will lend.)
        The results indicate that hypnosis and meditation are effec-
        tive treatments for lowering both state and trait anxiety.

D180   Rose, Donna S. "The Transcendental Meditation Movement:
        The Creation, Development and Institutionalization of a
        World View." DAI, 37 (1977), 6075A (Ph.D. Southern
        Illinois University at Carbondale. Will lend.)
        This investigation is a detailed history of the TM movement.

D181   Rosenthal, J.M. "The Effect of Transcendental Meditation
        on Self-Actualization, Self-Concept, and Hypnotic Sus-
        ceptibility." (M.A. Thesis. University of Hawaii, 1974.)

D182   Russel, Norris M. "The Effects of Biofeedback and Relaxa-
        tion Response Training on Submaximal Exercise." DAI,
        42 (1981), 601A (Ed.D. East Texas State University.
        Will lend.)
        Findings varied among the four test groups.

D183   Russie, Roger E. "The Influence of Transcendental Medita-
        tion on Positive Mental Health and Self-Actualization; and
        the Role of Expectation, Rigidity, and Self-Control in the
        Achievement of These Benefits." DAI, 36 (1976), 5816B
        (Ph.D. California School of Professional Psychology, Los
        Angeles. Will lend.) Tentatively scheduled for inclusion
        in Scientific Research on the Transcendental Meditation
        Program: Collected Papers, Vol. 2. Rheinweiler, West
        Germany: Maharishi European Research University Press,
        (in press).
        Significant positive results were found in some but not all
        relationships.

D184   Salsbury, Janice C. "Relaxation Response: An Evaluation
        of a Technique for Anxiety Reduction Among College
        Graduate Students." DAI, 40 (1979), 2415A (Ed.D.
        Montana State University. Will lend.)
        The investigation failed to show that Relaxation Response
        reduced anxiety.

D185   Sanford, David E. "Inspiration in the Creative Process and
        Meditation." DAI, 39 (1975), 2481B (Ph.D. Johns Hop-
        kins University. Will lend.)
        The evidence suggests that the meditation procedure used in
        the experiment promotes originality but not fluency, flexibil-
        ity, or elaboration.

D186   Schackmann, R. "Verhalten von Atemzugvolumen, Herzschlag-
        frequenz, Atemgaszusammensetzung bei Sportstudenten
        während der Ausübung der TM im Vergleich zu nicht-
        meditierenden Sportstudenten." [Activity of Inhalation
        Volume, Heartbeat Frequency, Inhalation Gas Components
        of Sports Students During the Practice of TM in Compari-
        son with Non-Meditating Sports Students.] (Diplomarbeit.
        Berlin, 1976.)

D187   Schulze, V. "Zur Starkung der Identität durch Entspan-
        nungsubungen am Beispiel der TM mit möglichen Auswir-
        kungen im Alltagsleben." [More Strength of the Identity
        Through Relaxation Techniques: TM Used as an Example
        with Effects in Day to Day Life.] (Diplomarbeit für
        Handelslehre. Kassel, 1976.)

D188   Schwartz, Eric. "The Effects of the Transcendental Medita-
        tion Program on Strength of the Nervous System, Per-
        ceptual Reactance, Reaction Time and Auditory Thres-
        hold." (M.S. Thesis. University of Massachusetts,
        1979.) Tentatively scheduled for inclusion in Scientific
        Research on the Transcendental Meditation Program:
        Collected Papers, Vol. 2. Rheinweiler, West Germany:
        Maharishi European Research University Press, (in press).
        Longitudinal increases in sensitivity and flexibility of the
        nervous system were found in practitioners of the Transcen-
        dental Meditation technique.

D189   Scott, Cora A. "Self-Realization and Personality Change."
        DAI, 35 (1975), 4634B (Ph.D. University of Massachu-
        setts. Will lend.)
        Results indicate that the workshop program incorporating
        meditation would not by itself be useful as a therapeutic
        procedure for subjects having greater than average problems
        of adjustment.

D190   Scott, Linda J. "Transcendental Meditation: Effect of Pre-
        treatment Personality and Prognostic Expectancy Upon De-
        gree of Reported Personality Change." DAI, 38 (1977),
        2383B (Ph.D. George Washington University. Will lend.)
        Tentatively scheduled for inclusion in Scientific Research
        on the Transcendental Meditation Program: Collected Pa-
        pers, Vol. 2. Rheinweiler, West Germany: Maharishi
        European Research University Press, (in press).
        Results indicated that significant psychological change oc-
        curred.

D191   Scuderi, Richard J. "The Effects of Meditation on General
        Anxiety, Test Anxiety, and Non-Verbal Intelligence."
        DAI, 38 (1978), 5930-5931A (Ph.D. University of South-
        ern California. Will lend.)

Because no significant difference between experimental and control group scores could be found, no support was shown that the meditation treatment itself was responsible for significant improvements.

D192　Sereda, Lynn. "Some Effects of Relaxative and Meditative States on Learning, Memory and Other Cognitive Processes." DAI, 38 (1978), 4697-4698A (Ph.D. University of California, Berkeley. Will lend.)
As a whole, analysis showed significantly more positive effects than regressive effects.

D193　Shackman, S. "The Effect of Two Relaxation Techniques on Anxiety, Self-Concept, and Personality Growth." (Senior Thesis. Princeton University, 1974.)

D194　Shapiro, Dean H., Jr. "The Effects of a 'Zen Meditation-Behavioral Self-Management' Training Package in Treating Methadone Addiciton: A Formative Study." DAI, 34 (1973), 2952-2953B (Ph.D. Stanford University. Will lend.)
The acquisition of meditative behavior and techniques of behavioral self-management in lowering subjects' methadone dosage was achieved. Difficulties arose in attempting to maintain those behaviors in subjects' natural environment.

D195　Shapiro, Jonathan S. "The Relationship of Selected Characteristics of Transcendental Meditation to Measures of Self-Actualization, Negative Personality Characteristics, and Anxiety." DAI, 36 (1975), 137A (Ph.D. University of Southern California. Will lend.)
A group of individuals that practiced TM changed very significantly in its level of self-actualization and in its level of negative personality characteristics and anxiety.

D196　Shaw, Robert L. "The Short and Long Term Effects of Rest on the Reduction of Stress." DAI, 39 (1979), 3594-3595B (Ph.D. University of Texas at Austin. Will not lend.)
Experienced practitioners of the Transcendental Meditation technique and novice meditators were tested to assess the cumulative effects of rest.

D197　Shecter, Howard E. "A Psychological Investigation Into the Source of the Effect of the Transcendental Meditation Technique." DAI, 38 (1978), 3372-3373B (Ph.D. York University, Canada.)
Results indicated that the actual practice of TM is the source of its effectiveness. The potential value of the practice of TM on measures of anxiety, creativity, intellectual performance, complexity, conformity, energy level, innovation, self esteem, and tolerance were investigated.

D198   Shellman, Herbert F. "Efficacy of Electromyographic Biofeed-
        back and the Relaxation Response in the Treatment of
        Situation-Specific Anxiety." DAI, 40 (1980), 5831-5832B
        (Ph.D. University of Rochester. Will not lend.)
        Measures produced no significant difference between any
        groups. Analyses did show significant decreases across the
        groups.

D199   Sherman, Benna Z. "Attentional Style in Undergraduates
        as a Function of Experience with Transcendental Medita-
        tion." DAI, 40 (1979), 1342B (Ph.D. University of
        Pennsylvania. Will lend.)
        Results imply that TM experience has neither beneficial nor
        harmful attentional effect.

D200   Silver, Joel. "The Effects of Transcendental Meditation and
        Masker Uncertainty on the Detection of a Masked Psycho-
        acoustic Signal: A Selective Attention Theoretical Ap-
        proach." DAI, 37 (1977), 4167B (Ph.D. Purdue Uni-
        versity. Will lend.)
        The practice of TM, while reducing trait and state anxiety,
        did not significantly enhance performance on any of the
        three masker pairs.

D201   Sisley, R.C. "The Effects of Sleep Deprivation on the Physi-
        ological Changes Induced by Transcendental Meditation."
        (Postgraduate Diploma in Arts in Psychology Thesis.
        University of Otago, 1971.)

D202   Slobodin, Paula. "A Comparison of the Effectiveness of
        Progressive Relaxation Training and the Relaxation Re-
        sponse Technique as a Function of Perceived Locus of
        Control of Reinforcement in Tension Reduction." DAI,
        39 (1979), 6167B (Psy.D. Rutgers University, The State
        University of New Jersey, Graduate School of Applied and
        Professional Psychology. Will not lend.)
        Subjects receiving Progressive Relaxation training did signifi-
        cantly better than subjects receiving Relaxation Response
        training in lowering frontalis muscle tension levels.

D203   Smail, Kenneth H. "Runners, Meditators, Weightlifters and
        Skydivers: A Comparison of Psychological Characteris-
        tics." DAI, 41 (1980), 1527-1528B (Ph.D. University
        of Georgia. Will not lend.)
        No significant differences were found between groups on
        measures of depression, creativity, or the hypothesized
        values. However, meditators were significantly less anxious
        than the other groups.

D204   Smith, Jonathan C. "Meditation as Psychotherapy." DAI,
        36 (1975), 3073B (Ph.D. Michigan State University.

Will lend.) Also reported in the Journal of Consulting and Clinical Psychology, 44 (1976): 630-637. [Cf. A764]
The conclusion is that the critical therapeutic agent in TM is something other than the TM meditation exercise.

D205   Snyder, Lee D.   "Wessel Gansfort and the Art of Medita-
            tion." (Ph.D. Harvard University, 1966. Will not lend.)
        A study of Johannes Wessel Gansfort, Dutch theologian, phi-
        losopher, & humanist, 1419-1489; (at times called a precursor
        of the Reformation) and his works on meditation.

D206   Sternberg, Marc B.   "Man, Mind and Meditation." DAI, 35
            (1974), 2449B (Ed.D. University of Northern Colorado.
            Will lend.)
        It was concluded that the Hindu and Buddhist traditions
        utilizing techniques such as Yoga-breathing exercises have
        much to offer the mental health field.

D207   Stewart, C.R.   "Self Actualization and the Transcendental
            Meditation Technique." (Master's Thesis. University of
            Missouri, Columbia, 1977.)

D208   Stiffler, Paul.   "Meditation: Practical Settings in an Age of
            Need." (D.Min. Bethany Theological Seminary, 1982.
            Will not lend.)

D209   Suarez, Verna W.   "The Relationship and Practice of Tran-
            scendental Meditation to Subjective Evaluation of Marital
            Satisfaction and Adjustment." (Master's Thesis. Univer-
            sity of Southern California, 1976.) Tentatively scheduled
            for inclusion in Scientific Research on the Transcendental
            Meditation Program: Collected Papers, Vol. 2. Rhein-
            weiler, West Germany: Maharishi European Research Uni-
            versity Press, (in press).
        Couples who practiced the TM technique were found to have
        more well-adjusted and happier marriages.

D210   Sullivan, Russell H.   "Reading, Anxiety and Behavioral
            Management as Functions of Attention and Relaxation
            Training." DAI, 41 (1980), 1960-1961A (Ph.D. Uni-
            versity of Missouri, Columbia. Will not lend.)
        This study investigated the effects of attention (meditation)
        or of relaxation training upon reading achievement, level of
        anxiety, and problem behavior of third and fourth grade
        students.

D211   Sultan, S.E.   "A Study of the Ability of Individuals Trained
            in Transcendental Meditation to Achieve and Maintain
            Levels of Physiological Relaxation." (Master's Thesis.
            U.S. International University, San Diego, 1975.) [Cf.
            A791]

D212   Suzuki, Takao J. "Psychophysiological Effects of Meditation
         on Test-Anxious Male Youthful Prisoners." DAI, 38
         (1978), 6629A (Ph.D. Florida State University. Will
         lend.)
         It was concluded that meditation had a positive impact on
         test-anxiety but not on test-performance nor respiratory and
         heart rates.

D213   Törber, S. "Befindlichkeitswirkungen der TM." [Effects of
         TM on Health.] (Diplomarbeit. Universität Köln, 1976.)

D214   Trausch, Clarence P. "Psi Training Through Meditation, and
         Self-Actualization as Related to Psi Performance." DAI,
         42 (1981), 1531A (Ed.D. Northern Illinois University.
         Will not lend.)
         Results indicated that meditation significantly increased self-
         actualization. There was uncertainty regarding the facilitat-
         ing of ESP performance.

D215   Traynham, Richard N. "The Effects of Experimental Medita-
         tion, Relaxation Training, and Electromyographic Feedback
         on Physiological and Self-Report Measures of Relaxation
         and Altered States of Consciousness." DAI, 38 (1977),
         2386-2387B (Ph.D. University of Arkansas. Will not
         lend.)
         Five different hypotheses were tested for the effects of medi-
         tation, biofeedback, and relaxation training within the psy-
         chology of consciousness and transpersonal psychology.

D216   Tsakanos, Frances A. "The Response of Obese and Non-
         Obese Women to Meditation." DAI, 37 (1977), 3636-3637B
         (Ph.D. City University of New York. Will lend.)
         Results showed that obese subjects could meditate as well as
         non-obese subjects.

D217   Valois, M.G.L. "The Effects of Transcendental Meditation
         on the Self-Concept as Measured by the Tennessee Self-
         Concept Scale." DAI, 37 (1976), 208A (Ph.D. Univer-
         sity of Kansas. Will lend.)
         Significant differences were indicated for the factors of age,
         marital status, and TM. Self-concept was also studied.

D218   Van Esterik, John L. "Cultural Interpretation of Canonical
         Paradox: Lay Meditation in a Central Thai Village."
         DAI, 38 (1978), 6205A (Ph.D. University of Illinois at
         Urbana-Champaign. Will lend.)
         This study argues that participants in lay meditation in a
         Central Thai village have found this religious behavior a way
         to recoup loss of face.

D219   Vogt, A. "Die Aktualität der Überlegungen Diderot zum

Problem der Intuition: ihre zentrale Funktion für alle
Wissensgebiete und systematische Erlernbarkeit im Rahmen
der WKI." [The Topicality of the Thoughts of Diderot in
Regard to the Problem of Intuition: Its Central Function
for All Disciplines and the Possibility of Learning It Systematically Through the Scope of SCI.] (Zulassungsarbeit
zur Erlangung des Magistergrades. Freie Universität Berlin, 1977.)

D220   Wachsmuth, D. "Zur Psycho-Physiologie ruhevoller Wachheit,
EEG und subjektives psychologisches Befinden während
der Ausübund der TM im Vergleich mit den Schlafstadien
dierselben Versuchspersonen." [The Psychophysiology
of EEG and Subjective Psychological Health During the
Practice of TM in Comparison with Sleepstates of the
Same.] (Dissertation. Johann Wolfgang Goethe Universität, Frankfurt, West Germany, 1978.) Tentatively
scheduled for inclusion in Scientific Research on the
Transcendental Meditation Program: Collected Papers,
Vol. 2. Rheinweiler, West Germany: Maharishi European
Research University Press, (in press).
An analysis of the EEG and EKG patterns during TM, wak-
ing, and sleep states for five meditators showing unique
neurophysiological functioning.

D221   Walder, Jeffrey M. "The Effects on a Measure of Self-
Actualization of Adding a Meditation Exercise to a Sensitivity Group--Group Facilitator Training Program."
DAI, 36 (1976), 6533-6534A (Ph.D. University of Maryland. Will lend.)
The hypothesis predicted that the practice of meditation
would significantly affect the self-actualization sub-test
scores of workshop participants. It was not supported.

D222   Wallace, Robert K. "The Physiological Effects of Transcen-
dental Meditation: A Proposed Fourth Major State of
Consciousness." DAI, 31 (1971), 4303B (Ph.D. Univer-
sity of California, Los Angeles. Will lend.) Also published by the Students' International Meditation Society,
Los Angeles. See Books section. Extracted in Scientific
Research on the Transcendental Meditation Program: Col-
lected Papers, Vol. 1, 2nd ed., Weggis, Switzerland:
Maharishi European Research University, 1977. pp. 43-78.
Physiological effects of Transcendental Meditation are used
to distinguish meditation from other states of consciousness.
Suggests that meditation produces a fourth major state of
consciousness which may have practical clinical applications.
[Cf. A845, B951]

D223   Wampler, Larry D. "Transcendental Meditation and Assertive
Training in the Treatment of Social Anxiety." DAI, 39

(1979), 5598B   (Ph.D.   Vanderbilt University.   Will lend.)
It is concluded that TM produces the better outcome in the
treatment of social anxiety.   [Cf. A860]

D224   Warrenburg, William S.   "Meditation and Hemispheric Special-
        ization."   DAI, 40 (1979), 2892-2893B   (Ph.D.   University
        of Washington.   Will lend.)
        The hypothesis that meditation facilitates information proces-
        sing specialized in the right hemisphere of the brain, and
        impairs left hemisphere specialized processing was tested.

D225   Warshal, D.   "The Temporal Effects of the Transcendental
        Meditation Technique on Fractionated Reflex and Reaction
        Time."   (Master's Thesis.   University of Massachusetts,
        1977.)

D226   Weiner, Arnold J.   "Attention and Expectations: Their Con-
        tribution to the Meditation Effect."   DAI, 33 (1973), 5528-
        5529B   (Ph.D.   New York University.   Will not lend.)
        The study attempts to objectively determine some of the situ-
        ational factors that contribute to the meditation effect.

D227   Weiner, Donald E.   "The Effects of Mantra Meditation and
        Progressive Relaxation on Self-Actualization, State and
        Trait Anxiety, and Frontalis Muscle Tension."   DAI, 37
        (1977), 4174B   (Ph.D.   University of Texas at Austin.
        Will not lend.)
        The only hypothesis which was confirmed was that both
        meditation and relaxation training significantly reduced state
        anxiety.

D228   Weiss, C.   "Der Kurzzeiteffekt der TM und theoretische
        Überlegungen zur Psychologie und Physiologie der sub-
        jektiven Benfindlichkeit."   [The Short Term Effect of TM
        and the Theoretical Considerations of the Psychology and
        Physiology Underlying the Subjective Experience.]   (Dip-
        lomarbeit.   Universität Saarbrücken, 1975.)

D229   West, M.A.   "Psychophysiological and Psychological Corre-
        lates of Meditation."   (Ph.D.   University of Wales Insti-
        tute of Science and Technology, 1978.)

D230   Willis, Clara L.R.   "Transcendental Meditation and Its Influ-
        ence on the Self-Concept."   DAI, 36 (1975), 139A   (Ph.D.
        Texas A&M University.   Will lend.)   Tentatively scheduled
        for inclusion in Scientific Research on the Transcendental
        Meditation Program: Collected Papers, Vol. 2.   Rhein-
        weiler, West Germany: Maharishi European Research Uni-
        versity Press, (in press).
        Positive results reported were increased self confidence,
        calmness, comprehension, and energy.

D231   Wood, Daniel T. "The Effects of Progressive Relaxation,
       Heart Rate Feedback, and Content-Specific Meditation on
       Anxiety and Performance in a Class Situation." DAI, 39
       (1978), 3458A (Ed.D. University of Toledo. Will lend.)
Results showed that all three groups indicated each technique
was effective in reducing anxiety. There was no difference
between groups.

D232   Yoder, Nanci S. "Changes in Suggestibility Following Alert
       Hypnosis and Concentrative Meditation." DAI, 43 (1982),
       2013B (Ph.D. California Institute of Asian Studies.
       Now, California Institute of Integral Studies. Will lend.)
There was statistically significant gain in suggestibility for
the meditation and hypnosis groups that was substantially
the same.

D233   Yoon, Byung-Yul. "A Study of an Extended Concept of
       Human Intrapsychic Capacity as Expressed in D.T. Suzu-
       ki's Zen Buddhism." DAI, 40 (1979), 2346-2347B (Ph.D.
       United States International University. Will lend.)
Indicates that the supplementary side of the human intrapsychic capacity is possible and necessary with the practice
of Zen in order to extend our concept of perception.

D234   Zeff, Ted. "The Psychological and Physiological Effects of
       Meditation and the Physical Isolation Tank Experience on
       the Type A Behavior Pattern." DAI, 41 (1981), 3877B
       (Ph.D. California Institute of Asian Studies. Now,
       California Institute of Integral Studies. Will lend.)
The findings lend some support regarding the effects on
Type A behavior pattern in the reduction of heart rate.
There was no significant reduction of blood pressure or state
anxiety.

D235   Zweigenhaft, Richard L. "Modern Transcendentalists and
       Modern Empiricists: A Social Psychological Comparison."
       DAI, 35 (1975), 4156B (Ph.D. University of California,
       Santa Cruz. Will lend.)
The two groups are compared in religion, life style, and
susceptibility to hypnosis. Profiles indicated the transcendentalists to be more creative, but less socialized, less self-
accepting and less socially mature than the empiricists.

▪ MOTION PICTURES ▪

M1   The Art of Meditation [Motion Picture]. Cos Cob, Conn.:
       Hartley Productions, 1972, 1 reel, 28 min., sd., col., 16
       mm. LC 79-700773/F Also issued as a videorecording,
       Westport, Conn.: Videorecord Corp. of America, 1971, and
       New York: Cine Magnetics Video, 1971, 1 cassette no. 406,
       25 min., sd., col., 3/4 in., U standard.
   Alan Watts, accompanied by nature photography and natural
   sounds gives advice on means of meditation. Produced by Irving and Elda Hartley. Label on Videorecord Corp. of America
   cassette: Primary Communications, Inc., 136 East Pennsylvania
   Ave., Southern Pines, N.C., 28387.

M2   The Bird on the Mast [Motion Picture]. Pacific Palisades,
       Calif.: Paulist Productions, 1971, 1 reel, 29 min., sd.,
       16 mm. LC 71-713925
   A dramatization about a young executive who finds in meditation
   an inner freedom he needed after an unhappy life. From the
   Insight Series.

M3   The Flow of Zen [Motion Picture]. Cos Cob, Conn.: Hartley
       Productions, 1969, 1 reel, 14 min., sd., col., 16 mm. LC
       79-703346
   Discusses the philosophy of Zen Buddhism. Shows how Buddhist chants synchronized with striking psychedelic pictures,
   turn the mind inward and induce a state of meditation which
   is basic to Zen teaching. From the Great Minds of Our Times
   Series. Script and narration by Alan Watts.

M4   The Holy Assassins [Motion Picture]. Toronto: Canadian
       Film-Makers' Distribution Centre, 1974, 1 reel, 65 min.,
       sd., col., 16 mm. LC 75-701032/F
   A science fiction story about a metaphysical criminal from
   another dimension who is wanted for an act of interstellar
   piracy. Shows that after being defeated by Earthmen, he
   chooses to live a spiritual life of discipline and meditation in
   an attempt to reach the ultimate goal, a return to Divine Unity. Produced by Infinity Studio in Canada.

M5   Holy Men of India: The Sadhus [Motion Picture]. Santa Ana,
        Calif.: International Communications Films, 1968, 1 car-
        tridge, 10 min., sd., col., super 8 mm. Also 1 reel, 16
        mm. LC 75-703274
The day of a holy man is covered. A series of yoga practices,
as an example of one of the disciplines needed in the study of
the Hindu religion, is shown. Produced and narrated by Lew
Ayres. From the Religions of the Eastern World Series.

M6   Lapis [Motion Picture]. Santa Monica, Calif.: Pyramid Films,
        1972, 10 min., sd., col., 16 mm. LC 75-701555/F
An abstract art film composed of images produced by an analog
computer. The shifting kaleidoscopic patterns, mandalas, and
starbursts trace a patterning of mystic meditation, accompanied
by sitar music of Ravi Shankar. Produced by James Whitney
in 1956.

M7   Learn to Live with Stress: Programming the Body for Health
        [Motion Picture]. Toronto: Hobel Leiterman, Ltd., 1976;
        Also, New York: Document Associates, 1976, 1 reel, 19
        min., sd., col., 16 mm.
Dr. Hans Selye and Dr. Herbert Benson discuss stress and
how it affects the health of a person. Stress is described as
a killing disease which causes heart problems, hypertension,
and other types of threats to a person. Using the job of air
traffic controller as an example, Dr. Selye explains how man
is affected by high pressured stress jobs.

M8   Living Yoga: Four Yokes to God [Motion Picture]. Cos Cob,
        Conn.: Hartley Productions, 1977, 1 reel, 20 min., sd.,
        col., 16 mm. LC 77-700747/F
Discusses the everyday practices of Hatha, Raja, Bhakti, and
Karma Yoga. Explains various Yoga postures, correct breathing, diet, meditation, and the concepts of selfless service and
true devotion. Produced by Reuben Aaronson.

M9   Maharishi Mahesh--Jet Age Yogi [Motion Picture]. New York:
        Center for Mass Communication of Columbia University
        Press, 1 reel, 28 min., sd., 16 mm.
Transcendental meditation is covered. Shows the Maharishi
Mahesh Yogi arriving home by helicopter to the foothills of the
Himalayas and an interview at his ashram. The spiritual re-
generation movement is discussed. From the Faces of India
Series.

M10   Master Kiteman [Motion Picture]. Pasadena, Calif.: Barr
        Films, 1975, 1 reel, 12 min., sd., col., 16 mm. LC 75-
        700271/F
Presents the ideas and philosophy of Dinesh Bahadur, who discusses his feelings about kites and reveals how kites help him
meditate and discover his inner self. Produced by Murray
Mintz.

M11   Meditation [Motion Picture]. Bloomington, Ind.: Indiana University Audio-Visual Center, 1973, 1 reel, 29 min., sd., b&w., 16 mm. LC 73-703034/F
Indian spiritual leader Jiddu Krishnamurti explains the process of meditation, which he defines not as concentration or self-stimulation, but as the acute awareness of a quiet mind. Sets forth the philosophy that man can free himself from his troubled image of himself by finding life beyond daily existence through meditation. Produced and directed by Richard Moore at television station KQED, San Francisco.

M12   Meditation [Motion Picture]. Santa Monica, Calif.: Pyramid Films, 1971, 1 reel, 6 min., sd., col., 16mm. LC 72-700568/F
An experimental film in which a variety of abstract images and circular shapes expand to the sound of a gong. Without narration. Produced by Jordan Belson.

M13   Meditation Crystallized   Lama Govinda on Tibetan Art [Motion Picture]. Cos Cob, Conn.: Hartley Productions, 1973, 1 reel, 14 min., sd., col., 16 mm. LC 73-700376/F
Lama Govinda, artist, author, and one of the world's foremost interpreters of Tibetan Buddhism, discusses Tibetan art as an expression of the deepest and most meaningful levels of the human psyche and a crystallization of centuries of meditation.

M14   Meditation in Motion [Motion Picture]. New York: National Film Board of Canada, 1979, made 1978, 1 reel, 11 min., sd., col., 16 mm. LC 79-701522/F. Also issued as a videorecording, 1 cassette, 11 min., sd., col., 3/4 in. LC 79-707445/F
An introduction to a Chinese system of meditation and exercise known as Tai Chi Ch'uan, which aims at attaining calm and developing the mnd and body harmoniously. Directed and written by Irene Angelico.

M15   Meditation: The Inward Journey [Motion Picture]. Cos Cob, Conn.: Hartley Productions, 1977, 1 reel, 20 min., sd., col., 16 mm. LC 77-701611/F
Defines meditation as an inward power, as a journey which, when successful, enables the traveler to see himself as if he were someone else and others as if they were himself. Produced by Elda Hartley.

M16   Meditation: Yoga, T'ai Chi and Other Spiritual Trips [Motion Picture]. New York: Document Associates, 1976, 1 reel, 18 min., sd., col., 16 mm.
Includes a visit to the School of Hatha Yoga; an interview with Alan Watts; and a look at theater students working on traditional T'ai Chi forms. Includes interviews with Colin Wilson and persons who view yoga as possibly helpful in dealing with

alcoholism and drug addiction; others claim it is a perfectly
safe cure for all mental and physical illness.

M17   Meditations [Motion Picture]. Columbus, Ohio: Lewis, 1977,
        1 reel, 14 min., sd., col., 16 mm. LC 77-702106/F
      Looks closely at the normally overlooked beauties and meanings
      in everyday life. Intended to communicate the experience of
      adjustment to a new lifestyle. Produced by Brian Scott Lewis.

M18   Mohawk [Motion Picture]. Pacific Palisades, Calif.: Paulist
        Productions, 1974, 1 reel, 27 min., sd., col., 16 mm. Al-
        so issued in b&w. LC 75-700941/F
      Presents a drama about an angry Mohawk Indian who decides
      to meditate before the doors of St. Patrick's Cathedral. Deals
      with his confrontation with a policeman and with a priest and
      attempts to answer questions about meditation and prayer.
      From the Insight Series. Produced by John Meredyth Lucas.

M19   Relaxation Techniques [Motion Picture]. Beverly Hills, Calif.:
        American Educational Films, 1978, 1 reel, 11 min., sd.,
        col., 16 mm. Also issued in super 8 mm., and 8 mm., and
        as a videorecording. LC 78-701903/F
      Presents methods of meditation, biofeedback, and relaxation
      therapy that are effective means of reducing stress and keep-
      ing its negative effects to a minimum. From the Stress and
      You Series. Produced by Neil Mawby Productions.

M20   Requiem for a Faith [Motion Picture]. Cos Cob, Conn.: Hart-
        ley Productions, 1968, 28 min., sd., col., 16 mm. Also
        issued as a videorecording, 1 cassette, 27 min., sd., col.,
        3/4 in.
      Surveys Buddhist practices and explains the role of Tibetan
      lamas in developing the extremely religious nature of Tibetan
      culture. From the Great Minds of Our Times Series. Produced
      by Elda Hartley. Written by Huston Smith.

M21   Science of Zen [Motion Picture]. Tokyo: Orient Film Assoc.,
        1 reel, 30 min., 16 mm.
      Both the Soto and Rinzai sects are discussed. The medical
      and psychological aspects of meditation are presented by Dr.
      Akira Kasamatsu and Dr. Tomio Hirai of the department of
      neuropsychiatry at the University of Tokyo.

M22   The Search for Alternate Life-Styles and Philosophies [Motion
        Picture]. Studio City, Calif.: FilmFair Communications,
        1973, 1 reel, 20 min., sd., col., 16 mm. LC 73-701224/F
      Explores some of the efforts which are being made today for
      attaining personal harmony and a fulfilling life-style. Examines
      a cooperative village in the Sierras which follows a yoga phi-
      losophy. Discusses other approaches both within and outside
      conventional society: Zen, Tai Chi, Transcendental Meditation,
      and Biofeedback.

M23 The Search for Faith [Motion Picture]. Pacific Palisades,
Calif.: Paulist Productions, 1973, 12 min., sd., col., 16
mm. LC 73-701995/F
Presents three examples of how individuals receive faith. God
is discovered by a teenage girl in the wisdom of an old Navajo,
by a disillusioned advertising executive through meditation,
and a jaded rock star in writing a Jesus song. From the Vig-
nettes Series. Produced by Michael Rhodes.

M24 The Silent Mind [Motion Picture]. Bloomington, Ind.: National TV, Indiana University, 1958, 1 reel, 29 min., 16
mm., Kinescope.
The value of Hindu and Buddhist meditation is examined. Discusses ways in which consciousness or the mind is used. Produced by television station KQED-TV, San Francisco, Calif.
From the Eastern Wisdom and Modern Life Series.

M25 Sumi [Motion Picture]. Santa Monica, Calif.: Pyramid Films,
1971, 1 reel, 7 min., sd., b&w., 16 mm. LC 72-714093
A film poem which uses ink paintings to portray the relationship between art, nature, and meditation. Produced by David
Lawrence.

M26 Two Communities [Motion Picture]. Portland, Oregon: Oregon
State System of Higher Education Film Library, 30 min.,
sd., 16 mm.
Monks at Mount Baldy Zen Center in California are shown during an intensive week of meditation. Life in an Episcopal
monastery in San Francisco's Mission District is also shown.
From the Devout Young Series.

M27 Urvasi [Motion Picture]. New York: Artscope, 1972, 1 reel,
10 min., sd., col., 16 mm. Also issued in b&w. Also issued in 35 mm. in col, or b&w. LC 72-701949/F
A dramatization of a meeting between a Buddhist disciple, Muni,
and a dancing girl, Urvasi. Urvasi attempts to disrupt Muni's
meditations, but fails, and ultimately joins Muni as a disciple
of Buddha. Music by Ragunath Seth. Made by Amin Chaudhri.

M28 Vejen [Motion Picture]. New York: Carousel Films, Inc.,
1971, 1 reel, 22 min., sd., col., 16 mm. LC 77-713869
The principle of Eastern stoicism, meditation, and impermanence
are presented by following the daily rounds of a Buddhist
priest and his acolyte. Produced by Per Holst teknish cam-
pagni in Copenhagen, Denmark.

M29 The Wind and the River [Motion Picture]. New York: Contemporary Films, 1951, 1 reel, 10 min., sd., 16 mm. LC
fia64-1377
A holy man meditating on a secluded mountain is set in con-

trast to a cross section of Kashmiri Valley life with its beauti-
ful vistas and its economically poor villagers. Produced by
Arne Sucksdorff for the Swedish Film Industry, Stockholm,
Sweden.

M30 Your Own Worst Enemy [Motion Picture]. Long Beach, Calif.:
Southerby Productions, 1977, made in 1976, 1 reel, 26
min., sd., col., 16 mm. LC 77-702308/F
Explains what stress is, how to handle it, and how to use it
beneficially. Produced by Fiveson Productions, Universal City,
Calif.

M31 Zen in Ryoko-in [Motion Picture]. Ruth Stephan Films, 1971,
1 reel, 71 min., sd., col., 16 mm. LC 72-702164/F
An examination of Zen Buddhism through glimpses of the daily
life of the abbot, his family, and students in Ryoko-in, the
Zen Buddhist temple in the Daitokuji compound in Kyoto, Japan.
Produced by Ruth Stephan.

M32 Zen Master [Motion Picture]. Santa Barbara, Calif.: Image
Associates, 1966, 1 reel, 3 min., sd., b&w., 16 mm. LC
79-700701/F
Focuses on Zen Buddhist master Roshi Josho Sasaki, showing
him doing everyday chores and conducting Zen meditation sessions. Written, produced and directed by Frank Lisciandro.

■ RECORDINGS ■

R1   The Art of Meditation [Sound Recording]. Sausalito, Calif.:
     MEA, 1973, 1 sound cassette, 40 min., 1 7/8 ips, 2 track,
     mono. (Yoga)

R2   Beede, Norman. Clouds: Music for Relaxation [Sound Record-
     ing]. New York: Folkways Records, 1981, 1 sound disc,
     33 1/3 rpm, mono., 12 in. Also, Clouds: New Music for
     Relaxation.

R2K Benson, Herbert. Relaxation & Meditation: Peace Without
     Pills [Sound Recording]. North Hollywood, Calif.: Center
     for Cassette Studies, n.d., 1 cassette, 52 min., 2-track
     mono.

R2T _____. The Relaxation Response: An Innate Capacity for
     Dealing with Stress [Sound Recording]. New York: Bio-
     monitoring Applications, Inc., 1978, 1 cassette, BMA series
     no. T-170, 55 min. 36 sec., 2-track mono. Sold by ISHK
     Book Service, P.O. Box 176, Dept. T-5, Los Altos, CA
     94022

R3   Bez, Edward. Christian Meditation [Sound Recording].
     Broken Arrow, Okla.: Charles Trombley Ministries, 1980?,
     1 sound cassette, 55 min., 1 7/8 ips, mono.

R4   Bloomfield, Harold H. The TM Program: Releasing Stress and
     Finding Happiness [Sound Recording]. Perceptive, 1975, 1
     disc no. PC-903. 33 1/3 rpm., stereo.
     Lecture and questions and answers by the author. Recorded
     at Camp Colomby, New City, New York.

R5   _____. Transcendental Meditation: An Adjunct to Psycho-
     therapy [Sound Recording]. Los Angeles: Audio-Digest
     Foundation, 1976, 1 cassette.
     This is a recording of an article from Psychiatry, v.5, no.1,
     Jan. 26, 1976. Harold Bloomfield is Director of the Institute
     of Psychophysiological Medicine, San Diego.

R6   Carlson, Ronald L. Transcendental Meditation [Sound Record-

ing]. Richfield, Mn.: Wooddale Baptist Church, 197-?,
1 sound cassette, 30 min., 1 7/8 ips, mono.

R7   Carrington, Patricia. Learning to Meditate: The Instructor's
Course [Sound Recording]. Kendall Park, N.J.: Pace
Educational Systems, Inc., date? (Also sold by Yes!
Bookshop, Washington, D.C.)
This set contains both the Self-Regulated Course (with work-
book and three cassettes) and an Instructor's Course (with
three one-hour cassettes and manual). Both courses are
boxed together.

R8   _____. Learning to Meditate: Self-Regulated Course
[Sound Recording]. Kendall Park, N.J.: Pace Educational
Systems, Inc., date? (Also sold by Yes! Bookshop, Wash-
ington, D.C.)
This consists of three one-hour long cassettes and a work-
book.

R9   Chinmoy, Sri. Music for Meditation [Sound Recording]. New
York: Folkways Records, 1976, 1 disc no. FR 8935, 12
in., 33 1/3 rpm., mono.
Sung by Sri Chinmoy, with esraj or portable organ accompaniment.

R10   Cosmic Consciousness: Transcendental Meditation [Sound Re-
cording]. Toronto: CBC Learning Systems, 1972, 1 audio
tape cassette, 30 min., 1 7/8 ips.
Discusses sources of meditation.

R11   Easwaran, Eknath. Meditation [Sound Recording]. Petaluma,
Calif.: Nilgiri Press, 1968, 1 disc. no. F 9001, 33 1/3
rpm., microgroove, monaural, 12 in. (Also sold by Yes!
Bookshop, Washington, D.C.)
Discourse by the author on the three stages of meditation and
instruction in meditation. (Hinduism)

R12   _____. Meditation Instruction [Sound Recording]. Berkeley, Calif.: Blue Mountain Center of Meditation and Petaluma, Calif.: Nilgiri Press, 1975, 4 cassettes, 2-track,
mono. (Also sold by Yes! Bookshop, Washington, D.C.)
The first two tapes explain the theory and practice of meditation; the third and fourth describe the application of spiritual disciplines to daily life. With manual. (Gandian philosophy)

R13   Fisichella, Anthony J. Meditation [Sound Recording]. Hicksville, N.Y.: Kosmic Kassattes, 1976, 4 sound cassettes,
1 7/8 ips.

R14   Fryling, Vera. Autogenic Training: Relaxation Reinforcement

<u>Exercises</u> [Sound Recording]. Belmont, Calif.: Halpern
Sounds and Palo Alto, Calif.: Spectrum Research Institute, 1978, 1 sound cassette, 60 min., 1 7/8 ips, stereo.
Dr. Fryling presents the classic method for relaxation and
stress reduction in combination with Dr. Halpern's stress-
reducing music.

R15   Goleman, Daniel. <u>Meditation: An Instructional Cassette</u>
[Sound Recording]. New York: Psychology Today, 1975,
1 cassette no. 36, 30 min.

R16   Gunther, Bernard. <u>Sensory Awakening: Allowing & Chanting</u>
[Sound Recording]. San Rafael, Calif.: Big Sur Recordings, 1967, 1 cassette no. 2226, 1 hr. Also issued on
reel, mono. or stereo. LC 78-740958
A program presenting techniques for allowing one's inner
creativity and energy flow out into the external environment
producing a harmonious balance between one's inner and outer
existence. Also offers exercises in chanting which result in
total body relaxation and an increased breathing capacity.

R17   Halpern, Steven. <u>Ancient Echoes</u> [Sound Recording]. To-
panga, Calif.: Heru Records and Palo Alto, Calif.:
Halpern Sounds, 1978, 1 cassette no. SRI 783, stereo.
(Also sold by Yes! Bookshop, Washington, D.C.)
Sounds and instrumental music intended to aid in relaxation
and meditation. All compositions written by Steven Halpern
and Georgia Kelly.

R18   _____. <u>Centerscape</u> [Sound Recording]. Palo Alto, Calif.:
Spectrum Research Institute, 1977, 1 cassette, 4-track,
stereo.
Side 1, Steven Halpern "Live" at Findhorn, was recorded in
the meditation sanctuary at Findhorn, Scotland, on May 7,
1977. Side 2, Steven Halpern "Live" in Palo Alto, was recorded during "A concert for the sound health" in Palo Alto
on April 5, 1977.

R19   _____. <u>Comfort Zone: The Anti-Frantic Alternative; Music</u>
<u>for Relaxation, Self-Healing, and Pure Listening Pleasure</u>
[Sound Recording]. Belmont, Calif.: Halpern Sounds,
1980, 1 sound cassette, 60 min., 1 7/8 ips, stereo. (Also
sold by Yes! Bookshop, Washington, D.C.)

R20   _____. <u>Eastern Peace</u> [Sound Recording]. Palo Alto,
Calif.: Halpern Sound, 1978, 1 cassette no. HS-782, 4-
track, stereo. Also issued as 1 sound disc., 50 min.,
33 1/3 rpm, stereo. (Also sold by Yes! Bookshop, Washington, D.C.)
Music to help attain a relaxed, meditative state of consciousness. With program notes. From the Anti-Frantic Alternative
Series.

R21 _____. Hear to Eternity [Sound Recording]. Belmont,
Calif.: Halpern Sounds, 1979, 1 cassette no HS 793, 4-
track, stereo. (Also sold by Yes! Bookshop, Washington,
D.C.)
Music to help attain a relaxed, meditative state of consciousness. Featuring Victor Spiegel, percussion ensemble. With
program notes.

R22 _____. "I": A Cosmic Attunement [Sound Recording].
Palo Alto, Calif.: Spectrum Research Institute, 1977, 1
cassette no. SRI-771C, 4-track, stereo.
Suite relating the twelve chromatic tones of the musical octave
to the twelve signs of the Zodiac; designed to tune ourselves
in to ourselves, and thus, to the music of the spheres. With
program notes. Later released as Zodiac Suite.

R23 _____. Letting Go of Stress [Sound Recording]. Palo
Alto, Calif.: Spectrum Research Institute and San Jose,
Calif.: Arkay Records, 1980, 1 sound cassette, 20 min.,
1 7/8 ips, stereo.
Techniques of getting rid of stress and tension, narrated in
a manner to encourage relaxation and accompanied by suitable
music.

R24 _____. Organ of Perception [Sound Recording]. Palo Alto,
Calif.: Spectrum Research Institute, 197-?, 1 sound cas-
sette, 30 min., 1 7/8 ips, stereo.
Organ music designed to assist the listener in relaxing.

R25 _____. Prelude [Sound Recording]. Belmont, Calif.:
Halpern Sounds, 1980, 1 sound disc., 50 min., 33 1/3
rpm., stereo. (Also sold by Yes! Bookshop, Washington,
D.C.)
Music to help attain a relaxed, meditative state of conscious-
ness. From the Anti-Frantic Alternative Series.

R26 _____. The Rain Meditation [Sound Recording]. Palo Alto,
Calif.: Spectrum Research Institute, 1977, 1 cassette,
4-track, stereo.
Music to focus collective powers of concentration and deliver
rain at the right time to the right place. Title on container:
The Universality of Music. Vocals and harmonium by Sunil
K. Bose.

R27 _____. Rings of Saturn [Sound Recording]. Palo Alto,
Calif.: Spectrum Research Institute, 197-?, 1 sound cas-
sette, 20 min., 1 7/8 ips, stereo. (Also sold by Yes!
Bookshop, Washington, D.C.)
Celestial music for meditation and listening pleasure.

R28 _____. Serenity Suite: The Breath of Life [Sound Record-

ing]. Palo Alto, Calif.: Spectrum Research Institute,
1978, 1 cassette, 4-track, stereo.
A program of stretching, relaxing, breathing, and visualizing
to help lead the listener into a state of serenity. Narrated by
Mark and Yamuna Becker with electronic music. From the
Anti-Frantic Alternative Series.

R29 _____. Spectrum Suite [Sound Recording]. Palo Alto,
Calif.: Spectrum Research Institute, 1976, 1 disc no.
SRI-770, 33 1/3 rpm., stereo. Also issued as 1 cassette,
4-track, stereo. (Also sold by Yes! Bookshop, Washington, D.C.)
Music to help attain a relaxed, meditative state of consciousness. With 7 slides in the seven colors of the spectrum,
each corresponding to a musical key. Disc from the Soundscape TM Series, I.

R30 _____. Spectrum Suite, Extended Play [Sound Recording].
Belmont, Calif.: Halpern Sounds, 1979, 1 sound cassette,
60 min., 1 7/8 ips, stereo., Dolby processed. (Also sold
by Yes! Bookshop, Washington, D.C.)
Instrumental music with wind and ocean sounds, designed to
create an aura of uplifting relaxation. From the Anti-Frantic
Alternative Series. With program notes.

R31 _____. Starborn Suite: Extended Play [Sound Recording].
Belmont, Calif.: Halpern Sounds, 1980, 1 sound disc no.
HS-780, 33 1/3 rpm, stereo. Also issued as 1 cassette
no. HS-780-X, 4-track, stereo. (Also sold by Yes! Book-
shop, Washington, D.C.)
Music to help attain a relaxed, meditative state of conscious-
ness. Cassette from the Anti-Frantic Alternative Series.
Disc from the Soundscape TM Series, Ill.

R32 _____. Steven Halpern in Concert [Sound Recording].
Belmont, Calif.: Halpern Sounds, 1978, 1 sound cassette,
60 min., 1 7/8 ips, stereo, Dolby processed.
The composer playing flute, piano, organ and guitar.

R33 _____. Tuning the Human Instrument (an Owner's Manual)
[Sound Recording]. Palo Alto, Calif.: Spectrum Research
Institute, 1978, 1 cassette no. SRI-776-C, 4-track, stereo.
Talk, with background music, about the ways in which our
bodies are subtly manipulated by our acoustic environment.
Offers principles that can bring your own soundscape into
harmony with your needs. With notes.

R34 _____. Zodiac Suite [Sound Recording]. Palo Alto, Calif.:
Spectrum Research Institute, 1977-78, 1 cassette, no. HS-
774, 42 min., 1 7/8 ips. Also released as 1 sound disc,
33 1/3 rpm, stereo. (Also sold by Yes! Bookshop, Wash-

ington, D.C.)
Part of a series of specially composed musical environments
designed to enhance and serve that part of you that is na-
turally tranquil and peaceful. Previously released as "I": A
Cosmic Attunement. Cassette from the Anti-Frantic Alternative Series. Disc from the Soundscape TM Series, II.

R35   Health and Wholeness [Sound Recording]. Surrey, England:
       Crusade for World Revival, 1981, 1 sound cassette, 1 7/8
       ips, mono.
       From a weekly broadcast: Design for Living; Crusade for
       World Revival. Discusses healing and meditation. From the
       Christian Counselling Series.

R36   Hills, Christopher B. Meditation [Sound Recording]. San
       Rafael, Calif.: Big Sur Recordings, 1970, on side 2 of 1
       cassette no. 6430, 2-track, mono. Also issued on reel,
       3 3/4 ips, mono., or stereo. LC 78-740787
       Christopher Hills conducts an experimental meditation session.
       Recorded in Amsterdam in 1970. With: A Theoretical Model
       of Humanism, by M. Allen; The Psychology of Inward Infinity,
       by A.J. Brodbeck; and The Relationship of Science, Intellect
       & Mind, by A. Wolf.

R37   Huxley, Laura A. Meditation on a Flower [Sound Recording].
       San Rafael, Calif.: Big Sur Recordings, 1 sound cassette
       no. 3010, 1 hr. LC 78-740476
       As a method for contacting one's own inner world, Laura Hux-
       ley conducts a demonstration of meditation on a flower for
       listener participation. Recorded in Big Sur Calif. in 1965.

R38   _____. Recipes for Living & Loving [Sound Recording].
       San Rafael, Calif.: Big Sur Recordings, 197-?, 1 cas-
       sette no. 1000. Also issued on reel, 3 3/4 ips, mono. or
       stereo. LC 78-740267
       The author presents two meditational exercises intended to
       supplement the "31 recipes for living and loving" in her book,
       You Are Not the Target.

R38K   Jacobson, Edmund, and Frank J. McGuigan. Principles and
       Practice of Progressive Relaxation: A Teaching Primer
       [Sound Recording]. New York: BMA Audio Cassettes,
       1982, 4 sound cassettes, 234 min. 1 7/8 ips, mono. + 2
       pamphlets. 1. Progressive relaxation: origins and criti-
       cal concepts. 2. Essentials of progressive relaxation
       training: clinician's guide. 3. Learner's guide to pro-
       gressive relaxation (1): Introduction and step-by-step
       instruction. 4. Learner's guide to progressive relaxation
       (2): Timed instructions for localized tension reduction.
       For sale by ISHK Book Service, P.O. Box 176, Dept. T-5,
       Los Altos, CA 94022

R39   Kannellakos, Demetri, and Walter Bellin. Meditation: A Psy-
       chophysiological Experience & Its Implications [Sound Re-
       cording]. San Rafael, Calif.: Big Sur Recordings, 1972,
       1 cassette no. 6850, 1 hr., 30 min. Also issued on reel,
       3 3/4 ips, mono. or stereo. LC 78-740573
       Discusses transcendental meditation as a means to the inte-
       grated development of all aspects of life. Examines the be-
       havioral effects of TM and surveys recent psychological studies
       which indicate that TM results in decreased drug abuse and
       improved physical and mental health. Recorded in Squaw
       Valley, Calif., on Sept. 8, 1972.

R40   Khan, Pir Vilayat Inayat. Sufi Meditation [Sound Recording].
       San Rafael, Calif.: Big Sur Recordings, 1971, 1 sound
       cassette, 60 min., 1 7/8 ips, mono. (Also sold by Yes!
       Bookshop, Washington, D.C.)
       This is a tape for listener participation in Sufi meditation.
       Includes exercises for centering.

R41   Khan, Ustad Ali Akbar. Music for Meditation [Sound Record-
       ing]. New York: Connoisseur Society, 1974, 1 disc no.
       2063, 33 1/3 rpm., stereo.
       Indic music with sarod and tamboura. With program notes.

R42   Knippschild, Ernestine. Rainbows of Love: Introductions
       for Meditation and Relaxation [Sound Recording]. New
       York: Folkways Records, 1980, 1 disc, 33 1/3 rpm, mono.
       (Also sold by Yes! Bookshop, Washington, D.C.)
       Instructions in color meditation and deepened relaxation.

R43   LeShan, Lawrence L. How to Meditate: A Guide to Self-
       discovery [Sound Recording]. Washington, D.C.: Li-
       brary of Congress, Div. for Blind & Physically Handi-
       capped, 1974, 2 discs, 8 rpm.
       Explains the reasons for meditating; how to meditate; and
       what meditation does psychologically and physiologically.
       Provides specific exercises and programs. Produced by the
       American Foundation for the Blind. Narrated by Arnold Moss.

R44   Lilly, John C. Meditative Exercises [Sound Recording]. San
       Rafael, Calif.: Big Sur Recordings, 1970, 1 cassette no.
       4360, 1 hr., 30 min. Also issued on reel, 3 3/4 ips, mono.
       or stereo. LC 78-740356
       Intended to bring awareness of the existence of our own re-
       peating loops, our unfinished business, by demonstrating
       phenomena that appear when attention wanders or wears out.
       Thus the alternatives of stored material in our biocomputers
       can begin to emerge.

R45   Mahesh Yogi, Maharishi. Maharishi Mahesh Yogi: Deep Medi-
       tation [Sound Recording]. Los Angeles: World Pacific

Records, date?, 1 sound disc, 33 1/3 rpm.
The Maharishi discusses the basic thesis and techniques of
the Spiritual Regeneration Movement.

R46 _____. Maharishi Mahesh Yogi: The Master Speaks
[Sound Recording]. Los Angeles: World Pacific Records,
197-?, 1 sound disc no. WPS-21446, 50 min., 33 1/3 rpm,
stereo.
Side 1, Love. Side 2, The Untapped Source of Power that
Lies Within.

R47 _____. Toward "Pure Awareness." [Sound Recording].
North Hollywood, Calif.: Center for Cassette Studies, 1974,
1 cassette no. 33844, 2-track, mono.
Maharishi Mahesh Yogi explains Transcendental Meditation.
Includes a bibliography.

R48 Majumdar, Sachindra Kumar. Yoga [Sound Recording].
Huntington Station, N.Y.: Golden Crest, 197-?, 1 sound
disc, 33 1/3 rpm.
Presents yoga for meditation and relaxation. Notes on slip-
case. From the Spoken Word Series.

R49 Martin, Walter R. Transcendental Meditation [Sound Record-
ing]. Santa Ana, Calif.: One Way Library, 1975, 1 sound
cassette, 1 7/8 ips, mono.

R50 Maupin, Ed. Guided Meditation on Body Awareness [Sound
Recording]. San Rafael, Calif.: Big Sur Recording,
196-?, 2 cassettes no. 347, 2 hr. Also issued on reel,
3 3/4 ips, mono. or stereo. LC 78-740530
Dr. Maupin conducts a workshop on the techniques of meditation on body awareness, first describing his own experiences with the practice, then conducting exercises with the
audience. He explains that the way a person feels about
himself is directly related to how he feels about his body.

R51 May, Rollo. Meditation as an Aspect of Spirit [Sound Record-
ing]. San Rafael, Calif.: Big Sur Recordings, 1970, 1
cassette no. 4284, 1 hr. Also issued on reel, 3 3/4 ips,
mono. or stereo. LC 78-740230
Lecture read by the author. He offers explanations and de-
scriptions of his personal experiences with meditation. Dr.
May relates violence to nonbeing coming into being.

R52 _____. The Oedipus Myth & Meditation [Sound Recording].
San Rafael, Calif.: Big Sur Recordings, 1966, 1 cassette
no. 3254, 1 hr. Also issued on reel, 3 3/4 ips, mono. or
stereo. LC 78-740409
Lecture read by the author. The author explores various
dimensions of consciousness disclosed by an inquiry into the

Oedipus myth and meditation. Recorded in Big Sur, Calif., Aug. 5, 1966.

R53   McKay, Matthew, and Patrick Fanning. Autogenics [and] Meditation [Sound Recording]. Oakland, Calif.: New Harbinger Publications, 1982?, 1 sound cassette, 1 7/8 ips, 2-track, mono.
Training techniques for autogenics and meditation are given. Narrated by Jerry Landis.

R54   Meditation: A Way of Life [Sound Recording]. Atascadero, Calif.: Forces of Change, 1971, 1 sound cassette, 13 min., 1 7/8 ips.
Considers group meditation as a service to mankind rather than used for personal benefit. Read by Mary Bailey. Produced by Lucis Trust in New York.

R55   Miller, Emmett E. Rainbow Butterfly [Sound Recording]. Menlo Park, Calif.: E. Miller, 1979, 1 sound cassette, 1 7/8 ips, stereo. (Also sold by Yes! Bookshop, Washington, D.C.)
A combination of harp music and meditations. Music by Georgia Kelly.

R56   Mind as Healer, Mind as Slayer [Sound Recording]. Berkeley, Calif.: Extension Media Center, University of California, 1975, 5 cassettes no. AT 257-AT 260, 2-track mono. (Title on container spine: Holistic Medicine.)
Derived from a conference presented by University of California, Extension Symposium, 1975. Includes: The Role of Stress in the Psychogenesis of Disease, by K.R. Peletier; Uses of Self-Regulation Techniques in Alleviating Stress Disorders and Promoting Healing, by A. Green and E. Green; Reorganization in Psychotic Turmoil, by J.E. Perry; and Belief Systems and Cancer, by C. Simonton and S. Simonton.

R57   Murphy, Michael. Survey of Human Growth Movement [Sound Recording]. San Rafael, Calif.: Big Sur Recordings, 197-?, 1 cassette no. 220, 1 hr., Also issued on reel, 3 3/4 ips, mono. or stereo. LC 78-740600
Michael Murphy talks about current approaches to fostering human growth, including encounter groups, sensory awareness, Gestalt therapy, fantasy exploration, and meditation.

R58   Ornstein, Robert Evans. Meditation and Consciousness (I): Robert Ornstein on Opening the Mind to the Intuitive [Sound Recording]. Center for Cassette Studies, 1974, 1 cassette, 41 min., 2-track, mono.

R59   _____. Meditation and Consciousness (II): Robert Ornstein on Learning from Consciousness Change [Sound

Recording]. Center for Cassette Studies, 1974, 1 cassette no. 35772, 40 min., 2-track, mono.
Dr. Ornstein explains how a person can use the meditative state to observe himself objectively and he discusses the function of the teaching story using ancient tales which merge psychotherapy with Eastern mystical systems. Includes a bibliography.

R60 _____. On the Psychology of Meditation [Sound Recording]. San Rafael, Calif.: Big Sur Recording, 1971, 1 cassette no. 2810, 1 hr., 30 min., Also issued on reel, 3 3/4 ips, mono. or stereo. LC 78-740326
Dr. Ornstein discusses various systems of meditation including his three main methods: concentration techniques, opening techniques, and teaching stories. Also gives detailed instructions on Zen meditation.

R61 _____. A Scientific View of Meditation [Sound Recording]. London: Seminar Cassettes, Ltd. and New York: Psychology Today, Seminar Cassettes, 1973 (Dist. in U.S. by Jeffrey Norton Publishers, New York. Also sold by Yes! Bookshop, Washington, D.C.) 1 cassette, 2-track, mono.
Lecture read by the author. Recorded in 1973. Discusses whether meditation is suppressing ordinary thought so that other functions of the mind can appear and if there is a physiological basis for this concept.

R62 Prabhavananda, Swami. Meditation: Why and How? [Sound Recording]. Hollywood, Calif.: Vedanta Press, 1971, 1 cassette, 55 min.
Recorded at the Vedanta Temple, Hollywood, California.

R63 Procter, Judith. Breathing and Meditative Techniques [Sound Recording]. New York: Bio-Monitoring Applications, Inc., 1 cassette, 1 7/8 ips.
Instructions for relaxation therapy. From the Biofeedback Techniques in Clinical Practice, Vol. 1 Series.

R64 Ram Dass. One Man's Journey to the East [Sound Recording]. San Rafael, Calif.: Big Sur Recordings, 1970, 3 cassettes no. 3281-3282, 4 hr., 15 min., LC 78-740536. Also issued on 4 reels, 3 3/4 ips, mono. or stereo. LC 78-752243
The former Richard Alpert tells the story of his journey from professor at Harvard, through psychedelia, to meeting his guru in the East, and the continuing changes in his life. He discusses forms of yoga and meditation, reincarnation, and the problem of desire.

R65 _____. Yoga of Daily Life [Sound Recording]. San Rafael, Calif.: Big Sur Recordings, 1970, 1 cassette no. 3300, 1 hr. Also issued on reel, 3 3/4 ips, mono. or stereo. LC 78-740500

Lecture read by the author. Explains the principles of yoga and shows how we limit ourselves in everyday life and how meditation enables us to see ourselves without attachment, to have compassion for ourselves and others, and to see the world as it really is. Recorded in West Franklin, N.H., 1970.

R66 Rama, Swami. First Step Towards Advanced Meditation [Sound Recording]. Honesdale, Pa.: Himalayan International Institute of Yoga Science and Philosophy, date?, 1 cassette, 22 min., 2-track, mono. (Also sold by Yes! Bookshop, Washington, D.C.)
Instructions on breathing techniques are given and the importance of the chakras is discussed.

R67 _____. A Guide to Intermediate Meditation [Sound Recording.] Honesdale, Pa.: Himalayan International Institute of Yoga Science and Philosophy, date?, 1 cassette, 2-track, mono. (Also sold by Yes! Bookshop, Washington, D.C.)
Guidance is provided for deepened meditation.

R68 _____. Guided Meditation for Beginners [Sound Recording]. Honesdale, Pa.: Himalayan International Institute of Yoga Science and Philosophy, date?, 1 cassette, 20 min., 2-track, mono. (Also sold by Yes! Bookshop, Washington, D.C.)
Explains the purposes and benefits of meditation. Provides a method of meditation describing how to sit, when to meditate, and how to calm the mind and body.

R69 _____. Meditation for Initiates [Sound Recording]. Honesdale, Pa.: Himalayan International Institute of Yoga Science and Philosophy, 197-?, 1 cassette, 1 7/8 ips, mono. (Also sold by Yes! Bookshop, Washington, D.C.)
Advanced meditation instruction for experienced meditators.

R70 Rozman, Deborah. Meditating with Children [Sound Recording]. Boulder Creek, Calif.: University of the Trees Press, date?, 1 cassette. (Also sold by Yes! Bookshop, Washington, D.C.)
This tape can be used with the author's book of the same title or by itself. For children.

R71 _____. Meditation and Children [Sound Recording]. San Francisco: New Dimensions Foundation, 1979, 1 cassette no. 1187, 1 hr., 2-track, mono.
Deborah Rozman is interviewed about contemporary child education and its relation to violence in society. Meditation (defined as concentrating, sharing, and expanding the self) is seen as a chance to release their psychic tensions. Transcription of a New Horizons radio broadcast.

R72 Shapiro, Dean H. Clinical Applications of Meditation & Be-

havioral Self-Control Strategies [Sound Recording]. New
York: Biomonitoring Applications, Inc., 1977, 1 sound
cassette no. T-128, 1 7/8 ips, mono.

R73   . Meditation and Behavioral Self-Management Instructions [Sound Recording]. New York: Biomonitoring Applications, Inc., 1977, 1 cassette no. T-128B, 1 7/8 ips,
2-track, mono.
Shows how meditating can help reduce excessive stress and
tension and enhance self-awareness.

R74 Shealy, C. Norman. Deep Relaxation: The Biogenics Approach [Sound Recording]. Palo Alto, Calif.: Spectrum
Research Institute, 1979, 1 sound cassette, 45 min., 1 7/8
ips, stereo.
Music by Steven Halpern. Narration by C. Norman Shealy.

R75   . Relaxation Meditation: Biogenic Exercises [Sound
Recording]. Palo Alto, Calif.: Spectrum Research Insti-
tute, 1976, 1 cassette no. SRI-775, 2-track, mono.
Narration by C. Norman Shealy with background music by
Steven Halpern.

R76 Shore, Jon, and Frank Smith. Meditation 1: Meditation 2
[Sound Recording]. Phoenix, Ariz.: Light Unlimited
Publishing, date?, 1 cassette. (Also sold by Yes! Book-
shop, Washington, D.C.)
Gives a basic breathing meditation technique for relaxation
and stress reduction accompanied by appropriate music.

R77   , and   . The Mirror: Morning in the Garden
[Sound Recording]. Phoenix, Ariz.: Light Unlimited
Publishing, date?, 1 cassette. (Also sold by Yes! Book-
shop, Washington, D.C.)
This tape suggests the subject use a large mirror during the
guided meditation. Side two is a journey through a garden.

R78 Sippel, Mary O'Brien. Revitalization, and End of the Day
Relaxation, by Donald A. Tubesing [Sound Recording].
Duluth, Minn.: Whole Person Associates, 1982, 1 sound
cassette, 37 min., 1 7/8 ips, mono.
Relaxation techniques narrated in a manner to encourage relaxation, with suitable musical accompaniment by Steven Halpern.

R79 Sivananda Radha, Swami. Guided Meditation [Sound Record-
ing]. Porthill, Idaho: Timeless Books, date?, 1 cassette.
(Also sold by Yes! Bookshop, Washington, D.C.)
A Hindu meditation technique is explained. Focuses on light
and the image of Siva.

R80 _____. Mantras [Sound Recording]. Porthill, Idaho:
    Timeless Books, date?, 1 cassette. (Also sold by Yes!
    Bookshop, Washington, D.C.)
    This cassette contains classical mantras and Sanskrit songs
    sung by Swami Sivananda Radha.

R81 _____. Power of Mantras [Sound Recording]. Porthill,
    Idaho: Timeless Books, date?, 1 cassette, 90 min. (Also
    sold by Yes! Bookshop, Washington, D.C.)
    The use of mantras is explained in step-by-step guidance.

R82 Smith, Huston. Journeys Into Civilization [Sound Recording].
    San Rafael, Calif.: Big Sur Recordings, 1968, 2 cas-
    settes nos. 3051-3052, 3 hrs. Also issued on reel, 3 3/4
    ips, mono. or stereo. LC 78-740263
    Lectures read by the author. Recorded in San Francisco,
    Aug. 21, 1968. In the first part, Dr. Smith describes his
    experiences with yoga, Zen meditation, and a unique form of
    chanting. In the second part, he describes his view of the
    characteristics of the major civilizaitons, and how these char-
    acteristics of the West, East Asia, and India will be combined
    to make a new civilization.

R83 Sohn, Robert, and Steven Halpern. Musical Sleep Induction
    [Sound Recording]. Palo Alto, Calif.: SRI Records,
    1978, 1 sound cassette, 1 7/8 ips, stereo.

R84 Sufi Meditation [Sound Recording]. San Rafael, Calif.: Big
    Sur Recordings, date?, audio tape, 60 min., 3 3/4 ips,
    2-track.
    Includes physical exercises for centering, chanting, and a
    series of meditations on light.

R85 Sutphen, Dick. Eagle Meditation: Eagle and Multi-Worlds
    [Sound Recording]. Malibu, Calif.: Valley of the Sun,
    date?, 1 cassette. (Also sold by Yes! Bookshop, Washing-
    ton, D.C.)
    The listener is hypnotized and instructed to fly free like an
    eagle to the meditative background music.

R86 _____, and Treena Sutphen. Chakra Balancing and Ener-
    gizing: Chakra Meditation [Sound Recording]. Malibu,
    Calif.: Valley of the Sun, date?, 1 cassette. (Also sold
    by Yes! Bookshop, Washington, D.C.)
    The listener is hypnotized and a golden light of life energy
    is directed through the chakras. Each chakra is discussed.
    The listener experiences cleansing and balancing through
    breathing exercises.

R87 Sutphen, Treena. Color Therapy Meditation: By the Ocean
    Meditation [Sound Recording]. Malibu, Calif.: Valley of

the Sun, date?, 1 cassette. (Also sold by Yes! Bookshop, Washington, D.C.)
The listener is guided into a deep meditation using images of color and the ocean.

R88   Swann, Ingo, and Steven Halpern. Star Children: Turn on Your Drive [Sound Recording]. Belmont, Calif.: Swann Halpern Records and Tapes, 1979, 1 sound cassette, 1 7/8 ips, stereo.
This musical recording can be used for relaxation.

R89   Thurston, Mark. How to Meditate: The A.R.E. Meditation Course [Sound Recording]. Virginia Beach, Va.: A.R.E. Press, date?, 6 cassettes. (Also sold by Yes! Bookshop, Washington, D.C.)
The tapes have an accompanying workbook and a copy of Meditation and the Mind of Man, by Herbert Puryear and Mark Thurston. Based on the teachings of Edgar Cayce.

R90   Trungpa, Chögyam. Buddhism and Meditation [Sound Recording]. San Rafael, Calif.: Big Sur Recordings, 1970, 2 cassettes nos. 1881-1882, 2 hrs. Also issued on reel, 3 3/4 ips, mono. or stereo. LC 78-740233
Lecture read by the author. Recorded in San Francisco, June 11, 1970. The author discusses the place of meditation in Buddhism and the creation of a silent space in which one can be alone with one-self. Paradoxically, the creation of such a silence also aids communication, as one is then free to hear another person without the defensive interference of ego.

R91   Watts, Alan. Cycles in Buddhist Philosophy [Sound Recording]. Toronto: CBC Learning Systems and North Hollywood, Calif.: Center for Cassette Studies, 1975, 1 cassette no. CBC508, 30 min.
Alan Watts discusses the view of cycles held in Buddhist philosophy and examines the theology of the Tibetan Book of the Dead and various aspects of meditation.

R92   _____. The Silent Mind: Alan Watts Discusses the Oriental Concept of Meditation [Sound Recording]. North Hollywood, Calif.: Center for Cassette Studies, 1972, 1 cassette no. 5134, 2-track, mono.
Alan Watts discusses the Hindu and Buddhist concept of meditation, the exercise by which man transcends the world of abstract thought and enters a timeless realm of unfiltered experience. Includes a bibliography.

R93   _____. Zen: The Eternal Now [Sound Recording]. London: Seminar Cassettes Ltd. and New York: Psychology

Today, Seminar Cassettes, 1977, (Distributed in the U.S. by Jeffrey Norton Publishers, New York.), 1 cassette no. 527, 47 min., 1 7/8 ips, 2-track, mono.

■ SOCIETIES AND ASSOCIATIONS ■

Selections made from ENCYCLOPEDIA OF ASSOCIATIONS, edited by Denise S. Akey (copyright © 1959, 1961, 1964, 1968, 1970, 1972, 1973, 1975, 1976, 1977, 1978, 1979, 1980, 1981, 1982 by Gale Research Company; reprinted by permission of the publisher), seventeenth edition, Gale, 1983. For information about other groups, see The Encyclopedia of American Religions, by J. Gordon Melton, Wilmington, N.C.: McGrath Publishing Co., 1978.

S1 AGNI YOGA SOCIETY (Eastern Philosophy)
319 W. 107th St.   Phone: (212) 864-7752
New York, NY 10025   Mrs. Sina Fosdick, Pres.
Founded: 1946. "Promotes study and research in Eastern philosophy and comparative religion." Promotes study of esoteric literature and Eastern sources. Associated with the Nicholas Roerich Museum. Publishes books and reprints.

S2 AMERICAN ASSOCIATION OF PHYSICIANS PRACTICING THE
    TRANSCENDENTAL MEDITATION AND TM-SIDHI PROGRAMS
P.O. Box 836
Palo Alto, CA 94302   Daniel Liebowitz, M.D., Pres.
Founded: 1978. Staff: 1. Physicians; auxiliary members are students and non-physician health care professionals; honorary members are outstanding scientists elected by the board. Encourages physicians to develop within themselves the "highest ideal of the perfect physician." Assists physicians in: encouraging patients to utilize TM programs to prevent disease and develop "perfect" health; improving doctor-patient relationships; bringing "perfect" health to society. Acts as clearinghouse for information exchange among physicians and professionals and to make information available to the medical community and the general public. Promotes research of physiological effects of the TM programs. Maintains speakers bureau; offers specialized education; compiles statistics. Utilizes resource library at Maharishi International University. Publication: Directory, quarterly; also publishes Scientific Research on the Transcendental Meditation Program, Collected Papers:

311

Volume One. Affiliated with: World Government of the Age
of Enlightenment (parent). Also known as: United States Association of Physicians. Convention/Meeting: annual national
conference; also conducts quarterly regional meetings.

S3　AMERICAN CONFERENCE OF THERAPEUTIC SELFHELP/SELF-
　　HEALTH SOCIAL ACTION CLUBS
　　Ross Towers, Apt. B 1104
　　710 Lodi St.　　　　　　　　　　Phone: (315) 471-4644
　　Syracuse, NY 13203　　　Shirley Mae Burghard, R.N., Exec.Dir.
　　Founded: 1960. Members: 2000. Subscribers to the organization's magazine are considered members. Distributes social activities information and encourages formation of therapeutic groups
concerned with mental and physical health and with helping themselves and others develop "wholeness of body, mind and spirit
through forms such as poetry, music, dance, Zen and other meditation." Encourages members to correspond with each other and
with persons confined in hospitals, nursing homes and prisons.
Publications: Constructive Action for Good Self Health, monthly.
Formerly: (1969) American Conference of Therapeutic Selfhelp/
Social Clubs; (1973) American Conference of Therapeutic Psychiatric Selfhelp/Selfhealth Social Clubs; (1977) American Conference of Therapeutic Selfhelp/Selfhealth Social Clubs. Conven-
tion/Meeting: annual--1982 Toronto, ON, Canada.

S4　ANANDA MARGA (Yoga)
　　North American Headquarters
　　854 Pearl St.　　　　　　　　　Phone: (303) 832-6465
　　Denver, CO 80203　　　　　　　P.R. Sarkar, Pres.
　　Founded: 1955. Regional Groups: 16. State Groups: 44.
Local Groups: 100. Ananda Marga is "a dynamic socio-spiritual
philosophy which teaches that it is the duty of every individual
to use all of his or her potential for the all-around advancement
of one's self and the society as a whole." Provides free instruction in meditation and yoga practices. Service projects
have included extensive disaster relief locally and globally in
cooperation with the American Red Cross (see separate entry)
and other agencies including long-term assistance; community
food and nutrition projects; prison projects; group homes for
teenagers and women ex-offenders; recreation for all ages; co-
ops and schools. Provides traveling missionaries and teachers
of meditation and related spiritual practices. Sponsors speakers
bureau, placement service and children's services. Maintains
library of 2500 volumes on spirituality, humanities and arts and
sciences. Committees: Artists and Writers Association; Disaster
Relief; Education; Permanent Relief; Prevention of Cruelty to
Animals and Plants; Social Security; Women's Welfare. Depart-
ments: Education; Relief and Welfare. Publications: (1)
Trishula, monthly; (2) Crimson Dawn, monthly; (3) Renaissance
Universal Journal, quarterly; has also published Cooking for
Consciousness, What's Wrong With Eating Meat, The Spiritual
Philosophy of Shrii Shrii Anandmorti, and The Circle of Crea-

tion, Mamami Krsna Sundaram. Formerly: (1974) Ananda Marga Yoga Society.

S5   AQUARIAN RESEARCH FOUNDATION (Social Change)
      5620 Morton St.   Phone: (215) 849-3237
      Philadelphia, PA 19144   Art Rosenblum, Dir.
      Founded: 1969. Conducts research in discovering ways people can help bring a new age of love and peace into the world. Provides printing apprenticeships to peace activists. Publications: Newsletter, monthly; has also published Natural Birth Control Book, Unpopular Science (book) and new developments in alternative methods.

S6   ARCANA WORKSHOPS (Spiritual Meditation)
      407 N. Maple Dr., Suite 214   Phone: (213) 273-5949
      Beverly Hills, CA 90210   Frederick Rompage, Pres. of Bd.
      Founded: 1961. A training center which applies the writings from Alice A. Bailey (1880-1949) books to the development of human relations skills and other disciplines necessary for competent, responsible community and public service. Teaches principles of meditation that relate the individual's spiritual goal and particular talents to community needs. Considers the highest human creative capacity to be the insight and skill to solve urgent community problems. Aims are to apply what is learned through study and meditation to the daily life; to express through publications and other communications media, the insights gained from meditation; to provide a group channel for the manifestation of new ideas and ideals. Maintains speakers bureau; offers Correspondence Courses; Library; Mail Order Book Sales; Public Lectures; Seminars; Training Workshops. Publications: (1) Thoughtline, monthly; (2) Full Moon Magic, annual; also publishes pamphlets and monographs. Convention/ Meeting: monthly Community Meditation Meetings; also holds annual Three Linked Festivals.

S7   THE ASSOCIATED READERS OF TAROT INTERNATIONAL
          (Fortune-Telling)
      Box 174, Dept. EA
      Brockway, PA 15824   L. D. Worley, Pres.
      Founded: 1972. Members: 850. Staff: 3. Local Groups: 6. Liberal, "New Age" thinkers who have an interest in the Tarot and who wish to learn to master the art of divination with Tarot as well as the art of meditation using Tarot. (Tarot cards are a set of 78 cards bearing allegorical representations used for divination.) Objectives are: to provide local lodge fellowship for initiates; to train persons interested in learning to use Tarot; to bring the art of reading to a professional standing; to enlighten legislators about Tarot and provide an information bureau about Tarot; to encourage readers in the art by providing achievement awards for which members may work. Offers a complete correspondence course in

Tarot. Maintains noncirculating occult research library.
Grants awards of achievement and merit. Donates books on
occult matters to public libraries; loans audiovisual program
on Tarot to public libraries; loans audiovisual program on
Tarot to interested groups.

S8   ASSOCIATION FOR RESEARCH AND ENLIGHTENMENT (Para-
      psychology)
      215 67th St.   Phone: (804) 428-3588
      Virginia Beach, VA 23451   Charles Thomas Cayce,
                                       Ph.D., Pres.
Founded: 1931. Members: 30,000. Staff: 130. Seeks to
give physical, mental, and spiritual help through investigation
of the 14,256 "readings" left by Edgar Cayce (1877-1945), a
clairvoyant diagnostician who is said to have "possessed an
utterly amazing ability to describe, in a kind of self-imposed
hypnotic sleep, individuals and events which he had never
seen." Coordinates medical research program with ARE Clinic,
Phoenix, AZ. In regard to medical data from the Cayce readings, ARE recommends that except for non-critical home reme-
dies, all medical information should be used under supervision
of a licensed physician. Sponsors lectures, symposia, psychic
research, prayer and meditation workshops, a summer camp,
and over 1750 international study groups. Maintains Therapy
Department and 30,000 library on metaphysics, psychic phenomena and related subjects. The Edgar Cayce Foundation has
custody of the readings and conducts continuous program of
indexing, extracting, microfilming, and otherwise organizing
the material in the files; all data files are open to the public.
Makes loans to members through circulating files department of
readings on several hundred subjects or ailments. Publications: (1) Cayce Readings Extracts, monthly; (2) Covenant,
monthly; (3) Newsletter, monthly; (4) Perspective on Consciousness and Psi Research, monthly; (5) Prayer Leaflets,
monthly; (6) Journal, bimonthly; also publishes, through ARE
press, books, booklets, and studies based on or related to the
readings. Convention/Meeting: annual congress--always Virginia Beach, VA.

S9   BUDDHIST VIHARA SOCIETY
      5017 16th St., N.W.   Phone: (202) 723-0773
      Washington, DC 20011   Mahathera H. Gunaratana,
                                      Pres.
Founded: 1966. Members: 600. "To provide a religious and
educational center to present Buddhist thought, practice and
culture and more broadly, to aid cross-cultural communication
and understanding--prerequisites for a peaceful world."
Formed by the Most Venerable Madihe Pannaseeha, Maha Naya-
ka Thera, of Sri Lanka, who noted a serious and growing interest in Buddhism in the U.S. after he visited this country
in 1964. The Society offers the perspective of Theravada

Buddhism which it claims is "the oldest continuous school of
Buddhism that today characterizes the cultures of Burma, Laos,
Cambodia, Sri Lanka and Thailand." Conducts Sunday services, operates a bookstore and mail order service, holds discussions, provides lecturers, conducts classes on Buddhism
and meditation for adults and children, and organizes celebra-
tions on days of special Buddhist significance. The Society is
headquartered in the Washington Buddhist Vihara (Temple)
which also houses a shrine room, a meditation room, a library
of 3000 volumes on Buddhism and related subjects, a garden
and the bookstore. Committees: Book Service; Publications.
Publications: Washington Buddhist (newsletter), quarterly;
also publishes brochures and a devotional handbook. Con-
vention/Meeting: annual--always first Sunday in December,
Washington, DC. Also holds bimonthly and special meetings.

S10   CALIFORNIA YOGA TEACHERS ASSOCIATION
      c/o Yoga Journal
      2054 University Ave.   Phone: (415) 751-1912
      Berkeley, CA 94704   Judith Lasater, Pres.
      Founded: 1975. Members: 120. Yoga centers, teachers and
      practitioners. To contribute toward the advancement of yoga
      education. Conducts workshops on yoga and related discip-
      lines; maintains resource file of doctors and other professionals
      working with the principles of yoga. Publications: The Yoga
      Journal, bimonthly. Convention/Meeting: annual.

S11   CULTURAL INTEGRATION FELLOWSHIP (Asia)
      3494 21st St.   Phone: (415) 648-6777
      San Francisco, CA 94110   Mrs. Bina Chaudhuri,
                                                Pres.
      Founded: 1951. Members: 300. Staff: 10. Individuals in-
      terested in the concepts of universal religion, cultural har-
      mony and creative self-fulfillment. Promotes intercultural un-
      derstanding between Asia and America; emphasizes the "spirit-
      ual oneness of the human race"; and applies fundamental
      spiritual principles in daily living. Activities include weekly
      lectures and study groups, a summer seminar on Oriental phi-
      losophy and a student essay contest. Operates bookstore.
      Committees: East-West Research; Essay Contest; India Cul-
      ture; Yoga and Meditation. Divisions: Center of India Cul-
      ture; East-West Research Centers; Publication Center; Univer-
      sal Religion. Publications: (1) Ashram Bulletin, quarterly;
      (2) Special Cultural Events, quarterly; also sponsors and pub-
      lishes books and monographs. Convention/Meeting: semian-
      nual--always August and October, San Francisco, CA.

S12   FIRST ZEN INSTITUTE OF AMERICA (Buddhist)
      113 E. 30th St.   Phone: (212) 684-9487
      New York, NY 10016   Mary Farkas, Sec.
      Founded: 1930. Carries on program of daily life, with medi-

tation practice in the Rinzai tradition. <u>Publications</u>: Zen Notes, 10/year.

S13 FOUNDATION OF HUMAN UNDERSTANDING (Meditation)
8780 Venice Blvd.   Phone: (213) 559-3711
Los Angeles, CA 90034   Roy Masters, Pres.
<u>Founded</u>: 1961. <u>Staff</u>: 25. Religious/educational organization. Provides instruction, through books and recordings, in a Judeo-Christian meditation exercise. Operates a call-in radio program nation-wide and throughout Europe and Canada known as "How Your Mind Can Keep You Well." Maintains ranch-retreat in Oregon where spiritual guidance and training in practical skills are provided. Offers recorded lectures and books (by Roy Masters) on subjects such as "controlling negative emotions and healing through understanding one's relationship to stress."

S14 HIMALAYAN INTERNATIONAL INSTITUTE OF YOGA SCIENCE
AND PHILOSOPHY OF THE U.S.A. (Human Development)
RD 1, Box 88   Phone: (717) 253-5551
Honesdale, PA 18431   Rudolph M. Ballantine,
                                                      M.D., Pres.
<u>Founded</u>: 1971. <u>Members</u>: 2300. <u>Staff</u>: 75. <u>Regional</u>
<u>Groups</u>: 20. People of all ages, walks of life and faiths. Purpose is to help people understand themselves in every way; to teach holistic health care based on a synthesis of Eastern and Western knowledge techniques; and to further the personal growth of modern man and his society. Offers courses and seminars whose underlying philosophy is the practice of "Superconscious Meditation," a systematic method for developing every level of one's consciousness, and the belief that everyone has the power to recreate his life and realize his inner potential through study and practice. Imparts techniques which can be applied to daily life including techniques for regulation of the various aspects of body, mind and emotions; conducts research to establish scientific basis for these techniques. Offers stress management programs, training programs for counselors, therapists and physicians, diet and nutrition programs and training in combined therapy. Sponsors weekend seminars on a wide variety of personal growth topics. Maintains speakers bureau; operates a children's school and a graduate school which offers masters degrees in Eastern Studies and Comparative Psychology. Has established the Eleanor N. Dana Research Laboratory and the Himalayan Institute Teachers Association, which certifies yoga teachers. Maintains library of 20,000 volumes. <u>Divisions</u>: Publishers and Distributors. <u>Publications</u>: (1) Himalayan News, bimonthly; (2) Dawn Magazine, quarterly; (3) Research Bulletin of the Himalayan International Institute/Eleanor N. Dana Laboratory, quarterly; also publishes over 50 books and tapes. <u>Convention/Meeting</u>: annual--always June, New York City.

S15　INNER PEACE MOVEMENT (Leadership Training)
　　　5103 Connecticut Ave., N.W.　　　Phone (800) 424-3670
　　　Washington, DC 20008　　　Francisco Coll, Founder
　　　Founded: 1964. Members: 300. A leadership training pro-
　　　gram designed "to help man identify and balance the physical,
　　　mental and spiritual forces in life so he can mold his own des-
　　　tiny and become the architect of his own success." Believes
　　　that meditation and inner guidance will help individuals make
　　　mature decisions. Holds local and national workshops for ad-
　　　vanced training. The nature of the program evolves with the
　　　changing needs of the members. Publishes Expression Maga-
　　　zine.

S16　INTERNATIONAL ORDER OF KABBALISTS (Mysticism)
　　　25 Circle Gardens, Merton Park
　　　London SW19 3JX, England　　　J. Sturzaker, Principal
　　　Founded: 1959. Members: 3000. Individuals interested in
　　　developing the hidden faculties of man, and helping human be-
　　　ings "evolve on a spiritual path" through Kabbalah, an ancient
　　　philosophical system which "brings together all related occult
　　　subjects in a comprehensive manner." Areas of study and
　　　practice include meditation, tarot, astrology, mythology, "eso-
　　　teric colour" and Kabbalistic Ritual. Offers a correspondence
　　　course and produces cassette recordings. Maintains speakers
　　　bureau. Publications: The Kabbalist, quarterly; and pub-
　　　lishes books.

S17　INTERNATIONAL SOCIETY FOR KRISHNA CONSCIOUSNESS
　　　3764 Watseka Ave.　　　Phone: (213) 559-2874
　　　Los Angeles, CA 90034　　　David M. Schiller, Jr.,
　　　　　　　　　　　　　　　　　Exec. Officer
　　　Founded: 1966. Members: 65,000. Regional Groups: 100.
　　　State Groups: 40. Local Groups: 85. Individuals interested
　　　in Krishna, Non-sectarian, cultural, religious, philosophical
　　　and educational movement which represents tradition rooted in
　　　ancient India. Dedicated to teaching self-realization and
　　　Krishna consciousness worldwide through the practice of
　　　Bhakti-yoga and meditation on the various names of Krishna.
　　　Maintains multimedia diorama museum. Sponsors cultural festi-
　　　vals throughout the year. Divisions: Bhaktivedanta Book
　　　Trust; Bhaktivedanta Scientific Institute; Food Relief and
　　　Agricultural Development; Gurukla System (for young people);
　　　International Life Membership Trust; Television. Publications:
　　　(1) Back to Godhead (magazine), monthly; (2) Report (media
　　　newsletter), monthly; (3) World Review (newspaper), monthly;
　　　also publishes Bala Books (children's stories), Bhaktivedanta
　　　Scientific Institute Monograph Series, a cassette tape ministry,
　　　religious music on tape, documentary/educational films and
　　　videotapes on ISKCON; and over 200 volumes on the philo-
　　　sophical and spiritual classics of India. Convention/Meeting:
　　　semiannual.

S18 KRISHNAMURTI FOUNDATION OF AMERICA (Human Develop-
       ment)
     P.O. Box 216   Phone: (805) 646-2726
     Ojai, CA 93023   Erna Lilliefelt, Adm.
                                        Officer
     Founded: 1968. Staff: 1. Individuals interested in the
     teachings of J. Krishnamurti, Indian author, lecturer, and
     educator, who believes that the "general disorder and con-
     fusion that pervades the consciousness of mankind" can be
     dispelled through meditation, which brings order to the activ-
     ity of thought. "As such order comes, the noise and chaos
     of our consciousness die out." To sponsor public talks of
     Krishnamurti and to disseminate information on his teachings,
     his repudiation of all connections with organized religions and
     ideologies, and his concern with "setting men absolutely and
     unconditionally free." Has established an elementary school
     in Ojai, CA. Conducts seminars and discussion groups and
     produces and distributes films, video, and audio recordings
     on Krishnamurti's teachings. Maintains library of 300 volumes.
     Publications: Bulletin, 2/year; also publishes pamphlets and
     books.

S19 LAMA FOUNDATION (Human Development)
     Box 444
     San Cristobal, NM 87564   Kim Myers, Coordinator
     Founded: 1968. Members: 30. Staff: 30. Individuals will-
     ing to live in and work full time wherever needed, participate
     in group meetings and decisions and cooperate in fund-raising
     ventures. United to work for the awakening of higher con-
     sciousness. Conducts program of regular meditation, group
     meetings, communal meals, work projects, farming and garden-
     ing and book publishing. Intensive Study Center houses 12
     students and one teacher in intensive practices and studies.
     Plans seminars for music study, vipassana, meditation, study
     of various religious traditions. Maintains library. Publishes
     books. Convention/Meeting: annual--always summer, San
     Cristobal, NM.

S20 LIGHT OF YOGA SOCIETY
     2134 Lee Rd.   Phone: (216) 371-0078
     Cleveland Heights, OH 44118   Patricia Hammond,
                                         Contact
     Founded: 1968. Members: 250. Staff: 37. To promote the
     practice of yoga as a practical and effective tool for physical,
     mental and emotional health and well-being. Teaches all facets
     of classical yoga with emphasis on breathing, exercise and
     relaxation/meditation. Has specially designed programs for the
     elderly ("Easy Does It" Yoga), and for children as well as
     adapted courses for prisoners, alcoholics, drug addicts, learn-
     ing-disabled children, kidney dialysis patients, and other spe-
     cial populations. Through its division, Systems for Management

Effectiveness, offers a Stress Management Program to businesses and organizations throughout the country. Conducts classes, seminars, lectures, workshops, retreats and extensive teacher training programs. Offers free introductory classes to interested groups. Distributes instructional materials on teaching safe beginner yoga practices and practical nutrition. Has engaged in local, state and federally funded research to evaluate the effects of classical yoga practice. Makes available documentary film and videotapes on yoga instruction. Maintains center in India, Switzerland and Sarasota, FL. Publications: Yoga in America, quarterly; has also published the LYS Beginner's Manual and books.

S21   NATIONAL FEDERATION OF SPIRITUAL HEALERS
       Old Manor Farm Studio
       Church St.   Audrey Copland, Sec.
       Sunbury-on-Thames, Middlesex TW16 6RG, England
       Founded: 1955. Spiritual healers, trainees and fellowship supporters from 61 countries. Federation is established for the promotion and encouragement of the study and practice of the art and science of spiritual healing, including all forms of healing of the sick in body, mind or spirit, by means of the laying-on of hands or by either prayer or meditation, whether or not in the actual presence of the patient. Federation aims, in particular, at: safeguarding the interests of healers in general and affording protection for them and their patients during treatment; raising the standard of healership; giving recognition to the status of the qualified healer in the community; acting as a representative body for healers in all matters pertaining to spiritual healing. Conducts: classes for meditation and healing development; conferences, lectures and seminars; mail study courses. Bestows certificate to all healer members, and special certificate to elected Fellows. Conducts research programs. Maintains national referral service for patients. Publications: Healing Review, quarterly. Convention/Meeting: annual--1982 October.

S22   PANSOPHIC INSTITUTE (Human Development)
       P.O. Box 42324   Phone: (503) 235-8250
       Portland, OR 97242   Dr. Simon Grimes, Dir. Gen.
       Founded: 1973. International education organization of persons interested in expanding their knowledge in the spiritual field. To promote "clear awareness" in humanity through the goals of global unity, spiritual enlightenment and the conservation of resources. Believes that "an awakening humanity can solve world problems and begin to think, feel and act on a planetary level." Sponsors School of Universal Religion and Philosophy which offers courses related to the New Age consciousness movement; Church of Universal Light, which provides a program of ministerial education and ordination; and Structural Unitism Society, which is based on "a social and spiritual ideol-

ogy designed for the Macro society of the New Age." Maintains library of 3000 volumes on metaphysical, philosophical and social sciences. Committees include Committee for Investigation of Extra-Tellurian Intelligence; Humanology and Company; Mahamudra Society; and Tibetan Students Fund. Publications: (1) Clear Light, quarterly; (2) Programs (directory), quinquennial; also publishes books on Buddhism and religious psychology.

S23 SANATANA DHARMA FOUNDATION (Yoga)
3100 White Sulphur Springs Rd.   Phone: (707) 963-9487
St. Helena, CA 94574   Yogeshwar Muni, Spirit-
                                                        ual Head
Founded: 1975. Members: 450. Staff: 22. The "founding and supervising organization for Sanatana Dharma in the Western World." Sanatana Dharma means the Path of Eternal Truth or the way of living as determined by the way things actually are. Was originally organized by Charles Berner, now known as Yogeswhar Muni. Conducts: Dyad School of Enlightenment; Energy Mastery Program: Sanatana Dharma Spiritual Community; Vyasa School of Sanskrit; School of Yogic Music and Dance; G.C. Berner Library of Spiritual Sciences. The schools are attended by sincere students who wish to become teachers and practitioners of the Sanatana Dharma. The various schools conduct retreats, month long sessions, yoga training and various types of enlightenment sessions. Maintains Spiritual Sciences Library (7000 volumes) including scriptures of all religions and hundreds of hours of recorded tape. Publications: Vishvamitra, quarterly. Absorbed: Institute of Ability.

S24 SELF-REALIZATION FELLOWSHIP (Yoga)
3880 San Rafael Ave.   Phone: (213) 225-2471
Los Angeles, CA 90065   Daya Mata, Pres.
Founded: 1920. Persons interested in scientific practice of yoga "to attain direct personal experience of God." Maintains temples and centers throughout the world; trains SRF teachers in monastic order, supples 3 1/2 year series of lessons to members; operates day and residential grade schools, high schools, colleges, free medical dispensary and hospital in India. Students make Braille copies of some books for the blind. Publications: (1) Self-Realization Fellowship Lessons, weekly; (2) Service Readings, monthly; (3) Center Bulletin, quarterly; (4) Self-Realization Magazine, quarterly; (5) Yogoda Magazine (published in India), quarterly; (6) Annual Journal (in German and Spanish); also publishes books and recordings by Paramahansa Yogananda and Daya Mata. Convention/Meeting: annual.

S25 TAOIST SANCTUARY
c/o Virgilius Kasper

4400 Melbourne Ave.   Phone: (213) 660-8569
Los Angeles, CA 90027   Virgilius Kasper, Exec. Officer
Founded: 1971. Offers instruction in traditional Taoist disciplines to provide open consciousness. Works toward inner
harmony and external poise through acceptance of the total
self. Expounds no creed, dogma, theology or other divisive
philosophy. Encourages the fulfillment of each individual's
recognized potential. Maintains the International I Ching
Studies Institute offering courses in T'ai Chi Ch'uan, Kung Fu,
Taoist meditation and Chinese Wholistics. Publications: Tao
and Change, quarterly; also publishes numerous brochures.
Also known as: Hsien Tzu Kuan.

S26   THEOSOPHICAL SOCIETY IN AMERICA
      1926 N. Main St.   Phone: (312) 668-1571
      Wheaton, IL 60187   Dora Kunz, Pres.
      Founded: 1886. Members: 6000. Staff: 40. Local Groups:
      150. "To form a nucleus of the universal brotherhood of hu-
      manity without distinction of race, creed, sex, caste or color;
      to encourage the study of comparative religion, philosophy and
      science; to investigate unexplained laws of nature and the
      powers latent in man." Maintains 20,000 volume library. De-
      partments: Education; Information; Publications; Publicity and
      Public Relations; Theosophical Publishing House. Publications:
      (1) The American Theosophist, monthly; (2) Directory, annual.
      Convention/Meeting: annual.

S27   3HO FOUNDATION (Yoga)
      1620 Preuss Rd.   Phone: (213) 550-9043
      Los Angeles, CA 90035   Shakti Parwha Kaur
                                               Khalsa, Exec. Dir.
      Founded: 1969. Members: 265,000. Operates 108 centers
      in the U.S., Canada, Puerto Rico, Japan, South America,
      Australia, Europe and Mexico. Students and teachers of
      Kundalini Yoga, which includes all types of Yoga and who
      practice the "Healthy, Happy, Holy way of life" as taught by
      Yogi Bhajan. Provides nursery school education; sponsors
      special teacher training courses. Is developing elementary
      schools in Phoenix, AZ, Washington, DC and Los Angeles,
      CA. Operates speakers bureau; provides lectures and demon-
      strations of the Kundalini Yoga technique; teaches gourmet
      vegetarian cooking. Sponsors drug rehabilitation programs at
      regional centers. Operates Kundalini Research Institute to
      investigate all aspects of the drug rehabilitative and other
      beneficial aspects of Kundalini Yoga. Also offers legal services
      and operates free food kitchens. Has women's division,
      GGMWW or Grace of God Movement (see separate entry),
      "for the uplift of the dignity and respect of womanhood."
      Publications: (1) Beads of Truth, quarterly; (2) Journal of
      Science and Consciousness for Living in the Aquarian Age,
      quarterly; also publishes Peace Lagoon, a translation of the

sacred writings of the Sikhs; Guru Nanak, Guru for the Aquarian Age; Teachings of Yogi Bhajan and Experience of Consciousness. Convention/Meeting: semiannual--always June or July, Espanola, NM and December, Orlando, FL. Also holds annual 6-week training camp for women--always summer, Espanola, NM.

S28   TIBETAN AID PROJECT (Relief)
      2425 Hillside Ave.   Phone: (415) 548-5407
      Berkeley, CA 94704   Tarthang Tulku, Pres.
      Founded: 1974. A project of the Tibetan Nyingma Relief
      Foundation. Offers assistance to Tibetan refugees in India,
      Nepal, Bhutan and Sikkima. Conducts Tibetan Pen Friend
      Program; sponsors relief distribution to communities for sup-
      port of religious and community activities. Organizes benefits
      of all types, including seminars on Tibetan meditation and
      physical yoga. Maintains speakers bureau. Publishes bro-
      chures and booklets; plans to publish a book.

S29   WORLD GOVERNMENT OF THE AGE OF ENLIGHTENMENT--U.S
         (Meditation)
      17310 Sunset Blvd.
      Pacific Palisades, CA 90272   Thomas A. Headley, Pres.
      Founded: 1965. Purpose is to teach Science of Creative In-
      telligence, the TM-Sidhis program and the Transcendental
      Meditation program and to thereby accomplish the seven goals
      of the World Plan, which are: to develop the full potential
      of the individual; to improve governmental achievements; to
      realize the highest ideal of educaiton; to eliminate the age-old
      problem of crime and all behavior that brings unhappiness to
      the family of man; to maximize the intelligent use of the en-
      vironment; to bring fulfillment to the economic aspirations of
      individuals and society; to achieve the spiritual goals of man-
      kind in this generation. ("The TM program is a natural, ef-
      fortless procedure which allows the individual to contact the
      inner field of pure consciousness and thus live a happier, more
      progressive and problem-free life; the TM-Sidhis program is a
      more advanced technology which allows the individual to draw
      more dynamically upon that inner field of all possibilities.")
      Maintains statistics demonstrating beneficial effects resulting
      from participation in TM. Bestows annual Maharishi Award to
      ten outstanding members of the community. Maintains six edu-
      cational services: Students' International Meditation Society
      (offers courses to students and young people); International
      Meditation Society (offers courses to the general public);
      American Foundation for the Science of Creative Intelligence
      (conducts courses for business, industry and government);
      Spiritual Regeneration Movement (offers courses to individuals
      specifically interested in personal development in the context
      of a spiritual, holistic approach to knowledge); Institute for
      Social Rehabilitation; International Center for Scientific Re-

search. Has trained over 10,000 teachers who have instructed over 2,000,000 individuals in the TM and TM-Sidhis programs. Publications: World Government News, quarterly. Formerly: (1979) World Plan Executive Council.

S30 YASODHARA ASHRAM SOCIETY (Yoga)
Box 9   Phone: (604) 227-9224
Kootenay Bay, BC, Canada   Swami Sivananda-Radha,
   VOB 1X0   Founder
Founded: 1957. Members: 15. To investigate the nature of human consciousness; to establish research facilities and educational programs; to coordinate existing knowledge; to certify teachers and establish branches for instruction and research in spiritual practices. The Ashram functions as a yoga retreat and study center that is open to anyone and that requires no conformity to any particular religious teaching. It offers workshops and courses throughout the year, including an annual three month Yoga Teacher Training Course with certification and Yoga Intensive Courses for self-development. Maintains library of 5000 volumes on Yoga and metaphysical subjects. Publications: Ascent, 3/year; also publishes books, tapes and records. Affiliated with: Association for Development of Human Potential. Convention/Meeting: annual.

S31 YOGA RESEARCH FOUNDATION
6111 S.W. 74th Ave.   Phone: (305) 595-5580
Miami, FL 33143   Swami Jyotir Maya Nanda,
                                             Pres.
Founded: 1969. An international movement in "elevating the consciousness, alleviating suffering and enriching the lives of all humanity: through Integral Yoga. (Integral Yoga, a modern method for integrating the personality, combines the practices of the four major yogas: Raja Yoga, the Yoga of Meditation; Bhakti Yoga, the Yoga of Devotion; Karma Yoga, the Yoga of Action; and Jnana Yoga, the Yoga of Wisdom.) The foundation believes that Integral Yoga can provide "a basis for upgrading the cultural growth of humanity while bringing about a worldwide level of social and religious harmony." Conducts regular classes in teaching of yoga, vedanta and Indian philosophy. Maintains library of over 50 books and 200 cassette lecture topics on yoga. Sponsors children's yoga classes. Publications: International Yoga Guide, monthly; also publishes books.

S32 ZEN STUDIES SOCIETY (Buddhist)
Dai Bosatsu Zendo, Kongo-Ji
Beecher Lake, Star Rte.   Phone: (914) 439-4566
Livingston Manor, NY 12758   Eido Tai Shimano, Roshi
                                             (Abbot)
Founded: 1965. Members: 210. To provide Zen Buddhist training, practice and retreats. Maintains Temple (New York

Zendo) and Lay Mountain Monastery (Dai Bosatsu Zendo) in New York state. Also maintains 1200 volume library on Zen Buddhism and related subjects. <u>Publications</u>: Namu Dai Bosa, quarterly; also produces books and cassettes.

Aaronson, Bernard S.   A1
Aaronson, Reuben   M8
Abbas, K.A.   A806
Abdullah, Syed   A2
Abrams, Allan I.   A3-A5, A448,
  D1
Abramson, Pamela   A908
Abulafia, Abraham ben Samuel
  B511
Addington, Cornelia   B1, B2
Addington, Jack Ensign   B1,
  B2
Adkins, Joyce   A17
Adriance, Wayne   A917
Aerthayil, James   A6
Agard, Roy   B3
Agarwal, B.L.   A7
Agnihotri, S.N.   B238
Ahuja, M.M.S.   A8
Aïvanhov, Omraam M.   B4, B5
Ajaya, Swami   B6, B515
Akers, Thomas K.   A9
Akins, W.R.   B7
Akishige, Yoshiharu   A9K
Albert, Ira B.   A10
Alberts, Ton   B8
Albrecht, Alois   B9
Alder, Vera S.   B11
Aldrich, Virgil C.   A11
Alexander, C.N.   A12, A171,
  A617, D2
Allan, John   B13
Allen, Christine P.   D3
Allen, Don   A13
Allen, M.   R36
Allen, Mark   B14
Allen, Robert L.   A61
Allen, Roger J.   D4
Allison, John   A14
Almeida, Elza M.   B143
Alpert, Richard   see   Ram Dass
Alschuler, Alfred S.   B15
Amaldas, Brahmachari   B16
Amira, Stephan B.   A860
Anand, B.K.   A15, A16

Ananda Vandana, Ma   B671
Anchor, Kenneth N.   A17
Anderson, Douglas J.   A18
Anderson, Hilary   D5
Andrews, Gavin   A19
Angelico, Irene   M14
Antes, Michael   B17, D6
Antes, Peter   B18
Appelkvist, Claes   B19
Appelle, Stuart   A20
Ardhapurkar, Indubala   A829K
Argüelles, José   B21
Argüelles, Miriam   B21
Arintero, Juan G.   B22
Armstrong, Carol A.   B95
Armstrong, P.F.   D7
Arnáiz Barón, Rafael   B23
Arnold, E.   A877
Arnold, Seraphin   B24
Arns, Patricia A.   A62, A367
Aron, Arthur   A21-A25, A199, A448,
  A872
Aron, Elaine N.   A21, A23-A25
Arthur, Gary K.   A609
Arya, Usharbudh   B26-B28
Ashbrook, James B.   A26
Atkinson, William W.   B29
Atlanteans   B30
Atmananda, Swami   B31
Aubin, L.X.   B456
Aufderbeck, Hugo   B32
Austin, Anne   A19
Avila, Donald   A27
Aygen, Maurice M.   A151, A152
Ayres, Lew   M5

Bache, Christopher M.   A28
Bacher, Paula G.   D8
Badaoui, K.   A29, A610, A696
Badaracco, Marie R.   A30
Badzong, Hans-Joachim   B33
Bagga, O.P.   A31
Bahadur, Dinesh   M10
Bahrke, Michael S.   A32, A33, D9

Bai, A. Jhansi Lakshmi A676
Bailey, Alice A. B34-B37
Bailey, Judi A34
Bailey, Mary R54
Bain, Alexander B732
Bainbridge, William S. A35, A36
Baird, Robert D. A37
Baker, Douglas B38, B39
Baker, John B921
Baker, Mary Ellen Penny B40, B41
Bakker, Robert A38
Balan, George B42
Balasooriya, Somaratna A495
Bali, Lekh R. A675
Ball, Orlow E. A617, D10
Ballentine, Rudolph B895
Ballou, David A39
Balsamo, Ignatius B43
Baltazar, Eulaio R. A40
Bamrungtrakul, Ratna A41
Banquet, Jean-Paul A42-A47
Barber, Theodore X. A167
Bardet, Vincent B200
Barish, J. D11
Barmark, Susanne A. A48
Barnes, Michael A49, A50
Barnes, Ronald D12
Barozzi, Ronald L. D13
Barr, William H. D14
Barrabino, J. A463
Barrios, René C. B247
Bartels, Wayne J. D15
Barth, Friedrich K. B44
Bartholomae, Wolfgang B45
Barton, Winifred G. B46, B47
Barwood, T.J. A51
Bass, Barry A. A777
Bassford, R.D. D16
Battelle, Phyllis A52 see also
  Van Horn, Phyllis Battelle
Bauer, T.W. A200
Bauhofer, U. A53, D17
Baxter, Elizabeth S. D18
Bean, L.H. A862
Beard, Rebecca B48
Beary, John F. A54, A63
Beck, Sharon E. A17
Becker, David E. A55
Becker, Mark R28
Becker, Yamuna R28
Beckwith, L.L. D19
Beede, Norman R2
Beier, Peter B49
Beiman, Irving A55K, A664
Belle, Jack van B1008
Bellin, Walter R39

Bélorgey, Godefroid B50
Belson, Jordan M12
Benares, Camden B51
Bendrath, Detlef B685
Bennett, James E. A56
Bensch, C. A642
Benson, Herbert A54-A73, A127, A324, A367, A464-A469, A846, A847, B51K, B52, B52K, M7
Benz, Ernst B53
Berg, C.G. A82
Berg, Ruth E. D20
Berg, William P. van den A74
Berger, Ralph J. A917
Bergfalk, Lynn A75
Berker, Ennis A76
Berkowitz, Alan H. D21
Berlin, T. D22
Bernard, Dahme A679
Bernard, Theos B54
Bernoff, Noj B14
Berrettini, R.B. A77
Berry, George C. D22K
Besnard, Albert-Marie A78, A79
Besseghini, Italo A923
Betz, Otto B55, B56
Bevan, A.J.W. A80-A83
Beyer, Stephan V. A84, A85
Bez, Edward R3
Bhajanananda, Swami A86
Bhaktivendanta Swami, A.C. B59
Bibbee, Richard A87
Bielefeldt, Carl W. D23
Biesinger, Albert B61
Bill, Josef B62
Bingay, James S. A150
Birmingham, Frederic A. A88
Bitter, Wilhelm B63, B64
Bitting, Anthony L. D24
Bjornstad, James B65
Black, Henry R. A89
Blackwell, Barry A90, A91
Blantz, Larry T. D25
Blasdell, Karen S. A92, D26
Blavatsky, Helen P. B66, B67
Bleistein, Roman B68-B70
Block, Bruce A93
Blofeld, John E.C. B71-B74
Bloomfield, Harold H. A94, B75-B82, R4, R5
Bloomfield, Saul S. A90, A91
Blümlein, W. D27
Boals, Gordon F. A95
Boden, Liselotte M. B83, B84
Bodmershof, Wilhelm B85
Boeckel, Johannes F. B86
Boissennault, L. D19

Bokert, Edwin   A619, A620
Bole, David N.   D28
Bolen, Jean S.   A96
Bolley, A.   A97
Bonarjee, Hector   B87
Bond, Nigel W.   A196
Bonilla, John of   B628
Bono, Joseph, Jr.   A97K
Borelli, Marianne D.   D29
Borkovec, T.D.   A353
Borland, C.M.   A238
Borland, Candace   A98
Börne-Kray, Brunhild   B88
Boros, Ladislaus   B57
Bose, Sunil K.   R26
Boswell, Philip C.   A99
Boudreau, Leonce   A100
Bourne, Peter G.   A101
Bourzeix, J.C.   A44
Bowers, Margaret   B89
Bowker, John   A102
Bowman, Mary L.   A677
Bowness, Charles   B90
Boxerman, David   B91
Boylan, M. Eugene   B50, B92
Braden, Klaus   B93
Bradley, B.W.   A103
Bradshaw, David   A104
Braidwood, M.   A189
Bralley, J.A.   A656
Brandon, Jeffrey E.   D29K
Brandrud, Rolf   B853
Braud, W.G.   D89
Bräutigam, Eva   A105
Brenot, P.   A642
Bridgewater, Michael J.   D30
Bright, Deborah   A106
Bristol, John   A615
Brodbeck, A.J.   R36
Broeck, José van den   B383
Brofman, Martin   A107
Bronson, Edward C.   A201
Brooke, Avery   B94, B95, B96
Brosse, Jacques   B97
Brown, Clinton C.   A108
Brown, Daniel P.   A109, A109K,
   A110, D30K
Brown, Melanie   D31
Brubaker, Paul   A22
Bruijn, Erik   B98
Bruner, Richard L.   D32
Bruno, Vincenzo S.J.   B99
Brunton, Paul   B100-B113
Buccola, Victor A.   A106
Buchanan, Franklin R.   A112
Buchinger, Otto   B114
Buckler, W.   A113

Buckley, Peter   A277
Buckminster Fuller, R.   see   Fuller,
   R. Buckminster
Budberg, Kurt   B115
Buddhaghosa   B166
Bugault, Guy   B117
Bühler, M.   D33
Bühler, Walther   B118
Bujatti, M.   A114
Buksbazen, John D.   B119
Bumpus, Ann K.   A768
Bunk, Brian E.   D34
Burgin, Victoria D.   D35
Burns, Douglas   A115
Burns, John E.   A116
Busby, Keith   A117
Buttrick, George A.   A118
Byles, Marie B.   B120, B121
Bynum, Jack L.   D36
Byrne, D.G.   A19

Caballero, Nicolás   B122-B124
Cain, Michael P.   B75, B76, B79
Cairns, Grace E.   A119
Calandra, Alexander   A120
Calian, Carnegie S.   A121
Calquist, Jan   B125
Cammer, L.   A674
Campbell, Anthony   B126, B127
Campbell, Colin   A122
Campbell, Ken   A286
Campbell, Richard E.   D37
Candelent, Gillian   A123
Candelent, Thomas   A123
Cappo, Bruce M.   A369
Caprile, Giovani   B128
Cara, Arthur J.   D38
Carlsen, Robin W.   B129
Carlson, Mary L.   A620
Carlson, Ronald L.   B130, R6
Carmody, J.   A124
Carol, Mark P.   A63
Carpenter, J. Tyler   A125
Carr-Kaffashan, Lucille   A126, A910
Carrey, Normand J.   B625
Carrington, Patricia   A127, A128,
   A465, A533, B131, B132, R7, R8
Carrol, Frieda   B989
Carruthers, M.   A640
Carsello, Carmen J.   A129
Carson, Linda G.   D39
Caruso, John L.   A371
Case, David B.   A656
Casper, Marvin   B921
Cassel, Russell N.   A130, A131
Castillo, J.A.   A132

Cataldi, Oscar B., Jr. B133
Cauthen, Nelson R. A133
Cayce, Charles T. A666
Cayce, Edgar B134, B650, B651
Cayce, Hugh L. B41
Center for Self Sufficiency B135
Chailak, Seumor D. A134
Chaitow, Leon B136
Chaman Lal B137
Chandra, A. A475
Chandraprabhsagar, Muni B138
Chaney, Robert G. B139
Chang, Lit-sen B140
Chang, Suk C. A135
Chantal, Jeanne F. B141
Chao Khun, Sobhana Dhammasudhi
  B142
Chapman, A.H. B143
Chapman, Jeffrey C. B143
Charles, B. A877
Chase, Loriene B144
Chaube, Shakuntala A795
Chaudhri, Amin M27
Chaudhuri, Haridas B145
Chen, C.M. A136, B146
Chenard, J.R. A137
Chentanez, T. A436
Chermol, Brian A219
Chetanananda, Swami B939
Chethimattam, John B. A138
Chhina, G.S. A15, A16
Ch'ien, Anne A139
Chihara, T. A319
Chih-i B147
Childs, John P. A140, D40
Chilson, Richard B148
Chin, N. A862
Chinmayananda, Swami B149,
  B973
Chinmoy B150-B156, R9
Chitrabhanu, Gurudev S. B138
Chiu, John T. A901
Chögyam Trungpa, T. see
  Trungpa, Chögyam
Christensen, Chuck B157
Christensen, Winnie B157
Christine, Shirley A141
Chuang, Chou B160
Churches' Fellowship for Psychical
  and Spiritual Studies B161
Claiborn, Charles D. A291
Clark, Matt A142
Clarke, W. Norris A143
Clasper, P.D. A144
Clements, Geoffrey A145, A610,
  A877
Clowney, Edmund P. B162

Clutterback, David A146
Cognet, Louis A147
Cohen, Daniel B163
Cohen, Irving J. A148
Cohen, Mariam C. A273
Cole, Jean W. A127
Coleman, John E. B164
Collier, Roy W. A149
Collings, Gilbeart H., Jr. A127
Collins, Betty B457
Collons, Roger D. A150
Comer, James F. D41
Conze, Edward B166
Cooke, Grace B167-B169
Cooper, Joan B170
Cooper, Michael J. A151, A152
Corbin, Henry B356
Corby, James C. A153
Corcoran, Kevin J. A154
Corey, Paul W. A155
Corless, Roger B171
Corlin, Claes A156
Cossio, Claudia B271
Costa, Eugenio A157
Costain, Edward E. B172
Cotter, Deborah M. B51
Cousins, Ewert A158, A315
Cousins, L.S. A159
Cowger, Ernest L. A160, D42
Cox, Harvey A161, B173
Craig, Philippa B174
Crasset, Jean B175
Crassweller, Karen D. A67
Creaser, James W. A129
Credidio, Steven G. A162
Crom, Scott B176
Cumming, Diana B538
Cummins, Norbert A163
Cunis, David A230
Cunningham, Monte A164
Curran, Jo B177
Curtin, Thomas G. D43
Curtis, Miriam J. D44
Curtis, William D. A165
Cuthbert, Bruce A166, D45
Cuvelier, André B178

Dalai Lama B834
Dalal, Abdulhusein S. A167
Dancer, Jay B179
Daniels, D. A168
Daniels, Lloyd K. A169
Darcourt, G. A463
Dardes, J.A. A170
Dash, P. A171
Datta, G.P. A172

Davidson, Julian M. A173
Davidson, Richard J. A174, A175, A175K, A717
Davies, John A176
Davies, Stevan L. A177
Davis, Roy Eugene B180-B188
Day, Judith A178
Day, Richard C. A179
Daya, A. A728
Dean, P.J. D46
Deatherage, Gary A180
DeBlassie, Paul A., III D47
Déchanet, Jean Marie B189-B192
Deckarm, R. D48
Dees, Joly B124
DeFrutos, Ricardo B196
DeGrâce, Gaston A181
Dehne, Matthias B884
Dehof, K. A455
Deichgräber, Reinhard B308
Deikman, Arthur J. A182, A183, A183K, A194
Deissler, R. A668
DeKoninck, Joseph A117
DelCor, Christa B194, B195
Deleo, James A784
Delitz, Antonio J. A184
Delmonte, M.M. A185-A189
DeLyzer, A. A320
Denmark, Ted H. D49
Denniston, Denise B196, B197, B273
Denny, Mary C. D50
Depping, F. D51
Desbuquoit, Achille M. B198
Deshimaru, Taisen B199, B200
Deshpande, R.R. B201
Dessauer, Phillip B202, B203, B204
Devas, Dominic B628
DeVol, Thomas I. A190
Dhammaratana, U. B205
Dhammasudhi, Chao Khun Sobhana see Phra Sobhana Dhammasudhi
Dhanaraj, V.H. A191, A192
Dhavamony, Mariasusai A193, A194
Dhiravamsa B206, B207, B208
Dice, Marvin L., Jr. D52
Dick, Leah D. A195, D53
Dickins, J.A. A83
Dieball, Werner B209
Diefenbach, Gabriel B210
Dieterle, W. D54
Diger, Michael J. D55
DiGiusto, Eros L. A196

Dillbeck, Michael C. A197-A203, A611, A617, A668, A848-A850, D56
Dillbeck, Susan L. A199
Dilley, John R. A204
DiNardo, Peter A. A205
Diner, Martin D. D57
Dinklage, H.A. A206
Diskin, Eve B213
Docherty, Edward M. A426
Dodds, Dinah A207
Doerr, Edd A208, A209
Dolley Diddee B666
Domash, Lawrence H. A210
Domino, George A211
Domiter, Paul J. D58
Don, Norman S. A212
Donahue, Charles B482
Doner, David W. A213
Donohue, John W. A214
Donovan, Dale A215
Donovan, Kevin A157
Doongaji, D.V. A829K
Doren, David M. A216
Dorje, Konchok B214
Dormitor, Paul J. A302
Dostalek, C. A217
Douglas, Donald B. A753
Douval, H.E. B215
Dowman, Keith B216, B544
Downing, George B217, B218
Downing, Jim B219
Doxley, N.C.S. D59
Dreher, John A218
Drennen, William A219
Dreskin, Thomas A591
Driscoll, Francis A220
Dryer, Thomas A64
Dubin, Louis L. A571-A574
Duck, Brigitte A612
Dukhan, Hamlyn A221
Dumitresca, Ioan F. A222
Dumoulin, Heinrich B220
Dupree, Judy B860
Duquoc, Christian A78
Durand, A. B141
Dürckheim, Karlfried G. B221, B222
Durham, Robert A898
Dutta, Rex B223
Dwivedi, K.N. A223
Dworkin, Susan A224
Dyke, Ron A647

Earle, Jonathan B. A224K
Eastcott, Michael J. B224, B225
Easwaran, Eknath B226-B229, R11, R12

Ebon, Martin B230, B908
Eddy, Glen B921
Edmiston, Susan A225
Edwards, Francis H. B231
Edwards, John T. D60
Edwards, Mark R. A702
Edwards, Tilden B232
Egan, James M. A226
Egdom, Richard van B233
Egenes, Thomas A510
Eggiman, Ernst B234
Ehrlich, Milton P. A227, A228
Elegant, John I. D61
Ellis, Albert A229K
Ellis, George A. B235
Ellwood, Robert S. B235K
Elson, Barry D. A153, A230
Emery, P. A231
Emery, Pierre Y. B236
Emmons, Michael L. B237
Empson, J.A. A51
Engel, Allison A232
England, Kathleen B658
Engler, Jack A109K, A110
Enomiya-Lassalle, H.M. <u>see</u>
    Lassalle, Hugo
Ephron, Harmon S. A128
Epstein, Mark D. A68, A314
Eriksson, C.G. A812
Erskine-Milliss, Julie A233
Esser, P. D62
Eyerman, James A235

Faber, J. A217
Faber, Phillip A. A236
Fabick, Stephen D. D63
Fadeuilhe, A. A463
Fagerstrom, M.F. D64
Falconi, Juan B239
Falk, William A237
Fanning, Patrick R53
Farge, E.J. A238
Farley, Frank H. A426
Farrow, John T. A239, A240,
    A460, A548, B789
Farwell, Lawrence A460
Fast, Howard M. B240
Faulkner, Michael H. D65
Faure, J.M.A. A642, A643
Fehr, Terry B629
Fehr, Theo A241, A242
Feldman, Christina B907
Fenhagen, James C. B241
Fenn, Mair B242
Fenton, J.C. A243
Fenwick, P.B. A244

Ferguson, Phillip C. A245-A247,
    B386, D66
Ferguson, R.E. A248
Fichtl, Friedemann B243
Fiebert, Martin S. A249, A250
Fine, Lawrence B. D67
Firkel, Eva B245
Fischella, Anthony J. R13
Fischer, R. A108
Fischer, Roland A251-A254
Fish, Sharon B506
Fisher, David B700
Flanagan, Finbarr A255
Fling, Sheila A256
Flor, Margherita B246
Floyd, W.T. A257
Flurer, James A. D68
Flygare, Thomas J. A258
Forem, Jack B247, B248
Forte, Michael A. D69
Fossage, James L. B317
Fox, Matthew A259
Francis, Anthony A898
Frank, Kenneth A. B317
Frank, Marion R. D70
Frankel, Bernard L. A260
Franklin, Lavelle A609
Franklin, R.L. A261, A262
Franks, Cyril M. A910K
Frederick, A.B. A263
French, Alfred P. A264
French, Phyllis E.W. D71
Frew, David R. A266, A267, B250
Friede, Martin B251
Friedewald, William T. A260
Friend, Kenneth E. A268-A270
Fritz, George D72
Fröbe-Kapteyn, Olga B252
Fromm, Erika A271, A272
Frumkin, Kenneth A273
Frumkin, Lynn R. A274, A511, A627
Fryling, Vera R14
Fuchs, Joseph B254
Fujimoto, Rindo B255
Fuller, R. Buckminster B75, B77,
    B78
Fulton, Robert B. A275
Funderburk, James B256
Furst, Merrick L. A570-A575
Fuson, J.W. A276

Galanter, Marc A277, A785
Gallaher, Michael A256
Gandhi, A. A31
Ganguli, H.C. A278
Gannon, Linda A279

Garde, Margaret A596, A597
Gardner, Adelaide B257
Gardner, Kenneth R. A260
Garfield, Charles A. A280
Garrison, J. A281, A282
Gartside, Peter A90, A91
Gash, Arnold A283
Gaunitz, Samuel C. A48
Gaus, Hans B258
Gawain, Shakti B14, B259
Gaylin, Jody A284
Gayten, Warren D73
Geffré, Claude A78
Geisler, M. A285, A708, D74
Geller, Barry B196, B197
Gellhorn, Ernst A286
Gent, John B260
Gerberding, Kieth A. B261
Gersten, Dennis J. A287
Gerus, Claire A288
Gibbons, Gerald A289
Gibbons, Richard B99
Giber, David A742
Gibson, William B262
Gijsen, Wim B263
Gilbert, Albin R. A290
Gilbert, Gary S. A291, A633,
  A634
Giles, S. A292
Gill, Andrew A367
Gill, Jean B264
Gilles, Anthony A293, A294
Gillies, Jerry B265
Ginder, Richard A295
Girodo, Michel A296
Glasenapp, Sigrid von B275
Glasser, William B266
Glassman, Bernard R. B602
Globus, Gordon G. A296K
Glueck, Bernard C. A297, A297K,
  A297R, A786K, B82
Godrèche, Dominique B269
Goichon, Amélie M. B270
Goldberg, Jordon A575
Goldberg, Lois S. A298
Goldberg, Phil A299
Goldberg, Phillip B271, B272
Goldberg, Richard J. A300
Goldhaber, Amos N. A301
Goldhaber, Nat B273
Goldman, Barbara L. A302, D75
Goldman, Ralph F. A68
Goldsmith, Joel S. B274-B278,
  B973
Goldstein, Jeffrey A. A177
Goldstein, Joseph B279, B280
Goleman, Daniel J. A174, A175,

A303-A316, A717, A858, B281,
  B676, D76, R15
Gómez, Elfas B239
Good, Michael I. A793
Goodman, George J.W. see Smith,
  Adam
Goosen, Marilyn M.M. B282
Gopi Krishna A317, B283, B973
Gordin, Richard D. D77
Gordon, Rikki L. D78
Gössmann, Wilhelm B284
Gotami, Li B286
Gottlieb, Jack A770, A771
Gouillard, Jean B631
Govinda, Amagarika B. B285-B289,
  B884, M13
Gowan, John A247, A318
Goyeche, John R. A319
Graham, Aelred B203
Graham, John R. A69
Graham, Lewis E. A55K
Graham, T. A320
Granieri, Barbara A613
Grassi, Joseph A321
Greaves, George A322
Green, A. R56
Green, Alyce B290, B291
Green, David B. D79
Green, E. R56
Green, Elmer B290, B291
Greenberg, Jeffrey L. A369
Greenberg, Jerrold S. A323
Greenfield, Thomas K. D80
Greenspan, Brian A575
Greenwood, Martha M. A65, A67,
  A70, A324
Gregg, Richard B. B292
Gregorius I. B293
Griffiths, Paul A325, A326
Griffiths, Thomas J. D81
Griggs, Steven T. D82, D83
Grim, Paul F. A327
Grubb, P.H.W. A328
Gruber, Louis N. A329
Gstrein, Heinz B294
Guenther, H.V. A330, B402, B884
Guillerand, Augustin B295
Guimarães, Iris F. B296
Gunaratana, Henepola D84
Gunther, Bernard B297, R16
Gupta, N.C. A331
Gupta, V.M. A223
Gutfeldt, H. A332

Haack, Friedrich-Wilhelm B298
Haas, Harry B299

Haddon, David A333, A334, B89, B300, B301
Haendler, Otto B302
Hafner, R. Julian A335
Hahn, H.R. A336
Haich, Elisabeth B996-B999
Haimes, Leonard A337
Haines, Aubrey B. A338
Haines, John L. D85
Hall, Joseph B352
Hall, Manly Palmer B303
Hall, Robert B279
Halpern, Steven B304, R14, R17-R34, R74, R75, R78, R83, R88
Hamilton, David W. A851
Hamilton, Vail B301
Hamilton-Merritt, Jane B305, B306
Hampton, Peter J. A339
Handmacher, Barbara D86
Hanenson, Irwin A90, A91
Hanley, Charles A. A340
Hanschen, G. D87
Hansen, Celia B39
Hanson, Bradley A341, B307
Hanson, Judith B407K
Hanson, Mervin V. B544
Hanson, Virginia B20
Hanssen, Olav B308
Happold, Frederick C. B309, B310
Harder, Hugo B270
Harding, S.D. A342
Harf, Anneliese B254
Hari Dass, Baba B311
Harkins, S.W. A511
Harrington, Beth A848
Harrington, John B312
Harris, R. Baine A687
Harris, T. George A761
Harrison, Alan B313
Harrison, Alton, Jr. B314
Harrow, R.J. D88
Hart, Daniel J. A343
Hartgrove, J.L. D89
Hartley, Elda M1, M15, M20
Hartley, Irving M1
Hartley, L. Howard A64
Hartmann, R. A696
Hartung, G.H. A238
Hassett, James A344
Hatch, Jeffrey M. D90
Hatchard, G. A345
Hattauer, Edward A. D91
Hauri, Peter A230
Hauth, Rüdiger B315
Hayden, Eric W. B316

Haynes, C. A45
Haynes, Christopher T. A346, A473, A610, A614
Haynes, J. A257
Heaton, Dennis P. A347
Hebert, J. Russell A240, A346, A348, A349, A473, A616
Hedgepeth, William A350
Heery, Myrtle A351
Heide, Frederick J. A352-A354, D91K
Heidelberg, R. A355
Heidelberg, Rainer B318, D92
Heifetz, Harold B1007
Heigham, John B43
Heil, John D93
Heimler, Adolf B319
Heinrichsbauer, Johannes B320
Heinz, Brad R. D94
Heitmann, Claus B321
Helleberg, Marilyn M. B322
Helminiak, Daniel A. A356, A357
Hemingway, Patricia D. B323
Hemmerle, Klaus B268
Hendlin, Steven L. A358
Hendricks, C.G. A359
Hendricksen, Norman E. D95
Henry, David A422
Henry, James P. A360
Herbert, P.G. A895
Herbst, Winfrid A361
Herring, John B328
Hertner, H.D. D96
Hertzog, Stuart P. B325
Herz, Stephanie M. B326
Hesse, Gisela B881
Hewitt, James B327-B329
Hewitt, Jay A362
Heyes, Anthony D. A363
Hickman, James L. A364, A775
Hiesel, E. A824
Higgins, Paul L. B253
Higuchi, Annete A. D97
Hilarion see Schmidt, Karl O.
Hills, Christopher B. B330, R36
Hills, John B731, B722
Himber, Jane A. B703
Hindmarsh, Roland B189
Hintersberger, Benedikta B331
Hirai, Tomio A406, B332-B334, M21
Hirss, Jean R. D98
Hittleman, Richard B335-B337
Hjelle, Larry A. A365
Hlastala, Michael A863
Ho, Van H. B338
Hobson, Douglas P. A792
Hodes, Robert A166
Hodgson, Joan B339

Hof, Hans B340
Hoffer, William A366
Hoffman, John A367
Hoffman, John W. A62
Hoffmann, B. D99
Holeman, Richard A368
Hollander, Sandra B760
Hollandsworth, James G. A421
Hollings, Robert B342
Holmes, David S. A369
Holmes, Stewart W. B343
Holmgren, Carl A. A370
Holt, William R. A371
Honsberger, Ronald W. A372,
  A373, A901
Hopkins, Jeffrey A68, B834, B835
Hoppenworth, Klaus B344
Horbat, Irene B363
Horioka, Chimyo B343
Horn, Paul A374
Horowitz, Mardi J. A403
Horrom, N. A108
Horwitz, David A260
Houston, Jean A315
Howald, W. D100
Howard, Jane A376
Hritzuk, J. A827
Hsüan-chüeh B199
Hübener, Christian B345
Huber, Jack T. B346, B347
Huber, M.J. A543
Huelsman, Richard J. B348
Hufnagel, Pat A434
Hulme, William E. B349
Humphreys, Christmas B351
Huntley, Frank L. B352
Huxley, Laura A. R37, R38
Hyatt, Christopher S. B353

Ibish, Yusuf B165, B909
Ichazo, Oscar B354
Imbert, Jean C. B355
Inayat Khan, Vilayat B356
Incorvaia, Joel A377
Ingalls, Elizabeth A264
Ingleside, John J. A378
Ingraham, E. B357
Inoue, Tetsuya B255
Iranschähr, Hossein K. B358
Isaacs, Ken A379
Isbert, Otto A. B359-B363
Isherwood, Christopher B364,
  B365
Israelson, Kathy A630
Ital, Gerta B366, B367
Ivarsson, Henrik B125

Jackson, Daniel H. A35
Jackson, Yvonne D101
Jacobe, Eliha A848, A849
Jacobs, Jane A. D102
Jacobson, Edmund B367K, R38K
Jaffe, Dennis T. B75, B76, B79
Jaffe, Robert D. A732-A734
Jain, Prabhachandra K. D103
James, Nancy A. A380
Janakananda Saraswati, Swami B368
Janby, Jørn A381
Jans, Franz X. B341
Javalgekar, R.R. A382
Jefferson, William B369
Jenkins, D.A. A840
Jerome, Jim A383
Jeste, D.V. A829K
Jevning, Ron A384-A395
Johansson, F.P. A396
Johne, Karin B370, B371
Johnson, Janis A397
Johnson, Stephen J. A55K, D104
Johnson, Willard L. B372
Johnston, A. A398
Johnston, William A399, B332, B373-
  B375
Jones, Roger C. D105
Jones-Ryan, Maureen B376
Jonsson, C. A400
Jorban, E. B377
Joscelyn, Lela A. D106
Joseph, Arthur B. D107
Joubert, L.E. B378
Juan de la Cruz, Saint B293
Jungclaussen, Emmanuel B379, B380
Jungmann, Ruy B828
Justin Lucian, Bro. A401
Jyotirmayananda Saraswati, Swami
  B381, B382

Kabat-Zinn, Jon A402
Kadloubovsky, E. B990
Kamalasila B383
Kamen, Randy A922
Kamholtz, John D. D108
Kamiya, Joe A582
Kampf, Harold B384
Kanas, Nick A403
Kanellakos, D. A404, B385-86, R39
Kantipalo, B. B146
Kaplan, Aryeh B387, B511
Kaplan, Stephen A405
Kapoor, S.N. A829K
Kapur, Teg B. B388
Karg, Cassian B389
Karliner, Joel S. A283

Karmarkar, M.G. A8
Kasamatsu, Akira A406, M21
Kasdin, Simon B390
Katz, David A407
Kaufmann, W. A455
Kaushik, R.P. B391, B392
Kauz, Herman B393
Keating, Thomas A408, A409
Keck, L. Robert B394
Keefe, Jeffrey A410
Keithler, Mary A. D109
Kelly, Georgia R17, R55
Kelly, Hugh A411
Kelsey, Morton A412, B395
Kelton, Jeffrey J. D110
Kemmerling, T. A413, D111
Kennedy, Raymond B. A414
Kenton, Leslie A415
Keshavadas, Swami B396
Khamashta, Karen A630
Khan, Pir Vilayat I. R40
Khan, Ustad Ali A. R41
Khantipalo, Bhikshu B397
Kharbanda, A. A7
Kiehlbauch, John A615
Kiely, William F. A286
Kikoler, Charlotte Minoga B75
Kim, Young M. A416
Kimball, Chase P. A755
Kindler, Herbert S. A417, D112
Kindlon, Daniel J. D113
King, Clifton W. B144
King, Jeanne W. D114
King, Winston L. A418-A420,
  B398
Kirkland, Karl A421, D115
Kirpal Singh B399
Kirsch, Irving A422
Kirschner, Sam D116
Kirtane, L.T. A423
Kitagawa, Joseph M. A424
Kiyota, Minoru B479
Klang, Gary B400
Klein, Aaron E. B401
Klein, Cynthia B401
Klemchuk, Helen P. A54, A65,
  A69K, A70
Klemons, Ira M. A425
Kline, Kenneth S. A426, D117
Klipper, Miriam Z. A66, B51K,
  B52
Klon-chen-pa Dri-med-od-zer
  B402
Klosterman, Christl B723
Knippschild, Ernestine R42
Kniffki, Christa B403, D118
Knight, Harry G. B404

Kobal, G. A427
Kobayashi, Kazuo D119
Koch, Walter A164
Koh, T.C. A428
Kohler, Mariane B405
Kohn, Michael H. B249
Kohr, Richard L. A429, A430
Kolb, David A616, A747
Kollander, Cielle B406
Kollander, Kathy B406
Kolswalla, Maharukh B. A431
Kongtawang, Thanom D120
Kongtrul, Jamgon B407, B407K
Kopell, Bert S. A153
Kornfield, Jack A432, A858, B408,
  B409, D120K
Kory, Robert B. A433, A434, B75,
  B77-B79, B82, B410
Koseki, Aaron K. A435
Köster, Peter B411, B412
Kotch, Jamie B. A67
Kotchabhakdi, N. A436
Kraft, Charles G. D121
Krahne, W. A437, D122
Kral, Mary A438, A439, A440
Kamen, Randy A922
Kramer, Joel B413
Kranenborg, R. B414
Kras, Diana J. A441
Krasa, H. A217
Kravette, Steve B415
Kretschmer, H. D123
Krieger, Joan A692, A767
Kripalvanandji, Swami B416
Krippner, Stanley A442
Krishna, Gopi see Gopi Krishna
Krishna Bharti, Swami B297
Krishnamurti, Jiddu B417-B419, M11
Krishnananda, Swami B420
Kristeller, Jean A166
Kriyananda Saraswati, Swami B667
Kroll, Una M. A443, B421, B422
Krueger, Robert C. D124
Krüger, M. D125
Kubose, Sunnan A. A444, A445
Kühlewind, Georg B423
Kukulan, J.C. A448
Kulandai, Victor A449, A450
Kuna, Daniel J. A451
Kuoni, Alfred B533
Kurtz, Waldemar B424
Kushi, Michio B425
Kvapil, Mary A. D126

Labes, Gertrud B37
LaFarge, Sheila B368

Lahr, J.J. A452
Lakshmi, Vinay B212
Lalita B426
Lalitananda, Swami B427
LaMore, George E. A453
Lamott, Kenneth C. B428
Landers, R.L. B611
Landis, Jerry R53
Landrith, Garland A98, A202,
    A454, A611, D127
Landsberg, Lewis A367
Lang, Peter J. A166
Lang, R. A455
Langdon, Joe B582
Langen, Dietrich B429
Lanphear, Roger G. B430
Lanza del Vasto, Joseph J. B431
Lapauw, Camillus B432
Lapham, Lewis H. A456
Laragh, John H. A656
Larkin, Vincent A457
Lasden, Martin A458
Lassalle, Hugo B433-B442
Laurie, Gina A459
Laurie, James R. D128
Laurie, Sanders G. B443
Lavely, Richard A. A732-A734
Lawrence, David M25
Lay, Rupert B444
Lazar, Zoe A460
Lazarus, Arnold A. A460K, A461
Leclerc, Claude B793
Leen, Edward B445
Lefebvre, Georges B292
Lefferts, Barney A462
LeGrand, P. A463
Lehmann, D. A349
Lehmann, John W. A68, A464
Lehner, Francis C. B527
Lehodey, Vital B446
Lehrer, Paul M. A127, A465,
    A911
Leighton, Sally M. A466
Leiste, Heinrich B447
Lercaro, Giacomo, Cardinal B448,
    B449
Lerner, Eric B450
Leseure, N. A44
Lesh, Terry V. A467, B451,
    D129
LeShan, Lawrence A468, A713,
    B452, B453, R43
Lester, David A470
Leung, Paul A469K
Levander, V.L. A469
Levin, Susan A471, D130
Levine, Paul H. A472, A473

Levine, S. A395
Levine, Stephen B454
Levitt, Zola B966
Lewis, Brian S. M17
Lewis, Gordon R. B455
Lewis, Jerome B131
Lewis, John D132
Lewis, Shawn A474
Leypold, Annemarie B183
Lhundup Sopa, Geshe see Sopa,
    Geshe Lhundup
Lichtveld, Noni B98
Liquori, Alfonso Maria dé, Saint
    B456
Lilly, John C. R44
Lin, M.T. A475
Linden, William A476, D133
Lindenberg, Wladimir B457, B458
Ling, Paul K. D134
Link, Mark J. B1006
Linnewedel, Jürgen B459
Linssen, Robert B460
Lintel, Albert G. A477
Lionel, N.D. A478
Lisciandro, Frank M32
Lister, S.G. A51
Livingston, Diane D. A688
Lock, Mary C. A479
Lodge, B. A896
Loeckle, Werner B461
Loewen, D.R. A726
Löffler, Johann H. B462
Long, Barry B463
Loori, John Daido B119
Lotz, Johannes B. B464-B468
Lounsbery, Grace C. B469, B470
Lourdes, P.V. A480, D135
Love, Mike A481
Lovell-Smith, H. David A482
Lu, K'uan Y. B471, B472
Lucas, John M. M18
Luis de Granada B473
Luk, Charles see Lu, K'uan Y.
Lukas, Jerome S. A483, B385
Lukoff, David G. D136
Lundy, Richard M. A354
Luria, Isaac ben Solomon B511
Lutyens, Mary B418
Lyman, Frederick C. B474
Lysebeth, André van B475

MacCallum, Michael J. A484
MacCormick, Chalmers A485
MacHovec, Frank J. B476
MacIntosh, G.R. D137
MacMahon, S.W. A19

Macrae, Janet A. D137K
Madsen, W.C. A486
Maezumi, Hakuyu T. B602
Magarey, Christopher A487
Magenheim, Herbert A90, A91
Maharishi International University B477, B478
Maher, Michael F. D138
Mahesh Yogi, Maharishi B82, B480–B488, B789, R45–R47
Main, J. A488
Main, John B489, B490
Maitland, Robert B491
Majestic, Henry W. A55K
Majumdar, Sachindra K. A489, R48
Makarios, Saint B244
Malec, James A491
Malhotra, M.S. A68
Maliszewski, Michael A270, A442, D139
Malone, A. Hodge B492
Malvea, Bonnie P. A69
Manchester, Harland A492
Mandus, Brother B493, B494
Mangalo, Bhikkhu B495
Mangoldt, Ursula von B356, B496–B498, B915, B961
Manickam, P. Kambar A493
Mano, D. Keith A494
Maquet, Jacques A495
Maraldo, John C. A496
Marchand, Roger A497
Marcia, James A. A601
Marculescu, Ileana B165
Marcus, Jay B. A498–A500, B499
Marcus, Steven V. D140
Marechal, Paul A501
Markos, Saint B631
Marks, E.J. A12
Marks, Leonard M. B138
Marks, P. A108
Marlatt, C. Allan A501K
Marr, S. D141
Marron, Jay P. D142
Marshall, James P. D143
Martin, John S. A571–A574
Martin, Walter R. R49
Martinetti, Raymond F. A502
Marzetta, Barbara R. A69K
Massa, Willi B341, B500
Masters, Roy B501
Matas, Francine A503
Matheson, Charles M. D144
Matthew, Father B502
Matthiessen, Peter B119

Maupin, E.W. A504, D145, R50
Mawbry, Neil M19
May, Gerald B503, B504
May, Rollo R51, R52
Mayer, Elizabeth L. D146
Mazzarella, Pat A505
McAlpine, Campbell B505
McBride, Alfred A506
McCann, Barbara S. A911
McCann, Daisy S. A543, A544
McCanne, T.R. A103
McCormick, Anne A507
McCormick, Thomas B506
McCuaig, Larry W. A508
McDonagh, John M. A509, A510
McDonald, R. A680
McEvoy, T.M. A511
McGeveran, William A. A512
McGuigan, Frank J. R38K
McIntyre, Mary E. A513
McKay, Matthew R53
McKenzie, N.C. D147
McLaughlin, Mary A514
McLeod, John A515
McNeece, Barbara A10
McNulty, Terrance F. A910
McPherson, Klim A806
McQuade, Walter A516
McSorley, Joseph B507
McWilliams, Peter B196, B197, B273, B508
Mead, Travis M. A250
Means, John R. A343
Meany, John O. A517
Meares, Ainslie A518–A531, B509, B510
Mehta, Rohit B517
Meilwes, Margret B132, B534
Melançon, Ovila B518
Meldau, Rudolf B586
Melton, J. Gordon B519
Meltzer, Gloria A298
Melzer, F. A535, B520–B526
Menédez, Iris B51K
Mengel, Gail S.E. D148
Mertesdorf, F. A824
Merton, Thomas A536–A540, B528–B535
Meserve, Harry C. A541, B536
Meuhlman, Mac A58
Meurer, K.A. A455
Meyer, Richard A542
Michael, Russ B537
Michaels, Ruth R. A543, A544
Michaëlle B538, B539
Miele, Philip B810, B811
Mikulas, William L. A545, A546

Mildenberger, Michael B159, B540
Miller, Alan L. A547
Miller, Calvin B541
Miller, Emmett E. R55
Miller, John P. B542
Miller, Kevin B426
Miller, Ralph A362
Mills, Gary K. A286
Mills, Paul J. A849, A850
Mills, Walter W. A548
Milstein, Stephen L. A145
Minelli, Paul B190
Minger, Fritz B543
Mintz, Murray M10
Mi-pham-rgya-mtsho, Jam-mgon
  'Ju B216, B544, B545
Miro, B. D149
Miskiman, Donald E. A551-A555
Misra, L.K. B25
Mitchell, Elsie P. B255
Mitchell, Kenneth R. A556
Mitchell, Mairin B23
Miura, Isshu B546
Moffatt, Doris B547
Moffett, James A557, A558
Mojica Sandoz, Luis B548
Mokusen, Miyuki A559
Moles, Edward A. D150
Molina, Antonio B549
Molinero, José R. B550, B551
Möller, S. D151
Moltmann, Jürgen A560
Monahan, Raymond J. A561
Monléon, Jean de B552
Monnot, Janine B200
Monroe, Sylvester A142
Montgomery, Randal A562
Moore, Richard A615, D151K, M11
Moore, Stewart A835
Morando, Dante A563
Morel, H.V. B743
Morgan, Douglas A650, A651
Morgan, William P. A33
Morler, Edward E. D152
Morris, J.D. A221, A691
Morris, Joseph A564
Morris, R.L. A221, A691
Morse, D.R. A565-A576
Morton, M.E. A386, A393
Moser, Georg B553
Moth, Hanne B. A783
Mountain, Marian B554
Mouradian, Kay B555
Muinz, Arthur J. A577
Mukerji, A.P., Swami B556
Muktananda Paramhamsa, Swami
  B557-B559

Mulder, B. A74
Müller-Elmau, Bernhard B560, B561
Muller-Kainz, E. D153
Munk, H. D154
Muñoz Malagarriga, Concepción B563
Muppathyil, Cyriac B564
Murdock, Maureen H. A578
Murphy, Carol R. B565, B566
Murphy, Martha J. D155
Murphy, Michael A364, R57
Murphy, Suzanne A579
Murray, Edward J. A99, A302
Murray, John B. A580
Musial, Diann B314

Nadel, Gerry A581
Nagel, Hajo B567
Nagel, Hans B93
Naifeh, Kaifeh A582
Nanda, Jyotir Maya, Swami B568-
  B571
Nantel, Linda B793
Naranjo, Claudio A583, B572, B573,
  B973
Narayanananda, Swmai B574
Narayanaswami Aiyar, K. B575
Nash, Carroll B. A584
Nataraj, P. A585
Nath, S. Ravindra A829K
Nathan, Robert J. A273
Nayak, Anand B576
Nearing, Peter A586
Nebelkopf, Ethan A587
Neidenbach, S.L. D156
Nelson, Harold R. A588
Nenadavic, P. A83
Neptune, Calvin D157
Nerstheimer, Uwe A242
Nevins, Albert J. A589
Newhouse, Flower A.S. B577, B578
Nhat, Thich Nhat B579, B580
Nicet Joseph, Brother A590
Nichols, Ted B581
Nicodemus see Nikodemus Hagioreites
Nidich, Sanford I. A90, A91, A591,
  A592, D158, D159
Nikodemus Hagioreites B244, B631
Nishijima, Gudo B582
Nivaldi, Mauro B583
Nolly, Gerald A. D160
Nordberg, Robert A. A594
Norris, Hugh A828
Norvell B584, B585, B586
Norwood, Jean E. D161
Nourse, James C. D162
Novey, Harold S. A901

Nowak, W. D163
Noyes, Humphrey F. A595
Nuernberger, Edwin P. D164
Null, Gary B587, B588
Null, Steve B587, B588
Nummela, Renate A27
Nurnberg, E. George B7
Nyanaponika B589, B590, B591
Nyanasamvara B592
Nystul, Michael S. A596, A597

Oakley, E.M. A598
Oates, Bob A599, B593
Oberhammer, Gerhard B594
O'Brien, Bartholomew J. A600, B595
O'Brien, Justin B238
O'Connell, James A609
Odier, Daniel B596
Oehlschlager, Stephen B597
O'Haire, Trula D. A601
O'Halloran, J.P. A384K, A390
O'Hanlon, Daniel J. A602, A603
Ohayv, Ron J. A115, A604
Oki, Masahiro B598
Olausson, Ingrid B599
Oldfield, Richard R. D165
Oliver, Fay Conlee B600
Olsen, Paul B317
Olson, Helena B601
Olson, Steven D. A605
Oparil, Suzanne A755
Orme-Johnson, David W. A22, A29, A202, A203, A346, A347, A606-A617, A849, B789
Ornstein, Robert Evans B572, B603, B604, R58-R61
Orsy, Ladislas M. A618
Orth, Deborah K. D166
Osbelt, U. D167
Osis, Karlis A619, A620
Oswald, Lawrence E. A20
Otis, Leon A344, A620K, A621
Ott, Ulrich B605
Ottens, Allen J. A622, D168
Overbeck, K.D. A624, A625, B606, D169
Owens, Claire M. A626

Pagano, Robert R. A274, A627, A628, A863
Palmer, D.K. A629
Palmer, G.E.H. B990
Palmer, John A630, A776
Palmer, Susan A631

Pálos, Stephan B607
Pandit, Madhav P. B608-B610
Pandita, Indiradevi B611
Pantas, Lee A503
Papentin, Frank B612
Paramananda, Swami B613, B614
Parampanthi, Puragra, Swami B615
Paratparananda, Swami B632
Parker, Jerry C. A291, A633, A634, D170
Parmisano, A. Stanley A635
Parra, Juan A544
Pas, Julian F. A636
Patel, Chandra H. A637-A640
Patel, Dali J. A260
Paton, Susan B729
Patricca, Nicholas A. A641
Patton, John E. B617
Paty, J. A642, A643
Paulauski, M.T. B654
Payne, Buryl B618, B619
Pe Maung Tin B620
Pearce, Joseph C. B621
Peck, Robert L. B622
Peeke, Harmon V. A675
Peerbolte, M. Leitert A644
Peet, Malcolm A806
Pelletier, Kenneth R. A645, A646, B623, B624, R56
Penner, Wes J. A647
Pensa, Corrado A858
Perry, J.E. R56
Persinger, Michael A. B625
Peter of Alcantara, Saint B626-B628
Peters, Ruanne K. A648
Petersen, W. B629, B630
Peterson, J.W. A865
Peterson, Norman H. A70
Pfaltzgraff, Rogério B632
Phelan, Michael A649
Philippi, Jakob B175
Phillips, Chris A415
Phillips, Susan K. D171
Phra Sobhana Dhammasudhi B633, B634
Pieper, Josef B636
Piggins, David A650, A651
Pinart, Robert B94
Pine, Devera A652
Pipkin, H. Wayne B637
Pirkle, H.C. A385
Pirot, Michael A653
Plattig, K.-H. A427, A861
Podgorski, Frank A654
Poeppig, Fred B638-B641
Pohlmann, Constantin B642
Polidora, Jim A655

Poling, Donald R. B799
Pollack, Albert A. A656
Polowniak, William D172
Pomerans, A.J. B690
Pond, Kathleen B22
Popenoe, Chris B643, B644
Pouliot, Elise B793
Prabhavananda, Swami R62
Prabhu Ashrit, Swami B645
Prasad, S.C. A759
Preston, David L. A658, A659
Preston, Paul A660
Price, John F. A661
Prince, Raymond A662
Procter, Judith R63
Procter, William B52K
Progoff, Ira B648
Prout, Maurice F. A273
Prymak, Carole A. A133
Pseudo-Dionysius B948
Puente, Antonio E. A55K, A663,
  A664, D173
Puligandla, R. A665
Pulley, William S. B649
Puranas B59
Puri, Irpinder A672
Puryear, Herbert B. A666, B650,
  R89
Puryear, Meredith A. B651
Puthiadam, Ignatius B652

Qian, Xue Sen A667
Quiery, William H. B653

Rabinoff, R. A668
Rabten, Geshe B654, B655
Radford, John A669
Radhamani, M.G. A585
Radtke, H. Loraine A772
Radtke-Bodorik, H. Loraine A773
Raeburn, John M. A722
Raghunathrao, Sadashivrao B656
Ragland, Robert E. A195
Raguin, Yves B657, B658
Rahav, Giora A670
Rajagopalachari, P. B659
Rajaneesh, Acharya B660-B674
Ram Chandra B675
Ram Dass B279, B676, R64, R65
Rama, Swami, B238, B512, R66-
  R69
Ramacharaka, Swami see Atkin-
  son, William W.
Ramachandra Rao, Saligrama K.
  B677

Ramakrishna Vedanta Centre B678
Ramirez, J. A671
Rankin, G. D174
Rao, K. Ramakrishna A221, A672,
  A673
Rao, P.V. Krishna A673
Rao, V. Raghavender A676
Rappaport, A.F. A674
Raskin, Marjorie A675
Ray, David A692, B679
Raymond, Jayne B. A205
Reber, B. A45
Reber, William A346
Reddish, P.S. A896
Reddy, M. Kesav A676, D175
Reddy, S. A8
Redfering, David L. A677
Reed, Henry A678
Reed, Jeanette D176
Regardie, Israel B680
Reichelt, Karl L. B681
Reitano, Carmen T. B619
Reiter, Udo B682-B685
Reller, Horst B324
Remscheid, Gilda B889
Reynolds, David K. B687
Reynolds, John B544
Rhodes, Michael M23
Richter, Rainer A679
Riddle, Alexander G. D177
Riederer, P. A114
Riedesel, Brian C. A680, D178
Rieker, Hans-Ulrich B688, B689,
  B690
Riemkasten, Felix B691, B692
Riepe, Dale A681
Rigby, Byron P. A682, A683, A877
Riley, James B. A371
Rimol, Andrew G.P. A684
Rinpoche, Namgyal B693
Rinpoche, Sogyal B694, B695
Rios, Robert J. D179
Rittelmeyer, Friedrich B696-B698
Ritter, Gerhard B699
Rivers, Steven M. A685, A770-A773
Robbins, Jhan B700, B701
Robertson, Debra W. A686
Robertson, Irvine B702
Robins, Alan B703
Robinson, Ann A90
Robinson, Gweneth E. B704
Robinson, Harry A127
Roche, Lorin A859
Rodenberg, Jennifer C. A783
Rodhe, Sten B705
Rodier, David F.T. A687
Roebuck, Julian B. A87

Rofidal, Jean B706-B708
Rogan, John B709
Rogers, Cecil A. A688
Roggenbuck, Peggy A689
Rohrbach, Peter T. B710
Roldan, E. A217
Roll, W.G. A221, A690-A692,
  A767
Romney, Rodney R. B711
Roof, Simons L. B712
Rooney, Anthony J. A911, A912
Roost, Jean G. B713
Rooy, J. de B714
Ropp, Robert de B973
Roquette, Nelly B889
Rose, Donna S. D180
Rose, Richard M. A628
Rosenberg, Alfons B715, B716
Rosenthal, J.M. A693, D181
Roshi, Chotan A. B119
Rosner, Bernard A. A69K
Ross, Jean A694
Roth, Ephrem B717
Roth, Randy S. A9
Roth, Walton T. A153
Rotthaus, Erich B718
Rötting, Gerhard J. B719
Routt, Thomas J. A695
Roux, Georges B720
Rouzere, A.M. A29, A696
Rowan, John A697
Rozman, Deborah B721-B723, R70,
  R71
Rubottom, Al E. A698
Rudhyar, Dane B724
Rudolph, Hermann B725
Ruhbach, Gerhard B267, B726
Rupp, Walter B727
Russel, H. A45
Russell, Kenneth C. A699
Russell, Marjorie B728
Russell, Norris M. D182
Russell, Peter B729, B730
Russie, Roger E. D183

Saayman, Graham S. A236
Sabel, Bernhard A. A700
Sabha-pati Svami B731, B732
Sacks, Howard L. A701
Sadek, Samia N. A179
Sadhu, Mouni B733-B737
Sailer, Heather R. A702
Sailhan, Maurice A46, A47
St. John, John R. B738
Sallis, James F. A703, A704
Salsbury, Janice C. D184

Samendra, Anand B739
Sampaio, André L. B740
Sanford, David E. D185
Sanjoy B741
Sarason, Irwin G. A404
Sarasvati, Satya P., Swami B742
Saraydarian, Torkom B743-B746
Sarojani, N. B755
Sartory, Thomas B747
Sasaki, Josho M32
Sasaki, Ruth B546
Satchidananda, Swami B748, B749
Sathya Sai Baba B750
Satprakashananda, Swami B751
Satya Bharti, Ma B669, B670, B752,
  B753
Satyanand Agnihotri B754
Satyananda Rao, Vedula B755
Satyananda Saraswati, Swami B756,
  B757
Satyavan B758
Sauer, Joseph B268, B686
Sauls, Lynn B759
Sax, Saville B760
Saxena, R.P. B212, B761
Sayadaw, Mahasi B762
Scabelloni, Antoni M. B763, B764
Scarf, Maggie A705
Schachter, Zalman M. A177
Schackmann, R. D186
Schacterle, George R. A575
Schaeffer, Edith A706, A707
Schamoni, Wilhelm B765
Scharf, Siegfried B766, B767
Scheihing, Theresa O. B768
Schenkluhn, Hartmut A708
Scherer, Georg B769
Schilling, Peter B. A709
Schimmel, David A710
Schinle, Gertrudis B770
Schlacter, John A702
Schlereth, Albert B258
Schlingloff, Dieter B116
Schmid, Albert C. A264
Schmidt, Heinz G. B535
Schmidt, Karl O. B771-B775
Schmitt, Winfried B776, B777
Schoicket, Saundra A465
Schöll, Albrecht B540
Scholtz-Wiesner, Renate F. von
  B778, B779
Schonell, Malcolm A233
Schreiner, Lothar B159
Schucman, Helen A2
Schulte, Nico B780-B782
Schulte, Therese B783
Schultz, Edward L. A711

Schultz, Terri A712
Schulz, Chrysostomus B784
Schulze, V. D187
Schur, Edwin A713
Schuster, Richard A714, A715
Schwäbisch, Lutz B785
Schwartz, Eric D188
Schwartz, Gary E. A175, A175K, A316, A716, A717
Schwarz, J. Conrad A926, A927
Schwarz, Jack B786, B787
Schwemer, Hermann B788
Sciacca, Michele F. A718
Scott, Cora A. D189
Scott, Linda J. D190
Scott, Patricia A282
Scott, R.D. B792
Scuderi, Richard J. D191
Scully, Malcolm A719
Seader, Ruth B399
Sechrist, Elsie B794
Seeman, William A591, A592, A720, A862
Seer, Peter A721, A722
Seferovich, S.I. A200
Seibert, Donna B482
Seibert, Mary A592
Seifert, Harvey B795, B796
Seiler, Gary A368, A724
Seiler, Victoria A724
Seitz, Manfred B324
Sekida, Katsuki B797
Sekiguchi, Shindai B798
Selye, Hans B75, B77, B78, M7
Sereda, Lynn A920, D192
Sethi, Amarjit S. A725-A728
Severeide, C.J. A729
Sexton, Thomas G. B799
Shackman, S. D193
Shafii, Mohammad A730-A734
Shah, Douglas B800
Shainberg, David A735
Shainberg, Lawrence A736
Shankar, Ravi M6
Shapiro, David A55, A793
Shapiro, Deane H., Jr. A314, A737-A745, A858, B801, B802, D194, R72, R73
Shapiro, Jonathan A746, D195
Sharma, K.N. A759
Shastri, Hari P. B803, B804
Shattock, Ernest H. B805
Shaw, Robert A747, D196
Shea, Gordon F. A748
Shear, Jonathan A749, A750
Shealy, C. Norman R74, R75
Shecter, Howard A751, D197

Shedd, Charlie W. B806
Shellman, Herbert F. D198
Shepherd, Massey H. A752
Sherman, Benna Z. D199
Shimano, Eido T. A753
Shimizu, H. A319
Shore, Jon R76, R77
Shyam, Swami B807
Siddheswarananda, Swami B808, B809
Siddhinathananda, Swami B616
Siegel, Larry M. A4, A5
Sieveking, Nicholas A17
Silva, José B810, B811
Silver, Joel A850, D200
Silverman, Franklin H. A513
Silverman, M.S. A480
Simard, Jean-Paul B812
Sime, Wesley E. A754
Simon, David B. A755
Simon, Jane A756
Simons, Robert A166
Simonton, C. R56
Simonton, S. R56
Sinari, Ramakant A758
Singh, Baldev A16
Singh, Charan B813, B814
Singh, Mohan A192
Sinha, S.N. A759
Sippel, Mary O. R78
Sipprelle, Carl N. A491
Sisley, R.C. D201
Sivananda, Swami B815-B822
Sivananda Radha, Swami B823, R79-R81
Slade, Herbert E.W. B824
Slater, Victor W. B825
Slobodin, Paula D202
Smail, Kenneth H. D203
Smedt, Marc de B826, B827
Smith, Adam A760, A761
Smith, Bradford B828, B829
Smith, Frank R76, R77
Smith, Huston M20, R82
Smith, J. Holland B203
Smith, Jonathan C. A762-A764, D204
Smith, Malcolm B830
Smith, Terrance R. A765
Smith, W.R. A386, A391-A393
Snell, Vincent A766
Snyder, Lee D. D205
Sober, Victoria Parker B831
Sobhana Dhammasudhi, Phra, Chao Khun see Phra Sobhana Dhammasudhi
Sohn, Robert R83

Solfvin, Gerald F. A691, A692, A767
Solomon, Earl G. A768
Solomon, Sheldon A369
Somdet Phra see Nyanasamvara
Soni, R.L. B832
Sonnet, André B833
Söpa, Geshe Lhündup B834, B835
Sorensen, Connie B406
Soskis, David A. A769
Spachtholz, Otto J. B836
Spanos, Nicholas P. A685, A770–A773
Spates, James L. A340
Speeth, Kathleen R. A774
Speyr, Adrienne B837
Spiegel, Victor R21
Spielberger, Charles D. A404
Spink, Peter B838
Spino, Mike A364, A775
Splett, Ingrid B840
Splett, Jörg B840
Sprenger, Werner B842
Stachel, Günter B562, B843
Staehelin, Balthasar B844, B845
Staff, Vera Stuart B846
Stahl, Carolyn B847
Stainbrook, Gene L. A367
Stam, Hendrikus J. A772
Stanford, Rex G. A776
Stanietz, Walter B848
Stark, Rodney A36
Steggles, Shawn A773
Steinbrecher, Edwin C. B849
Steiner, Rudolf B850
Steinert, Roger F. A70
Steinfeld, Ludwig B851
Steinmetz, Franz–Josef B62
Stek, Robert J. A777
Stephan, Ruth M31
Stern, Maureen A778
Sternbach, Richard A. A279
Sternberg, Marc B. D206
Stevens, Clifford A779
Stevens, Edward B852
Stevens, Mary M. A780
Stewart, C.R. D207
Stewart, Robert A. A781, A782
Stiffler, Paul D208
Stigsby, Bent A783
Stinissen, Wilfrid B340
Stivers, Robert M. A628
Stokes, M. A320
Stone, Justin F. B854–B857
Stone, Richard A. A784
Stone, William J. A106
Story, Francis B858

Strassman, R.J. A785
Straughn, R.A. B859
Street, Noel B860
Strenski, Ivan A786
Strobel, Urs A473
Stroebel, Charles F. A297, A297K, A297R, A786K
Stuhr, Chris B368
Stürmer, Ernst B861
Suarez, Verna W. D209
Subrahmanyam, Sarada A787, A788
Subramuniya, Master B862–B867
Sucksdorff, Arne M29
Sudbrack, Josef A789, B868–B870
Suess, Lynn A. B625
Suflita, Jeanette A790
Sujata, Anagarika B871
Sullivan, Russell H. D210
Sultan, S.E. A791, D211
Surwillo, Walter W. A792
Surwit, Richard S. A793
Susek, James A575
Sutphen, Dick R85, R86
Sutphen, Treena R86, R87
Sutton, David B. A795
Suzuki, Daisetz T. B872
Suzuki, Shunryu B873
Suzuki, Takao J. D212
Swan, Narmacaláya B115
Swann, Ingo R88
Swearer, Donald K. A794, B874
Swiecinski, David A575
Swinyard, Chester A. A795
Symons, R.G. A82

Tabak, Lawrence A796
Taimni, Iqbal K. B875
Takeuchi, Yoshinori B876
Tambiah, S.J. A797
Tanigawa, Yoshihiko B255
Target, George W. B877
Tart, Charles T. A798, B878–B881
Tarthang Tulku B544, B882–B884
Tasler, Susan A799
Tauler, Johannes B379, B380
Taylor, Rodney L. A800, A801
Teahan, John F. A802
Tebbetts, Charles B885
Tebecis, Andris K. A803
Techow, Ernst G. B225
Tellenbach, Hubert B686
Temple, Sebastian B886
Tenoli, G. A437
Tepperwein, Kurt B887
Teresia (a Matre Dei et Sanctissimo Vultu) B433, B888

Thaker, Mahendra H. B664
Thaker, Vimala B889-B894
Thelle, Notto R. A805
Thomas, Anne A256
Thomas, D. A806
Thomas, Jesse J. B896
Thomas, Klaus B897
Thomas, Steven N. B311
Thompson, Era B. A807
Thoreson, Richard W. A634
Throll, D.A. A808-A811
Throll, L.A. A811
Thubten Yeshe B898, B899
Thurston, Mark A. A666, B650, R89
Thyagarajan, V.A. B808
Tibblin, Gösta B812
Tilley, A.J. A51
Tilmann, Klemens B900-B906
Titmuss, Christopher B907
Tjioe, Robert The Tjong B935
Tjoa, André A813, A814
Toane, E.B. A822
Tönnies, S.E. A625
Toohey, Jack V. A106
Törber, Sibille A242, A824, D213
Torrance, E. Paul A160
Toubol, M. A463
Touyz, Stephen W. A236
Trausch, Clarence P. D214
Travis, Frederick A826
Traynham, Richard N. D215
Trende, Wulf B910
Trinder, John A56
Troeger, Thomas H. B911
Trotter, William D. A513
Truch, Steve A647, A827, B912
Trudinger, Ron B913
Trungpa, Chögyam B249, B407K, B914-B921, B973, R90
Trupo, Anthony see Norvell
Tsakonas, Frances A. D216
Tson-kha-pa Blo-bzan-grags-pa B922, B923
Tubesing, Donald A. R78
Tucker, Melvin J. B443
Tucker, Non M. A9
Tupin, Joe P. A265
Turnbull, Michael J. A828
Tyson, Paul D. A829
Tyson, Richard A337, B924, B925

Uchiyama, Kosho B926
Udupa, K.N. A223
Uellenberg, Gisela B881
Ugarte, Isabel B77

Umemoto, Takao A445
Unde, Bernhard B18
Upadhyay, R.K. A172

Vahia, N.S. A829K
Vajiranana, Parawahera B928
Valois, M.G. D217
Van de Wetering, Janwillem B929
van den Berg, W.P. see Berg, Willem P. van den
Van Dusen, Wilson A830
Van Esterik, John L. D218
Van Horn, Phyllis B. A831 see also Battelle, Phyllis
Van Nuys, David A832, A833
Van Over, Raymond B930
Vander, Arthur J. A544
VanderLaan, Eileen F. A394, A395
Varadachari, K.C. B931-B933
Varenne, Jean M. B827
Varni, James W. A834
Vattano, Anthony J. A835
Vaughan, Frances B58
Vele, F. A217
Vellal, B.G. B934
Verwaal, Ernst B935
Vianney, Jean B.M. B936
Vickerman, B.L. A897
Vidiloff, John S. A9
Vieg, Elizabeth L. A836
Vincent, J.D. A643, A643
Vining, Elizabeth G. B936K
Vishadananda, Swami B937
Vishnudevananda, Swami B938
Vivekananda, Swami B939-B944
Vizbara-Kessler, Barbara A837
Viziale, Enrica B945
Vogt, A. D219
Volin, Michael B946
Volk, Georg B947
Völker, Walther B948
Vonnegut, Kurt, Jr. A838
Vrolijk, Arie A839

Waalmanning, H.J. A840
Wachsmuth, D. D220
Wadler, Joyce A841
Wadlington, W.L. A354
Wagman, A.M.I. A108
Wagoner, Dale E. A850
Wainwright, Loudon A842
Waldemar, Charles B949
Waldenfels, Hans B950
Walder, Jeffrey M. D221
Walker, C.R. A843

Walker, Jay R. B924, B925
Wallace, Robert K. A71, A72,
  A203, A469, A610, A611, A617,
  A628, A844-A850, B951, D222
Walrath, Larry C. A851
Walsh, Roger N. A314, A852-
  A859, B58, B802
Walter, Eugen B952
Walter, Silja B953
Wampler, Larry D. A860, D223
Wandhoefer, A. A427, A861
Wangchuk, Anangavajra K. see
  Govinda, Anagarika
Wangyal, Geshe B954, B955
Warm, J.S. A862
Warrenburg, Stephen A628, A863
Warrenburg, William S. D224
Warshal, Debra A864, A865, D225
Washburn, Michael C. A866
Watts, Alan B956, B957, M1, M3,
  M16, R91-R93
Waxman, Jerry A867
Wayman, Alex A868
Webb, Jeffrey R. B138
Webb, R. A320
Weber, Michael A. A656
Webster, Nell B958
Wedemeyer, Inge von B959
Wedgwood, James I. B960
Weidelener, Herman B962, B963
Weinberger, David A869
Weiner, Arnold J. D226
Weiner, Donald E. D227
Weinless, M. A870
Weiss, Bardo B964
Weiss, C. A871, D228
Weiss, Hartmut B965
Weldon, James T. A872
Weldon, John A873, B966
Weldon, Wilson O. B970
Wellby, M.L. A82, A83
Welwood, John A874-A876, B516
Werner, O. A877
Weschke, Eugen B967
Wessberg, Harold W. A165
Wessler, Daniel B. B968
Wessler, M. Jenelyn B968
Wessling, N.F. A862
West, Michael A878-A883, A899,
  D229
West, Serene B969
Westcott, Mark A884
Wetering, Janwillem van de see
  Van de Wetering, Janwillem
Whalen, T.E. A336
Whalen, William J. A885
Wheeler, R.C. A469

Whelan, Joseph A886
White, John A887, B971-B973
White, Ken D. A888
White, Ronald G. A556
White-Eagle B167
Whitehead, Carleton B974
Whitehill, James B975
Whitman, Ardis A889
Whitman, Evelyn Ardis B976
Whitney, James M6
Wieck, Carl E. B977
Wienpahl, Paul A890, B978
Wijngaards, N.M. B979, B980
Wiking, Philippa B79
Wilberforce, Bertrand A.H. B981
Wilcox, Gregory G. A891
Wilcox, James M. A576
Willett, Robert F. B982
Williams, Gurney A892, A893
Williams, L.R. A894-A897
Williams, Lillian B983
Williams, Paul A898, A899
Willis, C.E. B37
Willis, Clara L.R. D230
Willis, D. A320
Willis, Janice D. B984
Willis, Robert J. A900
Wilson, Archie F. A372, A373, A385-
  A395, A847, A901
Wilson, Bradford A902
Wilson, Bryan A35
Wilson, Colin M16
Wilson, Jim B985
Wilson, Peter L. B909
Wilson, Robert A. B51
Winquist, W. Thomas A903
Wise, Charles C. B986
Wittenberg, Stephen A923
Witzenmann, Herbert B987
Wolf, W. R36
Wolkomir, Richard A904
Wong, Martin R. A905
Wood, Daniel T. D231
Wood, Ernest B988
Wood, Loring W. A127
Woodrum, Eric A906, A907
Woods, Marcella A863
Woodward, Kenneth L. A908
Woolfolk, Robert L. A126, A127,
  A465, A909-A912
Woolley-Hart, Ann A913
Wortz, Edward A914
Wunderli, Jürg B991, B992, B993

Yaego, David A915
Yamaoka, Haruo B994

Yang-ming, Wang A890
Yatiswarananda, Swami B995
Yergin, Daniel A916
Yesudian, Selva R. B996-B999
Yoder, Nanci S. D232
Yoga Cinmaya, Swami B664, B674
Yoga Laxmi B662, B666
Yogananda, Paramhansa B1000-B1003
Yogiji, Harbhajan S.K. B1004, B1005
Yoon, Byung-Yul D233
Young, James B. A367
Young, P.M. A83
Younger, Joel A917
Younts, Lee A692
Yu, Chun-Fang A919
Yuille, John C. A920

Zaffarano, Joan A921
Zaichkowsky, Leonard D. A922
Zamarra, John W. A923
Zarafonetis, Chris J.D. A72
Zarcone, Vincent P. A153
Zeff, Ted D234
Zeiger, B.F. B403
Zeiger, Berndt B790
Zifferblatt, Steven M. A744, A745
Zigler, Ronald A90
Zimmerman, W. A924
Zingle, Harvey W. A647
Zullo, Allan A925
Zurhausen, Herman B175
Zuroff, David C. A926, A927
Zweigenhaft, Richard L. D235

Abhidarma: A Cross-Cultural Model for the Psychiatric Application of Meditation A785
Abridgement of Meditations B99
Academic Psychology Bulletin A272
Academy of Management Journal A266
Accumulative Effects of Periodic Relaxation A688
Achtung, Mitmensch. Wohlstandsgesellschaft herausgenfordert B93
Acta Medica Scandinavica Supplementum A812
Activas Nervosa Superior A217
Active and Placebo Effects in Treatment of Moderate and Severe Insomnia A126
Acute Effects of Transcendental Meditation on Selected Psychophysiological Parameters and Athletic Performance D175
Adaptive and Therapeutic Aspects of Meditation A730
Addictive Behaviors A21, A633
Administrative Management A599, A921
Adrenocortical Activity During Meditation A389
Advantages of Meditation A590
Adverse Effects of Transcendental Meditation A620K
Agency Sales Magazine A339
Airway Conductance and Oxygen Consumption Changes Associated with Practice of the Transcendental Meditation Technique A155
Aktive Meditation B914
Aktive Meditation: Tibet Weisheit B915
Aktualität der Überlegungen Diderot zum Problem der Intuition D219
Alien Methods of Meditation A635
All About You B493
Alles über TM, Transzendentale Meditation B971
Alone with God B505
Alpha Enhancement as a Treatment for Pain A279
Alpha-Wellen B91
Als Mönch in Burma B649
Alterations in Blood Flow During Transcendental Meditation A386
Altered Attention Deployment in Meditation B23
Altered Awareness Activities for Receptive Learning B314
Altered Red Cell Metabolism in Transcendental Meditation A387
Altered States of Consciousness B878
Altered States of Consciousness and Hypnosis A271
A.M.: Anthrocentric Meditation B581
America A214, A229, A294, A399, A408, A602
American Benedictine Review A802
American Corrective Therapy Journal A32
American Ecclesiastical Review A243
American Journal of Chinese Medicine A101, A428
American Journal of Clinical Biofeedback A17

American Journal of Clinical Hypnosis   A167, A169, A519, A576, A851
American Journal of Medicine   A89
American Journal of Physiology   A393, A847
American Journal of Psychiatry   A18, A287, A414, A732, A739, A753, A852, A859, A927
American Journal of Psychoanalysis   A756
American Journal of Psychotherapy   A125, A135, A265, A306, A768
American Meditation and Beginning Yoga   B622
American Psychologist   A745
American School Board Journal   A710
American Scientist   A67
American Society for Psychical Research Journal   A630
American Theosophist   B20, S26
Analysis of Decreased Crime Trends in 56 Major U.S. Cities Due to the Transcendental Meditation Program   A292
Analysis of Sleep in Altered States of Consciousness by Classical Electro Encephalogram and Coherence Spectra   A45
Ancient Echoes   R17
Andacht   B696
Angenommen, Sie fühlen sich elend   B206
Anleitung zum innerlichen Gebet mit einer neuen Art von Betrachtungen B175
Anleitung zur Meditation   B520
Anleitungen zur Meditation   B308
Annals of Internal Medicine   A283, A300
Annals of the National Academy of Medical Sciences   A788
Annals of the New York Academy of Sciences   A57, A735, A795
Anthrocentric Meditation   B581
Anti-Frantic Alternative Series   R19, R20, R25, R28, R30, R31
Anweisungen für eine esoterische Schulung   B859
Anxiety Management in Alcoholics   A633
Anxiety Reduction Associated with Meditation   A666
Anxiety Reduction by Self-Regulation   A300
Anxiety Reduction Following Exercise and Meditation   A33
Application of Awareness Methods in Psychotherapy   A914
Applied Clinical Combination of Zen Meditation and Behavioral Self-Control Strategies   A744
Appraisal of Psychological Approach to Meditation   A405
Approach to Zen   B926
Approaches de la vie intérieure   B431
Approaches to Meditation   B20
Approaches to Self-Realization in Adult Education Through Meditation   D49
Appunti su l'orazione mentale   B128
Archaische Ekstase und asiatische Meditation mit ihren Beziehungen zum Abendland   B429
Archives de Sciences Sociales des Religions   A649
Archives of General Psychiatry   A153, A403, A675, A742, A909
Archives of Physical Medicine and Rehabilitation   A281
A.R.E. Journal   S8
Arrow-Dot Scores of Drug Addicts Selecting General or Yoga Therapy   A298
Art and Science of Meditation   B25
Art of Christian Alchemy   B171
Art of Christian Meditation   A588, B679
Art of Concentration and Centering   B722
Art of Contemplation   B956
Art of Divine Meditation   B352
Art of Ecstasy   B669

Art of Meditation   A889, B274, B276, M1, R1
Art of Meditation as Defined by the Hesychasts from the Critical Perspective of Psychology   D20
Art of Zen Meditation   B240
Arte da meditação   B828
Ascent   S30
Ashram Bulletin   S11
Asian Journal of Thomas Merton   B528, B535
Assessment of the Possible Relationship of the Practice of Meditation to Increases in Attentiveness in Learning   A370
Association Management   A366, A660
Ästhetischer Zustand und Transzendentales Bewusstsein   D163
Astrological Themes for Meditation   B724
At Your Own Pace Bibliography on Meditation   B135
Atavistic Regression as a Factor in the Remission of Cancer   A518
Atem und Meditation   B607
Atembuch   B691
Atlantean Meditation Course   B30
Atlantic   A760
Att komma till sig själv   B705
Attention and Expectations: Their Contribution to the Meditation Effect   D226
Attention au mystère   B657
Attention Style in Undergraduates as a Function of Experience with Transcendental Meditation   D199
Attention to the Mystery   B658
Attentional and Affective Concomitants of Meditation   A175
Au bout de la pensée   B378
Auditory Evoked Potentials and Transcendental Meditation   A51
Auditory Thresholds in Advanced Participants in the Transcendental Meditation Program   A145
Auf dem Wege zu Satori   B366
Aufbruch zur Ruhe   B18
Aufruf zur Meditation   B843
Aus der Mitte leben   B62
Australian Family Physician   A521, A526, A527, A531
Auswirkungen der Technik der TM auf den Muskeltonus   D111
Auswirkungen der TM auf die psychische und psychosomatische Befindlichkeit   D169
Auswirkungen der Transzendentalen Meditation auf die psychische und psychosomatische Befindlichkeit   B606
Autogene Meditation   B851
Autogenic Training   R14
Autogenics [and] Meditation   R53
Autonomic Correlates of Meditation and Hypnosis   A851
Autonomic Functioning in Subjects Practicing the Transcendental Meditation Technique   A891
Autonomic Responses to Stress   A103
Autonomic Stability and Transcendental Meditation   A606
Autorrealizacion   B682
Autre et les autres   B190
Available Mind   B565
Awakening of a New Consciousness in Zen   B872
Awakening of Kundalini   B283
Awakening of Zen   B872

Back to Godhead S17
Bala Books S17
Basic Fundamentals of Mind Control and Transcendental Meditation A130
Be Still and Contemplate A143
Beads of Truth S27
Becoming a Zen Practitioner A658
Befindlichkeitswirkungen der TM D213
Before You Reach Your Breaking Point A458
Beginning to Meditate
Beginning to See B871
Behavior Therapy A674, A744, A834, A910
Behavioral Alteration of Plasma Phenylalamine Concentration A385
Behavioral and Attitudinal Changes Resulting form a Zen Experience Workshop
    and Zen Meditation A737
Behavioral Increase of Cerebral Blood Flow A388
Behaviour Research and Therapy A162, A324, A465, A911
Behebung einiger sozialerzieherischer Probleme in der Schule D51
Belief Systems and Cancer R56
Beneficial Factors for Meditation B142
Beschauliches Leben inmitten der Welt B270
Beschouwend gebed B529
Best's Review A150
Beten, leben, meditieren B727
Betrachten. Ansätze, Erfahrungen u. Entfaltungen B952
Betrachtung des Körpers B592
Bewusstseinserweiterung durch Meditation B57
Beyond Biofeedback B290, B291
Beyond Ego B58
Beyond Health and Normality A314
Beyond Self and Time B597
Beyond the Physical Limits A775
Beyond the Relaxation Response B52K
Beyond TM B322
Beyond Transcendental Meditation B600
Bhagavad-Gita B482
Bhaktivedanta Scientific Institute Monograph Series S17
Bhavana in Contemporary Sri Lanka A495
Bible Tells You How B219
Biblical Appraisal of TM and Eastern Mysticism B541
Biochemical Effects of the TM and TM-Sidhi Program A436
Biochemische und physiologische Auswirkungen der Transzendentalen Medita-
    tion D149
Biofeedback-Aided Relaxation and Meditation in the Management of Hyperten-
    sion A637
Biofeedback and Meditation A922
Biofeedback and Meditation in the Treatment of Psychiatric Illness A297
Biofeedback and Self-Regulation A103, A274, A335, A582, A627, A637, A663,
    A912
Biofeedback, eine neue Moglichkeit zu heilen B291
Biofeedback, Fasting and Meditation B587, B588
Biofeedback Techniques in Clinical Practice R63
Bioinformacion, ayuno y meditacion B588
Biological Psychology A244
Bio-Meditation B567, B619
Biotranszendenz B209
Birds on the Mast M2
Bishop Joseph Hall and Protestant Meditation in Seventeenth-Century England

B352
Blair and Ketchum's Country Journal A111
Blindness and Yoga A363
Body Temperature Changes During the Practice of G Tum-mo Yoga A68
Bond of Power B621
Book of the Secrets B660
Books for Inner Development B643
Bouncing Up the Road to Nirvana A869
Bo[u]quet of Love B611
Brain Electrical Activity During Prayer A792
Breath Meditation in Treatment of Essential Hypertension A674
Breath Suspension During the Transcendental Meditation Technique A240
Breathing and Meditative Techniques R63
Brief Account of Zazen B987
Brief Guide to Meditation Temples of Thailand B408
Briefe zur geistigen Schulung B638
British Journal of Psychiatry A879
British Journal of Psychology A828
British Journal of Social and Clinical Psychology A882
British Medical Journal A19, A638, A806
British Psychological Society Bulletin see Bulletin of the British Psycho-
    logical Society
Bronchial Asthma in Adults A679
Brothers Speak A598
Buch der Besinnung. Anregungen zu Betrachtung u. priesterl. Werk B320
Bücher der flammenden Herzens. Meditation u. Kontemplation als Führer
    kosmischen Bewusstseins B771
Buddha-Invocation (Niem-Fo) as Koan A919
Buddha on Meditation and States of Consciousness, Part I A303
Buddha on Meditation and States of Consciousness, Part II A304
Buddhism: A Modern Perspective A84, A85
Buddhism and Behavior Modification A545
Buddhism and Meditation R90
Buddhism in the Life and Thought of Japan B872
Buddhist Devotion and Meditation B620
Buddhist Jhana A159, A325
Buddhist Meditation B166, B858
Buddhist Meditation and Christian Contemplative Prayer A178
Buddhist Meditation and the Middle View, from the Lam Rim Chenmo Tson-
    kha-pa B922
Buddhist Meditation in the Southern School B469, B470
Buddhist Meditation in Theory and Practice B928
Buddhist Meditation, Systematic and Practical B146
Buddhist Metaphysics and Existential Meditation A330
Buddhist Monastery as a Total Institution A547
Buddhist Philosophy and Its Effects on the Life and Thought of the Japanese
    People B872
Buddhist Studies in Honour of Walpola Rahula A495
Buddhist Transformation of Yoga B398
Buddhistisches Yogalehrbuch B116
Bulletin of the American Protestant Hospital Association A588
Bulletin of the British Psychological Society A881
Bulletin of the Psychonomic Society A10, A862
Business Week A234, A375
By the Ocean Meditation R87

Call of Silence B307
Calm and Clear B216, B544
Calm and Insight B397
Calming the Mind and Discerning the Real B922
Camino de la libertad B122, B123, B124
Can a Christian Practice TM A218
Can Intelligence Be Taught B799
Can Meditation Improve Your Management Performance A479
Can TM Work for You A841
Canadian Business Magazine A799
Canadian Journal of Public Health A726
Canadian Medical Association Journal A113, A822
Carmino derecho para el cielo B239
Cartography of the Ecstatic and Meditative States A251
Case Against TM in the Schools B617
Case for Extrovert Meditation A259
Case for Meditation A468
Catechist A410, A790
Caution: Meditation Can Hurt A344
Cayce Readings Extracts S8
Celebrating the Dawn B593
Cells for Life B913
Censurs of Certaine Propositions B99
Centering: The Power of Meditation B443
Centering, Your Guide to Inner Growth B443
Centerscape R18
Cerebral Laterality and Meditation A224K
Cerebral Lateralization, Bimodal Consciousness, and Related Developments in
    Psychiatry A2
Ceylon Medical Journal A478
Chain of Compassion B872
Chakra Balancing and Energizing R86
Chakra Meditation R86
Challenge of Eastern Meditation A789
Change A232
Change in Cardiac Output During Transcendental Meditation as Measured by
    Noninvasive Impedance Plethysmography A865
Changes in Alveolar Carbon Dioxide Tension During Meditation A582
Changes in Inflammation in Persons Practicing the Transcendental Meditation
    Technique A425
Changes in Psychological Functioning Through Contemplative Meditation
    D151K
Changes in Skin Resistance in Subjects Resting, Reading, Listening to Music,
    or Practicing the Transcendental Meditation Technique A878
Changes in Subjective Meditation Experience During a Short-Term Project
    A429
Changes in Suggestibility Following Alert Hypnosis and Concentrative Medita-
    tion D232
Chave dos mistérios B115
Chemistry A550
Cheops Pyramidal Form: Its Influence Upon Alpha and Theta Production
    During Meditation D90
Chief Guru of the Western World A462
Child's Garden of Yoga B311
Choose Your Own Mantra B426
Christentum in der antiken Welt B158
Christian Alternative to Transcendental Meditation B806

Christian Century A40, A75, A118, A204, A275, A338, A397, A453
Christian Growth Through Meditation B600
Christian Meditation B162, B489, D47, R3
Christian Meditation and Biofeedback as Psychotherapeutic Agents in the
    Treatment of Essential Hypertension D36
Christian Meditation, Its Art and Practice B637
Christian Meditation: It's the Real Thing A438
Christian Meditation the Better Way B547
Christian Ministry A711
Christian Mysticism B282
Christian Response to Transcendental Meditation B301
Christian Yoga B189
Christian Zen A399, B373
Christianity Today A333, A334, A706, A707, A817
Christliche Bildmeditation B714, B715
Christliche Meditation B167
Christliche Meditation für alle B194
Christliche Tiefenmeditation B432
Christus und die Gurus B159
Church and State A209
Ciena de la meditación B743
Circle of Creation S4
Cistercian Studies A147, A488, A501
Clairvoyance and the Transcendental Meditation Sidhi Program D82
Classic Perspectives of Meditation A737K
Clear Light S22
Clear Light Series B407K
Clergy Review A193, A255
Client and Audience Cults in America A36
Climb the Joyous Mountain B854
Clinical and Biochemical Effects of the TM Program A787
Clinical and Experimental Pharmacology and Physiology A80
Clinical Applications of Meditation and Behavioral Self-Control Strategies R72
Clinical Research A372
Clinical Treatments of Depression D166
Clinical Use of "Mindfulness" Meditation Techniques in Short-Term Psycho-
    therapy A180
Clinically Standardized Meditation (CSM) and Counselor Behavior D91
Clouds: Music for Relaxation R2
Clouds: New Music for Relaxation R2
CM, Christian Meditation B162
Cognitive Therapy and Research A33
Coherent Field Effects in Collective Consciousness Measured by the EEG
    A611
Collected Writings on Shin Buddhism B872
College English A558
College Student Development and Transcendental Meditation D14
College Student Journal A22
Color Therapy Meditation R87
Comfort Zone R19
Comme une terre desséchée B178
Comment méditer B172
Comment on Samatha, Samapatti, and Dhyana in Ch'an A136
Commerce America A819
Common Mystic Prayer B210
Commonweal A586
Comparative Effectiveness of Patterned Biofeedback Versus Meditation Train-

ing on EMG and Skin Temperature Changes   A162

Comparative Effects of Training in External and Internal Concentration on Two Counseling Behaviors   A469K

Comparative Effects of Zen Focusing and Muscle Relaxation Training on Selected Experimental Variables   D124

Comparative Evaluation of Three Relaxation Training Procedures   D29K

Comparative Multidisciplinary Investigation Into Three Hypothetical Altered States of Consciousness   D59

Comparative Study of the Effect of Transcendental Meditation (T.M.) and Shavasana Practice on Cardiovascular System   A31

Comparison Between Meditating Subjects and Non-Meditating Subjects on Time Experience and Human Field Motion   D137K

Comparison of a Holistic and a Social Skills Training Program for Schizophrenics   D136

Comparison of Aerobic Exercise, Anaerobic Exercise and Meditation on Multidimensional Stress Measures   D105

Comparison of Cardiovascular Biofeedback, Neuromuscular Biofeedback, and Meditation in the Treatment of Borderline Essential Hypertension   A793

Comparison of Exercise and Meditation in Reducing Physiological Response to Stress   A754

Comparison of Heart Rate, Respiration, and Galvanic Skin Response Among Meditators, Relaxers, and Controls   A165

Comparison of Self-Concepts of Transcendental Meditators and Nonmeditators A596

Comparison of Somatic Relaxation and EEG Activity in Classical Progressive Relaxation and Transcendental Meditation   A863

Comparison of the Effectiveness of Progressive Relaxation Training and the Relaxation Response Technique as a Function of Perceived Locus of Control of Reinforcement in Tension Reduction   D202

Comparison of the Transcendental Meditation Technique to Various Relaxation Procedures   A168

Comparison of the Usefulness of Self-Hypnosis and a Meditational Relaxation Technique   A73

Comparison of Theravada and Zen Buddhist Meditational Methods and Goals A418

Comparison of Transcendental Meditation and Progressive Relaxation in Reducing Anxiety   A806

Comparison of Two Types of Meditation to Reduce Stress in a Teaching Population   D98

Comparisons of Feelings During and After Long Periods of Transcendental Meditation   D127

Compassionate Teacher   B542

Complete How-To Guide to the Famous TM Method of Total Relaxation   B701

Complete Meditation   B415

Complete Yoga Book   B327

Comprehensive Psychiatry   A297

Comprehensive Treatise on Mantra-Sastra   B818

Computer Decisions   A458

Concentration, a Guide to Mental Mastery   B733, B735

Concentration: An Approach to Meditation   B988

Concentration, an Outline for Practical Study   B733

Concentration and Meditation   B350, B568, B613, B815

Concentration or Insight   A326

Concept of Practice in San-lun Thought   A435

Conference Board Record   A267

Confinia Psychiatrica   A254

Congressional Record   A301

Consciousness Alteration and Fear of Death   A280
Consciousness Disciplines and the Behavioral Sciences   A852
Constructive Action for Good Self Health   S3
Contemplation and Action in World Religions   B165
Contemplation Is Companionship   A886
Contemplative Meditation for All   B502
Contemplative Prayer   B530, B534
Contemplative Prayer in the Christian Tradition   A408
Contemporary Review   A178
Contingent Negative Variation in Meditation   A463
Contingent Negative Variation Studies During Meditation   A643
Continuous Measurement of O_2 Consumption and CO_2 Elimination During a
    Wakeful Hypometabolic State   A70
Control and Freedom   A794
Control of Migraine Headache by Behavioral Self-Management   A556
Controlled Study of the Influences of Transcendental Meditation on a Specific
    Value of the H-Reflex (Hoffmann) Recruitment Curve and the Surface
    EMG   A137
Conversation with Christ   B710
Cooking for Consciousness   S4
Coping with Stress   A415
Coronary Risk Factor Reduction Through Biofeedback-Aided Relaxation and
    Meditation   A640
Corrective and Social Psychiatry and Journal of Behavior Technology, Meth-
    ods and Therapy   A470
Cosmic Consciousness   R10
Cosmological and Performative Significance of a Thai Cult of Healing Through
    Meditation   A797
Cosmopolitan   A337
Cost Effective Stress Management Training   A748
Council on the Study of Religion Bulletin   A412
Course in Meditation   B351
Course on Direct Enlightenment   B330
Court Challenge to TM   A397
Covenant   S8
Creating an Ideal Society   B480
Creative and Altered States of Consciousness   A756
Creative Child and Adult Quarterly   A160
Creative Intelligence and the Teaching of Maharishi Mahesh Yogi   B127
Creative Meditation   B974
Creative Meditation and Multi-Dimensional Consciousness   B285
Creative Self-Transformation Through Meditation   B615
Creative Visualization   B259
Creativity and the Zen Koan   A445
Criminal Justice and Behavior   A4, A5, A670
Crimson Dawn   S4
Critical Analysis of the Jhanas in Theravada Buddhist Meditation   D84
Cross and Crown   A635
Cross Currents   A161
Cultivating Contemplation   A602
Cultural Interpretation of Canonical Paradox: Lay Meditation in a Central
    Thai Village   D218
Culture, Medicine, and Psychiatry   A797
Curé d'Ars, sa pensée, son coeur   B936
Currents in Theology and Mission   A605
Cycle of Process Meditation   B648
Cycles in Buddhist Philosophy   R91

Dagende niets B 929
Darshana International A 644
Dawn Magazine S 14
Dawn of a New Age B 703
Dawn of the Age of Enlightenment A 607
Dawn Series B 25
Dbu ma'i lta khrid zab mo B 216
De la méditation orientale à l'oraison chrétienne B 178
Decreased Alcohol Intake Associated with the Practice of Meditation A 57
Decreased Blood Pressure in Hypertensive Subjects Who Practiced Meditation A 71
Decreased Blood Pressure in Pharmacologically Treated Hypertensive Patients Who Regularly Elicited the Relaxation Response A 69K
Decreased Drug Abuse with Transcendental Meditation A 72
Decreased Drug Use and Prevention of Drug Use Through the Transcendental Meditation Program A 407
Decreased $\dot{V}O_2$ Consumption During Exercise with Elicitation of the Relaxation Response A 64
Decreased Respiratory Rate During the Transcendental Meditation Technique A Replication A 38
Deep Relaxation R 74
Dental Hygiene A 780
Dental Student A 569
Dental Survey A 567
Descriptive Study of Beginning Transcendental Meditators D 64
Dev Shastra B 764
Develop Spiritually, Unfold Psychically B 860
Development and Personality in Practitioners of the Transcendental Meditation Program in Comparison to Members of Other Programs in a Male Inmate Population A 12
Development of a Christian Approach to Sport Meditation D 68
Development of the Transcendental Meditation Movement A 906
Devout Young Series M 26
Dhyana B 608
Dhyana Mandala B 388
Dhyana, the Yoga of Meditation B 260
Dhyana Vahini B 750
Dhyana, Wege d. Versenkung B 609
Dhyana Yoga B 816
Dhyanayoga in the Bhagavadgita B 201
Dialog A 341, A 915
Dialogue on Meditation B 510
Diamond Light B 984
Diamond Light of the Eastern Dawn B 984
Die to Live B 813
Differential Effects of Meditation and Systematic Desensitization on Specific and General Anxiety D 57
Difficulties in Mental Prayer B 92
Dimensionality in Meditative Experience A 430
Dimensionless Dimension B 661
Dimensions in Health Service A 727, A 728
Dimensions of the Meditative Experience A 620
Directory of Ashrams in India and Abroad B 212
Discipleship in the New Age B 35, B 37
Discourses on "Vigyana Bhairava Tantra" B 660
Discover Yourself B 100, B 101, B 104, B 107
Discovering Christian Meditation B 307

Discriminating Groups of Hypnotized and Meditating Subjects from Normal
    Subjects with the Altered States of Consciousness Inventory D22K
Disharmony About TM A118
Do-It-Yourself Book of Instruction in Varied Meditation Techniques B855
Doctor's View of TM A443
Doctrine and Life A163, A411
Doctrine of Meditation in the Hinayana A84
Doctrine of Meditation in the Mahayana A85
Does an In-Depth Transcendental Meditation Course Effect Change in the
    Personalities of the Participants A647
Does Transcendental Meditation Training Affect Grades A129
Do-in B706
Do-in: Eastern Massage and Yoga Techniques B707
Do-in: The Philosophy B708
Doing Something About Stress A516
Door of Liberation B954, B955
Doorway to Meditation B94, B96
Double Mantra Technique A509
Dpyad sgom 'khor lo ma B216
Drug Abuse A72
Drug Forum A498, A715
Drunk on the Divine B752
Durch die Sinne zum Sinn B462
Durch Krankheit zur Genesung B251
Durch Yoga zum eigenen Selbst B475
Dying for Enlightenment B297
Dynamic Way of Meditation B207
Dynamics of Jain Meditation B138
Dynamics of Meditation B662, B669

Eagle and Multi-Worlds R85
Eagle Meditation R85
East Asian Pastoral Review A41
Eastern and Western Approaches for Mind-Body Integration D121
Eastern Buddhist A496, A559
Eastern Churches Review A121
Eastern Peace R20
Eastern Toe in the Stream of Consciousness A305
Eastern Wisdom and Modern Life Series M24
Easy Guide to Meditation B180, B181
Easy Method of Mental Prayer B981
Eating and Living the TM Way B958
Ebony A474, A807
Ecstatic Pentecostal Prayer and Meditation A190
Education Digest A209
Education: Meditation/Contemplation/Recollection A563
Educational Horizons A837
Educational Technology A199
EEG Analysis of Spontaneous and Induced States of Consciousness A46
EEG and Meditation A42
EEG and Transcendental Meditation A437
EEG Coherence During the Transcendental Meditation Technique A473
EEG in Meditation and Therapeutic Touch Healing A108
EEG Response to Photic Stimulation in Persons Experienced at Meditation
    A899
Effect of a Three Month Residence Course Upon the Personalities of Experi-

enced Meditators A811

Effect of Benson's Relaxation Response on the Anxiety Levels of Lebanese Children Under Stress A179

Effect of Coherent Collective Consciousness on the Weather A668

Effect of Explicit Expectations on Initial Meditation Experiences A912

Effect of Hypnosis and Meditation on State and Trait Anxiety and Locus of Control D179

Effect of Meditation on Serum Cholesterol and Blood Pressure A151

Effect of Spiritual Exercises on the Integration of Self-System A701

Effect of Stress and Meditation on Salivary Protein and Bacteria A575

Effect of Tai Chi Ch'uan Meditation on the Presence of Facilitative Factors in the Psychotherapist D55

Effect of the Practice of Meditation by Eight to Eleven Year Old Children on Their Trait Anxiety and Self-Esteem D29

Effect of the Practice of the Transcendental Meditation Program on the Degree of Neuroticism as Measured by DMT (Defense Mechanism Test) A396

Effect of the Regular Practice of the Transcendental Meditation Technique on Behavior and Personality A709

Effect of the Relaxation Response on the Positive Personality Characteristics of Paraprofessional Counselors D28

Effect of the Science of Creative Intelligence Course on High School Students A434

Effect of the Transcendental Meditation Program on Compensatory Paradoxical Sleep A551

Effect of the Transcendental Meditation Program on Self-Actualization, Self-Concept, and Hypnotic Susceptibility A693

Effect of the Transcendental Meditation Program on Short-Term Recall Performance A77

Effect of the Transcendental Meditation Program on Sleeping and Dreaming Patterns A276

Effect of the Transcendental Meditation Program on the Organization of Thinking and Recall A552

Effect of the Transcendental Meditation Program Upon University Academic Attainment A149

Effect of the Transcendental Meditation Technique on Anxiety Level A197

Effect of Transcendental Meditation on Heart Rate Response to a Startle A320

Effect of Transcendental Meditation on Iconic Memory A274

Effect of Transcendental Meditation on Language Learning and GPA A207

Effect of Transcendental Meditation on Mild and Moderate Hypertension A7

Effect of Transcendental Meditation on Muscle Tone A413

Effect of Transcendental Meditation on Right Hemispheric Functioning A627

Effect of Transcendental Meditation on Self-Actualization, Self-Concept, and Hypnotic Susceptibility D181

Effect of Transcendental Meditation on Trait Anxiety and Self-Esteem D21

Effect of Transcendental Meditation Upon Bronchial Asthma A372

Effect of Transcendental Meditation Upon Modifying the Cigarette Smoking Habit A622, D168

Effect of Two Relaxation Techniques on Anxiety, Self-Concept and Personal Growth D193

Effect of Zen Meditation on the Valence of Intrusive Thoughts D119

Effective Test Taking A421, D115

Effectiveness of Meditation on Selected Measures of Self-Actualization D52

Effects of a Group Meditation Technique Upon Degree of Test Anxiety and Level of Digit-Letter Retention in High School Students D131

Effects of a Meditative-Relaxation Exercise on Non-Attending Behaviors of Behaviorally Disturbed Children A677

Effects of a Stress Reduction Program on Type A Behavior Pattern, Blood Pressure, Muscle Tension, and Relaxation Practice Time D108

Effects of a Transcendental Meditation Program on Personality and Arousal D117

Effects of a Trans-rational Training Program on Affective Sensitivity D85

Effects of a Western Meditation on a Measure of Self-Actualization D15

Effects of a 'Zen Meditation-Behavior Self-Management' Training Package in Treating Methadone Addiction D194

Effects of Behavior Therapy, Self-Relaxation, and Transcendental Meditation on Cardiovascular Stress Response A664

Effects of Biofeedback and Relaxation Response Training on Submaximal Exercise D182

Effects of Experimental Meditation, Relaxation Training, and Electromyographic Feedback on Physiological and Self-Report Measures of Relaxation and Altered States of Consciousness D215

Effects of Hatha Yoga and Mantra Meditation on the Psychological Health and Behavior of Incarcerated Males D34

Effects of Hypnosis, Relaxation Training, or Music on State Anxiety and Stress in Female Athletes D77

Effects of Induced Affect and Relaxation Response Training on the Self-Management of Cigarette Smoking D60

Effects of Intensive Meditation on Sex-Role Identification A743

Effects of Mantra Meditation and Progressive Relaxation on Self-Actualization, State and Trait Anxiety, and Frontalis Muscle Tension D227

Effects of Meditation and Relaxation Upon Alcohol Use in Male Social Drinkers A501K

Effects of Meditation on Anxiety and Chemical Dependency A905

Effects of Meditation on Brain-Stem Auditory Evoked Potentials A511

Effects of Meditation on Elementary School Students D1

Effects of Meditation on General Anxiety, Test Anxiety, and Non-Verbal Intelligence D191

Effects of Meditation on Personality and Values A181

Effects of Meditation on Psychological and Physiological Measures of Anxiety A99

Effects of Meditation on Selected Measures of Human Potential D165

Effects of Meditation on Self-Concept D120

Effects of Meditation Upon Peer Counselor Effectiveness D72

Effects of Meditation Versus Professional Reading on Students' Perceptions of Paraprofessional Counselors' Effectiveness A343

Effects of Meditation (Zazen) Upon Selected Dimensions of Personal Development D42

Effects of Progressive Relaxation and Meditation on Cognitive and Somatic Manifestations of Daily Stress A911

Effects of Progressive Relaxation and Meditation on Mood Stability and State Anxiety in Alcoholic Inpatients D95

Effects of Progressive Relaxation, Heart Rate Feedback, and Content-Specific Meditation on Anxiety and Performance in a Class Situation D231

Effects of Progressive Relaxation Training and Meditation on Autonomic Arousal in Alcoholics D170

Effects of Selected Elements of Meditation on Self-Actualization, Locus of Control, and Trait Anxiety D177

Effects of Self-Induced Relaxation on Autonomic Responses and Subjective Distress of High- and Low-Neuroticism Scorers to Aversive Baby Cries D97

Effects of Sensitivity Training and Transcendental Meditation on Perception of Others A368

Effects of Short-Term Meditation Practice on Hypnotic Responsivity A770

Effects of Sleep Deprivation on the Physiological Changes Induced by Transcendental Meditation   D201

Effects of the Age of Enlightenment Governor Training Courses on Field Independence, Creativity, Intelligence, and Behavioral Flexibility   A613

Effects of the TM-Sidhi Program on Rigidity-Flexibility   D6

Effects of the TM Technique on Concept Formation, Autonomic Stability and EEG Coherence   D46

Effects of the TM Technique on Fractionated Reflex and Reaction Times   D88

Effects of the Transcendental Meditation and TM-Sidhi Program on the Aging Process   A848

Effects of the Transcendental Meditation Program on Anxiety, Drug Abuse, Cigarette Smoking, and Alcohol Consumption   A460

Effects of the Transcendental Meditation Program on Anxiety, Neuroticism, and Psychotocism   A694

Effects of the Transcendental Meditation Program on Athletic Performance   A676

Effects of the Transcendental Meditation Program on Drug Abusers   A105

Effects of the Transcendental Meditation Program on Levels of Hostility, Anxiety, and Depression   A336

Effects of the Transcendental Meditation Program on Perceptual Style   A645

Effects of the Transcendental Meditation Program on Strength of the Nervous System, Perceptual Reactance, Reaction Time and Auditory Threshold   D188

Effects of the Transcendental Meditation Program on the Exercise Performance of Patients with Angina Pectoris   A923

Effects of the Transcendental Meditation Program on Trait Anxiety   A778

Effects of the Transcendental Meditation Program on Work Attitudes and Behavior   A268

Effects of the Transcendental Meditation Technic on the Psychological and Psychosomatic State   A624

Effects of the Transcendental Meditation Technique on a Measure of Self-Actualization   D106

Effects of the Transcendental Meditation Technique on Mood and Body Sensation   A824

Effects of the Transcendental Meditation Technique on Normal and Jendrassik Reflex Time   A864

Effects of the Transcendental Meditation Technique on Visual Perception and Verbal Problem-Solving   D56

Effects of the Transcendental Meditation Technique Upon a Complex Perceptual-Motor Task   A92

Effects of the Transcendental Meditation Technique Upon Adolescent Personality   A808

Effects of the Transcendental Meditation Technique Upon Auditory Discrimination   A653

Effects of TM on Concurrent Heart Rate, Peripheral Blood Pulse Volume, and the Alpha Wave Frequency   A483

Effects of Transcendental Meditation and Masker Uncertainty on the Detection of Masked Psychoacoustic Signal   D200

Effects of Transcendental Meditation and Muscle Relaxation on Trait Anxiety, Maladjustment, Locus of Control, and Drug Use   A926

Effects of Transcendental Meditation, Electromyographic (EMG) Biofeedback Relaxation, and Conventional Relaxation on Vasoconstriction, Muscle Tension, and Stuttering   D3

Effects of Transcendental Meditation on Anxiety and Self-Concept   A331

Effects of Transcendental Meditation on Blood Pressure   A91

Effects of Transcendental Meditation on Fine Motor Skill   A897

Effects of Transcendental Meditation on Periodontal Tissue   A724

Effects of Transcendental Meditation on Rotary Pursuit Skill A896
Effects of Transcendental Meditation on Self-Identity Indices and Personality A828
Effects of Transcendental Meditation on Several Psychological Variables Associated with Teacher Effectiveness A827
Effects of Transcendental Meditation on the Physiological Functions in Chinese People A475
Effects of Transcendental Meditation on the Reading Achievement of Learning Disabled Youngsters D148
Effects of Transcendental Meditation on the Self-Concept as Measured by the Tennessee Self-Concept Scale D217
Effects of Transcendental Meditation (TM) and the TM Sidhis Program on Verbal and Figural Creativity (TTCT), Auditory Creativity (S & I), and Hemispheric Dominance (SOLAT) D10
Effects of Transcendental Meditation Upon Ego Permissiveness, Anxiety and Neuroticism D78
Effects of Transcendental Meditation Versus Resting on Physiological and Subjective Arousal A369
Effects of Two Selected Relaxation Techniques on Levels of Anxiety, Stress, and Underwater Performance of Beginning SCUBA Diving Students D81
Effects of Yoga-Therapy on Conflict Resolution, Self-Concept, and Emotional Adjustment D104
Effects of Zen Meditation on Anxiety Reduction and Perceptual Functioning A302
Effects on a Measure of Self-Actualization of Adding a Meditation Exercise to a Sensitivity Group--Group Facilitator Training Program D221
Effekt der Transzendentalen Meditation auf Adipositas D153
Efficacy of Electromyographic Biofeedback and the Relaxation Response in the Treatment of Situation-Specific Anxiety D198
Efficacy of Meditation of Reported Anxiety with Controls for Expectancy D75
Efficacy of Progressive Relaxation in Systematic Desensitization and a Proposal for an Alternative Competitive Response A324
Efficacy of Raj Yoga in the Light of Sahaj Marga B675
Ego Development, Personality and Behavioral Change in Inmates Practicing the Transcendental Meditation Technique or Participating in Other Programs D2
Einfache Einführung in die Meditation B181
Einfluss der Meditation auf die Veränderung psychotherapeutisch relevanter Persönlichkeitsmerkmale D123
Einfluss der TM auf die Faktoren der mensclichen Arbeitskraft D96
Einführung in die Meditation B962
Einführung in die Musikmeditation B42
Einsatz von TM in der Rehabilitation Strafgeganger D151
Einstellungs und Verhaltensänderung bei Drogenkonsumenter nach TM D74
Einübung ins Meditieren am Neuen Testament B464, B465
Elected Silence: New Jersey School Meditation A229
Electroencephalographic Findings During Mantra Meditation A783
Electroencephalographic Phase Coherence, Pure Consciousness, Creativity, and Transcendental Meditation Sidhi Experiences A614
Electroencephalographic Study of the Zen Meditation (Zazen) A406
Electroencephalography and Clinical Neurophysiology A16, A42, A43, A45, A51, A349, A463, A643, A783, A899
Electronographic Study of Psychic States Obtained by Yoga A222
Electrophysiological Changes During Periods of Respiratory Suspension During the Transcendental Meditation Technique A29
Electrophysiological Characteristics During Transcendental Meditation and Napping A171

Electrophysiology of Transcendental Meditation A642
Elementary Guide to Vipassana Meditation, Preferably for Beginners B142
Empathy and Mindfulness A714
Encyclopedia of American Religions B519
End of the Day Relaxation R78
Endocrine Changes in Relaxation Procedures A83
Endocrine Changes in Transcendental Meditation A80, A81
Endocrinological Changes Following Instruction in the TM-Sidhi Program A877
Energy Beyond Thought B391
English Recusant Literature, 1558-1640 B43, B99
Enlightenment in Nursing Through Transcendental Meditation A682
Enlightenment of the Mind and Total Fitness B338
Enseigmement oral du bouddhisme au Tibet B654
Entdecke dich selbst B101
Entdeckungen d. inneren Welt nach Johannes Tauler B380
Enter the Quiet B975
Entspannung, Sammlung, Meditation B947
Epistemologia A661
Erfahrungen eines Christen mit der Zen-Meditation B433
Erfahrungen mit dem TM-Sidhi-Program B403
Erfahrungen mit Meditation B747
Ergebnisse meditativer Arbeit B963
ERIC A207, A211, A263, A370, A483, A507, A703, A740, A754, A860, B15
Erlösung im Lotussitz B683
Erwachen der Seele. Meditation u. Kontemplation als Führer zum neuen Leban
  B772
Escape from Stress B428
ESP and Changed States of Consciousness Induced by Meditation A619
ESP Ganzfeld Experiment with Transcendental Meditators A630
Esquire A237, A838
Essays in Zen Buddhism B872
Essence of Buddhism B872
Essentials of Meditation B491
Essentials of Zen Buddhism B872
Eternal Message B663
Ethiek van verlichting B780
Ethnos A156
Etre Jésus B827
Evaluation of Transcendental Meditation as a Method of Reducing Stress
  A543
Evangelical Religion and Meditation A277
Everyone's Way to Meditation B975
Everything Is Within You B863
Everything You Want to Know About TM, Including How to Do It B971, B972
Evolution of the Human Soul B937
Evolutionary Model of Meditation Research A852K
Evolutionsstrategie D125
Examination of the Teaching of Maharishi Mahesh Yogi B127
Excerpt from The Guide Meditation B849
Executive's Guide to Living with Stress A234
Exercise and Meditation as a Lifestyle Intervention for Addictive Behaviors
  D144
Exercise, Meditation and Anxiety Reduction A32
Exercises of Personality B465
Expectation and Meditation A185
Experience in Buddhist Meditation A419
Experience, Knowledge and Understanding A424

Experience of Insight B279
Experiences in an American Zen Community B929
Experientia A392, A508
Experiential Empathy A154
Experiment in Mindfulness B805
Experimental Analysis of the Effects of the Transcendental Meditation Technique on Reaction Time A616
Experimental Investigation Into the Effectiveness of Some Yogic Variables as a Mechanism of Change in the Value-Attitude System A431
Experimental Investigation of Psychological Aspects of Meditation A444
Experimental Meditation A182
Experimental Neurology A849
Experimental Study of Cognitive Control and Arousal Processes During Meditation A759
Exploration de la conscience B355
Exploration of the Social Consequences and Implications of a Revelationary Movement D143
Explorations in East/West Psychology B516
Explorations in Meditation and Contemplation B795
Explorations in the Use of Group Meditation with Persons in Psychotherapy D155
Exploratory Study of Individual Differences in Response to a Zen Meditation Exercise D145
Exploratory Study of the Use of Meditation Alone and in Combination with Hypnosis in Clinical Dentistry A565
Exposition of the Gayatri B645
Expository Times A843
Extent to Which Relaxation Techniques Are Taught at Community Colleges in California A507
Eye Movement During Transcendental Meditation A803

Face à Dieu B295
Face to Face B694
Faces of India Series M9
Faces of Meditation B238
Facilitation of Creativity Through Meditational Procedures A318
Facing God B653
Facts on Transcendental Meditation A122, A621, A716
Family Meditation A227
Fate A562
Federal Court Upholds Minute of Silent Prayer or Meditation in Public Schools A258
Federation Proceedings A469
Field Interview with a Theravada Teaching Master A604
Field of Zen B872
Fields Within Fields A887
Fifth Dimension B11
Fifth Dimension and the Future of Mankind B11
50 techniques de méditation B526
Filocalia B244
Finale Mensch B844
Finding the Quiet Mind B235K
Finding Your Way to the Real World B193
Fine Art of Meditation A779, B864
Finite State Model for Meditation Phenomena A867
First Step in God Realization B59

First Steps Towards Advanced Meditation R66
Five Great Mantrams of the New-Age B744
Flight of the Alone to the Alone B664
Flow of Zen M3
Folia Psychiatrica et Neurologica Japonica A803
Form of Intensive Meditation Associated with the Regression of Cancer A519
Fortune A516
Fostering Transcendental Meditation Using Bio-Feedback Eliminates Hoax and
    Restores Creditability to Art A131
Foundations of Mindfulness B249
Foundations of Practical Magic B680
Foundations of Tibetan Mysticism B286
Four Noble Truths of Buddhism Related to Behavior Therapy A546
Four Yogas B31
Fourteen Lessons in Raja Yoga B817
Franciscan Meditation A158
Frankfurter Paradiesgärtlein als Meditationsbild B461
Franziskanische Meditation B642
Freedom from Crime Through the TM-Sidhi Program B430
Freedom in Meditation B131, B132
Friheten är din B19
From India with 'Shakti' A383
From Intellect to Intuition B34
From Meditation to Contemplation A618
From Zen to the Cloud of Unknowing A506
Frontal EEG Coherence, H-Reflex Recovery, Concept Learning, and the TM-
    Sidhi Program A203
Frontier A443
Frontiers of the Spirit B253
Führung der Kinder zur Meditation B900
Führung zur Meditation B901, B904
"Fukan Zazen-Gi" and the Meditation Teachings of the Japanese Zen Master
    Dogen D23
Full Moon Magic S6
Further Examination of the Quality of Changes in Creative Functioning Re-
    sulting from Meditation (Zazen) Training A160
Further Experience with Therapy Based Upon Concepts of Patanjali in the
    Treatment of Psychiatric Disorders A829K
Future of Mankind B11

Garuda B249
Gateway to Light B794
Gateway to Wisdom B71, B73
Gateways Into Light B577
Gayatri B875
Gayatri Mantra B758
Gayatri Rahasya; or, An Exposition of the Gayatri B645
Gebet und Hingabe, Ausführungen der Heiligen B765
Gedrag A74, A813, A839
Geheimnis der Meditation B688, B690
Geheimnis der Stille B692
Geheimnis des Kaiser-Yoga B949
Geheimnisse der chinesischen Meditation B471
Geheimnisvolle Helfer in dir B773
Geist, der in uns lebt B275
Geist der Wahrheit B652

Geistestraining durch Achtsamkeit B589
Geistheilung durch sich selbst B887
Geistige Fundament des Schulungsweges. Wie stärken wir unser Ich B638
Geistige Versenkung, eine Studie B85
Geistige Vertiefung und reliogiöse Verwirklichung durch Fasten und meditative Abgeschiedenheit B114
Geistliche Stunde. Ein Weg z. Bildung d. Gemeindekernes B32
Gelebte Wahrheit B321
General Dentistry A566
General Hospital Psychiatry A402, A464
General Systems Approach to Consciousness, Attention, and Meditation A829
Genetic Psychology Monographs A580
Geschenk des Geistes B148
Gestalt Conference Talk 1981 A583
Gestalt Journal A583
Gestalt Therapy, Non-Western Religions, and the Present Age B896
Gesture of Balance B882
Getting There Without Drugs B618
Getting Through to the Wonderful You B806
Gifted Child Quarterly A578
Gifts of Silence B968
Glaube, Erfahrung, Meditation B267
Glaubenserfahrung und Meditation B268
Glimpse of Nothingness B929
Glück und Kontemplation B636
Glückspotential B81
God's Power and You B394
Golden Treatise of Mental Prayer B626
Good Housekeeping A581
Gott in dir B771
Gott is da B45
Gradual Awakening B454
Gradual Enlightenment, Sudden Enlightenment and Empiricism A786
Grail A466
Great Challenge B665
Great Exposition of Secret Mantra, 2 and 3 B923
Great Minds of Our Times Series M3, M20
Greatness of Being B712
Grosse Buch der Herzensmeditation B766
Grosse Buch der Meditation B132
Grossen Liebenden B771
Group ESP Scores, Mood, and Meditation A692
Group Self-Care Approach to Stress Management A282
Group Treatment of Test Anxiety in College Students by Undergraduate Group Leaders D35
Growth Exercises in Meditation and Action B796
Growth of Affective Learning in the Light of the Science of Creative Intelligence D19
Growth Process Inventory D18
Grundlagen des meditativen Lebens B778
Grundlagen tibetischer Mystik B286, B287
Guía de la meditación transcendental B563
Guide-Lines for Meditation B161
Guide Meditation B849
Guide Through Visuddhimagga B205
Guide to Awareness, Selfhealing, and Meditation B882
Guide to Beginner-Intermediate Meditation B712

Guide to Buddhist Meditation B495
Guide to Christian Meditation A439, B395
Guide to Increase Your Personal Awareness of God B679
Guide to Intermediate Meditation R67
Guide to Liberation Through Marananussati Mindfulness of Death B693
Guide to Meditative Therapy B237
Guide to Self-Discovery B452
Guide to Successful Meditation B384
Guide to Yoga Meditation B335
Guided Imagery Meditation on Scripture for Individuals and Groups B847
Guided Meditation R79
Guided Meditation and the Teaching of Jesus B170
Guided Meditation for Beginners R68
Guided Meditation on Body Awareness R50
Guru als Seelenführer B521
Guru Nanak, Guru for the Aquarian Age S27

Habituation of Alpha Blocking During Meditation A352
Hadassah Magazine A224
Handbook of Christian Meditation B728
Happiness: The TM Program, Psychiatry, and Enlightenment B82
Harnessing Pegasus B936K
Harper's Magazine A916
Harvard Business Review A60, A61, A648
Hatha Yoga. Ein Erfahrungsbericht aus Indien und Tibet B54
Have Mantra Will Meditate A916
Headache A556
Healing and Meditation in Medical Practice A487
Healing as a State of Consciousness A252
Healing Implications for Psychotherapy B317
Healing Potential of Transcendental Meditation B421
Healing Review S21
Healing Through Meditation A328
Healing Through Meditation and Prayer B651
Health A652
Health and Wholeness R35
Health Instruction Packages A457
Hear to Eternity R21
Heart of Buddhist Meditation B590
Heilkraft im Yoga für Körper und Geist B359
Helps for the Daily Quiet Time B157
Hemispheric Laterality and Cognitive Style Associated with Transcendental
     Meditation A56
Hemispheric Symmetry of the EEG During the Transcendental Meditation
     Technique A884
Herausforderung religiöse Erfahrung B324
Herausgefordert zur Meditation B868
Hermeneutics of Practice in Dogen and Francis of Assisi A496
Hermit in the Himalayas B102
Hermit in the House B601
Herr, führe mich in die Stille B125
Hesychasm and Transcendental Meditation A121
Hesychast Method of Prayer A6
Hidden in Plain Sight B95
Hidden Teaching Beyond Yoga B103, B105
High Amplitude Fronto-Central Alpha and Theta Activity During the Tran-

scendental Meditation Technique A696
Higher Education for Higher Consciousness D31
Higher States of Consciousness A610
Higher States of Consciousness Through the Transcendental Meditation Programme A683
Himalayan News S14
Hindu Upasana Vis-a-vis Christian Meditation A86
Historical and Clinical Considerations of the Relaxation Response A67
Historical View of Theories of the Soul B732
History of Clinical Biofeedback A17
History of Meditation from Shamanism to Science B372
History of Religions A418, A636
History of the Koan and Koan Study in Rinzai (Lin-chi) Zen B546
Hoffen und Erkennen B779
Höhles des Herzens B341
Hol mich herein B953
Holistic Approach to Preventing Stress Disorders B624
Holistic Programs for the Drug Addict and Alcoholic A587
Holy Assassins M4
Holy Men of India M5
Holy Path B399
Hormones and Behavior A389
Hospital and Community Psychiatry A123
House and Garden A579
How Companies Cope with Executive Stress A375
How I Learned to Meditate B830
How I Stopped Worrying A146
How Is Meditation Prayer A356
How Much Stress Is Too Much A61
How to Actually Meditate B695
How to Control Your Emotions B501
How to Converse Continually and Familiarly with God B456
How to Do Everything by Learning to Do Nothing A380
How to Enjoy the Rest of Your Life B197
How to Find Peace of Mind Through Meditation B908
How to Harness the Healing Power of Your Personal Beliefs B52K
How to Listen When God Speaks B157
How to Meditate A337, B172, B198, B452, B453, B886, R43
How to Meditate Perfectly B860
How to Meditate: The A.R.E. Meditation Course R89
How to Meditate Without Attending a TM Class B7
How to Meditate Without Leaving the World B96
How to Practice Zazen B582
How to Respond to Transcendental Meditation B261
How to Stop Smoking Through Meditation B924
How to Stop Tension and Start Living B323
How to Succeed in Yoga and Other Talks B748
How to Teach and Learn with Your Whole Self B542
How to Teach Children to Meditate A790
How to Teach Yourself Meditation B581
How to Unlock Your Soul B377
How Transcendental Meditation Changed Our Family's Life A831
How You Can Use the Technique of Creative Imagination B182, B184, B188
Human Miracle: Transcendent Psychology B144
Human Process of Enlightenment and Freedom B354
Human Relations A278
Humanistic Psychology A714

Humanist A208
Humanitas A595
Hypertension Comparison of Drug and Nondrug Treatments A19
Hypnosis and Transcendental Meditation as Inducers of ESP A584
Hypnotic Induction of the Void A1
Hypnotic Responsivity as a Predictor of Outcome in Meditation A354
Hypnotic Responsivity, Meditation, and Laterality of Eye Movements A771

"I": A Cosmic Attunement R22, R34
Ich bin da, vor Ihm B784
Ich gebe euch ein neues Herz B411
Illustrated Guide to Zen Meditation B119
I'm the Maharishi: Fly Me A284
Imagery and the Autonomic Nervous System A196
Images of My Self B264
Immediate Aftereffects of Meditation on Perceptual Awareness D160
Immediate Effect of the Transcendental Meditation Technique and Theoretical
    Reflections Upon the Psychology and Physiology of Subjective Well-Being
    A871
Immediate Effects of the Transcendental Meditation Technique A381
Impact of Transcendental Meditation on Cognitive Flexibility, Field Depend-
    ence, and Directional Priorities in Attention Deployment D176
Impact of Zen Meditation B554
Implication of Liturgical Prayer for Personal Meditation and Contemplation
    A752
Implications of Experimentally Induced Contemplative Meditation A183
Implications of the Transcendental Meditation Program for Counseling D135
Importance of Meditation A315
Improved Dream Recall Associated with Meditation A678
Improved Quality of City Life Through the Transcendental Meditation Pro-
    gram A98
Improved Quality of Life During the Rhode Island Ideal Society Campaign
    from June 12 to September 12, 1978 A924

In Days of Great Peace B734
In Defense of Meditation A411
In Search of Serenity B384
Inc. A148
Increased Forearm Blood Flow During a Wakeful Hypometabolic State A469
Indian Heart Journal A31
Indian Journal of Medical Research A8, A15
Indian Journal of Medical Sciences A223
Indian Journal of Psychiatric Social Work A172
Indian Philosophical Influences on Recent American Thought and Life-Styles
    A681
Individual Differences and Mystical Experience in Response to Three Forms
    of Meditation D80
Individual Differences in Response to a Zen Meditation Exercise A504
Industrial Management A116, A415
Industry Week A532
Influence of a Meditation-Relaxation Technique on Group Problem-Solving Ef-
    fectiveness A417, D112
Influence of a Meditation Technique and an Eastern Ideology on the Value
    Orientations of College Students D13
Influence of Acute Physical Activity and Non-Cultic Meditation on State Anxi-
    ety D9

Influence of One Form of Zen Meditation on Levels of Anxiety and Self-
 Actualization D107
Influence of Asiatic Methods of Meditation A78
Influence of the Transcendental Meditation Program and Personality Variables
 on Auditory Thresholds and Cardio-Respiratory Responding D109
Influence of the Transcendental Meditation Program on Crime in Major U.S.
 Cities A870
Influence of the Transcendental Meditation Program on Crime Rate A345
Influence of the Transcendental Meditation Program on State Anxiety A592
Influence of the Transcendental Meditation Program on the Marital Dyad
 D140
Influence of Transcendental Meditation A591
Influence of Transcendental Meditation on a Measure of Self-Actualization
 A720
Influence of Transcendental Meditation on Anxiety A257
Influence of Transcendental Meditation on Drug Abuse A191
Influence of Transcendental Meditation on Perceptual Illusion A502
Influence of Transcendental Meditation on Positive Mental Health and Self-
 Actualization D183
Influence of Transcendental Meditation Upon Autokinetic Perception A646
Initial Meditative Experience: Part I A853
Initial Meditative Experience: Part II A854
Initial Zen Intensive (Sesshin) A358
Inleiding tot Zen-meditatie B98
Innenschau B745
Inner Development B643
Inner Guide Meditation B849
Inner Reality B100, B104
Inner Source B237
Inner Way B139
Innere Beten B24
Innerlijke grond B379
Innerung. Stufen und Wege der Meditation B522
Inside Folsom Prison B235
Insight Meditation A689, B633
Insight Series M2, M18
Insights Into the Devotional Life B970
Inspiration in the Creative Process and Meditation D185
Inspired Analgesia Through Transcendental Meditation A629
Instruction How to Pray and Meditate Well B43
Instructions for a Training Package Combining Formal and Informal Zen
 Meditation with Behavioral Self-Control Strategies A738
Instructions in Meditation B226
Instructions on Vision in the Middle Way B544
Integrative Meta-Analysis of Psychological Studies Investigating the Treatment
 Outcomes of Meditation Techniques D66
Intensive Buddhist Meditation Retreat and the Self D134
Intensive Insight Meditation A432
Interciencia A416
Interface Journal A299
Interior Prayer B465
International Journal of Clinical and Experimental Hypnosis A48, A62, A109,
 A174, A271, A354, A772, A832
International Journal of Neuroscience A201, A203, A511, A611, A614, A848
International Journal of Psychiatry in Medicine A65
International Journal of Psycho-Analysis A731
International Journal of Psychoanalytic Psychotherapy A730

International Journal of Social Psychiatry   A785
International Journal of the Addictions   A561
International Management   A146
International Philosophical Quarterly   A194
International Review of Missions   A144, A535, A873
International Yoga Guide   S31
Intersubject EEG Coherence   A611
Into Meditation Now   B330
Introduction to Christian Meditation   A488
Introduction to Ethical Meditation   B404
Introduction to Maharishi's Theory of Creativity   A23
Introduction to Meditation   A887, B224
Introduction to Meditation: From the Teachings of Namgyal Rimpoche   B325
Introduction to Mental Prayer   B710
Introduction to Oriental Mysticism   B852
Introduction to Qabalistic, Magical and Meditative Techniques   B680
Introduction to Tibetan Buddhist Meditations   B984
Introduction to TM   B242
Introduction to Transcendental Meditation and the Teachings of Maharishi
     Mahesh Yogi   B730
Introduction to Zen Buddhism   B872
Introduction to Zen for Beginners   B797
Investigation Into the Changes in Skin Resistance During the Transcendental
     Meditation Technique   A459
Investigation Into the Compatibility of Existential-Humanistic Psychotherapy
     and Buddhist Meditation   D8
Investigation of a Zen Meditation Procedure and Its Effect on Selected Per-
     sonality and Psychotherapeutic Variables   D161
Investigation of Physiological Changes During the Practice of Tai Chi Ch'uan
     D73
Investigation of the Effect of Meditation Training in a Cigarette Smoking Ex-
     tinguishment Program   D157
Investigation on Yogic Claiming to Stop Their Heartbeats   A15
Invitation to Instant Bliss   A842
Invitation to Meditation   A466
Inward Art   B829
Inward Revolution   B670
Islamische Sufi-Meditation für Christen   B294
Issues in the Therapeutic Use of Meditation   A703
It Will Help You Cope   A581
It's About Meditation   B983

Japa (Mantra Yoga)   B610
Japanese Buddhism   B872
Japanese Religions   A805
Japanese Spirituality   B872
Je perfectionne mon yoga   B475
Jewel in the Lotus   B168
Jewish Digest   A224
Jews Who Seek Eastern Mysticism   A224
Journal d'un yogi   B190, B192
Journal for the Scientific Study of Religion   A28, A701
Journal of a Lonely Exile   B102
Journal of Abnormal Psychology   A175, A771
Journal of Altered States of Consciousness   A108, A165, A212, A245, A252,
     A253, A312, A317, A429, A626, A651

Journal of Analytical Psychology A236
Journal of Applied Behavioral Science A417
Journal of Applied Psychology A129, A211, A920
Journal of Behavior Therapy and Experimental Psychiatry A100, A279, A296
Journal of Behavioral Medicine A722, A863
Journal of Chinese Philosophy A800, A890
Journal of Chronic Diseases and Therapeutics Research A25
Journal of Clinical Child Psychology A677
Journal of Clinical Psychiatry A235
Journal of Clinical Psychology A27, A181, A197, A256, A291, A664, A678, A809, A810
Journal of College Science Teaching A120
Journal of Comparative Sociology A725
Journal of Consulting and Clinical Psychology A99, A126, A133, A205, A302, A316, A353, A421, A422, A476, A491, A634, A763, A764, A793, A926
Journal of Consulting Psychology A504
Journal of Contemporary Psychotherapy A93, A509
Journal of Counseling Psychology A469K, A591, A720
Journal of Creative Behavior A23, A318, A750, A826
Journal of Crime and Justice A202
Journal of Dharma A6, A37, A86, A138, A139, A158, A308, A315, A654, A919
Journal of Drug Education A905
Journal of Ecumenical Studies A485
Journal of Experimental Child Psychology A179
Journal of Experimental Psychology A166
Journal of Family Counseling A227
Journal of Family Practice A329
Journal of General Psychology A426
Journal of Holistic Health A222
Journal of Human Psychology A467
Journal of Human Stress A64, A70, A152, A568, A575
Journal of Humanistic Psychology A219, A247, A515, A697, A737, A856
Journal of Indian Psychology A431, A442, A672
Journal of Molecular and Cellular Cardiology A382
Journal of Nervous and Mental Diseases A182, A183, A277, A286
Journal of Neural Transmission A114
Journal of Occupational Medicine A127
Journal of Orthomolecular Psychiatry A184
Journal of Parapsychology A673, A692, A767
Journal of Pastoral Counseling A228, A358, A902
Journal of Personality and Social Psychology A369
Journal of Personality Assessment A238, A270
Journal of Psychedelic Drugs A499
Journal of Psychiatric Nursing and Mental Health Services A282
Journal of Psychoactive Drugs A587
Journal of Psychology A340, A597
Journal of Psychosomatic Research A679, A883
Journal of Religion A419
Journal of Religion and Health A541, A542, A769, A900
Journal of Religious Studies A547
Journal of School Health A106, A323, A622
Journal of Science and Consciousness for Living in the Aquarian Age S27
Journal of Special Education A246
Journal of Sports Medicine and Physical Fitness A686
Journal of the American Academy of Psychoanalysis A30, A128
Journal of the American Academy of Religion A326, A420

Journal of the American Association of Nephrology Nurses and Technicians
 A213
Journal of the American Institute of Hypnosis   A406
Journal of the American Society for Preventive Dentistry   A206
Journal of the American Society for Psychical Research   A619
Journal of the American Society of Psychosomatic Dentistry and Medicine   A1,
 A522, A528, A530, A565, A570, A572, A573, A574, A724
Journal of the Association of Physicians of India   A7
Journal of the Israel Medical Association   A151
Journal of the Royal College of General Practitioners   A640
Journal of Transpersonal Psychology   A95, A110, A115, A180, A224K, A280,
 A303, A304, A307, A311, A359, A430, A432, A495, A578, A604, A620,
 A774, A798, A833, A853, A854, A855, A857, A858, A866, A874, A875,
 A876, A914
Journey Into Burmese Silence   B120
Journey Inward   B309
Journey of Awakening   B676
Journey of Insight Meditation   B450
Journey of the Soul   B831
Journey to Inner Space   B711
Journey to the Self   B976
Journeys Into Civilization   R82
Joy of Meditation   B1
Joys of Meditation   B855
Jung Menschen meditieren   B68
Jüngerschaft im Neuen Zeitalther   B35
Jungian Depth Psychology and Transcendental Meditation   D132

Kabbalah of the Nations   A177
Kabbalist   S16
Karme-Choling   A111
Key to Expanded Consciousness   B316
Key to Personal Freedom   B193
Kindly Bent to Ease Us   B402
Klang der Stille   B374
Kleine Geheimnis   B389
Kleinod in der Lotos-Blüte   B424
Know Thyself   B177
Kontemplation und Ekstase bei Pseudo-Dionysius Areopagita   B948
Kontemplation und Meditation, die Stufen des Resenkreuzerweges   B638
Kontemplative Leben. Kurze Betrachtungen   B770
Konventionelle und quantitative EEG-Analyse bei TM   D122
Konzentration, Meditation, Kontemplation   B523
Konzentration und Meditation   B822
Konzentration und Meditation. Eine Einf   B358
Konzentration und schöpferisches Denken. Praktische Übungswege   B360
Konzentration und Verwirklichung   B735
Konzentration. Vom Wege, von d. Nachfolge, vom lebendigen Wort   B524
Kraft der Stille   B889
Kräfte aus der Stille   B560
Kreislaufphysiologischen Auswirkungen bei der Transzendentalen Meditation
 D17
Kreuzmeditation   B716
Krishnamurti Foundation of America Bulletin   S18
Kundalini Meditation Manual for Intermediate Students   B1004
Kundalini Yoga   B756

Kunst, Blumen zu stecken B 284
Kunst der Meditation B 276
Kunst der Versenkung B 147
Kurze Anleitung zum Meditieren B 466
Kurzzeiteffekt der TM und theroetische überlegungen zur Psychologie und
    Physiologie der subjektiven Befindlichkeit D 228

Ladies' Home Journal A 52, A 831
Lama and the Jumbo-Jet A 156
Lamp A 682
Lancet A 14, A 90, A 639, A 656
Language Arts A 557
Lapis M 6
LaSallian Digest A 590
Lasst alles völlig neu für Euch sein B 907
Learn to Live with Stress M 7
Learning A 564
Learning Disorders and the Transcendental Meditation Program D 101
Learning to Meditate: Self-Regulated Course R 7, R 8
Learning to Meditate: The Instructor's Course R 7
Lebe bewusst B 160
Leben aus der Fülle B 561
Leben aus der Tiefe B 902, B 903
Leben heisst sehen B 308
Leben meditieren B 55
Leben wird es geben B 299
Lebenshilfen durch Geistesschulung. Wege zur Pflege d. inneren Lebens
    B 639
Lebensorientierung an der Bibel B 412
Lebensweiser zur Selbst- und Schicksalsmeisterung. Handbücher d. Erfolgs-
    Psychologie B 774
Lecture Given by Lama Thubten Yeshe at the 7th Meditation Course B 898
Lecture Given by Lama Thubten Yeshe at the 8th Meditation Course B 899
Lectures on Sahaj Marg B 931
Let the Spirit In B 349
Letters on Occult Meditation B 36
Letting Go of Stress R 23
Leven dat het een lieve lust is. Kruiden, homeopathie, makrobiotiek, yoga,
    meditatie B 263
Leven vanuit de dipte B 903
Liberation of Life B 796
Libro de la TM (meditación transcendental) B 196
Licht der Gewissheit B 407
Licht der Seele B 771
Licht und die Bilder. Elemente d. Kontemplation B 837
Life A 376, A 842
Life as Yoga B 890
Light from the East A 49, A 50
Light of Exploration B 392
Light on the Path B 557
Liguorian A 289, A 497, A 918
Limitations of Transcendental Meditation in the Treatment of Essential Hyper-
    tension A 656
Listener A 102
Living Buddhist Masters B 409
Living by Zen B 872

Living from Within B174
Living in the Light of Eternity B872
Living Simply Through the Day B232
Living the Life of a Zen Monk A112
Living the Meditative Way B854
Living with Bhagwan Shree Rajneesh B297
Living Yoga M8
London Quarterly and Holborn Review A328
Long Distance Running as Meditation A735
Long-Term Effects of the Transcendental Meditation Program in the Treatment of Insomnia A553
Longitudinal Effects of the TM-Sidhi Program on EEG Coherence, Creativity, Intelligence and Moral Reasoning A617
Longitudinal Study of the Effect of the Transcendental Meditation Program on Changes in Personality A241
Longitudinal Study of the Influence of the Transcendental Meditation Program on Drug Abuse A708
Look A350, A374
Look at Higher Consciousness and the Enlightenment Industry B972
Love and God B481
Low Normal Heart and Respiration Rates in Individuals Practicing the Transcendental Meditation Technique A695
LSD: A Shortcut to False Samadhi B666
Lumen Vitae A97, A231
Lure of Novel Religious Forms A836

Ma Bell Gets De-Stressed A141
Macht der Seele als erlebte Wirklichkeit B183
Macht der süssen Worte B540
Macleans A288, A869
Mademoiselle A380, A821
Mahabarata. Bhagavadgita B482
Mahamudra, der Weg zur Erkenntnis der Wirklichkeit B655
Mahamudra Meditation-Stages and Contemporary Cognitive Psychology D30K
Maharaj Charan Singh Answers Questions on Meditation B813
Maharishi at '433' B601
Maharishi Effect and Invincibility A454
Maharishi International University A299
Maharishi International University Mixes Meditation and Education A232
Maharishi Mahesh: Jet Age Yogi M9
Maharishi Mahesh Yogi and the TM Technique B593
Maharishi Mahesh Yogi: Deep Meditation R45
Maharishi Mahesh Yogi og transcendental meditation B246
Maharishi Mahesh Yogi: The Master Speaks R46
Maharishi Mahesh Yogi y la ciencia de la intellegencia creativa B247
Maharishi Over Matter A908
Maharishi, Plato, and the TM-Sidhi Program on Innate Structures of Consciousness A749
Maharishi: The Founder of Transcendental Meditation B230
Maharishi U. A719
Maharishi U.: Learning to Levitate in Fairfield, Iowa A796
Maharishi's Spiritual Novocaine A505
Mahayana Buddhist Meditation Theory and Practice B479
Main Currents in Modern Thought A595
Major Change in Intermediary Metabolism by Behavioral Rest States A384
Making Brain Waves A490

Mamami Krsna Sundaram S4
Man, Mind and Meditation D206
Manage A479
Management and Meditation A728
Management of Stress B250
Management World A433
Mandala B21
Mandala: Meditationsgedichte und Betrachtungen B288
Mantra and Meditation B26
Mantra, Kirtana, Yantra and Tantra B569
Mantra Yoga B390
Mantra Yoga, the Music of the Mind B260
Mantram Handbook B227
Mantras R80
Mantras: Sacred Words of Power B72
Mantras: Words of Power B823
Manual for Living Creatively with One's Self B413
Manual of Mind Development B350
Manual of Zen Buddhism B872
Manual on Meditation B580
Manuale pratico della meditazione B763
Märchen von der Freiheit und der Weg der Meditation B916
Marketed Social Movement: A Case Study of the Rapid Growth of TM A398
Marriage A925
Marxismus und Meditation B214
Massage and Meditation B217, B218
Massage & [und] Meditation B218
Master Course, Part One B865
Master Kiteman M10
Mastermind B807
Matching Relaxation Therapies to Types of Anxiety A175K
Materialien zur Bildmeditation B243
Matter of Zen B978
McCalls A514
Meaningful Silence A718
Mechanics of Enlightenment B127
Mechanix Illustrated A904
Medical Journal of Australia A487, A518, A523, A524, A525
Medieval and Renaissance Texts and Studies B352
Medieval Dynamic Understanding of Meditation A699
Meditação; ensaio B740
Meditación en accion B917
Meditación según la más antiqua tradición budista B548
Meditación transcendental B247, B563
Meditación: Un paso al más allá con Edgar Cayce B40
Meditación: una téchnica oriental y un contenido cristiano B123
Meditate B558
Meditate the Tantric Yoga Way B381
Meditating for Self Realisation B388
Meditating on Stress A148
Meditating with Children B722, R70
Meditation A124, A147, A295, A830, A879, B38, B167, B169, B258, B328,
    B345, B402, B678, B957, M11, M12, R11, R13, R36
Meditation: A Discriminating Realization A138
Meditation: A Foundation Course B463
Meditation: A New Dimension B667
Meditation: A Practical Guide to a Spiritual Discipline B506

Meditation: A Practical Study with Exercises B257
Meditation: A Psychological Approach to Cancer Treatment A520
Meditation: A Psychological Experience and Its Implications R39
Meditation, a Step Beyond with Edgar Cayce B40, B41
Meditation: A Way of Life B891, R54
Meditation According to Spanish Mystics A632
Meditation According to Yoga-Vedanta B808
Meditation: Action and Union A536
Meditation: Affair of the Heart A440
Meditation als Erkenntnisweg B118
Meditation als Lebenshilfe B453
Meditation als Lebenspraxis B302
Meditation als Weg zur Gotteserfahrung B434
Meditation: An In Depth Study A570
Meditation: An Instructional Cassette R15
Meditation: An Introduction and Review A855
Meditation: An Open Way to Serenity of Mind and Body A489
Meditation: An Outline for Practical Study B736
Meditation and Academic Performance A250
Meditation and Archetypal Content of Nocturnal Dreams A236
Meditation and Astral Projection B46
Meditation and Behavior Therapy A910K
Meditation and Behavioral Self-Management Instructions R73
Meditation and Behavioral Therapy A416
Meditation and Biofeedback D24
Meditation and Cancer A913
Meditation and Children R71
Meditation and Consciousness A306
Meditation and Consciousness (I) R58
Meditation and Consciousness (II) R59
Meditation and Empathetic Behavior D178
Meditation and ESP A691, A767
Meditation and ESP Scoring A221
Meditation and Flexibility of Visual Perception and Verbal Problem Solving
    A198
Meditation and Health A541
Meditation and Hemispheric Specialization D224
Meditation and Its Methods According to Swami Vivekananda B939
Meditation and Kabbalah B511
Meditation and Life B149
Meditation and Mankind B457
Meditation and Mantras B938
Meditation and Marijuana A732
Meditation and Medicine A478
Meditation and Ministry A711
Meditation and Piety in the Far East B681
Meditation and Prayer B231, B277
Meditation and Prayer in Merton's Spirituality A802
Meditation and Prayer in Theological Education in South-East Asia A144
Meditation and Problem Solving A150
Meditation and Progressive Relaxation in the Treatment of Test Anxiety D41
Meditation and Psychoanalysis A128
Meditation and Psychotherapeutic Effects A742
Meditation and Psychotherapy in the Treatment of Cancer A96
Meditation and Rituals in Neo-Confucian Tradition A139
Meditation and Self-Actualization A704
Meditation and Self-Examination A915

Meditation and Self Exploration Through the Jungian Imagery of the Gospels B264

Meditation and Self-Realization A641

Meditation and Spiritual Life B995

Meditation and Stress Reactivity D76

Meditation and Surfing A215

Meditation and Sustained Attention A862

Meditation and the Art of Dying B27

Meditation and the Bible B387

Meditation and the Creative Process A442

Meditation and the EEG A880

Meditation and the Enhancement of Focusing Ability D114

Meditation and the Flexibility of Constructions of Reality A486

Meditation and the Fulness of Life B985

Meditation and the Mind of Man B650, R89

Meditation and the New Church A332

Meditation and the Prevention of Alcohol Abuse A733

Meditation and the Search for God A226

Meditation and the Unconscious A874

Meditation and Well-Being A314

Meditation and Work A451

Meditation as a Path to God-Realization B564

Meditation as an Adjunct to Medical and Psychiatric Treatment A287

Meditation as an Adjunct to Psychotherapy A322

Meditation as an Aspect of Spirit R51

Meditation as an Intervention in Stress Reactivity A316

Meditation as Discrimination Training A359

Meditation as Meta-Therapy A307

Meditation as Psychotherapy A762, D204

Meditation as Re-Minding Oneself A644

Meditation: Aspects of Research and Practice A858

Meditation at the Telephone Company A512

Meditation, Attention, and Hypnotic Susceptibility A832

Meditation: Betrachtungen u. Hinweise B88

Méditation bouddhique B470

Meditation Can Solve Race Problem A807

Meditation: Classic and Contemporary Perspectives A9K, A16, A43, A55K, A56, A69K, A72, A97K, A109, A109K, A153, A173-A175K, A183K, A224K, A229K, A244, A296K, A297K, A297R, A303, A304, A316, A384K, A406, A430, A460K, A467, A469K, A476, A491, A501K, A571, A620K, A627, A628, A646, A717, A737K, A739, A739K, A742, A745, A762-A764, A784, A786, A829K, A847, A851-A854, A899, A909, A909K, A910K, B802

Meditation: Commonsense Directions for an Uncommon Life B228

Meditation: Concentration and Insight A308

Meditation Crystallized M13

Méditation dans le Bhâgavata-Purana B576

Méditation de l'Ecriture B236

Meditation der Gemeinsamkeit. Aspekte e. ehel. Anthropologie B840

Meditation der Liebe B195

Meditation, der Weg nach innen B467

Meditation: die Kunst, zu, sich selbst zu finden B668

Meditation Diet B925

Meditation Disciplines and Personal Integration B303

Meditation: e. Weg in d. Freiheit B553

Meditation, Eine Libenshilfe B525

Meditation-Encounter-Growth Group D172

Meditation, Endocrine Glands, Prayer, and Affirmations B134

Meditation: Escape to Reality B911
Meditation, Esoteric Traditions A125
Méditation et action B918
Méditation et la projection astrale B47
Meditation: Excerpts from Talks B749
Meditation, Expectation and Performance on Indexes of Nonanalytic Attending A772
Meditation Experience B694
Meditation for Beginners B960
Meditation for Children B721
Meditation for Healing B856
Meditation for Initiates R69
Meditation for Managers A532
Meditation for Self-Development B687
Meditation for Young People B451
Meditation für Kranke B370
Meditation: Future Vehicle for Career Exploration A594
Meditation Game A760
Meditation: Gateway to Light B794
Meditation Gets an A-Okay in Ma Bell Tryout A533
Meditation: Glück in eigener Regie B700
Meditation: God Speaks and I Listen B150
Meditation: God's Blessing-Assurance B151
Meditation: God's Duty and Man's Beauty B152
Meditation: Guidance of the Inner Life B697
Meditation Gut Enlightenment B944
Meditation Hall and Ideals of the Monkish Discipline B872
Meditation Handbook B503
Meditation; Heilkraft im Alltag B496
Meditation Helps Break the Stress Spiral A309
Meditation, Hilfe im Alltag B991
Meditation: How to Do It B709
Meditation: Humanity's Race and Divinity's Grace B153
Meditation, ihre angsttherapeutischen und angstprophylaktischen Wirkungen, dargestellt am Beispiel der TM D100
Meditation im Alltag B468
Meditation im christlichen Dasein B202
Meditation im Religionsunterricht B61
Meditation in Action B915, B917, B918, B919
Meditation in Christianity B512
Meditation in Christianity and Other Religions A868, B513
Meditation in Contemporary Sri Lanka A495
Meditation in Dentistry A566
Meditation in Depth B904
Meditation in Forschung und Erfahrung, in weltweiter Beobachtung und praktischer Anleitung B897
Meditation in General Practice A638
Meditation in Ming Neo-Orthodoxy A800
Meditation in Motion M14
Meditation in Ost und West B526
Meditation in Religion und Psychotherapie B63
Meditation in Religion und Psychotherapie; ein Tagungsbericht B64
Meditation in the Classroom A564
Meditation in the Service of Theological Training A535
Meditation in the Silence B357
Meditation in the Treatment of Psychiatric Illness A297K
Meditation Instruction R12

Meditation: Is It Always Beneficial A317
Meditation: Its Process, Practice, and Culmination B751
Meditation: Its Theory and Practice B420, B803
Meditation: Journey to the Self B976
Meditation: Let's Sleep on It A534
Meditation Made Easy B629
Meditation: magi eller terapi B599
Meditation: Man-Perfection in God-Satisfaction B154
Meditation Manual B229
Meditation: Man's Choice God's Voice B155
Meditation: Medicine A652
Meditation Merges with the Mainstream A237
Meditation mit offensen Augen B234
Meditation Movement A87
Meditation, Musik und Tanz B53
Meditation, Neuroticism and Intelligence A813
Meditation och mystik B340
Meditation ohne Geheimnis B543
Meditation on a Flower R37
Meditation on the New Theory and Practice of Meditation A11
Meditation One: Meditation Two R76
Meditation or Meditation A706
Meditation, Ost und West B950
Meditation: Paths to Tranquility B729
Meditation, Personality and Arousal A881
Meditation: Philosophy and Practice in a Drug Rehabilitation Setting A715
Meditation: Practical Setting in an Age of Need D208
Meditation Practice and Research A856
Meditation, praktisch B605
Meditation, Prayer, Healing, and the Psychic B986
Meditation, Prior to the ESP Task A776
Meditation Program and Modern Youth A278
Meditation, Protein, Diet, and Mega-Vitamins in Treatment of a Progressive,
    Iatrogenic Cardiac and Psychotic Condition A184
Meditation: Psychologically and Theologically Considered A357
Meditation Research: Three Observations on the State-of-the-Art A762K
Meditation: Self-Regulation Strategy and Altered States of Consciousness
    B801
Méditation selon le Yoga-Védânta B809
Meditation: Some Psychological Speculations A662
Meditation Starting from the Word A79
Meditation: Stress Reduction Aid for Management A921
Meditation Techniques of the Kabalists, Vendantins and Taoists B859
Meditation: The Art of Ecstasy B669
Meditation: The Bible Tells You How B219
Meditation: The Doorway to Wholeness A595
Meditation: The Inward Art B828, B829
Meditation: The Inward Journey M15
Meditation: The Key to Expanded Consciousness B316
Meditation: The Problems of Any Unimodal Technique A460K
Meditation: The Way to Attainment B578
Meditation: Theorie und Praxis B804, B869
Meditation Therapy A142
Meditation to Fit the Person A900
Meditation Took Me Past Cancer A107
Meditation Training and Essential Hypertension A722
Meditation Training as a Treatment for Insomnia A910

Méditation transcendantale B400, B422
Meditation: 12 Briefe über Selbsterziehung B698
Meditation: Ubungen zur Selbstgestaltung B689
Meditation und Kontemplation aus christlicher Tradition B497
Meditation und pädagogische Praxis B83
Méditation véritable B460
Meditation: Versuche-Wege, Erfahrungen B726
Meditation Versus Relaxation A133
Meditation, Weg zur Mitte B514
Meditation: Wege zum Selbst B682, B684
Meditation: What It Can Do for You B163
Meditation: What? Why? How? A321
Meditation: Why and How R62
Meditation: Wiederentdeckte Wege zum Heil B685
Meditation with Young Children A578
Meditation Without Frills B376
Meditation Without Mystery A310
Meditation-World B156
Meditation Yoga B598
Meditation: Yoga, T'ai Chi and Other Spiritual Trips M16
Meditation, Zen und TM D62
Meditation Therapy B515
Meditationen B417
Meditationen aus dem Geist des Zen B367
Meditationen. Ein theosoph. Andachtsbuch nebst Anleitung z. Meditation
    B725
Meditationen eines Einsiedlers B531
Meditationen. I B977
Meditationen zur Selbslverwirklichung B1001
Meditations M17
Meditations of Maharishi Mahesh Yogi B483
Meditations from the Tantras, with Live Class Transcriptions B757
Meditationsgottesdienste B49
Meditationspraxis B86
Meditationstechniken für Manager B444
Meditationstexte zur Selbstfindung B842
Meditative Approach to Increasing Sensual Pleasure B265
Meditative Exercises R44
Meditative Ritual Practice and Spiritual Conversion-Commitment A659
Meditative States in the Abhidharma and in Pseudo-Dionysius A687
Meditative Way B892
Meditator B866
Meditators B800
Meditator's Diary B305, B306
Meditator's Guidebook B676
Meditazione e miracolo B764
Meditazione e posizioni yoga per un perfetto equilibrio fisco e mentale B583
Meditazione transcendentale B945
Mediteren B714
Meditieren im Alltag B254
Meditieren, sich entfalen B84
Meditieren, wozu und wie B221
Meet Your Guru B377
Meeting Christ Through Daily Meditation B326
Meeting of the Ways B516
Meeting Schools of Oriental Meditation B824
Meister B659

Meister in dir B379, B380
Memory and Cognition A198
Mending the Ragged Edges B492
Menschheit betet B457, B458
Menschlichkeit probieren B44
Mental Exercises and Meditative Practices for Personal Growth B946
Mental Health and Meditation A493
Mental Health in Classical Buddhist Psychology A311
Mental Prayer and Modern Life, a Symposium B527
Metabolic and EEG Changes During Transcendental Meditation A244
Metabolic Effects of Transcendental Meditation A384K
Metaphysical Meditations B1000, B1001
Method of Phenomenological Reduction and Yoga A758
Methode der Ideenfindung zur Lösung von Gestaltungsprobleme D54
Méthode d'oraison avec une nouvelle forme de méditation B175
Methods of Mental Prayer B448
Metodi di orazione mentale B448, B449
Metodo Silva de control mental B810
Michio Kushi's Do-in-buch B425
Mind as Healer, Mind as Slayer B624, R56
Mind Control Techniques for a Small Planet in Space B930
Mind Field B603
Mind Is It B986
Mind Over Drugs A549
Mind Over Matter A550
Mind Trips B401
Minnesota Law Review A825
Miracle of Being Awake B579
Miracle of Mindfulness B580
Miracle Power of Transcendental Meditation B584, B586
Mirror: Morning in the Garden R77
Miscellany on the Shin Teaching of Buddhism B872
Mit Kindern meditieren B723
Mit Jugendlichen meditieren B331
Model for Enabling Persons in the Spiritual Disciplines of Prayer and Medita-
    tion D126
Model for Teaching Meditation Classes in a Christian Context D128
Model for the Levens of Concentrative Meditation A109
Model for Viewing Meditation Research A857
Modern Transcendentalists and Modern Empiricists D235
Modification of the Paired H Reflex Through the Transcendental Meditation
    and TM-Sidhi Program A849
Möglichkeiten und Grenzen der TM zur Behebung schulischer Insufficienzen
    im educaktiven Bereich D99
Mohawk M18
Moment A796
Momentum A506
Mon coeur et Dieu B190
Mon corps et moi B190
Monastic Studies A789
Monatliche Geisteserneuerung und Vorbereitung auf den Tod B717
Month A49, A50
More on the Reliability of the Kinesthetic Aftereffects Measure and Need for
    Stimulation A270
More than 150 Scientific Prayers that Will Work for You B2
More than Wanderers B241
Movement Exploration and Zazen Meditation D138

Moving Meditation B338
MT [i.e. Meditação transcendental]: Descoberta da energia interior e domínio
  da tensão B75
Mudra B920
Munen musō B562
Muscle and Skin Blood Flow and Metabolism During States of Decreased Acti-
  vation A390
Muscle Biofeedback and Transcendental Meditation A675
Music and Liturgy A157
Music and Meditation A157
Music for Meditation R9, R41
Musical Sleep Induction R83
My Guru and His Disciple B364
My Master B659
My Search to Find Happiness in 40 Minutes a Day A227
My Words are Spirit and Life B326
Mystical States of Consciousness A286
Mystical Teachings of Yoga, Meditation, and Love B396
Mysticism: Christian and Buddhist B872
Mystik, Meditation, Yoga, Zen B459
Myth of Freedom, and the Way of Meditation B921

Nach innen weggetreten B910
Naikan Psychotherapy B687
Namu Dai Bosa S32
National Review A494
Nation's Business A757
Natural Birth Control Book S5
Natural Meditation B203
Natural Unfolding B279
Naturale Meditation B203, B204
Nature A68
Need for Stimulation D139
Neoplatonism and Indian Thought A687
Neue Heilswege aus Fernost, Hilfen oder Gefahren B344
Neuronumoral Correlates of Behaviour A788
Neurological and Behavioral Aspects of Transcendental Meditation Relevant to
  Alcoholism A795
Neurophysiology of Enlightenment A844
Neuwerden aus seinem Wort B9
New Catholic World A143, A886
New-Church Magazine A332, A830
New Directions in Psychotherapy B317
New Earth B4
New England Journal of Medicine A58, A59, A784
New Jersey Education Association Review A577
New Jersey Mantra A214
New Life B399
New Light on TM A497
New Mode of Meditation A586
New Outlook for the Blind A363
New Plant Thrives in a Spiritual Desert A333
New Realities A141, A598, A823
New York Times Magazine A462, A705, A736
New Zealand Dental Journal A629
New Zealand Family Physician A482

Newsweek A142, A490, A657, A908
Nirvana in a Dank, Dark Tank A593
Nirvana Tao B596
No Effect of Transcendental Meditation on Left Ventricular Function A283
Non-Drug Turn-On Hits Campus A350
Non-Pharmacological Approaches to the Treatment of Drug Abuse A101
Non-Surgical Endodontic Therapy for a Vital Tooth with Meditation-Hypnosis as the Sole Anesthetic A576
Nonanalytic Attending, Hypnotic Susceptibility, and Psychological Well-Being in Trained Meditators and Nonmeditators A773
Nonpharmacologic Control of Essential Hypertension in Man A273
Nonpharmacological Therapy for Hypertension A89
Note Upon Steady Visual Fixation and Repeated Auditory Stimulation in Meditation and the Laboratory A650
Notion de "Prajna" ou de sapience selon les perspectives du "Mahayana" B117
Nouvelle terre B4, B5
Novel Technique for Studying Attention During Meditation A833
Nursing Mirror A766, A913

O Inward Traveller B566
Observations Relevant to a Unified Theory of Meditation A866
Occasional Meditations B352
Oedipus Myth and Meditation R52
Of Prayer and Meditation B473
Offering to Ramanachala B656
Ökumenische Meditationsbriefe B371
OM: A Guide to Meditation and Inner Tranquility B476
On Images and Pure Light A253
On Indian Mahayana Buddhism B872
On Meditation and Self-Parenting A902
On Meditation and Sensory Awareness A517
On Psychotherapeutic Attention A774
On Research in Zen A753
On Starting a Study Group with Practice of Meditation B846
On Taking New Beliefs Seriously A261
On the Aesthetic Education of Man D163
On the Emergence of Perinatal Symptoms in Buddhist Meditation A28
On the Psychological Nature of Resistances to Meditation Which Arise During the Meditation Process D146
On the Psychology of Meditation B572, B573, R60
On Zen Practice B602
Onderwijs voor verlichting B781
One Man's Exploration of Encounter Groups, Meditation, and Altered States of Consciousness B738
One Man's Journey to the East R64
Only Revolution B418
Only Way to Deliverance B832
Open Way B503, B504
Opening to God B847
Openness Mind B883
Oraison catholique et les techniques orientales de méditation B518
Ordnung, Intelligenz und Evolution B612
Organ of Perception R24
Organizational Development Through the Transcendental Meditation Program A400

Oriental Mysticism B852
Origins of Meditation D94
Östliche Meditation und chrisliche Mystik B220
Östliche Meditation und westliche religiöse Erneuerung B788
Östliche und westliche Meditation B498
Other Side of Silence B395
Other Ways, Other Means B314
Our Catholic Faith: Saint Ignatius Loyola on Meditation A623
Our Sunday Visitor A218, A438, A439, A440, A589, A623, A779
Our Treasured Heritage B768
Outlines on Mahayana Buddhism B872
Outpatient Program in Behavioral Medicine for Chronic Pain Patients Based on
    Practice of Mindfulness Meditation A402
Over het TM [i.e. Transcendente Meditatie] progama en het TM-Sidhi pro-
    gramma B979
Overcoming 'Practice Stress' via Meditation and Hypnosis A567
Overview: Clinical and Physiological Comparison of Meditation with Other
    Self-Control Strategies A739

Pacific Sociological Review A398
Paired-Associate Learning and Recall A3
Parapsychology Review A584
Parent's Magazine A713
Participant Characteristics and the Effects of Two Types of Meditation Versus
    Quiet Sitting A256
Passionate Mind B413
Passive Meditation A786K
Pastoral Life A361
Pastoral Psychology A357
Patanjali Raja Yoga B742
Path of Action B786
Path of Purity B166
Path of the Mystic B838
Paths of Meditation B616
Paths to Inner Calm B121
Paths to Inner Power B90
Patterning of Cognitive and Somatic Processes in Self-Regulation of Anxiety
    A717
Pax animae B628
Peace Lagoon S27
People A383
Perception of Depth and Illusions During a Transcendental State D89
Perceptual and Cognitive Processes in Meditation D110
Perceptual and Motor Skills A20, A117, A196, A249, A250, A298, A365,
    A368, A371, A477, A502, A513, A601, A646, A650, A666, A688, A700,
    A864, A867, A894, A895, A897, A898, A917, A922
Perceptual Phenomena Resulting from Steady Visual Fixation and Repeated
    Auditory Input Under Experimental Conditions in Meditation A651
Performance on a Learning Task by Subjects Who Practice the Transcendental
    Meditation Technique A554
Performance Practice in Meditation Rituals Among the New Religions A631
Periodic Suspension of Respiration During the Transcendental Meditation
    Technique A348
Personal Adjustment and Perceived Locus of Control Among Students Inter-
    ested in Meditation A777
Personal and Corporate Benefits of Inner Development B499

Personal Discipline and William Law   A843
Personal Experience of the Buddha's Way   B450
Personal Freedom   B193
Personal Prevention: Meditation May Be the Answer   A206
Personal Variables Predicting Voluntary Participation in and Attrition from a
    Meditation Program   A685
Personality and Autonomic Changes in Prisoners Practicing the Transcendental
    Meditation Technique   A615
Personality and Meditation   A898
Personality Changes as a Function of Two Different Meditative Techniques
    D25
Personality Characteristics and Regularity of Meditation   A186
Personality Correlates of Continuation and Outcome in Meditation and Erect
    Sitting Control Treatments   A763
Personality Correlates of EEG Change During Meditation   A9
Personnel   A702
Personnel and Guidance Journal   A680
Perspective on Consciousness and Psi Research   S8
Perspectives in Biology and Medicine   A173
Petite Philocalie de la prière du coeur   B631
Pfad der Meditation im Spiegel einer universalen Kunst   B959
Pflüger's Archiv   A427, A437, A861
Phenomenological Approach to Self-Knowledge   D162
Phenomenological Reduction and Yogic Meditation   A665
Phi Delta Kappan   A220, A258, A472, A815
Philosophie der Wahrheit   B105
Philosophy and Practice of TM and Its Relationship to Self-Actualization   D11
Philosophy and Psychology of the Oriental Mandala   A119
Philosophy and Science of Vedanta and Raja Yoga   B731
Philosophy East and West   A119, A136, A435, A665, A758, A786, A794, A801
Philosophy of Meditation   B145
Philosophy of Nature   B754
Philosophy of Truth and Falsehood   B754
Philosophy Today   A563, A718
Physiologic Correlates of Meditation and Their Clinical Effects in Headache
    A69
Physiological and Clinical Investigation of Muscular States and Their Signifi-
    cance in Psychology and Medical Practice   B367K
Physiological and Phenomenological Aspects of Transcendental Meditation
    A729
Physiological and Subjective Effects of Zen Meditation and Demand Character-
    istics   A491
Physiological and Subjective Evaluation of Meditation, Hypnosis, and Relaxa-
    tion   A571
Physiological and Subjective Evaluation of Neutral and Emotionally-Charged
    Words for Meditation   A572, A573, A574
Physiological Anxiety Response in Transcendental Meditators and Nonmedita-
    tors   A477
Physiological Cardiovascular Effects of the Transcendental Meditation Tech-
    nique   A53
Physiological Changes Associated with Transcendental Consciousness, the
    State of Least Excitation of Consciousness   A239
Physiological Changes in Yoga Meditation   A230
Physiological Effects of Meditation   A882
Physiological Effects of Transcendental Meditation   A845, B951, D222
Physiological Responses to Clicks During Zen, Yoga, and TM Meditation   A55
Physiologist   A388

Physiology and Behavior   A385, A390
Physiology of Meditation   A846
Physiology of Meditation and Mystical States of Consciousness   A173
Pilot Study of Conditioned Relaxation During Stimulation Meditation   A187
PK Experiment Comparing Meditating Versus Non-Meditating Subjects   A503
Place of Meditation in Cognitive-Behavior Therapy and Rational-Emotive
    Therapy   A229K
Planetary Harmonies   B339
Plasma Amino Acids During the Transcendental Meditation Technique: Com-
    parison to Sleep   A391
Plasma Prolactin and Cortisol During Transcendental Meditation   A395
Plasma Prolactin and Growth Hormone During Meditation   A394
Poesien aus religiöser Innenschau mit einstimmenden Akkorden in Prosa
    B836
Pool of Narcissus   A161
Popular Science   A379
Positive Addiction   B266
Positive Effects of Meditation   A920
Posture of Contemplation   B474
Potential Contributions of Meditation to Neuroscience   A296K
Potentiels évoques et états de vigilance induits qu' cours d'épreuves de temps
    de réaction de choix   A44
Power of Mantras   R81
Power of Mindfulness   B591
Power of Positive Non-Thinking   A657
Powers of Mind   A760, A761
Practical Guide to Meditation   B6
Practical Guide to the Lost Traditions of Christian Meditation   B322
Practical Insight Meditation   B762
Practical Meditator   B536
Practical Teaching Strategies for the Use of Relaxation, Imagery, Dreams,
    Suggestology-Hypnosis, Meditation   B314
Practical Techniques in Teaching the Art of Prayer   A600
Practice and Theory of Tibetan Buddhism   B834, B835
Practice of Awareness as a Form of Psychotherapy   A542
Practice of Christian Meditation   B95
Practice of Insight Meditation   B208
Practice of Meditation   B90, B905
Practice of Mental Prayer   B50
Practice of Process Meditation   B647
Practice of Recollection   B495
Practice of Yoga   B819
Practices in Prayer and Meditation Throughout the World   B457
Practicing Christian Devotional Meditation   B349
Practicing of Meditation by School Children and Their Levels of Field De-
    pendence-Independence, Test Anxiety, and Reading Achievement   A476
Practicing the Presence   B275, B278
Practitioner   A520, A529
Praktische Hilfen zum Gebet   B245
Prana   B646
Pratique du Zen   B200
Praxis der Herzensmeditation   B767
Praxis der Konzentration und Meditation   B833
Praxis der Meditation   B382
Pray: Participant's Handbook   B348
Prayer   B489

Prayer and Meditation B 310
Prayer and Meditation for Spiritual Growth B 704
Prayer and Spirituality A 409
Prayer for Beginners and Those Who Have Forgotten How B 1006
Prayer Leaflets S 8
Prayer Life A 78
Prayer, Meditation and Religious Experience D 147
Prayer of the Presence of God B 295
Praying for the Spirit A 26
Precipitation of Acute Psychotic Episodes by Intensive Meditation in Individu-
   als with a History of Schizophrenia A 859
Preliminary Report on Some Physiological Changes Due to Vipashyana Medita-
   tion A 223
Preliminary Study Into the Effects of Transcendental Meditation on Empathy
   D 83
Preliminary Study of the Effects of Transcendental Meditation on Selected
   Dimensions of Organization Dynamics D 152
Prelude R 25
Presuppositions to Meditation A 537
Prevention A 107
Prevention of Hypertension A 812
Prière pure et pureté du coeur B 293
Priest A 378
Priest and His Daily Meditation A 361
Priestly Meditation and Theology A 243
Primärtherapie und Transzendentalen Meditation Vergleichende Untersuchung
   über Methoden, Theorien, therapeutische Effekte D 154
Primary and Secondary Process in Waking and in Altered States of Conscious-
   ness A 272
Primer for Christian Meditation B 982
Primer of Prayer B 507
Principles and Practice of Progressive Relaxation R 38K
Principles of Psychology of Zen A 9K
Probleme der Versenkung im Ur-Buddhismus B 876
Proceedings of the Australian Society for Medical Research A 81
Proceedings of the Endocrine Society of Australia A 82, A 83
Proceedings of the Parapsychological Association A 503
Proceedings of the University of Otago Medical School A 840
Process of Meditation and the Retraining of Attention D 69
Processes of Western Meditation B 577
Procura do deus interno no yoga B 550
Profitable Meditation A 378
Programma di MT, meditazione transcendentale B 271
Progress Through Mental Prayer B 445
Progression dans la méditation B 383
Progressive Relaxation B 367K
Pseudo Mind-Expansion Through Psychedelics and Brain-Wave-Programming
   Versus True Mind-Expansion Through Life Conditioning to the Absolute
   A 290
PSI Research A 667
Psi Training Through Meditation, and Self-Actualization as Related to Psi
   Performance D 214
Psychiatric Journal of the University of Ottawa A 662
Psychiatric Problems Precipated by Transcendental Meditation A 461
Psychiatry A 63, R 5
Psychic A 96, A 690
Psychische Energie durch inneres Gleichgewicht B 884

Psycho-Yoga   B699
Psychoanalysis as Altering States of Consciousness   A30
Psychobiology of Transcendental Meditation   A245, B385
Psychobiology of Transcendental Meditation: An Annotated Bibliography
   B386
Psychodynamics of Buddhist Meditation   A559
Psychologia   A290, A327, A444, A445, A669, A704, A738, A741, A759, A782
Psychological and Physiological Effects of Meditation and the Physical Isolation
   Tank Experience on the Type A Behavior Pattern   D234
Psychological Assessment of Transcendental Meditation   A97K
Psychological Bulletin   A721, A762
Psychological Change Through the Spiritual Teacher   D102
Psychological Changes Associated with the Practice of Transcendental Medita-
   tion and Personality Characteristics of Self-Selected Meditators   A170
Psychological Changes in Meditating Western Monks in Thailand   A115
Psychological Control of Essential Hypertension   A721
Psychological Investigation Into the Source of the Effect of the Transcendental
   Meditation Technique   D197
Psychological Medicine   A880
Psychological Record   A545, A546, A770, A829
Psychological Reports   A9, A24, A185, A186, A187, A188, A189, A343, A362,
   A461, A596, A685, A743, A777, A792
Psychological Research on the Effects of the Transcendental Meditation Tech-
   nique on a Number of Personality Variables   A74
Psychological Testing of MIU Students   A612
Psychological Treatment of Cancer   A521
Psychological Treatment of Essential Hypertension   A335
Psychologie der Meditation   B573
Psychologist's Experience with Transcendental Meditation   A798
Psychology   A131
Psychology of Consciousness   A135, B604
Psychology of Inward Infinity   R36
Psychology of Mindfulness Meditation   D120K
Psychology of the Esoteric   B670
Psychology Today   A122, A284, A305, A309, A310, A313, A344, A621, A716,
   A761
Psychonomic Society Bulletin   see   Bulletin of the Psychonomic Society
Psychophysical Transformations Through Meditation and Sport   A364
Psychophysiological and Cognitive Responses to Stressful Stimuli in Subjects
   Practicing Relaxation and Clinically Standardized Meditation   A465
Psychophysiological and Psychological Correlates of Meditation   D229
Psychophysiological Correlates of Meditation   A909
Psychophysiological Correlates of Meditation: EEG Changes During Meditation
   A297R
Psychophysiological Correlates of the Practice of Tantric Yoga Meditation
   A153
Psychophysiological Effects of Meditation on Test-Anxious Male Youthful Pris-
   oners   D212
Psychophysiological Investigation on Transcendental Meditation   A663, D173
Psychophysiology   A55, A56, A230, A352, A384, A386, A387, A888
Psychophysiology and Its Therapeutic Effects on Stress   B133
Psychophysiology of Advanced Participants in the Transcendental Meditation
   Program   A346
Psychophysiology of Zen   B332
Psychosomatic Medicine   A54, A91, A233, A240, A260, A360, A394, A544,
   A548, A571, A606, A717, A850
Psychosomatics of Meditation   A883

Psychosomatische Christus B845
Psychotherapeutic Control of Hypertension A784
Psychotherapeutic Effects of Transcendental Meditation with Controls for Expectation of Relief and Daily Sitting A764
Psychotherapeutischen Wirkungen der TM D48
Psychotherapie, Psychosomatik, Medizinische, Psychologie A624
Psychotherapy A875
Psychotherapy and Meditation B346
Psychotherapy and Psychosomatics A73
Public Funding for TM A275

Quaker Worship and Techniques of Meditation B176
Quality of Meditation Effect in the Regression of Cancer A522
Quantified EEG Spectral Analysis of Sleep and Transcendental Meditation A47
Quest of the Overself B106, B110
Quênte du gourou B405
Quiet Hour B946
Quiet Mind B164

Rain Meditation R26
Rainbow Butterfly R55
Rainbows of Love R42
Raja Yoga B361, B570, B825, B867, B868, B996, B997
Raja-yoga; mit den Yoga-aphorismen des Patanjali B940
Raja-Yoga: or, Conquering the Internal Nature B941
Raja-Yoga, or Occultism B66
Raja yoga ou occultisme B67
Raja yoga secreto B551
Raja Yoga: The Yoga Aphorisms of Patanjali B942
Raja yoga, yoga royal B998
Ramakrishna and His Disciples B365
Reaction Time Following the Transcendental Meditation Technique A747
Reactions of Transcendental Meditators and Nonmeditators to Stress Films A403
Reader's Digest A492, A889
Reading and Writing as Meditation A557
Reading Anxiety and Behavioral Management as Functions of Attention and Relaxation Training D210
Reading Guide to the Biology of the Mind/Body A655
Real Self and Mystical Experiences A697
Real Way to Awakening B634
Réalité intérieure B107
Reality of Occult, Yoga, Meditation, Flying Saucers B223
Reality of Zazen B926
Realize What You Are B138
Recent Research Into the Psychology of God-Consciousness in Meditation A97
Recipes for Living and Loving R38
Records and Cassettes B644
Redbook A225
Reduced Sympathetic Nervous System Responsivity Associated with the Relaxation Response A367
Reduction in Metabolic Rate During the Practice of the Transcendental Meditation Technique A192
Reduction of Anxiety and Tension States Through Learning the Relaxation Response D32

Reduction of Autonomic Arousal in Alcoholics A634

Reflection on Psychotherapy, Focusing, and Meditation A875

Reflective Meditation B555

Reflexion, Meditation, Gebet B769

Regression of Cancer After Intensive Meditation A523

Regression of Cancer of the Rectum After Intensive Meditation A524

Regression of Osteogenic Sarcoma Metastases Associated with Intensive Meditation A525

Regression of Recurrence of Carcinoma of the Breast at Mastectomy Site Associated with Intensive Meditation A526

Relajación B51K

Relation Between the Practice of Meditation by School Children and Their Levels of Field Dependence-Independence, Test Anxiety and Reading Achievement D133

Relations Between Interpersonal Styles and Mood States D103

Relationship and Practice of Transcendental Meditation to Subjective Evaluation of Marital Satisfaction and Adjustment D209

Relationship Between Bimodal Consciousness, Meditation and Two Levels of Death Anxiety D44

Relationship Between Experience in Transcendental Meditation and Adaption to Life Events and Related Stress A452

Relationship Between Meditation Practice and Components of Anxiety and Creativity D113

Relationship Between Transcendental Meditation and Adoptive Regression D43

Relationship Between Transcendental Meditation and Dogmatism D61

Relationship Between Zen Meditation and the Development of Accurate Empathy D129

Relationship of a Counselor-Guided Meditation to Counselor Presence as Defined in Psychosynthesis D79

Relationship of Arica Training to Self-Actualization and Interpersonal Behavior D37

Relationship of Client Characteristics to Outcome for Transcendental Meditation, Behavior Therapy, and Self-Relaxation A55K

Relationship of Science, Intellect and Mind R36

Relationship of Selected Characteristics of Transcendental Meditation to Measures of Self-Actualization, Negative Personality Characteristics, and Anxiety D195

Relationship of the Transcendental Meditation Program to Self-Actualization and Negative Personality Characteristics A746

Relative Effectiveness of Progressive Relaxation, Meditation, and GSR Biofeedback for Reducing Psychophysiological Stress D4

Relative Effectiveness of Systematic Desensitization, Cognitive Modification, and Mantra Meditation in the Reduction of Test Anxiety D63

Relative Effects of Meditation Versus Other Activities on Ratings of Relaxation and Enjoyment of Others A362

Relative Efficacy of Meditation in Reducing an Induced Anxiety Reaction D30

Relax Today, Tomorrow the World A288

Relax with Transcendental Meditation A925

Relax Your Way to Better Health A66

Relaxation and Meditation R2K

Relaxation and Meditation Techniques B136

Relaxation and Placebo-Suggestion as Uncontrolled Variables in TM Research A219

Relaxation-Induced Anxiety A353, D91K

Relaxation Meditation R75

Relaxation, Meditation, and Insight A327

Relaxation Methods and the Control of Blood Pressure   A360
Relaxation Response   A63, A66, B51K, B52
Relaxation Response: An Evaluation of a Technique for Anxiety Reduction
   Among College Graduate Students   D184
Relaxation Response: An Innate Capacity for Dealing with Stress   R2T
Relaxation Response and Hypnosis   A62
Relaxation Response: Psychophysiologic Aspects and Clinical Applications
   A65
Relaxation Technique in the Management of Hypercholesterolemia   A152
Relaxation Techniques   M19
Relaxation Therapy in Asthma   A233
'Relaxit', and Get Fit   B494
Release and Cure of Pain and Suffering   B207
Relief of Anxiety Through Relaxing Meditation   A527
Religion   A159, A325
Religion and Society   A493
Religion in Life   A26
Religions of the Eastern World Series   M5
Religiöse Themen der Gegenwart   B686
Religious or Non-Religious: TM in American Courts   A37
Religious Organizational Change   A907
Religious Studies   A262, A424
Remission of Massive Metastastis from Undifferentiated Carcinoma of the Lung
   Associated with Intensive Meditation   A528
Renaissance Universal Journal   S4
Renin, Cortisol, and Aldosterone During Transcendental Meditation   A544
Rentoudu   B76
Reorganization in Psychotic Turmoil   R56
Report on a Mental Health Center Transcendental Meditation Program for Staff
   A269
Reported Sleep Characteristics of Meditators and Nonmeditators   A10
Requiem for a Faith   M20
Research Bulletin of the Himalayan International Institute/Eleanor N. Dana
   Laboratory   S14
Research Communications in Psychology, Psychiatry and Behavior   A2
Research in Parapsychology   A221, A691, A776
Research Quarterly   A896
Resources in Education   see   ERIC
Respiratory Changes During Transcendental Meditation   A14
Response of Obese and Non-Obese Women to Meditation   D216
Responsiveness to an Introductory Meditation Method   A249
Reunion, Tools for Transformation   B14
Révélation de la joie, technique de la méditation   B720
Reversal of Biological Aging in Subjects Practicing the Transcendental Medi-
   tation and TM-Sidhi Program   A848
Review for Religious   A356, A401, A517, A618, A699
Review of Religious Research   A907
Revitalization   R78
Revolution durch Meditation   B419
Revolutionary World   A681
Revue d'Electroencephalographie et de Neurophysiologie Clinique   A44, A46
Richard Hittleman's Guide to Yoga Meditation   B335
Richard Hittleman's 30 Day Yoga Meditation Plan   B336
Riding the Ox Home   B372
Rings of Saturn   R27
Rise and Fall of Transcendental Meditation   A35
Role of Attention in Meditation and Hypnosis   A174

Role of Stress in the Psychogenesis of Disease R56
Role of the Transcendental Meditation Program in the Promotion of Athletic Excellence D175
Rorschach Study of the Stages of Mindfulness Meditation A109K
Ruhig und klar B545
Runners and Meditators A238
Runners, Meditators, Weightlifters and Skydivers: A Comparison of Psychological Characteristics D203
Runner's World A775
Running Meditation Response A768

Sacred Words of Power B72
Sadhana B363
Sahaj Marg and Personality and Yoga Psychology and Modern Physiological Theories B932
St. Anthony Messenger A34, A321
St. Chantal on Prayer B141
St. LaSalle and Transcendental Meditation A401
Salivary Electrolytes, Protein and Ph During Transcendental Meditation A508
Salivation A888
Samadhi B737
Samadhi Yoga B820
Samkhya-Yoga Meditation A654
Sampling of the New Religions A873
San Diego Law Review A377
Sanfte Weg B504
Santana B269
Satipatthana sutta B832
Satori B366
Satori: ou, Un début en zazen B97
Saturday Evening Post A88, A456
Saturday Review A468
Saturday Review of Education A719
Scandinavian Review A216
Schleichwege zum Ich B842
Schöpferische Meditation und multidemensionales B285
Schöpferische Meditation und multidemensionales Bewusstsein B289
Schritte nach innen B992
Schweigen und Wort B500
Science A251, A367, A543, A628, A845
Science and Meditation A120
Science de l'etre et l'art de vivre B484
Science Digest A892, A893
Science Looks at the Occult A690
Science News A534
Science of Being and the Art of Living B484, B485, B486
Science of Creative Intelligence as a Theory of Education D158
Science of Creative Intelligence for Secondary Education First-Year Course B477
Science of Creative Intelligence for Secondary Education: Three-Year Curriculum B478
Science of Creative Intelligence--Transcendental Meditation: A Correlated Study with the Art of Violin Playing D65
Science of Meditation B375, B416, B517, B743, B746
Science of Pure Consciousness A262
Science of Zen M21

Science Studies Yoga B256
Scientific American A846
Scientific Approach to Zen Practice B333
Scientific Healing Affirmations B1002, B1003
Scientific Research on the Transcendental Meditation Program: Collected Papers, Vol. 1 A3, A14, A20, A38, A39, A42, A43, A46, A47, A71, A72, A74, A76, A91, A92, A94, A98, A105, A140, A149, A155, A164, A176, A192, A195, A210, A239, A241, A242, A247, A266, A268, A346-A348, A365, A372, A373, A381, A391, A395, A407, A425, A434, A441, A459, A460, A469, A473, A484, A510, A513, A551-A555, A591, A592, A606, A607, A609, A610, A612, A613, A615, A616, A645-A647, A653, A676, A684, A694, A695, A708, A709, A720, A732, A733, A746, A747, A751, A755, A765, A777, A778, A813, A814, A844-A847, A872, A878, A884, A891, A899, A901, A903, A923, B789, D40, D159, D222, S2
Scientific Research on the Transcendental Meditation Program: Collected Papers, Vol. 2 A4, A5, A7, A12, A24, A29, A44, A45, A53, A56, A77, A81-A83, A90, A114, A123, A132, A134, A137, A151, A152, A168, A170, A171, A191, A197, A200, A202, A213, A235, A248, A257, A269, A270, A276, A285, A292, A316, A320, A331, A336, A340, A342, A345, A349, A355, A371, A385-A389, A393, A394, A396, A400, A413, A423, A436, A448, A452, A454, A455, A463, A471, A475, A480, A486, A502, A508, A511, A548, A561, A585, A596, A608, A611, A617, A625, A627, A642, A661, A668, A671, A693, A696, A729, A734, A749, A787, A791, A808, A811, A824, A826, A827, A848, A849, A864, A865, A870, A871, A877, A924, B790, D1, D2, D26, D31, D56, D66, D83, D86, D101, D140, D143, D175, D183, D188, D190, D220, D230
Scientific Research on the Transcendental Meditation Programme B791
Scientific View of Meditation R61
Scientific Way to Use the Energy of Your Mind B619
Scottish Journal of Theology A560
Scripture Meditated A231
Se concentrer pour être heureux B810
Se guérir soi-même B793
Search for Alternate Life-Styles and Philosophies M22
Search for Faith M23
Search in Secret India B108
Search Within B351
Season in Heaven B262
Secondary Prevention of Drug Dependence Through the Transcendental Meditation Program in Philadelphia A561
Secret of Meditation B690
Secret Path B109, B111
Secrets of Chinese Meditation B471, B472
Secrets of Mind-Control B574
Secrets of the Lotus B874
Secular Selling of a Religion A453
Seed Thoughts for Meditation B37
Seelische Selbsthilfe durch Yoga und Meditation B776
Seer of Flying A723
Seins-Prinzipien B33
Seins-Strukturen ins Ur; Der Weg zum Logos-Bewusstein; Weisheit des Logos B33
Selbst-Erkenntnis, Bewusstseins-Lenkung, Lotusblumen-Kraftzentren B33
Selbstentfaltung durch Meditation B785
Selbsterfahrung und Glaube B319
Selbstheilung durch die Kraft der Stille B73
Selbstverwirklichung. (Diene, liebe, meditiere, verwirklich.) Die Ges. vom

göttl. Leben   B821

Selected Papers from the Rothko Chapel Colloquim "Traditional Modes of Contemplation and Action"   B165

Self-Acceptance and Meditation   A228

Self-Actualization and the Transcendental Meditation Technique   D207

Self-Concepts of Regular Transcendental Meditators, Dropout Meditators, and Nonmeditators   A597

Self-Control Meditation and the Treatment of Chronic Anger   A909K

Self-Cultivation by Mind Control as Taught in the Ch'an Mahayana and Taoist Schools in China   B472

Self-Desensitization and Meditation in the Reduction of Public Speaking Anxiety   A422

Self-Enquiry Retreat, Sora, Italy, 1975   B391

Self-Help Through a System of Relaxing Meditation   B509

Self Hypnosis and Other Mind Expanding Techniques   B885

Self-Hypnotic Absorption and Affective Change in a Program of Spiritual Exercises   D50

Self-Induced Depersonalization Syndrome   A414

Self-Introspection and Meditation   B399

Self-Management Procedures for Coping with Stress   A835

Self-Realisation Through Soham Sadhana   B934

Self-Realization and Personality Change   D189

Self-Realization as the Basis of Psychotherapy   A781

Self-Realization Fellowship Lessons   S24

Self Realization: Induced and Spontaneous   A626

Self-Realization Magazine   S24

Self-Regulation Strategy and Altered States of Consciousness   B801

Self-Regulation Technique in the Management of Chronic Arthritic Pain in Hemophilia   A834

Self-Transcendence   B292

Senior Scholastic   A481

Sensory Awakening: Allowing and Chanting   R16

Serenity Suite   R28

Series of Lessons in Raja Yoga   B29

Serotonin, Noradrenaline, Dopamine Metabolites in Transcendental Meditation-Technique   A114

Sets of Arrows   A661

Seven Pillars of Ancient Wisdom   B38

Seven States of Consciousness   B126

Seventeen   A841

Shan-Tao's Interpretation of the Meditative Vision of Buddha Amitayus   A636

Shin Buddhism   B872

Sho do ka, chant de l'immédiat satori   B199

Short and Long Range Effects of the Transcendental Meditation Technique on Fractionated Reaction Time   A686

Short and Long Term Effects of Rest on the Reduction of Stress   D196

Short-Term Effects of Strategies for Self Regulation on Personality Dimensions and Dream Content   A117

Short-Term Endocrine Changes in Transcendental Meditation   A82

Short-Term Longitudinal Effects of the Transcendental Meditation Techniques on EEG Power and Coherence   A201

Siddha Meditation   B559

Siddhi's zweven naar ideaal leven   B782

Sign   A505

Sikh Meditation   A725

Silence   A605

Silence as Yoga   B614

Silence in Action   B893
Silence in the Service of Ego   A731
Silent Mind   M24, R92
Silent Music   B374, B375
Silent Path   B224, B225
Silva Mind Control Method   B810, B891
Simple, Cost-Free and Comfortable Way to Combat Job Tension   A757
Simple Introduction to the Practice of Contemplative Meditation by Normal
    People   B309
Simple Psychophysiologic Technique Which Elicits the Hypometabolic Changes
    of the Relaxation Response   A54
Simple Reaction Time as a Function of Alertness and Prior Mental Activity
    A20
Simple Techniques to Relieve Anxiety   A329
Simulation and Games   A364
Sit Back, Close Your Eyes, Turn Off   A892
Six Lessons on Raja Yoga   B943
Sleeping During Transcendental Meditation   A628, A917
Slow Me Down Lord   A34
So kannst Du Deine Träume verwirklichen   B184
Social Behavior and Personality   A781
Social Context of TM   A515
Social Education   A112, A698
Social Impact of New Religious Movements   A35
Social Justice Review   A449, A450
Social Work   A835
Sociological Analysis   A36, A659
Sociological Effects of the TM-Sidhi Program in Thailand   A134
Sociological Studies of the TM and TM-Sidhi Program in the Philippines   A132
Somatics   A655
Some Aspects of Electroencephalographic Studies in Yogis   A16
Some Aspects of Zen Buddhism   B872
Some Effects of Relaxative and Meditative States on Learning, Memory and
    Other Cognitive Processes   D192
Some Effects of Transcendental Meditation on Children with Learning Problems
    A625
Some Evidence that the Transcendental Meditation Program Increases Intelli-
    gence and Reduces Neuroticism as Measured by Psychological Tests   A814
Some Observations on the Uses of the Transcendental Meditation Program in
    Psychiatry   A94
Some Personality Characteristics Associated with Ananda Marga Meditators
    A601
Some Theoretical Ideas on the Development of Basic Research in Human Body
    Science   A667
Song of Awakening   B693
Sonne um Mitternacht   B771
Soundings   A836
Soundscape TM Series   R29, R31, R34
Special Cultural Events   S11
Spectral Analysis of the EEG in Meditation   A43
Spectrum Suite   R29
Spectrum Suite, Extended Play   R30
Speelse geweten   B233
Spirit of Synergy   B394
Spiritual Community Guide   B839
Spiritual Direction and Meditation   A532, A536
Spiritual Disciplines for Christian Ministry   B241

Spiritual Discourses B814
Spiritual Exercises A701
Spiritual Exercises Toward Learning the Lesson of Penitance and Humiliation at the Foot of the Cross B877
Spiritual Life A600
Spiritual Life: Meditation A589
Spiritual Philosophy of Shrii Shrii Anandmorti S4
Spiritual Science B937
Spiritual Survival in a Complex Age B232
Spirituality Today A259
Sponsa Regis A124, A295, A536, A537, A538, A539, A540
Sport Is a Western Yoga A761
Spotlights on Purity, Knowledge, and Raja Yoga B841
Spurs to Meditation B595
Sri Prabhuji's Lectures Divine on the Theory, Practice, and the Technology of the Science of Rajayoga B755
Srimad Bhagavatam B59
Stability of Skin Resistance Responses One Week After Instruction in the Transcendental Meditation Technique A76
Stages in Prayer B22
Stages of Mindfulness Meditation A110
Star Children R88
Starborn Suite R31
State-of-the-Art Meditation A183K
States of Consciousness B879
States of Human Realization A782
Step Beyond with Edgar Cayce B41
Steven Halpern in Concert R32
Still Mind B3
Still sein, schauen, Christ sein. Einf. in d. Stille B719
Stillhetens psykologi B853
Stimulus-Linked DC-Shift and Auditory Evoked Potentials in Transcendental Meditation A861
Story of Consciousness-Raising Movements B401
Story of Maharishi Mahesh Yogi's First Visit to the United States B601
Story of the Maharishi B369
Strategies for Coping with Stress A660
Strategies of Arousal Control A166
Stress and Anxiety A404
Stress and Bruxism A568
Stress and Meditation A410
Stress and You Series M19
Stress, Causes, Consequences, and Coping Strategies A702
Stress Coping A726
Stress Management Training for the Handicapped A281
Stress, Meditation and the Regression of Cancer A529
Stress, Relaxation, and the Health Educator A323
Stressbewältigung und Transzendentalen Meditation D167
Structure and Dynamics of Attainment of Cessation in Theravada Meditation A420
Strukturen yogischer Meditation B594
Studia Liturgica A752
Studia Missionalia A868, B513
Studia Mystica A177
Studies in Buddhist Meditation B874
Studies in Formative Spirituality A79
Studies in Religion A330, A631

Studies in the Lankavatra Sutra B 872
Studies in Truth B 185, B 187
Studies in Zen B 872
Study in the Spiritual Teachings of Swami Prabhavananda and His Assessment of Christian Spirituality B 564
Study of an Extended Concept of Human Intrapsychic Capacity as Expressed in D.T. Suzuki's Zen Buddhism D 233
Study of Infra-Human Relationships B 754
Study of Meditation in the Science of Counseling D 53
Study of Personality Changes Resulting from the Transcendental Meditation Program A 242
Study of the Ability of Individuals Trained in the Transcendental Meditation Technique to Achieve and Maintain Levels of Physiological Relaxation A 791, D 211
Study of the Principles and Methods of Self-Integration in Integral Yoga D 5
Study of the Psychological Structures of Transcendental, Yoga, and Ignatian Meditation as Applied Phenomena D 12
Study of the Relationship of Transcendental Meditation to Kohlberg's Stages of Moral Reasoning D 159
Study of the Transcendental Meditation Program in the Service of Counseling A 195
Study to Investigate the Effects of Meditation in Reducing Attentional Deficits in a Thirteen-Year-Old Male D 71
Stufen einer Meditation. Nach Zeugnissen der Sufi B 356
Subject of Meditation A 538
Subsensory Perception (SSP), Extrasensory Perception (ESP) and Transcendental Meditation (TM) A 672
Sudden/Gradual Paradigm and Neo-Confucian Mind-Cultivation A 801
Sufi Meditation R 40, R 84
Suggestibility and Meditation A 188
Sumi M 25
Superconscious Meditation B 28
Superconsciousness Through Meditation B 39
Superthinking A 399
Supervisory Management A 500
Supreme Court A 710
Surfer A 215
Survey of Human Growth Movement R 57
Survival Kit B 1005
Sympathetic Activity and Transcendental Meditation A 455
Systematic Hypertension and the Relaxation Response A 58
Systems Approach to Meditation Research A 739K
Systolic Blood Pressure and Long-Term Practice of the Transcendental Meditation and TM-Sidhi Program A 850
Systolic Blood-Pressure and Pulse-Rate During Transcendental Meditation A 840

Tai Chi Chuan A 428
Tai Chi Handbook: Exercise, Meditation, and Self Defense B 393
Take a Relaxation Break A 579
Taking a Flier with TM A 338
Taking Knowledge: A Sociological Approach to the Study of Meditation and the Divine Light Mission D 7
Talks on Meditation, San Francisco, 1975 B 392
Talks on Sri Ram Chandra's Efficacy of Raj-Yoga B 933
Tantra of Kundalini Yoga B 756

Tantric Mysticism of Tibet   B74
Tao and Change   S25
Taoist and Buddhist Contemplative and Healing Yogas Adapted for Western
    Students of the Way   B71
Taxonomy of Meditation-Specific Altered States   A312
Teach Your Child Transcendental Meditation   B585
Teach Yourself Meditation   B328
Teacher Burnout   B15
Teaching Adults   A104
Teaching Christian Meditation to Children   B768
Teaching Meditation to Medical Students   A769
Teaching Religious Experience Through Meditation   A412
Teaching Transcendental Meditation in a Psychiatric Setting   A123
Teaching Transcendental Meditation in Public Schools   A377
Teachings of Ir-a-qi, the Persian Mystic   B704
Teachings of Kirpal Singh   B399
Teachings of William Joseph Chaminade on Mental Prayer   B312
Teachings of Yogi Bhajan   S27
Technique of Spiritual Self-Discovery for the Modern World   B109
Techniques and Theories for the Expansion of Consciousness   B618
Techniques de méditation   B596
Techniques of Mystical Meditation for Achieving Prophecy and the Holy Spirit
    in the Teachings of Isaac Luria and Hayyim Vital   D67
Teilhard and the Maharishi   A293
Teilhard Review   A293
Temperament and Meditation   A539
Tempest Over TM: Questions of TM Courses in the New Jersey Schools
    A804
Temporal Effects of the Transcendental Meditation Technique on Fractionated
    Reflex and Reaction Time   D225
Tension Literature   A263
Testing TM   A707
Theological Studies   A603
Theology of Mystical Experience   A560
Theoretical Model for Humanism   R36
Theorie-Praxis Verhältnis in der Wissenschaft der Kreativen Intelligenz   D87
Theory and Practice of Meditation   B38, B895
Theoria to Theory   A261
Therapeutic Application of a Simple Relaxation Method   A265
Therapeutic Effects of Transcendental Meditation on Drug Users   A285
Theravada Meditation   B398
There Once Was a Guru from Rishikesh   A456
There's No Use Talking to Me--I'm Meditating   A88
Theta Bursts: An EEG Pattern in Normal Subjects Practising the Transcen-
    dental Meditation Technique   A349
30 Day Yoga Meditation Plan   B336
Thirty-Two Vidyas   B575
This Is Reality   B183, B186
This Is Wisdom   B396
This Very Body, the Buddha   B671
Thomist Reader   A226
Thoughtline   S6
Three Modes of Meditation   A294
Through an Eastern Window   B347
Tibetan Book of the Dead   R91
Tibetan Meditation: Theory and Practice   B677
Tibetische Buddhismus   B835

Tibetische Meditationen B 955
Tiefgang-Reihe B 719
Time A 549, A 593, A 723, A 804, A 816, A 818, A 820
Time in Meditation and Sex Differences Related to Intrapersonal and Inter-
     personal Orientation D 86
Time Out From Tension A 648
TM: A Cosmic Confidence Trick B 13
TM: A Prescription to Cure Stress A 799
TM: A Signpost for the World B 421
TM: An Alphabetical Guide to the Transcendental Meditation Program B 273
TM: An Investment with Positive Returns A 433
TM and Business B 499
TM and Cult Mania B 625
TM and Rehabilitation A 670
TM and Science A 562
TM and Stress (Physiological and Subjective), Internal Versus External Locus
     of Control and Self-Concept D 16
TM and Sun Myung Moon B 89
TM and the Nature of Enlightenment B 127
TM and the Religion-In-School-Issue A 40, A 75
TM and the Salesman A 339
TM as a Secondary School Subject A 220
TM at Folsom Prison A 13
TM Book B 196, B 197
TM Comes to the Heartland of the Midwest: Maharishi International Univer-
     sity A 204
TM Course Entangles Church, State A 815
TM Craze A 816
TM*: Descubrimiento de la energía interna y superacíon del stress B 77
TM: Discovering Inner Energy and Overcoming Stress B 75, B 76, B 77, B 78,
     B 79, B 80
TM: Expensive Meditation A 885
TM Goes to School A 208
TM Grounded A 817
TM: How to Find Peace of Mind Through Meditation B 908
TM in Court B 927
TM in the Pen A 818
TM Is for Kids Too B 406
TM: Management Finds a New Technique to Increase Productivity A 819
TM, meditación transcendental B 196
TM Opponents A 75
TM or CM B 759
TM Program B 271, B 272, B 508
TM Program, Psychiatry, and Enlightenment B 82
TM Program: Releasing Stress and Finding Happiness R 4
TM: Self-Transcendence or Self-Deception A 255
TM: Some Preliminary Findings A 247
TM Technique B 730
TM Technique and the Art of Learning B 912
TM: The Drugless High A 820
TM, Transcendental Meditation B 630
(TM) Transcendental Meditation: Hur man finner den inre energin och över-
     vinner stress B 79
TM und Industriegesellschaft D 22
TM Versus RR A 52
TM Wants You B 301
To Ease Your Mind A 821

To Forget the Self B119
To Know How to Wait B23
To Shine During Meetings, Enliven the Mind A599
Today's Catholic Teacher A409
Today's Health A712
Tonic of Wildness A216
Tools for Meditation B714
Tools for Transformation A823
Torch of Certainty B407K
Total Meditation B930
Toward a Cognitive Reconceptualization of Meditation A95
Toward Full Development of the Person A680
Toward "Pure Awareness" R47
Traditional Modes of Contemplation and Action B165, B909
Training A533
Training and Development Journal A748
Training of the Student in the Life of Prayer A163
Training of the Zen Buddhist Monk B872
Traité sur l'oraison B552
Tranquility Without Pills B700, B701
Transactional Analysis and Meditation Training as Interventions in Teacher Education D70
Transcendence Is as American as Ralph Waldo Emerson A122
Transcendent Psychology B144
Transcendental Consciousness A404
Transcendental Explosion B966
Transcendental Hesitation B541
Transcendental Meditation A113, A172, A193, A301, A474, A481, A492, A494, B485, B486, B702, R6, R10, R49
Transcendental Meditation: A Christian View B300
Transcendental Meditation: A Clinical Evaluation D142
Transcendental Meditation, a Multipurpose Tool in Clinical Practice A423
Transcendental Meditation: A Mystic Cult of Self-Intoxication B140
Transcendental Meditation: A New Method of Reducing Drug Abuse A498
Transcendental Meditation: A Psychological Interpretation A27
Transcendental Meditation: A Revitalization of the American Civil Religion A649
Transcendental Meditation: A Scientific Approach B761
Transcendental Meditation, Altered Reality Testing, and Behavioral Change A264
Transcendental Meditation: An Adjunct to Psychotherapy R5
Transcendental Meditation: An Analysis of the Rhetoric of a Social Movement as Innovation D38
Transcendental Meditation: An Introduction to the Practice and Aims of TM B342
Transcendental Meditation and Assertive Training in the Treatment of Social Anxiety A860, D223
Transcendental Meditation and Asthma A901
Transcendental Meditation and Christian Prayer A289
Transcendental Meditation and Concentration Ability A700
Transcendental Meditation and Creativity A211
Transcendental Meditation and Dental Hygiene A780
Transcendental Meditation and Dianetics A839
Transcendental Meditation and Fine Perceptual-Motor-Skill A895
Transcendental Meditation and Heterohypnosis as Altered States of Consciousness A48
Transcendental Meditation and Its Influence on the Self-Concept D230

Transcendental Meditation and Its Potential Application in the Field of Special Education A246

Transcendental Meditation and Its Potential Uses for Schools A698

Transcendental Meditation and Its Potential Value in the Monastic Life A501

Transcendental Meditation and Meaning of Religion Under Establishment Clause A825

Transcendental Meditation and Mental Retardation A235

Transcendental Meditation and Mirror-Tracing Skill A894

Transcendental Meditation and Productivity A266

Transcendental Meditation and Progressive Relaxation: Their Physiological Effects A809

Transcendental Meditation and Progressive Relaxation: Their Psychological Effects A810

Transcendental Meditation and Psychological Health A365

Transcendental Meditation and Rehabilitation at Folsom Prison A4

Transcendental Meditation and Selected Life Attitude D137

Transcendental Meditation and Social Psychological Attitudes A340

Transcendental Meditation and Stuttering A513

Transcendental Meditation, and the Great Night Festival of Shiva, March 11, 1975 A449

Transcendental Meditation and the Science of Creative Intelligence A472

Transcendental Meditation and the Self-Reported Incidence of Psychosomatically Related Symptoms B156

Transcendental Meditation and the Tonic Vibration Reflex D26

Transcendental Meditation and TM-Sidhi Program B235

Transcendental Meditation and Yoga as Reciprocal Inhibitors A100

Transcendental Meditation as a Means of Trait Anxiety Reduction in a Correctional Setting D141

Transcendental Meditation as a Reciprocal Inhibitor in Psychotherapy A93

Transcendental Meditation as an Alternative to Heroin Abuse in Servicemen A18

Transcendental Meditation: Can It Fight Drug Abuse A893

Transcendental Meditation Challenges the Church A334

Transcendental Meditation: Consciousness Expansion as a Rehabilitation Technique A499

Transcendental Meditation: Effect of Pretreatment Personality and Prognostic Expectancy Upon Degree of Reported Personality Change D190

Transcendental Meditation Experience B179

Transcendental Meditation Goes Public A313

Transcendental Meditation Goes to School A209

Transcendental Meditation in Correctional Settings A470

Transcendental Meditation in Hypertension A90

Transcendental Meditation in the Boardroom A116

Transcendental Meditation in the Management of Heart Failure A382

Transcendental Meditation in the Obstetrical Psychoprophylaxis A355

Transcendental Meditation in Treating Asthma A373

Transcendental Meditation: Maharishi Mahesh Yogi and the Science of Creative Intelligence B248

Transcendental Meditation Movement D174, D180

Transcendental Meditation Primer B323

Transcendental Meditation Program A822

Transcendental Meditation Program and a Basic Paradigm Shift in Science and Psychotherapy A480

Transcendental Meditation Program and Academic Achievement A347

Transcendental Meditation Program and Children's Personality A448

Transcendental Meditation Program and Cigarette Smoking A734

Transcendental Meditation Program and Creativity A484

Transcendental Meditation Program and Crime Rate Change in a Sample of Forty-Eight Cities A202

Transcendental Meditation Program and Drug Abuse A903

Transcendental Meditation Program and Essential Hypertension A755

Transcendental Meditation Program and Its Effects on Psychological Functionings in Secondary School Students of a Rural Indian High School A585

Transcendental Meditation Program and Marital Adjustment A24

Transcendental Meditation Program and Normalization of Weight A872

Transcendental Meditation Program and Progressive Relaxation A176

Transcendental Meditation Program and Rehabilitation A164

Transcendental Meditation Program and Rehabilitation at Folsom State Prison A5

Transcendental Meditation Program as a Possible Treatment Modality for Drug Offenders A671

Transcendental Meditation Program as a Predictor of Crime Rate Changes in the Kansas City Metropolitan Area A200

Transcendental Meditation Program as an Education-Technology-Research and Applications A199

Transcendental Meditation Program at MCI Walpole A248

Transcendental Meditation Program at Stillwater Prison A39

Transcendental Meditation Program for Business People B410

Transcendental Meditation Program for the Reduction of Stress-Related Conditions A25

Transcendental Meditation Program in British Secondary Schools A342

Transcendental Meditation Program in the Classroom A751

Transcendental Meditation Program in the College Curriculum A22

Transcendental Meditation Program: New Dimension in Living for the Dialysis/Transplant Client A213

Transcendental Meditation Program's Effect on Addictive Behavior A21

Transcendental Meditation: Relaxation or Religion B130

Transcendental Meditation, Self-Actualization, and Global Personality A426

Transcendental Meditation: Some Implications for Education A577

Transcendental Meditation: Stressing Natural Harmony A766

Transcendental Meditation Technique, Adrenocortical Activity, and Implications for Stress A392

Transcendental Meditation Technique and Acute Experimental Pain A548

Transcendental Meditation Technique and Creativity A826

Transcendental Meditation Technique and Drug Abuse Counselors A609

Transcendental Meditation Technique and EEG Alpha Activity A441

Transcendental Meditation: Technique and Interpretation A341

Transcendental Meditation Technique and Its Effects on Sensory-Motor Performance A684

Transcendental Meditation Technique and Quantum Physics A210

Transcendental Meditation Technique and Skin Resistance Response to Loud Tones A765

Transcendental Meditation Technique and Temperature Homeostasis A510

Transcendental Meditation Technique in Secondary Education A471, D130

Transcendental Meditation TM Book B197

Transcendental Meditation: Treating the Patient as Well as the Disease A482

Transcendental Meditation Versus Muscle Relaxation A927

Transcendental Meditation Versus Pseudo-Meditation on Visual Choice Reaction Time A371

Transcendental Mirage B65

Transcendental Misconceptions B792

Transcendental Sex B265

Transcendente meditatie B414

Transfiguring the Ordinary Through Holistic Meditation B171
Transformation of Conscious Experience and Its EEG Correlates A212
Transformations of Consciousness A254
Transpersonal Dimensions in Psychology B58
Transpersonal Psychologies B880
Transpersonal Psychology and Snydic Energy A644
Transpersonale Psychologie B881
Transpersonalizing Education in the '80s A837
Transzendentale Meditation B80, B298
Transzendentale Meditation in der geburtshilflichen Psychoprophylaxe B318,
    D92
Transzendentale Meditation, neue Wege zum Heil B315
Transzendentale Meditation, TM-Sidhi-Programm und Rigidität-Flexibilität
    B17, D6
Transzendentale Meditation und Autogeneses Training B403, D118
Transzendentale Meditation und wohin sie führt B783
Transzendentalen Meditation D33
Trap: Transcendental Meditation A450
Tratado de la oración y meditación B627
Travels in Inner Space B738
Treatise of Mental Prayer B549
Treatise on Prayer and Meditation B628
Treatment of Anxiety A73
Treatment of Hypertension with Biofeedback and Relaxation Techniques A260
Treatment of Insomnia by the Transcendental Meditation Program A555
Treatment of Psychophysiological Disorders and Severe Anxiety by Behavior
    Therapy, Hypnosis and Transcendental Meditation A169
Treatment of Retarded Ejaculation with Psychotherapy and Meditative Relaxa-
    tion A189
Trishula S4
TSH, LH, Cortisol Response to TRH and LH-RH and Insulin Hypoglycaemia
    in Subjects Practising Transcendental Meditation A8
Tua mente é um foco irradiante B296
Tuning Down with TM A705
Tuning the Human Instrument B304, R33
Türen nach innen B69, B70
Turning East: The Promise and Peril of the New Orientalism B173
Turning East: Why Americans Look to the Orient for Spirituality, and What
    that Search Can Mean to the West B173
Turning In B672
12-Month Follow-Up of Yoga and Bio-Feedback in the Management of Hyper-
    tension A639
Two Communities M26
Two Concentration Methods A319
Two Faces of Meditation A713
Two New Cults B89
Two Studies of Extrasensory Perception and Subliminal Perception A673

Über die asthetische Erziehung des Menschen D163
Überselbst B110
Übung des Leibes auf dem innern Weg B222
Übungen zur gegenständichen Meditation B967
Übungen zur Konzentration und Meditation B822
Übungsbuch zur Meditation B905, B906
Ultimate Risk B751, B753
Undoing Yourself with Energized Meditation and Other Devices B353

Unique Way to a Better Life A904
Universal Principles for a Universal Religion B937
Universal Structures and Dynamics of Creativity A750
Universality of Music R26
Unpopular Science S5
Unsichtbare Kirche B771
Unstressing the Stressed Up Executive A267
Urvasi M27
U.S. Catholic A885
Use of Meditation in the Treatment of Alcoholism D164
Use of Meditation Techniques for the Management of Stress in a Working
 Population A127
Use of the Transcendental Meditation Program as a Therapy with Juvenile
 Offenders A140
Use of Transcendental Meditation as Therapy with Juvenile Offenders D40
Uses of Self-Regulation Techniques in Alleviating Stress Disorders and Pro-
 moting Healing R56
Using Meditation in Stress Situations A727
Using TM at Work B250

Varieties of the Meditative Experience A310, B281
Variety, Exercise, Meditation Can Relieve Practice Stress A569
Vedanta Kesari A632
Vedantic Philosophy of Religion A194
Vedantic Raj Yoga B732
Vejen M28
Veränderungen spezifischer bzw. spezieller Leistungen (Aufmerksamkeit) und
 des subjektiven Erlebens nach Ausübung der Technik der TM in Vergleich
 zu einfacher Entspannung D27
Verhalten von Atemzugvolumen, Herzschlagfrequentz, atemgaszusammensetzung
 bei Sportstudenten während der Ausübung der TM im Vergleich zu nicht-
 meditierenden Sportstudenten D186
Verweilen vor Gott B888
Verwirklichung der idealen Gesellschaft B487
Very Practical Meditation B969
Vie contemplative est-elle possible dans le monde B270
View, Meditation and Action B695
Vignette Series M23
Violence of Just Sitting A736
Vipassana-Meditation B280
Vishvamitra S23
Vision of Possibilities Suggested by the Teaching of Maharishi Mahesh Yogi
 B126
Visit with India's High-Powered New Prophet A374
Visual Imagery Change During Relaxation-Meditation Training D93
Vivid Visualization and Dim Visual Awareness in the Regression of Cancer in
 Meditation A530
Vocational Guidance Quarterly A451, A594
Vogue A489
Voices: The Art and Science of Psychotherapy A322
Voie du silence B189, B191
Voies de l'oraison mentale B446
Voluntary Controls B787
Voluntary Slowing of Heart Rate D45
Vom Sinn der Kontemplation B533
Vom Wesen der Meditation B447

Vom Wesen und Wert des meditierenden Übens in der Psychotherapie. Vortrag
B718
Vrai Zen, source vive, révolution intérieure B199
Vulnerability and Power in the Therapeutic Process A876

Wagnis Orange, Bhagwan Shree Rajneesh B753
Wahrhaftig beten B534
Wahrheit tun B423
Wahrheitsstudien B187
Wake the Dragon B760
Wakeful Hypometabolic State A847
Wandlung durch Meditation B306
Wang Yang-Ming and Meditation A890
Was ist Meditation B673, B987
Was jedermann sucht B48
Washington Buddhist S9
Wat is transcendente meditatie B980
Watch and Pray B313
Watch with Me B877
Way and the Goal of Raja Yoga B741
Way of Compassion B872
Way of Hara B994
Way of Non-Attachment B208
Way of Zazen B255
Way to Cope with Executive Stress A366
Way to Freedom B124
Way to Fulfillment B272
Ways of Mental Prayer B446
Wealth Within B509
Weg der Stille B225
Weg ins Leben B964
Weg nach innen B111
Weg van zazen B98
Weg zur Vollendung B774, B775
Wege der Meditation heute B961
Wege zu einem meditativen Leben B640
Weisheit des Überselbst B112
Well and the Cathedral B648
Welt meditieren B56
Wereld in ons innerlijk ontdekken aan de hand van Johan Tauler B379
Wessel Gansfort and the Art of Meditation D205
Western Humanities Review A11
Western Psychologist A647
Western Woman's Unique Experiences in Thailand Monasteries B305
Wharton Magazine A512
What Can the Cancer Patient Expect from Intensive Meditation A531
What Can We Learn from Zen A669
What Everyone Should Know About Transcendental Meditation B455
What Is Contemplation B532, B533
What Is Enlightenment B129
What Is Meditation A540, A887, B673, B674, B973
What Is Meditation? Does It Help A580
What Is Zen B872
What School Physicians, Nurses and Health Educators Should Know About
Transcendental Meditation A106
What Science Is Discovering About the Potential Benefits of Meditation A712

What the Supervisor Should Know About Transcendental Meditation   A500
What's Wrong with Eating Meat   S4
When Doctors Meditate   A351
When Fires Burn   B970
Who Are You   B177
Why and How of Meditation   B537
Why Meditation   B894
Why Pay to Meditate   A514
Wie der Mond stirbt   B535
Wie Sie die Technik der schopferischen Imagination anwenden können, um
   Ihre Träume zu verwirklichen   B188
Wiedergeburt durch innere Sekretion   B215
Wind and the River   M29
Wisdom of the Overself   B112, B113
Wissenschaftliche Heilmeditationen   B1003
Woman's Workbook   B376
World Government News   S29
World Peace Project   A608
Worldwide Directory of Meditation and Yoga Retreats   B989
Word Into Silence   B490
World Review   S17
Worlds of Faith   A102
Worte sind Brücken   B870
Writing, Inner Speech and Meditation   A558
Writings from the Philokalia on Prayer of the Heart   B990

Year of the Guru   A376
Yes, We Have No Nirvanas   A838
Yoga   A104, R48
Yoga and Contemplation   B16
Yoga and God   B192
Yoga and Meditation   B329
Yoga and Meditation for Everyone   B611
Yoga and Prayer   B538
Yoga, Arbeit am Selbst   B362
Yoga Asanas   B488
Yoga de meditação de Maharishi Mahesh Yogi   B632
Yoga en meditatie   B8
Yoga et prière   B538, B539
Yoga for Beginners   B758
Yoga for Drug Abuse   A59
Yoga in America   S20
Yoga in den zwei Welten   B996, B997, B998, B999
Yoga Journal   A351, A689, S10
Yoga Lessons for Developing Spiritual Consciousness   B556
Yoga Meditation   B213, B965
Yoga Meditation and Flooding in the Treatment of Anxiety Neurosis   A296
Yoga Meditation Effect on the EEG and EMG Activity   A217
Yoga Mystic Songs for Meditation   B427
Yoga Mysticism for Modern Man   B87
Yoga oder Meditation, der Weg des Abendlandes   B641
Yoga of Breathing, Yoga of Posture, and Yoga of Meditation   B327
Yoga of Daily Life   R65
Yoga of Meditation   B137
Yoga of Tibet   B923
Yoga Philosophy and Meditation   B337

Yoga pratiques (Karma, Bhakti, Raja) B944
Yoga Psychology B6
Yoga Psychology and Dimensions of Counseling Practice B171
Yoga, science et connaissance de l'homme B713
Yoga Seeker B260
Yoga, Tantra and Meditation in Daily Life B368
Yoga, Tantra and Meditation in Your Daily Life B368
Yoga, tanra och meditation i min vardag B368
Yoga und Meditation im Osten und im Western B252
Yoga und Medizin B993
Yoga Uniting East and West B996
Yoga 'Yogic Feats', and Hypnosis in the Light of Empirical Research A167
Yoga, Zen, Meditation B777
Yogi Philosophy B29
Yogoda Magazine S24
You Are Not the Target R38
You Book B739
You Can Change Yourself and the World with Christian Asian Meditation A41
You: Prayer for Beginners and Those Who Have Forgotten How B1006
Youniverse B896
Your Innate Asset for Combating Stress A60
Your Needs Met B2
Your Own Worst Enemy M30
Your Very Own Meditator A379
Youth Discovers Meditation A918

Za-Zen: la pratique du Zen B200
Zauberkraft der transzendentalen Meditation B586
Zeitschrift für Klinische Psychologie A285
Zen B435
Zen: A Manual for Westerners B798
Zen and Hasidism B1007
Zen and Japanese Buddhism B872
Zen and Japanese Culture B872
Zen and the Mind B333
Zen and the Spiritual Exercises A603
Zen Art for Meditation B343
Zen Buddhism and Its Influence on Japanese Culture B872
Zen Buddhism and Psychoanalysis B872
Zen Buddhism, Selected Writings B872
Zen Catholicism of Thomas Merton A485
Zen Doctrine of No-Mind B872
Zen Dust B546
Zen Environment B554
Zen for Missionaries A805
Zen in Ryoko-in M31
Zen Master M32
Zen-Meditation B436
Zen Meditation: A Broad View B857
Zen Meditation: A Study of Regression in Service of the Ego D150
Zen Meditation and Behavioral Self-Control A740, A745
Zen Meditation and Behavioral Self-Control Strategies Applied to a Case of
    Generalized Anxiety A741
Zen Meditation and the Development of Empathy in Counselors A467
Zen Meditation: eine Einfuhrung B436
Zen Meditation, Expectancy, and Their Relative Contributions to Changes in

Perceptual Flexibility   D58
Zen Meditation for Christians   B437
Zen-Meditation für Christen   B435, B438
Zen Meditation in the Elderly   D39
Zen Meditation Therapy   B334
Zen Meditators: A Clinical Study   D116
Zen Mind, Beginner's Mind   B873
Zen Monk's Life   B872
Zen Notes   S12
Zen: The Eternal Now   R93
Zen Training   B797
Zen, un camino hacia la propia identidad   B439
Zen unter Christen   B440
Zen: Way to Enlightenment   B441
Zen, Weg zur Erleuchtung   B439, B441, B442
Zen Without Zen Masters   B51
Zen Writings Series   B119
Zen. Zauber oder Zucht   B861
Zetetic   A906
Zienswijze op occultisme, meditatie, spiritisme, reincarnatie, ufo's   B1008
Zodiac Suite   R22, R34
Zomaar een glimach. Chinese Zenmeditatie   B935
Zum Paradies des Menschen   B848
Zur Psycho-Physiologie ruhevoller Wachheit, EEG und subjektives psycho-
    logisches Befinden während der Ausübung der TM im Vergleich mit den
    Schlafstadien dierselben Versuchspersonen   D220
Zur Starkung der Identität durch Entspannungsubungen am Beispiel der TM
    mit möglichen Auswirkungen im Alltagsleben   D187
Zygon   A405

Abhidharma A306, A311, A785
Absolute A290
Absorption A770
Academic achievement A129, A149,
    A207, A250, A347, A434,
    A751, D1, D57, D101
Accidents A134, A454
Acoustic stimulation A55
ACTH A877
Action A259, B165, B909, B914,
    B915, B917, B919
Activeness A871
Actualism meditation A250
Acupuncture A101, A587, A667
Adipositas D153
Administrators see Executives
Adolescents A715, A808, D101
Adrenal cortex hormones A392
Adult Education D49
Advaita Vedanta A138
Aerobic exercise D105
Aesthetics D163
Affection D86
Age D217
Age of Enlightenment A607
Age of Enlightenment Governor
    Training Courses A613
Aged D39
Aggression A242, A671, A746,
    A787, A788, D165, D195,
    see also Hostility
Aging A848
Agni Yoga Society S1
Ahamgrahopasana A86
Alcohol drinking and
    Evangenlical religion A277
    Exercise D144
    Meditation A501K, D144
    Transcendental Meditation A57,
        A72, A407, A460, A709,
        A733
Alcoholics Anonymous and Medi-
    tation A905
Alcoholism and
    Meditation A291, A634, A905,

    D95, D164, D170
    Progressive relaxation D95, D170
    Relaxation techniques A633, A634
    Self-regulation strategies A739
    Transcendental Meditation A795
Aldosterone A544
Alertness A20, A42, A400, A871,
    A899
Aletheia Psycho-Physical Foundation
    B519
Alice Bailey Movement see Bailey,
    Alice B.
Alpha waves A56, A153, A279, A352,
    A441, A465, A473, A483, A696,
    A846, A899, D90, D224
Altered states of consciousness see
    Consciousness states
Altered States of Consciousness In-
    ventory D22K
American Association of Physicians
    Practicing the Transcendental
    Meditation and TM-Sidhi Pro-
    grams S2
American Conference of Therapeutic
    Selfhelp/Selfhealth Social Action
    Clubs S3
American Foundation for the Science
    of Creative Intelligence S29
American Sufi Order A631
Amino acids A385, A391
Amita meditation A636
Amitayur-Buddhanusmrti-sutra A636
Anaerobic exercise D105
Ananda Marga Yoga A153, A230,
    A601, B684, D192
Ananda Marga Yoga Society B519, S4
Ananda Meditation Retreat B519
Anecdotes B51
Anger A400, A824, A909K
Angina pectoris A423, A923
Anglican Church B241
Anthroposophy B423, B447
Anxiety A263 see also Test anxiety
Anxiety and
    Alcoholism A291, A633, A905, D95

Assertive training A860, D223
Athletes D77, D81, D203
Behavior therapy A169
Biofeedback training A300,
  A675, A739, D24, D198
Blindness A363
Blood pressure A73, A633
Chemical dependency A905
Children A476, A625, D29
Christian meditation D47
Clinically Standardized Medita-
  tion A256, A465
Cognitive meditation D63
Contemplation D151K
Counselors A609
Dentistry A565
Desensitization A835, D57, D63
Exercise A32, A33, A717, D9,
  D105, D121
Flooding A296
Gestalt therapy A329, D121
Heart rate D231
Hypnosis A73, A169, A457,
  A565, A739, D77, D179
Juvenile offenders D40
Meditation A99, A175, A300,
  A355, A429, A666, A717,
  A739, A763, A835, A905, D9,
  D24, D29, D30, D34, D57,
  D63, D91K, D95, D98, D105,
  D113, D170, D177, D179,
  D191, D203, D212, D227,
  D234
Mental ataraxis A527
Music D77
Open Focus A256
Prisoners D34, D141, D212
Progressive relaxation A176,
  A291, A353, A465, A739,
  A806, A810, D91K, D95,
  D170, D227, D231
Public speaking A422
Quiet sitting A256, A291, A621,
  A763, D9
Relaxation response A33,
  A179, D32, D184, D198
Relaxation techniques A32,
  A73, A117, A175K, A265,
  A300, A457, A675, A835,
  A926, D30, D77, D81, D124,
  D193
Rest D30
Scuba diving D81
Self-concept A331
Self-hypnosis A73, A457
Social relations A860, D223
Teachers A827, D98

Transcendental Meditation A5, A39,
  A90, A91, A117, A123, A164,
  A169, A176, A197, A213, A242,
  A245, A247, A248, A257, A331,
  A336, A365, A381, A404, A423,
  A460, A477, A554, A565, A592,
  A609, A621, A625, A675, A694,
  A764, A778, A806, A810, A811,
  A824, A827, A860, A926, D21,
  D40, D78, D100, D140, D141,
  D142, D177, D195, D197, D200,
  D223
  Workers A451 see also Business;
    Executive stress
Yoga A296, A363, D34, D121
Zen meditation A302, A329, A741,
  D42, D75, D107, D124
Aquarian Research Foundation B519,
  S5
Arcana Workshops B519, S6
Arica Institute B354
Arica training D37
Arithmetic D101
Arousal A46, A114, A166, A369,
  A570, A739, A881, A912, D117,
  D173
Art B715, M13, M25
Arthritis A423, A834
Arunachala Ashrama B519
Ashrams B212, B519, B676, B989
Asia S11
Assertiveness A860, D223
Associated Readers of Tarot Interna-
  tional S7
Association for Development of Human
  Potential S30
Association for Research and Enlighten-
  ment S8
Association for the Understanding of
  Man A598
Asthma and Transcendental Meditation
  A233, A372, A373, A423, A679,
  A901
Astral projection B46, B47
Astrology A690, B339, B724, D235
Athletes A676, D77, D175, D203
Atlanteans B30
Attention [see also Concentration]
  Anxiety D210
  Behavioral management D210
  Buddhism A84
  Children A476, A677, D71
  Exercise A677
  Expectations A772, D226
  Hypnosis A48, A174, A772, A773,
    A832
  Learning A370, A554

Locus of control A205
Meditation A174, A175, A205,
    A476, A772, A773, A829,
    A832, A833, A920, B257,
    B522, B812, B988, D69, D71,
    D110, D114, D210, D226, R44
Performance A772
Reading A476, D210
Relaxation techniques A677,
    D29K, D210
Students D199
Transcendental Meditation A48,
    A554, B623, D27, D176,
    D199, D200
Vipashyana meditation A759
Workers A451
Zen meditation A319, A370,
    D119, D145
Attitudes A340, A431, A737,
    D137, D142
Attrition A186, A685
Auditory acuity A475
Auditory discrimination A653
Auditory evoked potentials A51,
    A55, A427, A511, A861
Auditory perception D10
Auditory stimulation A650, A651
Auditory thresholds D109, D188
Aum Temple of Universal Truth
    B519
Aurobindo, Sri A836, D5
Autogenic training A252, A260,
    B344, B403, B699, B851,
    B885, D118, R14, R53
Automobile accidents A454
Autonomic changes A615
Autonomic functioning A891
Autonomic nervous system and
    Transcendental Meditation
    A76, A196, A455
Autonomic stability A76, A168,
    A606, D46
Awareness A47, A135, A174,
    A517, A542, A610, A750,
    A759, A794, A914, B882,
    D160, R16, R44, R57
Awareness meditation A402

Bahadur, Dinesh M10
Bailey, Alice B. B519, S6
Barnet, Vermont A111
Beatles A456
Behavior A738, A740, A741, A744,
    A745
Behavior disorders A677

Behavior modification A234, A264,
    A545, A737, D2
Behavior therapy A55K, A169, A546,
    A910K
Behavioral flexibility A613
Behavioral management D210
Behavioral relaxation training D29K
Benson, Herbert see Relaxation
    response
Bhagavadgita B201
Bhagavatapurana B576
Bhakti A919
Bhaktivedanta, Swami A376
Bible A231, A538, A540, A706, A707,
    B96, B157, B219, B236, B387
Bibliographies A263, A655, B60,
    B133, B135, B385, B386, B643,
    B802
Bimodal consciousness D44
Bioenergetic exercise D121
Biofeedback training A17, B587,
    B588, B619, M22
Biofeedback training and
    Academic performance D231
    Arousal control A166
    Asthma A233
    Anxiety A300, A675, D81, D198,
        D231
    Athletes D81
    Blood pressure A360, A640,
        D108
    Christian meditation D36
    Consciousness states D215
    Creativity A756
    Drug abuse A101
    Executives A234, A375
    Exercise D182
    Heart rate D45
    Hypertension A19, A89, A260,
        A273, A335, A637, A639, A721,
        A793, D36
    Imagery A196
    Intelligence B799
    Locus of control A922
    Meditation A162, D81
    Mental illness A297
    Muscle tension A922, D3, D108
    Passive meditation A786K
    Relaxation response D182, D198
    Relaxation techniques D108, D215,
        M19
    Self-regulation A781
    Stress A234, A516, A748, B133,
        B428, D4, D81, D108
    Stuttering D3
    Transcendental Meditation A130,
        A131, D45

Type A behavior   D108
Vasoconstriction   D3
Biophysics   A210
Birth trauma   A28, A355
Blind   A363
Blood   A245, A387, A436
Blood flow   A386, A393, A469,
     A483, D17
Blood lactate   A846
Blood plasma   A367, A385, A389,
     A394
Blood pressure   see also   Hyper-
     tension
Blood pressure and
   Autogenic training   D108
   Biofeedback training   A640,
     D108, D182
   Breathing   A674
   Exercise   B182
   Hypnosis   A62, A73
   Isolation tank   D234
   Meditation   A73, A142, A335,
     A640, A652, A722, A846,
     D108, D234
   Progressive relaxation   D108
   Relaxation response   A62,
     A69K, A367, D182
   Relaxation techniques   A335,
     A360
   Rest   A369
   Self-hypnosis   A73
   Transcendental Meditation   A7,
     A31, A53, A71, A90, A91,
     A151, A369, A455, A755,
     A840, A847, A850, B951,
     D222
   Type A behavior   D234
Blue Mountain Center of Meditation
     B519
Bodaiji Mission   B519
Bodhi   A547
Body awareness   R50
Bonaventure, St.   A158
Brain   A114, A210, A274, A511,
     A617, A627, A661, A826,
     A884, D224   see also
     Cerebral hemispheric domi-
     nance
Breath suspension   A29, A240
Breathing   A155, A337, A348,
     R63
Breathing exercises   D206
Breathing meditation   A674, A914,
     R76
Brotherhood of the Sun   B519
Bruxism   A568
Buddha, Gottama   A303, A304

Buddhism   B116, B269, B347, B548,
     B596, B693, B876, M28
   Abhidharma psychology   A306,
     A311, A687, A785
   Attention   A84
   Behavior modificaiton   A545, A546
   Bodhi   A547
   Burma   A419, B120
   Calmness   A84, B121, B397
   Chinese meditation   B471, B472
   Christian prayer   A178
   Concentration   A308, A312, B350
   Consciousness states   A303, A304,
     A312
   Freedom   A794
   Healing   B71, B207
   Hypertension   A784
   Insight   A308, B279, B397
   Insight meditation   A689, B208,
     B633, B634, B450, B762
   Jhanani   A325
   Koans   A919
   Lay meditation   D218
   Mahayana meditation   B117, B479
   Meditation   A303, A304, A306,
     A330, A545, B146, B164, B350,
     B351, B383, B620, B858, D8,
     M24, M27, R90, R92
   Meditation centers   A419
   Mental health   D206
   Metaphysics   A330
   Mindfulness meditation   A180,
     A305, A312, A547, B249
   Monasteries   A495, A547, B305
   Neoplatonism   A687
   Prajna   B117
   Pseudo-Dionysius   A687
   Psychotherapy   A125, A306, B346,
     D8
   Samadhi   A547
   Samkara   A138
   Sarvastivadin meditation   B166
   Satipatthana meditation   B495,
     B589, B805, B832
   Self-concept   D134
   Self-control   A546, A794
   Southern school   B469, B470
   Sri Lanka   A495
   Thailand   B305, D218
   Theravada meditation   A159, A178,
     A689, B166, B398, B409, B874,
     B928, D84, D134, S9
   Trance   A84
   United States   B454
   Vipassana meditation   A689, B207,
     B208
   Visuddhimagga   B205

Buddhist Association of the United States B519
Buddhist Vihara Society S9
Burma A419, B120
Burnout B15
Business see also Executive stress
Business and
Behavior modification A234
Biofeedback training A234, A375, A516
Clinically Standardized Meditation A127, A141, A533
Encounter groups A234
Meditation A375, A479, A660, D112
Progressive relaxation A127
Relaxation response A61, A757
Transactional analysis A234
Transcendental Meditation A116, A146, A234, A266, A267, A339, A366, A415, A433, A458, A500, A516, A532, A599, A799, A819, A921, B410, B499
Yoga A234
Zen meditation A516

Cabala A177, B387, B511, B680, B859, D67, S16
California Yoga Teachers Association S10
Callisthenics B4
Calmness A84, D230
Cambridge Buddhist Association B519
Canada A869
Cancer A96, A107, A518, A519, A520, A521, A522, A523, A524, A525, A526, A528, A529, A530, A531, A913, R56
Carbon dioxide A54, A70, A244, A582
Cardiac output A53, A245, A865
Cardiovascular system A283
Career development A594
Carrington, Patricia A141, A512, A533
Cassettes B644
Catholic authors B23, B99, B268, B431, B528, B626, B843
Catholic Church A485, B99, B210
Cayce, Edgar A430, A678, B40,

B41, B650, B651, B794, R89, S8
Center of India Culture S11
Centering A294, A507, A655, A768, A902, B443, B760, R40, R84
Cerebral hemispheric dominance A2, A56, A274, A360, A617, A826, D10, D224
Cerebral hemispheric functions A224K, A627, A662
Chakras R66, R86 see also Kundalini
Chaminade, William J. B312
Chanting M3, R16, R40, R82, R84
Cheops pyramidal form D90
Chickering, Arthur D14
Childbirth A355, D92
Children A179, 448, A578, A625, A677, A790, B585, B768, D29, R70, R71 see also Juvenile literature
Children of God A873
Chinese people A475
Chi-Tsang A435
Cholesterol A151, A152
Christian life A241, B264, B278
Christian meditation A26, A79, A295, A321, A438, A440, A439, A488, A718, B95, B194, B307, B349, B490, B547, B637, B657, B684, B697, B728, B902, B982, B985, D208, R3, S13
Christian meditation and
Anxiety D47
Asian meditation A41, A78, A253
Athletes D68
Awareness A517
Biofeedback training D36
Breathing A34, A588
Children B768
Eastern mysticism B309
Eucharist A635
God A536, A886, B679
Groups A586, B846, B913
Guigo II A699
Hindu meditation A86
Hypertension D36
Jesus Christ B170, B326
John Cassian B489
Light A253
Liturgical texts A538
Monasteries M26
Neurosis D47
Oriental meditation A635
Other religions A868
Penitence B877
Personality D103

Prayer A124, A356, A409,
    A466, A590, A600, A779,
    B911, D147
Psychology A357, B395
Priests A243, A378
Quiet sitting A143
Religious orientation D47
St. Loyola A623
Scripture A231, A540, A706,
    B96
Secular meditation A635
Self-examination A915
Soul A147
Spiritual life A226, A411, A412,
    A466, A589, A699, A711,
    B658
Sports D68
Teachers A535
Temperament A539
Theology A357
Transcendental Meditation A193,
    A255, A334, A450, A453,
    A505, A707, A918, B300,
    B301, B322, B421, B600,
    B759, B806
Yoga A78, B911
Zen A78, A789
Christianity A341, A443, B159,
    B161, B162, B174, B373
Christward Ministry B519
Chung Fu Kuan B519
Church of One Sermon B519
Church of Tzaddi B519
Church of Universal Light S22
Church state separation see
    Court litigation
Cigarette smoking A72, A460,
    A622, A734, B924, D60,
    D144, D157, D168
Circle of Inner Truth B519
Circulatory system see Blood
    flow
Civilization R82
Clairvoyance D82
Claustrophobia A100
Cleveland A345
Clinical meditation A281, A282
Clinically Standardized Meditation
    A237, A256, A512, A533,
    B131, B132, D91, D178
Cognitive control A759
Cognitive development A12, D1
Cognitive modification A229K,
    D63
Cognitive processes A95, A717,
    D110, D150, D192
Cognitive style A56, D176

Cold tolerance A475
College curriculum A22, A199, A299,
    A507
College students A22, A129, A149,
    A350, A421, D13, D14, D31,
    D35
Color R87
Color meditation R42
Color visualization D80
Committee for Investigation of Extra-
    Tellurian Intelligence S22
Community colleges A507
Computers M6
Concentration A308, A444, A469K,
    A564, A700, B350, B358, B360,
    B524, B568, B613, B733, B735,
    B774, B815, B822, B988, D50,
    R60 see also Attention
Concentrative meditation A104, A866,
    D232
Conceptualization A583, D46
Conditioned responses A187
Conflict resolution D104
Conformity D197
Consciousness A317, A829, B58,
    B233, B391, B516, B618, B621,
    B760, B896, M17
Consciousness and
    Abhidharma psychology A306
    est B401
    Meditation A737K, B316, B355,
        B604, R58, R59
    Oedipus myth R52
    Plato A749
    Prisoners A12
    Social disorder A611
    Sufism B603
    Transcendental Meditation A12,
        A244, A262, A480, A611, A614,
        A729, A749, B82, B401, B781
Consciousness states A852, B738,
    B879, D59
Consciousness states and
    Abhidharma psychology A311
    Biofeedback training D215
    Buddha A304
    Buddhism A312
    Cerebral hemispheric dominance
        A2
    Concentration A109
    Creativity A610
    Death attitudes A280
    Ecstasy D20
    EEG A212, A610
    ESP A619
    Glossolalia A190
    Healing A252

Hesychasm D20
Hypnosis A48, A174, A271
Meditation A70, A135, A173,
    A174, A272, A307, A414,
    A628, A651, A737K, A742,
    B878, D215
Neurophysiology A286
Physiology A173
Psychoanalysis A30
Relaxation techniques D215
St. John D20
St. Teresa D20
Sufism D20
Tai Chi Chuan D73
Theravada Buddhist meditation
    A252
Transcendental Meditation A43,
    A46, A48, A607, A782, B126,
    B951, D222
Yoga A109, A254, A286, B878,
    D20
Zen meditation A254, A286,
    A782, B878, D20
Contemplation A183, B309, B474,
    B497, B502, B522, B530,
    B532, B533, B636, B771,
    B772, B774, B795, B837,
    B909, B948, B956
Contemplation and
    God A886, B653
    Healing A328
    Light A253
    Meditation A618
    Prayer A408, A409, B529,
        B534
    Religion B165
    Religious life A408
    Retreats A602
    Scripture A752
    Seminaries A408
    Yoga B16
    Zen meditation B373
Contingent negative variation
    A463, A643
Control A794
Conversion A658, A659
Cookery B958
Coronary risk factor A640
Correctional rehabilitation A5,
    A13, A25, A670 see also
    Prisoners
Cortisol A81, A83, A395, A787,
    A877
Cosmology A797
Cost effectiveness A748
Counseling A27, A129, A195,
    A343, A469K, A515, D53,
D135
Counselors A467, A609, D28, D72,
    D79, D85, D91, D138, D171
Counter culture A907
Courses A507
Court litigation and
    Silent prayer A258
    Transcendental Meditation A37,
        A40, A75, A208, A209, A214,
        A229, A275, A377, A397, A710,
        A804, A815, A817, A825, B617,
        B927
Creativity B621, D235
Creativity and
    Athletes D203
    Biofeedback training A756
    Dreams A756
    Hypnosis A756
    Meditation A442, A444, A811,
        D113, D185, D203
    Runners D203
    Skydivers D203
    Students A751
    Therapy A756
    Transcendental Meditation A23,
        A211, A241, A318, A346, A472,
        A484, A610, A613, A614, A617,
        A750, A751, A826, D10, D52,
        D197
    Weightlifters D203
    Zen koans A445
    Zen meditation A160, D42
Crime and Transcendental Meditation
    A98, A132, A134, A140, A200,
    A202, A292, A345, A454, A870,
    B430
Crisis intervention A876
CSM see Clinically Standardized
    Meditation
Cults A36, B159, B401
Cultural Integration Fellowship S11

Death A280, A521, A531, B27, B693,
    D44, D39
De-automatization A182
Defense mechanisms D150
Dentistry A206, A425, A565, A566,
    A567, A569, A575, A576, A629,
    A724, A780
Depersonalization A414
Depression A247, A336, A746, A824,
    D86, D166, D195, D203
Desensitization A422, A835
Desire R64
Devotion B2

Dharmadatu A631
Dhyana yoga A136, B260
Diabetes A423
Diamond Sangha B519
Dianetics A839
Diderot, Denis D219
Diets B925
Dimensionality A430
Dinkar, Yogi A376
Directories B839
Discrimination training A359
Divine Light Mission A277, D7
Doctors A351, A443, A487, A728,
    S2
Dodecahedral meditation structure
    A379
Dogen D23
Dogen Kingen Zenji A496
Dogmatism D61
Dominance A181
Dreams A10, A117, A236, A276,
    A678, A756, B144, B314,
    B951, D222
Drug abuse and
    Meditation A549, A879
    Transcendental Meditation A18,
        A21, A25, A72, A101, A105,
        A191, A285, A407, A460,
        A498, A499, A561, A609,
        A671, A708, A709, A808,
        A811, A893, A903, D74
    Yoga A59
    Zen meditation A744
Drug addiction and
    Acupuncture A101
    Biofeedback training A101
    Electrosleep A101
    Hypnosis A101
    Meditation A905
    Transcendental Meditation A21,
        A101
    Zen meditation A194
Drug rehabilitation and
    Meditation A287, A715
    Transcendental Meditation A561
    Yoga A298
Drug usage and
    Evangelical religions A277
    Transcendental Meditation
        A926, D40
Drugs and Meditation A290
Dunlop, Marian A328
Dyad School of Enlightenment S23
Dying see Death

East-West Research Centers S11
Eastern States Buddhist Association
    of America B519
Eating patterns A184
Edgar Cayce Foundation S8
Education see also Learning
Education and
    Meditation A563, A564, A837, D1
    Transcendental Meditation A22,
        A40, A106, A199, A208, A220,
        A232, A246, A333, A342, A434,
        A471, A472, A507, A577, A585,
        A698, A719, A769, A827, B477,
        B478, B912, D1, D14, D19, D31,
        D51, D99, D158
    Zen meditation A506
Ego A12, A645, A731, D2, D78
Ejaculation A189
Electroencephalography and
    Cerebral hemispheric dominance
        D224
    ESP A776
    Focusing A212
    Healing A108
    Meditation A9, A290, A297R, A582,
        A643, A776, A880, D224
    Sleep A917
    Transcendental Meditation A29,
        A42, A43, A46, A47, A56, A131,
        A171, A203, A239, A240, A244,
        A346, A349, A352, A385, A427,
        A437, A441, A473, A610, A611,
        A614, A617, A628, A661, A663,
        A783, A791, A792, A845, A847,
        A863, A867, A880, A884, A899,
        A917, B951, D46, D122, D220,
        D222
    Yoga A16, A153, A230
    Zen meditation A406
Electroluminescence A222
Electrolytes A508
Electromyography A131, A137, A162,
    A187, A300, A385, A491, A663,
    A922, D3, D45, D81, D215
Electonography A222
Electrooculography A385, A582, A917
Elementary school students A476,
    A564, D1, D133, D210
Emerson, Ralph Waldo A122
Emotional adjustment A777, D104,
    D116
Emotional stability A242, A624, A671,
    D95
Emotions B413, B501, D103, D127
Empathy A154, A467, A714, D83,
    D85, D129, D178
Empiricism A786

Empiricists D235
Encounter groups A234, B738, R57
Endocrine changes A80, A877
Endocrine system A81, A82, A83
Energy A609, B77, B78, D197, D230
Energy Mastery Program S23
Enlightenment A495, A786, B97, B129, B439, B441, B442
Epilepsy A787, A788
Episcopal monasteries M26
Epistemology A665
Ergotopic arousal A251
ESP see Extrasensory perception
est A234
Etherian Religious Society of Universal Brotherhood B519
Ethical meditation B404
Eucharist A635
Euphoria D103
Evolution D125
Ewan Choden B519
Executive stress see also Business
Executive stress and
  Behavior modificaiton A234
  Biofeedback training A234, A375, A748
  Encounter groups A234
  est A234
  Exercise A748
  Meditation A375, A479, A660, A727, A728
  Progressive relaxation A748
  Relaxation for Living A415
  Relaxation response A61
  Self-hypnosis A748
  Transactional analysis A234
  Transcendental Meditation A116, A146, A234, A267, A366, A415, A433, A458, A532, A748, A921, B410
  Yoga A234, A748
  Zen A748
Exercise A19, A32, A33, A64, A89, A564, A717, A748, A754, A812, D9, D121, D136, D144
Existential meditation A330
Existenz D162
Expectations A103, A185, A764, A772, A912, D58, D75, D139, D183, D190, D226
Experience A424
Expression Magazine S15

External locus of control see Locus of control
Extrasensory perception A221, A584, A619, A620, A630, A667, A672, A673, A690, A691, A692, A767, A776, D214
Extraversion A256, A400, A813, A828, A898
Extrovert meditation A259
Eye movement A45, A117, A650, A651, A771, A803, A917

Faith M23
Faith healing see Mental healing
Family meditation A227
Fantasy A564, A837, R57
Far East B681
Fasting A859, B587, B588
Fatigue A400, A824
Federal Correctional Institution at Lompoc, California A164
Federal courts see Court litigation
Fellowship of Meditation A328
Fellowship of the Inner Light B519
Field dependence D176
Field independence A613, A645, D133, D161
Finite state model A867
Fires A454
First Zen Institute B519
First Zen Institute of America S12
Flexibility A624, B17, D6
Float tanks see Isolation tanks
Flooding A296
Flying see Levitation
Flying saucers B223, B1008
Focusing A212, A875, D114, D124
Folsom State Prison A4, A5, A13, A670, B235
Formational problems D54
Fortune telling S7
Foundation of Human Understanding S13
Francis of Assisi, St. A496
Franciscan Order A158
Freedom A794, B921
Freiburger Personality Inventory A241, A242
Friends of Buddhism, Washington, D.C. B519
Friends, Society of B176
Fright A320

G Tum-mo yoga A68
Galvanic skin response A103, A165, A606, A663
Gandian philosophy R12
Gansfort, Wessel D205
Gardens R77
Gayatri B645, B758, B875
Gedatsu Church of America B519
Gestalt therapy A329, A583, B896, D121, D138, R57
Glossolalia A190
God A97, B59, B481
Grades see Academic achievement
Group counseling D138
Group dynamics A417
Group for Creative Meditation B519
Group relations training R57
Group therapy D35, D155
Groups A282, B913
Growth Process Inventory D18
Guigo II A699
Gurus A376, B364, B409, B621

Habits D56
Haikim International Meditation Society B519
Haiku B343
Hall, Joseph B352
Hallucination A251
Hallucinogenic drugs A290, B118, B666 see also Lysergic Acid Diethylamide
Handicapped A235, A246, A281
Hanuman Foundation B519
Happiness A871, B82
Hare Krishna Movement see International Society for Krishna Consciousness
Harp music R55
Harvard meditation technique A120
Hasidism B511, B1007
Hatha yoga see Yoga
Headache and Transcendental Meditation A69, A297, A556
Healing A108, A328, A487, A655, A797, B856, B882, B1002, R35, S21 see also Mental healing
Healing and Transcendental Meditation B421
Health A541, D213
Health education A106
Health educators A323
Hearing and Transcendental Meditation A145, A653, D109
Heart A15, A283, A640, A664, A865
Heart attacks A423
Heart disorders A184
Heart failure A382
Heart rate D231
Heart rate and
Biofeedback training D45, D182
Clinically Standardized Meditation A465
Exercise D182
Expectancy A103
Hypnosis A62, A166
Meditation A103, A165, D212, D234
Muscle relaxation A165
Progressive relaxation A103, A465, A809
Relaxation response A62, A103, A367, D182
Sports D186
Transcendental Meditation A29, A31, A53, A155, A239, A240, A320, A369, A455, A483, A548, A663, A695, A729, A809, A845, B951, D45, D186, D222
Type A behavior D234
Yoga A166
Zen meditation A491
Hemispheric dominance see Cerebral hemispheric dominance
Hemodialysis A213
Hemophilia A834
Herbs A587
Hermeneutics A496
Heroin addiction A18 see also Drug addiction
Hesychasm A6, A121, D20
High blood pressure see Blood pressure; Hypertension
High school students A342, A434, A471, A585, A751, D130, D131
Higher education D31 see also College curriculum
Himalayan International Institute of Yoga Science and Philosophy B519, S14
Hinayana A84
Hinduism B149, B201, B521, B575, B663, B670, B661, B672, B678, B750, B754, B757, B934, B937, B995
Christian meditation A86
Gayatri Rahasya B645
Meditation M24, R92
Mental health D206
Sadhus M5
Vedanta B808

Hoffmann reflex A137, A849
Holistic medicine B171, R35
Holy Grail Foundation B519
Holy men M5
Holy Order of Ezekiel B519
Holy Order of Mans B519
Holy Spirit D67
Home of the Dharma B519
Homeopathy B263
Hopping see Levitation
Hormones A80, A81, A82, A389,
    A392, A394, A544, A877
Hostility A5, A248, A336, D86
    see also Aggression
Hsien Tzu Kuan S25
Human field motion D137K
Humanology and Company S22
Husserl, Edmund A665, A758
Hydrocortisone A389, A544
Hypertension see also Blood
    pressure
Hypertension and
    Biofeedback training A19, A89,
        A273, A335, A637, A639,
        A640, A739, A793, D36
    Breathing A674
    Christian meditation D36
    Drugs A19, A69K
    Exercise A89, A464, A754,
        A812
    Hypnosis A739
    Meditation A19, A142, A335,
        A464, A637, A638, A640,
        A674, A721, A722, A754,
        A784, A793, A812, A879
    Muscle relaxation A19
    Progressive relaxation A739
    Relaxation response A65, A69K,
        A648, B52
    Relaxation techniques A89,
        A273, A464, A721
    Salt A19, A89, A464, A812
    Smoking A640
    Transcendental Meditation A7,
        A71, A89, A90, A423, A656,
        A722, A755
    Weight reduction A19, A89,
        A464, A812
    Yoga A19, A639
Hypnosis A167, B885, D235, R85
Hypnosis and
    Anxiety A73, A169, D77,
        D179
    Athletes D77
    Attention A174, A772, A773,
        A832
    Consciousness states A48,

    A271, A768, B951, D22K, D222
    Creativity A756
    Dentistry A566, A567, A576
    Drug abuse A101
    ESP A584
    Eye movement A803
    Learning B314
    Locus of Control D179
    Meditation A188, A354, A567,
        A571, A576, A584, A770, A771,
        A832, A851, D50
    Mysticism A1
    Relaxation response A62, A63,
        A457
    Relaxation techniques A571
    Running A768
    Stress A748, B428, D77
    Suggestibility D232
    Transcendental Meditation A565,
        A566, A693, A768, A803, D181
    Zen meditation A406
Hypometabolism A847, D182

Iconic memory A274
Idealization D134
Identity B516
IES test A298
Ignatian meditation see Loyola, Ig-
    natius, St.
Illusions D89
Imagery A110, A196, A834, A888,
        B314, D93, D150
Imagination A771, B182
Immortality B27
Incentives A166
India A493
Indian philosophy A681
Indians of North America M18
Individual differences D145
Induced affect D60
Industrial personnel see Business;
    Executive stress
Industrial society D22
Infinite Way B519
Inner direction D161
Inner Light Foundation B519
Inner Peace Movement S15
Innovation D197
Insight A84, A308, A327
Insight meditation A104, A432, A853,
        A854 see also Vipassana medi-
        tation
Insomnia A5, A123, A126, A423,
        A553, A555, A739, A879, A910
Inspiration B2

Institute for Social Rehabilitation
S29
Institute of Ability B519 S23
Institute of Cosmic Wisdom B519
Institute of Esoteric Transcen-
dentalism B519
Institute of Mentalphysics B519
Instructions for Practical Living
A890
Intelligence A235, A613, A617,
A813, A814, D191, D192,
D197
Internal locus of control see
Locus of control
International Babaji Kriya Yoga
Ashram B519
International Buddhist Meditation
Center B519
International Center for Scientific
Research S29
International Dai Bosatsu Zendo
A736
International Health Conference
A351
International I Ching Studies In-
stitute S25
International Meditation Society
S29
International Order of Kabbalists
S16
International Society for Krishna
Consciousness A681, B344,
S17
Interpersonal relations A362,
D37, D40, D86, D102,
D103, R57
Intraversion A256, A898
Intuition A256, D219, R58
Isolation tanks A593, D234

Japa yoga A662, B818
Japan B687, B872
Jesus Prayer A662
Jews A224, A796
Jhanas A159, D84
Jainism B138
Jesus Christ B827
Job satisfaction A268, A269,
A799 see also Business;
Executive stress
Jogging see Running
John of the Cross, St. A632,
B282
Judaism A796, B173, B387,
B511, B1007

Jung, Carl G. A559, A750, D132
Juvenile literature B163, B311, B401,
B406, B451, B629, B721, B831
Juvenile offenders and Transcendental
Meditation A140, D40

Kabbala see Cabala
Kansas City A200
Kao P'an-lung A800
Karma Dzong B519
Kashmir M29
Kidney disease A213
Kirlian photography A222
Kites M10
Knowledge A424
Koans A919, B546 see also Zen
Buddhism
Kohlberg, Lawrence D159
Kreuz, Johannes von B888
Kripalu Yoga Ashram B519
Krishna Consciousness see Interna-
tional Society for Krishna Con-
sciousness
Krishna Foundation of America S18
Krishnamurti, Jiddu B656, S18
Kundalini A358, B192, B283, B662,
B669, B756, B1004, S27
Kung Fu S25
Kwan Yin Zen Temple, Inc. B519

Lama Foundation B519, S19
Lamaism B216, B286, B883, B898,
B899, B984
Language instruction A207
Lapland A216
Large type books B52, B78
LaSalle, St. A401
Lassale, Hugo B562
LaTuna Federal Penitentiary A615
Law, William A843
Lawsuits see Court litigation
Lay Mountain Monastery S32
Leadership D221, S15
Learning A250, A837
Learning and
Transcendental Meditation A3,
A198, A203, A207, A554, A625,
B912, D19, D101, D148, D192
see also Education and Tran-
scendental Meditation
Zen meditation A370
Lebanon A179
Legal problems see Court litigation

Levitation and Transcendental
    Meditation A261, A284,
    A338, A723, A869, B782
Light A253, R79, R84
Light of Yoga Society A519, S20
Lighted Way B519
Listening A770
Listening meditation A914
Little Synagogue B519
Locus of control A205, A256,
    A365, A777, A922, A926,
    D16, D34, D161, D177, D179
Loneliness B391
Lord's Supper B686
Loss of face D218
Love B396, B481, R46
Loyola, Ignatius, St. A294,
    A603, A623, A701, B411,
    B412, D12, D50
LSD see Hallucinogenic drugs;
    Lysergic Acid Diethylamide
Luria, Isaac D67
Lysergic Acid Diethylamide A28,
    B666

Macrobiotics B263
Maggidism D67
Magic B680
Mahamudra meditation D30K
Mahamudra Society S22
Maharishi Effect A200, A202, A292,
    A454, A870 see also Crime
Maharishi International University
    A22, A199, A204, A232,
    A299, A719, B60, D31
Mahayana Buddhism A85, B117,
    B479, B834
Mahesh Yogi, Maharishi A374,
    A376, A449, A462, A842,
    B126, B230, B246, B247,
    B369, B593, B601, B632,
    B730, B780, B782, B979, M9
Mahesh Yogi, Maharishi and
    Beatles A456
    Creativity A23, A750, B248
    Kurt Vonnegut, Jr. A838
    Levitation A284
    Pierre Teilhard de Chardin
        A293
Maheshwarananda, Swami A217
Maladaptive behavior A730
Maladjustment A926
Mamopasana A86
Managers see Business; Execu-
    tive stress

Mandalas A119, A322, B21, B288,
    B388, M6, M12
Mantras A509, B26, B72, B227,
    B228, B341, B426, B744, B758,
    B823, B875, B938, R80, R81
Mantras and
    Anxiety D63, D227
    Christian meditation A488
    Emotions A572, A573, A574
    Muscle tension D227
    Mysticism D80
    Relaxation techniques A187
    Self-actualization D227
    Stress D98
    Transcendental Meditation A841
    Yoga B260, B390, B569, B610,
        B818, D34
Marihuana A732, D144
Mark-Age B519
Marriage and Transcendental Meditation
    A24, D140, D209, D217
Masking D200
Maslow, A.H. A704, B126
Massachusetts A258
Massage B217, B706, B707, B708
Mathematics A661, D101
Maturity A671, D235
Medical students A769
Medicine and Transcendental Meditation
    A478, A482
Meditation centers B989
Meditation Group of the New Age
    A519
Meditation groups B913
Meditation International Center B519
Meditation movement A87
Meditation structure A379
Meditations B99, B305, B473, B483,
    R37
Memory A274, A920, D192 see also
    Recall
Mental ataraxis A527
Mental disorders A25, A306, A426,
    A461, A739, A829K
Mental healing B52K, B253, B492,
    B493, B986, B1002, R35, R56,
    S21 see also Cancer
    Edgar Cayce B651
    Prayer B394
    Psychotherapy B317
    Touch A108
    Transcendental Meditation B421
Mental health A170, A311, A314,
    A342, A451, D183, D206
Mental illness A297K, A423, A859
Mental prayer A124, A536, A537,
    A540, B312

Mental retardation A235, A787,
    A788
Merton, Thomas A485, A802
Metabolic rate and Transcendental
    Meditation A192, A239,
    A475
Metabolism A54, A244, A384,
    A384K, A388, A393, A809,
    A847
Metabolites A114
Metaphilosophy A749
Metaphysics A330
Meta-therapy A307
Methadone A744, D194
Methodist Church B394
Military A18
Mills, Porter A328
Mind A323
Mind and body B251
Mind control A130
Mind emptying D80
Mindfulness meditation A109K,
    A110, A180, A305, A402,
    A547, A714, D120K
Ministry A711
Mirror-tracking skill A894
Mirrors R77
Mishnah D67
Models A460K, A857, A867
Monasteries A111, A501, A756,
    M26
Monasticism A547, B120, B121
Monks A112, A115, A495
Montreal A631
Mood changes A291
Moon, Sun Myung B89
Moral development D159
Moral reasoning A617
Motion D137K
Motivation A166, A278, A583,
    D116, D139, D142
Motor ability B623
Motor reactions A926
Movement exploration D138
Moving meditation B338
Muktananda, Swami A383
Muktananda Paramhamsa, Swami
    B621
Multiple sclerosis A287
Muscle relaxation A19, A165,
    A165, A265, A297, A465,
    A926, A927, D30 see also
    Progressive relaxation
Muscle tension D3, D202
Muscles A137, A413, A675,
    A926, A922, D111
Music B304, D224, R18, R33,

    R55
Music and
    Athletes D77
    Christian meditation A157
    Hypnosis R85
    Meditation B42, R2, R9, R27, R41
    Rain R26
    Relaxation R17, R19, R20, R21,
        R24, R25, R28, R29, R30, R31,
        R32, R74, R75, R76, R78, R88
    Sanskrit songs R80
    Skin resistance A878
    Sleep R83
    Stress D77, R14, R23
    Transcendental Meditation D65
    Zodiac R22, R34
Mysticism B253, B324, B379, B380,
    B459, B814, B827
Mysticism and
    Christian meditation B452
    ESP A690
    God A560
    Hesychasm D20
    Judaism B452
    Meditation A697, B34, B220, B340,
        D80
    Neurophysiology A286
    Perception A182
    Physiology A173
    Prayer B210, B446
    St. John D20
    St. John of the Cross A632, B282
    St. Teresa D20
    St. Theresa of Jesus A632
    Self-actualization A697
    Sufism D20
    Transcendental Meditation B541
    Yoga A286, B252, D20
    Zen meditation A286, A626, B435,
        B437, D20

Naikan psychotherapy B687
Nam A725
National Federation of Spiritual Healers
    S21
Naturopathy B251
Neo-Confucianism A139
Nervous system D188
Neuromuscular recovery A346
Neurophysiology A286, A296K, A384K
Neuroticism and
    Children A342
    Christian meditation D47
    Divine Light Mission A277
    Flooding A296

Meditation D97
Prisoners A5
Progressive relaxation D97
Satipatthana A180
Transcendental Meditation A5,
 A241, A342, A396, A694,
 A746, A813, A814, A898, D78,
 D130, D195
Yoga A296
New Age Teachings B519
New Angelus B519
New Church A332
New Jersey A40, A208, A214,
 A229, A815, A817, B929
New Thought B274, B519
New York Telephone Co. A127,
 A141, A512, A533
Nicholas Roerich Museum S1
Nien-fo A919
Noise A511, A765
Nonpharmacologic interventions
 A89, A101, A273, A464
Norepinephrine A367, A652
Novelty D142
Nurses A682
Nutrition A184, A587
Nyingma Order A156

Oasis Fellowship B519
Obesity D216
Occult sciences A690, B11, B34,
 B36, B37, B66, B115,
 B959, B1008
Occupational guidance A594
Ocean R87
Oedipus complex R52
Ontology B484, B485
Open focus A256, D72
Opening techniques R60
Open-mindedness A431, A486
Openness D24
Organization dynamics D152
Organizational change A907
Organizational development A400
Orthodox Eastern authors B244,
 B631, B990
Osis, Karlis A430
Otis, Leon A344
Oxygen A64, A70, A244, A245,
 A845, A847
Oxygen consumption A54, A155,
 A192, A846, A863, B951,
 D222

Pain A265, A279, A355, A358, A402,
 A475, A531, A548, A565, A576,
 A629, A834
Painting B343
Pali Suttas A794
Panosophic Institute B519, S22
Paradox D218
Paraplegia A287
Parapsychology A630
Participation A186, A685
Passive meditation A786K
Patanjali A665, A749, A758, A829K,
 B574, B941, B942
Peace A608
Peace of mind B164
Pen pals S28
Pentecostal prayer A190
Pentecostals B830
Perception and
 Attention B623
 ESP A673
 Expectancy D58
 Light A253
 Meditation A182, A253, A327,
  A650, A651, B623, B110,
  D151K, D160, D224
 Mindfulness meditation A110
 Progressive relaxation A327
 Sound A650, A651
 Transcendental Meditation A198,
  A270, A502, A645, A646, A653,
  A673, D10, D56, D89, D188
 Visual fixation A650, A651
 Yoga A650
 Zen meditation D58, D233
Perceptual motor coordination A894,
 A895
Perceptual motor learning A896
Perceptual motor skills A92
Perfect Liberty B519
Periodontal tissue A425, A724
Personality and
 Arica training D37
 Autogenic training D118
 Children A448
 Elderly D39
 Jungian psychology D132
 Meditation A9, A468, A570, A601,
  A685, A763, A788, A811, A881,
  A883, D57, D123, D151K
 Prisoners D2
 Relaxation techniques D193
 Students A471
 Transcendental Meditation A170,
  A186, A241, A242, A245, A247,
  A270, A426, A448, A471, A647,
  A746, A808, A828, D2, D18,

D101, D103, D109, D118,
D123, D132, D139, D142,
D183, D190, D195
Vipassana meditation A854
Yoga A298, A788
Zen meditation D39, D161
Personality change A74, A115,
A879, A905, D25, D189, D190
Personality traits A74, A181,
A238, A898, D86, D108,
D117, D197, D235
Personnel management A141, B250
see also Business
Perspiration A100
Phenomenological reduction A665,
A758
Phenylalamine A385, A391
Phenylalantine A385
Philadelphia A561
Philosophy A749
Phobias A169
Photic stimulation A899
Physicians see Doctors
Physics A210
Physiological correlates A782,
A909
Physiological psychology D173
Physiology A173, A845
Pilgrims B686
Placebo suggestion A126, A219
Plasma cortisol see Cortisol
Plasma prolactin see Prolactin
Plasma phenylalamine concentration
see Phenylalamine
Plato A749, A750
Potential D165
Prabhavananda, Swami B364,
B564
Prajna B117
Pratikopasana A86
Prayer A102, A590, B22, B43,
B50, B92, B128, B178,
B210, B232, B253, B313,
B348, B445, B446, B448,
B449, B507, B527, B529,
B530, B534, B769, B911,
B981, B1006, D126, D147
Prayer and
Contemplation A408
Court litigation see Court
litigation
Daily life B94
Edgar Cayce B134, B651
Eucharist A635
Glossolalia A190
God A886, B295
Healing B651, B986

Ir-a-qi B704
Light A253
Meditation A356, B231, B264,
B277, B310, B457, B458, B473,
B506
St. Chantal B141
St. Gregorius I B293
St. John of the Cross B293
St. Loyola A623, A701
St. Peter of Alcantara B626,
B627, B628
St. Teresa of Avila B710
Scripture A752
Seminaries A600
Students A163, A258, A600
Transcendental Meditation A50,
A289, B806
William Joseph Chaminade B312
Yoga A78
Zen meditation A78
Prayer in the schools issue see
Court litigation
Prayers B2, B134, B310, B744
Pregnancy A189, A355
Priests A243, A361, A378
Primal therapy D154
Prisoners A4, A5, A12, A13, A39,
A164, A245, A248, A615, A670,
A671, A818, B235, D2, D34,
D141, D151, D212
Prisoners and
Meditation D34, D212
Transcendental Meditation A4,
A5, A12, A13, A39, A164,
A245, A248, A615, A670, A671,
A818, B235, D2, D141, D151
Yoga D34
Prisons A470, A818
Problem solving A150, A198, A417,
D56, D112
Process meditation B647, B648
Productivity A266, A267, A532,
A799, A819
Progoff, Ira B647
Progressive relaxation A337, B367K,
R38K
Progressive relaxation and
Alcoholics A291, A633, A634,
D95, D170
Anxiety A176, A291, A353, A527,
A633, A806, A810, D30, D91K,
D95, D227, D231
Arthritis A834
Autonomic arousal D170
Blood pressure A634
Desensitization A324
Handicapped A281

Hypertension A260, A273
Imagery A196, A327
Meditation A739
Metabolism A809
Mood stability D95
Muscle tension D202, D227
Relaxation response D202
Self-actualization A176, D227
Stress A103, A281, A282,
    A465, A533, A748, A863,
    A911, B133, D4, D97, D108
Transcendental Meditation
    A176, A806, A809, A810,
    A863
Prolactin A394, A395, A877
Prophecy B11, D67
Prophets B387
Proteins A184, A508
Pseudo-Dionysius A687, B948
Psi training D214
Psychedelic drugs see Hallu-
    cinogenic drugs; Lysergic
    Acid Diethylamide
Psychiatry A123, B346
Psychical research A598, A630,
    B164, B253, B314, B986
Psychoanalysis A30, A128, A272,
    A423, A730, A731, A785,
    D146
Psychobiology A245
Psychodynamics D203
Psychokinetic phenomena A503
Psychological change D102
Psychologists A798
Psychology A27, A161, A314,
    A405, B572
Psychomotor skills A896
Psychopathology A12, A874
Psychophysiology A65, A247,
    A279, A297R, A364, A483,
    A739, D173, D234
Psychoses A184, A264, A694,
    A859, R56
Psychosocial development D172
Psychosocial functioning A709
Psychosomatic medicine A1,
    A2, A298, B624, D156, D169
Psychosynthesis D79
Psychotherapists D55
Psychotherapy and
    Abhidharma psychology A306
    Biofeedback training A781
    Buddhist meditation D8
    Creativity A756
    Evangelical religion A277
    Group meditation D155
    Healing B317

Meditation A95, A96, A125, A287,
    A297, A322, A468, A542, A703,
    A704, A742, A762, A914, B63,
    B64, B317, B346, B684, B687,
    D123, R59
Running A768
Satipatthana meditation A180, A305
Spiritual teachers D102
Sufism B603
Transcendental Meditation A93,
    A94, A128, A172, A245, A480,
    A764, A781, B81, D48, D135,
    D139, D204
Yoga D104
Zen meditation D161
Public speaking A422
Pure Land Buddhism A919
Pyramidal form D90

Qabalah see Cabala
Qigong meditation A667
Quality of life A531, A924
Quantum physics A210
Quiet sitting A256, A291, A621,
    A762, A800, A801, D9

Race problem and Transcendental
    Meditation A807
Racquetball D105
Radha Soami Satsang Beas B831
Rahner, Karl A497
Rain making R26
Rainbow Family of Living Light B519
Raja yoga B29, B31, B66, B67,
    B215, B359, B361, B362, B363,
    B551, B557, B570, B571, B598,
    B675, B713, B731, B732, B741,
    B742, B755, B817, B820, B825,
    B841, B867, B931, B932, B933,
    B940, B941, B942, B943, B944,
    B949, B996, B998 see also
    Yoga
Rajneesh, Acharya B297, B752,
    B753
Rajneesh Meditation Center B519
Ram Chandra B659
Ramakrishna B365
Ramana, Maharshi B656
Ramanuja A194
Rational-emotive therapy A229K
Reaction time A20, A44, A371, A616,
    A686, A747, D188
Reading A343, A476, A557, A585,

A878, A920, D101, D133, D148, D192, D210
Reality B621
Reality testing A264, D150
Recall see also Memory
Recall and
  Satipatthana meditation B495
  Transcendental Meditation A3, A77, A552
Receptive meditation A866
Reciprocal inhibition therapy A93, A100
Recordings B644
Reducing diets B925
Reflexes A203, A346, A849, A864, D88, D225
Regression A518, D43, D145
Rehabilitation programs A5
Reincarnation B1008, R64
Relaxation A655, R42, B233, B429
Relaxation and
  Anxiety A421
  Biogenics R74, R75
  Breathing R76
  Chanting R16
  Client characteristics A55K
  Hypertension A721
  Learning D192
  Meditation A133, A162, A187, A316, A417, A421, A638, A721, A837, A882, A883
  Memory D192
  Music R17, R19, R20, R25, R29, R30, R31, R34, R55, R74, R75, R78, R83, R88
  Phenylalamine A385
  Skills acquisition A421
  Stress A316, A664, R14
  Students A837
  Stuttering D3
  Transcendental Meditation A46, A81, A201, A385, A413, A609, A716, A791, A831, B701, D27, D211
Relaxation for Living A415
Relaxation response A65, A66, A67, A313, A549, A581, A757, B51K, B52
Relaxation response and
  Anxiety A33, A179, D32, D47, D184, D198
  Arousal D173
  Blood pressure A69K, A142
  Central nervous system A63
  Children A179
  Clinically Standardized Medi-
    tation A237
  Counselors D28, D72
  Exercise D182
  Healing B52K
  Hypertension A58
  Hypnosis A62, A457
  Karl Rahner A497
  Locus of control A922, D202
  Metabolism A54
  Muscle tension A922, D202
  Neurosis D47
  Oxygen consumption A64
  Personality D28
  Progressive relaxation A324, D202
  Religious orientation D47
  Smoking D60
  Stress A60, A61, A148, A367, A702, B15, R2K, R2T
  Students D184
  Transcendental Meditation A120, A497, A514, A885, D173
Relaxation techniques A570, A571, A579, D29K, M19, R28, R63
  Alcohol usage A501K
  Anxiety A32, A175K, A300, D77, D81, D91K, D193
  Asthma A233
  Athletes D77, D81
  Blood pressure A360
  Community colleges A507
  Consciousness states D215
  Endocrine changes A83
  Hypertension A89, A273, A464, A637
  Learning B314
  Meditation A95
  Music R78
  Personality D193
  Prisoners A469
  Self-concept D193
  Sleep R83
  Stress A127, A323, A835, D77, D81
  Students A507
  Transcendental Meditation A117, A168, A219, A362, A469, A688, A878
Religion B63, B64, B82, B346, D235
Religions B519
Religious orientation D47, D61
Religious psychology B319
Reprints B60
Resistance D146
Respiration and
  Meditation A70, A165, A846
  Relaxation response A54, A62, A64

Transcendental Meditation A14,
A38, A240, A348, A663,
A695, A729, D17, D109,
D186, D212
Respiratory "one" method A533
Rest A543, A878, D9, D30, D175,
D196 see also Quiet sitting
Retention A3, D131
Retreats A602
Revelationary movements D143
Rhode Island A924
Rigidity B17, D6, D183
Rimpoche, Namgyal B325
Rinpoche, Lama Duchung A156
Rinzai-Ji, Inc. B519
Ritual A139
Roerich, Nicholas S1
Rorschach test A109K, A110
Roshi, Joshu Sasaki A358
Rosicrucians B519
Rotary pursuit A895, A896, A897
Running A238, A364, A735,
A768, A775, B266, D105,
D166, D203
Ryoko-in M31

Sabian Assembly B519
Sadhus M5
Salesmen A339
Salivation A508, A575, A888
Salt A19, A89, A464, A812
Samadhi A547, B734, B736,
B737
Samapatti A136
Samatha A136
Samkara A138
Sanatana Dharma Foundation S23
Sanatana Dharma Spiritual Com-
munity S23
Sankara A194
Sankhya A654
San-lun thought A435
Sant Mat B814
Sasaki, Josho M32
Satchidananda, Swami A376
Satipatthana A180, A714, B495,
B590, B805
Satipatthana sutta B589, B832
Satori B366
Savitria B519
Schiller, Freidreich D163
Schizophrenia A859, D136
School health services A106
School of Hatha Yoga M16
School of Truth B519

School of Universal Religion and Phi-
losophy S22
School of Yogic Music and Dance
S23
Science A480, A562
Science fiction M4
Science of Creative Intelligence A23,
A577, B612, D19, D65, D87,
D135, D158, D219
Scientology A873
Scuba diving D81
Secondary education A342, A471,
A585, A751, D130
Secularization A907
Seicho-No-Ie B519
Self B597, B661, B663
Self-acceptance A105, A228, A559,
D235
Self-actualization B58, B177, B266,
B760
Self-actualization and
Arica training D37
Biofeedback training D24
Exercise D121
Gestalt therapy D121
Juvenile offenders D40
Movement exploration D138
Meditation A249, A697, A704,
A837, D15, D24, D49, D70,
D121, D172, D177, D189, D221,
D227
Progressive relaxation A176, D227
Psi training D214
Relaxation response D28
Students A837
Teachers A827
Transactional analysis D70
Transcendental Meditation A74,
A176, A247, A365, A426, A591,
A612, A693, A720, A746, A808,
A827, D11, D40, D51, D52,
D106, D162, D177, D181, D183,
D195, D207
Yoga D121, D172
Zen meditation D42, D107, D138
Self-awareness A517, A583, A595,
R73
Self-concept and
Concentration D172
Drug offenders A671
Meditation D34, D120, D134, D165,
D172
Naikan psychotherapy B687
Prisoners D34
Relaxation techniques D193
St. Loyola A701
Students A471, D130

Teachers A827
Transcendental Meditation
A331, A340, A471, A596,
A597, A671, A693, A827,
A828, D16, D52, D130,
D181, D217, D230
Yoga D34, D104, D172
Self-confidence A400
Self-control A130, A205, A422,
A483, A546, A717, A738,
A740, A741, A744, A745,
A835, A888, A902, B787,
D45, D97, D150, D168,
D183
Self-control and
Anxiety A422
Buddhist psychology A546
Desensitization A835
Exercise A717
Meditation A205, A717, A835,
A902, B787, D97
Mental health D183
Muscle relaxation D97
Relaxation techniques A835
Self-actualization D183
Smoking D168
Transcendental Meditation
A130, A483, D45
Zen meditation A738, A740,
A741, A744, A745, D150
Self-defense B393
Self-enlightenment D143
Self-esteem A763, A773, D1, D21,
D24, D29, D39, D197
Self-evaluation D18, D162
Self-examination A915
Self-hypnosis A769, A851, D50
Self-identity A828
Self-knowledge A139
Self-love D134
Self-parenting A902
Self-perception A212, A659, B413,
B738, D53, D130, D189, R73
Self-realizaiton A139, A626,
A641, A781, A782, B59,
B138, B182, B185, B330,
D132, D189
Self-Realizaiton Fellowship S24
Seminarians A701
Seminaries A600
Sensitivity D85, D178
Sensitivity training A368, D172,
D221
Sensory awareness A564
Sensory-motor performance A684
Serotonin A436
Servicemen A18

Set theory A661
Sex A189, B265
Sex differences A898, D86, D120
Sex roles A743
Shan-tao A636
Shavasana and Transcendental Medita-
tion A31
Shingon Mission B519
Siddha meditation A614, B559, D98
Siddha Yoga Dham Foundation A351
Sikh Dharma B519
Sikh meditation A725
Sikhism B399
Silence A605, A718, B357, B614
Silva Mind Control Method B811
Sino-American Buddhist Association
B519
Siva R79
Sivananda Yoga Society A631
Sixth Annual Conference of the As-
sociation for Transpersonal
Psychology A858
Skills acquisition A421, D115
Skin conductance see Galvanic skin
response
Skin resistance A76, A239, A369,
A381, A459, A548, A615, A729,
A765, A845, A846, A891
Skin temperature A162, A510
Skydivers D203
Sleep see also Insomnia
Sleep and
Meditation A10
Music R83
Prisoners A248
Transcendental Meditation A45,
A46, A47, A171, A248, A276,
A386, A390, A437, A534, A551,
A628, A642, A783, A917, D26,
D201, D220
Zen meditation A406
Smoking see Cigarette smoking
Sociability A340
Social adjustment A860
Social anxiety D223
Social behavior A39, A164, A235,
A241, A242, A248, A709,
D40, D143 see also Inter-
personal relations
Social disorder A608, A611
Social environment A515
Social movements D38
Social perception A368
Social relations A362
Social skills D136
Social status A181
Social well being A924

Societas Rosicrucian in America
  B519
Society A25, A87, A607, B480,
  D22
Society for the Teaching of the
  Inner Christ, Inc. B519
Society of Friends B176
Sociological analysis A658
Somatic relaxation A863
Songs B427
Sonorama Society B519
South-East Asia A144
Space 735
Special education A246, D148
Speech A422, A513, D3
Spiritual direction B532
Spiritual Exercises A603, A701,
  D50
Spiritual Frontiers Fellowship
  B253
Spiritual life B23, B109, B149,
  B171, B244, B431, B528,
  B538, B539, B547, B796,
  B974
Spiritual meditation S6
Spiritual Regeneration Movement
  R45, S29
Spiritual teachers D102
Spiritualism B1008
Sports A215, A364, A676, A761,
  D68, D77, D81, D175,
  D186, D203
Sri Chinmoy Centers B519
Sri Lanka A495
Sri Ram Ashrama B519
Stanford, Ray A598
State church separation see
  Court litigation
States of consciousness see
  Consciousness states
Stein, Edith B888
Steiner, Rudolph B118
Stillpoint Institute B519
Stillwater Prison A39
Stimulation D139
Stress B428, B624, M7, M30
  Autogenic training D108
  Behavior therapy A664, B133
  Biofeedback training A375,
    A516, A748, B133, D4,
    D81, D108, M19
  Bruxism A568
  Cancer A529
  Clinical meditation A281, A282
  Clinically Standardized Medita-
    tion A141, A512
  Desensitizaiton A835

Dental caries A575
Exercise A569, A748, A754, B1005,
  D105
Expectancy A103
Handicapped A281
Hypnosis A748
Meditation A150, A309, A316,
  A375, A451, A479, A529, A568,
  A569, A570, A702, A726, A727,
  A728, A754, A835, A883, A911,
  B133, B515, B1005, D4, D29K,
  D76, D81, D97, D98, D105,
  D108, M19, R73, R76
Music R23
Progressive relaxation A103, A281,
  A282, A748, A911, B133, D4,
  D97, D108, D202
Relaxation A316, A323
Relaxation response A60, A61,
  A67, A103, A148, A367, A648,
  A702, A757, B15, B52, D202
Relaxation techniques A127, A664,
  A835, B133, D29K, M19
Self-control A741, R56
Teachers B15
Transcendental Meditation A25,
  A80, A245, A263, A267, A362,
  A366, A381, A392, A395, A396,
  A403, A404, A415, A452, A458,
  A516, A532, A543, A544, A606,
  A664, A748, A799, B75, B76,
  B77, B78, B79, B80, B250,
  B323, B912, D16, D167, D196
Yoga A748, B515
Zen meditation A516, A741, A748
Stress Management Training A281,
  A282
Structural Unitism Society S22
Students A163, A577, D1, D101
Students' International Meditation So-
  ciety S29
Stuttering A513, D3
Subconsciousness B177
Subliminal perception A673
Subramuniya Yoga Order B519
Subsensory perception A672
Substance abuse see Alcoholism;
  Drug abuse
Sufi meditation A792
Sufism B294, B452
Suggestibility A188, D232
Suggestion B430
Sumie B343, M25
Surfing A215
Suzuki, D.T. D233
Sweating A100
Swedenborg, Emanuel A830

Sympathetic nervous system A67,
A367, A455
Systematic desensitization therapy
D57, D63
Switzerland A156

Tai Chi Chuan A428, A631,
B393, D55, D73, M14, M16,
M22, S25
Tantra B368, B381
Tantric Buddhism B74, B285
Tantrism A153, B660, B757
Taoism B71, B471, B596, S25
Taoist Sanctuary S25
Tarot S7
Tauler, Johannes B379, B380
Taxonomies A312
Teachers A535, A827, B15,
D70, D98, D102
Teaching A299, B542
Teaching meditation D128
Teaching stories R49, R60
Teeth grinding A568
Teilhard de Chardin, Pierre A293
Telephone companies see New
York Telephone Co.
Temperament A539
Temple of Cosmic Religion B519
Temple University School of Medi-
cine A769
Temples B408
Tennessee Self-Concept Scale
D217
Tension see Stress
Teresa of Avila B888
Test anxiety A179, A421, A476,
A625, D35, D41, D57, D63,
D115, D131, D133, D191,
D212
Testosterone A389
Thailand A115, A134, A604,
A797, B408, D218
Theological educaiton A144
Theosophical Society of America
B519, S26
Theosophy B36, B223, S26
Theravada Buddhism A110,
A159, A326, A418, A420,
A432, A604, D84, D120K,
D134, S9
Theravada Buddhist meditation
A178, A252, B398
Theresa of Jesus, St. A632
Theresia Lisieux B888
Theta waves A153, A349, A473,

A696, D90
3HO Foundation S27
Tibet B54, B74, B286, B287, B402,
B407K, B654, B915, B954,
B955, M20, S28
Tibetan Aid Project S28
Tibetan art M13
Tibetan Book of the Dead R91
Tibetan Buddhism A156, B249, B544,
B654, B834, B835, M13, R91
Tibetan Buddhist meditation A68,
A109, A280, B285-B289, B677
Tibetan Buddhist Meditation Center
A111
Tibetan Nyingma Relief Foundation
S28
Tibetan Nyingmapa Meditation Center
B519
Tibetan Pen Friend Program S28
Tibetan Students Fund S22
Tidal volume A192
Time A735, D137K
Time competence D161
Time perspective D124
TM see Transcendental Meditation
TM-Sidhi program A749, A848, A849,
A850, B430, D82, D109, S29
Tobacco see Cigarette smoking
Tolerance D197
Tonic vibration reflex D26
Touch healing A108 see also Mental
healing
Transactional analysis A234, D70
Transcendental Meditation A11, A36,
A44, A55K, A83, A88, A92,
A97K, A113, A114, A118, A149,
A185, A187, A195, A204, A210,
A224, A225, A227, A235, A264,
A274, A288, A294, A299, A301,
A313, A341, A344, A350, A355,
A371, A374, A376, A384, A387,
A389, A391, A393, A394, A398,
A401, A416, A436, A443, A449,
A456, A459, A461, A462, A463,
A470, A474, A481, A486, A492,
A494, A510, A511, A513, A550,
A553, A555, A562, A608, A616,
A620K, A624, A629, A630,
A649, A657, A676, A681, A682,
A683, A684, A685, A686, A696,
A700, A712, A734, A747, A765,
A766, A777, A798, A816, A820,
A821, A836, A838, A839, A842,
A844, A848, A849, A861, A864,
A871, A872, A873, A877, A882,
A891, A892, A894, A895, A896,
A906, A907, A908, A909, A916,

A922, A923, A924, A927,
B7, B13, B17, B19, B38,
B60, B65, B89, B127, B130,
B133, B140, B143, B163,
B179, B197, B242, B246,
B247, B248, B261, B262,
B265, B266, B271, B272,
B273, B296, B298, B315,
B318, B323, B342, B344,
B355, B369, B376, B386,
B400, B403, B406, B414,
B422, B455, B484, B485,
B486, B508, B540, B560,
B561, B563, B584, B585,
B586, B593, B599, B612,
B625, B630, B684, B701,
B702, B703, B730, B761,
B780, B783, B789, B790,
B791, B792, B800, B853,
B908, B945, B958, B966,
B971, B972, B980, D3, D6,
D22, D33, D38, D43, D53,
D61, D64, D65, D66, D82,
D83, D86, D87, D88, D92,
D96, D111, D125, D127,
D137, D143, D149, D152,
D153, D154, D156, D159,
D163, D168, D169, D174,
D175, D180, D187, D213,
D225, D228, M9, M22, R4,
R5, R6, R10, R39, R46, S2,
S29 see also Transcendental
Meditation combined with oth-
er subjects
Transcendentalists D235
Transpersonal psychology B881,
D215
Traumas A730
Trophotropic arousal A251
Trüodothyronine A81
Trungpa, Chögyam A111
Truth B754
Type A behavior pattern D234
Typhoons A132
Tyrosine A436

Unconscious A874
Unification Church A873, B89
Unified meditation A866
United States Association of
Physicians S2
University of California, Berkeley
D31
University of Notre Dame A412
Unrealistic experience D145

Values A181, D13
Vasoconstriction D3
Vedanta A49, A138, A194, B678,
B808, D94
Verbal ability A235, D224
Verbal behavior A198
Vigyana Bhairava Tantra B660
Violence A608, R51, R71
Violin playing D65
Vipassana meditation A115, A223,
A432, A689, A759, A853, A854,
B142, B207, B208, B279, B454
see also Insight meditation
Visual discrimination A371
Visual fixation A651
Visual imagery D93
Visual perception D56, D58
Visual stimulation A899
Visualization B259, B542, D80
Visuddhimagga A303, A304
Vital, Hayyim D67
Vitamins A184, A587
Vocational adjustment A451
Void experience A1
Vyasa School of Sanskrit S23

Walking meditation A216
Washington Buddhist Vihara S9
Weather and Transcendental Meditation
A132, A668
Weight A19, A89, A464, A812, A872
Weightlifters D203
White Star B519
Wholeness A902
Wilderness A216
Wisdom B117
Workers see also Business; Execu-
tive stress
Workers and Transcendental Meditation
A268, A269, A451, B250
Workshops D221
World Catalyst Church B519
World Government of the Age of En-
lightenment S2, S29
World Plan Executive Council B519,
S29
Writing A557, A558

Yang-ming, Wang A890
Yasodhara Ashram Society S30
Yen-yang B706, B707, B708
Yihudim D67
Yoga A49, A109, A153, A317, A655,

A909, B54, B100, B101,
B102, B103, B104, B105,
B106, B107, B108, B109,
B110, B111, B112, B113,
B190, B223, B254, B263,
B327, B344, B368, B396,
B429, B452, B459, B475,
B488, B550, B556, B569,
B622, B646, B664, B665,
B707, B708, B748, B777,
B814, B999, M8, M16, M22,
R64, R65, R82, S4, S10,
S14, S20, S23, S24, S27,
S28, S30, S31 see also
    Raja yoga
Yoga and
    Anxiety   A296, B515, D34,
        D121
    Awareness   A650
    Biofeedback training   A17,
        B290, B291
    Blindness   A363
    Body temperature   A68
    Cardiovascular system   A31
    Children   B311
    Christianity   B512
    Concentration   B733, B815
    Conflict resolution   D104
    Consciousness states   A55,
        A222, A286
    Contemplation   B16
    Counseling   D171
    Dhyana   B608, B816
    Dreams   A236
    Drug addicts   A298, B515
    Dying   B27
    EEG   A792
    Enlightenment   B31
    Gayatri   B758, B875
    God   B192
    Headaches   B515
    Healing   B71, B993
    Health   D121
    Hypertension   A19, A273
    Jnana   B734
    Kundalini   B192, B283, B756,
        B886
    Learning   D192
    Locus of control   D34
    Mantras   B390, B610, B758,
        B818, B823, B875
    Maturity   A431
    Medicine   B993
    Meditation   B8, B90, B137,
        B213, B252, B260, B329,
        B335, B336, B337, B416,
        B427, B491, B512, B568,

    B583, B594, B598, B611, B662
    B669, B684, B691, B736, B749,
    B793, B815, B819, B859, B886,
    B911, B965, B992, B1000, D12,
    R1
    Memory   D192
    Mental health   D206
    Mysticism   A286, B87
    Pain   A279, A402
    Perception   A254
    Personality   D25
    Phenomenological reduction   A665,
        A758
    Physiological changes   A230
    Prayer   A78, B189, B191, B538,
        B539
    Prisoners   D34
    Psychotherapy   A322
    Retreats   A602
    Sadhus   M5
    St. Loyola   D12
    Samadhi   A167, B737
    Samkhya   A654
    Schizophrenics   D136
    Science   B256
    Self-actualization   D121, D172
    Self-concept   D172
    Self-control   A431
    Self-realization   D5
    Songs   B427
    Spiritual teachers   D102
    Stress   A748, B515
    Students   A507
    Tai Chi Chuan   D73
    Tantrism   B381
    Transcendental Meditation   A352,
        D12
Yoga Research Foundation   S31
Yoga retreats   B989
Yogananda, Paramahansa   S24
Yoganta Meditation Center   B519
Yogis   A15, A16, A279
Youth   A278

Zen breathing   A337
Zen Buddhism   A9K, A17, A658,
    A736, B51, B199, B332, B333,
    B347, B439, B441, B442, B452,
    B459, B546, B579, B671, B707,
    B708, B797, B798, B861, B872,
    B873, B874, B926, B929, D233,
    M3, M21, M22, M26, M31, M32,
    R82, R93, S12, S32
Zen Buddhism and
    Behavioral change   A669

Catholicism A485
Chinese monks A919
Christianity A805
Creativity A445
Hasidism B1007
Jews A224
Missionaries A805
Pure Land Buddhism A919
Satori B97
Students D13
Thomas Merton A485
Value orientation A181, D13
Zen Buddhist Temple of Chicago
B519
Zen Center of Los Angeles B519
Zen meditation A49, A112, A136,
A317, A358, A380, A490,
A491, A504, A753, A909,
B98, B119, B200, B240,
B255, B424, B436, B471,
B472, B491, B554, B562,
B580, B582, B602, B684,
B777, B854, B857, B926,
B978, R60
Zen meditation and
Anxiety A302, A329, D42, D75,
D107, D124
Athletes A761
Attention A370, A504, D119,
D145
Behavioral change A416, A737
Christian meditation A399,
A789, B373, B433, B435,
B437, B438, B440
Concentration A319
Consciousness states A55,
A286
Counselors A467, D85
Creativity A160, D42
Death attitudes A280
Dogen D23
Ecstasy A251, A254

EEG A406, D25
Emotional problems D116
Empathy A154, A467, D85,
D129
Fukan Zazen-gi D23
Hypnosis A406
Jungian psychology A559
Learning A370
Muscle relaxation D124
Mysticism A286, A626, B437
Perception A251, A254, A302,
D58
Personality D25, A161
Prayer A78
Psychotherapy A322, B334
St. Francis of Assisi A496
St. Loyola A603
Satori A366
Seizures A28
Self-acceptance A559
Self-actualization D42, D107, D138
Self-control A738, A740, A741,
A744, A745, D194
Self-realization A626, A641, A781,
A782, D150
Sleep A406
Spiritual conversion A659
Sports A761
Stress A516, A748
Students A506
Tai Chi Chuan D73
Theravada meditation A418
Transcendental Meditation A55,
A352, A782, D62
Yoga A55, A254
Zen Meditation Center of Rochester
B519
Zen Mission Society B519
Zen painting B343
Zen Studies Society B519, S32
Zikr A662
Zodiac R22